MW01120607

HUMBER LIBRARIES LAKESHORE CAMPUS
3199 Lakeshore Blvd West
TORONTO, ON.   M8V 1K8

International Development Governance

PUBLIC ADMINISTRATION AND PUBLIC POLICY

A Comprehensive Publication Program

Executive Editor

JACK RABIN
Professor of Public Administration and Public Policy
School of Public Affairs
The Capital College
The Pennsylvania State University—Harrisburg
Middletown, Pennsylvania

Assistant to the Executive Editor
T. Aaron Wachhaus, Jr.

Available Electronically

International Development Governance

edited by

Ahmed Shafiqul Huque
McMaster University
Hamilton, Ontario, Canada

Habib Zafarullah
University of New England
Armidale, New South Wales, Australia

Taylor & Francis
Taylor & Francis Group
Boca Raton   London   New York

A CRC title, part of the Taylor & Francis imprint, a member of the
Taylor & Francis Group, the academic division of T&F Informa plc.

HUMBER LIBRARIES LAKESHORE CAMPUS
3199 Lakeshore Blvd West
TORONTO, ON.   M8V 1K8

Published in 2006 by
CRC Press
Taylor & Francis Group
6000 Broken Sound Parkway NW, Suite 300
Boca Raton, FL 33487-2742

© 2006 by Taylor & Francis Group, LLC
CRC Press is an imprint of Taylor & Francis Group

No claim to original U.S. Government works
Printed in the United States of America on acid-free paper
10 9 8 7 6 5 4 3 2 1

International Standard Book Number-10: 1-57444-556-1 (Hardcover)
International Standard Book Number-13: 978-1-57444-556-5 (Hardcover)
Library of Congress Card Number 2005046272

This book contains information obtained from authentic and highly regarded sources. Reprinted material is quoted with permission, and sources are indicated. A wide variety of references are listed. Reasonable efforts have been made to publish reliable data and information, but the author and the publisher cannot assume responsibility for the validity of all materials or for the consequences of their use.

No part of this book may be reprinted, reproduced, transmitted, or utilized in any form by any electronic, mechanical, or other means, now known or hereafter invented, including photocopying, microfilming, and recording, or in any information storage or retrieval system, without written permission from the publishers.

For permission to photocopy or use material electronically from this work, please access www.copyright.com (http://www.copyright.com/) or contact the Copyright Clearance Center, Inc. (CCC) 222 Rosewood Drive, Danvers, MA 01923, 978-750-8400. CCC is a not-for-profit organization that provides licenses and registration for a variety of users. For organizations that have been granted a photocopy license by the CCC, a separate system of payment has been arranged.

Trademark Notice: Product or corporate names may be trademarks or registered trademarks, and are used only for identification and explanation without intent to infringe.

Library of Congress Cataloging-in-Publication Data

Handbook of international development governance / edited by Ahmed Shafiqul Huque, Habib
    Zafarullah.
        p. cm. -- (Public administration and public policy ; 117)
    Includes bibliographical references and index.
    ISBN 1-57444-556-1
    1. Economic development--Handbooks, manuals, etc. 2. Sustainable development--Handbooks,
manuals, etc. 3. Economic policy--Handbooks manuals, etc. 4. Corporate governance--Handbooks,
manuals, etc. 5. Globalization--Handbooks, manuals, etc. I. Huque, Ahmed Shafiqul. II. Zafarullah,
Habib Mohammad. III. Series.

HD82.H2753 2005
338.94'068--dc22

2005046272

---

informa

Taylor & Francis Group
is the Academic Division of Informa plc.

Visit the Taylor & Francis Web site at
http://www.taylorandfrancis.com

and the CRC Press Web site at
http://www.crcpress.com

Dedication

This book is dedicated to those who are committed to the promotion of good governance and development in the less fortunate parts of the world

Preface

This book has two objectives. The first is to weave together the concepts of 'development" and "governance" by examining a range of issues and problems faced by developing countries in establishing a system of sustainable governance. It also takes a look at a number of tools that can contribute to the process. The second one is to initiate discussions on the concept of development governance in an international context. The surge of interest in governance among various quarters has generated considerable debates, and attention has shifted to the nature of relationships within and between governments, agencies and other key institutions and citizens in their efforts to effect improvements in a number of areas.

The book is, in some ways, the culmination of our efforts over a long period of time to understand, analyze and explain the basis, strategies and outcome of development plans and programs. The establishment of good governance remains a major challenge for the developing world as imperfections in, and the absence of, the appropriate tools of this desirable objective continue to place governments and citizens in a difficult position. An even bigger challenge seems to be the inability of developing countries to sustain the limited progress achieved through developmental efforts. The benefits of development are lost without a firm foundation to launch the next round of efforts. Thus a compilation on development governance is expected to shed light on the achievement of progress as well as ways to sustain and build on them.

There are numerous studies on development and governance, yet few make a serious effort to bring together the two critical concepts. Both are considered important, but the linkages between them are not made obvious. There are some overlaps between the elements of development and governance, and there is a need to weave them in an overarching framework in order to identify the way forward. Further, the existing studies often focus on specific aspects or geographical regions rather than encourage discussions on a conceptual level that could lead to productive deliberations. Therefore, it is useful to consider these concepts in the international context.

This book makes an attempt to fill the prominent gap in the literature by drawing upon the experience and expertise of scholars from a broad spectrum of specialization. Their views on the context of development and governance help understand the issues and problems with reference to a number of tools that could help establish "development governance" and sustain it. In-depth examinations of a number of development sectors add to the value of the book. The outcome of our efforts has been a compendium suitable for use by academics, public officials, policy makers, consultants and students of development. We hope this will generate more discussions on the critical issue of development governance, and contribute to the betterment of life of citizens in developing countries.

A number of people have helped make this book a reality. Jack Rabin, executive editor of the series, has provided encouragement, advice and help from the conception of the idea to the final preparation of the manuscript. The contributors to this volume deserve to be thanked first for their initiative, enthusiasm and commitment, and we are grateful for their input. One of our contributors, Professor Sanjaya Lall of Oxford University passed away during the final stages of the production process of this volume. The development studies community will miss the erudite ideas and thoughts of this eminent development economist. We would also like to register our gratitude to Russell Dekker for help in initiating the project, and Taylor & Francis for bringing it to fruition.

Finally, our sincere thanks go out to our families for their support and cooperation.

About the Editors

Habib Zafarullah teaches political science and public policy at the University of New England, Australia. He previously served as professor and chair of the Department of Public Administration at the University of Dhaka in Bangladesh. His expertise and research interests cover democratic governance, public policy, and development management with a focus on South and Southeast Asia. He has been associated with several international development agencies and non-governmental organizations as a consultant.

Dr. Zafarullah has published widely on political, administrative, and development issues. He has authored or edited several books including *Politics and Bureaucracy in a New Nation: Bangladesh* (1980), *Rural Development in Bangladesh* (1981), *The Decentralized Planning Process in Bangladesh* (1988), *Policy Issues in Bangladesh* (1994), *The Zia Episode in Bangladesh Politics* (1996), and *The Bureaucratic Ascendancy* (2005) and published numerous chapters in edited volumes and articles in refereed journals. He served as the editor of *Politics Administration and Change* for twenty-five years. He was also the regional editor (Asia) of the *Development Policy Newsletter*, published by the Policy Studies Organization, and has been on the editorial boards of *Public Organization Review and South Asia*.

Ahmed Shafiqul Huque teaches in the Department of Political Science at McMaster University. His research interests are in the areas of public policy and administration, governance, and development studies. He has served as consultant for several international agencies on development-related projects. Dr. Huque is a past vice president of the Hong Kong Public Administration Association and has served as the editor-in-chief of the journal *Public Administration and Policy* (1993–2005). He is a contributing editor for the on-line *Encyclopedia of Public Administration and Public Policy* (New York: Marcel Dekker).

Dr. Huque has published extensively on policy and administrative issues in developing countries and the problems and challenges of introducing reforms in transitional societies. His books include *Public Service in a Globalized World* (2004), *Managing Public Services* (2000), *The Civil Service in Hong Kong* (1998), *Social Policy in Hong Kong* (1997, translated in Chinese in 2002), *Public Administration in the Newly Industrializing Countries* (1996), *Development Through Decentralization in Bangladesh* (1994), *Paradoxes in Public Administration* (1990), and *Politics and Administration in Bangladesh* (1988).

Contributors

Senyo Adjibolosoo
Fermanian School of Business
Point Loma Nazarene
  University
San Diego, California, U.S.A.

C. J. Barrow
School of Environmental and
  Social Studies
University of Wales
Swansea, Wales, U.K.

Jo Beall
Development Studies Institute
  (DESTIN)
London School of Economics
London, U.K.

James Warner Björkman
Institute of Social Studies
The Hague
  and
Department of Public
Administration
Leiden University
Leiden, The Netherlands

Harry Blair
Department of Political
  Science
Yale University
New Haven, Connecticut, U.S.A.

Tim Bowyer
Centre for Development
  Studies
University of Wales
Swansea, Wales, U.K.

Derick W. Brinkerhoff
Research Triangle Institute
Washington, D.C., U.S.A.

Gerald E. Caiden
School of Policy, Planning, and
  Development
University of Southern California
Los Angeles, California, U.S.A.

Terrance Carroll
Department of Political Science
Brock University
St. Catharine's, Ontario, Canada

Anis Chowdhury
School of Economics and Finance
University of Western Sydney
Campbelltown, NSW, Australia

Gerard Clarke
Centre for Development Studies
University of Wales Swansea
Singleton Park, Swansea, U.K.

William D. Coleman
Department of Political Science
McMaster University
Hamilton, Ontario, Canada

Richard Common
The Business School
University of Hull
Hull, U.K.

Diana Conyers
Institute of Development Studies
University of Sussex
Brighton, U.K.

Andrea Cornwall
Institute of Development Studies
University of Sussex
Brighton, U.K.

Ali Farazmand
School of Public Administration
Florida Atlantic University
Ft. Lauderdale, Florida, U.S.A.

Shelley Feldman
Department of Development
    Sociology
Cornell University
Ithaca, New York, U.S.A.

Jean-Claude Garcia-Zamor
School of Policy and Management
Florida International University
Miami, Florida, U.S.A.

Des Gasper
Public Policy and Management
Institute of Social Studies
The Hague
The Netherlands

John Gaventa
Institute of Development Studies
University of Sussex
Brighton, U.K.

M. Shamsul Haque
Department of Political Science
National University of Singapore
Singapore

Niels Hermes
Faculty of Management and
    Organisation
University of Groningen
Groningen, The Netherlands

Peter Hills
Centre of Urban Planning and
    Environmental Management
The University of Hong Kong
Hong Kong, P. R. China

Ian Holliday
Faculty of Humanities and
    Social Sciences
City University of Hong Kong
Hong Kong, P. R. China

Kempe Ronald Hope, Sr.
Secretariat
United Nations
New York, New York, U.S.A.

Akhtar Hossain
Faculty of Business and Law
University of Newcastle
Callaghan, Australia

Ahmed Shafiqul Huque
Department of Political
  Science
McMaster University
Hamilton, Ontario, Canada

Michiyo Iwami
University of Warwick
Coventry, U.K.

R. B. Jain
Indian Institute of Public
  Administration
New Delhi, India

Michael Jennings
Centre for Development
  Studies
University of Wales
Swansea, Wales, U.K.

Donald E. Klingner
Graduate School of
  Public Affairs
University of Colorado at
  Colorado Springs
Colorado Springs, Colorado, U.S.A.

Sanjaya Lall
International Development
  Centre
Oxford University
Oxford, U.K.

Laurids S. Lauridsen
Department of Geography and
  International Development
  Studies
Roskilde University
Roskilde, Denmark

Adrian Leftwich
Department of Politics
University of York
York, U.K.

Robert Lensink
Faculty of Economics
University of Groningen
Groningen, The Netherlands

Ian Marsh
Research School of Social
  Sciences
The Australian National
  University
Canberra, Australia

Geoffrey Meads
University of Warwick
Coventry, U.K.

Kristen Nordhaug
Deparment of Geography and
  International Development
  Studies
Roskilde University
Roskilde, Denmark

Isabel Ortiz
Poverty Reduction Unit
Asian Development Bank
Manila, The Philippines

Jan Nederveen Pieterse
Sociology Department
University of Illinois
Urbana, Illinois, U.S.A.

Joanna R. Quinn
Department of Political Science
The University of
  Western Ontario
London, Ontario, Canada

Dennis A. Rondinelli
Kenan-Flagler Business School
University of North Carolina
Chapel Hill, North Carolina, U.S.A.

Susan Rose-Ackerman
Law School and Department of
    Political Science
Yale University
New Haven, Connecticut, U.S.A.

Alan Thomas
Centre for Development Studies
University of Wales
Swansea, Wales, U.K.

Mark Turner
School of Business and
    Government
University of Canberra
Canberra, Australia

Roger Wettenhall
Centre for Research in Public
    Sector Management
University of Canberra
Canberra, Australia

Joanna S. Wheeler
Development Research Centre on
    Citizenship, Participation, and
    Accountability
Institute of Development Studies
University of Sussex
Brighton, U.K.

Habib Zafarullah
School of Social Science
University of New England
Armidale, Australia

Table of Contents

GOVERNANCE AND DEVELOPMENT: CONTEXTUAL ISSUES

I

Chapter 1

Introduction: Challenges of Governing Development

Ahmed Shafiqul Huque and Habib Zafarullah

CONTENTS

I. Introduction

The literature on social sciences in general, and public policy and administration in particular, is replete with long lists of unattained objectives and failures of government policies and programs. Efforts aimed at correcting faults in the system, redressing grievances, and improving conditions often fail to make the desired impact. Several factors can be attributed to such outcomes. The state may not have the capacity to identify problems accurately and adopt the best method for dealing with them; the selected solutions may not be suitable for particular social and political systems; the priorities may be misleading; policies may be inappropriate; or the governmental framework in which the system operates may not be consistent with the adopted strategies. Many of these cases of failure can be related to countries which have been going through the process of "development."

Development has remained one of the most slippery concepts in social sciences for decades, and is yet to be defined precisely. It has been defined in terms of rationalization (Sutton, 1961), modernization (Eisenstadt, 1963), and socio-economic progress (Esman, 1966). Earlier studies sought to view any positive change as development, and bundled "economic" (increasing per capita income or gross national product) and "political" (enhanced ability to make decisions involving value choices and legitimize changing power relationships) aspects together (Riggs, 1966). A variety of approaches to development were tried in many countries across the world since the conclusion of the Second World War, but instances of system failure and nonachievement of these efforts remain alarmingly high. Haque (1999: 157) summarized the overall impact of development efforts, and stated that it has various "adverse implications, including the perpetuation of academic hegemony, legitimation of socio-economic domination, erosion of indigenous culture and identity, and destruction of environment and ecology."

The crises of development prompted the rethinking over existing knowledge and reassessment of development programs and priorities. Meanwhile, major changes were taking place at two levels. At the state level, governments came under pressure to deal with the problems that remained unresolved due to ineffective development programs and also to bring about improvements in a wide range of areas. At the international level, new ideas and strategies acquired prominence as the world underwent significant changes since the mid-20th century. A large number of countries achieved or were granted independence and struggled to adopt appropriate strategies and ideologies for organizing governmental activities and pursuing the goals of development.

Approaches to development were influenced by a number of factors. The emergence of major powers led to the division of the world into distinct camps. In their efforts to win over the loyalty of new and weaker states, the major powers propagated the virtues of capitalist or socialist models of development, giving rise to tension and debates over the suitability of a decentralized model as opposed to the benefits of central planning.

The capitalist approach prevailed in most areas, thanks to the support from a number of international agencies created for this purpose. The United Nations and World Bank played a major role in propagating a uniform approach to development, and the results were far from impressive. Within a few decades, the futility of pursuing the goals of development in isolation from the indigenous economic, cultural, social, and environmental conditions began to be recognized. This prompted debates and discussions regarding the premises, approaches, strategies, and outcomes of development.

II. Governance as Panacea

Rhodes (1997: 15) claimed that governance generally refers to "a new process of governing." Despite the ambiguity over the use of the term "governance" and its essential features, it has entered the discourse of Western political science and has permeated discussions of a new role for political and social institutions in a more fragmentary, globalized world. The notion of governance appeared in the late 1980s when cracks began to appear in the consensus on a reduced role for the government in the economy, achieved mainly by privatization. In other words, "governance" stands between state and market in the organization of economic, political, and social life. Governance can thus be understood as the exercise of democratic government, which guarantees the dominance of the rules of economics over those of politics (Frischtak, 1994). In this sense, governance implies the realization of a much wider range of "desired outcomes" than those provided by the state or traditional development programs.

Good governance has emerged as perhaps the most desired value among governments in recent years. Over the past two decades, governance has gradually established itself in the mainstream study of public policy and administration as well as politics. Many governments, international agencies, and researchers and scholars are in agreement that the development of good governance is essential for eliminating a range of problems related to public administration, policy and the community. The qualifying word "good" appears redundant since "governance" is expected to connote a collection of features that contribute to a positive finale. The concept of governance attained ready acceptance across the developing world, mainly due to the unsuccessful attempts to achieve development by following the traditional models.

Accountability, efficiency, equity, rule of law, transparency, and a number of similar features are the hallmarks of governance, but earlier efforts at development often focused on different aspects. Traditionally, the objectives of development were limited to nation-building and socio-economic progress (Esman, 1966: 59). Understandably, the attempts at development concentrated on the alleviation of poverty and disparity, the provision of facilities for improving the quality of life, and facilitating access to the services provided by the state. Over the years, emphasis has changed, priorities rearranged, and several new dimensions of development have been identified. Consequently, human and social capital have acquired importance in the development literature, and it has been acknowledged that considerable improvements are required to allow citizens to participate in the political process and perform their duties.

Governance has a critical role to play in the process of development and is required as an essential tool in striking a balance between the diminishing role of governments and the threat of an increasingly powerful private sector. This is of great importance in the developing world where many governments appear to have failed in performing their duties, and major changes were considered necessary for arranging new patterns of inter-actions between the government and citizens. The need for improving governance has received increased attention in view of a high level of corruption and authoritarian rule in many countries. The key elements of governance — constitutionalism and rule of law, decentralization and participation, transparency and accountability, predictability and policy consensus, equity and inclusiveness, and efficiency and effectiveness — encompass a comprehensive set of values that could serve as the guiding principles for developing countries. These emerge as critical factors to sustain the benefits achieved through socio-economic progress. Therefore, states must proceed to attain a sound system of governance in order to sustain the benefits of development.

III. Development Governance

As is the case with the concept of development, "governance has been var-iously defined as the exercise of authority or the distribution of power. In essence it is related to the notions of order and decision making" (Valaskakis, 2001: 46). Uniting the concepts of "development" and "govern-ance" is a difficult yet essential task. In the past, development was viewed as a combination of concrete goals that were measurable with reference to a set of arbitrarily determined standards. These criteria were quite simplistic in nature and would reflect a misleading picture with reference to the amount of wealth, rate of employment, percentage of literacy, infrastruc-tural facilities, and similar items. The statistics could appear quite impress-ive, yet they would disclose nothing about the real state of affairs in a country. In most cases, a small privileged group exercised control over the resources and key institutions, while the vast majority of citizens were deprived of all the benefits of state and developmental activities. Thus, the key objectives of development remained unattained, while superficial progress was claimed by the elite who continued to be the main beneficiaries and exercised effective control over the country.

Several factors contributed to the skewed outcome of developmental efforts in most countries. State power was often captured through unconstitutional means and retained through authoritarian methods. This, in effect, disenfranchised a large number of citizens who had no means of participating in the process. The regimes were preserved through dispensation of favors to selected groups and individuals, corruption and repression, thus negating the prospect of an effective opposition that is crucial for providing checks and balances. The civil society was relegated to the background and the governmental system deprived of inputs from significant groups and stakeholders.

In order to sustain and effectively distribute the benefits obtained from various programs of economic, political and social development, there is no alternative to the following activities identified in an OECD report: raising awareness and making commitments; developing coherent approaches and responses throughout the government machinery; and adopting a holistic — as opposed to sectoral — approach to policies (OECD, 2002: 11–21). In addition, a number of basic reforms are required to ensure an appropriate framework within which development efforts can be undertaken.

IV. Plan of the Book

This book undertakes a thorough examination of "governance" in light of its role in, and relevance to, "development," and highlights the idea of "development governance." There is a need to develop the idea by combining the concepts of "democratic governance," "development administration," and "sustainable development." In the process, the book examines the role of the "developmental" state, political institutionalization and democratization, human rights, civil society and social capital, human development, globalization, policy transfers, administrative reform, capacity building, development planning and implementation, integrity management, gender, and similar other issues as well as explores selected development sectors. This is expected to enlighten the readers on the ongoing debates and deliberations in governance and development issues.

The book is divided into four parts. The first part deals with a number of contextual issues in development and governance. Zafarullah and Huque provide an explanation of the background, evolution and current state of the yet unformulated concept of development governance. Leftwich finds the prospects of adopting the "developmental state" model for newly developing countries feasible, although they will always need state involvement to stay on course. Coleman offers a framework for analyzing the relationship between globalization and development and for trying to determine the impacts of globalization on states seeking to advance economic and social development and concludes that it will be an extremely difficult undertaking. Pieterse considers the growing impacts of neoliberal policies and details the economic and political shift that has taken place. Marsh explores the link between economic and democratic development with reference to the experience of seven states in Asia and finds that Western templates of democratic development are not applicable there. Adjibolosoo makes his case for improving the quality of the human factor in development in the context of democratic development governance and examines the attributes of both the positive and negative climate of governance and shows how the human factor can be engineered for better results. Quinn elaborates on the concept of human rights from various perspectives and the application of the structures of governance to this critical area. Hermes and Lensink seek to draw lessons from the outcomes of empirical research and examine the effectiveness of aid and argue that, the aid community should reassess their stance and policies toward aid-recipients. Haque provides a general overview of the sustainable development paradigm and applies various measures of governance in analyzing sustainable development in Southeast Asia. The final chapter in this part by Nordhaug explores the parameters of the development state in the context of East Asia and, drawing from the experience of the financial crisis of the late 1990s, considers the debate on the decline of the development state.

Part Two concentrates on the issues and problems encountered in operationalizing development governance. Ortiz examines several issues relating to poverty alleviation and argues for a multidimensional approach by national governments and international agencies to effectively contain the problem. Carroll emphasizes the importance of the role to be played by civil society in development, and proposes various methods for strengthening it. Chowdhury focuses on macroeconomic management and analyzes the economic determinants of growth. He highlights the need for adopting balanced fiscal and monetary policies to prevent countries from falling into a "stabilization trap" as well as to protect them from economic dangers. Brinkerhoff presents accountability as another critical component of governance and underscores the need for appropriate structures and rules that support it. Rose-Ackerman's chapter evaluates the causes and consequences of corruption and their relevance to governance and suggests appropriate measures to curb the malaise. On a similar subject, Caiden cautions the reader of the flaws in the current anticorruption campaigns around the world and argues for a more realistic approach to deal with this problem.

Garcia-Zamor explores the intricate relationship between governance and administrative ethics using the former East German experience as a case, and concludes that it could take quite a bit of time for the bureaucracy to fully adopt Western norms and values. Taking health as the focus of his study, Bowyer accents the significance of social capital as an effective mechanism to fight the dilemmas of ill-health in developing nations. Wheeler elaborates on the various ways in which gender can play an important role in governance for development and argues for substantive citizenship since ignoring the issue may lead to an incomplete approach.

The third part of the book takes a look at various tools of development governance. Decentralization has been at the centre of debates for several decades, and Rondinelli explores the perceived and actual benefits of this strategy in supporting economic and political development and considers the conditions necessary for its success. Cornwall and Gaventa focus on participation as a tool and examine the challenges encountered in extending its scope and reach in governance which can be overcome by more deliberation and consultation and participatory rights assessment. NGOs are undoubtedly an essential tool of governance. Clarke and Thomas provide an overarching view of non-governmental development organizations from the perspective of civil society and governance. They identify challenges and dilemmas these entities face and project future scenarios for them. Feldman reports and analyzes the shifting role of NGOs and emphasizes the values outlined in an alternative development paradigm and identifies key interests, contradictions and tensions. Small funds at the microlevel can help overcome some of the problems associated with large financial grants and Beal considers this as an effective tool for development agencies to reach the poor and aid local governance. It helps to prevent the delay experienced in anticipation of trickling down of resources and enhance the level of accountability.

Privatization may be a contemporary issue in governance, but Wettenhall traces its historical dimensions and the variations they presented to place the ongoing phenomenon in perspective and establishes the practicalities of privatization from current initiatives in developing countries and prescriptions from developing agencies. With evidence from an Asian case, Hills examines the concept of governance *vis-à-vis* environmental planning and the design and implementation of policies for sustainable development and highlights the implications of social and institutional transformations for the transition to new modes of environmental governance. Holliday explores the potential of new technology in reviewing the state of e-government and some plans and documents to draw attention to the need for adapting e-government to the needs and capacities of the user community for it to be effective. The bureaucracy occupies a central position in the development literature owing to the key position it occupies

in developing countries. Jain examines the role of this institution and recommends ethical sensitivity and creative intelligence in order to serve
public interest for achieving good governance. Related to this subject is
public sector reforms, and Farazmand takes a hard look at the trends and
impact of major administrative reform attempts across the developing
world. He is concerned at the emergence of the new "welfare-corporate
state" and highlights a number of implications that appear to forecast a
return to a rigid and uniform pattern of administrative arrangements in the
public sector, and hints at several options for dealing with the challenges.
With reference to public service reform, Caiden dissects the problem
from a discursive standpoint. Taking lessons from past reform movements,
he points to the fact that there is no universal recipe for reform and only a
pragmatic approach is expected to provide effective results.

Developing the capacity of institutions and people is another important
element of development governance. Apart from public managers who contribute to policy formulation, implementation, and evaluation, those directly
involved with development in the field are also significant. Hope reviews
the conceptual dimension of capacity development, establishes its objectives and principles and calls for designing sustainable capacity development initiatives. Jennings embarks on an evaluation of development
processes during the 20th century. He raises the critical issue of the
integration of developing regions, but finds little evidence of substantial
progress. Judging the experience of Africa, Conyers investigates the
causes of failure of interventions and concludes that radical changes are
required in development management. Turner considers development
planning as an important development management tool and analyzes its
strategic aspects. Focusing on project planning and its flaws, he discusses
alternative approaches. Klingner regards program implementation as
another key area in development governance and emphasizes clarification
of concepts, understanding of issues, and specific sector applications. He
urges capacity building and recognizes factors such as natural and social
capital. Policies being an integral part of development governance, a
sound system of evaluation is critical. Gasper examines some methods of
policy evaluation that are prominent in developing countries and finds
that interactions between markets and their social, political, and natural
environments; an appropriate political infrastructure; and the inclusion of
all citizens are vital for the fruition of this exercise. Learning from the
experience of other countries can be extremely valuable in areas of policy
evaluation and in policy formulation and implementation, particularly for
countries with little or limited success to build upon. Common explores
the popularity of the idea of policy learning, and uses the U.K. as an
example to argue that it can only be effective if the institutional context is
fully understood.

In the final part, the book moves on to some selected development sectors to consider the state of governance. Each of these sectors contributes to economic growth and provides inputs to social development. Lall focuses on the industry sector and shows the impact of technological change and globalization on industrial structures and production and argues for a cautious approach to the designing of industrial policies. Lauridsen provides the rationale for adopting appropriate institutional measures for an adequate technological policy that would support advanced and competitive industrial structures. Barrow's examination of water resource management recognizes the increasing demand for water and makes some concrete suggestions for overcoming hindrances emanating from poor management. Hossain reviews a number of agricultural policies and issues in Asia to arrive at some policy lessons in view of contemporary issues and challenges. Bjorkman discusses health policy with reference to the process of relevant actors and their role in governance. His suggestions for overcoming health inequalities consequential of socio-economic structures includes, developing appropriate health policies and implementing them effectively. Meads and Iwami draw upon their fieldwork in 20 countries to examine the modernization of health care systems and find them to be fragmented and dysfunctional. They emphasize the quality of collaboration and framework of local governance for harmonizing the available resources. Many countries have pursued the goal of rural development over decades, and it is considered one of the core programs essential for development. Blair recollects the themes of rural development and draws attention to the promises and pitfalls encountered in attaining good governance.

References

Eisenstadt, S.N., Bureaucracy and political development, in *Bureaucracy and Political Development*, LaPalombara, J., Ed., Princeton University Press, Princeton, NJ, 1963, pp. 96–119.

Esman, M.J., The politics of development administration, in *Approaches to Development: Politics, Administration and Change*, Montgomery, J.D. and Siffin, W.J., Eds., McGraw-Hill, New York, 1966, pp. 59–65.

Frischtak, L., *Governance Capacity and Economic Reform in Developing Countries*, The World Bank, Washington, DC, 1994.

Haque, M.S., *Restructuring Development Theories and Policies: A Critical Study*, State University of New York Press, Albany, NY, 1999.

OECD, *Governance for Sustainable Development: Five OECD Case Studies*, OECD, Paris, 2002.

Rhodes, R., *Understanding Governance*, Open University Press, Buckingham, 1997.

Riggs, F.W., Administrative development: an elusive concept, in *Approaches to Development: Politics, Administration and Change*, Montgomery, J.D. and Siffin, W.J., Eds., McGraw-Hill, New York, 1966, pp. 225–255.

Sutton, F.X., Planning and rationality in the newly independent states of Africa, *Econ. Develop. Cult. Change*, 10, 44, 1961.

Valaskakis, K., Long-term trends in global governance: from "Westphalia" to "Seattle", in *Governance in the 21st Century*, OECD, Paris, 2001.

Chapter 2

Understanding Development Governance: Concepts, Institutions, and Processes

Habib Zafarullah and Ahmed Shafiqul Huque

CONTENTS

I. Introduction

The decolonized developing nations in Asia, Africa, and Latin America have been struggling since the end of World War II to overcome the scourge of poverty and human misery and to lift living standards to reasonable and satisfactory levels. Post-colonial development strategies generally faltered in attacking poverty and were only partly productive in alleviating social malaise. For several decades, development was equated with economic growth measured purely in terms of economic variables such as GDP, per capita income, rate of investments, or industrial productivity, yet the masses of the poor or the impoverished rural areas were virtually excluded from the benefits that flowed from such piecemeal economic growth. The lacuna between the rich and the poor nations widened as the latter fell prey to the dynamics of the rapidly emerging "integrated" global economic system and the accumulating burden of debt caused by massive borrowing for financing welfare and development programs, enormous trade deficits, plummeting foreign exchange reserves, commodity price falls, and so on.

On the contrary, inappropriate state policies, deprioritization of key sectors, cost overruns and inefficient management of the public sector, and political and bureaucratic corruption further intensified the financial woes of the developing countries (DCs). The increased dependency of the DCs on the affluent nations hindered their attempts to attain development goals. This enlarged the disparity between the two groups of nations and further reinforced the dependency syndrome.

On a different level, the political leadership in many DCs and least developed countries, sometimes unsure of the correct route to development, has remained bewildered by conflicting approaches or strategies pursued elsewhere (perhaps with some success) and generally has had to rely on the advice of governments in the advanced countries or the international development/funding community for directions. However, such counsel has not always been rewarding and is often bereft of altruism. The adopted approaches or models of development, based on western precepts, practices, and experiences, often seemed incompatible with local needs or value systems and generated mixed results. In addition, development aid from overseas is, rarely if ever, separated from political and other conditionalities. Apparently, these bite through a recipient nations' "sovereignty" as they accede to the policy dictates of lenders and comply with their demands for radical political and economic restructuring with unwarranted social costs. Nonetheless, such aid can also impact positively insofar as it fosters democratic development, promotes human rights, and builds the capacity of state institutions to perform efficiently.

On pragmatic grounds, DCs cannot remain isolated from mainstream global trends, insulate themselves from external shocks, or make social and economic progress without external support in an increasingly changing and interdependent world. Undeniably, the context of development for the southern or developing nations or those in transition has been rapidly changing with the incursion of neoliberal ideas and approaches, the exploits of market-based economic systems, the rise of regional cooperation, the globalization of culture and democracy, the universalization of human rights, and the push for a nondirigiste state and decentralized governance.

In this shifting scenario, a broad consensus among social scientists, development practitioners, and funding agencies has evolved over the past few decades. This places a premium on sound policies based on rational choices factored by feasibility, appropriateness, and efficiency, and has been developed by democratic political institutions with the support of a responsible and accountable public bureaucracy in conjunction with civil society and other stakeholders. This complements the general ethos of "good governance," which in recent times has become the acknowledged *mantra* in development praxis and the basis of external aid and support policies of western governments, the United Nations agencies, and international lending institutions.

Global bodies such as the World Bank, the International Monetary Fund, the World Trade Organization (WTO), and the various regional development banks (Asian Development Bank [ADB], African Development Bank [AfDB], and Inter-American Development Bank [IDB]) as well as national funding agencies based in the northern hemisphere have proposed several policy ideas and prescriptions relating to development goals and the methods and instruments of achieving them. However, the application of pure management-based techniques in the allocation of resources and in planning, implementing, and administering development activities in the DCs have provided only partial results in the past.

Bounded by the notion of a value-free, scientific and apolitical administration, the framework of "development administration," constructed and refined by Western intellectuals and practitioners, was circumscribed by bureaucratic or technical determinants and largely delinked from *realpolitik* or from societal imperatives (Dwivedi, 1994: 10–20). Even after its metamorphosis into "development management," which has implanted best practices in managing development and welfare and redefined the policy–administration nexus, the development policy process and the execution of development programs remain to be fully embedded into the holistic governance framework. We argue that the technical aspects of managing development cannot be discrete from social–political realities and moral issues impinging upon governance. The development policy cycle and the management of development programs must be apportioned an important slot within the governance framework and intricately linked to social–cultural, political, legal, economic, and technological issues if development has to have any positive impact upon society and liberate the people from social and economic indigence.

The purpose of this chapter is to delineate a framework of "development governance" by conjoining the architecture of governance to the development management paradigm. On the basis of current knowledge and practice, we attempt to find the correlation between various elements of governance and development management, how they influence and interact with one another, mainly in conjunction with other factors, to produce effective results. A coherent structure of development governance can be expected to play a strategic part in interconnecting several social and economic sectors that are critical in a DC's strides towards the goals of development as well as creating relationships between and among a range of instruments (social, economic, political, etc.) to facilitate the attainment of goals.

II. Approaches to Development

The dominant development paradigm until the end of the 1960s was influenced by Western thinking of the role of state and approaches to development. The traditional view was influenced by a positive Western vision of the less developed or developing nations' capacity to tread on the same path as advanced countries in reaching the desired levels of development by utilizing imported strategies, methods, and tools with little cognizance of local circumstances. The focus was on "modernization," political and economic, postulated and prescribed by industrialized countries of the West and the international development community (IDC) and essentially thrust upon underdeveloped economies. The assumption was that both groups of countries shared common policies and interests and that social change was predictable and easily induced by eclectic ideas and practices (Dwivedi and Nef, 1982: 60). A belief in "the universality and inevitability of the spread of Western values and practices such as instrumental rationality, secularism, individualism, and science-based enlightenment" (Esman, 1988: 126) crept into development thinking and infiltrated the mindset and predilections of political and administrative elites in the developing world and infused in them a sense of blind optimism about the success of derived development strategies for their countries.

The dependence of poor countries on Western donors became an inevitable and a routine matter; overseas aid in various forms and arrangements, in cash or kind, was eagerly sought after by recipient countries. Such aid, however, was motivated by political motives or compulsions. The West's fear of the spread of communism in the impoverished countries increased its drive to enlarge the quantum of aid. For the recipient countries, this exponentially increased the burden of debt thereby debilitating efforts in alleviating poverty among the majority of their populations or advancing their social and economic status.

In the 1950s and 1960s, development came to be equated with economic growth; industrialization, import substitution, and urbanization became the preferred route to economic success. For the DCs, the linear-stages approach influenced by Rostow's stages of economic growth and the Harrod–Domar growth model became the acknowledged development strategy from the Western standpoint. A strategy of rapid economic growth or "capital fundamentalism" emphasized investment, foreign aid, and savings that would provide a "trickle down" effect and was expected to relieve the common people from poverty. This, however, remained an implausible proposition as abject poverty continued to grip the developing world and the gap between the rich and poor nations widened alarmingly (Lewellen, 1995: 59). Massive transfer of capital and technical assistance to the DCs generally proved counterproductive for the ordinary citizens.

Since the 1970s, development discourses and development practices began changing, with several shifts often random and overlapping. The modernization thesis of the 1960s, emphasizing borrowing of extraneous political and economic principles and putting them into practice, gradually lost its relevance because of endogenous social–cultural factors. The prime focus moved towards internal mechanisms of structural change and greater dependency on Western governments and international donors for development support. Domestic polices favored diversity in urban-based industrialization and emphasized on a manufacturing and service economy rather than ameliorating traditional agricultural practices for providing direct benefits to the rural sector and to a major portion of the poor population. The offshoot of such a strategy was population shift to the urban areas, a swift transformation of production modes, and changes in the composition of consumer demands (Ray, 1998: Chapters 2–4; Rapley, 2002; Todaro and Smith, 2002: Chapters 3 and 4; Chang, 2003: 21–40).

The dependence models of development highlight the unequal relationship of the DCs with countries in the West — a relationship of exploitation of the former by the latter (Cohen, 1973). Inappropriate policies, based on external expertise, that are insensitive to local factors, generally turned out to be counterproductive and sustained the pattern of underdevelopment in a dichotomous social–political environment that fostered the traditional–modern, rich–poor, healthy–diseased, educated–illiterate, and privileged–disadvantaged divide. Bureaucratic collectivism was often seen as a development alternative, but this simply contravened people's enterprise and bottom–up initiatives in development wherever they were attempted. Egalitarian approaches to counter mal-development, such as poverty alleviation, generating diversified employment opportunities, and reducing income inequalities, were advanced by the dependence theorists. However, before their ideas could be fully tested or provide benefits to the people, the push for neoliberal, free market-based open economics began to penetrate the South and the state gradually began to roll back.

Neoliberalism, which became the catch phrase in development discourse from the 1980s, "highlights freedom, including freedom from responsibility, and derives welfare from individual rationality ... [and is] based on market failure" (Gaspar et al., 2003: 589). Full-fledged state intervention in economic as well as social matters is an aberration in this development paradigm, which underscores the diminishing role of the public sector in managing development and prescribes market-led outward development strategies. Among an array of economic measures, the thrust is specifically on financial liberalization, deregulation, withdrawal of capital controls, privatization of state enterprises, and corporatization of public utilities (Jilberto and Mommen, 1996; Savin and Savas, 2000; Kessides, 2003; for Korea's experience, see Jwa and Chwa, 2001). Complementing public choice theory, the proponents of neoliberalism view the state, its bureaucratic apparatus, and its relationship with citizens as culpable because, as they argue, providers of public services (politicians and civil servants) abuse their positions to maximize their self-interest and recipients (private bodies and citizens) apply inordinate influence on public personnel to obtain undue benefits. State caprice is considered to be the root cause of misgovernment and worthy of being restrained; shrinking state control and jurisdiction over development initiatives are seen as the way out by neoliberal advocates.

A clear outcome of neoliberalism in the DCs "has been the radical weakening of the state, which has been increasingly subordinated to the interests of the dominant classes and has relinquished important areas of national sovereignty to the imperial superpower, the big transnational bourgeoisie, and its 'institutional' guards: the IMF, the World Bank" (Boron, 1996: 309). These multilateral bodies along with other aid and lending institutions have adopted the neoliberal dogma complemented by the "Washington consensus" (Williamson, 1990) as the basis for governance structures and practices insofar as they relate to development policy formulation, implementation, administration, and appraisal. Accordingly, with the infusion of neoliberalism into the developing world, there have been significant shifts in national economic management as the state is forced to redefine its role in development.

The state is hard pressed to not only release its firm grip on economic management but also to partly relinquish its direct involvement in social/ human development matters. The goals of development and the indicators of acceptable performance have also changed. Neoliberal advocates no longer acknowledged centralized planning as the panacea for economic problems or the preferred route to development. Apparently, "stronger, more effective institutions were urgently needed to complement macroeconomic policy changes" in those DCs and transitional economies embracing the new approach to development (Naim, 2000).

The economic theories of development generally underscore the importance of instruments and yardsticks to measure economic growth. The focus has invariably been on structural/institutional issues and on policies targeting monetary and fiscal sectors. The basic assumption was that the common people would indirectly benefit from the gains of economic growth and problems would be solved by default. Even the "redistribution from growth" alternative paid little attention to the problems directly associated with the people — such as poverty, malnutrition and health hazards, unemployment, inadequate education facilities, inhospitable habitats, social discrimination, degrading environment, and so on (Seers, 1969; Goulet, 1971; Brinkman, 1995). Development, however, is "the movement upward of the entire social system" including in its fold non-economic components directly relevant to society (Myrdal, 1974: 729). The wholeness of development obviously incorporates cultural variables, which are essential in understanding the nature and pattern of a society's pursuit for advancement.

Thus, it is important to view development as inevitably culture-bound and therefore intricately linked to the society where it is pursued. All western models of development including those sympathetic toward the poorer nations have been intrinsically "westrocentric" or based on European and Western views of development (Cooper, 1979: 247) that barely recognize historical, social, political, economic, and other ground realities prevailing there (Apter, 1987: 26). Undeniably, the historical process through which the West gained social and economic progress cannot be replicated in the Third World due to considerable differences they represent in social, political, economic, and behavioral terms (Haque, 1999: 141). This is also true for the way they are governed.

The contextualization of development governance is therefore central in judging the appropriateness of development strategies and the instruments for realizing them. Neither theoretical models identified above provide precise solutions to the problems of social–economic backwardness of the developing societies or the east European countries in transition. On the other hand, elements of each of these models pertinent to requirements of these countries can balance deficiencies and provide a more appropriate framework to attack poverty and social deprivation. The classical and neo-classical theories, interventionist strategies, and neoliberal approaches were/are fundamentally geared toward economic growth and mainly prof-fered economic determinants and instruments to attain development. The need for refining, synthesizing, and extending them in the typical Third World situation thus becomes essential and this is why notions of human development become so profoundly significant. Indeed, there are strong arguments highlighting the human side of development and the need to harness human potential for the composite well being of individuals.

III. Human Development

The dependency theorists identified social and economic differences between the nations of the North and South and proposed remedies for nar-rowing the gap through economic strategies. However, similar differences exist within nations and need to be addressed. Benefits of lop-sided devel-opment resulting from strategies of the economic kind have normally reached the affluent classes, which they have utilized to advance on the social scale leaving the poor to languish in worsening poverty. Access to education, healthcare, housing, information, technology, and so on has been easier for the economically well-off while the poor, denied of these, has also had to bear the brunt of social instability, environmental hazards, public bads,[1] and other forms of reversals (UNDP, 1998). Yet, the socially and economically disadvantaged people are worthy of not only enjoying the fruits of development but also participating in and contributing to the process of development. The "right to development" thesis evolved from the "Universal Declaration of Human Rights" and won the overwhelming support of the DCs that were at the receiving end of the negative impact of economic development on human conditions. The logic for such a right was premised on ethical and legal factors. It was argued that "development is the condition of all social life, the international duty of solidarity, the duty of reparation for colonial and neocolonial exploitation, increasing moral interdependence, economic interdependence, and the cause of world peace, which is threatened by underdevelopment" (quoted in Nanda, 1993: 43). While this view highlighted the plight of the developing/transitional countries *vis-à-vis* the role and responsibility of the international community and especially the developed nations, by the early 1990s, the human element came to be recognized as critically significant in the development process within nations. The UN advanced the notions of access, participation, fair share, equity, and group solidarity in development. It asserted:

> The right to development is the right of individuals, groups and peoples to participate in, contribute to, and enjoy continuous economic, social, cultural and political development, in which all human rights and fundamental freedoms can be fully realized. This includes the right to effective participation in all aspects of development and at all stages of the decision-making process; the right to equal opportunity and access to resources; the right to fair distribution of the benefits of development; the right to respect for civil, political, economic, social and cultural rights, and the right to an international environment in which all these rights can be fully realized (UN Document E/CN.4/1990/9/ Rev. 1, 26 September, 1990, 42, paragraph 143, quoted in Nanda, 1993: 258).

The United Nations Development Programme (UNDP) made a more concrete move to bring this undeniable right to the focal point of development discourse by releasing its first "human development" report in 1990. People were repositioned in the centre of development to enable them to enhance their capabilities within the gamut of freedom and rights. As Sen argued, "Economic growth cannot be sensibly treated as an end in itself. Development has to be more concerned with enhancing the lives we lead and the freedoms we enjoy" (Sen, 2000: 14). A distinction emerged in development parlance — between economic growth, which now came to be viewed as an *instrument*, and human prosperity as the *target* of development. Both human development and economic growth being integral to all-round development, balance, association, and even fusion between social and economic programs are essential. Undue emphasis on economic growth (a general tenor of the past) produced adverse impact on the people, communities and the environment, and thereby obviated human progress. Only appropriate strategies reconciling the instrument with the target can serve worthy purposes. The emphasis ought to be upon the "structure and quality" of economic growth rather than a set of impressive figures to complement human progress (UNDP, 1996: 1). Subsequently, a new shibboleth — "human development" entered the development lexicon and became the rallying point for those who decried the economic-only strategies. It is, nonetheless, not a novel concept as ideas of "human good," justice and people's prosperity have been in existence since ancient times.

Human development entails two complementary dimensions — one deals with "the *process* of widening people's choices" and the other with "the *level* of their achieved well-being" (UNDP, 1990: 10, emphasis in original). Distinguishing but not entirety dissociating the concept from other relevant development approaches,[2] the concept (UNDP, 1990: 11) accents the "expansion and use of human capabilities" within the framework of production and distribution cogently theorized by Sen (1985). Thus human development embodies three principal targets — *longevity* through a healthy life, *knowledge* through organized education, and a decent *living standard* through access to resources and services. Complementing these goals is an array of social, political, and economic freedoms and opportunities for enhancing creativity and productivity to enjoy "personal self-respect and guaranteed human rights" (UNDP, 1996: 10). Obviously, to realize these goals a structure and environment of democratic governance is *de rigueur.*

IV. Donor Strategies for Development

Several international funding and development agencies have proposed paradigms of development that take account of contemporary ideas and common problems and needs of developing and transitional countries. A proposal of the World Bank — the "comprehensive development framework" or CDF is designed to stimulate development from within by entrusting the responsibility of attacking poverty and undertaking social development programs by these countries themselves rather than, in the Bank's view, forever depending upon external support. The notion of ownership, the involvement of civil society, and the need to build social capital and use it as an instrument of social–economic development are tied to this framework. The principal objectives of CDF are: "to sharpen the focus on the major goals of development, to highlight the integrated nature of policy-making, to emphasize the institutional processes required to sustain development, and to coordinate development efforts" (World Bank, 1999a: 3). The World Bank also addresses the problem of ownership by encouraging DCs to prepare long-term strategies toward social–economic development using the CDF as an exemplar rather than as an absolute blueprint for change.[3] Thus emerged a new development plan mechanism — the Poverty Reduction Strategy Papers (PRSP), which in many countries replaced the time-honored "5-year plans." The Bank's proposal that these PRSPs "should be country-driven, be developed transparently with broad participation of elected institutions, stakeholders including civil society, key donors, and regional development banks" appears to have been enthusiastically received by country governments as until mid-2004 nearly 50 countries have adopted the CDF as the basis for their PRSPs and many are about to do so. Nonetheless, while the WB has proclaimed its desire to relinquish its influence on DC policy making, it expects the PSRPs to "have a clear link with the agreed international development goals — principles that are embedded in the Comprehensive Development Framework" (World Bank, 1999b). Apart from the World Bank, other regional lending institutions also have their own schemas for specific development sectors, which they insist should be pursued. Thus, with major funding for development programs and projects coming from the international lending agencies, national governments cannot but conform to external directives. Herein rests the crux of the dilemma surrounding policy ownership.

The poverty reduction strategies advanced by the ADB, the AfDB, and the IDB are basically similar. The ADB emphasizes:

- Pro-poor — sustainable economic growth to reduce poverty by generating income among the poor and fostering equitable development with, and for, the poor.
- Social development — ensuring comprehensive social protection and providing access to basic necessities — such as education, primary health care, and water and sanitation; and promoting social institutions and the social capital of vulnerable groups.
- Good governance — public policies that encourage the inclusion of the poor and other vulnerable groups in the development process. This involves pro-poor public expenditures, social services that are nearer to the users and have more relevance for the poor, policies that generate equity and access to socio-economic assets, and enhanced social relations — including gender equity and the improved status of women (ADB, 2000).

Given the unique conditions of the African continent, the AfDB emphasizes infrastructure building, agriculture, and rural development as strategic areas for tackling the problems of inequity and poverty. Indeed, the improvement of access to productive assets, technology, information, and social services (such as health and education) would create opportunities for the poor. Accelerated and sustainable economic growth can come about through the development of the private sector as a complementing force to public sector initiatives. Clearly, the components of good governance need to be embedded within the state framework (AfDB, 2003).

The IDB, like its counterparts in Asia and Africa, prioritizes income-earning opportunities for the poor as a key to total development. Hence, the emphasis is on agriculture and micro-enterprises as well as infrastructure development and export-led manufacturing using labor-intensive technology. Additionally, to augment human capital emphasis is placed on improving education and health standards, widening the web of social investment and social safety, and mainstreaming women and indigenous groups into the development process (IDB, 1997).

Clearly, these institutions underscore the imperative to adopt the multi-sectoral approach to addressing developmental issues and problems and the several sets of strategies they advance complement the Millennium Development Goals (MDGs) set forth by the United Nations. Endorsing "the principles of human dignity, equality, and equity at the global level," these goals are directed at achieving holistic development for the developing nations by facing the challenges of globalization and the tribulations of social and political conflicts. Premised on the values of freedom, equality, solidarity, tolerance, respect for nature and shared responsibility, the MDGs can be achieved through democratic governance supporting participatory structures, gender equality and empowerment, better health and education facilities, environmental sustainability and global partnership for development (United Nations, 2000). Unmistakably, the MDGs complement human development and these have been linked to all sectors of development and all UN agencies have directed their attention toward their accomplishment insofar as each relate to their own areas of specialism.

Essentially, the onus to realize development goals (human development targets and MDGs) has fallen on the state but it cannot achieve them alone or within a specified time frame. Thus, the involvement of civil society, non-governmental organizations, and international development agencies becomes vital. Working in concert, the state and the nonstate entities need to chart the route and determine the appropriate tasks and instruments for reaching these goals. Consequently, the role, structure, and functions of governments need to be reconfigured within the framework of democratic governance.

V. Democratic Governance

The nexus between democratic governance and effective development management is vital for accomplishing the goals of social advancement and economic progress within the dynamic and complex international political and economic arrangements and changing patterns of domestic interrelationships. With the advent of democratic politics in most DCs, people's expectations about the performance of elected governments have risen. They crave for productive results from social and economic policies framed by their political institutions and implemented by responsive and transparent state agencies with competence and integrity. With the strengthening of credible electoral practices, gradual political institutionalization, and accountable management of development initiatives, the state in most of these countries has gained legitimacy at home and abroad, providing it with the authority and capacity to play a prominent role in its negotiations with foreign governments and more importantly with funding agencies to support social and economic programs. Such legitimacy may also clothe them with the clout to develop their policies based on local needs, using domestic expertise and resources and with minimal external intervention. Public and civil society confidence in the effectiveness of their governments pursuing deliberative policy making is very critical in the success of development (UNDP, 2002: 63–64), and for this reason the development policy space demands the entry of nonstate stakeholders such as nongovernmental organizations, community groups, research bodies, and private sector concerns into its fold.

Good governance, defined as "the exercise of political power to manage a nation's affairs" (World Bank, 1989a) embodies two sets of attributes. The qualitative attributes concern the political makeup of the state — such as political pluralism, constitutionalism and rule of law, liberal economic arrangements, administrative efficiency and effectiveness, governmental integrity, judicial autonomy, empowered local governance, and free media. Less government (a smaller public sector and bureaucracy), more government (for social protection) and wider government (better social and economic services) have a quantitative dimension (see Osborne, 1993; Lowenthal and Dominguez, 1996: 3–8; Linz and Stepan, 1996; Zafarullah, 1999: 182–184).

When the elements of governance are correctly combined with those of democracy, we secure democratic governance. This enlarged concept of governance is based on democratic values, human rights, and productive state–society interrelationship that builds social capital and allow for popular participation in public affairs and development enterprise.

VI. Development Governance

In the 1960s, "development administration" was basically a technocratic process trapped in bureaucratic structures and regulations and, to a large measure, not directly reflective of social and political realities (see Dwivedi, 1994: 26). Although its goals were equated with "nation building[4] and socio-economic progress" (Esman, 1966: 69) to be achieved exclusively by the state mainly using external resources in the form of commodity and project aid and technical assistance, the focus was on the policy cycle[5] and how best to realize development policy targets (Stone, 1966), and the principal instruments used were organized planning mechanisms and institution building devices (Swerdlow, 1975). Administrative system change was a crucial variable; public organizations needed the capacity to centrally manage change (Diamant, 1966; Riggs, 1966) through "increased differentiation and coordination, together with appropriate accompanying specialization" (Weidner, 1970: 8). Essentially, development administration was concerned with planned directional economic growth with or without system change and the application of "discretionary social decisions" by public administrators using certain specialized institutions and instruments for that purpose (Weidner, 1970: 10ff; Riggs, 1966: 72; Gant, 1979; Siffin, 2001).

The early theorists of development administration were not totally oblivious of the cultural, social, and political perspectives of managing development. Riggs, for instance, pointed to the significance of "freedom, justice, security, and the basic integrity of man as a human being" as issues in development and underscored the relevance of participation in a polyarchical form of decision making (Riggs, 1966: 62–69). They also postulated decision-making systems factored by bureaucratic roles and choices as well as public demands and perception of decisions affecting community development (Friedman, 1966: 256–258). Nonetheless, the "the centralist hierarchical–bureaucratic organizational modality" of administering development until the 1980s was more suited in achieving economic growth rather than holistic development (Wunsch, 1999: 243). The cardinal features of development administration of the time perpetuated existing administrative dysfunctions, sustained social anomalies and uneven power relationships, and deterred creativity and innovation in government and public engagement in development. To a large extent, the rich–poor divide endured and even widened, decentralization was partially implemented, administrative reforms resisted by self-serving bureaucrats, the policy process captured by political and administrative elites, and people's participation neutralized by overarching control (Korten and Alfonso, 1983; Rondinelli and Cheema, 1984; Uphoff, 1986; Wunsch 1999).

"Development administration" or "development management" (as it came to be known later) in its existing form is no longer reliable as a mechanism for steering development in a democratizing and globalizing environment in which most DCs are currently placed. Its features require refinement and extension and complete coalescence with the norms of democratic governance to give the process a humane dimension and a proper social, political, legal, and economic perspective. Thus, the concept "development governance" has emerged.

Sound development governance is about harmonizing and integrating economic growth, human advancement, and sustainable development. Based on the norms of democracy, the values of governance, and the standards of environmental sustainability, it signifies a composite process that synthesizes social, political, and economic goals of a nation by forging a productive synergy between the state, civil society, the people, and global development regimes. It influences and is itself influenced by a development culture and a governance regimen that facilitate the realization of society's material needs and the promotion of people's intrinsic potentials. Development governance is also about linking various institutions, instruments, actors, and transactions relevant to development for the explicit purpose of meeting the common needs of society and bringing about stable livelihood for its citizens.

For such a form of governance to be effective in delivering worthwhile services to the community, an efficient, accountable, and honest public management system (PMS) is required. Likewise, to reach the goals of development smoothly or with minimal disruption, PMS depend upon renewal and impregnation with best practices borrowed from the private sector. The public policy space needs opening up to permit the entry of different stakeholders to work in concert with or provide vital inputs to agenda setting, policy formulation, adoption, implementation, evaluation, and administration. Sound policy-making calls for the reconciliation of political and bureaucratic inputs and top–down and bottom–up approaches conjointly with the lateral infusion of ideas and support from the outside.

Development governance is a dynamic process encompassing vertical and horizontal linkages within public organizations and exchanges with nonstate entities. The effectiveness of development planning and execution is a product of synergy between a host of institutions and actors (both state and nonstate) and coordination of discrete activities that add up to program success. Sound policy coordination and collaborative decision making enable optimum resource mobilization and utilization, inhibit duplication and overlapping of activities, timely completion of projects, and efficient and economic management of programs. Total development demands include civic participation and people's empowerment through decentralized structures and the continued interplay between the state and the people. Positive state–people, government–private sector, and political society–civil society interface can stall state domination and advance social capital — an important aspect of development governance (AfDB, 2002: 7–8). Consolidated democracy provides the institutional framework and legitimizing force for development governance to deliver gainful products to society via genuine partnership between citizens, their governments, and the international community.

ADB identifies four basic governance elements that are directly relevant to the development process: accountability, transparency, predictability, and participation (ADB, 1997: 9). Their symbiotic relationship has implications for successful implementation of development policies and programs, and each of these has a bearing on the social, political, legal, and ethical dimensions of development governance. Their relevance is also applicable to the role of the state, its relationship with civil society, and hence the building of social capital through civic engagement in public affairs. Accountability of public institutions and officials associated with development programs is essential to ensure effective policy formulation and implementation, efficient use of resources, proficient accounting, budgeting and expenditure controls, and in meeting performance standards. Access of citizens to and disclosure of information by public bodies on policies, rules, and decisions pertinent to development support accountability mechanisms and the transparency of the development process help abate incertitude from the policy process and serve as a deterrent to rent-seeking and corruption. A transparent governmental framework also complements predictability, which implies primacy of a comprehensive rule-based system to regulate development, safeguard citizens' rights, and resolve conflicts arising from contentious policies and their application. A well-constructed legal–rational structure supports growth and development as the rational assessment of business risks is ensured, transaction costs kept low, and governmental caprice attenuated. Stakeholder participation is essential for the development process to assume a legitimate and credible locus in governance. Citizens' involvement or input in the policy phenomenon creates in them a sense of ownership and widens the scope for program success. Such citizen engagement also props the other three elements of governance (ADB, 1997).

Another critical element of development governance is empowerment of the people, particularly the poor and those marginalized at the grassroots, by expanding their capabilities and enlarging the domain of their participation in and influence over the process of development. Empowerment is about making choices and converting them into desired outcomes and utilizing these for building individual or collective assets. It enables the people to "participate in, negotiate with, influence, control, and hold accountable institutions that affect their lives" (World Bank, 2002a: 11). Empowerment has both instrumental and intrinsic dimensions. Asset building is essential for material well-being, while capabilities can reinforce innate human faculties, enable people to fulfill their social needs and partake in public affairs.[6] Obviously, the state (along with the political institutions), civil society, and markets can create opportunities for social action and for expanding human capabilities (Sen, 2000: 39, 144).

VII. Institutions of Development Governance

A. The Development State

The image of the development state, known for its interventionist attributes in the past, has been changing with the democratizing effect, the entry of free-market principles, and globalization having wider ramifications in the lives of people. The development state[7] sustained by "bureaucratic authoritarianism" served the purposes of development but only to a limited compass in some countries (such as the newly industrializing countries of Asia or parts of Latin America) (see O'Donnell, 1973; Collier, 1990). In its place is emerging the "democratic development state" which combines "the basic elements of democracy with the continuity and coherence of policy... required for sustained development" (Leftwich, 1996: 293). The primary purpose of this type of state is to augment its developmental capacity through sound policies dictated by informed, responsible, and representative political institutions and put in effect by a committed political leadership with the support of an efficient, transparent, accountable, and responsive administrative apparatus. It must undertake three basic socioeconomic functions — *regulative*: to preside over macroeconomic management and facilitate "the functioning of complex market economies," *infrastructural*: creating both physical and social support systems, and *redistributive*: "to tackle absolute poverty and ameliorate morally repugnant and social destructive forms of social inequality" (Robinson and White, 1998a: 29). The state's development performance is largely governed by *consensual autonomy*, which affords state institutions and the political elite to determine and put in place development policies, and *inclusive embeddedness* that creates a nexus between the state and social forces to further the development process" (Robinson and White, 1998a: 30–31; see also Evans, 1996a).

The bureaucracy is a vital component in the development machine. In spite of the vagaries and pathologies of most bureaucratic systems, especially in the DCs, it can play a significant role in serving as a catalyst for change holding, as it does, "accurate intelligence, inventiveness, active agency and sophisticated responses to a changing economic reality" (Evans, 1992: 148). However, it might require restructuring and reorientation to prepare it to work in a democratic development framework. The cultural distance between the bureaucracy and politics and bureaucracy and society must be narrowed.

The developmental state can approach the function of development in a variety of ways and utilize a range of institutions to enhance its capacity and credibility in development. To create an enabling development environment, there is need for political, legal, administrative, and policy reforms that would usher in political stability, useful linkages between the state, political society, and civil society as well as rewarding government–business relations. The state, obviously, has a crucial role in all this (White, 1995) and also to thwart its capture by strong social groups (if any). In contrast, state predation needs to be counterbalanced by civil society and all the paraphernalia necessary to make it robust and vibrant.

B. Political Institutions

Institutions are important in any human endeavor. According to Ostrom (1990: 51), institutions are "the sets of working rules that are used to determine who is eligible to make decisions in some arena, what actions are allowed or constrained, what aggregation rules will be used, what procedures must be followed, what information must or must not be provided, and what payoffs will be assigned to individuals dependent on their actions." The democratic development state needs strong and stable political institutions to achieve development goals. These institutions need to work in harmony as a coherent enterprise within a constitutional framework supporting the rule of law, the preservation of fundamental rights and civil liberties, and upholding the moral obligations of the state. Operating in unique cultural, social, and political settings, these "reflect not just legal forms but also normative understandings and expectations" (Rockman and Weaver, 1993: 10) about development issues.

The legislature, the executive, the judiciary, the bureaucracy, and subnational governments are key political institutions that are associated either directly or indirectly with the governing of development. Their relationship will differ with the type of political system in place and so will the development performance. The primacy of the legislature determines how effectively it is able to deliberate and make laws relevant to different development sectors, the intent and commitment of the political executive guide their adoption and the capacity and efficiency of the bureaucracy measure implementation and outcome. Reciprocal intergovernmental relations within a decentralized system facilitate smooth development project completion and program management, while an independent judiciary reviews and resolves legal differences with fortitude. Political institutions provide scope for policy innovation and entrepreneurship and for the acquisition, evaluation, and utilization of development ideas from the outside. Bureaucratic discretion and intra-bureaucratic politics, which have implications for policy coordination and implementation, can be offset by sound executive–legislative interface.

For best results, institutions engaged in development planning and implementation are expected to work in conjunction or liaise with a variety of nonstate actors, both domestic and external, involved in or associated with development at different levels. Institutions enhance the effectiveness of the government by creating and applying internal rules and restraints, promote "voice" and partnership at the community level and provide for competition for the efficient delivery of services to the people (World Bank, 2000a; xiv). In the new democratic environment, DC governments, perhaps under donor pressure, have been particularly conscious of the need for structural reforms and have had to overcome social and political barriers to do so (Haggard, 1997).

C. Civil Society

An important element of democratic governance is political socialization not only to provide legitimacy to political decisions and actions but also to construct new forms of social relationships or to realign relations between the state and the market and most importantly between these entities and civil society or "that sector of social reality in which human interests ... seek to affirm themselves and defend their rights and prerogatives" (Ana, 1994: 3). Civil society, which was at the forefront of the "third wave" of democratization (Huntington, 1993) "has become the cutting edge of the effort to build a viable democratic order" (Diamond et al., 1988: 26). Indeed, it can be a catalyst in circumscribing the power of a predatory or coercive state (Harbeson, 1994; Fukuyama, 2000) and in potentially addressing the problems of the excluded or marginalized sections of society, who in many cases might have been denied appropriate state attention insofar as policies and decisions that affect them.

The correlation between an autonomous civil society along with its constituents — the nongovernmental organizations, voluntary bodies, or other associational forms — and development is suggestive of its significance in democratic governance. As an essential vehicle for social development, civil society supports participation and hence enables civic engagement and promotes empowerment at the lowest levels of governance. Its actors can play an active role in enhancing local organizational capacity, gathering, processing, and disseminating information for policy development and evaluation, performing social audits and strengthening accountability mechanisms, endorsing citizen action programs, and influencing global policy regimes. Apart from maintaining their presence in the domestic policy arena, civil society organizations (CSOs) from DCs can work concertedly in putting pressure on international organizations to review and redesign their policies that have implications for their nations, such as globalization and environmental policies. Civil society has challenged authoritarian governments as well as powerful global agencies such as the Bretton Woods institutions and the WTO.

However, confrontation works alongside cooperation. The governments of the DC and the IDC can enter into a productive relationship with CSOs in pursuing development goals. CSO interventions, advocacy, and consultations have occurred across social and economic sectors, particularly in relevance to poverty reduction strategies (see World Bank, 2004). Strengthening CSOs have been an important concern for the IDC (see IDB, 1994; Synergos Institute, 1996; Nelson, 2000). Although a robust civil society is crucial for democracy to consolidate and the development process to strengthen, it should be an equally significant concern for development governance to curb the growth of errant CSOs. As Fukuyama (2000: 8) has argued, "There is no guarantee that self-styled public interest NGOs actually represent real public interests. It is entirely possible that too active an NGO sector may represent an excessive politicization of public life, which can either distort public policy or lead to deadlock."

D. The Market

The structures and mechanisms of the market and its performance effectively contribute to the success or failure of economic development and, perhaps by default, social progress. However, the social impact of market forces can have wide repercussions, especially if these broaden income differentials and living standards both globally and domestically. The uncertainties of the global capital markets can trigger financial crises in underdeveloped regions; global competition for resources and markets for goods and services may put intense pressure upon local industries and firms to the extent of causing liquidation and job losses, and the globalization of economic processes may engender diverse regulatory and administrative problems, thus deterring the development process. As the 1999 *Human Development Report* commented: "Competitive markets may be the best guarantee of efficiency, but not necessarily of equity. Liberalization and privatization can be a step to competitive markets — but not a guarantee of them. And markets are neither the first nor the last word in human development" (UNDP, 1999: 2).

However, markets can be effectively utilized to work for human progress and the benefits of globalization channeled to the poverty-stricken regions of the world. Expansions in trade, technology, communication, investment, and environmental upkeep have the potential to energize both economic growth and human development. The responsibility to regulate the market in a way that would promote growth with equity, social and human advancement, and sustained development rests with the state, the civil society, the private sector, and the global development agencies. The "fiscal squeeze on public goods, a time squeeze on care activities and an incentive squeeze on the environment" (UNDP, 1999: 2) need gradual containment. Trade liberalization, deregulation, privatization, export expansion, price controls, etc. have to be managed efficiently.

DC governments have a stake in macroeconomic management. The behavior of the market and of firms within it must be placed within stipulated limits and its processes need to be monitored and evaluated for misdemeanor. Like public bodies, business organizations should embrace higher ethics of corporate responsibility and come clean about their operations and impact on society and environment (Repetto and Austin, 2000). For competitive markets to thrive in a hassle-free environment, bureaucratic hindrances need to be removed, economic incentives need to be offered, and rent seeking and corruption need to be curbed.

Markets and businesses, however, cannot be spared from their social responsibility obligations. They cannot remain insensitive to the public interest and must be accountable to their communities for their actions and consequences. In many ways, the emerging economic order influenced by trade agreements and dominated by global financial institutions and transnational corporations pose threats to the poorer nations and the people living therein. Countervailing measures need to be in place to offset its adverse effects. It is also incumbent upon the market and its supportive institutions to supplement public efforts in providing safety nets for the affected. Similarly, social vulnerabilities caused by market failures or external economic shocks have to be dealt with by governments through social protection programs. Therefore, sound development governance has to have embedded within it mechanisms to counter the problems associated with market failure and attendant consequences.

VIII. Building Capital

Various forms of capital bear direct relevance to growth and social progress, as they are like concrete and steel in the edifice of development. These include natural capital, physical capital, human capital, social capital, organizational capital, and financial capital (see Viederman, 1996: 47) and they are all important aspects of a nation's wealth and well-being. Nature's resources, both renewable and nonrenewable, ranging from intangible public goods (atmosphere, living organisms) to production-related divisible assets (land, water, forests, minerals) are the constituents of *natural capital* and these needs protection from the blight of exponential population increases and the adverse offshoots of economic growth. Thus, the principal objective of sustainable development is the protection of the world's ecological system and the establishment of conditions for the better management of the natural environment. The depletion of nature's limited assets on the pretext of economic development requires a halt through a range of interventions by the institutions of development governance and a sound regulatory framework guaranteeing environmental protection. Natural capital can be built by "the integration of environmental considerations into economic planning, mitigation of the effects of environmental degradation, and prevention of future degradation, particularly in the interests of the poorest people" (DFID, 1997: 42).

Beyond natural capital is *physical capital* (physical infrastructure such as roads, bridges, dams, irrigation systems, buildings, capital equipment, etc.) used in generating economic growth and providing human welfare. Infrastructure development is essential in facilitating communications, in providing shelter and housing to people, in creating educational and healthcare opportunities, in applying new technologies, and in carrying out the business of government. Maintaining physical capital for productive purposes can be a difficult task and governments must efficiently plan infrastructure development, as costly investment in physical capital may not always produce desired social and economic results (Dompere and Ejaz, 1995: 130). The accumulation of physical capital becomes more daunting during macroeconomic crises with adverse impact upon the poor population's ability to break free from poverty (World Bank, 2000b: 162).

Likewise, *human capital*, the set of "knowledge, skills, and experience of people that make them economically productive," is a key to alleviating poverty. It has also been argued that "societies that invest more in human capital than physical capital have a higher rate of economic growth" (Dompere and Ejaz, 1995: 130). The command of disadvantaged segments of the populations (for instance, women) over physical and human capital can improve their access to resources and services, thus "allowing them to undertake higher-risk, higher-return activities" (World Bank, 2000b: 148). The east-Asian countries have shown the efficacy of human capital investments in contributing to both human and economic development.

Social capital has become a catch phrase in development discourse. Indeed, almost all aspects of development governance have been tied to this concept, and it is perceived to be a crucial element in fostering participation in communities and in empowering individuals to achieve their social, political, and economic goals. As an attribute of social organization, it can both build and bridge social networks that are essential in contributing to policy formation and execution (Putnam, 2000). "Instantiated" and "informal" norms and networks enable individuals within a social structure (institutions, relationships) to work collectively to achieve common objectives engendered by civic engagement, social trust, and reciprocal obligations (Coleman, 1990; Kentworthy, 1997; Fukuyama, 2000).

As a tool in development governance, social capital performs several functions. Apart from creating horizontal and vertical linkages for social action, social capital helps in the creation of human capital, produces public order, enhances people's participation, creates partnerships, and contributes to social and economic well-being and sustainable development (Coleman, 1988; Brown, 1991; Thomas, 1996; Isham et al., 2002; Holm, 2004).

From an economic standpoint, social capital lowers transaction costs and generates greater efficiency of governmental tasks. Politically it "produces a dense civil society" and deepens democracy (Fukuyama, 2000). Civil society and social capital are interlinked and citizen interactions through social networks have a positive impact on macroeconomic policy development and hence in devising strategies to alleviate poverty (Hyden, 1997; Brinkerhoff and Goldsmith, 2003). Social capital fosters a participative policy process, lowers the incidence of corruption, and gives governance a human dimension.

Both human capital and social capital work conjointly to build *organizational capital*, which is fundamental to boosting the performance of development agencies. Cultivated through processes of socialization and training, harmonious organizational relationships enable the meeting of agency goals for efficiency. Organizational capital leads to proper coordination of programs, information upkeep and sharing, rational decisions, and better appreciating of the needs of the community (see Tomer, 1999). Renewed organizational structures and processes for development along with sound integrity management, incentive systems, and the use of informational technology or e-governance can vastly improve agency performance (Brynjolfsson et al., 2002) and hence help attain development objectives.

Economic growth rests on the rate of capital formation. The acquisition and maintenance of physical and human capital depend on *financial capital* represented by wealth (money and property), and a sound financial system is imperative for supporting the development process. Through efficient regulation, and sometimes its appropriate deregulation, governments can create avenues for savings and investment, which are essential for supporting both economic and social development. As the 1989 *World Development Report* suggested:

> Conditions that support the development of a more robust and balanced financial structure will improve the ability of domestic financial systems to contribute to growth. By restoring macroeconomic stability, building better legal, accounting, and regulatory systems, specifying rules for fuller disclosure of information, and levying taxes that do not fall excessively on finance, governments can lay the foundations for smoothly functioning financial systems (World Bank, 1989b: 1).

Despite the ongoing neoliberal push for economic liberalization around the world, government intervention in development remains embedded in statecraft. What is important, however, is the quality of that intervention, rather than its extent (Bardhan, 1990: 4). Rather than simply generating a plethora of regulations, it becomes important to see how these can be effectively enforced to make the economy healthy and supportive of both economic growth and social development. Microeconomic stabilization, which is conditioned by both internal and external factors, is imperative although its realization may be daunting for DCs. Sound economic management should provide the lever for efficient implementation of carefully framed fiscal and monetary policies and the prudent allocation of resources. The appropriate institutions and instruments to build financial capital must be put in place and a favorable economic environment created for commercial activities to thrive and provide gainful results. Market failures have to be addressed discreetly by the government or it will itself be liable for failure (Krueger, 1990).

Each of these forms of capital can support *capacity development* — defined as "strengthening the national framework ... that affects the direction, management and sustenance of the development process in the sector and the economy as a whole" (ADB, 1998: 36–37). It is basically about strengthening organizations, both public and nongovernmental to realize the goals of development. Vigorous capacity building hinges upon the reform of the core institutions of government, including the civil service, strengthening policy, and decision processes within public agencies, establishing proper audit, financial and procurement management strategies, and preparing public administrators to take on the tasks of development. A range of areas/themes are covered by capacity building in both public and private sectors including personnel, infrastructure, technology, and financial, program, and process management (Horton et al., 2003).

IX. Sustainable Development

As indicated earlier, a key issue confronting our planet is the sustenance of its natural resources and their proper utilization for growth and development. Sustainable development is defined as a development approach that "meets the needs of the present without compromising the ability of future generations to meet their own needs" (WCED, 1987: 43). It is a function of "market-friendly, people-friendly, and environment-friendly policies" (Picciotto, 1997: 343) framed by eco-sensitive governments and supported by an attentive public. As a development governance stratagem, sustainable development needs refabrication of the value system *vis-à-vis* the environment and the creation or redesign of new institutions for sustainability. It is important for the state to ensure the equitable use of scarce natural resources to sustain growth and development.

Realizing sustainable development is a challenge for all developing or transitional countries with high population growth, rapid urbanization, food shortages, depletion of forest resources, natural disasters, industrial pollution, and energy deficiencies. A combination of political, economic, management, and technological factors is needed to consolidate sustainable development initiatives (WCED, 1987). Global eco-regimes have emerged to respond to environmental problems, which are no longer country-specific and are tied with other trans-border issues and therefore need to be addressed on regional and international basis.

Yet, the role of the state remains crucial in environmental planning and management, which in the new framework of governance, has to be more pro-people, participative and transparent and involve a host of nonstate actors (Litfen, 1993: 98). *Agenda 21* of the United Nations Conference on Environment and Development (UNCED) urges states to develop and implement economic policies conducive to sustainable development and augment multilevel governmental capacity to design, implement, and manage environmental programs. It calls for the "integration of economic, social, and environmental considerations in decision-making at all levels and in all ministries," broadening public participation in decision making, and providing individuals, groups, and organizations "access to information relevant to environment and development . . . and environmental protection measures" (UNCED, 1992: Chapter 8).

Sustainable development needs an enabling institutional environment that will *"pick up signals* about needs and problems . . . *balance interests* . . . [and] *execute* and *implement solutions"* (World Bank, 2002b: 37). This calls for enhancing the capacity of development institutions both within government and civil society. All forms of assets — financial, intellectual, human, social, organizational, and environmental — require responsible management, and the institutions of development governance must display genuine practical commitment towards protecting the environment and forge a functional rapport for that purpose. Environmental norms and standards must be carefully stipulated and the instruments devised and applied in practice. Depending on the circumstances, regulatory and market-based instruments for enforcing compliance to environmental standards need to be balanced. A mix of instruments is more useful than relying on any one type. The environment being "an overarching sector that addresses the dynamic interactions among other sectors" (Schramm and Warford, 1989: 59), the necessity for incorporating environment impact assessment for economic development policies becomes preeminent and the confluence of environmental issues with those relating to infrastructure, industrial, and water resources development becomes critical. Coordination among agencies, transparency of operations, and the accountability of participants are also important concerns.

X. Participation, Partnership, and the Policy Process
A. *Participation*

For development in general and sustainable development in particular to generate maximum human welfare, an inclusive participatory praxis encompassing social, political, and economic structures is indispensable. Democratic development governance would be a fallacy without the spontaneous yet conscious and organized participation of the common people and CSOs as well as the altruistic engagement of external development agencies. Described as a "transformative movement," total development requires the rejection of the traditional ways of dealing with problems, a change of perceptions and attitudes, and embracing of new ideas and methods to attack social and economic indigence (see Stiglitz, 2002: 164–165). Participation takes place in social settings and is collective action for gaining and exercising greater control over resources, institutions, and policies or decisions (see Stiefel and Wolfe, 1994: 5). Participatory development and partnership are coterminous as both are premised on deliberative discourse and negotiations among stakeholders without being ruffled by outside maneuvers (Rudqvist and Woodford-Berger, 1996: 12).

In development governance, participation can be useful in designing, implementing, and evaluating development policies and programs through consultation and monitoring and information generation and diffusion (Cohen and Uphoff, 1977; Zazueta, 1995: 22; Brinkerhoff, 1996). These lead to greater collaboration between the state and other stakeholders and empower the common people at the local level to influence and even control the development process. The more intense the degree of participation, the greater the movement toward citizen power and democracy (Arstein, 1969; Pateman, 1970). The inclusive approach to participation has transformed citizens from being mere beneficiaries of development to becoming partners in the process (Cornwall, 2000).

Participation for the poor, marginalized, and disadvantaged has many positive benefits. Apart from providing them the access to resources and a voice to ventilate their grievances and place their demands, it facilitates social interactions and help build social capital, transforms their mindset, enhances their confidence, improves their self-esteem, expands their assets and capabilities, and accords them the leverage to influence the outcome of development initiatives (Oakley and Clayton, 2000; World Bank, 2002a). State–citizen relationship, strengthened by participation, have significant implications for transparency and accountability providing legitimacy to government actions, improving the quality and effectiveness of governance, and enhancing "the quality of representative democracy" (OECD, 2001: 73–74). Participation also replaces or complements top–down development strategies by grassroots groups and CSOs contributing to agenda setting in the policy process. Thus, the links between participation and empowerment are obvious.

B. Engendering Development

The prospect for gender equity is advanced by participatory approaches to development. Women who were, in the past, discriminated against and excluded from the development process or were relegated to a secondary position are now playing or are expected to play a more prominent role either as beneficiaries of development programs or more so as active participants. A shift from welfare to empowerment is noticeable. Yet, gender-related barriers still remain and need to be removed and opportunities need to be created for women to be in the government and at the center of development. The rights of women need to be promoted. The UN's conceptualization of gender mainstreaming — "a strategy for making women's as well as men's concerns and experiences an integral dimension of the design, implementation, monitoring, and evaluation of the policies and programs in all political, economic, and societal spheres so that women and men benefit equally and inequality is not perpetuated" (UN Economic and Social Council, E. 1997, line 10, Paragraph 4 quoted in UNDP 2003: 3) can serve as the premise for engendering development. Strategies for mainstreaming gender are now being developed both by DC governments and funding or development agencies mainly in partnership with CSOs and these focus on welfare, anti-poverty, efficiency, equity, and empowerment of women (Moser, 1993). Nonetheless, more has to be done to gradually diminish the gender imbalance.

C. Development Synergy

The success of development governance will depend on building coalitions and partnerships between the institutions involved in the process and those within them. Building synergies is a key task in development governance (Evans, 1996b: 1130). Such partnerships evolve out of the need for stakeholder participation in development and for building issues networks for policy development and renewal. These partnerships may be activated at the global, regional, national, and local levels vertically, horizontally, and laterally and covering the range of development sectors. Global partnerships are essential to promote sustainable development and accomplish its mission as the environment transcends national boundaries and the cooperation of neighboring countries can solve common problems.

In the domestic front, as well, government departments, community-based organizations, research institutions, and donor agencies need to work together toward common objectives. Collaborative processes involving both public and private organizations can also be productive in providing a wide array of social services to the community (Robinson and White, 1998b). The existing state–community hiatus in many countries can be substantially closed by "generating developmental state–community synergy [which] is greatly enhanced by interventions which reduce serious power imbalances within communities ... [and] reduces poor people's dependence on local elites, helping prepare communities for initiating collective action, and for collaborating among themselves and with government agencies" (Gupta et al., 2004: 29).

D. Expanding the Policy Space

The policy space in the developing world thus far has been the domain of the state and its institutions; external inputs to policy making and implementation were thus severely limited. Participation and partnerships provide the rationale for unlocking the gates of the policy arena to admit multiple stakeholders to interact, deliberate, and proffer new ideas or solutions to problems. The advent, restoration, or consolidation of democracy in many developing nations has increased the opportunities for nonstate actors to partake in the process. Depending on its policy stance, the state may adopt either the society-centered (pluralist) or the state-centered (corporatist) mode in policy development (Brinkerhoff and Goldsmith, 2003). The former is particularly useful in involving minor actors in the policy process and drawing on their ideas and interests in framing development policies and programs in general, while the corporatist mode is more functional in framing macroeconomic policies, with the state playing a more dominant role and major civil society groups providing gainful inputs. In either mode and in different phases of the policy cycle, CSOs as policy entrepreneurs can serve as informed monitors, advocates, innovators, and service providers (Najam, 1999: 152–153).

"Policy regimes," created around specific issues can play a constructive role in shaping or reviewing policies. With their distinctive advocates and interest articulators, they are in a position to influence agenda setting and policy development and stipulate the rules of implementation (Wilson, 2000: 257–260). These regimes can liaise with international policy regimes in the same policy area and quite freely borrow ideas for implantation in the domestic arena. Globalization has spurred the phenomenon of policy transfers or the "export of policy solutions" as development policies are increasingly conditioned by global factors and affords policy actors to play a more objective role autonomous of the state (Nedley, 2000). The "multilayered web of governance" caused by globalization "is linked and articulated through a complex of public and private processes and institutions" (Cerny, 2001: 398). The transfer of policy ideas and institutional arrangements for policy implementation have merits as they initiate a "policy learning" process and diffuse innovation enhancing policy development in DCs. However, with the principal roots of policies lying outside national boundaries, the question of policy ownership becomes critical. Thus, it is judicious for governments to balance borrowed policy prescriptions and local policy determinants for their policies to have a positive impact on society and cause fewer disruptions to social and economic well being of the people. But with coercive policy transfers at the behest of the Bretton Woods institutions dominating the policy arena, aid-dependent countries have little choice but to oblige donors.

This contentious issue aside, apart from encouraging issues networks, policy subsystems, advocacy coalitions, etc. to enter the policy domain, the governments of DCs will need to reform the policy process itself by setting the modalities of agenda setting and policy formulation and decision-making methods, synthesizing top–down and bottom–up approaches to policy implementation and clearly stipulating the instruments for addressing policy problems. The changes have to be brought about within a comprehensive public management reform program that would also have capacity building as a key component.

Communications and information technology (ICT) or e-government has a significant part in enriching the policy process. Indeed, ICT can be at the core of development governance as it has the potential to strengthen communication by storing, processing, helping retrieve information essential for policies to be planned, put into effect, and evaluated. An inclusive people-centered communication approach will foster social capital, ensure participation, and generate a sense of ownership among the people and can contribute to democratic governance (Weigel and Waldburger, 2004).

XI. Conclusions

It has been a tortuous and complex transition toward development for many countries, following decolonialization. While the aims and objectives of development appeared to be relatively clear, the strategies shifted over the years as governments, experts, scholars, and international agencies struggled to arrive at a consensus and determine the best way for achieving them. In the early days of decolonization, development packages were externally determined along with the material, financial, and human resources in the form of aid and assistance and international consultants or technical advisers. Such an approach was soon found to be unsuitable as most of the objectives remained unattained and eventually, the emphasis shifted to capacity building through human and institutional resources in DCs. Thus, the strategy changed from one of complete domination by, and dependence on, external agents to that of limited involvement by indigenous agents and institutions.

Continued problems and obstructions in the way of achieving the goals of development prompted serious rethinking, and attention was diverted to other problems facing the main sponsors of development. The western world was affected by financial stress emanating from major changes in the world economy as well as the extravagant policies pursued in the previous decades. Naturally, the level of enthusiasm in assisting development efforts and the capacity to support them underwent changes among the sponsors, and the emergence of neoliberal ideas provided the scope for exercising influence over DCs through major international institutions. The trend continued throughout the decades that followed, and the subsequent experiences have highlighted the need to reconsider the aims and objectives of development and expanding its scope to include a number of critical elements that were neglected in earlier conceptualizations. These will need to be subsumed under the label of "development governance."

The experience of DCs and the outcome of decades of efforts at transforming them have led to the idea that mere strengthening of institutions or the development of capacity is not helpful unless there are arrangements to sustain the improvements. As a result, development governance can be postulated as an essential condition for achieving the desired outcome in DCs. Attention should be paid to the development state, political institutions, civil society, and the market and its performance to ensure improvement in a wide variety of areas. Efforts need to be directed toward building the capital in various forms and to ensure the conditions for sustainable development. The process is dependent on fostering effective participation by the various stakeholders and institutions in the policy process. In spite of the major shifts in strategies and expected consequences of development, human and social capital remains critical to the process and must be supported by appropriate institutional framework. There can be no substitute for interconnection between social, political, and economic sectors and long-standing relationships between the key institutions and actors that will constitute the base of actions for attaining developmental goals.

Notes

1. Kaul et al. (1999: 6) uses the term "public bad" to denote goods and activities providing negative utility as distinct from "public good."
2. These include GNP growth, theories of human capital formation and human resources development, human welfare, and the basic needs approach.
3. The question of ownership became a contentious issue ever since international lending agencies and Western governments began providing technical assistance and transferring policy ideas to the DCs. The altruism of these agencies became suspect and the demand for ownership of development policies and implementation grew.
4. Esman defined "nation-building" as "the deliberate fashioning of an integrated political community within fixed geographic boundaries in which the nation state is the dominant political institution" (Esman, 1966: 69).
5. Stone conceived it as "the continuous cycle of formulating, evaluating and implementing interrelated plans, policies, programs, projects, activities and other measures to reach established development objectives in a scheduled time sequence" (Stone, 1966: 4). For Friedman (1966: 254), development administration has two components: "the implementation of programs designed to bring about modernity and ... the changes within an administrative system which increase its capacity to implement such programs."
6. According to the World Bank (2002a: 11), "Human capabilities include good health, education, and production or other life-enhancing skills. Social capabilities include social belonging, leadership, relations of trust, a sense of identity, values that give meaning to life, and the capacity to organize. Political capability includes the capacity to represent oneself or others, access information, form associations, and participate in the political life of a community or country."
7. Leftwich (1996: 284) defined a "development state" as one "whose internal politics and external relations have served to concentrate sufficient power, authority, autonomy, competence and capacity at the centre to shape, pursue and encourage the achievement of explicit developmental objectives, whether by establishing and promoting the conditions of economic growth, or by organizing it directly, or a varying combination of both."

References

ADB, *Governance: Promoting Sound Development Management*, Asian Development Bank, Manila, 1997.

ADB, *Key Themes and Priorities for Governance and Capacity Building in the Asian and Pacific Region*, Asian Development Bank, Manila, 1998.

ADB, *Fighting Poverty in Asia and the Pacific*, Asian Development Bank, Manila, 2000.

AfDB, *Policy on Good Governance*, African Development Bank, Abidjan, 2002.

AfDB, *A Re-invigorated Bank: An Agenda for Moving Forward*, African Development Bank, Abidjan, 2003.

Ana, J., The concept of civil society, *Ecumenical Rev.*, 46 (1), 3–9, 1994.

Apter, D., *Rethinking Development*, Sage, Beverly Hills, CA, 1987.

Arstein, S., A ladder of citizen participation, *J. Am. Inst. Plann.*, 35, 216–224, 1969.

Bardhan, P., Symposium on the state and economic development, *J. Econ. Perspect.*, 4 (3), 3–7, 1990.

Boron, A., Governability and democracy in Latin America, *Soc. Justice*, 23 (1–2), 303–337, 1996.

Brinkerhoff, D., Process perspectives on policy change: highlighting implementation, *World Dev.*, 24 (9), 1395–1401, 1996.

Brinkerhoff, D.W. and Goldsmith, A.A., How citizens participate in macroeconomic policy: international experience and implications for poverty reduction, *World Dev.*, 31 (4), 685–688, 2003.

Brinkman, R., Economic growth versus economic development: toward a conceptual clarification, *J. Econ. Issues*, 29, 1171–1188, 1995.

Brown, D., Bridging organizations and sustainable development, *Hum. Relat.*, 44 (8), 807–831, 1991.

Brynjolfsson, E., Hitt, L.M., and Yang, S., Intangible assets: computers and organizational capital, *Brookings Papers on Economic Activity*, Brookings Institution, Washington, DC, 2002.

Cerny, P., From "Iron Triangles" to "Golden Pentangles?" globalizing the policy process, *Global Governance*, 7 (4), 397–411, 2001.

Chang, H.-J., *Rethinking Development Economics*, Wimbledon Publishing Company, London, 2003.

Cohen, B., The Question of Imperialism: The Political Economy of Dominance and Dependence, Basic Books, New York, NY, 1973.

Cohen, J.M. and Uphoff, N.T., *Rural Development and Participation: Concepts and Measures for project Design, Implementation and Evaluation*, Cornell University Rural Development Committee, Ithaca, NY, 1977.

Coleman, J., Social capital and the creation of human capital, *Am. J. Sociol.*, 94 (Suppl.), 95–120, 1988.

Coleman, J., *Foundations of Social Theory*, Harvard University Press, Cambridge, MA, 1990.

Collier, D., Ed., *New Authoritarianism in Latin America*, Princeton University Press, Princeton, NJ, 1990.

Cooper, R.N., Developed country reactions to calls for a New International Economic Order, in *Toward a New Strategy for Development*, Colloquium, R.C., Ed., Pergamon, New York, NY, 1979, pp. 243–274.

Cornwall, A., *Beneficiary, Consumer, Citizen: Perspectives on Participation for Poverty Reduction, SIDA Studies 2*, SIDA, Stockholm, 2000.

DFID, *Eliminating World Poverty: A Challenge for the 21st Century*, Department for International Development, London, 1997.

Diamant, A., Political development: approaches to theory and strategy, in *Approaches to Development: Politics, Administration and Change*, Montgomery, J.D. and Siffin, W.J., Eds., McGraw-Hill, New York, NY, 1966, pp. 15–47.

Diamond, L., Linz, J., and Lipset, S.M., Eds., *Democracy in Developing Countries*, Vol. 2, Africa, Lynne Rienner Publishers, Boulder, CO, 1988.

Dompere, K.K. and Ejaz, M., *Epistemics of Development Economics: Toward a Methodological Critique and Unity*, Greenwood Press, Westport, CT, 1995.

Dwivedi, O.P., *Development Administration: From Underdevelopment to Sustainable Development*, St. Martin's Press, New York, NY, 1994.

Dwivedi, O.P. and Nef, J., Crises and continuities in development theory and administration: First and Third World perspectives, *Public Adm. Dev.*, 2 (1), 59–77, 1982.

Esman, M., The maturing of development administration, *Public Adm. Dev.*, 8 (2), 125–134, 1988.

Esman, M., The politics of development administration, in *Approaches to Development: Politics, Administration and Change*, Montgomery, J.D. and Siffin, W.J., Eds., McGraw-Hill, New York, NY, 1966, pp. 59–87.

Evans, P., The state as problem and solution: predation, embedded autonomy, and structural change, in *The Politics of Economic Adjustment*, Haggard, S. and Kaufman, R.R., Eds., Princeton University Press, Princeton, NJ, 1992, pp. 139–179.

Evans, P., Introduction. development strategies across the public-private sector divide, *World Dev.*, 24 (6), 1033–1038, 1996a.

Evans, P., Government action, social capital and development: reviewing the evidence on synergy, *World Dev.*, 24 (6), 1119–1132, 1996b.

Friedman, H., Administrative roles in local governments, in *Development Administration in Asia*, Weidner, E.W., Ed., Duke University Press, Durham, NC, 1966, pp. 251–276.

Fukuyama, F., Social capital and civil society, *IMF Working Paper WP/00/74*, International Monetary Fund, Washington, DC, 2000.

Gant, G.F., *Development Administration: Concepts, Goals, Methods*, University of Wisconsin Press, Madison, WI, 1979.

Gaspar, T., Gervai, P., and Trautmann, L., The end of neoliberal history: the future of economics, *Futures*, 35 (6), 589–608, 2003.

Goulet, D., *The Cruel Choice: A New Concept in the Theory of Development*, Atheneum, New York, NY, 1971.

Gupta, D.M., Grandvoinnet, H., and Romani, M., State-community synergies in community-driven development, *J. Dev. Stud.*, 40 (3), 27–58, 2004.

Haggard, S., Democratic institutions, economic policy, and development, in *Institutions and Economic Development: Growth and Governance in Less-Developed and Post-Socialist Countries*, Clague, C., Ed., Johns Hopkins University Press, Baltimore, MD, 1997, pp. 121–149.

Haque, M.S., Restructuring Development Theories and Policies: A Critical Study, SUNY Press, New York, NY, 1999.

Harbeson, J.W., Civil society and political renaissance in Africa, in *Civil Society and the State in Africa*, Harbeson, J.W., Rothchild, D., and Chazan, N., Eds., Lynne Rienner, Boulder, CO, 1994, pp. 1–29.

Holm, A., A (social) capital idea: making development work, *Harv. Int. Rev.*, 25 (4), 24–33, 2004.

Horton, D. et al., *Evaluating Capacity Development: Experiences from Research and Development Organizations Around the World*, International Service for

National Agricultural Research (ISNAR), The Netherlands; International Development Research Centre (IDRC), Canada; ACP-EU Technical Centre for Agricultural and Rural Cooperation (CTA), The Netherlands, 2003.

Huntington, S.P., *The Third Wave: Democratization in the Late 20th Century*, University of Oklahoma Press, Norman, OK, 1993.

Hyden, G., Civil society, social capital, and development: dissection of a complex discourse, *Studies in Comparative International Development*, 32 (1), 3–30, 1997.

IDB, *A Strategy for Poverty Reduction*, Inter-American Development Bank, Washington, DC, 1997.

IDB, *Summary Report of the Conference on Strengthening Civil Society*, Inter-American Development Bank, Washington, DC, 1994.

Isham, J., Kelly, T., and Ramaswamy, S., *Social Capital and Economic Development: Well-being in Developing Countries*, Edward Elgar, London, 2002.

Jilberto, A.E. and Mommen, A., Eds., *Liberalization in the Developing World: Institutional and Economic Changes in Latin America, Africa and Asia*, Routledge, London, 1996.

Jwa, S.-H. and Chwa, S.-H., *New Paradigm for Korea's Economic Development: From Government Control to Market Economy*, Palgrave Macmillan, New York, NY, 2001.

Kaul, I., Grunberg, I., and Stern, M.A., *Global Public Goods: International Cooperation in the 21st Century*, Oxford University Press, Oxford, 1999.

Kentworthy, L., Civic engagement, social capital, and economic cooperation, *Am. Behav. Sci.*, 40 (5), 646–657, 1997.

Kessides, I., *Reforming Infrastructure: Privatization, Regulation, and Competition*, World Bank, Washington, DC, 2003.

Korten, D. and Alfonso, F., *Bureaucracy and the Poor: Closing the Gap*, Kumarian Press, West Hartford, CT, 1983.

Krueger, A.O., Government failures in development, *J. Econ. Perspect.*, 4 (3), 9–23, 1990.

Leftwich, A., Two cheers for democracy? Democracy and the developmental state, in *Democracy and Development*, Leftwich, A., Ed., Polity Press, Cambridge, 1996, pp. 279–296.

Lewellen, T.C., *Development and Dependency: An Introduction to the Third World*, Bergin & Garvey, Westport, CT, 1995.

Linz, J.J. and Stepan, A., Toward consolidated democracies, *J. Democracy*, 7 (2), 14–33, 1996.

Litfen, K., Ecoregimes: playing tug of war with the nation-state, in *The State and Social Power in Global Environmental Politics*, Lipschutz, R.D. and Conca, K., Eds., Columbia University Press, New York, NY, 1993, pp. 94–117.

Lowenthal, A. and Dominguez, J., Eds., *Constructing Democratic Governance*, Johns Hopkins University Press, Baltimore, MD, 1996.

Moser, C., *Gender Planning and Development: Theory, Practice and Training*, Routledge, London, 1993.

Myrdal, G., What is Development?, *J. Econ. Issues*, 8, 729–736, 1974.

Naim, M., Washington Consensus or Washington confusion?, *Foreign Policy*, Spring, 86–103, 2000.

Najam, A., Citizen organizations as policy entrepreneurs, in *International Perspectives on Voluntary Action: Reshaping the Third Sector*, Lewis, D., Ed., Earthscan, London, 1999, pp. 142–181.

Nanda, V.P., The right to development: an appraisal, in *World Debt and the Human Condition: Structural Adjustments and the Right to Development*, Nanda, V.P., McCarthy-Arnolds, E., and Shepherd G.W., Jr., Eds., Greenwood Press, Westport, CT, 1993, pp. 41–62.

Nedley, A., Policy transfer and the developing-country experience gap: taking a southern perspective, *ESRC Research Seminar, Studying Policy Transfer: Insider and Outsider Perspectives*, University of York, Heslington, 2000.

Nelson, P., Whose civil society? Whose governance? Decisionmaking and practice in the New Agenda at the Inter-American Development Bank and the World Bank, *Global Governance*, 6 (4), 405–416, 2000.

O'Donnell, G.A., *Modernization and Bureaucratic–Authoritarianism: Studies in South American Politics*, Institute of International Studies, University of California, Berkeley, CA, 1973.

Oakley, P. and Clayton, A., *The Monitoring and Evaluation of Empowerment: A Resource Document*, INTRAC, Oxford, 2000.

OECD, *Citizen as Partners: Information, Consultation and Public Participation in Policy-Making*, Organisation for Economic Cooperation and Development, Paris, 2001.

Osborne, D., Good governance initiatives in the global context, *Hong Kong Public Adm.*, 2, 107–116, 1993.

Ostrom, E., *Governing the Commons*, Cambridge University Press, Cambridge, 1990.

Pateman, C., *Participation and Democratic Theory*, Cambridge University Press, Cambridge, 1970.

Picciotto, R., Putting institutional economics to work; from participation to governance, in *Institutions and Economic Development*, Clague, C., Ed., Johns Hopkins University Press, Baltimore, MD, 1997, pp. 343–367.

Putnam, R., *Bowling Alone: The Collapse and Revival of American Community*, Simon and Schuster, New York, NY, 2000.

Rapley, J., *Understanding Development: Theory and Practice in the Third World*, Lynne, Rienner, 2002.

Ray, D., *Development Economics*, Princeton University Press, Princeton, NJ, 1998.

Repetto, R. and Austin, D., *Coming Clean: Corporate Disclosure of Financially Significant Environmental Risks*, World Resources Institute, Washington, DC, 2000.

Riggs, F.W., The idea of development administration, in *Development Administration in Asia*, Weidner, E.W., Ed., Duke University Press, Durham, NC, 1966, pp. 25–72.

Robinson, M. and White, G., *The Democratic Developmental State: Politics and Institutional Design*, Oxford University Press, Oxford, 1998a.

Robinson, M. and White, G., Towards synergy in social provision: civic organisations and the state, in *Beyond the New Public Management. Changing Ideas and*

Practices in Governance, Minogue, M.C., Polidano, C., and Hulme, D., Eds., Edward Elgar, Cheltenham, U.K./Northampton, MA, 1998b, pp. 94–116.

Rockman, B. and Weaver, K., *Do Institutions Matter? Government Capabilities in the United States and Abroad*, Brookings Institution, Washington, DC, 1993.

Rondinelli, D. and Cheema, S., *Decentralization in Developing Countries: A Review of Recent Experience*, World Bank, Washington, DC, 1984.

Rudqvist, A. and Woodford-Berger, P., *Evaluation and Participation: Some Lessons*, SIDA Studies in Evaluation 96/1, SIDA, Stockholm, 1996.

Savin, E.S. and Savas, E.S., *Privatization and Public–Private Partnerships*, Seven Bridges Press, New York, NY, 2000.

Schramm, G. and Warford, J.J., Eds., *Environment Management and Economic Development*, John Hopkins University Press, Baltimore, MD, 1989.

Seers, D., The meaning of development, *Int. Dev. Rev.*, 11, 2–6, 1969.

Sen, A., *Commodities and Capabilities*, North Holland, Amsterdam, 1985.

Sen, A., *Development as Freedom*, Anchor/Random House, New York, 2000.

Siffin, W.J., Problem of development administration, in *Handbook of Comparative and Development Public Administration*, Farazmand, A., Ed., Marcel Dekker, New York, NY, 2001, pp. 1–8.

Stiefel, M. and Wolfe, S., *A Voice for the Excluded: Popular Participation in Development Utopia or Necessity?* Zed Press, London, 1994.

Stiglitz, J., Participation and development: perspectives from the comprehensive development paradigm, *Rev. Dev. Econ.*, 6 (2), 163–182, 2002.

Stone, D., Tasks, precedents and approaches to education for development administration, in *Education for Development Administration*, Stone, D.C., Ed., IIAS, Brussels, 1966.

Swerdlow, I., *The Public Administration of Economic Development*, Praeger, New York, NY, 1975.

Synergos Institute, How governments and multi-lateral donors can form large-scale partnerships with civil society organizations: reflections from three Latin American countries. *Synergos Institute Working Paper*, Synergos Institute, New York, NY, 1996.

Thomas, C., Capital markets, financial markets and social capital: an essay on economic theory and economic ideas, *Soc. Econ. Stud.*, 45 (2–3), 1–23, 1996.

Todaro, M.P. and Smith, S.C., *Economic Development*, 8th ed., Addison-Wesley, Reading, MA, 2002.

Tomer, J., Social and organizational capital, in *Encyclopedia of Political Economy*, O'Hara, P., Ed., Routledge, London, 1999, pp. 1049–1051.

United Nations, *United Nations Millennium Declaration*, United Nations, New York, 2000.

UNCED, *Earth Summit: Agenda 21*, United Nations Conference on Environment and Development, New York, NY, 1992.

UNDP, *Human Development Report: Concept and Measurement of Human Development*, Oxford University Press, New York, NY, 1990.

UNDP, *Human Development Report: Economic Growth and Human Development*, Oxford University Press, New York, NY, 1996.

UNDP, *Human Development Report: Consumption for Human Development*, Oxford University Press, New York, NY, 1998.

UNDP, *Human Development Report: Globalisation with a Human Face*, Oxford University Press, New York, NY, 1999.

UNDP, *Human Development Report: Deepening Democracy in a Fragmented World*, Oxford University Press, New York, NY, 2002.

UNDP, *Transforming the Mainstream: Gender in UNDP*, UNDP, New York, NY, 2003.

Uphoff, N., *Local Institutional Development: An Analytical Sourcebook with Cases*, Kumarian Press, West Hartford, CT, 1986.

Viederman, S., Sustainability's five capitals and three pillars, in *Building Sustainable Societies: A Blueprint for a Post-Industrial World*, Pirages, D.C., Ed., M.E. Sharpe, Armonk, NY, 1996, pp. 45–54.

WCED, *Our Common Futures*, UN, World Commission on Environment and Developments, New York, 1987.

Weidner, E.W., The elements of development administration, in *Development Administration in Asia*, Weidner, E.W., Ed., Duke University Press, Durham, NC, 1970, pp. 3–24.

Weigel, G. and Waldburger, D., *Connecting people for a Better World*, Swiss Agency for Development and Cooperation and Kuala Lumpur, Global Knowledge Partnership, Berne, 2004.

White, G., Towards a democratic developmental state, *IDS Bull.*, 26 (2), 27–36, 1995.

Williamson, J., The progress of policy reform in Latin America, in *Policy Analyses in International Economics*, Vol. 28, Institute for International Economics, Washington, DC, 1990.

Wilson, C.A., Policy regimes and policy change, *J. Public Policy*, 20 (3), 247–274, 2000.

World Bank, *Sub-Saharan Africa: From Crisis to Sustainable Growth*, World Bank, Washington, DC, 1989a.

World Bank, *World Development Report: Financial Systems and Development*, World Bank, Washington DC, 1989b.

World Bank, *World Development Report: Entering the 21st Century*, World Bank, Washington, DC, 1999a.

World Bank, *Development Committee Communiqué*, Available at http://web. worldbank.org/WBSITE/EXTERNAL/PROJECTS/STRATEGIES/CDF/0,,con tentMDK:20072662~menuPK:60746~pagePK:139301~piPK:139306~the SitePK:140576,00.html (accessed on 24 September 2004), 27 September, 1999b.

World Bank, *Reforming Public Institutions and Strengthening Governance*, World Bank, Washington, DC, 2000a.

World Bank, *World Development Report: Attacking Poverty*, World Bank, Washington, DC, 2000b.

World Bank, *Empowerment Sourcebook*, World Bank, Washington, DC, 2002a.

World Bank, *World Development Report: Sustainable Development in a Dynamic World*, World Bank, Washington, DC, 2002b.

World Bank, *Partnerships in Development: Progress in the Fight Against Poverty*, World Bank, Washington, DC, 2004.

Wunsch, J., Institutional analysis and decentralization: developing an analytical framework for effective third world administrative reform, in *Polycentric Governance and Development*, University of Michigan Press, McGinnis, M.D., Ed., Ann Arbor, 1999, pp. 243–268.

Zafarullah, H., Consolidating democratic governance: one step forward, two steps back, in *Development, Governance and the Environment in South Asia: A Focus on Bangladesh*, Alauddin, M. and Hasan, S., Eds., Macmillan, London, 1999, pp. 182–184.

Zazueta, A., *Policy Hits the Ground: Participation and Equity in Environmental Policy-Making*, World Resources Institute, Washington, DC, 1995.

Chapter 3

Changing Configurations of the Developmental State

Adrian Leftwich

CONTENTS

I. Introduction

Since the late 1980s, a new orthodoxy has dominated much of the theory and practice of development governance. Generally (and incorrectly) referred to as "The Washington Consensus," the regime which it entails has often been associated with theoretical and philosophical positions such as "neoconservatism," "neoliberalism," and even "market fundamentalism" (Williamson, 1997, 2000). In terms of the governance of economic matters, this new orthodoxy has meant a commitment to more rather than less free markets. It is also usually associated in political terms with a strong preference for representative liberal democratic politics as the institutional means whereby governments and bureaucracies are held accountable for the residual and facilitating role allocated to them in some versions of the neoliberal theory, usually the provision of the institutional and infrastructural framework for economic activity and growth (World Bank, 1997: 111). In short, at the heart of this current (2004) and continuing (though modifying) orthodoxy is the claim that the economic and political institutions of liberal democratic capitalism, with a limited, noninterventionist but efficient state, deploying a competent and noncorrupt bureaucracy, is (and always has been) the most effective model of development governance.

While there may be a case (often a fiscal one) to be made today for rebalancing the state–society or public–private relationship in promoting economic and social welfare in the industrially advanced OECD (the Organisation for Economic Co-operation and Development) countries (Giddens, 1998), the state played a central role in the critical early stages of their industrial development. Indeed, most of the now developed industrial countries and most of the successful developing countries of the second half of the 20th century have all shown the importance and effectiveness of state involvement, direction and management in the governance of development, especially in "catch-up" development. In particular, the history of Japan from the 1870s and of Korea, the Republic of China (Taiwan), Singapore, and some other south-east Asian countries in the postwar era (as well as outliers such as Botswana and Mauritius) illustrate the centrality of the state (and especially the "developmental state" in its various forms) as an essential and effective agency of "late" development.

But, given the current orthodoxy, what prospects are there for other newly developing countries to adopt or adapt the "developmental state" model? I shall argue that, for the moment at least, the prospects are not good. Nonetheless, there will always be the need for state involvement, especially in "catch-up" development, and it will once again return to the agenda. In the following, I will first clarify the central concepts and terms to be used — especially those of development and governance — and I will argue that development governance is essentially a *political* not an administrative or managerial matter, and that politics determines both the form and limits of such governance. The central elements of the current orthodoxy and how much of this was absent in the now developed countries when they were pushing ahead with their industrial transform-ations are then outlined. This will be followed by an account of the model of the "developmental state," based on its East Asian manifestations, showing how central, effective, and pervasive it has been in promoting some of the most astonishing transformations of the 20th century. I return finally to the neoliberal foundations of contemporary globalization and suggest that the intellectual, ideological, and political pressures which emanate from it offer little hope for the replication of the developmental state model of development governance, but only in the short run.

II. Concepts and Terms: "Development," "Governance," and "Development Governance"

Often associated with the idea of "progress" in the history of the social sciences (Arndt, 1981; Leftwich, 2000), the concept of "development" can be understood in the context of a variety of different approaches, which include development:

- as the economic core of historical "progress"
- as the conscious exploitation of natural resources (as in "to develop the Sahara")
- as the planned promotion of economic and (sometimes) social and political advancement (by the state)
- as a condition (like maturity or even old age, i.e., something to be reached)
- as a process (i.e., an on-going process of positive change for which there is no limit)

- as economic growth (usually measured in gross national product [GNP] per capita)
- as structural change (for instance, through industrialization)
- as modernization (usually referring primarily to secular capitalist or socialist democracy)
- of the forces of production (Marxism) and associated "modes of production"

The gist all the above approaches has been a common concern for *economic* transformation (in the form of growth in GNP, modernization, structural change, and enhancing the forces of production). But in the second half of the 20th century these concerns widened to include other noneconomic goals and values (Huntington, 1987) such as "social development," the satisfaction of basic human needs, "freedom," the expansion of choice (Sen, 1999), and "sustainable" development (Redclift, 1987).

However, the slow progress of "development" in many parts of the world gave rise to a more critical view of the concept, especially by some third-world theorists. Some began to see "development" as little other than western domination in practice (certainly in its globalizing manifestation), or as a disguise for a discourse of economic, political, and intellectual domination (Said, 1978; Esteva, 1992; Escobar, 1995). These criticisms have unquestionably helped to expand the conception of development to include social objectives such as greater equality (both economic and social, for instance, in relation to gender), widespread education, and the elimination of poverty, as expressed in the Millennium Goals (UNDP, 2003). Nonetheless, there can be little doubt that few of these broader social goals of development can be achieved nationally without the resources, which only economic growth can generate. In addition, emerging evidence suggests strongly that the incomes of the poor increase with increasing average income (Dollar and Kraay, 2001).

So economic growth, as a necessary (but not sufficient) means to achieve a wide range of developmental goals, remains at the heart of most schools of theory and policy when it comes to devising the institutions of developmental governance to carry it through. And the processes of growth-based development have long been understood, on both the left and the right, to involve a shift from societies based primarily on agrarian economies to those based on the application of science to production for industrial purposes (Kitching, 1982; Munck, 2000; Stiglitz, 2003). In the 19th century, Marx (as with many other theorists of social development) understood this to mean that "the country that is more developed industrially only shows to the less developed, the image of its own future" (Marx, 1976: 91), and in the early 21st century Joseph Stiglitz (2003: 77) talks simply of nothing less than the "transformation of society." These transformative processes have everywhere required immense changes in the structure of societies, and they have commonly involved profound human suffering, social costs and environmental damage (something which contemporary schools of development hope can be reduced, if not avoided), and inevitably political turbulence. Nonetheless, in terms of its achievements with respect to infant mortality, life expectancy, containment of disease, choice and freedom, knowledge and understanding, the process of growth-based development has been profoundly beneficial. That these benefits have also been unevenly distributed both *within* countries (grotesquely so, e.g., in Brazil, South Africa, and the Philippines) and *between* countries, represents not simply a failure of "development," but of its governance or, more sharply, its politics, both nationally and internationally. And this, too, is something which contemporary theorists of development are concerned to change (Stiglitz, 2002, 2003).

So the term "development" in this chapter means the processes of sustainable economic growth through science-based industrialization, the purpose of which is the expansion of human welfare, as measured by increasing life expectancy, education, security, freedom, and choice; and by the reduction of poverty, vulnerability (both social and natural), disease, and inequality.

A. Governance

What is clear, however, is that economic growth, on its own, has never achieved any of these other noneconomic "goals of development" (Huntington, 1987; North, 1997), nor could it. The context, direction, and pattern of growth, whether successful or not, and also the distribution of its costs and benefits have always and everywhere been a function of politics and the institutions devised through political processes, where institutions are understood to mean rules, routines, and procedures (North, 1989). In the broadest sense, these structures and relations of institutions of course constitute the *governance* of a society, a concept that is wider than that of *government*. The former — governance — denotes the overarching structure of political and economic institutions, that is the principles, procedures, relationships, and rules, by which the total social, political, and economic life of a society is governed; whereas the latter refers to the formal institutional structure and location of authoritative decision-making in the modern state (Frischtak, 1994: 4).

B. Development Governance

Markets, on their own, however, cannot by definition set or prioritize collective *economic* developmental goals (such as rural development, import substitution, export orientation, the establishment of export processing zones, the layout of transport infrastructure, or the attraction or repulsion of direct foreign investment). Nor can markets set, let alone achieve, *social* developmental goals (such as educational or welfare provision, poverty reduction, or gender equality). Only states, or the governments within them, can do so by setting goals and devising the institutional constraints and incentives that they believe will promote the achievement of such goals (Peters, 2004: 26). This is essentially what governments do; simply stated, it is the politics of what development governance is all about. In short, development governance may be defined as the political processes and institutional arrangements, which are dedicated and devoted to the purposeful promotion of economic growth and the distribution of its costs and benefits. In other words, development is not simply a matter of economics and economic policy, but fundamentally a matter of political economy.

Moreover, the important point here is that the modern state arose as the macroinstitutional agency of development governance. To be precise, the (varying) institutions of the modern state — in its European provenance from the 17th century, and especially in the 19th century, which have been borrowed and adapted so widely around the world from Latin America to Japan — arose, essentially, as the agency of and for industrial transformation, commonly spurred in this purpose by economic and military rivalry and war, or the preparation for war (Tilly, 1975, 1992; Bates, 2001). In its provenance and evolution, *the fundamental defining role and function of the modern state has been to promote, organize, protect, and sustain the economic and social transformation to industrialism — and beyond into the so-called postindustrial era*. It is fair to say that in both the 19th and 20th century history of the now industrial powers, and in the more recent modern history of the contemporary developing world, *successful and effective modern states and successful economies have gone together* (Leftwich, 2004a). Nothing encapsulates this relation better than the slogan of state purpose and the rallying cry of the modernizers in post-Meiji Japan after 1870: "Fukoku Kyōhei," that is "National Wealth and Military Strength!" (Crump, 1983: 4), often translated as "Rich country, Strong army."

It should be clear that the World Bank's notion of governance as "the exercise of political power to manage a nation's affairs" (World Bank, 1989: 60) and of "good" governance as "sound development management" (World Bank, 1992: 1) has been all too simple, too superficial, too technicist, and too managerial in conception and approach. For if politics is understood to consist of all the activities of conflict, cooperation, and collaboration in the use, production, and distribution of resources (Leftwich, 2004: 103), then nothing could be more political than "development," involving as it does the structuring, restructuring, and institutionalization of new ways of producing, using, and distributing resources, inevitably involving new winners and new losers. So, to understand development governance properly, we have to understand it *politically*, not simply managerially or administratively. And, as will become clear, nothing illustrates this better than the rise and characteristics of the "developmental state" as a *political* phenomenon.

III. Neoliberalism and Development Governance

The rise of neoliberalism in the 1980s — the so-called "counter-revolution in development theory and policy" (Toye, 1987) — has been well described and analyzed elsewhere (Colclough and Manor, 1993); as has the way in which it underpinned the structural adjustment programmes, which accompanied it (Nelson, 1989; Mosley et al., 1991). The aim of the counter-revolution was to shatter the dominant postwar state-led and state-planned development paradigms and to overcome the problems of developmental stagnation (which were very serious, especially in Africa) by promoting open and free competitive market economies on a global scale, supervised by minimal states. In the words of one of the most persuasive advocates of markets as engines of development: an "imperfect market mechanism" is likely to perform better in practice than an "imperfect planning mechanism" (Lal, 1983: 106), or, in short, "imperfect markets are better than imperfect states" (Colclough, 1993: 7; World Bank, 1997).

The general pattern of structural adjustment packages has usually involved two main stages: "stabilization" and "adjustment," often deployed by the IMF and the World Bank, working in tandem. Stabilization has normally meant immediate devaluation and often quite drastic public expenditure cuts. At the national level, adjustment followed and sought to transform economic structures and institutions through varying doses of deregulation, devaluation, privatization, dismantling or downsizing allegedly oversized and rambling public bureaucracies, reducing subsidies and tariffs, and encouraging realistic prices to emerge as a stimulus to greater productivity, especially for export. The overall thrust of these packages was to encourage enterprise-driven growth (and especially export-oriented growth) in open economies, to give security to property rights, and to attract direct foreign investment, with few constraints. At the international level, the multilateral organizations of development, finance, and trade — the World Bank, the International Monetary Fund, the World Trade Organization, and regional organizations of governments and banks — have sought to promote new sets of rules to free up the movement of goods, capital, and labor. As the then Foreign Secretary of the United Kingdom, Douglas Hurd, put it in 1990: ". . . free markets, open trade and private property are the best ways known to mankind for improving its standard of living" (Hurd, 1990: 4).

A. The Washington Consensus

It was in the context of such broad almost philosophical announcements that the so-called Washington consensus emerged (Williamson, 1990). It was "invented," as its author describes it, to refer to "the lowest common denominator of policy-advice being addressed by the Washington-based institutions to Latin American countries in 1989" (Williamson, 2000: 251). There were ten propositions which, in Williamson's view, summed up the consensus on economic governance (Williamson, 2000: 252–253). These were:

- Fiscal discipline
- A redirection of public expenditure to areas, which could promote growth and improve income distribution (such as primary health care and education and infrastructure)
- Tax reform to lower marginal rates and broaden the base
- Liberalization of interest rates
- A competitive exchange rate
- Trade liberalization
- Liberalization of rules governing foreign direct investment (FDI)
- Privatization
- Deregulation to encourage enterprise
- Secure property rights

Williamson has maintained throughout that this list represents nothing more than a realistic assessment of the lowest common denominator which the Washington-based institutions would agree on and that, properly applied, would contribute to both growth and redistribution. A more recent list (Williamson, 1997: 58) adds strengthening institutions (central banks, budget offices, and judiciaries) and increasing educational and social expenditure. In addition, it is clear that in the 1990s there has been some retreat from the more extreme and quasi-libertarian forms of neoliberalism and market fundamentalism. To illustrate, major Western governments, the UN and international institutions, like the World Bank, have once again started to show concern with pro-poor policies, as reflected in the Millennium Goals. Moreover, a growing realization of the importance of the role of institutions in development has acted not only to modify the extremes of neoliberal notions of development governance, but also to spawn very interesting research[1] on the role of institutions in development (Zysman, 1994; World Bank, 2002; DfID, 2003; Rodrik, 2003).

Nonetheless, despite this reemergence of concern for pro-poor policies and institutions, the emphatic and central thrust of official policy in the west, generally, has remained consistently sceptical of states and governments as agents of development governance. In addition, this has been reflected in a general model of governance that represented a contemporary version of liberal governmental minimalism in a context of secure property rights.

B. Neoliberal Development Governance

What was this model of governance that went with the ascendance of neoliberal economics? In a series of definitive statements, the World Bank (followed by most of the developed OECD countries through their national overseas aid agencies) identified four main principles of development governance, which would enhance the new regime of market-led economic growth (World Bank, 1992, 1994). They were: (i) accountability, which in essence meant holding governments responsible for their actions; (ii) a legal framework for development, which meant a structure of rules and laws which would secure property rights and provide clarity, predictability, and stability for the private sector, and which would be impartially and fairly applied to all, providing the basis for conflict resolution through an independent judicial system; (iii) information, by which was meant that information about economic conditions, budgets, markets, and government intentions would be reliable and accessible to all, something which is crucial for private sector calculations; (iv) finally, insistence on transparency as a call for open government, to enhance accountability, limit corruption, and stimulate consultative processes between government and private interests over policy development. It will be clear that the postwar preoccupation in the theory and practice of development governance with planning, infant industry protection, import substitution, tariffs, subsidies and general state protection and promotion of the national economy through full or partial nationalization and control or management of finance (on which topic, for Korea, see Woo, 1991), constraints on foreign investment and state involvement in infrastructural development are entirely absent from the agenda of the neoliberal political economy of development.

Moreover, though institutions like the World Bank are forbidden (by its Articles of Agreement in the case of the Bank) to discuss "politics," or to use political considerations in loan decisions, many of the major Western governments interpreted the new model to include democratic, or "polyarchical" (Robinson, 1996) reform, and indeed exercised their influence through aid conditionality (and more recently coercion) to bring this about, as the classic cases of Kenya and Malawi in the early 1990s illustrated (Bratton and van der Walle, 1997: 182–183). These concerns, in turn, stimulated a renewed debate and fresh research about the relationship of democracy and development, and a flurry of publications (see Przeworski et al., 2000, for a good recent example), with some arguing that democracy was an outcome of development and others arguing that it was a condition of democracy.

In short, the nub of the neoliberal prescription for both the economics and politics of development governance was essentially to leave productive activities, and increasingly many aspects of welfare provision from health to pensions (Haagh and Helgø, 2002), to the efforts of domestic and foreign entrepreneurs and investors working in largely open national and international markets, while requiring of the state that it provide the legal and institutional framework to permit and promote this, with particular reference to property rights.

IV. Developmental Antecedents

Was this how the now developed (OECD) societies managed their own transitions to industrialism before and during the 18th and 19th centuries (Chang, 2002)? Did this model govern the way in which they later — in the 20th century — sustained, protected, and transformed that process through the consequences of war, the crises of inter-war depression, and postwar reconstruction (Shonfield, 1969)? Was this the way in which industrialization and modernization deepened in European late-developers such as Italy in the inter-war and post-war years (Gregor, 1979), or which Primo de Rivera and then, after him, Franco attempted in Spain from the late 1920s (Ben-Ami, 1983)? Is this how a process of industrial "modernization" in Turkey was initiated and sustained after its "elite revolution" from above in 1923 under Kemal Atatürk (Trimberger, 1978)? Did free markets alone in the factors of production — land, labor, and capital — shape the racist form of industrialization in South Africa for most of the 20th century, till the collapse of *apartheid* in 1990 (Yudelman, 1983; Moon, 2004)? Did these free market and minimalist state principles shape French policy and practice between the wars and, especially, after the Second World War (Shonfield, 1969; Loriaux, 1999)? And was it the model under which the remarkable East and South-east Asian economic transformations have taken place — in Japan from 1870, in Taiwan from 1949, in Korea after 1960 (Woo-Cumings, 1999), in Malaysia between 1970 and 1990 (Lall, 1995), and in Singapore (Huff, 1995) since its independence from Malaysia in 1965? Have Botswana (Taylor, 2004) and Mauritius (Bowman, 1991; Meisenhelde, 1995) achieved such remarkable developmental records under this free market model since the 1960s?

The answer to all these questions must be an emphatic "no." The historical practices of development governance (though not understood or called that everywhere all the time), both economic and political, which shaped these Euro-American and developing country histories bear little relationship to what is currently being advertised as the answer to third-world ills (Chang, 2002).

In mid-19th century, the German economist, List (1844), observed forcefully the need for a *national* (assisted and protected) economy to catch up with the leaders *before* entering open competition. Many other economic historians and historically grounded social scientists have shown how in many different ways the western developmental story is not simply about the growth of market-driven national economies in national states, but also of a variety of patterns of more or less active and pervasive state involvement (Polanyi, 1944; Gerschenkron, 1962; Senghaas, 1985; Tilly, 1992; Chang and Rowthorn, 1995; Kozul-Wright, 1995; Weiss and Hobson, 1995; Chang, 2002). This is not to say that state action was uniform everywhere in policy and practice over space and time. Nor is it to say that the now industrialized economies of the West had states remotely like the postwar developmental states of East Asia. However, what it is to argue is that the governments of most of the major industrialized economies, including the U.S.A. (Kozul-Wright, 1995), adopted a variety of *national* measures at key stages before during and after their industrial transformations to accelerate, protect, and recover growth. Tariff rates, for example, between 1820 and 1950 in selected developed countries (including the United States) were applied forcefully when and where necessary (Chang, 2002: 17). "European countries adhered to the principle of free trade only during the few years from 1860 to the second half of the 1870s" (Senghaas, 1985: 22). Thereafter, with the exception of England, up to the First World War and during the inter-war years, protection was not only widespread but also the norm.

But it was not only through tariffs that states intervened to bolster "their" economies, to favor certain sectors, and to protect the national interest. As so many of these accounts have shown in different ways, pervasive forms of planning leading to tax rebates, preventing the export of machines and skilled labor, espionage, industrial and agricultural training, schooling, export credits, establishing and funding research institutes, building infrastructure and utilities, prohibiting colonies from producing certain commodities and products, barring colonial imports, imposing free trade on others, and using but not respecting patents. There can be few better examples of the extent to which a major European state was an active partner in development processes than that of the French state as it deepened its industrialization after the First World War and rebuilt after the Second World War (Shonfield, 1969; Loriaux, 1999).

The key point to drive home here is that the governments of now developed societies used (and in some respect still use) a variety of measures under diverse circumstances to promote or protect their national economic interests. The dynamics of nationalism, from the 19th century in particular, sharpened state involvement in what Tilly (1992: 97) has referred to as "adjudication, production, and distribution" on a widespread basis — in the production and regulation of energy, transport, communication, food, and arms. He goes on to remind us that:

> All states intervened more generally in production as demands from workers and intellectuals for the checking of capitalist excesses became more effective; socialist states merely represent the extreme of a general tendency. Extraction, protection and adjudication intertwined, finally, to draw states into the control of distribution — first as a away of assuring state revenues from the flow of goods, then as a response to popular demands for correction of inequities and local shortages. Again, socialist states mark but the extreme version of a very general expansion in state activity outside the military realm. (Tilly, 1992: 98)

Policies of state-led capitalist development have been pervasive in the developing world from the inter-war years, especially in the now middle-income countries, ranging from Mexico in the 1930s and beyond (Espinosa-Coria, 2004) to Turkey after 1923 (Hale, 1981: 53–81; Keyder, 1987: 91–115). These developmental measures were, for a while, highly successful forms of development governance, promoting industrial development and change (for instance, through import substituting industrialization in Latin America), though not everywhere, as the grim record of Africa and parts of South Asia shows. But nothing quite compares to the rapid transformative capacity of the "developmental states" of East Asia, the model of which has been under attack for a decade.

V. Developmental State

Since Chalmers Johnson's original account (1982) of the developmental state in Japan, there has emerged a rich comparative literature on various aspects of this type of state, and this has been well surveyed recently (Woo-Cumings, 1999). I have elsewhere suggested (Leftwich, 1995) that the distinguishing characteristic of developmental states has been that their political purposes and institutional structures (especially their bureaucracies) have been developmentally driven, while their developmental objectives have been politically driven. At the heart of these states, fundamentally *political* factors have shaped the urgency, thrust, and pace of their developmental strategies through the structures of the state. These political factors have normally included intense nationalism, ideology, and a wish to "catch up" economically with the west or immediate neighbors. But the need for military preparedness has also been a powerful force in shaping developmental states, which has commonly been a consequence of their need to respond to regional competition and external threat, even more so than Tilly (1975) has argued for the link between state formation and warmaking in 19th century Europe. In short, a *necessary* combination of both economic and military nationalism ("Rich country, strong army") has been at the heart of the developmental state regime (Woo-Cumings, 1999a: 8).

Although, I have defined the developmental state at length elsewhere (Leftwich, 2000:167), for present purposes an operational definition of the developmental state will be sufficient. The developmental state is a state whose *politics* have concentrated sufficient determination, power, autonomy, capacity, and legitimacy at the center to shape, pursue, and encourage the achievement of explicit developmental objectives, whether by establishing, promoting, and protecting the conditions of economic growth (in the capitalist developmental states), by organizing it directly (in the "socialist" variants), or a varying combination of both.

In practical terms, developmental states have been characterized by a number of structural features, namely a dominant, determined and usually united elite, dedicated to the promotion of growth; relative autonomy of the state, either from democratic accountability or from capture by key interests, or both; a powerful, highly trained, competent, politically supported and insulated economic bureaucracy at the heart of developmental policy and planning; a relatively weak and subordinated civil society; the capacity for effective management of private economic interests; an uneasy mix of repression, poor human rights (especially in the nondemocratic developmental states), legitimacy, and performance. In addition, paradigmatic developmental states — like South Korea or Taiwan — have had the political backing and support of a major external power, or powers, such as the U.S.A. or Japan, as well as access to both economic and military aid to sustain their objectives.

These states have been remarkable in what they have achieved, as measured in terms of all the normal economic and social indicators such as growth rates, life expectancy, levels of education, and degrees of inequality. How did they do this?

A. Policy and Practice of Developmental States

The second slogan of the Meiji Restoration was *"shokusan kohgyo"* (promote industries) and first in the late 19th century and then again, crucially, before and after the Second World War, the Japanese state was single-minded in pursuing this objective, followed in the 1960s and beyond by other "newly industrializing economies" in East and South-east Asia, such as

Korea, Taiwan, Malaysia, Singapore, Thailand, and Indonesia. Throughout this period, all pursued various kinds of industrial (and agricultural) policies directed by a variety of administrative mechanisms (notably national 5-year "development plans") and tools. The varying mix of specific policies have included: active agricultural modernization (often involving land reform); control of financial institutions (as in Korea and Taiwan); the setting up and funding development banks; maintaining tariff walls to protect emerging industries as well as establishing import quotas or prohibiting the physical import of listed (and commonly luxury consumer) items; designating, targeting, and supporting key industries as leading agencies and establishing certain state-owned industries (for a while) as in textiles, glass, chemicals, iron, and steel; pursuing phases of import substitution, followed by export promotion and enhancement; providing tax exemptions and preferences as incentives for certain industrial lines; fixing prices; offering credit and export assistance to key industries; setting up export-processing zones; raising levels of education and industrial training while often maintaining repressive labor regimes to attract, under often close surveillance, foreign investment — and much more (Hale, 1981; Woo, 1991; Fields, 1995; Lall, 1995; Yamada and Kuchiki, 1997).

VI. Developmental Governance

The detail and the variety of developmental states, country by country, are well known. But under-girding the developmental strategies of these states has been a conception and practice of developmental governance — indeed of governance more generally — which has been very different to the liberal model with which western societies are familiar.

A. Western Model of Governance

In the western model of economic (and hence developmental) governance (and certainly in its neoliberal expression), state and society are set essentially in opposition to each other. Diverse interests compete against the state and against each other to extract the best possible policy output (for themselves) from the state, whether in terms of tax regimes, education and training, labor or export policy. In its pluralist and neoclassical forms, this model involves essentially a political market of interests — sometimes including that of the state — in which outcomes are the consequence of bargaining and deals between the interests and the state. Sometimes, as in the so-called "Swedish model," these relations of interests were contained within institutionalized bargaining structures of formalized cooperation, sometimes referred to as "corporatism" (Weiss and Hobson, 1995: 137; Rothstein, 2001). However in ideological terms, the ideal state was seen as, or required to be, distant, at best only governing the enabling institutional environment (courts, contracts, law and order, and defence) and sometimes providing physical and infrastructural development where the private sector would not go, but not setting or actively facilitating the achievement of stipulated developmental goals. Of course, the *actual* practices of western states in the crucial transformative years bear little relationship to this ideology for "states, not merely markets, are central to an historical understanding of national economic development" (Weiss and Hobson, 1995: 135).

B. Developmental State Model of Governance

However, the implicit model of governance in developmental states (and states with developmental determination) has been very different to this. The sharp antithesis (and suspicion) between society and state has not been the norm in their outlook or practice, at least not in the early phases of politically driven, defensive, and catch-up economic nationalism, which has been at the heart of their developmental preoccupations (Johnson, 1982: 24). Rather, the task of building a strong economy (and strong defensive capability which it finances) has been perceived as a collective or national project, best achieved by a collaborative division of labor between public and private elites. As Ding (1994: 317) indicates:

> In East Asia, the states are organizationally pervasive, without clear-cut boundaries. Their powers and functions are diffuse and they pay little respect to due process. Consequently the lines between public and private, political and personal, formal and informal, official and nonofficial, governmental and market, legal and customary, and between procedural and substantial, are all blurred.

When effective, and when not degenerating into clientelism or predatory behavior (Evans, 1995), this has usually generated, developmentally, a "synergy of state and market" (Weiss and Hobson, 1995: 135) in which the state (and key institutions within it, such as MITI in Japan and the Economic Planning Board in South Korea) had two overarching responsibilities: "managing capacity" and "coordination capacity" (Kim, 2000: 563). In pursuit of these policies of "governing the market" (Wade, 1990), most developmental states (even those outside East Asia, such as Botswana) built up impressive institutional capacities to steer, supervise, manage, and monitor their developmental trajectory (Chen et al., 1998; Evans, 1998; Weiss, 1998: 41–64; Chang, 2002: 69–121).

VII. Neoliberalism, Globalization, and the Developmental State

A. *Weakening of the Developmental States*

As mentioned earlier, the emerging neoliberal hegemony in domestic western political economy in the 1980s began to impact upon the development aid policies of the OECD countries, and came to be expressed in the new structural adjustment lending strategies. This was often justified (with good cause) by the clear failure of statist development strategy to promote growth and reduce poverty in much of Africa, many countries in Latin America, and parts of South Asia. But with the collapse of communism in 1990, the melting away of the Cold War, the rise to prominence of the World Trade Organization and its dedication to free trade, and the urge of global capital to find new havens for investment, and the ripples of liberal reform reached even the successfully performing developmental states. These external pressures to liberalize on imports and capital were intensified by internal demands from a burgeoning civil society for democratization (Potter, 1997) and financial liberalization, as well as by the increasing capacity of major industrial and financial interests in the developmental states to break free of developmental state supervision and surveillance or to achieve varying degrees of state "capture." South Korea (Kim, 2000) provides a classic example of how liberalization weakened the state and particularly its institutions of development planning, such as the dismantling of the Economic Planning Board in 1993, and financial regulation and control. At the same time, the process strengthened the capacity of vested interests to influence and hence reduce the autonomy of the state so that it succumbed to the crisis that struck in 1997 (Lee, 2000; Weiss, 2000).

B. *Containing New Developmental States*

The same political and economic forces which have acted to dilute the capacity of developmental states have also acted to preempt the emergence of new developmental states elsewhere. Such states, of course, cannot just be had to order and it is rare that the historical and internal socio-economic and political conditions have been present which would allow their formation. External threat (whether economic or political), a unified coalition of elites with both the political determination to promote growth and equity and the capacity and control (usually involving a close alliance with the military) to push it through have been the minimum internal requirements for developmental states to form, provided always that, externally, the international geo-political and ideological circumstances have been favorable, as they were during the postwar years.

Those circumstances obtain no longer. So the following wind — in aid or political and military support — which the developmental states of the 1960s and beyond received is no longer available. And short of the (now) rare socialist developmental velocity, which immediate postrevolutionary or postcoup regimes (China, Cuba, and Korea) can generate, it is hard to see the emergence of any newly determined statist development strategies, let alone the formation of new developmental states. And an interesting example of this problem can be found in the developments in post-apartheid South Africa after 1994.

C. South African Case

In 1994, the new ANC government (which was by far the most dominant party, enjoying massive legitimacy and support under President Mandela) adopted an economic policy and strategy known as the Reconstruction and Development Programme (RDP). Its aim was to correct the inequalities inherited from past racist policies and practices, to promote growth and ensure a more even distribution of wealth. In many ways, given the significant strategic role allotted to the state and the public sector, and a powerful redistributive thrust (Lodge, 2002), the RDP represented the most recent point in a lineage which went back to the Freedom Charter of 1955, which had set out the essentially democratic socialist vision and programme of the modern ANC. An attempt was made to institutionalize the RDP by locating its head office in the President's Office, with regional offices around the country (Webster and Adler, 1999; Moon, 2004).

But within 2 years the RDP had effectively given way to a new strategic policy — the Growth, Employment, and Redistribution (GEAR) programme, announced in 1996. While seeking rapid growth and redistribution, the means adopted veered quite sharply from those in the RDP by emphasizing much more standard neoliberal reforms — reduction of fiscal deficit, reducing the role of the state, lowering tariffs and relaxing exchange controls and tax reductions to encourage domestic investment and attract foreign investment. It is hardly surprising that the major trade union organization in South Africa, The Congress of South African Trade Unions (COSATU) was to describe GEAR as favoring "foreign and local capital" (cited in Lodge, 2002: 26).

Why the change of developmental direction from the social-democratic and statist traditions of the ANC to an essentially liberal approach?

Recent research (Bond, 2001; Lodge, 2002; Moon, 2004) has shown that both internal and external *political* factors must be central to any plausible explanation of the shift from RDP to GEAR. The absence of a clear developmental consensus within the dominant political alliance, and between it and the powerful institutions of both capital and labor in a burgeoning civil society, plus the insistent advice of World Bank, IMF, and other western government officials — through seminars, consultations, and study visits to Washington — all acted strongly to influence key players in the ANC government to downplay the role of the state in the developmental governance of post-apartheid development and give space to markets and free trade as RDP gave way to GEAR.

My point here is not that the RDP represented the typical blueprint for the classic developmental state strategy of state-managed economic catch-up. Rather, even in South Africa with a radical political movement enjoying great legitimacy and power, the shift to GEAR showed quite clearly that the international environment today is deeply inhospitable to policies and programmes which depart much from the prescriptions of the neoliberal orthodoxy. Under these circumstances — and given the absence of internal political coalitions determined to drive through late catch-up development — the prospects for new developmental statism elsewhere must currently be somewhat bleak.

VIII. Conclusions

Following Chang (2002) and others, the policy prescriptions of the current neoliberal orthodoxy bear little relationship to what the now developed OECD countries did in their formative years of industrial transformation, protection, and consolidation. Moreover, in the 20th century, following what had been happening in Japan, a relatively small number of developing societies elaborated, intensified, and institutionalized these essentially nationalist techniques in what have come to be called "development states," whose heyday was in the three decades between 1960 and 1990. Driven by the urgency of (usually external) threat and a powerful nationalist political determination to be rich and strong, all these states had as their key objective the development of policies and procedures that would enable them to "catch-up."

However, in the course of the 1980s and especially the 1990s, under the post-cold war pressure of external and internal demands for liberalization, many aspects of state management, surveillance, and involvement in development governance were greatly reduced, sometimes with catastrophic consequences (as in the crisis of 1997 in East Asia). More generally, in this global environment, intense political and economic pressures — through various aspects of aid conditionality, for example — have been applied to governments in the developing world to roll back the involvement of the state, to throw open markets, to lower trade barriers, and to promote greater political accountability through the introduction of democratic procedures. Where states had previously been predatory and oppressive, suffocating, distorting, or preventing the emergence of institutions, which might stimulate growth, this has had some beneficial effects in dismantling or displacing corrupt authoritarianisms. But where the private and public institutions have simply not been in place to allow this to become development — from Haiti to the Democratic Republic of Congo (Zaire as was) — there is the serious danger of a descent into "democratic" corruption and yet deeper economic malaise.

But even where liberal reforms have stimulated economic growth — for instance from Chile to China, and from Mexico to Malaysia — inequality has deepened quite sharply *within* these societies (Held, 2004: 37), while inequality *between* nation states continues to increase (Wade, 2001). There is some evidence to suggest that the international development and finance institutions have begun to recognize that though free markets may stimulate growth in some contexts, they are unable to solve the problems of inequality and poverty within and between countries. Hence the recent identification of the Millennium Development Goals and the necessarily enhanced interest in the institutional requirements for achieving them. There is now, moreover, widespread recognition that such inequalities and poverty have far-reaching implications for security issues on a national and global scale. Given this, there are grounds for cautious optimism that there will be a growing sense that it is time to "bring the state back in," provided it is capable of performing effectively in the field of development governance and, where it is not, of encouraging the political and economic institutions and conditions which will allow it to do so. This may not herald the resurgence of paradigmatic "developmental states" around the world — the internal political conditions seldom exist for that — but it may mean that, when thinking about development governance, greater recognition will once again be given to the central role of the state and public sector in both establishing the conditions for growth and ensuring that its benefits are more evenly distributed within developing societies. Ultimately this is a question of the internal politics of developing societies. But it is now unavoidable that this will also require a profound rethink and restructuring of the institutions and rules of governance of the global political economy in ways that will allow states in developing societies to respond flexibly and appropriately to the opportunities and constraints each faces in the light of their respective histories and endowments, instead of leaving them impotent and supine before the onward rush of markets (Held, 2004).

Note

1. Research conducted by the World Bank Development Research Group and the National Bureau of Economic Research (NBER) in the U.S.A. is illustrative of this work. Much of it is accessible through their respective Web sites.

References

Arndt, H.W., Economic development: a semantic history, *Econ. Dev. Cult. Change*, 29 (3), 457–466, 1981.

Bates, R.H., *Prosperity and Violence: The Political Economy of Development*, W.W. Norton, New York, 2001.

Ben-Ami, S., *Fascism from Above: The Dictatorship of Primo de Rivera in Spain, 1923–1930*, Clarendon Press, Oxford, 1983.

Bond, P., *Against Global Apartheid: South Africa Meets the World Bank, the IMF and International Finance*, University of Cape Town Press, Cape Town, 2001.

Bowman, L., *Mauritius: Democracy and Development*, Dartmouth, London, 1991.

Bratton, M. and van der Walle, N., *Democratic Experiments in Africa*, Cambridge University Press, Cambridge, 1997.

Chang, H.-J., *Kicking Away the Ladder: Development Strategy in Historical Perspective*, Anthem Press, London, 2002.

Chang, H.-J. and Rowthorn, R., Eds., *The Role of the State in Economic Change*, Clarendon Press, Oxford, 1995.

Cheng, T-J., Haggard, S., and King, D., Institutions and growth in Korea and Taiwan: the bureaucracy, *J. Dev. Stud.*, 34 (6), 87–111, 1998.

Colclough, C., Structuralism vs. neo-liberalism, in *States or Markets? Neo-liberalism and the Development Policy Debate*, Colclough, C. and Manor, J., Eds., Clarendon Press, Oxford, 1993, pp. 1–25.

Colclough, C. and Manor, J., Eds., *States or Markets? Neo-liberalism and the Development Policy Debate*, Clarendon Press, Oxford, 1993.

Crump, J., *The Origins of Socialist Thought in Japan*, Croom Helm, London, 1983.

DfID, *Better Government for Poverty Reduction: More Effective Partnerships for Change*, Consultation Document, Department for International Development, 2003.

Ding, X.L., Institutional amphibiousness and the transition from communism: the case of China, *Br. J. Polit. Sci.*, 24 (3), 293–318, 1994.

Dollar, D. and Kraay, A., Growth is good for the poor, Policy Research Working Paper 2587, The World Bank, Washington, 2001.

Escobar, A., *Encountering Development: The Making and Unmaking of the Third World*, Princeton University Press, Princeton, 1995.

Espinosa-Coria, H., The Politics of Tourism Development in Mexico, Ph.D. Thesis, Department of Politics, University of York, 2004.

Esteva, G., Development, in *The Development Dictionary*, Sachs, W., Ed., Zed, London, 1992, pp. 6–25.

Evans, P., *Embedded Autonomy. States and Industrial Transformations*, Princeton University Press, Princeton, 1995.

Evans, P., Transferable lessons? Re-examining the institutional prerequisites of East Asian economic policies, *J. Dev. Stud.*, 34 (6), 66–85, 1998.

Fields, K.J., *Enterprise and the State in Korea and Taiwan*, Cornell University Press, Ithaca, 1995.

Frischtak, L.L., *Governance Capacity and Economic Reform in Developing Countries*, World Bank Technical Paper 254, The World Bank, Washington, 1994.

Gerschenkron, A., *Economic Backwardness in Historical Perspective*, Harvard University Press, Cambridge, MA, 1962.

Giddens, A., *The Third Way*, Polity Press, Cambridge, 1998.

Gregor, A.J., *Italian Fascism and Developmental Dictatorship*, Princeton University Press, Princeton, 1979.

Haagh, L. and Helgø, C.T., Eds., *Social Policy Reform and Market Governance in Latin America*, Palgrave, Basingstoke, 2002.

Hale, W., *The Political and Economic Development of Modern Turkey*, St. Martin's Press, New York, 1981.

Held, D., *Global Covenant: The Social Democratic Alternative to the Washington Consensus*, Polity Press, Cambridge, 2004.

Huff, W.G., The developmental state, government and Singapore's economic development since 1960, *World Dev.*, 23 (8), 1421–1438, 1995.

Huntington, S.P., The goals of development, in *Understanding Political Development*, Weiner, M. and Huntington, S.P., Eds., Little Brown and Company, Boston, 1987, pp. 3–32.

Hurd, D., Promoting good government, *Crossbow*, Autumn, 4–5, 1990.

Johnson, C., *MITI and the Japanese Miracle*, Stanford University Press, Stanford, 1982.

Keyder, Ç., *State and Class in Turkey: A Study in Capitalist Development*, Verso, London, 1987.

Kim, H.-R., Korea's economic governance in transition: governance crisis and the future of Korean capitalism, *Korea Observer*, 31 (4), 553–577, 2000.

Kitching, G., *Development and Underdevelopment in Historical Perspective*, Methuen, London, 1982.

Kozul-Wright, R., The myth of Anglo-Saxon capitalism: reconstructing the history of the American state, in *The Role of the State in Economic Change*, Chang, H.-J. and Rowthorn, R., Eds., Clarendon Press, Oxford, 1995, pp. 81–113.

Lal, D., *The Poverty of Development Economics*, Institute of Economic Affairs, London, 1983.

Lall, S., Malaysia: industrial success and the role of government, *J. Int. Dev.*, 7 (5), 759–773, 1995.

Lee, Y., The failure of the weak state in economic liberalization: liberalization, democratization and the financial crisis in South Korea, *The Pacific Rev.*, 13 (1), 115–131, 2000.

Leftwich, A., Bringing politics back in: towards a model of the developmental state, *J. Dev. Stud.*, 31 (3), 400–427, 1995.

Leftwich, A., *States of Development*, Polity Press, Cambridge, 2000.

Leftwich, A., The political approach to human behaviour, in *What is Politics?* Leftwich, A., Ed., Polity Press, Cambridge, 2004, pp. 100–118.

Leftwich, A., The state in the developing world, in *Politics in the Developing World*, Burnell, P. and Randall, V., Eds., Oxford University Press, Oxford, 2004a.

List, F., *The National System of Political Economy*, A. M. Kelley, New York, 1844/1966.

Lodge, T., *Politics in South Africa*, David Philip, Cape Town, 2002.

Loriaux, M., The French developmental state as myth and moral ambition, in *The Developmental State*, Woo-Cumings, M., Ed., Cornell University Press, Ithaca, 1999, pp. 235–275.

Marx, K., *Capital I*, Penguin, Harmondsworth, 1976.

Meisenhelde, T., The developmental state in Mauritius, *J. Mod. Afr. Stud.*, 35 (2), 279–297, 1995.

Moon, S., Who can see clearly in the dark? The failure of developmental state construction in the South African Transition, 1990–1996, Unpublished Ph.D. Thesis, Department of Politics, University of York, UK, 2004.

Mosley, P., Harrigan, J., and Toye, J., *Aid and Power: The World Bank and Policy-Based Lending*, Routledge, London, 1991.

Munck, R., *Marx@ 2000*, Zed Press, London, 2002.

Nelson, J., Ed., *Fragile Coalitions: The Politics of Economic Adjustment*, Transaction Books, New Brunswick, 1989.

North, D.C., Institutions and economic growth: an historical introduction, *World Dev.*, 17 (9), 1319–1332, 1989.

North, D.C., The contribution of the new institutional economics to an understanding of the transition problem, WIDER Annual Lecture 1, World Institute for Development Economics Research (WIDER), Helsinki, 1997.

Peters, B.G., Politics is about governing, in *What is Politics?* Leftwich, A., Ed., Polity Press, Cambridge, 2004, pp. 23–40.

Polanyi, K., *The Great Transformation: The Political and Economic Origins of Our Time*, Beacon Press, Boston, 1944/1957.

Potter, D., Democratization at the same time in South Korea and Taiwan, in *Democratization*, Potter, D., Goldblatt, D., Kiloh, M., and Lewis, P., Eds., Polity Press, Cambridge, 1997, pp. 219–237.

Przeworski, A., Alvarez, M.E., Cheibub, J.A., and Limongi, F., *Democracy and Development*, Cambridge University Press, Cambridge, 2000.

Redclift, M., *Sustainable Development*, Routledge, London, 1987.

Robinson, W., *Promoting Polyarchy: Globalization, US intervention, and hegemony*, Cambridge University Press, Cambridge, 1996.

Rodrik, D., Ed., *In Search of Prosperity*, Princeton University Press, Princeton, 2003.

Rothstein, B., Social capital in the social democratic welfare state, *Politics Soc.*, 29 (2), 207–241, 2001.

Said, E., *Orientalism*, Pantheon, New York.

Sen, A., *Development as Freedom*, Oxford University Press, Oxford, 1999.

Senghaas, D., *The European Experience*, Berg Publishers, Leamington Spa, 1985.

Shonfield, A., *Modern Capitalism*, Oxford University Press, Oxford, 1969.

Stiglitz, J., *Globalization and its Discontents*, Penguin, London, 2002.

Stiglitz, J., Towards a new paradigm of development, in *Making Globalization Good*, Dunning, J.H., Ed., Oxford University Press, Oxford, 2003, pp. 76–107.

Taylor, I., Botswana's developmental state and the politics of legitimation, in *Global Encounters: International Political Economy and Globalization*, Harrison, G., Ed., Palgrave, Basinsgtoke, 2004, pp. 41–62.

Tilly, C., Ed., *The Formation of National States in Western Europe*, Princeton University Press, Princeton, 1975.

Tilly, C., *Coercion, Capital and European States, AD 990–1992*, Basil Blackwell, Oxford, 1992.

Toye, J., *Dilemmas of Development*, Basil Blackwell, Oxford, 1987.

Trimberger, E.K., *Revolution from Above: Military Bureaucrats and Development in Japan, Turkey, Egypt and Peru*, Transaction Books, New Brunswick, New Jersey, 1978.

UNDP (United Nations Development Programme), *The Human Development Report 2003*, Oxford University Press, New York, 2003.

Wade, R., *Governing the Market: Economic Theory and the Role of Governance in East Asian Industrialisation*, Princeton University Press, Princeton, 1990.

Wade, R., The rising inequality of world income distribution, 2001 (*Finance and Development* at: www.imf.org/external/pubs/ft/fandd/2001/12/wade/htm).

Webster, E., and Adler, G., Towards a Class Compromise in South Africa's "double transition", *Politics and Society*, 27 (3), 85–133, 1999.

Weiss, L., *The Myth of the Powerless State: Governing the Economy in a Global Era*, Polity Press, Cambridge, 1998.

Weiss, L., Developmental states in transition: adapting, dismantling, innovating, not 'normalizing', *The Pacific Rev.*, 13 (1), 21–55, 2000.

Weiss, L. and Hobson, J.M., *States and Economic Development: A Comparative Historical Analysis*, Polity Press, Cambridge, 1995.

Williamson, J., What Washington means by policy reform, in *Latin American Adjustment: How Much Has Happened?* Williamson, J., Ed., Institute for International Economics, Washington, DC, 1990, pp. 7–38.

Williamson, J., The Washington Consensus revisited, in *Economic and Social Development into the XXI Century*, Emmerij, L., Ed., Inter-American Bank, Washington, 1997, pp. 48–59.

Williamson, J., What should the World Bank think about the Washington Consensus? *World Bank Res. Observer*, 15 (2), 251–264, 2000.

Woo, J., *The Race to the Swift: State and Finance in Korean Industrialization*, Columbia University Press, New York, 1991.

Woo-Cumings, M., Ed., *The Developmental State*, Cornell University Press, Ithaca, 1999.

Woo-Cumings, M., Introduction: Chalmers Johnson and the politics of nationalism and development, in *The Developmental State*, Woo-Cumings, Ed., Cornell University Press, New York, 1999, pp. 1–31.

World Bank, *Sub-Saharan Africa: From Crisis to Sustainable Growth*, The World Bank, Washington, DC, 1989.

World Bank, *Governance and Development*, The World Bank, Washington, DC, 1992.

World Bank, *Governance. The World Bank's Experience*, The World Bank, Washington, DC, 1994.

World Bank, *World Development Report 1997: The State in a Changing World*, Oxford University Press, New York, 1997.

World Bank, *World Development Report 2002: Building Institutions for Markets*, Oxford University Press, New York, 2002.

Yamada, K. and Kuchiki, A., Lessons from Japan: industrial policy approach and the East Asian trial, in *Economic and Social Development into the XXI Century*, Emmerij, L., Ed., The Inter-American Bank, Washington, DC, 1997, pp. 359–402.

Yudelman, D. *The Emergence of Modern South Africa*, Greenwood Press, Westport, Conn, 1983.

Zysman, J., How institutions create historically rooted trajectories of growth, *Ind. Corporate Change*, 3 (1), 243–283, 1994.

Chapter 4

Globalization and Development

William D. Coleman

CONTENTS

I. Introduction

This chapter offers a framework for thinking about the relationship between globalization and development and for trying to determine what impacts globalization might have on states seeking to advance economic and social development. It begins by reflecting briefly on the meaning of the term globalization and suggests that contemporary globalization has deep historical roots. The chapter then turns to examine several defining characteristics of the contemporary phase of globalization by looking at the role of technology and its impact on capitalism. This analysis, in turn, helps us to understand a little better some of the changes globalization is bringing to the roles states can play in development. The chapter then concludes the analysis by looking at the relationships between sovereignty, individual and collective autonomy, and globalization. Based on this analysis, the chapter argues that globalization reinforces long-standing patterns of domination that hinder poorer countries interest in development. At the very end, it also notes some recent initiatives that may hold some promise for addressing these hindrances.

II. Defining Globalization

Globalization is typical of many concepts in the social sciences in that it carries considerable ideological baggage. Its meaning differs depending on whether one listens to protesters on the streets in Seattle during WTO meetings, or to global bankers talking about market structures, or to the governments of Zimbabwe or Zambia, which see globalization as a process that marginalizes and impoverishes their people. Not only does the term globalization carry considerable ideological baggage, but also it is a term at the center of a growing body of social theory that is challenging other theories and ways of understanding of the world in which we live. So like many other concepts in the social science disciplines — corporatism, autonomy, democracy, and human rights — globalization is both a theoretical tool and a term that has varied meanings among individuals and organizations that we study. In referring to it and using it in our research, accordingly, we need to proceed carefully.

Although, I recognize that ideologies which speak out for or against globalization are important for social analysis, I am also interested in the body of social theory, whose development has been sparked by a search for an understanding of what globalization entails and what it might mean for how we think about the world. Considerable, careful reflection on globalization has taken place in the social sciences since the early 1990s. After reviewing many of the competing definitions of globalization that emerged, the political scientist Jan Aart Scholte (2000: 46) suggests that globalization involves "the growth of 'supraterritorial relations' among people." Supraterritorial refers to relations that are somehow "above" territory, that is, they are relatively unconstrained by one's physical location. John Tomlinson (1999: 2), a sociologist, characterizes this "empirical condition" of supraterritoriality as one of "complex connectivity," a set of "connections that now bind our practices, our experiences and our political, economic and environmental fates together across the modern world." Associated with this change in the character of social relationships for both authors is "deterritorialization." The relative importance of physical location as a basis for building social relationships is declining as supraterritorial ties grow in significance. In this respect, globalization brings together far-reaching changes to the nature of social space: social space is less and less defined by the physical location in which we live.

A final characteristic of globalization is that many individuals are conscious of its occurring, and their imaginations are stimulated by these changes. Robertson (1992) refers to "an intensification of consciousness of the world" or increasing globality in many societies, where globality refers to the consciousness of the world as one place. Appadurai (1995: 31) comes at the same issue differently and speaks of a changing role for the imagination. He suggests that under present globalizing conditions, imagination becomes a social practice, "a form of negotiation between sites of agency (individuals) and globally defined fields of possibility." Hence individuals place themselves in a world context and imagine themselves doing new things in different ways than before.

With these points in mind, we can provide a working definition of globalization that will be used in this chapter. "Globalization is the growth of supraterritorial relations among people creating a complex series of connections that tie together what people do, what they experience, and how they live across the globe. In participating and acting in these connections, individuals and communities see the world increasingly as one place, and imagine new activities and roles for themselves in this world."

Defined in this way, historians remind us that globalization is not confined to the past 30 years. Supraterritorial relations have been growing to different degrees and in varying ways for over two millennia. The intensity and the global scope or extensity of these relations reached sufficient heights according to Hopkins (2002a, 2002b) and Bayly (2004) that we can begin to speak of globalization as a process as early as the beginning of the 15th century. They refer to the period between 1400 and 1600 as "archaic globalization." In this period, for example, cities became important nodes in global economic relations, migrant labor increased as did the presence and importance of diasporas, and systems of religious belief came to span continents. After 1600, archaic globalization gave way to "proto" globalization, a period characterized by an intensification of economic, social, and ideational relations across the globe, the emergence but not yet dominance of the nation-state, and a distinctly cosmopolitan world view among many elites.

After 1800, this phase, in turn, evolved into the period of modern globalization characterized by the appearance of two key elements: the rise of the nation-state and the spread of industrialization (Hopkins, 2002b). Hopkins adds that the cosmopolitanism that was a marked feature of the archaic and proto phases was "corralled, harnessed and domesticated to new national interests." Across the globe, land "was converted to property, property became the foundation of sovereignty; sovereignty, in turn, defined the basis of security." (Hopkins, 2002b: 6) Accordingly, in the period from 1800 to approximately 1950, the European states plus the USA and Japan, working through new forms of imperialism, began to impose a new pattern of internationalism on the old world order. The nation-state increasingly dominated global networks. "It imposed its system of more rigidly bound territories, languages, and religious conventions on all international networks" (Bayly, 2004: 234). The vast majority of developing countries, therefore, experienced modern globalization as colonialism.

In the current phase of globalization, which began in the postwar period, the colonial relations gave way to the globalization of the nation-state form, vastly increased integration in the world economy, the emergence of new organizational structures for transnational corporations, and an increased salience of global problems, whether related to the environment, security in the face of terrorism, or financial system instability. Developing countries took on the nation-state apparatus with varying degrees of success, especially given the complex populations they inherited within imperial territorial boundaries. And as they were adapting to this form of political structure, the nation-state itself became increasingly forced to take on a new role that involved extensive cooperation with other states to address many of the political challenges they faced. Although, the wealthier countries had the resources needed to participate in the emerging global governance networks, developing countries often did not. From their perspective, therefore, the old territorial empires were replaced by new forms of domination.

Held et al. (1999) suggested that one way of comparing the differences in these various phases of globalization is in terms of extensity, intensity, and velocity. By extensity, they refer to the global reach or the planet-wide inclusivity of supraterritorial relations. They hypothesize that these relations penetrate more parts of the world and link more people to one another in each successive phase. Intensity refers to the regularity and degree of importance of the relations in individual persons' lives. For example, the spice trade was globally extensive in the archaic period, but touched the lives of a limited number of persons and often in an irregular way. When one compares this trade to contemporary trade in processed foods, we can say that the latter commodities are much more regularly an important part of daily living for a more globally inclusive group than in the past. Velocity refers to the speed with which supraterritorial relations are sustained. If we were to measure the speed of communication between a

Dutch company and its traders in present-day Indonesia in the 18th century and compare it to the potential for communication with telephone and the internet today, we can see that the speed with which social relationships can evolve has increased dramatically. Increases in each of these three dimensions — extensity, intensity, velocity — of supraterritorial relations, Held et al. conclude, raise the overall impact of globalization on societies in the different time periods, with the impact being highest in the present day.

III. Globalization, Technology, and Capitalism

In discussions of the factors that favor the growth of supraterritorial relations over time, scholars usually single out changes in economic structures, particularly in the mode of production, changes in ideas and who promotes those ideas, and changes in technologies, especially those related to transportation and communication. Not surprisingly, therefore, analyses of the current phase of globalization tend to focus on changes in capitalism, the global influence of such ideas as neo-liberalism and of cultural commodities (movies, fast foods, and clothing), and on recent significant advances in information and communication technologies. The combination of these changes, in turn, has important implications for what states can and cannot do. The "role" of the state shifts in character, with some arguing that the change in role for developing countries is different from that of the more wealthy OECD countries.

Castells (1996) provides some useful analysis of the interaction between technological change and capitalism in the contemporary period. He begins by distinguishing between the mode of production (capitalism), and the mode of development, that is, "the technological arrangements through which labour works on matter to generate the product, ultimately determining the level and quality of surplus" (Castells, 1996: 16). Each mode of development is defined by the element that is central to the generation of productivity. Thus in the "industrialism" mode of development, Castells (1996: 17) states that the fundamental element is the introduction of new energy sources, particularly steam and electricity, and then the movement towards diffusing the use of these sources throughout the production and circulation processes. In the current "informationalism" mode of development, the core element is the technology of knowledge generation, information processing, and symbol communication. Again, as these elements penetrate all aspects of production and circulation, a new technological paradigm emerges fostering changes at the same deep levels as the first and second industrial revolutions.

Castells joins a number of observers of globalization to add that the interaction between this new mode of development and the capitalist mode of production brings forth a new form of capitalism. It is "global," Castells

(1996: 471) writes, in that for the first time in history, it shapes social relationships across the whole planet. Through the use of information and communication technologies, capital "works globally as a unit in real time; and it is realized, invested, and accumulated mainly in the sphere of circulation, that is as finance capital" (Castells, 1996: 471). Kellner (2002) speaks to these changes by coining the term "technocapitalism." He argues that technocapitalism leads to "a new configuration of capitalist society in which technical and scientific knowledge, computerization and automation of labour, and information technology and media play a role in the process of production analogous to the function of human labour-power, mechanization of the labour process, and machines in an earlier era of capitalism." In noting some of the implications of these developments, Mittelman (2000: 17) observes that they foster global "hypercompetition," which is accompanied by "a restructuring of production, including its spatial reorganization, which, is, in turn, facilitated both by technological advances and state policies. Global flows — labour, finance, trade, information and knowledge, and consumer goods and other cultural products — are thereby accelerated."

A number of globalization scholars observe that the structural changes accompanying the new form of global capitalism and the information technology revolution are redefining space or creating what Sassen (2000) calls new "spatiotemporal orders." Again, Castells is helpful here. He defines space as the "material support of time-sharing social practices" (Castells, 1996: 411). Traditionally, these social practices were heavily dependent on physical contiguity. In the present era, however, with the recent changes in technology, spaces can become less dependent on physical proximity to the point where Castells identifies a "space of flows" where flows are "purposeful, repetitive, programmable sequences of exchange and interaction between physically disjointed positions held by social actors in the economic, political, and symbolic structures of society" (Castells, 1996: 412). Such a space of flows is constituted in three layers: a circuit of electronic impulses; a series of nodes and hubs — places where strategically important functions are located; the spatial organization of dominant managerial elites. Sassen (2000) highlights the role of "global cities" in providing the nodes for the space of flows. Echoing Castells, she writes (Sassen, 2000: 226): "We see here a relation of intercity proximity operating without shared territory. Proximity is deterritorialized."

Castells (1996: 423–428) contrasts the space of flows with the "space of places." Most people, both in developed and developing countries, live in places and perceive their space as place-based. Nonetheless, because power and domination are increasingly organized in the space of flows, these places find their meanings and dynamics changed by the globalization of flows. Based on this analysis, Castells (1996: 476) offers a compelling hypothesis: "dominant functions are organized in networks pertaining to a space of flows that links them up around the world, while fragmenting subordinate functions, and people, in the multiple space of places, made of locales increasingly segregated and disconnected from each other." Hence while the informationalist mode of development permits an unprecedented concentration and globalization of capital, the opposite dynamic affects subordinate groups like labor and peasants. They are disaggregated in what they do, their traditional organizational bases of support fragment, and new divisions between one laboring place and another emerge. Often in this space of places, even usual nation-state rules are ignored or consciously over-ridden creating what Sassen refers to as "regulatory fractures": in-between spaces where one finds immigrant labor, displaced peasants, sex trade workers, and global crime syndicates among others.

IV. Globalization and the Role of the Nation-State

The space of flows is not bound by the territorial boundaries of nation-states, although the infrastructure for the flows is anchored in particular territories with the help of nation-state policies. Moreover, within any nation-state, there will be a selected elite that lives and works in the space of flows, with the vast majority of others continuing to live and work in the space of places. In noting the supraterritoriality of the space of flows, early observers of globalization like Ohmae spoke of the weakening of the state, perhaps even its end as a form of political organization. Subsequent analyses of globalization have moved well away from this position stressing the continued importance of the state, if not its centrality, in this era of globalization.

Debate about the state now focuses more on what changes globalization brings to the role of the state. Cerny (1997) coined the term "competition state" to emphasize that states have expanded their activities by pushing for marketization within their borders and re-regulating many sectors like financial services. These steps are designed to make economic activities within state boundaries more competitive in increasingly global, deterritorialized markets. In this respect, they are responding to the "hypercompetition" noted by Mittelman above.

This analysis is helpful but may fail to take account of new (or re-established old) hierarchies in the system of states. As Hedetoft (2003: 170) observes,

> The Global Order, an increasingly hegemonic system of dominance, has both a hierarchy and a center, and power resources and degrees of sovereignty are and will be distributed extremely

unevenly across the board. In other words, the many weak or cool states have, as their counterpart, other (fewer) states that must properly be designated as both "strong" and "hot", headed up, of course, by the USA, and assisted by a network of international and global institutions.

For developing countries, this position is a familiar one, even if the structures of domination and the roles they might be called upon to fulfill are new. The majority of developing states are called upon to play what Mittelman (2000: 25) terms a "courtesan role." "Broadly, a state in its capacity as a courtesan is beholden to more powerful interests in the global economy, submissive in its policies, not in rhetorical flourishes, because choice is constrained, and engaged in illicit relationships (although the line between licit and illicit is increasingly blurred."

The "new international order" or the "global order" is one being built on the recognition that addressing many of the most pressing problems of the age — environmental degradation, human security, increasing levels of financial systemic risk, continuing abuses of human rights — requires systematic interaction and cooperation between states. Slaughter (2004: 10) echoes many analysts when she notes that what is new is the "scale, scope, and type of transgovernmental ties." The resulting intergovernmental networks "are driven by many of the multiple factors that drive the hydra-headed phenomenon of globalization itself, leading to the simple need for national officials of all kinds to communicate and negotiate across borders to do business they could once accomplish solely at home" (Slaughter, 2004: 11).

Although, such imperatives are felt by all states, as Hedetoft's discussion of hierarchy indicates, not all states can or will respond to them in the same way. Grande and Pauly (2005) build a typology of states based on the capacity to respond to imperatives for transnational cooperation and on willingness to do so. They speak of four types of states:

- *Cooperative* states, those willing to engage in transnational policy-making and capable of doing so.
- *Autonomous* states, those unwilling to engage in transnational policy-making, although they are certainly capable of doing so. The US position on the UN Framework Convention on Climate Change or the positions of China and the US on the International Criminal Court illustrate this kind of state.
- *Weak* states, those willing to cooperate with other states, but which lack the personal, financial, technical, and other resources necessary to do so.
- *Rogue* states, those unwilling to cooperate and who do not have the necessary resources to do so.

Here again we should be cautious about assuming that states are one or the other of these types. In particular, capabilities will be variably distributed across states and within states. Accordingly, some will be capable of being cooperative states in virtually any policy area they deem important (the USA, Japan, and the EU). Others will be capable of participating in some policy areas but not in all that might be seen as being of strategic interest. Still others will be capable of participating in a few areas only, while being effectively excluded from the vast majority of policy realms of interest to them. Only the poorest developing countries will be pure "weak states."

A. Summary

Before moving to discuss development and globalization, it is important to review the implications of the analysis thus far. When one views globalization as the growth of supraterritorial relations and one makes the linkages between this growth and changes in capitalism and technology, we understand better how space is being ordered in new ways. There are spaces of flows, where information, capital, and select elites move relatively freely from the office towers in global cities to airports to conferences and meetings to other office towers and then back. Individuals and organizations living in such spaces *live* the world as one place and experience time as simultaneity or "timeless" (Castells, 1996: Chapter 7). These spaces of flows are more present in developed countries; nevertheless, they do incorporate elites from developing countries into the circuits of information and finance involved, with Brazil, China, and India being examples where this involvement is growing. Although, the conditions for the creation and growth of these spaces were created by states, are managed by a growing number of global institutions, and are sustained by state policies, spaces of flows are not easily controlled by states. They develop a logic and dynamism of their own that any state individually cannot control.

In contrast, spaces of places are filled with people who face increasingly impenetrable boundaries that stand in stark contrast to the fluidity of life in spaces of flows. These are the boundaries of poverty, boundaries that restrict movement to other states, boundaries that force movement from rural areas to urban poverty and slums, boundaries that limit access to wealth, education, and health. The coexistence of spaces of flows and of places in developing countries is accompanied by deepening social fractures and higher levels of inequalities within most such states. These spaces form within the territorial boundaries of states, are regulated by these states, and states remain the principal targets of those who wish assistance in breaking through these boundaries. Such spaces remain the predominant mode of living in developing countries but are matched by places in developed countries where living conditions have declined significantly over the past 20 year.

Global governance institutions have become more important for both types of spaces. For example, the various treaties under the jurisdiction of the World Trade Organization exist to regulate and promote the circuits of communication and exchange that constitute the infrastructure of the space of flows. Other sites of governance such as the UN High Commission on Human Rights, the Convention on Biological Diversity, the United Nations Development Program, and the UN efforts on AIDS have as their object the amelioration of some of the worst effects in the spaces of places. As noted above, however, such governance organizations rely heavily on the participation and cooperation of nation-states, a characteristic that tends to give OECD states a certain advantage.

Finally, the economic dynamism of spaces of flows puts intense pressures on developing countries to reshape policies to facilitate the participation of their economies in these spaces. The "structural adjustment" at the focus of these policy changes, however, may lead to the revocation of the very sorts of policies needed to address the worsening living conditions in spaces of places. In the following section, we examine this conundrum through the lens of the concept of autonomy.

V. Autonomy, Globalization, and Development

The notion of autonomy, like globalization, is a controversial and often contested term. For the purposes of this chapter, we will set aside these debates and offer definitions of these terms that help us understand the development conundrum faced by developing countries in the contemporary globalization period. The term autonomy is used in two ways. First, it refers to the situations of individual persons and usually to their capacity to shape the conditions under which they live (Held, 1995). It also is used in connection with collective bodies: nation-states, minority groups within states, indigenous peoples, and religious movements being the common examples. In this collective sense, autonomy usually means something closer to the Greek roots of the term: the capacity to give oneself laws. Individual and collective autonomy are linked and globalization shapes these linkages in important ways.

Building on the work of Sen (1985, 1999) and Nussbaum (2000) on the notions of "capabilities" and "functionings," Doyal and Gough (1991) offer a helpful approach to think about individual autonomy. They work with the notion of "need" as a particular category of goals, which are believed to be universalisable. If such needs are not satisfied, "harm" of some objective kind will follow. In particular, such harm is an impediment to successful social "participation." They suggest that participation in some form of life without serious arbitrary limitations, is "our most basic human interest" (Doyal and Gough, 1991: 55).

To pursue this universal goal of social participation, following from Kant, Doyal and Gough argue that there are two basic needs: health or physical capacity and mental capacity or autonomy. "To be autonomous in this minimal sense is to have the ability to make informed choices about what should be done and how to go about doing it" (Gough, 2003: 8). Here autonomy means being able to formulate aims and beliefs about how to achieve one's choices and to evaluate one's success based on empirical evidence, and working toward these aims.

Doyal and Gough (1991: 55–59) go on to identify three key factors that shape the degree to which individuals might enjoy autonomy. First, they must have the *cognitive and emotional capacity* to initiate action. They suggest (1991: 180) that across cultures one can identify a common set of disabling symptoms indicating weakness in this regard: hopelessness, indecisiveness, a sense of futility, and a lack of energy. Second, individuals must have *cultural understanding* that permits them to understand and situate themselves in their culture and to know what is expected of them in their daily life. Such understanding requires teaching and learning, whether in the family, through community practices and ceremonies, or in schools.

Finally, they refer to *critical capacity*, the ability "to compare cultural rules, to reflect upon the rules of one's own culture, to work with others to change them and, *in extremis*, to move to another culture" (Doyal and Gough, 1991: 187). To exercise this critical capacity, Doyal and Gough added that it requires some freedom of agency and political freedom. Held (1995: Chapter 8) adds to this point by listing some human rights necessary for such critical capacity: freedom of thought, freedom of expression, and freedom of association.

Weaknesses in these three factors have long been a concern for many in developing countries. The sources for these weaknesses are complex, with deep historical roots, making it difficult to speculate how globalization might contribute to their continued presence. If we consider the analysis of globalization presented in this chapter, we can make some preliminary observations. First, higher levels of individual autonomy are much more likely to characterize those living and working in spaces of flows than in spaces of places. The three factors Doyal and Gough postulate as critical to the fostering of individual autonomy are more likely to be present and available to individuals in spaces of flows. Hopelessness and depressive symptoms affecting mental and emotional capacity, and thus the ability to initiate action, are more likely to occur in response to the rigidity of boundaries found in spaces of places. Depressed economic conditions and the constant stress of finding means to subsist from one day to the next will undermine family structures and limit access to schooling, both key institutions for building cultural understanding. Weaknesses in these two capacities will inhibit critical capacity, an inhibition hindered further by the lack of civil and political rights found in the "regulatory fractures" (Sassen, 2000) that affect the lives of many in spaces of places. In short, to the extent to which globalization widens the gaps in these capacities between persons living in spaces of flows and those in spaces of places, it may reduce individual autonomy for many. Such a reduction in autonomy is bound to inhibit social and economic development, as Sen has argued persuasively for many years.

This analysis of individual autonomy cannot be divorced from collective autonomy, particularly the autonomy of states. Factors critical to individual autonomy remain by and large the concerns of states: health care, the conditions for economic self-sufficiency, stable social institutions, education, and the protection and enforcement of political and civic freedoms. Hence the extent to which globalization may restrict what states can or cannot do, will affect the levels of individual autonomy held by their citizens. In order to analyze this kind of impact of globalization, we need first to define what is meant by collective autonomy and to distinguish it from another common term, state sovereignty.

Cornelius Castoriadis (1991), a French philosopher of Greek origin, helps us to think about the meaning of collective autonomy, by recalling the Greek roots of the term: to give oneself laws. In this respect, autonomy is the opposite of heteronomy: being unselfconsciously subject to the power of another. To be collectively autonomous according to Castoriadis, a society has to have a place for "politics," public spaces where citizens are able freely to ask themselves "are the rules and the laws under which we exist the right ones?" "Are they just?" "Could they be better?" For Castoriadis, therefore, collective autonomy exists when a society is more reflexive, more able to look at itself critically, and where its members are free, have access to public spaces, and possess the resources, the understanding, and the education needed to interrogate itself and its laws.

What is also clear about autonomy in this sense is that it involves an act of the imagination. Castoriadis terms it the "radical imagination." Individuals and groups are able to imagine different futures, different ways of living, and different arrangements in their own lives. They are able to take an idea, talk about it, imagine how it might work in practice, and then take action to see if they can get it to work. In this respect, collective autonomy depends strongly on individual autonomy, particularly the third factor noted by Doyal and Gough: critical capacity. And the relationship is dialectical: sustaining individual autonomy requires collective autonomy over the longer term.

Defined in this way, collective autonomy should not be confused with state sovereignty. Following James (1999: 39), sovereignty is linked to constitutional independence. It consists of "being constitutionally apart, of not being contained, however loosely, within a wider constitutional scheme." James adds that sovereignty has three features. First, it is a legal condition, "founded on law inasmuch as a constitution is a set of arrangements that has the force of law" (James, 1999: 40). Second, sovereignty is an absolute condition, it is either present or absent. It is not possessed in terms of more or less. Finally, sovereignty is a unitary condition. Within the defined territory, only one authority, the state, is in the position of being formally able to take decisions.

Sovereignty typically implies or advances collective autonomy. The degree to which states can take advantage of this condition depends on certain anterior conditions. Within the given territory, there must be a polity, an imagined community in which sovereignty is vested through the constitution. The existence of such a socially integrated community has been problematic for many developing countries because of the haphazard definitions of territory bequeathed to them by departing imperial powers. There must also be a functioning state, capable of establishing authority in the territory backed by a monopoly on the legitimate use of coercion. The state must have a sufficiently effective bureaucracy that is able to implement laws and policies and to gather resources, particularly taxes. The territory in which the polity and the state exist must have sufficient resources both to maintain the state institutions and to provide for the economic and social well-being of the citizens concerned. If globalization makes it more difficult to construct a polity, to maintain a functioning state, or to sustain an effective bureaucracy, then the degree to which sovereignty might advance autonomy is less.

Sovereignty also implies that no external authority structures are active in the territory of a given state (Krasner, 2001: 10). This state of affairs is increasingly compromised under globalization because states find it more difficult, in some cases impossible, to control or regulate the movements of goods, capital, people, and ideas across their borders. Faced with these circumstances, states increasingly contract with other states to establish supranational authority structures to find ways to control and regulate such flows. The creation of the World Trade Organization and the revised system of international trading rules that accompanied its creation illustrate these processes. If we accept James's definition of sovereignty, such actions do not involve "giving up" sovereignty. The states concerned still have constitutional independence in a strict, legal sense. Rather, we might say that states are reducing their collective autonomy in terms of the range of options they can consider in giving themselves laws. In doing so, they may be placing themselves in a situation of increased heteronomy. In short, it might be said that sovereignty creates the possibility of making a claim to autonomy in a range of areas of life. Globalization may create situations where states find themselves required to accept a reduced number of options that might be included in such a claim.

In reflecting on these processes and their pertinence to developing countries, some initial hypotheses suggest themselves. Due to the intensification of inequalities arising from the reconstitution of social space into spaces of flows and spaces of places, developing countries may experience greater difficulty in creating political communities capable of creating and using public spaces. In the presence of a weakened polity, the resources of the state may be devoted more extensively to coercive and security measures, reducing their capacity to build individual autonomy. Second, the increased pressures for states to give up autonomy in cooperative arrangements with other states may be experienced more intensively by developing countries. They may have fewer resources for participating in this kind of global policy-making with the result that cession of autonomy may have more deleterious consequences on their powers. Finally, because developing countries may be in a weaker position in the first place to control the flow of goods, capital, persons, and ideas crossing their borders, any global policies agreed upon may be inadequate or poorly suited to their situations. A weakened polity and an ineffective state under globalizing conditions may lead developing countries to revert to "a *terra nullius*, in which local warlords make deals with intermediaries of the global economy, in a manner little different from that employed in the Third World prior to the imposition of colonial rule" (Clapham, 1999: 115). Under such conditions, of course, economic and social development become extremely difficult, if not impossible.

Current circumstances suggest, however, that developing countries can address some of these challenges by pooling their resources and their knowledge. Such a possibility is illustrated by the emergence of a bloc of developing countries challenging the long-standing dominant roles of the US, the EU, and Japan in the global trading system. Similarly, the building of new regional economic agreements by developing countries adds potential capacity, if not political weight, when those countries move into global policy-making forums. If cooperation is effective, it may permit participating states to compensate for limitations in their own resources and expertise. To use the categories of Grande and Pauly (in press), they may be able to move from the category of "weak states" to that of "cooperative states." Similarly, the growth of the World Social Forum with its emphasis on imagining alternative futures in a globalizing world gives rise to a new type of "space of flows" that links spaces of places. In the views of some, including Appadurai (2002), such linkages create the possibility for "deep democracy" on a global scale. Even here, however, states will remain important, providing the leaders hold power legitimately and have the diffuse support of their citizens. Such support will permit the redirection of resources from internal coercion and policing toward education and social policy. In such an environment, the social movements involved in grassroots globalization may be able to command the additional resources they need to succeed in building individual autonomy.

References

Appadurai, A., *Modernity at Large: Cultural Dimensions of Globalization*, University of Minnesota Press, Minneapolis, 1995.

Appadurai, A., Deep democracy: urban governmentality and the horizon of politics, *Public Cult.*, 14 (1), 21–47, 2002.

Bayly, C.A., *The Birth of the Modern World: 1780–1914, The Blackwell History of the World*, Blackwell Publishing, Oxford, 2004.

Castells, M., The rise of the network society, in *The Information Age: Economy, Society and Culture*, Vol. 1, Blackwell, Oxford, UK, 1996.

Castoriadis, C., *Philosophy, Politics, Autonomy: Essays in Political Philosophy*, Oxford University Press, New York, 1991.

Cerny, P.G., Paradoxes of the competition state: the dynamics of political globalization, *Government and Opposition*, 32 (2), 251–174, 1997.

Clapham, C., Sovereignty and the Third World state, in *Sovereignty at the Millennium*, Jackson, R., Ed., Blackwell Publishers, Oxford, 1999, pp. 100–115.

Doyal, L. and Gough, I., *A Theory of Human Need*, Guilford Press, New York, 1991.

Gough, I., *Lists and Thresholds: Comparing the Doyal–Gough Theory of Human Need with Nussbaum's Capabilities Approach*, ESRC Research Group on Wellbeing in Developing Countries, Bath, UK, 2003.

Grande, E. and Pauly, L., Conclusion: Complex sovereignty and the emergence of transnational authority, in *Complex Sovereignty: Reconstituting Political Authority in the Twenty-First Century*, Grande, E. and Pauly, L., Eds., University of Toronto Press, Toronto, 2005.

Hedetoft, U., *The Global Turn: National Encounters with the World*, Aalborg University Press, Aalborg, 2003.

Held, D., *Democracy and the Global Order: From the Modern State to Cosmopolitan Governance*, Stanford University Press, Stanford, CA, 1995.

Held, D., McGrew, A., Goldblatt, D., and Perraton, J., *Global Transformations: Politics, Economics and Culture*, Stanford University Press, Stanford, CA, 1999.

Hopkins, A.G., The history of globalization — and the globalization of history? in *Globalization in World History*, Hopkins, A.G., Ed., Pimlico, London, 2002a, chap. 2.

Hopkins, A.G., Introduction: globalization — an agenda for historians, in *Globalization in World History*, Hopkins, A.G., Ed., Pimlico, London, 2002b, chap. 1.

James, A., The practice of sovereign statehood in contemporary international society, in *Sovereignty at the Millennium*, Jackson, R., Ed., Blackwell Publishers, Oxford, 1999, pp. 35–51.

Kellner, D., Theorizing globalization, *Sociological Theory*, 20 (3), 285—305, 2002.

Krasner, S.D., Problematic sovereignty, in *Problematic Sovereignty: Contested Rules and Political Possibilities*, Krasner, S.D., Ed., Columbia University Press, New York, 2001, pp. 1–23.

Mittelman, J., *The Globalization Syndrome: Transformation and Resistance*, Princeton University Press, Princeton, 2000.

Nussbaum, M.C., *Women and Human Development: The Capabilities Approach*, Cambridge University Press, Cambridge, 2000.

Robertson, R., *Globalization: Social Theory and Global Culture*, Sage Publications, London, UK, 1992.

Sassen, S., Spatialities and temporalities of the global: elements for a theorization, *Public Cult.* 12 (1), 215–232, 2000.

Scholte, J.A., *Globalization: A Critical Introduction*, Macmillan, Basingstoke, UK, 2000.

Sen, A.K., *Commodities and Capabilities, Professor Dr. P. Hennipman Lectures in Economics*, Vol. 7, North-Holland, Amsterdam, 1985.

Sen, A.K., *Development as Freedom*, Knopf, New York, 1999.

Slaughter, A.-M., *A New World Order*, Princeton University Press, Princeton, NJ, 2004.

Tomlinson, J., *Globalization and Culture*, University of Chicago Press, Chicago, 1999.

Chapter 5

Neoliberal Globalization and the Washington Consensus

Jan Nederveen Pieterse

CONTENTS

I. Introduction

During the past two decades, neoliberal globalization has been the dominant approach, not in the sense that it is all there is to globalization but in the sense that it became a global regime. Most protest against globalization concerns neoliberal globalization and this is the actual problem, rather than globalization *per se*. Contemporary globalization can be described as a package deal that includes informatization (applications of information technology), flexibilization (de-standardization in the organization of production and labor), and various changes such as regionalization and the reconfiguration of states. Since the 1980s, the growing impact of neoliberal policies adds to the globalization package, deregulation (liberalization and privatization), marketization (unleashing market forces), financialization and securitization (conversion of assets into tradable financial instruments), and the ideology of lean government. This chapter considers how this has come about and focuses on the economic and political shift within the United States to the South, the connection between the cold war and neoliberalism, and the "Washington Consensus."

Studies generally explain the onset of neoliberalism as the confluence of the economic ideas of the Chicago school and the policies of Ronald Reagan and Margaret Thatcher. A further step is the Washington Consensus, the economic orthodoxy that guided the IMF and World Bank in their policies through the 1990s and turned neoliberalism into global policy.

Tickell and Peck (2003) discuss the development of neoliberalism in detail in three phases:

1. An early phase of proto-neoliberalism from the 1940s to the 1970s in which the main ideas took shape.
2. A phase of rollback neoliberalism in the 1980s when it became government policy in the United States and the United Kingdom.
3. A phase of roll-out neoliberalism in the 1990s when it became hegemonic in multilateral institutions.

Like many accounts, this focuses on economic ideas (of the Mont Pèlerin Society, Friedrich von Hayek, and Milton Friedman) and the policies of Reagan and Thatcher. However, by locating the origins of neoliberalism in the realm of ideas and the theories of the Chicago school, this overlooks the actual economic policies that shaped "real neoliberalism" already before the Reagan era. The low-taxes, low-services regime envisioned by free market advocates already existed in the American South. Real neoliberalism in the United States in the 1970s and 1980s meant the implementation of the low-wage, low-tax model of Southern economics. The political power of the Southern conservatives and the welcome mat of the anti-union South for corporations fleeing the Northeast are what gave the "Reagan revolution" its depth and punch. Eventually, this led to the rollback of the regulatory and social functions of the state as a national trend.

This is worth considering for several reasons. As we do not analyze Soviet society by reading the texts of Marx but by examining "real existing socialism," we should look at the material political economy of neoliberalism and not just its theoretical claims. Had the American South with its low wages, high exploitation, and reactionary culture been upheld as the model of economic growth, it would never have exercised the glossy appeal that the "free market" did in theory. The Chicago school provided an economic rationale and intellectual gloss to what was and remains a backward and impoverished economic condition. Revisiting Chicago economics to understand neoliberalism is largely revisiting smoke and mirrors. A further omission in most accounts of neoliberalism is that it ignores the setting of the cold war and glosses over the affinities between neoliberalism and the cold war. Both these elements are fundamental to understand the actual character of neoliberal globalization and its subsequent metamorphoses.

II. Dixie Capitalism

American politics has undergone a long conservative trend that has recently taken an aggressive turn; to understand this trend, we must go back several decades in American history. When, in response to stagflation in the 1970s, the U.S. Federal Reserve raised interest rates, it prompted the onset of the debt crisis in the global South, which led to the IMF imposing its financial discipline and eventually the regime of structural reform. Meanwhile in the United States, corporations sought to retain their profitability by moving to low-wage areas of operation, which they found first in the American South.

The economic strategy of the American South was based on low-wage, labor-intensive, high-exploitation production, and hostility to unions, and has its roots in the period following Reconstruction. During the New Deal in the 1930s, the agricultural South and West had been modernized through vast state-capitalist projects of which the Tennessee Valley Authority is best known. But its tax structures, labor laws, and institutions did not change and remained as conservative and illiberal as during the days of post-Reconstruction. In the 1970s, its industrial policy consisted of providing "a safe haven for 'footloose' capital seeking refuge from the regulatory and industrial relations regime and tax structures of the Northeast and Midwest." The South was committed to low taxes on capital and limited social services and had "a long tradition of using the law as a tool to build and protect a racialized political and economic order" (Wood, 2003: 24). This was the land of Jim Crow law.

During the liberal period of 1960s, the expectation was that Fordism would spread southward and this would result in the "Americanization of Dixie." What happened instead was the "Dixiefication of America." The Southern model not only survived but also became the way out of the 1970's economic crisis and the template for the Reagan revolution: "the economic development policies that we have implemented in the United States over the past three decades have taken on the characteristics of an up-to-date, modified version of those that have been in effect in the American South for decades" (Cummings, 1998: x). Southern economics has its roots in plantation economics with rural oligarchies and a low-cost workforce that performs manual labor — slaves, segregated blacks, right-less migrant workers from Mexico under the Bracero program, and after 1964, many illegal immigrants. According to Cummings (1998: 6), it is "the export of Southern and Republican conservative economic values to the nation that replaced the northern liberal values of the New Deal and the Great Society programs that set the country on the path to economic insecurity."

The Reagan reforms came with an antidemocratic cultural and racial backlash that had its beginnings in the 1960s with George Wallace in the South: "it was no accident that the groups Wallace attacked were the least powerful in society, such as welfare mothers and aliens — easy targets to scapegoat" (Cummings, 1998: 10). In 1971, the prison population in the South was 220% higher than in the Northeast; now nationwide incarceration rates began to approximate those that had long prevailed in the South. Within corporations, management became punitive — all elements that feed into a low-wage, high-exploitation accumulation strategy.

If the American South provided the material matrix, Chicago school economics provided the intellectual sheen. At a time of rapid technological change, a return to neoclassical economics offered a gloss of modernist minimalism. Hayek added a cybernetic twist by claiming that market forces, in contrast to state planning, provide superior circulation of information. Friedman's monetarism attacked Fordism and New Deal capitalism. The Laffer curve (tax cuts stimulate the economy and will yield more tax revenue) provided a rationale for rolling back government. Deregulation and tax cuts became bywords for achieving "competitiveness" and "flexibility," whereas in effect they converged on creating a low-wage, high-exploitation regime. As Hutton points out, the origin of what became the "Washington Consensus" lies in a Southern conservative campaign.

By 1979, when the Business Roundtable published its manifesto, essentially arguing for what was later to be dubbed the "Washington Consensus" (balanced budgets, tax cuts, tight money, deregulation, and antiunion laws), with the Moral Majority and the NRA campaigning hard on conservative social issues, the conservatives were on the move. The center of political and economic gravity was moving to the south and west (Hutton, 2002: 106).

Another variable is Wall Street, which had played a destructive role in the 1920s, leading to the 1929 crash. The Reagan administration dismantled the New Deal regulatory structure that had been put in place precisely to counteract the speculative financial practices of the 1920s and unleashed the financial sector. With the institutional restraints gone, the Wall Street-driven preoccupation with short-term stock value gradually transformed the character of American corporations. As corporations needed to show profits at the end of each quarter, the organizational weight within firms shifted to the financial department and elevated the status of financial over productive operations. The institutionalized obsession with earnings led to fraud and eventually culminated in Enron and the cascade of related scandals. Both forms of capitalism, the high-exploitation capitalism of the South and Wall Street financial engineering, are essentially predatory and profoundly different from the productive capitalism that had originally been the basis of American economic success.

The Bush II administration adds a Texan chapter to the magnolia model and reflects an ethos unlike any previous administration, which Lind describes thus: "Although Bush's ancestors were Northeastern, the culture that shaped him was made in Texas — a culture that combines Protestant fundamentalism and Southern militarism with an approach to economics that favors primitive commodity capitalist enterprises like cotton and oil production over high-tech manufacturing and scientific R&D" (Lind, 2003: 80).

While this sheds light on the Bush II administration, Lind easily lapses into schematic judgments, at times essentializes the South, assumes sweeping continuities over time, and dichotomizes Texas elites into modern and premodern factions. Applebome notes that "the South's stock in trade has been the myth and reality of its distinctiveness: the only part of the nation with institutionalized apartheid; the only part of the nation to know the crushing burden of losing a war" (Applebome, 1996: 10).

There is an American "Dixie industry" that produces a "Southern mystique," which operates as an "internal orientalism" within the United States (Zinn, 1964; Jansson, 2003). This comes with the usual North–South dichotomies of modern–traditional, rational–irrational, secular–fundamentalist, urban–rural, tolerant–racist that are familiar from other regions of the world. So while tucked within American exceptionalism, there is a "Southern exceptionalism," but this is not a simple matter. The South is internally differentiated and quite dynamic; for decades it has led the United States in population growth and economic growth. Traditional Southern elites represent a different political economy, but to classify it as "premodern" is too easy; it may well be considered an alternative modernity. This means to acknowledge that it has dynamics of its own and is not simply locked in a premodern pattern. So assessing the significance of the American South is not simply a matter of adding up stereotypes and indicators of regional uneven development, but of navigating representations and deciding what kernels to keep.

While avoiding the trap of "internal orientalism," a few points stand out when we seek to understand the ongoing changes in American policies.

The first is the empirical circumstance of the American South as a low-tax zone. The second is the leadership of Southern conservatives in American politics virtually since the 1970s. While Republicans also lead in the West and Northwest, the demographic center of the GOP is the much more densely populated South. The third circumstance is that over a long period Southern conservatives have consistently resisted the politics of the New Deal. "The Bush II administration was also the culmination of seventy years of a counter-revolution against the New Deal, in both domestic policy and foreign policy" (Lind, 2003: 81–82). Today the American South "has the largest concentration of low-wage jobs, its economy is dominated by externally owned branch plants...and is still dependent on natural resources, particularly oil and gas, just as it was a century ago" (Cummings, 1998: 117).

The United States has been subject to three decades of nonstop conservative onslaught coming from multiple sources. Southern conservatives pushed for dismantling the New Deal, bringing the country to the low-taxes, low-wages, and low-productivity level of the South. Chicago economics advocated the virtues of free markets and deregulation. Both agree on the conservative equation that "less regulation = more growth = more employment" (Cummings, 1998: 75). These socially reactionary changes were pushed through at a time of rapid technological change and presented as progressive measures, in keeping with the information society. New technologies were harnessed to achieve a fundamental change in the balance of forces between capital and labor, duly amplified by the spin of business media.

In Britain during the Thatcher era, the neoliberal package was welcomed as an attack on trade union power and New Labour continued this realignment. New Democrats in the United States accepted the tenets of the post-industrial society, flexibility and the new economy, abandoned the commitment to Fordism and the New Deal and went post-Fordist. The Democratic Party moved to the center right and, albeit for different reasons than the Southern conservatives, accepted major parts of Reaganomics. The Clinton administration institutionalized strands of Reaganomics as a bipartisan agenda — business deregulation, welfare reform, the "three strikes and out" regime — and exported it on an international scale. Instead of a democratic approach of stakeholder capitalism, New Democrats and New Labour adopted an authoritarian version of "flexibility."

How does Southern economics travel? The low-wage model increased the number of American families with two wage earners and lengthened working hours without a proportional increase of incomes. The single-minded pursuit of short-term profits and shareholder revenue eroded economic capacities to the extent that the main product of leading American enterprises has become financial engineering or paper entrepreneurialism, making sure that the books show higher numbers at the end of each quarter. The conservatives have been so busy dismantling government and the New Deal that they have paid little attention to the actual American economy, which has experienced a 30-yr decline. Long-term trends include massive deindustrialization, shrinking or inadequate investments in plants and equipment in many sectors, decline in research and development, and the growth of service jobs with low productivity, low wages, low job security and long working hours. Downsizing corporations has resulted in employee alienation and low morale. Income inequality has grown steadily.

The result of trying to be competitive on the cheap is that American industries have lost international competitiveness in several sectors (cf. Porter, 1990). This is reflected in the U.S. trade deficit and growing indebtedness at every level of the American economy, in households, corporations, cities, states, and the federal government. The bottom line is a current account deficit that has grown to unsustainable levels.

From time to time, various circumstances have boosted the numbers, such as financial crisis in other parts of the world (in part as an effect of American-induced liberalization of capital markets) and the new economy bubble of the Clinton years. What keeps the American economy going in a structural fashion is a combination of expansion, government deficit spending, and the influx of foreign funds. Expansion takes the form of corporations branching into other areas of business (as in conglomerates, frequently leading to business failure), waves of mergers and acquisitions (spinning fortunes in Wall Street while usually leading to less productive combinations), and opening up other markets by means of free trade agreements that liberalize capital markets and export American financial engineering overseas. The main form of government funding is the military–industrial complex. The inflow of foreign funds is a major cornerstone of the American economy. The influx of low-priced goods from China and Asia (and increasingly also services) keeps prices low as American incomes stagnate; also significant is the steady inflow of cheap migrant and immigrant labor, in particular from Mexico.

III. The Cold War and Neoliberalism

The postwar period of "proto-neoliberalism" coincides with the cold-war era. During these years, the infrastructure of neoliberalism was built in economic thinking and ideology (free market), think tanks and economic policy (the "Chicago boys" in Chile and Indonesia). In fact, could we consider neoliberalism as the sequel to the cold war?

Founding texts such as Friedrich von Hayek's *From Serfdom to Slavery* and Walt Rostow's *Take-off to Economic Growth* (subtitled *An*

Anti-Communist Manifesto) were originally anticommunist tracts. Over time anticommunist critique became "Free World" policy, cold-war geopolitics was converted into a global financial regime, and the erstwhile anticommunist alliance morphed into a free-market hegemonic compromise. Since the spoils come to the victor, the kind of capitalism that triumphed was Anglo-American "free enterprise" capitalism. As part of anticommunism, the United States actively undermined socialist forces throughout the world, pressured international labor unions, and blocked global alternatives such as a new international economic order. European social democracy and Asian state-assisted capitalism were similarly disparaged.

The affinities between the cold war and neoliberalism take several forms. The postwar modernization of Dixie capitalism in the nonunion Sunbelt was made possible by military tax dollars, so Dixiefication and the cold war were tandem projects. The American Sunbelt is now the most dependent on military contracts. The overseas network of security alliances built during the cold war was reproduced under the neoliberal dispensation with a new inflection. From the "Washington connection," it was a small step to the Washington Consensus. Now IMF conditionalities and World Bank structural adjustment programs disciplined unruly states. Applied to the USSR, Halliday (1986) refers to this process as the "second cold war." By undermining trade unions and nationalist governments in much of the global South, U.S. foreign policy helped create a favorable investment climate for American capital. American capital flight in turn weakened the hold of the New Deal within the United States, thus establishing an elective affinity between a domestic and transnational hegemony of similar inclination.

During the cold war, economic and security interests mingled in the military–industrial complex. If the Soviet Union had been economically exhausted by the arms race, so arguably was the United States, though this was masked by economic achievements. For the United States, the real burden of the superpower arms race was its growing path depending on the military–industrial complex. American economics, politics, and institutions have been huddled around the military–industrial complex for so long that it has become a functionally autonomous logic. American militarism has become entrenched in policy; as Johnson (2002) notes, this entails the formation of a professional military class, the preponderance of the military and the arms industry in administration policy, and military preparedness as the main priority of government policy. The end of the cold war, then, created an "enemy deficit" for how to sustain this gargantuan apparatus in the absence of a threat?

With the waning of the cold war, security interests slipped into the background and the Treasury and Commerce became the most salient government agencies, in cooperation with Wall Street and with the international

Table 5.1 Continuities/Discontinuities between Cold War and Neoliberal Globalization

Dimensions	Cold War	Neoliberalism
Ideology	Free world	Free market
	Open door	Free trade
	Anti-communism	Pro-American capitalism
Key state agencies	Pentagon, CIA	Treasury, Commerce
Economic center	Military–industrial complex, MNCs	MNCs, banks, Silicon Valley, telecommunications, media
Pressure on developing countries	Join Free World	Structural adjustment
Means of pressure	National security and economic incentives	Financial discipline and economic incentives
Agents of pressure	U.S. government, Pentagon	IMF, World Bank, WTO
Investments	Sunbelt	Third World made safe
Security	Strong U.S. military	Strong U.S. military
Politics of containment	Military intervention, covert operations	Humanitarian intervention, nation building
Allies	NATO, Israel, etc.	NATO, Israel, etc.
	Religious movements (Mujahideen, Hamas, etc.)	"Clash of civilizations": Islam as opponent

financial institutions based in Washington. So in the shift from the cold war to neoliberalism some elements remained constant — such as a strong U.S. military and support for strategic allies such as Israel — while in other respects there were marked shifts of emphasis (see Table 5.1).

IV. The Washington Consensus

Postwar American development policies in the global South favored nation building, "betting on the strong," Community Development that matched the American voluntary sector, and instilling achievement orientation — all strands of modernization theory in which modernization equals westernization equals Americanization. Policies such as the Alliance for Progress interacted with cold-war strategies and the "Washington connection."

The Washington Consensus that took shape in the late 1980s as a set of economic prescriptions for developing countries echoes the core claim of cold-war ideology: the free market and democracy go together. The main tenets of the Washington Consensus are monetarism, reduction of government spending and regulation, privatization, liberalization of trade and financial markets, and the promotion of export-led growth. A difference is that postwar modernization was a rival project, a contender in the cold war, while the Washington Consensus no longer looks to national security states to withstand communist pressure. Hence, if modernization theory was state-centered and part of the postwar governmental Keynesian consensus in development thinking, the Washington Consensus turns another leaf, to government rollback and deregulation, now elevated from domestic policy to international program. In this sense, the Reagan era was a foretaste and then consummation of American cold-war victory, acknowledging no rival, no competition. This imprint shows in the policies of the international financial institutions: "the end of the Cold War has been associated with the increasing politicization of the IMF by the United States. There is evidence that the United States has been willing to reward friends and punish enemies only since 1990" (Thacker, 1999: 70).

The 1990s has been described as a time of contestation between American and Asian capitalism, and American capitalism won (Hutton and Giddens, 2000). Speculative capital and hedge funds unleashed by Reagan deregulation played a major part in the Asian crisis of 1997 and subsequent financial crises. In the United States, the Asian crisis was hailed as an opportunity for the further Americanization of Asian economies (Bello, 2003).

The Washington institutions have been governed by the Wall Street–Treasury–IMF complex in accordance with American economic orthodoxy, so a shorthand account of neoliberal globalization is American economic unilateralism. These policies resulted in a rollback of developing country government spending and the growth and mushrooming of non-governmental organizations (NGOs).

Amid all the criticism of neoliberalism, little attention is given to the counter-revolution in the United States that prefigured the "counterrevolution in development." Changes in the United States prefigure those undertaken in the global South in the name of structural reform; in both, there is an attempt to dismantle the regulatory state. In the United States, government cutbacks were implemented through Reaganism; on a world scale the drive to liberalize and privatize economies was implemented by means of IMF stability lending and World Bank structural adjustment.

Through structural reform, the combination of Dixie capitalism and Wall Street financial engineering has been extrapolated on a global scale. Southern economics and its depth structure of plantation economics shed light on the realities of structural adjustment in the global South. Real neoliberalism, on display in the American South, is also known as "the Haitian road of development." So it is no wonder that during neoliberal globalization, development policies were a paradox, which is politely referred to as "policy incoherence": institutions matter, but governments are rolled back; capacity building is key, but existing public capacities are defunded; accountability is essential, but privatization eliminates accountability; the aim is "building democracy by strengthening civil society," but NGOs are professionalized and depoliticized (cf. Nederveen Pieterse, 2001).

Neoliberalism sought to do away with "development economics" and instead presented the free market as the answer to all economic questions. If we would consider only the economic theories of the free market advocates, there might be a rationale to this, even if at best half true; enough of a rationale to serve for a while as the basis of a transnational hegemonic compromise. During the Clinton years, the WTO became the overarching framework of neoliberal globalization. However, neither structural reform nor multilateral trade would conceal the actual character of neoliberalism as a high-exploitation regime. Stepping in as a debt collector for western lenders and investors, the IMF weakened states in the South. This is frontier capitalism that thrives on low wages and high exploitation.

Commenting on 9/11, Beck (2001) observes that "The terrorist attacks on America were the Chernobyl of globalization. Suddenly, the seemingly irrefutable tenets of neoliberalism — that economics will supersede politics, that the role of the state will diminish — lose their force in a world of global risks. . . . America's vulnerability is indeed much related to its political philosophy. . . . Neoliberalism has always been a fair-weather philosophy, one that works only when there are no serious conflicts and crises."

9/11 has shaken the "animal spirits" of late capitalism. An economy driven by replacement demand and consumer spending on status goods, kept going by marketing mood making, comes tumbling down like a house of cards once consumer confidence fades. Aviation, tourism, retail, stocks, banks, insurance, advertising, Hollywood, fashion, media — all sectors have been trembling and repositioning under the impact of 9/11. Global capitalism turns out to be as interconnected as network analysis has suggested and as vulnerable. With the exception of insurance rates, the economic impact of 9/11 has been temporary; the impact of the Enron episode is probably far more significant.

The fact that neoliberalism is crisis-prone rather than crisis-proof is no news to most of the world but a novel experience for the United States. There is a glaring inconsistency between federal government support for sectors hit by the 9/11 crisis — especially airlines and insurance — and the Washington Consensus which has been urging all governments, crisis or no, to liberalize economies and cutback spending. If the insurance industry would not receive government support, rates would increase, delaying economic recovery. Countries that have been lectured by Washington and the IMF on economic sanity may be surprised to learn that the United States does not follow its own counsel. This raises the wider question whether the Washington Consensus applies to Washington.

Williamson (1990) originally formulated the Washington orthodoxy in ten points. The first is fiscal discipline. In Washington, this applied during the 1990s, but not before or after. The second point is reordering public expenditure priorities in a pro-poor way. This has not been a Washington priority since the New Deal. Like the Reagan administration, the Bush II government uses deficit spending as a political instrument to cutback social spending (eventually heading for the privatization of social security). The third point is tax reform toward a system that combines a broad tax base with moderate marginal tax rates. The Bush II administration scrapped estate and dividend taxes and gives tax cuts disproportionally to the very affluent. States and cities are in financial crisis, cut support for education and services and will raise taxes, and so forth. Thus, of the ten points of Washington orthodoxy, it is practically only in privatization and deregulation that Washington follows the Washington Consensus.

For some time, the neoliberal project has been unraveling and the Washington Consensus faces mounting problems. The IMF handling of financial crises has lost credibility even in Washington and on Wall Street (e.g., Soros, 1998). Its reputation is now that of a "Master of Disaster" (Cassidy, 2002) and in Argentina it is the International Misery Fund. Congress has pressed the IMF for reforms of its operations since its recurrent failures in crisis management. In 2000, the Meltzer Commission examined the World Bank on behalf of the U.S. Congress and found that most of its projects have been unsuccessful and the bulk of its lending has gone to higher-income developing countries (which ensure a higher return on investment), so its impact on global poverty has been close to nil (Bello, 2003). Subsequently the World Bank made combating poverty its priority, but this does not sit well with the neoclassical orthodoxies of the Treasury, which has pressured the World Bank to the point of weakening its credibility.

The WTO is stalled by mounting public criticism and zigzagging American policies. It is no longer merely a tool of American power but also monitors the United States (on tax breaks, steel tariffs, and farm subsidies). Growing worldwide mobilization against the WTO, from the battle of Seattle to the World Social Forum, has made this an increasingly difficult and high-risk option. Earlier international NGOs blocked the Multilateral Agreement on Investments.

Arguably, there is no more Washington Consensus; what remains is a disparate set of *ad hoc* Washington agendas. In view of the disarray of the international financial institutions, the idea of a "post-Washington Consensus" papers over incoherence and improvisation (Stiglitz, 2002). In economics, the neoliberal orthodoxies are no longer broadly accepted; attention has long shifted from state failure to market failure, the importance of institutions and themes such as social capital. After decades of structural adjustment, most developing countries are worse off. As a development policy, neoliberalism has been an utter failure — not surprisingly because it is a regime of financial discipline.

As the Washington Consensus followed the compass of American neoliberalism, its status rises and falls with the success or failure of the American economy, which has been losing points in its own right. Signals of failure are the collapse of the new economy followed by the Enron series of corporate scandals, Wall Street decline, and recession. A reorientation of U.S. policies would be in the cards at any rate. The decomposition of the neoliberal order sheds light on the subsequent American turn to "permanent war."

Twenty years of rampant neoliberalism created a culture and habitus of neoliberalism. An anthropological study of the "meanings of the market" in western culture finds as the basic assumptions of the market model that the world consists of free individuals who are instrumentally rational and operate in a world that consists only of buyers and sellers (Carrier, 1997). The peculiar ethos of casino capitalism that neoliberal globalization unleashed on the world is ultimately an occidental cargo cult. Its secret rituals include Dixie capitalism, Wall Street wizardry, and cold-war strategy.

References

Applebome, P., *Dixie Rising: How the South is Shaping American Values, Politics and Culture*, Times Books, New York, 1996.

Beck, U., The Chernobyl of globalization, *Financial Times*, November 6, 2001.

Bello, W., *Deglobalization: Ideas for a New World Economy*, Zed, London, 2003.

Carrier, J.G., Ed., *Meanings of the Market: The Free Market in Western Culture*, Berg, Oxford, 1997.

Cassidy, J., Master of disaster, *The New Yorker*, July 15, 2002.

Cummings, S.D., *The Dixiefication of America: The American Odyssey into the Conservative Economic Trap*, Praeger, Westport, CT, 1998.

Halliday, F., *The Second Cold War*, Verso, London, 1986.

Hutton, W., *The World We're In*, Little, Brown, London, 2002.

Hutton, W. and Giddens, A., Eds., *Global Capitalism*, New Press, New York, 2000.

Jansson, D.R., Internal orientalism in America: W.J. Cash's the mind of the south and the spatial construction of American national identity, *Political Geogr.*, 22, 293–316, 2003.

Johnson, C., American militarism and blowback: the costs of letting the Pentagon dominate foreign policy, *New Political Sci.*, 24 (1), 21–38, 2002.

Lind, M., *Made in Texas: George W. Bush and the Southern Takeover of American Politics*, Basic Books, New York, 2003.

Nederveen Pieterse, J., *Development Theory: Deconstructions/Reconstructions*, Sage, London, 2001.

Porter, M.E., *The Competitive Advantage of Nations*, Free Press, New York, 1990.

Soros, G., *The Crisis of Global Capitalism*, Public Affairs, New York, 1998.

Stiglitz, J.E., *Globalization and its Discontents*, Norton, New York, 2002.

Thacker, S.C., The high politics of IMF lending, *World Politics*, 52, 38–75, 1999.

Tickell, A. and Peck, J., Making global rules: globalisation or neoliberalisation? in *Remaking the Global Economy: Economic-Geographical Perspectives*, Peck, J. and Cheung, H.W.-C., Eds., Sage, London, pp. 163–181, 2003.

Williamson, J., What Washington means by policy reform, in *Latin American Adjustment: How Much Has Happened?* Williamson, J., Ed., Institute for International Economics, Washington, DC, 1990, pp. 5–20.

Wood, P.J., The rise of the prison–industrial complex in the United States, in *Capitalist Punishment: Prison Privatization and Human Rights*, Coyle, A., Campbell, A., and Neufeld, R., Eds., Clarity Press and Zed, Atlanta, GA and London, 2003, pp. 16–29.

Zinn, H., *The Southern Mystique*, Knopf, New York, 1964.

Chapter 6

Economic Development and Democratic Consolidation: Patterns in East and Southeast Asian Countries

Ian Marsh

CONTENTS

I. Introduction

This chapter explores various aspects of the links between economic and democratic developments. These processes, and their linkage, have stimulated extensive, but mostly separate, theoretical and empirical literatures, for example, developmental approaches surveyed in Chilcote (2004) and democracy in Diamond (1999) and Grugel (2004). This chapter focuses particularly on the experience of seven countries in East and Southeast Asia: Korea, Taiwan, Singapore, Thailand, Indonesia, Malaysia, and the Philippines. Their economic modernization has surpassed that of other developing countries. In addition, they are also now (formally) democracies. Their recent history thus embraces both democratic transition and consolidation and economic takeoff and adaptation.

These seven countries form, along with Japan and China, a distinct economic region. In 2003, Asia accounted for 23% of world gross domestic product (GDP), Western Europe 29%, and North America 32.5%. Linkage between these countries has resulted primarily from the formation of regional production systems. Political regionalism has remained weak.

> The Asian financial crisis illustrates that Asian regionalism was not strong enough to prevent the establishment of beachheads in markets that used to be closed to foreign investors. An IMF-centred, global approach to the regional financial crisis rather than reliance on an Asian-centred, Japanese-led effort revealed the weakness of an exclusive and cohesive East Asian regionalism without U.S. involvement. (Katzenstein, 2000: 22)

These countries are more engaged in the international economy than their European Union (EU) counterparts (Fligstein and Merand, 2001). Economic prosperity remains much more dependent on U.S. and (to a lesser extent) EU markets. Other distinctions between individual countries are wide. Their colonial experience was varied (Japanese, British, American-Spanish, and Dutch). Religious–moral traditions were diverged (Islam, Confucian, Buddhist, Protestant, and Catholic). Nationalism is particularly strong in several countries (e.g., Korea and Thailand). Except Singapore and Malaysia (and to a lesser extent Indonesia), these are countries without significant ethnic divisions. Finally, social and economic differences are wide.[1]

There is a clear layering between these seven countries in the timing of economic and political developments. For example, Korea went from war-ravaged backwardness to membership of the OECD in 30 years. Taiwan and Singapore have achieved similar levels of economic growth. Following the Plaza Accords of the mid-1980s, economic development spread to the other four countries such as Malaysia, Thailand, the Philippines, and Indonesia. Their approaches to economic governance have however hitherto been less *dirigiste*. Meantime, on the political front, Malaysia and Singapore have been at least nominal democracies since their establishment in the 1960s. From the late 1980s, this regime spread to the other five countries, culminating in Indonesia's transition in 1998.

Their experience offers three broad lessons. First, it exemplifies linkages between economic and political processes. There is no necessary connection between economic development and democratization: these processes are independent and their conjunction is contingent. However, after democratization, the political system needs to facilitate continued economic adaptation. Political elites ultimately determine whether this happens. In the more successful countries, elites have preserved sufficient insulation from established economic interests to maintain a commitment to dynamic outcomes. Secondly, the experience of these seven countries illustrates a number of approaches to economic governance. In determining whether to pursue more or less ambitious goals, state capacity is the critical variable. In the absence of robust state capacities, individual states are obliged to accept relatively dependent incorporation into the international and regional political economy. Finally, their experience highlights on-going challenges that are associated with democratic consolidation. This involves above all the tensions between democratization as the development of a set of elite-dominated governing institutions and democratization as rule by the people.

Section I explores their varied experiences of economic modernization, and similarly, the Section II explores their varied experiences of democratic transition and consolidation. Section III explores linkages between these concepts and general lessons.

II. Economic Development

These countries can be classified into three groups: developmental (Korea, Taiwan, and Singapore), an intermediate group (Malaysia and possibly Thailand), and a dependent pair (Indonesia and the Philippines).

A. Developmental Countries

Korea, Taiwan, and Singapore exemplify a state-led approach to economic development. These are "strong" countries in the sense that they have a demonstrated capacity to define their national interests to an elaborated degree and then realize these purposes through appropriate strategies. This capacity is particularly critical in maintaining relatively independent engagement in economic globalization: the international political economy is hardly as benign as the doctrine of comparative advantage asserts (Cumings, 1999). These countries have displayed their strength through good times (e.g., 1988–1993) and bad (e.g., the 1997 financial crisis and the subsequent tech wreck).

The literature describes these countries as "developmental." Their distinct features have been analyzed extensively (Johnson, 1982; Wade, 1990; Evans, 1995; Weiss and Hobson, 1995; Weiss, 1998; 2003; Woo-Cumings, 1999; Painter and Pierre, 2005; for contrast views, see also Clifford, 1997; Lingle, 1998). One threshold condition and three basic governance capabilities have been identified. The threshold condition involves high saving rates. All these countries have been able to mobilize savings for developmental purposes, although the means used and the focus of investment have varied widely (Hamilton-Hart, 2002).

The first basic governance capability involves a consensus between political elites about an economic "vision," broad industry strategy and technological, structural, or other priorities. This has involved the development of industrial or structural capabilities, particularly high growth and high value sectors. The top leadership has united in adopting and implementing this strategy. This elite consensus has embraced political, official, and business groups. Until the early 1990s, it was realized through a soft authoritarian political framework. Thereafter, more or less democratic political regimes emerged at least in Korea and Taiwan.

The second basic governance capability involves the institutions that propose a (primarily technical) strategic vision and agenda and that coordinate implementation. Economic governance has been based on a meritocratic central bureaucracy with both the technical capabilities and the technical standing to provide strategic leadership. This is expressed in quasi-think tank organization (e.g., Council for Economic Planning and Development, Taiwan; Economic Development Board, Singapore). These bodies undertook the strategic structural and economic analyses that were required to operationalize the elite consensus. They enjoyed high standing in the overall structure of government.

The third capability involves the institutions creating sectoral or technological policy and implementation capacity. It includes the capability to design sectoral programs and to mobilize the collaboration necessary to implement them. It involves the ability to respond differentially to particular sectoral needs. Administrative capacity was based on the prestige of bureaucratic service, meritocratic recruitment, and insulation from particularist pressures. Rent seeking was thus minimized and the influence of sectional interests contained.

State capacity was also reflected in business–government relations, which were mediated by a variety of collaborative structures ("deliberation councils"). These arrangements have been associated with distinct patterns of business formation (Whitley, 1999; Redding, 2002). More recently, there have been experiments with corporatist-type structures in Taiwan and Korea. President Lee set up a National Affairs Conference in 1990 and a National Development Conference in 1996. Meantime, following his election in 1997, President Kim established a Tripartite Commission. The trade unions withdrew from this body in 1998 but rejoined in 1999. The influence of labor has however generally been contained. Korea has the most developed trade union movement but representation is split between two rival federations.

The requirements for economic governance have progressively changed and these states have a track record of adaptation. The developmental state literature originally described a world in which competitiveness was based on technology "catch-up" or "fast followership" (Matthews and Cho, 2000). It also described a world in which issues of structural adaptation were primary. Following an initial switch from agriculture to basic assembly industries, regional states progressively moved to more developed secondary industries. During the late 1980s, Korea, Taiwan, and Singapore moved progressively into advanced technology sectors in electronics. From the mid-1990s, their ambitions embraced other "knowledge-based" activities like biotechnology, nanotechnology, and new materials technology. They have also sought to establish a strong position in services (such as software and, in the case of Singapore, health and education). Weiss (1998) has christened this capability as "transformational."

However, these ambitions raise a host of new governance challenges. For example, in science-based industries, ownership of intellectual property is critical.[2] The frameworks available to guide the development of science-based industries involve attention to an ecology of market and nonmarket interactions (West, 2004). Similarly, the diffusion of knowledge to existing producers also involves an array of nonmarket institutions (Porter, 2003; Smith, 2004). Such approaches involve significant transaction costs, a legion of principal–agent issues, and problems of collective action (Doner and Ramsay, 2003: 211). There is evidence that these approaches are being adopted without dysfunctional consequences (Sturgeon and Lester, 2003; Boldeman, 2003). However, these new programs are in their early stages and detailed studies remain to be undertaken.

In summary, the developmental approach represented a distinct (and successful) bridling of market forces by political action in ways that reconciled economic development with improved income distribution. It was also a strategy for maintaining (relative) national economic independence in the international political economy. However, it remains particularly demanding of state capacity at political, policy, and administrative levels.

B. "Second-Tier" Countries: Thailand and Malaysia

Both Malaysia and Thailand have relied on foreign direct investment (FDI) as the primary engine of manufacturing development. Malaysia has gestured to the developmental approach, but this has been in conjunction with, and secondary to, efforts to extend Malay participation in the economy (Jomo and Felker, 1999; Jomo and Gomez, 2000). Thailand has not sought to manage structural outcomes. The financial crisis affected each of these countries differently and has elicited different responses.

1. Political Leadership and Consensus

Malaysia's Prime Minister Mahatir dominated his country's modernization from the early 1990s until his resignation in 2003 (Jomo and Felker, 1999: 21). The financial crisis had earlier disrupted Malaysia's ambitious developmental program and exposed weakness in both finance and manufacturing sectors. What began as a currency crisis quickly became a banking and corporate crisis (Cook, 2001: 16). On September 1, 1998, Mahatir fixed the value of the ringgit and imposed a ban for 12 months on short-term capital flows (Kaplan and Rodrik, 2001).

The government subsequently ordered the merger of the country's 54 banks and finance houses into ten banking groups. The economy recovered rapidly over the following 12 months. Stock market controls were eased in February 1999 when a graduated exit tax of 10% replaced the former ban on repatriation of funds. Assessments of Malaysian reform have been generally positive (e.g., according to the *Economist*, June 5, 2002, professional managers have largely replaced political appointees in state enterprises).

At the level of industry policy, the Malaysian government has been the most interventionist of the second-tier NICs and has exhibited the greatest strategic and sectoral ambitions. From the early 1990s, the Mahatir government introduced an industry strategy, which sought to accelerate development in the manufacturing sector, particularly electronics. Its model was the state-level Penang Development Corporation that had stimulated the development of an electronics cluster in the 1980s. Networking, clusters, and linkages between MNCs and indigenous firms were promoted. A hi-tech park at Kulim, on the model of the Hsinchu development in Taiwan, was foreshadowed. The CyberJaya Multimedia super corridor announced in 1996 was also an expression of this approach. A review in 2000, however, found the outcome fell far short of the promise (*Asian Wall Street Journal*, March 26 and April 1, 2001). In July 2003, a new industrial development strategy was announced the encouraged participation by local SMEs in multinational company (MNC) supply chains.

While the strategic framework for industry development has been put in place, sectoral capabilities have been found to be inadequate. In an evaluation of electronics developments, Matthews and Cho (2000: 276) question implementation capacities. "The direction toward upgrading is there but its execution has been slow, although much more advanced than in neighboring countries such as Thailand and the Philippines." Jomo and Felker (1999: 25) suggest that bureaucratic capacities for sectoral analysis and for monitoring implementation are inadequate. They suggest that state-led strategies approaches have not been backed by adequate analysis and oversight. "It is precisely the sparseness of . . . capacity for detailed, continuous sector-specific assessment of market and industry trends, which is the greatest constraint on effective industry implementation" (see also Dodgson, 2000). Doner and Ramsay (2003: 203–205, 213–214, 220–222) reached a similar conclusion in their comparative assessment of the development of the hard disk drive industry in Thailand, Malaysia, and Singapore. While Malaysia showed more strategic capacity than Thailand (although of course much less than Singapore), there was little evidence of ability to implement policy at the sectoral level — except the Penang Development Corporation, which was the model for the broader strategy.

In the case of Thailand, ownership of her domestic economic sector is highly concentrated. In 1998, 52% of publicly listed companies were family controlled when compared with 25% of that in Korea. Concentrated ownership is particularly prominent in the financial sector. This creates a particular context for economic governance in Thailand. Doner and Ramsay (2000, 2003) argue that the institutions that have spearheaded Thai economic development hitherto are inappropriately configured to meet prospective needs. Growth has been primarily based on structural adjustment. This has involved a switch of low-cost human resources from agriculture to manufacturing. Political institutions have (paradoxically) contributed positively to this outcome by promoting a kind of competitive clientelism. This has involved the development of (fragile) links between particular business promoters and particular political patrons. Political competition between these patrons limited predatory rent seeking. Meantime, the technocratic elite focused on macroeconomic stability, not on detailed intervention.

Thailand has the advantage of committed investors in electronics and automobiles sectors. It has much to gain by the liberalization of regional trading arrangements (Schwarz and Villinger, 2004). However, Thailand cannot compete with China for low-wage industries. The present necessity is to shift from a strategy based on low-cost manufacturing to one based on upgrading. This requires governance capabilities at systemic and sectoral levels. It requires institutions that can mediate human resource development, supplier linkages, technology development, and the introduction of advanced infrastructure. Doner and Ramsay (2003) illustrate particular patterns through analyses of electronics, textiles, and automobiles, all sectors in which Thailand has built a reasonably strong position. Evidence that weaknesses are being tackled is sparse.

In a detailed survey, Painter (2001) reached similar pessimistic conclusions about Thai institutional capacities. The track record of elected Thai governments in developing strategic policy frameworks and in achieving policy coherence was poor. In relation to administrative capacity, the author noted the considerable powers of delay and obstruction vested in senior civil servants, the politicization of appointments to the formerly meritocratic elite agencies, and the uneven quality of the overall service. Neither Malaysia nor Thailand has the political, policy, or administrative capacity to match their developmental cousins.

C. "Dependent" Countries: Indonesia and the Philippines

Indonesia and the Philippines, the third group of countries, have depended on FDI for their development. They have the least effective bureaucracies and the most unsettled political systems. Indonesia briefly gestured toward guided industry development, but enrichment of then President Suharto's family and their circle was another feature of the economic governance system (Dodgson, 2000: 248–251). The Philippines, like Thailand has sought, has primarily sought to manage macroeconomic outcomes and is plagued with problems of clientelism (Hutchcroft, 1999). The following paragraphs briefly review their experience.

As a result of the financial crisis, Indonesia experienced the largest economic reverse of any regional state, a situation that has not been improved by the ensuing political uncertainty. FDI fell from $34 billion in 1997 to $9 billion in 2001 (*Far East Economic Review*, December 19, 2002). Private consumption as a share of GDP increased from 64% in 1997 to 74% in 2002. Over the same period, investment dropped from 33 to 14%. The flirtation with "national champions" occurred while Habibie was industry minister (on the aircraft industry as a national champion see Dodgson, 2000: 248–251; also Keller and Samuels, 2003: 17). However, the state's licensing and regulatory powers were widely used as instruments of patronage. Following the financial crisis, the Indonesian Bank Restructuring Agency (IBRA) was established. However, its leadership changed seven times in 4 yr (*Economist*, June 15, 2002). No entrepreneurs have been prosecuted. The central bank governor was found guilty of corruption but not replaced. Banking sector reforms have been delayed and corporate debt issues remain unresolved. Indonesia's outlook remains the most insecure in Southeast Asia. Macintyre (2000) has argued convincingly that past structures facilitated economic development. However, there is now a clear mismatch between institutions and the requirements of economic governance with little immediate prospect of a satisfactory resolution.

In the case of the Philippines, clientelism and a predatory elite have undermined development. The Philippines is also characterized by highly concentrated wealth. Fifty-two percent of stock market capitalization was controlled by ten families (Cook, 2001: 7). The political standing of these families has biased policy toward the protection of privilege and weakened the extractive capacities of the state (tax revenues equal a very low percentage of GDP). The periodic need for external funding to avoid crisis has acted as a kind of countervailing influence. The external developmental agencies have supported the development of an economic technocracy. The Ramos presidency sought to liberalize the economy and weaken the economic dominance of the oligarchy. For example, the Philippines National Bank was privatized and foreign bank entry was permitted. By the time of the financial crisis, 19 foreign banks were active in the local market. "Technocratic actors within the state and its outside funders took advantage of the crisis to try to break the tight family control of local banks. Their objective is a banking sector dominated by a few large local and foreign players" (Cook, 2001: 20). This objective has been accomplished.

The government has sought to lead industry development by endeavoring to reconstitute the Board of Investment on the model of the Singapore EDB, but the contexts are completely different. It has also sought to develop an electronics cluster, modeled on the Penang and Hsinchu developments, at the former U.S. naval base site of Subic Bay. However, the overall outlook for the Philippines, as a base for low-cost manufacturing, has been undercut by the emergence of China. The prospects for a strategy of upgrading are bleak. Political and bureaucratic incapacity are both chronic problems (Hutchcroft, 1999; Painter, 2001).

III. Democratization

In five of the seven countries covered in this chapter, "soft authoritarianism" has given way to democracy over the past two decades. At least, formally, democratic regimes are now the norm. The pattern of regimes varies widely (Macintyre, 2003). Korea and Taiwan have adopted semipresidential systems. Thailand, Malaysia, and Singapore have parliamentary systems. The Philippines has a fully presidential system, modeled on that of its former colonial master, the United States. Indonesia's regime may be evolving from a fully presidential to a semipresidential pattern. Malaysia is the only federation in the region. Both Malaysia and Thailand are also constitutional monarchies, although the king is a significant political figure only in the latter.

The transitions of the 1990s displayed common features. Grugel (2004) identifies three areas that are salient in this development: the state, the international political economy, and civil society. Pressures can gather in each and, in the case of the five Asian countries, their conjunction facilitated a (more or less) peaceful transition. At the level of civil society, "people power" was an important catalyst. Demonstrations disclosed the temper of public opinion. External influences of different kinds were also prominent. Security dependence on the United States helped the transitions in Taiwan, Korea, and the Philippines. The United States promoted democracy to her clients. The financial crisis precipitated regime change in Indonesia and acceptance of a new constitution in Thailand. Meantime, the state was also an important catalytic agent. In each case, the ruling elite concluded state legitimacy required a new foundation. The conjunction of these elements precipitated the immediate democratic turn. However, democratic consolidation has posed a host of new issues. The following sections focus on the most critical, political socialization, and executive–legislative relations. The former is pertinent to the long-term development of democratic governance and the latter to its more immediate efficacy.

A. Representation, Mobilization, and Socialization: Democracy without Partisans?

The promise of democratic governance — citizens who freely determine their own constraints — remains an ideal that is far from realization in occidental states. However, the distance between the legal form and the democratic substance in regional states is (not surprisingly) very substantial. Political socialization is the process through which this gap might progressively close. One pattern of socialization was associated with western democratic development. What patterns might be emerging in the countries of East and Southeast Asia?

Attachment to the state remains primarily the result of nationalist sentiment (Sinnott, 2005). In contrast, such evidence as is available suggests that attachment to democratic norms and processes remains shallow

(Chu et al., 2001; Rose and Shin, 2001; Shin, 2003). How might such attachments develop? In western experience, mass political parties were the agents not only of democratic representation but also of democratic socialization. The causal sequence may have varied between countries. However, democracy was everywhere the fruit of a bottom-up agitation, based partly on the emergence of an industrial working class, partly on the development of trade unions, and partly on the ideologies of laborism, socialism, or communism. Coalitions with bourgeois, agrarian, or religious interests were variously formed. By such means, and also as a result of war and civil war, liberal or authoritarian political systems were progressively displaced by liberal democratic regimes.

In the literature on political development, the role of mass parties was critical. These bodies not only represented citizen views but also contributed to the formation of democratic citizens. In the process of mobilizing citizens, they developed citizen democratic orientations. Political parties augmented identities by politicizing them (Polanyi, 1949). Democracy is taking root in the Asian countries not only just without this phase but also without any immediate prospect of its occurrence. Except Taiwan and Malaysia, the cleavages — ideological, center-periphery, and religious — that in the west differentiated identities and constituted the essential foundation for party development either do not exist or do not have political salience.

Nor are the organizational forms that would provide a durable foundation for party development evident. Except UMNO in Malaysia, perhaps the major parties in Taiwan and the Democratic Party in Thailand and parties in the countries covered have no or very limited branch structures, no mass memberships, no internal policy development mechanisms, and virtually no or very limited durable organizations. Where a durable organization exists, its focus is on the leadership group rather than on the membership base. Nor are parties merely a legal artifact, the result of the rules of party competition, as in the United States (Katz and Kolodny, 1994). Rather, as Blondel (2005) has pointed out, they are primarily based on leaders with established national standing. These individuals can take a preexisting organization and remold it in their own image (Kim Dae Jung) or they can build a new organization (Thaksin; Roh Moon Hyun; Widhonyo). In either case, power flows outward and downward from the leader, not upward from a mass membership or local notables. Prime Minister Berlusconi provides a western analog for this particular pattern.

Top-down democratization has produced a superficially familiar formal structure, but the task of citizen-development remains. If political parties are not to be the immediate medium for these processes, are there alternatives?

1. Social Movements

Social movements are possible agents for representation and socialization. These meso-level formations could be catalysts in identity formation and advocacy. This outcome would be consistent with the evolution of western democratic practice. The trade union movement was central to western democratic development. More recently, the new social movements have extended and differentiated citizenship (Tarrow, 1998). Movements such as those championing women's rights, the environment, multiculturalism, antiglobalization, human rights, gay rights, and so on have proliferated in western states.

There are unfortunately no comprehensive comparative studies of the development of these intermediary political formations in East and South East Asia. Studies of developments in particular countries have been undertaken (Martin Jones, 1997), and there are also some more limited comparisons covering, for example, the environment movement (Hsiao, 1999, 2002). Interest groups and social movements are active in Korea (Moon and Sunghack, 2000: 8), Thailand, Taiwan, Indonesia, and the Philippines (Funston, 2003). Some restrictions on interest formation have been eased in Singapore (e.g., the gay movement has been allowed to organize). However, these formations are mostly in urban areas. Further, except Korea, trade union development is quite confined (Rowley and Benson, 2000). Non-governmental organizations (NGOs) have multiplied in a number of states. In Indonesia, according to Anthony Smith, "the burgeoning number of civil society groups . . . have been a notable feature of recent change. Independent unions have become more active in the workplace. A myriad of human rights groups has been established." Islamic organizations remain the largest NGOs including the 34 million strong Nahdatur Lama (NL) and the 28 million strong Muhammaduyah. In Malaysia, NGOs are constrained. One summary assessment suggests that "most NGOs . . . were effectively one-man outfits, reliant on external funding and small, mostly non-Malay memberships" (Abbott, 2001: 292) For its part, the Philippines has an extremely active civil society with some 27,000 individual groups identified in a 1996 survey. However, a substantial number are government initiated, particularly as a consequence of the 1991 Countryside Development Program. This was established by Congress to allow members to channel funds to local organizations. Finally, in the case of Thailand, Funston (2003: 358) notes that "the growth of civil society has been one of the most profound changes in Thai politics over the past three decades, disproving several learned works claiming public apathy and unwillingness to resist authority."

The dynamics of top-down democratic development in the countries of East and South East Asia may involve a long gestation in which social movements, not political parties, will prove to be critical agents.

B. Executive–Legislative Relations

Executive–legislative relations depend in the first instance on the nature of the regime. As noted already, three regime patterns are evident in these seven countries: presidential, semipresidential, and parliamentary. Except Malaysia and Singapore, the symptoms of tension are ubiquitous.

1. Semipresidential Systems

The semipresidential systems of Korea and Taiwan present the greatest opportunity for unstable interaction. This arises from the popular legitimization, which the presidency and the legislature derive independently. In both cases, these tensions are exacerbated because the elections for the assembly and the presidency are separated and because there is no runoff system: recent presidents have been elected by less than a plurality.

In the case of Korea, the president cannot dissolve the legislature. It has extensive formal powers of scrutiny and oversight. Against this, however, are the reserve and patronage powers of the presidency. In a review of developments, Park (1997; 2000) notes that Confucian traditions promote formalism over accommodation. These factors were all displayed in Kim Dae Jung's presidency and in that of his successor, Roh Moon-hyun. Reflecting popular disappointment with Kim Dae Jung, the opposition Grand National Party was four seats short of a majority in the 2000 assembly election. The president's party used procedures ruthlessly to force through its program. This provoked opposition counter-tactics: it occupied the rostrum, prohibited the speaker from calling or presiding over plenary sessions, blockaded the Assembly Hall and the surrounding corridors, and engaged in walkouts, and so on (Park, 2001).

Kim's successor, Roh, also inherited a hostile legislature, which ultimately ended in impeaching him. This maneuver, however, ultimately rebounded on his opponents. In the assembly elections of 2004, Roh's URI party won a majority of seats in a vote that also marked a first significant breach of regional voting patterns. Meantime, gestures toward a cross-party procedural consensus have been conspicuously absent.

In general, in Korea, the president has won out, but by strong-arm tactics. In the longer term, while confrontation will always be an option, day-to-day governance would seem to require the development of constructive relationships. The informal norms that might facilitate this outcome are not in prospect in South Korea. The executive's approach owes more to the authoritarian past than to a democratic future.

In Taiwan, the powers of the legislature were amended in 1999. The Legislative Yuan surrendered the right to affirm the prime minister but gained the power to pass no confidence motions in the latter and also to impeach the president. According to Gold (2000), it has become the focus of local factions, many with criminal connections, with around 60% of members owing primary allegiance to these groups. Legislative turnover is also high, inhibiting the development of stable procedures. In the 2001 election, 47% of the members were new. Conflicts between the legislature and the executive multiplied after the election of Chen Shui Ban in 2000. While the DPP won the presidency in a three-cornered race, the KMT maintained control of the legislature. A number of bruising tests of strength were ensued. Chen tried accommodation with his initial appointment of a prime minister sympathetic to the KMT. However, Tang Fei resigned after only 9 months in office. Subsequently, legislative posturing included moves to impeach the president and later to withhold approval from prime ministerial appointments. Meantime, conflict developed within the KMT about cross-straight relations. Former President Lee Teng-Hui was expelled in 2001 and founded a new party, the Taiwan Solidarity union, which contested the 2001 Legislative Yuan election. This election also left the executive in a minority in the legislature. Tensions have been exacerbated by the 2004 presidential election, which Chen Shui-Ban won by only a narrow margin after an assassination attempt, the authenticity of which was contested by the opposition KMT. As with Korea, the informal norms that might mediate relationships between these arms of government have yet to develop. According to Huang (2002: 18): "The problem of the Legislative Yuan is not lack of financial resources, equipment, staff or organisation ... (the key need is rather) to make the Legislative Yuan more accountable, responsive, representative and less corrupt."

2. Parliamentary States

The dynamics of executive–legislative relations are quite different in the parliamentary states where the prime minister and most ministers are drawn from the legislature. The dynamics are also influenced by other structural factors including the party system (multiparty or two party) and the formal powers of an upper house, if such exists. Of the three parliamentary countries, Malaysia, Singapore, and Thailand, the Thailand presents the most interesting example. The constitutional reforms of 1997 sought to enhance democratic consolidation. They included significant change in the composition and standing of the Senate (the upper house) and in the conduct of elections. A number of independent agencies were also established to uphold procedural integrity. These included a new Constitutional Court and independent Election and Anticorruption Commissions. According to Klein (2003: 48): "From the perspective of liberal reformers... the Constitutional Court has been conservative and disinclined to promote the protection of the rights of citizens over the powers of the state." Of four new justices appointed to the 15-member bench in 2003, three were closely associated with the prime minister.

Meantime, the Senate election in March 2000 was the first for this House. Senators were to be independent, free of party ties, and thus removed from the compromises and corruption associated with their lower house colleagues. The Thai Senate, while not realizing all expectations, has introduced a new element into the governance process. There are however signs of a pro-government majority emerging.

In Malaysia, the 193-member lower house is dominated by the BN coalition. Legislation usually awards ministers wide delegated powers and much of the state budget flows through the large state enterprises such as the oil company Petronas, whose accounts do not figure in the formal budget. There are few committees and minimal staff. The 69-member upper house is appointed by the states. It lacks the standing or the will to oppose government measures.

Singapore's parliament is unicameral. There have been moves to extend its representative role (e.g., through the appointment of "representative" MPs and the wider use of committee enquiries). However, these remain wholly peripheral to the basic structure of state power.

3. Presidential Regimes

There is one fully presidential regime, the Philippines and the ambiguous case of Indonesia. The Philippines congress enjoys substantial powers, including impeachment, which it exercised against former President Estrada in 2000. The bicameral legislature includes a Senate of 24 members (6-yr terms) and House of representatives of 250 members. Like the president, each senator is appointed on a national vote. Both chambers maintain extensive committee systems, which enhance their influence in the legislative and executive process. The congress has thwarted important elements of President Arroyo's program. The relatively stable patterns of executive–legislative relations that have evolved in the Philippines sustain the generally clientelist character of the regime. A reforming president faces the formidable obstacle of constructing legislative majorities.

Finally, in the case of Indonesia, parliament's role and procedures remain to be resolved. Majorities have been formed from ad hoc coalitions among the x-parties which compose it. It is divided into a number of commissions, which scrutinize executive activity. For example, Commission 9 is a 57-member grouping, which exercises oversight of the IBRA. The Commission's chair has played a significant role in policy decisions. He has orchestrated several blockages of proposed sales (*Far East Economic*

Review, August 2, 2001). Indonesia presents the most ambiguous example of unresolved executive–legislative relations. However, unique among the presidential states in Asia, a runoff system has been adopted for election of the president, which will ensure that the ultimate winner enjoys national legitimacy.

In summary, legislative–executive relations introduce a new arena to governance in five of the seven countries. In all these states, relations are either unsettled (Taiwan, Korea, and Thailand) or associated with dysfunctional governance patterns (Philippines and Indonesia). Elsewhere, Huntington has identified metrics (adaptability, complexity, autonomy, and coherence) by which legislative consolidation could be assessed (Park, 1997). The development of procedural norms is insufficiently advanced for even a rudimentary application of these measures.

IV. Democratization and Development

The economic and political developments of these seven countries must, in comparative terms, be accounted an extraordinary success. Their development has been guided by more or less "strong" states which have recently acquired democratic foundations. Elsewhere, White (1998) has outlined the patterning of what he terms a democratic developmental state. This ideal remains far from realization. The experience of the countries reviewed here rather illustrates the varied political and economic architectures by which development and democracy can be accomplished. It illustrates on-going issues associated with economic adaptation and democratic consolidation. It also illustrates the lack of any necessary linkage between these processes. The triggers for democratic transitions involved the conjunction of action on three distinct political planes, involving domestic political elites, civil society, and the international political economy. If economic development figured at all, it was solely as an indirect and background circumstance. Indeed, Singapore's persistence as a one-party state, despite the advanced economic development, demonstrates the contingent and indirect nature of the association.

In the case of economic development, two broad patterns are exemplified in the experience of these seven countries, namely a "bootstrap" approach and one that primarily depends on FDI. As we have seen, the former is demanding at both political and institutional levels. This capacity has also been attributed to background factors, such as culture (a Confucian inheritance), to colonial experience (both Taiwan and Korea were Japanese colonies), to external influences (their importance as frontline cold war states, or in the case of Singapore, to its location between Islamic states), or to institutions (the developmental state analysts). Whatever the causes, a bootstrap approach is clearly a viable but demanding pattern of economic governance, which is far from the orthodoxy championed by the international development agencies.

The FDI-driven pattern is a second-best approach, but one that asks much less initially of state capacity. It also illustrates the imperatives associated with cost-based competitiveness as a long-term developmental strategy. To avoid foot-loose investors, the development of local capabilities that tie international investors to the host economy becomes a requirement. Thus, the pressure to enhance state capacity is also strong in these countries. Where strong or medium state capacity has hitherto been present, this has been based on an elite consensus about the priority to be accorded economic growth. Indeed political (elite) division is arguably the root cause of weak state capacity in the Philippines and Indonesia. Partisan conflict or social movement contention has yet to pose a challenge to the elite consensus in the former countries. Democratic consolidation could, indeed should, create this outcome.

Of course, beyond these "national" considerations, it might be argued that regional location must be accounted an advantage and this has certainly been a major factor in the case of the takeoff of all the second-tier countries. Yet, others similarly located countries (e.g., Vietnam) have not experienced the same developmental surge. Meantime, in the case of the developmental states, Japanese success undoubtedly provided an initial example and inspiration, but their own acts of political will were decisive.

Turning to the lessons for democratic development, this is of course only a small sample of countries. They have variously adopted: presidential, semi-presidential, and parliamentary regimes. From the perspective of governance capacity, no regime type is unambiguously superior, although the familiar problem of presidential regimes in creating rival power centers is clearly evident. In a pioneering analysis, Macintyre (2003) has compared regimes not in terms of constitutional structure but in terms of veto points. This fruitful approach merits more extensive application. Similarly, Reilly (2003) has concluded that voting systems offer considerable scope for "constitutional engineering" to reconcile stability and political competition.

Western templates of democratic development are not applicable to these countries. The top-down nature of their transitions is wholly different from the bottom-up development that characterized the west. Equally, the Latin-American experience of many failed states or predatory regimes reflects another trajectory (Whitehead, 2002; Philip, 2004). Democracy in these seven Asian countries is in its infancy. Because it concerns the constitution of identity and purpose, this is ultimately a more significant development than their (prior) economic advance. The gravest immediate danger is that elite domination will staunch democratic socialization. Democratic forms could either be a veneer, beneath which monopolies of power and privilege are renewed, or a frame for the progressive assimilation of older norms and practices into "new modes and orders." The future patterning of political parties and social movements will be critical.

Notes

1. For example, participation in tertiary education in the relevant age cohort in South Korea increased from 9% in 1970 to 69% in 1997. In Singapore, the equivalent result was from 5 to 42%; in Thailand, it was from 2 to 21%; in the Philippines, it was from 18 to 30% (*The Economist*, November 10, 2001, p. 11). Despite the large differences in income per capita between individual countries, relative income equality ("shared growth") has been another feature of the economic development of regional states (Campos and Root, 1996). Income dispersion in these Asian countries is much less than that in Latin America and other developing regions (Kohli et al., 2003: 131).

2. U.S. Commerce Department data suggest value added by wages and salaries in disk drives equals 24%, in computers equals 11%, and in life sciences equals 7%. This compares with returns to wages and salaries of 67% in "old economy" industries such as precision engineering and specialty chemicals (West, 2001: 37).

References

Abbott, J., Vanquishing Banquo's ghost: the Anwar affair and its impact on Malaysian politics, *Asian Stud. Rev.*, 25 (3), 285–308, 2001.

Blondel, J., Political parties in East and Southeast Asia, in *Democracy, Governance and Regionalism in East and Southeast Asia*, Marsh, I., Ed., Routledge, London, 2005.

Boldeman, L., *Support for ICT Industry Development by the Taiwanese Government*, Department of Communications, Canberra, 2003.

Campos, E. and Root, H., *The Key to the Asian Miracle: Making Shared Growth Credible*, The Brookings Institution, Washington, DC, 1996.

Chilcote, R., Development, in *Encyclopedia of Government and Politics*, Hawkesworth, M., Ed., 2nd ed., Routledge, London, 2004.

Chu, W.-H., Diamond, L., and Shin, D., How people view democracy, *J. Democracy*, 12 (1), 122–136, 2001.

Clifford, M., *Troubled Tiger: Businessmen, Bureaucrats and Generals in South Korea*, M.E. Sharpe, New York, 1997.

Cook, M., Advancing State Projects: Malaysian and Philippine Banking Policy and Recent Financial Crises, Paper Prepared for the Australasian Political Studies Association Annual Conference, Brisbane, August, 2001.

Cumings, B., The Asian crisis, democracy and the end of 'late' development, in *The Politics of the Asian Economic Crisis*, Pempel, T.J., Ed., Cornell University Press, Ithaca, 1999, pp. 17–44.

Diamond, L., *Developing Democracy: Towards Consolidation*, Johns Hopkins University Press, Baltimore, 1999.

Dodgson, M., Policies for science, technology and innovation in Asian newly industrialized economies, in *Technology, Learning and Innovation: Experiences of Newly Industrialised Economies*, Kim, L. and Nelson, R., Eds., Cambridge University Press, New York, 2000, pp. 229–268.

Doner, R. and Ramsay, A., Rent-seeking and economic development in Thailand, in *Rents, Rent-Seeking and Economic Development: Theory and Evidence in Asia*, Khan, M. and Jomo, K.S., Eds., Cambridge University Press, Cambridge, 2000, pp. 145–181.

Doner, R. and Ramsay, A., The challenges of economic upgrading in liberalising Thailand, in *States in the Global Economy: Bringing Domestic Institutions Back in*, Weiss, Ed., Cambridge University Press, Cambridge, 2003, pp. 121–142.

Evans, P., *Embedded Autonomy, States and Industrial Transformation*, Princeton University Press, Englewood Cliffs, NJ, 1995.

Fligstein, N. and Merand, F., Globalization or Europeanisation? Evidence on the European Economy Since 1980, in Paper Prepared for the Conference "Shareholder Value Capitalism and Globalisation," Hamburg, Germany, May 10–12, 2001.

Funston, J., Ed., *Government and Politics in Southeast Asia*, Institute of South East Asian Studies, Singapore, 2003.

Gold, T., The waning of the Kuomintang State in Taiwan, in *State Capacity in East Asia*, Brodsgaard, K.E. and Young, S., Eds., Oxford University Press, chap. 5, 2000.

Grugel, J., Democratization, in *Encyclopedia of Government and Politics*, Hawkesworth, M., Ed., 2nd ed., Routledge, London, 2004, pp. 1115–1132.

Hamilton-Hart, N., *Asian States, Asian Bankers*, Cornell University Press, Ithaca, 2002.

Hsiao, M., Environmental movements in Taiwan, in *Asia's Environmental Movements*, Lee, Y.-S. and So, A., Eds., M.E. Sharpe, New York, chap. 2, 1999.

Hsiao, M., Coexistence and synthesis: cultural globalisation and localisation in contemporary Taiwan, in *Many Globalisations: Cultural Diversity in the Contemporary World*, Berger, P. and Huntington, S., Eds., Oxford University Press, New York, 2002, pp. 48–68.

Huang, S.-D., The new parameters of legislative politics, in Paper Prepared for the International Workshop on Challenges to Taiwan's Democracy, Taipei, June, 2002.

Hutchcroft, P., Neither dynamo nor domino: reforms and crisis in the Philippine political economy, in *The Politics of the Asian Economic Crisis*, Pempel, T.J., Ed., Cornell University Press, Ithaca, 1999, pp. 163–183.

Johnson, C., *MITI and the Japanese Miracle*, Stanford University Press, Stanford, 1982.

Jomo, K.S. and Gomez, E.T., The Malaysian development dilemma, in *Rents, Rent-seeking and Economic Development: Theory and Evidence in Asia*, Khan, M. and Jomo, K.S., Eds., Cambridge University Press, Cambridge, 2000, pp. 274–303.

Jomo, K.S. and Felker, G., *Technology, Competitiveness and the State, Malaysia's Technology Policies*, Routledge, London, 1999.

Jones, D.M., Democratization, civil society and illiberal middle class culture in Pacific Asia, *Comp. Politics*, 30 (2), 147–169, 1998.

Kaplan, E. and Rodrik, D., Did Malaysia's capital controls work? in Paper Prepared for NBER Conference on Currency Crises, NBER, Cambridge, MA, 2001.

Katz, R. and Kolodny, R., The United States, in *How Parties Organise: Change and Adaptation in Party Organisations in Western Democracies*, Katz, R. and Mair, P., Eds., Sage, London, 1994, pp. 23–51.

Katzenstein, P., Ed., *Asian Regionalism*, Cornell University Press, Ithaca, 2000.

Keller, W. and Samuels, R., *Crisis and Innovation in Asian Technology*, Cambridge University Press, Cambridge, 2003.

Kim, S., Ed., *Korea's Democratization*, Cambridge University Press, New York, 2003.

Klein, J., The Battle for the Rule of Law in Thailand: The Constitutional Court of Thailand, [http://www.cdi.anu.edu.au/thailand/thailand_downloads/ThaiUpdate_Klien_ConCourt%20Apr03.pdf].

Kohli, A., Moon, C.I., and Sorenson, G., *States, Markets and Just Growth*, United Nations University Press, Tokyo, 2003.

Lingle, C., *The Rise and Decline of the Asian Century*, Asia 2000 Limited, Hong Kong, 1998.

Macintyre, A., Funny money: fiscal policy, rent-seeking and economic performance in Indonesia, in *Rents, Rent-seeking and Economic Development: Theory and Evidence in Asia*, Khan, M. and Jomo, K.S., Eds., Cambridge University Press, Cambridge, 2000, pp. 248–273.

Macintyre, A., *The Power of Institutions, Political Architecture and Governance*, Cornell University Press, Ithaca, 2003.

Martin Jones, D., *Political Development in Pacific Asia*, Polity Press, Malden, Mass, 1997.

Matthews, J. and Cho, D.-S., *Tiger Technology: The Creation of a Semiconductor Industry in East Asia*, Cambridge University Press, Melbourne, 2000.

Moon, C.-I. and Sunghack, L., Weaving through Paradoxes: Democratisation, Globalisation and Environmental Politics in South Korea, in Paper Prepared for Eighteenth World Congress of the International Political Science Association, Quebec, Canada, 2000.

Painter, M., *Building Institutional Capacity in Asia: Public Sector Challenges and Government Reforms in South East Asia*, Project Commissioned by the Ministry of Finance, Japan, Research Institute of Asia and the Pacific, University of Sydney, 2001.

Painter M. and Pierre, J., Eds., *Challenges to State Policy Capacity*, Palgrave/Macmillan, London, 2005.

Park, C., The National Assembly in the consolidation process of Korean democracy, *Asian J. Political Sci.*, 5 (2), 96–113, 1997.

Park, C., Legislative–executive relations and legislative reform, in *Institutional Reform and Democratic Consolidation in Korea*, Diamond, L. and Shin, D., Eds., Hoover Institution Press, Stanford, 2000, pp. 73–95.

Park, C., The National Assembly of Korea, in *Parliaments in Asia*, Norton, P., Ed., Frank Cass, London, 2001, pp. 66–82.

Philip, G., Latin America, in *Encyclopedia of Government and Politics*, Hawkesworth, M., Ed., 2nd ed., Routledge, London, 2004, pp. 1209–1222.

Polanyi, M., *The Great Transformation*, The Free Press, Boston, 1949.

Porter, M., *UK Competitiveness: Moving to the Next Stage*, Department of Trade and Industry, London, 2003.

Redding, L.G., Alternative systems of capitalism, in *Emerging Market Democracies, East Asia and Latin America*, Whitehead, L., Ed., Johns Hopkins University Press, Baltimore, 2002, pp. 130–151.

Reilly, B., Political engineering for parties and party systems, paper prepared for the 2003 Annual Meeting of the American Political Science Association, 2003.

Rose, R. and Shin, D., Democratisation backwards: the problem of third wave democracies, *Br. J. Political Sci.*, 31, 331–354, 2001.

Rowley, C. and Benson, J., Eds., *Globalisation and Labour in the Asia-Pacific Region*, Frank Cass, London, 2000.

Schwarz, A. and Villinger, R., Integrating Southeast Asian economies, *McKinsey Quart.*, 1, 1–8, 2004.

Shin, D., Mass politics, public opinion and democracy in Korea, in *Korea's Democratization*, Kim, S., Ed., Cambridge University Press, New York, 2003, pp. 47–77.

Sinnott, R., Political culture and democratic consolidation in East and South East Asia, in *Democracy, Governance and Regionalism in East and Southeast Asia*, Marsh, I. Ed., Routledge, London, 2005.

Smith, K., The knowledge economy, in *Innovating Australia*, Marsh, I., Ed., Growth No. 53, Committee for the Economic Development of Australia, Melbourne, 2004.

Sturgeon, T. and Lester, R., The new global supply base: new challenges for local suppliers in East Asia, in Paper Prepared for World Bank Project on East Asian Futures, Industrial Performance Centre, Massachusetts Institute of Technology, 2003.

Tarrow, S., *Power in Movement, Social Movements and Contentious Politics*, Cambridge University Press, Cambridge, 1998.

Wade, R., *Governing the Market: The Role of the State in East Asian Industrialization*, Princeton University Press, Englewood Cliffs, NJ, 1990.

Weiss, L., *The Myth of the Powerless State: Governing the Economy in a Global Era*, Polity Press, Cambridge, 1998.

Weiss, L., Ed., *States in the Global Economy*, Cambridge University Press, Cambridge, 2003.

Weiss, L. and Hobson, J., *States and Economic Development in Comparative and Historical Perspective*, Polity Press, Cambridge, 1995.

West, J., The mystery of innovation: aligning the triangle of technology, institutions and organisations, in *Australia's Choices, Economic Strategies for a Prosperous and Fair Society*, Marsh, I., Ed., Australian Journal of Management, Special Issue, 2001, pp. 21–44.

West, J., Financing innovation: markets and the structure of risk, in *Innovating Australia*, Marsh, I., Ed., Growth No. 53, Committee for the Economic Development of Australia, Melbourne, 2004, pp. 12–35.

White, G., Constructing a democratic developmental state, in *The Democratic Developmental State*, Robinson, M. and White, G., Eds., Oxford University Press, Oxford, 1998, pp. 17–52.

Whitehead, L., Ed., *Emerging Market Democracies, East Asia and Latin America*, Johns Hopkins University Press, Baltimore, 2002.

Whitley, R., *Divergent Capitalisms: The Social Structuring and Change of Business Systems*, Oxford University Press, Oxford, 1999.

Woo-Cumings, M., Ed., *The Developmental State*, Cornell University Press, Ithaca, 1999.

Chapter 7

Laying a Propelling Foundation for Democratic Governance and International Development: The Role of Human Factor Engineering

Senyo Adjibolosoo

CONTENTS

I. Introduction

People of developing countries, global leaders, and representatives of the developed countries (DCs) and international development organizations, who are keen on improving the quality of the physical environment and the standard of living of people living in the least developed countries (LDCs), may have grandiose dreams that will never be realized in the long term. This opinion is based on the belief that these people are currently implementing their development programs and relief work as they did in the past. This repetition of personal attitudes, behaviors, and actions mostly leads to similar results (Adjibolosoo, 2004). In the case of international development programming and relief work, these results are nothing but miserable, painful failures, unleashing affliction and suffering of immeasurable proportions on the poor people in the LDCs.

From this perspective, therefore, if any of these individuals or groups of people are convinced that improving the quality of the physical environment and life can be achieved through rigorous and formal academic activities and other forms of development assistance — food aid, technical assistance, the supply of cheap generic pharmaceutical drugs, financial aid, the donation of used items, and so on — all aimed at improving the performance effectiveness of plans, policies, programs, projects (i.e., the 4Ps portfolio), systems, techniques, and processes, they will be setting themselves up for long-term disappointments and ultimate failures. These failures will in turn complicate the lives of the poor people who seem to have been permanently destined to a devastating plight of hunger, malnutrition, disease, and starvation.

Real-life data have shown that most international development programs and relief work in the LDCs, apart from their successes in providing temporary relief to the poor in the short term, have not necessarily improved the fetid conditions of people's physical environment and quality of life. In addition, until those involved in international development programs and relief work find better and more effective ways through which they can successfully transform the quality of life of the poor, their good intentions and humanitarian acts of global benevolence will always rob the disadvantaged and poor people of their right to survival and the ability to acquire the basic necessities of life. Therefore, to avoid these failures in the future, it is important that those involved in these programs search for, and discover, what they are doing wrong, change course, and refocus their philanthropic and humanitarian activities on laying a solid and propelling foundation on which the art of good governance and a veritable development process can thrive in the short term and then become fruitful in improving the quality of life of the poor people in the long term.

Attempts to improve the quality of the physical environment in which people dwell in the LDCs and their livelihood are not necessarily new. For many decades, experts from various fields, such as natural and social sciences, all over the world have tried to improve the standard of living and the quality of life in the poor countries. (prominent among these attempts are the efforts of leaders of the IMF, World Bank, United Nations, United Nations Development Program, USAID, Canadian International Development Agency, and OECD.) The primary reason for embarking on international development programs and relief work is to improve people's welfare and quality of life (Adjibolosoo, 2004).

The main objective of this chapter is to present and discuss the primary reasons for the failure of international development programs and relief works in detail. The critical human qualities that are necessary and sufficient to successfully improve the quality of the physical environment and life in the LDCs are then discussed. This chapter also highlights and discusses relevant ideas such as how international development agents can improve the physical environment, quality of life, democratic governance, and the results of international development programs and relief efforts.

To achieve these objectives, this chapter argues that the quality of the human factor (HF) of citizens, development programmers, relief workers, national and international leaders continuously exerts tremendous impact on the development process — be it positive or negative. From this, the primary idea of this chapter is: any program aimed at improving the quality of the physical environment and standard of living of the poor people in the LDCs through efforts of good governance and human-centered development must begin with massive and intensive HF engineering programs aimed at the development of the positive HF. The HF is:

> Spectrum of personality characteristics and other dimensions of
> human performance that enable social, economic, and political

> institutions to function and remain functional, over time. Such
> dimensions sustain the workings and application of the rule of
> law, political harmony, a disciplined labor force, just legal
> systems, respect for human dignity and the sanctity of life,
> social welfare, and so on. As is often the case, no social, econ-
> omic or political institutions can function effectively without
> being upheld by a network of committed persons who stand
> firmly by them. Such persons must strongly believe in and conti-
> nually affirm the ideals of society (Adjibolosoo, 1995: 33).

It will be difficult, if not impossible, to permanently improve the poor conditions of the physical environment, governance practices, human performance effectiveness, labor productivity, the standard of living, continuing
economic growth, human-centered development, and the quality of life of
the inhabitants of the LDCs until HF engineering programs are successfully
initiated and propelled to accomplish the goal of assisting people on the
receiving end of international humanitarian assistance. As successful economic reform programs in the LDCs require the development of the positive
HF, it is important that everyone interested in international development
and relief work understands that without the positive HF, no reform attempts
will work as effectively as proposed. We will discuss this issue later in detail.

The remainder of the chapter presents discussions and analyses of the
primary idea in detail. Section II presents the current state of the physical,
social, economic, and political environment within which the international
development program of activities and relief work take place in the LDCs. A
detailed evaluation of the quality of the environment of governance and
international development in the LDCs is also presented in this section.
The significance of the HF in terms of how to achieve and sustain good
governance, successful international development programming, and
productive relief work through effective HF engineering programs aimed
at improving the quality of the HF is discussed in Section III. The conclusions and recommendations for public policy are presented in Section IV.

II. Governance and Development: The Environment

Although democracy is not a term that is easily defined, many scholars have
agreed and believed that it is a vital prerequisite for international development. To examine this, it is important to highlight some views about what
democracy is and its acclaimed impact on international development.
Lipset (1960), writing about the meaning of democracy, observes that it is
"a political system which supplies regular constitutional opportunities for
changing the governing officials, and a social mechanism which permits
the largest possible part of the population to influence major decisions by

choosing among contenders for political office." Similarly, in the views of Held (1993: 220), "democracy refers to a form of government in which, in contradistinction to monarchies and aristocracies, the people rule. It entails a state in which there is some form of political equality among the people." To Jackson (2000: 342):

> In a workable democracy, the rulers are installed by the people who are the final source of authority in the state: this is popular sovereignty. Because it rests on the sanctity and inviolability of national populations, a world of democracies would be a world of general non-intervention and non-aggression. If democracy became an international norm as well as a domestic norm, that would raise even higher the barrier to external intervention *in democracies.* That is a basic premise of the democratic peace thesis (the emphasis is in the original; see also Doyle, 1983).

Many works have proved the critical role of democracy in the development of nations. Research works and heated debates that took place on this issue seem to have led to the conclusion that democracy causes ongoing economic growth and human-centered development: Rodrik, 2000; Scully, 1992; Slavenkov and Pisheva, 1990; and Grindle, 2000. We are not going to discuss this in detail (for details, refer Lipset, 1959; Prothro and Grigg, 1960; Dahl, 1961, 1971; McClosky, 1964; McCrone and Cnudde, 1967; Neubauer, 1967; Scully, 1992; Healy and Robinson, 1992; Przeworski and Limongi, 1993; Helliwell, 1994).

A. Democratic Governance and Development

A *good democratic governance* is defined as a cultural practice or process through which the supreme power to exercise authority on behalf of the people is entrenched or vested in the people and yet invoked and applied directly by their elected representatives in a free electoral system. The leaders who are entrusted with the authority and power are expected to govern with integrity, responsibility, and accountability as they engage in day-to-day activities of governance. These activities are aimed at bringing about a harmonious and peaceful community of people who pursue tranquility, justice, fairness, and equity as their primary goals. Each community member hopes that his or her quality of life will improve in the long term. Everyone involved in the process of democratic governance is expected to not only rule by the right of authority, but also act to influence others according to the dictates of the principles of the rule of law.

The citizens reserve the right to fully participate in the operation of the government, after having ceded power and authority to their elected representatives. They also expect and hope that they too will enjoy unlimited natural liberties. Similarly, they expect that there will not only be equality in its many forms — social, economic, political, and others — but also the opportunity and freedom to enjoy the fruits of their labor, and gain unhindered access to the administrative efforts and services of their representatives. Above all, they must always have the liberty to enjoy the freedoms and rights they are entitled to — religious, press, speech, information, and others. The human rights of each citizen and noncitizens must be upheld, protected, respected, and promoted regardless of which particular ideologues and political administrators are placed in charge of the administration of the day. The achievement of any of these desirable ends depends greatly on working with the right people — those who possess the positive HF.

As such, the process of democratization has little to do with the development process (Adjibolosoo, 1998). From this perspective, Das Gupta's (1990: 243) view that "political democratization, in order to endure, requires a rapid development of economic and social resources so that expanding public demands can be effectively satisfied" is seriously flawed and misleading. Other scholars who also have made misleading observations that have, however, become foundation pillars on which orthodox development plans and policies are based include but not limited to Goodwin and Nacht (1995: 1, 2, and 5), Boron (1995: 109 and 120), Dahrendorf (1990: 93), Slavenkov et al. (1990: 11–12), Pishev (1995: 180), Georgieva (1995: 281), Ray (1995: 8), Al-Suwaidi (1995: 90), Ostrom et al. (1993: 104 and 111), Scott (1995: 6 and 37), Huntington (1968: 27), Shivji (1976: 27–28), Picard (1994: 8), Snooks (1999: 60), and Shaw (1993: 145). A recent document with many such misleading views regarding development plans, policies, programs, and projects is the *Human Development Report 2003* (UNDP, 2003: 2, 4–6, 11).

From the HF perspective, the progress and advancement of the process of political democratization thrives on the shoulders of people who possess the positive HF (Adjibolosoo, 1998: 27–28). In addition, as long as the positive HF exists, social and economic progress will ensue as a natural by-product. However, when the positive HF is missing no amount of human energy and effort can bring about any forms of good governance and human-centered development in the long term. Therefore, it is the quality of the HF that determines the character of the environment and climate of democratic governance and development.

B. Environment and Climate of Democratic Governance and Development

By environment and climate of governance and development, we are referring to the aggregate of social, economic, political, cultural, intellectual, attitudinal, and behavioral conditions that originate from human beings that influence the personality, life, and performance effectiveness of everyone in and outside the locality of people who are at the receiving end of international development activities and relief work (i.e., the conditions people are surrounded with). Therefore, the character of the environment of governance and international development is determined by the climatic conditions the quality of the HF creates. The climate of the environment of governance and international development is, therefore, the aggregate of the prevailing set of human-induced conditions that influence the art of governance and the process of sustained economic growth and human-centered development. The quality of the environment of governance and development is reflected in the nature of its climate. The climatic factors of the environment of governance and development act upon citizens, leaders, and their external helpers and in so doing ultimately determine their level of successes or failures as they formulate policies, design plans, and implement them over time. Above all, the sole determinant of the nature of the environment of governance and development and the ambience of its corresponding climate is the quality of people's HF.

As the quality of the environment of governance and development affects the performance effectiveness of everyone involved in the art of governance, the process of development, and the performance of relief workers among the poor in the LDCs, it is more desirable to place those involved in an environment that is conducive to their success. However, to gain a deeper understanding of the quality of the existing environment of governance and international development in the LDCs, it is imperative to ask the local people to not only speak their minds about the pertinent problems, but also relate their experiences with the existing environment, its climate, and what they believe to be the primary factor that has created and perpetuated it.

Real-life experiences and data prove that the nature of the climate of governance and international development exerts a significant impact on the environment. Therefore, the nature of the environment of governance can be classified as being either (a) positive or (b) negative. Similarly, the character of the climate of governance and international development can be viewed as being either (1) propelling good governance and a virtuous cycle of development (i.e., fertile, conducive, growth producing, and progress sustaining) or (2) inhibiting good governance and continuing growth and development (i.e., bad and destructive).

Results from many years of formal and informal discussions with local people and personal letters, notes, and anecdotes received over the last two decades reveal local people's perception of what constitutes (i) a positive environment of governance and international development and (ii) an environment that inhibits. Deeper insights of these sources suggest that the nature of the environment — be it either positive or negative — is

HF-determined. As is clearly obvious from field information and communications with the inhabitants of the LDCs, these people spell out precisely what they view as constituting either a positive or a negative environment of governance and international development. The people's characterization of the various kinds of environment they find themselves in tells us about what they view as being either (a) an excellent or (b) a poor climate of governance and international development.

The local people who provided responses to the question "How does one characterize the currently existing climate of governance and international development in your country?" outline the primary characteristics in terms of what they either liked or disliked about the attitudes, behaviors, and actions of their leaders and personnel of international development organizations. From this, the characterization of the positive and negative environment and climate of governance and international development is presented in Section II.C (i.e., positive environment) and Section II.D (i.e., negative environment).

C. Characteristics of the Positive Climate of Governance and Development

A careful study and detailed analysis of information collected from field discussions and data reveal that according to the local people, the positive (desirable) environment and climate of good governance and a veritable international development process is:

1. *Safe and secure* — ensuring the feelings of being sheltered and protected.
2. *Nurturing* — promoting respect, caring, love, kindness, affirmation, and individual growth.
3. *Encouraging* — a lifestyle of cooperation, collaboration, sensitivity, questioning, patience, affirmation, and interaction.
4. *Inclusive* — engendering approval, belonging, and freedom.
5. *Stimulating* — creating opportunities for people to grow socially, intellectually, spiritually, morally, physically, aesthetically, and so on.
6. *Challenging* — encouraging intensity, tenacity, resilience, critical thinking, information processing, problem-solving, higher levels of imagination, full occupation of the mind, and applications of other learning faculties.

In the minds of the local people, these characteristics are *sine qua non* for the creation and establishment of a propelling climate for the art of good governance and the process of development to thrive.

D. Characteristics of the Negative Climate of Governance and Development

Regarding what constitutes a negative environment and climate of governance and development, local people mentioned various factors that work against the performance effectiveness of everyone who is involved. That is, the local people have together characterized the negative environment and climate of governance and development as being:

1. *Self-seeking* — infested with people who are selfish and corrupt.
2. *Discriminatory* — under the control of individuals who discriminate on the basis of blood, friendship, membership in professional associations, physical characteristics, and ethnicity.
3. *Deceptive* — shallow, fake, gloomy, hopeless, dishonest, and indecent.
4. *Disgraceful* — disrespectful, demeaning, and irreverent.
5. *Unsupportive* — lacking in encouragement, support, approval, affirmation, and nonstimulating.
6. *Barren and infertile* — empty of personal morality and filled with unethical attitudinal and behavioral practices.
7. *Paternal and pathetic* — sadly patronizing, apathetic, and over-possessive.
8. *Ignorant* — exhibiting the lack of education or knowledge. It is filled with misunderstanding, misdiagnoses, backwardness, stupidity, nonenlightening, unconsciousness, unfamiliarity, and primitive.
9. *Restrictive* — devoid of natural liberty and individual freedom.

From this, one of the most critical questions to ask relates to how people must go about to achieve good governance and a veritable development process. In other words, what are the necessary and sufficient conditions under which the pursuit of good governance can lead to the attainment of sustainable development? That is, in what ways can the people of the LDCs achieve and sustain sound and efficient macroeconomic management, effective governance, sound laws for protecting property rights and contracts, transparency in decision-making, successful public administrative reforms (Kmarck, 2000), institutional effectiveness, strong and workable judicial systems, democratic responsibility, accountability, and integrity?

It is impossible to achieve and sustain economic growth and development for the people in the LDCs, until this question is answered correctly. We present in the following section some detailed discussions and analyses of how local people and members of the global community can work together to foster good governance, continuing economic growth, and sustained human-centered development in the LDC.

III. HF: Its Significance and Engineering

The following questions are crucial to fully understand the HF perspective on the quality of the environment of governance and international development:

1. In what kinds of environment will those involved in the process of governance, international development programming, and relief work perform their best to achieve the goals and objectives of the people involved in the action and those who are being assisted to improve their quality of life?
2. What kinds of persons are preferable to engage in the creation and development of the requisite environment in which the art of good governance, a veritable international development programming, and successful relief work can take place?
3. What critical HF qualities must these players have to serve effectively and also perform efficiently in this environment?
4. What type of development education — HF engineering — curriculum would you prefer students, educators, administrators, relief workers, staff members that work at the governance and development offices, and local people have prior to their being invited to participate fully in the governance and development process?

From the HF perspective, until everyone involved in the process of governance and development programming comprehends fully the underlying philosophy, meaning, and implications of each of these questions, few people will be in the vantage position to improve the art and practice of governance and international development in the LDCs.

A. Key Clusters of the Positive HF: Laying a Propelling Foundation

As far as the international development process is concerned, to lay a propelling foundation is to establish a firm and permanent ground-level structure on which further additions can be made by the members of the current and future generations. This foundation is labeled as being propelling when its existence leads people to continuously drive — effectively and efficiently — their development forward — toward the desired goals and objectives. In terms of ongoing preparation for good governance and a fruitful international development process, the only true and powerful propellant of continuing advancement in the areas of social, economic, political, cultural, and technological progress is the positive HF. This is the case because people use their positive HF as the primary propelling agent through which they consciously take charge, tenaciously control, and relentlessly direct their development process toward an agreed upon destination and expected outcome. A person's positive HF does serve as a development oxidizer to guide, propel, and sustain good governance and the process of development along its intended course, just as explosives are used to propel projectiles from guns, for example.

Those who aim at improving the quality of life and the environment in the LDCs must be aware that the intellectual knowledge and skills they possess, though necessary, however, are not sufficient to bring the desired quality of governance and international development. This is the case because knowledge and skills (i.e., human capital) are nothing but a small segment of the HF (see information in Table 7.1). To be better positioned to achieve the intended changes in the environment, its climate, quality of life, and all dimensions of the HF must also be developed and used by the citizens, leaders, and external expert helpers involved (see Table 7.1). From this perspective, the primary propelling factor that is necessary and sufficient for carrying out continuous economic growth, sustaining good governance, and a veritable human-centered development is the positive HF. Those who have their positive HF developed or are working to make it perfect will possess its clusters that are *sine qua non* to good governance and long-term development. This is what they require to effect changes in their welfare, living standards, and quality of life.

With these concepts in mind, the key clusters of the positive HF that the citizens, leaders, and international development experts need to possess themselves and then initiate and foster to sustain and promote good governance and long-term development include:

1. *Integrity*: honesty, truthfulness, discernment, wisdom, accountability, selflessness, credibility, trustworthiness, and responsibility.
2. *Moral sentiment*: emotional intelligence, stability, and maturity, physical health and stamina, positive mental attitude, respect, empathy, desire, love, caring, and grace.
3. *Resilience*: persistence, decisiveness, self-confidence, dependability, tenacity, ability to weather storms, and loyalty.
4. *Courageousness*: valiance, dauntlessness, stoutheartedness, valor, fearlessness, and intrepidity.
5. *Knowledge and skills*: information, data, technical, conceptual, critical, thinking, analytic, and communications (i.e., human capital).

The development of each of these clusters is the primary task of the HF engineer. Thus, after having gained a deeper knowledge of and insight into the various clusters of the positive HF, the next thing to do is to find ways

Table 7.1 The Composition of the HF

HF (Type of Capital)	Description
Spiritual capital	It is the aspect of the human personality that is usually in tune with the universal laws and principles of human life; it equips the individual to see beyond what the five senses are able to grasp and also furnishes him or her with deeper insights into the nonmaterial world.
Moral capital	It represents habits and attitudes of the human heart that are based on universal principles regarding right or wrong; it refers to the qualities individuals possess that lead them to conform or not to conform to universal principles of life; its constituents include integrity, humility, justice, charity, patience, honesty, sensitivity, fairness, etc.
Aesthetic capital	A deep sense of and love for beauty; it includes a strong passion for music, art, drama, dance, and other artistic capacities (imagination and creativity are strong components).
Human capital	The know-how and acquired skills (i.e., technical, conceptual, intellectual, analytic, and communications); human experiences, knowledge, intelligence, physical well-being, emotional health, etc.
Human abilities	These constitute the power or capacity of an individual to competently undertake projects or effectively perform tasks requiring mental and physical effort; they are required for the effective use of human capital; examples include wisdom, vision, commitment, determination, diligence, courage, accountability, judgment, responsibility, competence, motivation, human energy, optimism, endurance, self-control, objectivity, reliability, and so on.
Human potentials	They are the human talents that may or may not be harnessed and employed for human utilization; these may be referred to as the yet undeveloped and unused dimensions of the HF.

Source: Adjibolosoo, S., *The Human Factor in Developing Africa*, Praeger, Westport, CT, pp. 33–38, 1995. With permission. The information in this table is also presented in a chapter entitled: *The Human Factor in Nation Building* (www.iihfd.com or www.iihfd.org).

and means through which people — especially children — which can be assisted to acquire the various elements of each cluster.

The successful development of the clusters of the positive HF will lead to the attainment of a great leap forward in good governance, continuing economic growth, and human-centered development in the long term. This is the case because as is implicitly stated in the definition for the HF presented earlier in this chapter, the positive HF promotes and sustains the workings and applications of the rule of law, political harmony, a disciplined labor force, just legal systems, respect for human dignity, and the sanctity of life, social welfare, and others. We will now see how the task of HF engineering can be successfully carried out.

B. HF Engineering: The Quality of the HF

To successfully realize any of these developmentally desirable goals and objectives, people must first initiate the HF engineering process with the primary objective of either removing or minimizing the impact of the dragon of human factor decay (HFD). In general, HFD·

> Refers to the phenomenon of negative attitudes, behaviors, and actions as evidenced in personal lack of accountability, integrity, honesty, responsibility, and caring. In its severest form, those who suffer from severe HFD engage in attitudes, behaviors, and actions that are contrary to principle-centeredness, moral injunctions, and ethical standards. People who suffer from this syndrome find it too difficult to make their development plans, policies, programs, and projects to function as effectively as expected. This is the case because these people are usually unable to successfully create, administer, and manage the development program. In addition, the people lack the requisite HF to support continuing economic growth and sustained human-centered development. To minimize problems of underdevelopment, people must begin with the appropriate education and training programs aimed at improving the quality of the HF (Adjibolosoo, 2003a: 108–109).

Indeed, good governance, a veritable development process, institutional development, capacity building, and all other items on the international development menu require the positive HF foundation to not only succeed temporarily, but also be sustained into the long term. That is, none of these desirable ideals listed in the ledger of international development will be achieved without having successfully minimized the influence of severe HFD through effective HF engineering activities. It is, therefore, a terrible mistake to ignore the development of the positive HF and yet think and believe that the art of good governance and the process of development can be successfully accomplished without it. This oversight is never developmentally innocuous. Instead, it is a sure recipe for disaster because real-life data and experiences have proven that in the past our 4Ps portfolio neither worked as successfully as proposed nor will they ever achieve any positive results. It is indeed time to transform our minds about what we have all along believed to cause good governance and development. In so doing we will successfully alter our existing course of action if in fact we are sincerely concerned with the plight of the poor and also genuinely interested in assisting them to improve their quality of life and longevity.

Though the elements of each of these clusters of the positive HF may not be easily manufactured in the factory of human wish or desire they will, however, emerge over the long term when people are committed to assisting children to become familiar with their significance through continuing socialization — modeling, nurturing, mentoring, role playing, and so on (Hirsch, 1996; Dill, 1998; Graham, 1998; Bennett et al., 1999; Avery, 2002; Beam, 2002). It is human desire backed with real-life action that will lead to the long-term emergence of each cluster of the positive HF in the environment of good governance and effective development and its associated climate. If the emphasis is on the children and youth, the whole program will take a period of one whole generation to begin to yield its expected fruits of good governance and development. The process requires the desire, willingness, and readiness to develop the positive HF in people — if we are willing and prepared to do so (see Owen, 1770–1857; Hutchins, 1968; Lickona, 1991).

As portrayed in Figure 7.1, the HF engineering process takes into account development education programs that concentrate on gaining the appropriate knowledge (i.e., knowing), reasoning ability (i.e., critical and analytical thinking), conscientizing (i.e., awakening, refurbishing, and enlivening), and learning to express personal emotional feelings (i.e., emotional growth and maturity) in a principle-centered manner (Tom, 1997; Mother Teresa, 1999; Owen, 1817). As shown in the upper portion of Figure 7.1, when the appropriate education programs and training activities are concentrated on principle-centeredness, children will not only be thoroughly bridled to engage in practices of sound reasoning and judgment, but also be able to arrive at reflective and thoughtful conclusions and principle-centered decisions (Dewey, 1897; Hutchins, 1968; Ichilove, 1999; Dworkin, 1959). These are the children who, as specified in Figure 7.1, will not only be productive in any endeavors they engage in, but also use their knowledge, understanding, and wisdom to be efficient, effective, and creatively constructive. Unfortunately, however, children whose education and training programs concentrate on activities and practices that are not principle-centered will give themselves to attitudes, behaviors, and acts of foolishness (see the bottom part of Figure 7.1). If this is the case, the natural outflow of a nonprinciple-centered lifestyle is the nursing of attitudinal and behavioral seeds that will finally bear the fruits of personal destruction, inefficiency, ineffectiveness, and barrenness in productivity

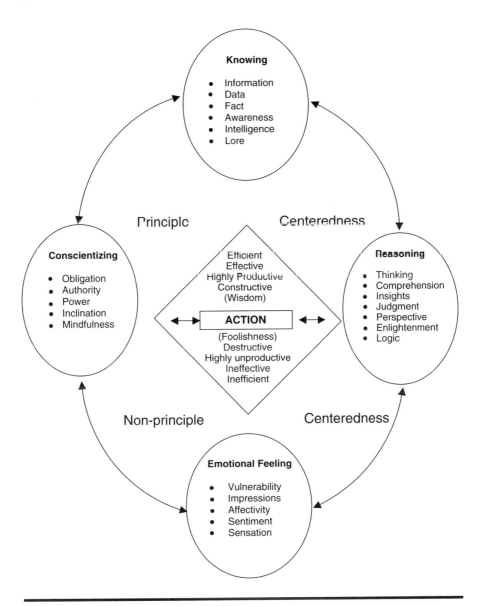

Figure 7.1   Engineering the quality of the HF. (From Adjibolosoo, S., Leadership qualities for improving the school environment: a parents' perspective, Unpublished Discussion Paper, Point Loma Nazarene University, San Diego, California, USA, 2003b. With permission.)

(Brown and Dugan, 2002; Hamburger and Schroeder, 2002; Maremont and Cohen, 2002; Solomon, Sandberg and Pullian, 2002; Hamburger, Hitt and Schroeder, 2002; Markon and Frank, 2002; Maremount and Cohen, 2003).

Another objective of the HF-centered reform program is to produce ethical and moral leaders who will gradually grow and mature in unconditional love, empathy, caring, respect, judgment, awareness, consciousness, trustworthiness, critical thinking, analytical abilities, diligence, logical reasoning, fair-mindedness, justice, responsibility, accountability, commitment, and self-control — just to list a few (Gandhi, 1959; Lincoln, 1970; Lickona, 1991; Mandela, 1997). Though the development of these qualities always poses a tremendous challenge to all humans and will take a generation or two to successfully accomplish the first time around, the applications of the HF-centered model of public school reform will facilitate children's abilities to acquire specific human qualities they need to be good leaders — husbands, wives, parents, teachers, administrators, professionals, laborers, and so on (see the presentation in Figure 7.1). Through *the creation and use of a hospitable academic and social environment*, children must be led to develop the necessary skills, qualities, and competencies with which to learn (i.e., to know), reason (i.e., to comprehend), and deal (i.e., to respond) appropriately with their emotional feelings, and also sharpen their conscience and habits of the human heart. Each of these is a key element in defining the quality and practice of moral character (see the center contents in Figure 7.1). By successfully accomplishing these goals and objectives, children will gradually grow in every dimension of the six aspects of the HF listed in Table 7.1 — spiritual capital, moral capital, aesthetic capital, human capital, human abilities, and the human potential.

Through the creation of an affable environment for good governance, development, and personalized professional guidance counseling, children will develop the ability to apply acquired knowledge (i.e., wisdom). Informed by principle-centeredness, children's attitudes, behaviors, and actions will lead them to pursue and do good works wherever they find themselves (see Figure 7.1). The long-term impact of these results will be the availability of a multitude of good citizens and leaders of integrity who are thoroughly prepared to deal effectively with complex social, economic, and political problems (see the upper middle portion of Figure 7.1). Alternatively, when children are placed in home and school environments that are devoid of practices of principle-centeredness, they will become unproductive in the short term and destructive in the long term. The bad habits they form will propel them toward poor attitudes, judgment, choices, behaviors, and wrong actions (see the lower middle segment of Figure 7.1).

Through *the use of creative projects in a hospitable classroom environment*, every academic subject being taught and learned must be used to develop the positive HF. Children's education must be unequivocally aimed at the effective applications of the various socialization techniques, training programs, mentoring activities, and modeling attempts to assist them to develop the positive HF at all levels of schooling. To be successful in doing so is to strategically place the nation on track toward long-term participation in global leadership. Otherwise, we must prepare ourselves for the abrupt and final demise of the human civilization — just as it was the case with the great civilizations of ancient Babylon, Egypt, Greece, Rome, and others. The final choice is ours and we must not mess it up — for time is truly running out for everyone — the poor and the rich alike.

IV. Conclusion: Recommendations for Public Policy

Though freedom of religion is better than its prohibition, neither of these causes good governance, continuing economic growth, and sustained human-centered development. Religion is only productive when people use its tenets to develop the positive HF rather than to destroy it — and hence perpetuating severe HFD. Truly, technological advancement and computer applications neither cause good governance nor promote economic growth and development in and by themselves. Similarly, capacity building and institutional development will never lead to good governance and development.

In the same way, chasing terrorist with the intent of destroying their network, pursuing dictators and their accomplishes, and marinating sovereign states with technologically smart bombs and then militarily occupying their land with the intent of forging democratic governance will only lead to emptiness in the long term — especially, when the bombs finally become silent and the occupancy is terminated. Truly, when the smoke clears, no long-term positive results would have been achieved for the simple reason that none of the applied solutions did anything to improve the people's quality of the HF. Billions of dollars and precious human lives would have been wasted. The only result to show forth for having applied the intended solution set is the serious devastation that occurred.

These techniques and programs are useless without the availability of the positive HF. In view of these conclusions, it goes without saying that in the presence of severe HFD, the people in the LDCs will never experience any forms of good governance, continuing economic growth, and long-term sustained human-centered development.

As Adjibolosoo (1995) observes, institutions, systems, techniques, procedures, and processes are inanimate. Therefore, from this angle, these things are neither able to operate by themselves nor attain performance optimality (i.e., effectiveness and efficiency) without having been operated and managed by a team of people who possess the positive HF in a high measure. This conclusion reveals that though attempts usually made to improve these things may result in some short-term improvements, these ameliorations are most frequently temporal.

From the HF perspective, therefore, the emphasis being placed on *the development and perfection of things* (i.e., systems, technology, techniques, processes, institutions, laws, regulations, etc.) today is a wrong one. As noted earlier, systems, institutions, technology, the 4Ps portfolio, and many others like these provide only guidance and assistance (see Adjibolosoo, 1999a). They are only *cooperant factors* in that they do not accomplish any goals and objectives by themselves. That is, until people put these to work in an intelligent and rational fashion, they will not achieve any long-term positive results when left on their own. However, by developing the positive HF, people using these things can achieve tremendous results in everything they put their hands to. This is the only true route to take if the people of the LDCs and their external helpers are sincerely interested in and committed to create the fertile and conducive environment and climatic conditions within which the art of governance and the process of development can flourish simultaneously.

Truly, while HF engineering leads to ongoing economic growth and human-centered development and HFD paves the way toward the city of underdevelopment, the absence of the positive HF leads to social decay, economic stagnation, political rot, and religious intolerance in the short term and socioeconomic suicide in the long term. To improve the environment of governance and development, those involved in international development must work with knowledgeable educators with well-developed positive HF to pursue programs and activities that are intentionally aimed at awakening and raising the human consciousness and conscience onto a higher plane where universal principles rule with noncompromising credence, authority, and power. Any successes attained in this exercise will bring positive improvements to the environmental conditions in which everyone can operate on a daily basis to promote good governance, economic growth, and development.

The expected transformation of the environment and climate of governance and development can be achieved through many HF-related programs of which the following are just but a selection of useful examples (see details in Adjibolosoo, 1999b). These are:

1. Learning about the universal principles, living by them, and striving against people's violation of their dictates. Pursuing continuing exhortation or counseling to live lives based on universal principles. People must know and comprehend that going against the authority of these principles will only lead them into a deep and darkened hole of misery and ultimate destruction.

2. Mentoring people who are struggling to live by principles, guiding, and directing them to the correct and narrow path of human life is critical. Living a life of continuing and complete subjection to the dictates of the principles is *sine qua non* to leadership development and performance effectiveness.

3. Teaching people to comprehend and learn that they too are expected to partake in the process of building sane and livable human communities is important. People must guard against wrong teachings and behaviors that have the potential to destroy their own society in the long term. People's reference point must be determined by the elements of the universal principles.

4. Pursuing personal peace and affable relationships with all people is an imperative. It is critical to not allow any seeds of personal dissatisfaction and bitterness to germinate, grow, and then destroy the expected long-term gains.

5. Demanding obedience, loyalty, respect, and honest living from all members of society must not be compromised — though this task must be carried out within the framework of democratic governance and rule of law — if they do exist.

6. The desire to learn and also be willing to give up one's rights in certain circumstances so as to preserve peace, tranquility, and good relationships in society must be lauded, promoted, and rewarded. This does not imply that wrongdoing should not be acknowledged and dealt with appropriately as per the laws of the nation. Instead, it calls to people to tamper justice with mercy as is deemed appropriate and timely.

The intention and seriousness with which educators pursue these activities will determine their degree of success in terms of improving the environment and its climate. The achievement of this goal will help us to produce the educated child (Bennett et al., 1999). This child will possess high qualities of the various dimensions of the HF (see details Table 7.1). Failure to do so will mean that there is no other way whereby the fertile environment and climate can be created and sustained — for good governance, economic growth, and sustained human-centered development.

References

Adjibolosoo, S., *The Human Factor in Developing Africa*, Praeger, Westport, CT, 1995.

Adjibolosoo, S., The human factor: foundation for development and democracy, in *The Human Factor Approach to Development in Africa*, Chivaura, V.G. and

Mararike, C.G., Eds., University of Zimbabwe Publications, Harare, Zimbabwe, 1998, pp. 11–33.

Adjibolosoo, S., *Rethinking Development Theory and Policy: A Human Factor Critique*, Praeger, Westport, CT, 1999a.

Adjibolosoo, S., The human factor in nation building, http://www.iihfd. org/intro.html, *Review of Human Factor Studies*, 5 (1 and 2), 1–20, 1999b.

Adjibolosoo, S., Ethnicity and the development of national consciousness: a human factor analysis, in *Critical Perspective on Political and Socio-Economic Development in Ghana*, Tettey, W.J., Puplampu, K. P., and Berman, B. J., Eds., Brill, Leiden, 2003a, pp. 107–132.

Adjibolosoo, S., Leadership qualities for improving the school environment: a parents' perspective, Unpublished Discussion Paper, Point Loma Nazarene University, San Diego, California, USA, 2003b.

Adjibolosoo, S., *The International Development Program: What are We Doing Wrong?* 1st Books Library, Bloomington, IN, 2004.

Al-Suwaidi, J., Arab and western conceptions of democracy: evidence from a UAE opinion survey, in *Democracy, War, and Peace in the Middle East*, Garnham, D. and Tessler, M., Eds., Indiana University Press, Bloomington, IN, 1995, pp. 82–115.

Avery, P.G., Teaching tolerance: what research tells us, *Soc. Educ.*, 66 (5), 270–275, 2002.

Beam, J.M., Toward education justice: can parents and community groups keep "the no child left behind act" on track? *Educ. Week*, 22 (4), 36, 38–39, 2002.

Bennett, W.J., Finn Jr., C.E., and Cribb Jr., J.T.E., *The Educated Child: A Parent's Guide from Preschool through Eight Grade*, The Free Press, New York, 1999.

Boron, A., Democratic citizens in wild markets: Menem's neoliberal experiment in Argentina, in *Beyond Government: Extending the Public Policy Debate in Emerging Democracies*, Goodwin, C.D. and Nacht, M., Eds., Westview Press, Boulder, CO, 1995, pp. 109–122.

Brown, K. and Dugan, I. J., Andersen's fall from grace is a tale of greed and miscues, *Wall Street Journal*, pp. A1 and A6, June 7, 2002.

Dahl, R. A., *Who Governs?* Yale University Press, New Haven, CT, 1961.

Dahl, R. A., *Polyarchy: Participation and Opposition*, Yale University Press, New Haven, CT, 1971.

Dahrendorf, R., *Reflections on the Revolution in Europe*, Chatto and Windus, London, 1990.

Das Gupta, J., India: democratic becoming and combined development, in *Politics in Developing Countries: Comparing Experiences with Democracy*, Diamond, L., Linz, J. J., and Lipset, S. M., Eds., Lynne Rienner Publishers, Boulder, CO, 1990, pp. 219–269.

Dewey, J., My pedagogic creed, *School J.*, 54 (3), 77–80, 1897.

Dill, V.S., *A Peaceful School: Cultivating a Culture of Nonviolence*, Phi Delta Kappa Educational Foundation, Bloomington, IN, 1998.

Doyle, M., Kant: liberal legacies and foreign affairs I and II, *Philos. Public Affairs*, 12, 205–236, 325–353, 1983.

Dworkin, M. S., *Dewey on Education: Selections with an Introduction and Notes*, Bureau of Publications — Teachers College, Columbia University, New York, 1959.

Gandhi, M., *Autobiography: The Story of my Experiments with Truth*, Navajin Publishing House, Ahmedabad, 1959.

Georgieva, K., Environmental politics and policy in Bulgaria: challenges and constraints to democratization, in: *Beyond Government: Extending the Public Policy Debate in Emerging Democracies*, Goodwin, C. D. and Nacht, M., Eds., Westview Press, Boulder, CO, 1995, pp. 265–285.

Goodwin, C. D. and Nacht, M., Eds., *Beyond Government: Extending the Public Policy Debate in Emerging Democracies*, Westview Press, Boulder, CO, 1995.

Graham, E., Values lessons return to the classroom, *The Wall Street Journal*, p. 25, September 26, 1998.

Grindle, M. S., Ready or not: the developing world and globalization, in: *Governance in a Globalizing World*, Nye, J. S. and Donahue, J. D., Eds., Brookings Institution Press, Washington, DC, 2000, pp. 178–207.

Hamburger, T., Hitt, G., and Schroeder, M., WorldCom scandal spurs congress: corporate-reform proposals, accounting legislation get boost from disclosures, *Wall Street Journal*, p. A9, June 27, 2002.

Healy, J. and Robinson, M., *Democracy, Governance, and Economic Policy: Sub-Saharan Africa in Comparative Perspective*, Overseas Development Institute, London, 1992.

Held, D., Democracy, in: *The Oxford Companion to the Politics of the World*, Krieger, J., Ed., Oxford University Press, New York, 1993, pp. 220–224.

Helliwell, J. F., Empirical linkages between democracy and economic growth, *Br. J. Political Sci.*, 24, 225–248, 1994.

Hirsch Jr., E. D., *The Schools We Need: Why We Don't Have Them*, Doubleday, New York, 1996.

Huntington, S. P., *Political Order in Changing Societies*, Yale University Press, New Haven, CT, 1968.

Hutchins, R. B., Education and the Socratic dialogue, in *The Human Dialogue: Perspectives on Communication*, Matson, F. W. and Montagu, A., Eds., The Free Press, New York, 1967, pp. 320–331.

Ichilov, O., Ed., *Citizenship Education in a Changing World*, Woburn Press, London, UK, 1998.

Jackson, R., *The Global Covenant: Human Conduct in a World of States*, Oxford University Press, New York, 2000.

Kamarck, E. C., Globalization and public administration reform, in *Governance in a Globalizing World*, Nye, J. S. and Donahue, J. D., Eds., Brookings Institution Press, Washington, DC, 2000, pp. 229–252.

Kauchak, D. P. and Eggen, P. D., *Learning and Teaching: Research-based Methods*, Allyn and Bacon, New York, 2003.

Kidder, R. M., Public concern for ethics rises, *The Christian Science Monitor*, 13, January 2, 1990.

Lickona, T., *Educating for Character: How Our Schools Can Teach Respect and Responsibility*, Bantam Books, New York, 1991.

Lincoln, C. E., Ed., *Martin Luther King Jr.: A Profile*, Hill and Wang, New York, 1970.

Lipset, S. M., Some social requisites of democracy: economic development and political legitimacy, *Am. Political Sci. Rev.*, 53, 69–105, 1959.

Lipset, S. M., *Political Man*, Doubleday, Garden City, NY, 1960.

Mandela, N., *Long Walk to Freedom*, Abacus, London, 1997.

Maremont, M. and Cohen, L. P., How Tyco's CEO enriched himself: Mr. Kozlowsky, ex-chief got secret loans, spent firm's cash as his own, *Wall Street Journal*, pp. A1 and A6, August 7, 2002.

Markon, J. and Frank, R., Five Adelphia officials arrested of fraud charges, *The Wall Street Journal*, pp. A3 and A6, July 25, 2002.

McClosky, H., Consensus and ideology in American politics, *Am. Political Sci. Rev.*, 58 (2), 361–382, 1964.

McCrone, D. J. and Cnudde, C. F., Toward a communications theory of democratic political development: a causal model, *Am. Political Sci. Rev.*, 61 (1), 72–79, 1967.

Mother Teresa, *Reaching Out in Love: Stories Told by Mother Teresa*, Continuum Publishing Group, New York, 1999.

Neubauer, D. E., Some conditions for democracy, *Am. Political Sci. Rev.*, 61 (4), 1002–1009, 1967.

Ostrom, E., Schroeder, L., and Wynne, S., *Institutional Incentives and Sustainable Development: Infrastructure Policies in Perspective*, Westview Press, Boulder, CO, 1993.

Owen, R., *A New View of Society*, Woodstock Books, New York, 1991 (originally published in 1817).

Picard, L. A., The challenge of structural adjustment, in *Policy Reform for Sustainable Development in Africa: The Institutional Imperative*, Picard, L. A. and Garrity, M., Eds., Lynne Rienner Publishers, Boulder, CO, 1994, pp. 1–17.

Pishev, O., The opening of public debate on economic policy in Bulgaria, in *Beyond Government: Extending the Public Policy Debate in Emerging Democracies*, Goodwin, C. D. and Nacht, M., Eds., Westview Press, Boulder, CO, 1995, pp. 165–181.

Prothro, T. W. and Grigg, C. M., Fundamental principles of democracy: base of agreement and disagreement, *J. Politics* 22 (2), 276–294, 1960.

Przeworski, A. and Limongi, F., Political regimes and economic growth, *J. Econ. Perspect.*, 7 (3), 51–69, 1993.

Ray, J. L., The future of international war: global trends and Middle Eastern implications, in *Democracy, War, and Peace in the Middle East*, Garnham, D. and Tessler, M., Eds., Indiana University Press, Bloomington, IN, 1995, pp. 3–33.

Rodrik, D., Governance of economic globalization, in *Governance in a Globalizing World*, Nye, J. S. and Donahue, J. D., Eds., Brookings Institution Press, Washington, DC, 2000, pp. 347–365.

Schauer, F., The politics and incentives of legal transplantation, in *Governance in a Globalizing World*, Nye, J. S. and Donahue, J. D., Eds., Brookings Institution Press, Washington, DC, 2000, pp. 253–268.

Scott, C. V., *Gender and Development: Rethinking Modernization and Dependency Theory*, Lynne Rienner, Boulder, CO, 1995.

Scully, G. W., *Conditional Environments and Economic Growth*, Princeton University Press, Princeton, NJ, 1992.

Shaw, T. M., *Reformism and Revisionism in Africa's Political Economy in the 1990s: The Dialectics of Adjustment*, St. Martin's Press, New York, 1993.

Shivji, I., *Class Struggles in Tanzania*, Monthly Review Press, New York, 1976.

Slavenkov, D. and Pisheva, G., *Economic Platform for the Transitional Period*, Information Publishing Company, Sofia, 1990.

Snooks, G. D., *Global Transitions: A General Theory of Economic Development*, St. Martin's Press, Inc., New York, 1999.

Solomon, D., Sandberg, J., and Pulliam, S., WorldCom angers regulators as accounting scandal widen, *The Wall Street Journal*, pp. A1 and A6, July 2, 2002.

Tom, A. R., *Redesigning Teacher Education*, State University of New York, New York, 1997.

UNDP, *Human Development Report: Millennium Development Goals, A Compact Among Nations to End Human Poverty*, Oxford University Press, New York, 2003.

Chapter 8

Human Rights and Governance

Joanna R. Quinn

CONTENTS

I. Introduction

Citizens of the modern world are by now largely familiar with the phrase *human rights*. It is common, for example, to hear people in Kampala,

Uganda, saying, "I know my rights." Similarly, whole countries have adopted bills of rights, which act as a formal template for legislation and the regulation of public and private activities, such as the Canadian Charter of Rights and Freedoms.[1] In fact, since World War II, the debate surrounding human rights has been made manifest in countries around the world through the proliferation of international human rights law and governance structures. The international solution of "never again," which was articulated at the Nuremberg Trials following the genocide of European Jews during World War II, has been writ large.

The same modern citizens, however, are also familiar with the abuses of human rights that continue to occur. At the time of writing, several long-standing conflicts that have caused the violation of the human rights of hundreds and thousands of people are still ongoing. Among these are escalating tension between Israelis and Palestinians, open hostility between Russia and the would-be breakaway Republic of Chechnya, and a heated confrontation between forces loyal to the Haitian government and various opposition forces. In each of these cases, a defined set of rules, although in diverse spheres and applied to various aspects, has been developed to mediate and solve such conflicts. These struggles and human rights abuses continue unabated. Clearly, then, there exists a tension between what *is* and what *ought to be*.

This chapter attempts to clarify what is meant by human rights, focusing on the principle of universality, inclusive of both civil and political rights as well as economic, social, and cultural rights, and the distinction between positive and negative rights. It also looks at how structures of governance can be applied to human rights. It also considers instruments and mechanisms of human rights, along with examples of their application.

II. Conceptions of Human Rights

Before moving ahead, it is important to understand exactly what is meant by the phrase "human rights," which is frequently used by different people in different contexts. The first, and perhaps most important element, is that human rights apply equally to all people, no matter in which political or legal jurisdiction they find themselves, or whether male or female, Buddhist or Christian, young or old. This is commonly called the principle of *universality*; that is, that one has human rights by virtue of the fact that one is a human being (Donnelly, 2003: 7, Chapters 1 and 2). Therefore, human rights are ascribed to individuals, and not to collective groups or communities.

It is also important to understand that human rights are not simply confined to the political sphere, as is sometimes understood to be the case in the literature emanating from many developed (and largely western) countries. Rather, human rights may be applied to a broad range of activities with which individuals are variously involved, including paid work, the ownership of property, voting and other civic activities, and education, to name only a few. Traditionally, people tend to think of human rights as being divided along two distinct lines. It is common to speak of "civil and political rights" and of "economic, social, and cultural rights," and, as will be discussed subsequently, the international covenants were divided on this basis. For the present purpose, however, it is sufficient to be aware that human rights are not simply about civil and political rights; economic, social, and cultural rights are every bit as important.

Human rights, however, are allocated to individuals in two very different ways. Here, the author refers to the distinction between "positive" and "negative" rights. "Negative" rights are granted to individuals not by any kind of overt action, but by a "forbearance on the part of others" (Donnelly, 2003: 30) "Positive" rights, on the other hand, necessitate an action on the part of others; they "require others to provide goods, services, or opportunities." Governance structures are often established to encourage the recognition of negative rights, and to enforce the promulgation of positive rights. Both are often required to ensure that individuals are able to enjoy the full spectrum of human rights (Donnelly, 2003: 30).

III. What Is Governance and How Does It Apply to Human Rights?

Kim Richard Nossal sets out a particularly useful definition of governance: "Governance involves establishing rules for a community, making allocative decisions for the community as a whole, settling conflicts over the rules, and mediating disputes between individuals and groups. Governance also involves the exercise of authority, that fascinating human practice of submitting obediently to the orders of others without having to be forced, coerced, induced, or persuaded to do so" (Nossal, 2003: 368). This definition, although surely not intended *only* to address the rules, decisions, and mediation central to the issue of human rights, does speak to the international struggle to uphold human rights.

It is important, however, to unpack Nossal's governance definition, for it contains a number of components which relate directly to the issue of human rights. The first element he mentions is the establishment of rules to manage relations within a community. This facet of governance is particularly applicable to the provision and upholding of human rights in any community, whether at a local, regional, national, or international level. What takes place in each jurisdiction, at a very basic level, is a series of interactions between individuals. In some cases, one or more of the individuals may have more power than another, and for this reason, communities have decided to enact a series of regulations that delineate how these interactions should proceed. These rules are effectively the governance of which Nossal speaks.

The second component of Nossal's definition involves "making allocative decisions for the community as a whole." Especially when looking at issues of development, it is easy to see that choices about who in the community should be allowed to partake in various goods and services can be of great importance. One recalls, for example, the devastating man-made famine in Ukraine which took place in 1932–1933, and the deliberate actions taken by the Soviet government under Stalin which "seized with unprecedented force and thoroughness the 1932 crop and foodstuffs from the agricultural population" (Mace, 1997: 78). This is, of course, a negative example of the kinds of "allocative decisions" that may be regulated by systems of governance. Nonetheless, it serves to illustrate the necessity of such rules.

A third feature of governance arises from the kinds of decisions discussed earlier. Settling conflicts which arise from the kinds of rules and regulations that are put in place is also an important feature of making sure that the individuals living and working within the different communities at local, regional, national, or international levels are able to do so in the manner they desire. This is not to suggest, of course, that individuals can and do act without any kind of restraint. Rather, in many cases, the enactment of governance systems means that individuals must sacrifice some degree of freedom for a corresponding degree of protection. So, when a disagreement occurs, the rules or governance structures must also have built in a mechanism to determine what should be done to settle the matter. Especially in the area of human rights, such mechanisms are important to ensure that such rights are upheld.

An especially important example of this is found in Nossal's reference to dispute mediation when conflicts arise between individuals and groups. In cases where individuals have been wronged by the state itself, and their human rights abrogated, such as the brutal violence perpetrated by the Pinochet government in Chile, such mediation becomes especially important. Or, conceivably, individuals may wrong the larger group, as happened when individuals pledging allegiance to Al-Qaeda flew planes into the World Trade Center in New York; in cases like this, instruments and mechanisms of governance must be able to deal sort out and mediate a satisfactory conclusion.

As Nossal points out, in all instances, governance also involves the exercise of authority, and we must be careful to recognize that authority (which equals power) may be harmless. At the same time, however, such authority can allow for heinous and despicable acts to occur, seemingly with no check on the exercise of that power. For this reason, structures and mechanisms of governance must be careful to provide such "checks" on the exercise of authority, which is meant, in the first place, to promote certain kinds of behaviors most favorable to those who live within their jurisdiction.

IV. International Instruments

Governance may take place at many different levels. Individuals may, in fact, belong to a series of hierarchical communities, ranging, broadly, from local to regional, to national, and to international levels. The governance of human rights, therefore, also occurs at each of these different levels. Human rights governance is meant to support the promotion and protection of human rights, both "positive" and "negative," as mentioned earlier. The following discussion attempts to provide an overview of what these kinds of instruments look like at the international level.

At the very highest level is the Universal Declaration of Human Rights. Following the atrocities committed by the Nazi regime in Germany and elsewhere during World War II, individuals and states from around the world decided that such wanton massacre should never again be allowed to take place. In response, in December of 1948, the emergent United Nations adopted the Universal Declaration of Human Rights. The preamble to the Declaration decrees "a common standard of achievement for all peoples and all nations ... [and strives] to promote respect for these rights and freedoms ... [through] their universal and effective recognition and observance ..." (United Nations General Assembly, 1948). It goes on to list a wide range of human rights, denoting "minimum conditions for a dignified life," (Donnelly, 2003: 15) to be upheld and promoted "by progressive measures, national and international, to secure their universal and effective recognition and observance, both among the Member States themselves and among the peoples of territories under their jurisdiction" (United Nations General Assembly, 1948).

A number of treaties, which are generally referred to as "instruments," have been enacted, and serve to strengthen and codify, thereby giving more force in international law, those rights set out in the Universal Declaration. Among these, and arguably two of the most important, are the International Covenant on Civil and Political Rights (ICCPR) and the International Covenant on Economic, Social, and Cultural Rights (ICESCR). Both of these were adopted by the United Nations General Assembly in December 1966. Each sets out a clear list of the types of rights and freedoms that individuals should be given.[2]

As suggested by their titles, each of the Covenants focuses on a particular set of rights that individuals should have the opportunity to enjoy. The ICESCR is a collection of guarantees that realizes a number of rights related to all things economic, social, and cultural. These include the right to work, the right to fair conditions in the workplace, protection of the family, the right to education, the recognition and protection of culture, the promotion of scientific progress, as well as many other protections. The ICCPR, accordingly, comprises a set of guarantees pertaining to civic and political matters. These include tenets regarding slavery, torture, and inhumane treatment, rights to liberty and against unlawful arrest or detention, freedom to choose one's own religion, and rules governing war propaganda, among others.

In addition, a number of other international treaties, covenants, and conventions, join with the Universal Declaration and the Covenants outlined earlier to form what is commonly known as an international bill of rights. Each different instrument carries with it a different set of conditions and obligations for those states that have become party to it. A covenant, for example, carries with it a set of legal obligations for states that have ratified it. This makes a covenant considerably stronger than a declaration. Also, each state may recognize a different level of binding authority of and adhesion to each treaty, declaration, or covenant; this is signaled in a state's willingness to sign or ratify these instruments. For this reason, the status of each of these bodies and their signatories is often complicated.

Many other international covenants and treaties have been enacted. One of these is the Convention on the Rights of the Child. Started in 1979, the International Year of the Child, the Convention is the result of cooperative efforts between UN agencies and others working on children's development. It outlines the basic rights and freedoms that children are meant to enjoy. And the Convention on the Rights of the Child holds a special status: "It has become the most rapidly and widely accepted covenant of human rights in history, ratified by every country but two (USA and Somalia)" (UNICEF Canada, 2004).

Another particularly important international treaty is actually a series of conventions known collectively as the "Geneva Conventions." These relate specifically to the protection of combatants, civilians, and journalists involved in an active theatre of war, and set out a set of rules to govern their treatment. There are four Geneva Conventions, signed in August 1949, and two additional Protocols, which were signed in June 1977.

One other, the Genocide Convention, attempts to define and also to prevent the occurrence of genocide. It was adopted in December 1949, immediately following World War II. The Genocide Convention is in place to give various United Nations bodies the authority to act to prevent or stop genocide from taking place.

These are just a small number of the many international treaties, conventions, and covenants that exist. While international agreements such as these also exist to regulate trade, finance, sport, and many other activities, the promulgation of such agreements is particularly strong in the area of human rights. In fact, these international treaties actually form the basis of national and domestic human rights protection.

V. International Mechanisms

Human rights abuses continue to occur, in spite of the proliferation of treaties for the protection of human rights. This has necessitated the development of various mechanisms, at the international and the national levels, to adjudicate in cases of abuse. These can take a variety of forms that we know as traditional, although new mechanisms, such as truth commissions, have also begun to emerge. As with the various treaties listed earlier, these mechanisms of enforcement and adjudication are somewhat piecemeal; together, however, they are capable of dealing with a wide variety of matters. The following discussion attempts to delineate the responsibilities of each as well as their relationship to one another.

The International Court of Justice dates to 1946, although its roots extend even earlier, to 1922, when it was an organ of the League of Nations. Today, the International Court of Justice is the primary justice mechanism of the United Nations. Its mandate is twofold: to adjudicate cases of international law brought by states; and to present advisory opinions on other matters of international law brought before it by international organizations which require further interpretation. Therefore, it deals mainly with disputes between states, and is not able to prosecute individual criminals. Since its most recent inception in 1946, the International Court of Justice has made 79 judgments in state matters, and has given 24 advisory opinions (ICJ, 2004).

Two specially appointed tribunals, however, have been established specifically to deal with the prosecution of individuals. The International Criminal Tribunal for the Former Yugoslavia was established in 1993 by United Nations Security Council Resolution 827, to prosecute individuals charged with having committed a variety of serious crimes in the former Yugoslavia from 1991 forward. The International Criminal Tribunal for Rwanda was established in 1994 by United Nations Security Council Resolution 955, to prosecute individuals involved in the Rwandan genocide. In 2005, both Tribunals continued to gather evidence and prosecute.

Outside of the United Nations framework, however, another judicial body has emerged. Created by an international treaty called the Rome Statute, which was signed by 120 states, the International Criminal Court entered into force in 2002. Importantly, several states, including the United States, did not become signatories to the Statute, which means that its jurisdiction will not apply to Americans or to citizens of other countries not signatories. The Court was created "to promote the rule of law and ensure that the gravest international crimes [including genocide, crimes against humanity, and war crimes] do not go unpunished" (ICC, 2004). It is intended as a fail-safe mechanism; that is, it will act when states themselves are unwilling or unable to prosecute such crimes. At the time of writing, the International Criminal Court had not yet been entirely created. It remains to be seen how effective the Court will be.

Apart from these kinds of international judicial mechanisms, there are a number of regional courts which also exist to adjudicate cases involving abuses of human rights. The European Court of Human Rights is perhaps the most far-reaching of these. It was established in 1953 under the European Convention on Human Rights, as a mechanism to enforce the human rights obligations to which states party to the Convention have agreed. The major impetus for the formation of such a mechanism, as elsewhere, was the realization of the events which had taken place during World War II. Under the terms of the Convention, European states must agree to "the partial surrender of sovereignty . . . to the regional and international human rights institutions" (Sikkink, 1993: 149–150). The Court hears cases brought by either states or individuals. As part of the broader European human rights regime, which also encompasses the European Human Rights Commission, the Court has been progressive in its decisions.

The European Court's American counterpart, however, has been decidedly less so. The Inter-American Court of Human Rights was created by the American Convention on Human Rights in 1969, although its statute was not approved until 1979. The Court's mandate is to interpret the American Convention on Human Rights on cases brought by states or by the Inter-American Commission on Human Rights, through either adjudication or advisory. "In contrast to the European human rights system, individual citizens of the [Organization of American States] member states are not allowed to take cases directly to the Court: individuals who believe that their rights have been violated must first lodge their cases with the Commission and have that body rule on the admissibility thereof."[3]

Other continental and regional organizations have not coalesced as enthusiastically around the issue of human rights. The Organization of African Unity adopted the African Charter on Human and Peoples' Rights (commonly referred to as the Banjul Charter) in 1981, which created the African Commission on Human and Peoples' Rights. In January 2004, an African Court on Human and Peoples' Rights was established (ACHPR, 2004); at the time of writing, it had not yet been created. Neither in Asia nor in the Middle East do any mechanisms of human rights governance exist. At the very most, the majority of the states within these regions are signatories to the Universal Declaration.

VI. Applications

As noted earlier, the kinds of mechanisms which form the backbone of human rights governance around the world are largely created in three ways: some follow from decisions of an organ of the United Nations; some are created by agreements among states (i.e., treaty); and some are an off-shoot of regional human rights commissions. Indeed, the earlier discussion has touched on the European Human Rights Commission, the Inter-American Court on Human Rights, and the African Commission on Human and Peoples' Rights. Although they are often involved in a variety of activities including the promotion of human rights through education, the European and Inter-American commissions (and eventually the African commission as well) acts mainly as a vetting agency in hearing cases, and determining their validity to be heard by their respective human rights courts. They are not alone in this activity.

Perhaps the largest and most comprehensive of such agencies is the office of the United Nations High Commissioner for Human Rights (UNHCHR). Established in 1983 by the United Nations General Assembly, the agency is mandated with the primary responsibility for and coordination of all human rights activities in the United Nations system. Primarily, the UNHCHR is involved in the protection and promotion of human rights, although it is often involved directly with state governments, and is sometimes asked to provide technical assistance in such matters.

Other states, however, have begun to implement national human rights commissions to further a variety of goals including auditing, monitoring, investigating complaints, and promoting and protecting human rights. In most cases, these commissions operate under the jurisdiction of that state. Canada is one of these. The Canadian Human Rights Commission was created upon the creation of the Canadian Human Rights Act in 1977, and began its work one year later.

In the late 1980s, the United Nations General Assembly began to discuss the utility of more such national human rights commissions. It felt that "priority should be accorded to the development of appropriate arrangements at the national level to ensure the effective implementation of international human rights standards" (United Nations General Assembly, 1993: Preamble). As a result, a number of states have begun to create national human rights commissions, and, at the time of writing, more were being created. India, for example, created its commission in 1993; South Africa in 1994; Thailand in 1999; Nepal in 2000; Mongolia in 2001; Japan in 2002; Republic of Congo in 2003.

One such example is the Uganda Human Rights Commission (UHRC), which was created in 1996 upon recommendation of the 1995 Constitution (Government of Uganda, 1995). The "permanent human rights commission," as it is often called, in many ways picks up where the truth commission[4] which had been active between 1986 and 1994, left off. As is often the case in countries where significant human rights abuses have taken place in the past, the UHRC is especially focused on two aspects in particular: investigations of complaints of abuse and promoting education and awareness. For example, the UHRC is active in the training of police officials throughout the country, providing them with information about human rights, and teaching them appropriate methods of dealing with human rights abuses. The Commission is also active in ratifying international human rights instruments.

VII. Conclusion

Human rights governance consists of a number of international human rights instruments, as well as largely juridical mechanisms meant to enforce them and a series of commissions who work to promote and protect these same universal rights. Taken together, they form a patchwork approach to the establishment of rules, allocative decision-making, conflict resolution and the mediation of disputes — each of which forms a key component of the definition of governance with which this chapter began. Indeed, the codification and enforcement of such human rights regimes is key to any kind of sustainable social and economic development. For the development of structures of equality and fairness, as represented in the enumerated lists of rights discussed earlier, can serve as a solid framework against which growth in every sector can take place. And, while not every human being yet lives in conditions which guarantee complete access to the enjoyment of human rights, the situation grows more favorable with each passing year. Still, however, there is much to be done.

Notes

1. The Canadian Charter of Rights and Freedoms was enacted as Schedule B to the *Canada Act 1982* (U.K.) 1982, c. 11, and came into force on April 17, 1982.
2. The origins of both Covenants arose from a political, cold-war era dispute between primarily Western and other states within the United Nations General Assembly. The Western states argued for the primacy of civil and political rights, while primarily Asian and African states argued for the primacy of economic social and cultural rights. Although this dichotomy was thought to be firmly entrenched, the U.S.A. and China, neither of which had signed both Covenants, finally did so in the 1990s. At the time of this writing, however, neither has ratified both Covenants.
3. Inter-American Court of Human Rights (article on-line). Available from http://encyclopedia.thefreedictionary.com/Inter-American%20Court%20of%20Human%20Rights; internet; accessed May 8, 2004.

4. The truth commission was formally known as The Commission of Inquiry into Violations of Human Rights. It was established in 1986 to consider all of the human rights abuses that had taken place since the country's independence in 1962. This included the atrocities committed under the regimes of both Idi Amin and Milton Obote. In all, nearly 1,000,000 people were tortured and killed during this period. The truth commission was appointed when Yoweri Museveni and the National Resistance Army seized power in 1986. It completed its work in 1994.

References

ACHPR (African Commission on Human and Peoples' Rights), 25th January 2004: A turning point in the history of the African System for the Protection of Human and Peoples' Rights (Press release online), Available at http://www.achpr.org/english/news/press_court_en.html, last accessed on May 8, 2004.

Donnelly, J., *Universal Human Rights in Theory and Practice*, 2nd ed., Cornell University Press, Ithaca, NY.

Government of Uganda, *The Constitution of Uganda*, Government of Uganda, Kampala, Uganda, 1995.

ICC (International Criminal Court), The ICC at a glance (online), Available at http://www.icc-cpi.int/ataglance/whatistheicc/history.html, last accessed on May 8, 2004.

ICJ (International Court of Justice), General information: the Court at a glance (online), Available at http://212.153.43.18/icjwww/igeneralinformation/icjgnnot.html, last accessed on May 8, 2004.

Mace, J.E., Soviet man-made famine in Ukraine, in *Century of Genocide*, Totten, S., Parsons, W.S., Charny, I.W., Eds., Garland, New York, NY, pp. 78–112, 1997.

Nossal, K.R., World politics: global anarchy, global governance, in *Studying Politics*, Dyck, R., Ed., Nelson, Toronto, pp. 368–388, 2003.

Sikkink, K., The power of principled ideas: human rights policies in the United States and Western Europe, in *Ideas and Foreign Policy: Beliefs, Institutions and Political Change*, Goldstein, J., Keohane, R.O., Eds., Cornell University Press, Ithaca, NY, pp. 139–172, 1993.

UNICEF Canada, U.N. Convention on the Rights of the Child Q&A (online), Available at http://www.unicef.ca/eng/special/questions_conv.html, last accessed on May 8, 2004.

United Nations General Assembly, *Universal Declaration of Human Rights*, United Nations, New York, NY, 1948.

United Nations General Assembly, *National Institutions for the Promotion and Protection of Human Rights*, United Nations, New York, NY, 1993.

Chapter 9

Does Aid Work?
New Evidence from
Recent Empirical Studies

Niels Hermes and Robert Lensink

CONTENTS

I. Introduction

In 1998, the World Bank published a report entitled *Assessing Aid: What Works, What Doesn't, and Why* (World Bank, 1998), in which it presented the results of an extensive investigation into the effectiveness of development aid. In one of the background papers to this report, by Burnside and Dollar (1997) (which was later published in the *American Economic Review* (Burnside and Dollar, 2000)), it was shown that development aid has a positive impact on growth in countries with good monetary, fiscal, and trade policies and little or no impact if these policies are poor.

Both publications, together with a follow-up paper by Collier and Dollar (2002), in which a poverty-efficient allocation of aid is proposed based on the idea that aid should be given to countries with good economic policies, have been enormously influential in setting the agenda of development aid policies, especially with respect to how development aid should be distributed among countries. Several donor countries have, at least partly, used the guidelines for aid distribution as suggested by the World Bank research outcomes.

The World Bank research has stimulated the discussion of the effectiveness of development aid in stimulating economic growth. Before the publication of these results, there had been a long-standing debate on the aid–growth nexus. This debate remained inconclusive, however.[1] The *Assessing Aid* report and its accompanying empirical studies seemed to provide a clear, simple, and policy-relevant answer: aid works, but only if recipient countries' policies are good. Yet, several researchers have recently contested the empirical outcome of the World Bank. Generally speaking, the research of these critics shows that aid does work. It also shows that the results of Burnside and Dollar (2000) and Collier and Dollar (2002) are less convincing than is claimed. The critics also show that good policies may not be the only, and perhaps not even the most important, prerequisite to make aid work.

This chapter reviews the outcomes of empirical research on the aid–growth nexus since the publication of the *Assessing Aid* report. The aim of this review is to see what policy lessons can be drawn from this research and to see whether there is a need for the donor community to reconsider aid policies in case they have been based on the results of the World Bank report.

The chapter is organized as follows. Section II provides a short description of the World Bank research results, and in particular of the Burnside–Dollar paper. Section III discusses the criticism of the Burnside–Dollar study, which has been raised in a number of studies. Section IV provides an overview of empirical studies that present alternative views on how aid may affect growth. Section V provides conclusions and a discussion of policy lessons.

II. *Assessing Aid:* A Brief Review[2]

There has been extensive empirical research on the macroeconomic effectiveness of development aid. Several authors have surveyed the empirical evidence on aid effectiveness that have been published before the *Assessing Aid* report. These authors do not agree on whether the effectiveness is generally positive or negative. Some conclude that the macroeconomic impact of aid has been minimal or that there has been no effect at all on economic growth. Mosley (1987: 139), for instance, points out that "there appears to be no statistically significant correlation in any post war period, either positive or negative, between inflows of development aid and the growth rate of GNP in developing countries when other causal influences on growth are taken into account." In his paper, he refers to the micro–macro paradox: most micro-project-related studies on aid are quite positive about the effectiveness of aid, whereas most macro-project-related studies do not find any evidence for the positive effects of aid. White (1992: 121) points out that "We know surprisingly little about aid's macroeconomic impact." and "The combination of weak theory with poor econometric methodology makes it difficult to conclude anything about the relationship between aid and savings [. . .] and aid and growth." Boone (1996), in an influential and extensive study, also expressed a rather pessimistic view on the effectiveness of aid. He found that aid increased government consumption rather than increasing investments or benefiting the poor. In contrast, Hansen and Tarp (2000) conclude that, based on an extensive survey of empirical studies that was conducted until the mid-1990s, there seems to be rather strong evidence for a positive effect of aid on investment and growth. They argue that the micro–macro paradox does not exist. In contrast to White's view, they argue that we can certainly learn something from the traditional macroeconomic aid studies: aid works, although not as well as we have sometimes hoped.

The publication of the *Assessing Aid* report (World Bank, 1998) provided a new stimulus to the discussion on the macro-economic effectiveness of development aid. The report contains an extensive analysis of aid effectiveness and is based on innovative macroeconometric research, as it is one of the first studies acknowledging that aid effectiveness may depend on specific circumstances in recipient countries. The analysis in the report fits well into a new wave of aid effectiveness studies that emerged since the mid-1990s. These studies are considerably different from the traditional aid effectiveness studies: they base their empirical analysis on a general equilibrium growth model, try to address the endogeneity of aid, deal with nonlinear effects of aid, and explicitly link the impact of aid to economic policies and the institutional environment in the recipient countries and to external conditions these countries are confronted with (Hansen and Tarp, 2000). Generally, models since the mid-1990s used (variants of) the following specification:[3]

$$y_g = \beta_1 A + \beta_2 A^2 + \beta_3 P + \beta_4 (A \times P) + \beta_5 Z + \varepsilon \qquad (9.1)$$

where y_g is the per capita growth rate, A the foreign aid flows, P a measure of the domestic policy and institutional environment, Z a vector of variables that are normally included in models explaining per capita growth, and ε an error term. The variable A^2 takes into account the nonlinearity of aid; the variable $(A \times P)$ deals with explicitly linking the impact of aid to economic policies and the institutional environment in the recipient countries and to external conditions these countries are confronted with.

The *Assessing Aid* report states that aid does help to increase growth, but only in countries with sound economic management, or "good governance." In the report, this is generally translated into "good" economic policies and building "strong" institutions. The main conclusion of the report is, therefore, that aid should be allocated based on selecting recipient countries according to their policy environment. In this sense, the report presents a clear message to aid policy-makers.

The claims of the *Assessing Aid* report with respect to the effectiveness of aid are mainly based on a number of background studies, especially the ones by Burnside and Dollar (2000) and Collier and Dollar (2002). In a cross-country regression analysis for 40 low-income countries and 16 middle-income countries over the 1970–1993 period (using six 4-yr averages), Burnside and Dollar estimate a neoclassical growth model in which they include aid and aid interacted with a policy index variable, together with a number of variables that are usually included in growth models. Thus, Burnside and Dollar use a specification similar to Equation (9.1), yet, without including the quadratic aid term. Table 9.1 provides a quick overview of the model specification of the Burnside–Dollar paper. They apply both the Ordinary Least Squares (OLS) and Two-Stage Least Squares (2SLS) models to take into account the possible endogeneity of aid. The policy index is a weighted index of the budget surplus to gross domestic product (GDP) ratio, the inflation rate, and an index reflecting trade openness as constructed by Sachs and Warner (1995). These variables are seen as proxies for fiscal, monetary, and trade policy, respectively. The weights are obtained from a growth equation, which includes these three measures as well as a number of other variables.[4] Burnside and Dollar show that aid has a positive impact on real GDP per capita growth, but only when aid is interacted with a policy index variable. In other words, aid may increase growth, but only when the government of a country carries out "good" fiscal, monetary, and trade policies. If aid is given to countries without these good policies, the aid flow can be considered wasted, because it will not stimulate higher economic growth.

Table 9.1 Overview of Empirical Studies on the Aid–Growth Relationship

Author(s)	A^{2a}	$A \times P^b$	$A \times X^c$	Results
Burnside and Dollar (1997, 2000)	—	Yes	—	Aid effectiveness depends on the policy environment
Durbarry et al. (1998)	Yes	—	—	Aid has diminishing returns
Collier and Dehn (2001)	—	Yes	Yes	Aid effectiveness depends on the policy environment
Dalgaard and Hansen (2001)	Yes	Yes	—	Aid is effective with diminishing returns and is independent from the policy environment
Guilleaumont and Chauvet (2001)	—	Yes	Yes	Aid effectiveness does not depend on the policy environment, but on climatic conditions
Hansen and Tarp (2001)	Yes	Yes	—	Aid is effective with diminishing returns and is independent from the policy environment
Hudson and Mosley (2001)	Yes	Yes	—	Aid is effective with diminishing returns and is independent from the policy environment
Lensink and White (2001)	Yes	Yes	—	Aid is effective with diminishing returns and is independent from the policy environment
Lu and Ram (2001)	Yes	Yes	—	Aid is effective with diminishing returns and is independent from the policy environment
Chauvet and Guilleaumont (2002)	—	Yes	Yes	Aid effectiveness depends on political stability
Collier and Dollar (2002)	Yes	Yes	—	Aid effectiveness depends on the policy environment
Islam (2002)	Yes	Yes	Yes	Aid effectiveness does not depend on the policy environment, but on political stability
Gomanee et al. (2003)	Yes	—	—	Aid is effective after a threshold value of growth has been reached
Jensen and Paldam (2003)	Yes	Yes	—	Aid is not effective in stimulating growth

(Continued)

Table 9.1 *(Continued)*

Author(s)	A^{2a}	$A \times P^b$	$A \times X^c$	Results
Kosack (2003)	—	—	Yes	Aid is effective in improving quality of life in democratic countries
Dalgaard et al. (2004)	Yes	Yes	Yes	Aid is effective with diminishing returns, is less effective in tropical regions, and is independent from the policy environment
Burnside and Dollar (2004)	Yes	Yes	Yes	Aid effectiveness depends on institutional quality
Easterly et al. (2004)	—	Yes	—	Aid effectiveness does not depend on the policy environment

[a]Quadratic aid term is included in the growth model specification.
[b]Interactive term of aid and a policy index is included in the growth model specification.
[c]Interactive term of aid and an indicator other than the policy index is included.

In their paper, Collier and Dollar determine the so-called poverty-efficient allocation of aid. According to them, re-allocating aid flows to poor countries with a good economic policy environment would reduce the number of poor people, with an extra 18 million people per year being helped out of poverty, when compared with the number based on the existing allocation of aid flows. The model specification of Collier and Dollar is similar to Equation (9.1), including both the quadratic aid term and the interactive aid-policy term (see Table 9.1).

III. The Critique

The *Assessing Aid* report was received quite well, especially in policymaking circles. This may be understandable, as the message of the report appeared to be simple, and it provided clear guidelines for policymakers who have to make difficult decisions with regard to disbursing scarce aid resources to a large number of recipient countries. However, the analysis of aid effectiveness in the report has also received major criticism, especially from academic circles. The critique focused on several issues such as the use of the concept of good governance, the suggestions of the report with respect to policy conditionality and aid selectivity, and the econometric specification of the aid effectiveness analysis.

In the remaining chapter, we will concentrate on the critique expressed regarding the econometric background papers to the *Assessing Aid* report, in particular the work of Burnside–Dollar. The results of this widely cited study have been used to support a redirection of aid policies by donor countries toward more selectivity when allocating aid to countries: aid should be allocated to countries which carry out good policies.[5] Such a redirection of policies may have a major impact on recipient countries and as this may be the case, many researchers have carefully evaluated the results of the Burnside–Dollar paper. If these results can be convincingly criticized, a policy of aid selectivity may be a wrong decision. As will be shown, the Burnside–Dollar results do not appear to be as strong as is suggested by the authors.

Several researchers have tried to redo the econometric analysis of the Burnside–Dollar paper. Dalgaard and Hansen (2001), Hansen and Tarp (2001), Lensink and White (2001), Jensen and Paldam (2003), and Islam (2002), among others, have analyzed the aid–growth relationship, using an interaction term between aid and a policy measure as suggested by Burnside–Dollar. Although these studies sometimes use different data sets and different model specifications, they all use variants of Equation (9.1). The differences mainly relate to whether they include A^2 and the variables they include in vector Z, and different econometric techniques, it is nevertheless surprising that none of these studies find the interactive term to be statistically significant. Dalgaard and Hansen (2001), for instance, show that the result that aid enhanced growth only in a good economic policy environment crucially depended on the fact that, Burnside and Dollar deleted five observations from the data set. Dalgaurd and Hansen (2001) also show that by deleting other combinations of observations, the opposite outcome can be produced, that is, that aid does stimulate growth irrespective of the policy environment. The results of this and other studies at least question the robustness of the Burnside–Dollar paper. Only one study (Collier and Dehn, 2001) lends support to the Burnside–Dollar theory on the importance of a good economic policy environment in determining the effectiveness of aid.

Perhaps the strongest attack on the robustness of the Burnside–Dollar results is presented in a paper by Easterly et al. (2004). They use the same data set, model specification, and econometric technique as Burnside–Dollar did and extend the data set using an additional 4 yr of data (until 1997). On the basis of their analysis, they conclude that the interactive term is no longer statistically significant.

Therefore, based on the work of those researchers who tried to redo Burnside–Dollar, it has to be concluded that the claims made on the importance of the policy environment for the effectiveness of aid are in fact rather fragile.

Several authors have also criticized the use and construction of the policy index as proposed by Burnside and Dollar. As discussed earlier, the policy index is a weighted index of the budget surplus to GDP ratio, the inflation rate, and a measure reflecting trade openness. One may, however, criticize the choice of variables to measure policies for various reasons.[6] First, the critics claim that measuring trade policy is very difficult. As Pritchett's (1996) study shows, there are several types of trade policy indices measuring different elements of policy. Moreover, Pritchett argues that different trade policies matter at different points of time. Not surprisingly, therefore, the different measures show very low correlation. The trade openness index of Sachs and Warner (1995) is a dummy variable, which takes into account various elements of trade policy. This makes it difficult to understand exactly how trade policy may affect growth, as the different effects of individual trade policy elements on growth may cancel out. Moreover, it is even more difficult to understand how trade policy influences the aid–growth relationship when using a constructed index.

Second, the use of inflation rate as a measure of monetary policy is problematic. To begin with, inflation rate is an outcome, rather than a policy in itself. The inflation rate may be influenced by policy measures of the government, for instance, by tight monetary policies. The inflation rate may also be determined by various other sources, such as changes in the domestic demand and supply conditions, and changes in the terms of trade. These sources of inflation are out of the direct control of the government. Therefore, the inflation rate may be a poor reflection of monetary policy. Moreover, the nature of the relationship between inflation and growth is unclear. Recent empirical studies show that this relationship is quadratic, rather than linear, which is the specification chosen by Burnside and Dollar. These studies stress that while low levels of inflation may stimulate growth, inflation has a negative impact on growth only after a threshold level has been passed.

Third, one may question the use of budget surplus as a measure of fiscal policy. Budget surplus results from different fiscal policy measures related to both government revenues and expenditures. These different policy measures may have a different impact on growth (Gemmell, 2004; Hermes and Lensink, 2004). Therefore, budget surplus, like the trade policy measure discussed earlier, is a composite measure of policies, which makes it difficult to exactly determine the relationship between policy and growth. In the literature, one generally finds budget surplus to be unrelated to growth (Levine and Renelt, 1992; Sala-i-Martin, 1997), which may be due to the fact that this is a composite measure of many different policies having different effects on growth.

Fourth, Burnside and Dollar use the same weights for the three policy measures when constructing the policy index for all the 56 countries in their data set. Yet, one may seriously question whether this is a correct assumption. Studies have shown that the impact of trade policies on growth may differ between countries, depending on the development of the domestic financial system (Berthelemy and Varoudakis, 1996). Similarly, it has been argued that fiscal policies have different effects on growth in different countries (Hermes and Lensink, 2004).

Finally, Burnside and Dollar do not really explain why they have left out other kinds of policy measures such as privatization, financial market liberalization, educational policies, tax reforms, etc. There is a huge empirical literature indicating that these measures also influence growth performance (see, e.g., Fry, 1995; Berthelemy and Dessus, 2000; Cook and Uchida, 2001). This makes the selection used by Burnside and Dollar to measure good policies rather arbitrary.

IV. Alternative Views on the Aid–Growth Relationship

The *Assessing Aid* report stimulated a huge amount of research in finding alternative explanations of the effectiveness of aid, as many researchers contested the explanation given by the World Bank research. A number of alternative views on the effectiveness of aid have been suggested. Basically, five main alternative views can be traced: aid has decreasing returns, aid effectiveness is influenced by the volatility of the aid flows, aid effectiveness is influenced by external and climatic conditions, aid effectiveness is influenced by political conditions, and aid effectiveness depends on institutional quality.[7]

A. Decreasing Returns of Aid

Several authors suggest that giving aid may have decreasing returns. They investigate this by adding a quadratic aid term to the growth model (see Equation (9.1)). This specification of the model tests whether the impact of aid on growth becomes negative after reaching a certain threshold level. There is an overwhelming amount of evidence for the existence of decreasing returns of aid. Most studies using this specification indeed find support for a negative effect of aid on growth after a certain threshold level (Durbarry et al., 1998; Dalgaard and Hansen, 2001; Hansen and Tarp, 2001; Hudson and Mosley, 2001; Lensink and White, 2001; Islam, 2002; Lu and Ram, 2001; Dalgaard et al., 2004). This threshold level of aid to GDP varies between 15 and 45% (Feeny, 2003). The decreasing returns of aid can be explained by pointing at the limited absorptive capacity of countries to take up large inflows of foreign capital and the problem of Dutch disease effects.

Only two studies do not find support for the decreasing returns of aid hypothesis. One study by Jensen and Paldam (2003) investigates the claim that giving aid has decreasing returns by simplifying the econometric model so that more observations can be taken into account than in the original data set used by most other empirical studies. They find decreasing returns of aid also for the extended data set. Moreover, this study carries out an out-of-sample replication of the aid–growth estimations with the extended data set. This exercise shows that quadratic aid term is no longer significant. A second study by Gomanee et al. (2003) shows that aid only becomes effective after the aid to GDP ratio has reached a threshold of 2%. However, they do not find evidence for aid having decreasing returns after this threshold level.

B. Aid Uncertainty

Some studies that investigated the patterns of aid flows have found these flows to be rather volatile. Buliř and Hamann (2003) show that aid flows are highly volatile; their volatility is even higher than the government's domestic budget revenues. They also show that the higher the volatility of aid flows is, the more the aid-dependent countries are. Next, they find that aid falls during periods in which domestic revenues of governments also fall and that the volatility of domestic revenues coincides with the volatility of aid flows. These findings do seem to suggest that although aid flows may increase the overall resources governments have, aid is currently disbursed "in a less than ideal manner" (Bulíř and Hamann, 2003: 83).

Lensink and Morrissey (2000) investigate the impact of volatile aid flows (or aid instability in their words) on the effectiveness of aid. In their analysis, the volatility of aid is seen as a measure of the uncertainty of aid flows of a recipient country. The uncertainty of aid flows is measured as the deviation of actual aid flows from expected aid flows, where expected flows are based on a simple autoregressive process (with or without a time trend). The reasons for aid flows being uncertain may be either explicit donor country policies or actions, or external shocks. In either case, aid uncertainty may have an adverse impact on government expenditures, and in particular on public investment. A reduction of public investment may in turn lead to lower private investment, and ultimately also to lower economic growth.

Lensink and Morrissey add their measure of aid uncertainty to a growth equation, which incorporates standard exogenous growth variables, including a measure of aid flows. They use data for a sample of 75 developing countries, using average values of variables for the period 1970–1995. The estimation results show that, while the aid uncertainty variable has a negative impact on growth, aid has a positive effect. This confirms the hypothesis that aid in itself contributes to higher growth, but that the effectiveness of aid is reduced when aid flows are more volatile. The authors therefore suggest that donors and recipients should develop more stable relationships to increase aid effectiveness.

C. Aid Effectiveness and External and Climatic Conditions

Some authors argue that aid effectiveness is crucially dependent on external and climatic factors, rather than on the economic policy environment, as is claimed by the *Assessing Aid* report. Examples of such factors are: long-term trade fluctuation terms, short-term export instability and floods, droughts, earthquakes, etc. Guilleaumont and Chauvet (2001) show that aid is more effective in raising income of the recipient country, the worse these external and climatic factors are. In their empirical analysis, they estimate a growth model, using a pooled cross-section time series analysis for the 1970–1993 period for 66 developing countries. The model includes the aid to GDP ratio, aid interacted with a policy index similar to the Burnside–Dollar paper, and aid interacted with a composite external environment indicator, incorporating different external and climatic factors.

The results of the analysis[8] show that the variable that combines aid with the external environment indicator has a statistically significant positive impact on growth. The variable that combines aid with the policy index is not statistically significant. Thus, they find no support for the claim that a good policy environment improves the effectiveness of aid. They do find, however, that the impact of aid is more positive for countries that are confronted with adverse external conditions. In particular, they show that aid stimulates growth only when countries are more vulnerable to external conditions. A plausible interpretation of this result is that aid has decreased the negative impact of adverse external conditions. Based on their analysis, Guilleaumont and Chauvet suggest that aid should be allocated based on a country's performance of economic policies, taking into account the impact of external and climatic factors on the country's growth performance.

Another paper that focuses on the effectiveness of aid, given external and climatic factors, is that of Dalgaard et al. (2004). In their paper, they focus on geography to assess the effectiveness of aid in enhancing growth. In particular, they take the fraction of land in the tropics and interact this variable with aid to evaluate the aid–growth relationship. Their reasoning to use a climate-related variable is two-fold. First, some studies have shown that tropical land area and tropical diseases may help to explain the differences in economic growth between countries (Bloom and Sachs, 1998; Gallup et al., 1999). Second, other studies suggest that geographical conditions determine the nature of institutions, which in turn influences economic growth (Acemoglu et al., 2001). Since climate-related circumstances are structurally different between countries, variables measuring these circumstances are interesting candidates for analyzing whether the impact of aid on growth differs between countries.

Dalgaard et al. (2004) add their climate-related variable, and this variable interacted with aid, to the Burnside–Dollar growth model specification. The result is that the policy index interacted with aid becomes insignificant. At the same time, however, aid and aid interacted with the climate-related variable are statistically significant and have a positive and negative sign, respectively. Their result thus shows that aid has a strong positive impact on growth of countries outside topical regions, whereas its impact decreases for countries in the tropics.

Collier and Dehn (2001) also contribute to the discussion on the role of climatic and external conditions in determining the effectiveness of aid. On the basis of the Burnside–Dollar specification, they add a measure of trade shocks, defined as the change in export prices. The results of the estimations show that, contrary to almost all other papers, the good policy index interacted with aid is positive and statistically significant, supporting the central message of the *Assessing Aid* report. However, they also show that aid may reduce the impact of negative price shocks on growth, a result similar to that of Guilleaumont and Chauvet (2001).

D. Aid and Political Instability

Some authors have investigated whether political instability in the recipient country matters for the effectiveness of aid. Political instability refers to irregular changes in the political system. The sources of instability may be two-fold. On the one hand, the political system may change regularly due to frequent elections. On the other hand, political systems may change due to political violence, such as riots, strikes, assassinations, etc. Frequent political instability, in turn, may lead to unpredictable changes in laws, regulations, government policies, taxation and expenditures, and property rights. The uncertainty created by these changes may reduce incentives for investment and consumption, leading to lower economic growth. In a similar vein, it may negatively affect the impact of aid on growth.

Islam (2002) investigates this issue by using annual data for a sample of 21 sub-Saharan African and 11 Asian countries for the period 1968–1997. He uses a measure of political instability that is based on De Haan and Siermann (1996), revised by using the freedom index scores from *Freedom in the World*, Freedom House, for the years 1993–1997. Adding the political stability measure, and its interaction with aid, to a Burnside–Dollar-type of growth model gives the result that the interactive term of aid and political stability is positive and statistically significant. In contrast, the interactive term of aid and the Burnside–Dollar policy index is not significant. Islam's results suggest that aid is only effective when the political situation of the recipient country is stable; in politically unstable environments, aid does not have any effect on growth.

Chauvet and Guilleaumont (2002) carry out a similar analysis. They estimate a growth model, using data for 53 countries for the period 1975–1999, and include a political instability measure, which is a composite of the number of coups d'états and a measure of regime changes obtained from Marshal and Jaggers (2000). Chauvet and Guilleaumont (2002) find evidence for the hypothesis that aid is more effective in politically stable environments, because aid interacted with the political instability variable is negative and statistically significant.

Another paper that is closely related to the work of the authors discussed here is that of Kosack (2003). This author investigates whether the effectiveness of aid depends on the political system. In particular, he investigates whether aid is able to improve the quality of life, which is measured by the human development index (HDI). Kosack uses a data set for 56 countries; the data are divided into three 4-yr periods (1974–1977, 1978–1981, and 1982–1985). He uses a simple HDI growth model in which aid to GDP and the interaction of aid to GDP with a measure of democratization are included, along with a list of variables that are normally used in growth models. His results show that, while aid does not generally improve the quality of life, it does lead to higher HDI growth rates when the extent of democratization is higher. In autocratic countries it is ineffective, and possibly even harmful. Kosack suggests that to make aid more effective, donor and recipient countries should at the same time aim at stimulating democratization.

E. Aid and Institutional Quality

Burnside and Dollar have not remained silent after their paper was published in 2000 and criticized by many researchers in the field of the economics of aid. In one paper (Burnside and Dollar, 2004b), they directly respond to the criticism brought forward by Easterly et al. (2004). In another paper, they contend that institutional quality is decisive in determining the effectiveness of aid (Burnside and Dollar, 2004a). In support of their view, Burnside and Dollar point out that most economists firmly believe that differences in institutions are the main determinants of differences in income levels between countries. In comparison with Burnside and Dollar (2000), in this paper they shift focus from government policies to institutions and investigate whether institutions enhance the effectiveness of aid.

They investigate this issue for 124 countries with a new data set by using a single cross-section for the 1990s. Their measure of institutional quality is based on a data set constructed by Kaufman et al. (1999). This data set contains an overall measure of institutional quality, summarizing various aspects of institutions and policies in one measure. In particular, this measure consists of four broad categories of variables measuring the institutional environment: government effectiveness, regulatory quality, rule of law, and control of corruption.[9]

Burnside and Dollar estimate a growth model similar to the specification they used in their previous paper, including an interactive term of aid and institutional quality, next to aid and the institutional quality measure separately. Using an instrumental variable estimation technique, Burnside and Dollar find strong evidence that institutional quality determines the effectiveness of aid. While aid in itself is not significantly related to growth, the interactive term is, indicating that institutions matter for aid effectiveness.

V. Concluding Remarks

The *Assessing Aid* report has stimulated the debate on aid effectiveness. This in itself is a major contribution of the report. On the one hand, it has stimulated a reevaluation of aid policies by donor countries, leading them to reconsider the use and distribution of aid among recipient countries. As was discussed earlier, this is understandable, as the message of the report appears to be simple. It provides clear guidelines for policymakers who have to make difficult decisions regarding disbursing scarce aid resources to a large number of recipient countries. The simple message of the report is that aid donations should become more selective, because it only leads to higher economic growth when the policy environment in the recipient country is good. Therefore, only countries with good policies should qualify for receiving development aid.

On the other hand, however, the analysis of aid effectiveness in the report has received major criticism, especially from academic circles. One of the main criticisms focuses on the econometric specification of the aid effectiveness analysis. This chapter has reviewed this criticism. It has been shown that many papers have repeated the econometric work of the background paper by Burnside and Dollar (2000), which contains the empirical support for the aid selectivity claim in the *Assessing Aid* report. Nearly all studies that redo the analysis in the Burnside–Dollar paper are unable to produce the same outcomes. Several papers explicitly show that the Burnside–Dollar results are dependent on the selection of the countries in the sample and the specification of the growth model. Therefore, we conclude that, based on the work of these critics, claims on the importance of the policy environment for the effectiveness of aid are in fact rather fragile.

Moreover, the manner in which Burnside and Dollar measured good policies has also received a lot of criticism. This adds to the scepticism we feel regarding the policy message of the *Assessing Aid* report. Therefore, we feel donor countries should be very careful in reevaluating their policies and turn them into a direction of aid selectivity based on good economic policies of recipient countries as measured by Burnside–Dollar. The evidence that good policies are decisive in making aid work is simply too weak.

Research has also shown that there may be other factors that influence the effectiveness of aid. We have reviewed papers that stress the importance of decreasing returns of aid and aid uncertainty, and the role of external and climatic conditions and political instability in influencing the effectiveness of aid. Although these studies provide interesting new insights into the understanding of how aid may have an impact on growth, we feel it is still too early to state that the debate on the aid–growth nexus is finalized. Also, these alternative views need further scrutiny before donor countries can confidently build their aid policies on them.

To conclude, the aid–growth debate is still continuing. The *Assessing Aid* report forwarded an interesting, yet weakly found hypothesis about how aid works in stimulating growth. The report's view on the importance of good economic policies is not the whole story. Other factors such as aid uncertainty, external and climatic conditions, political instability, institutional quality, and the absorptive capacity of recipient countries are probably more important. While initially the donor community may have thought that the *Assessing Aid* report provided something of a definitive answer to explain the aid–growth nexus, research since the publication of the report has increasingly questioned its claims. It seems that this leaves us where we were in 1998 before the World Bank report was published. Does aid work? Probably it does, but it is still unclear under which conditions this statement is true.

Notes

1. See White (1992) and Hansen and Tarp (2000) for extensive reviews of the aid–growth literature.
2. This section is partially based on Hermes and Lensink (2001).
3. This specification is borrowed from Feeny (2003: 26).
4. The specification of the equation of the policy index is as follows (Burnside and Dollar, 2000: 855): Policy $= 1.28 + 6.85 \times$ Budget surplus $- 1.40 \times$ Inflation $+ 2.16 \times$ Openness.
5. Feeny (2003: 28) states that currently most aid donors have embraced aid selectivity.
6. The discussion of the policy index is partly based on Lensink and White (2000).
7. See Table 9.1 for an overview of the results of studies analyzing the aid–growth relationship.
8. The analysis is based on a 2SLS specification to endogenize the policy and external environment variable.
9. For further details on the contents and construction of the data set, see the following World Bank Web site: http://worldbank.org/wbi/governance.

References

Acemoglu, D., Johnson, S., and Robinson, J.A., The colonial origins of comparative development: an empirical investigation, *Am. Econ. Rev.*, 91 (5), 1369–1401, 2001.

Berthelemy, J.C. and Dessus, S., Why doesn't human capital always contribute to growth? 2000. http://papers.ssrn.com/sol3/papers.cfm?abstract_id = 204828#PaperDownload.

Berthelemy, J.C. and Varoudakis, A., Financial development, policy and economic growth, in *Financial Development and Economic Growth: Theory and Experiences from Developing Countries*, Hermes, N. and Lensink, R., Eds., Routledge, London, 1996, pp. 66–93.

Bloom, D. and Sachs, J.D., Geography, demography and economic growth in Africa, *Brookings Pap. Econ. Activity*, 2, 207–273, 1998.

Boone, P., Politics and the effectiveness of aid, *Eur. Econ. Rev.*, 40 (2), 289–329, 1996.

Bulíř, A. and Hamann, J., Aid volatility: an empirical assessment, *IMF Staff Pap.*, 50 (1), 64–89, 2003.

Burnside, C. and Dollar, D., Aid, policies, and growth, World Bank Policy Research Working Paper 1777, The World Bank, Washington, DC, 1997.

Burnside, C. and Dollar, D., Aid, policies and growth, *Am. Econ. Rev.*, 90 (4), 847–868, 2000.

Burnside, C. and Dollar, D., Aid, policies and growth: revisiting the evidence, World Bank Policy Research Working Paper 3251, The World Bank, Washington, DC, 2004a.

Burnside, C. and Dollar, D., A reply to "New data, new doubts: a comment on Burnside and Dollar's 'Aid, policies and growth (2000)'", *Am. Econ. Rev.*, 94 (3), 781–784, 2004b.

Chauvet, L. and Guilleaumont, P., Aid and growth revisited: policy, economic vulnerability and political instability, in paper presented at the Annual Bank Conference of Development Economics, Oslo, 2002.

Collier, P. and Dehn, J., Aid, shocks and growth, Policy Research Working Paper 2688, The World Bank, Washington, DC, 2001.

Collier, P. and Dollar, D., Aid allocation and poverty reduction, *Eur. Econ. Rev.*, 46 (8), 1475–1500, 2002.

Cook, P. and Uchida, Y., Privatisation and economic growth in developing countries, Centre on Regulation and Competition Working Paper Series 7, University of Manchester, Manchester, 2001.

Dalgaard, C.J. and Hansen, H., On aid, growth and good policies, *J. Dev. Stud.*, 37 (6), 17–41, 2001.

Dalgaard, C.J., Hansen, H., and Tarp, F., On the empirics of foreign aid and growth, *Econ. J.*, 114 (496), F191–F216, 2004.

De Haan, J. and Siermann, C.L.J., New evidence on the relationship between democracy and economic growth, *Public Choice*, 86, 175–198, 1996.

Durbarry, R., Gemmell, N., and Greenaway, D., New evidence on the impact of foreign aid on economic growth, CREDIT Research Paper 98/9, University of Nottingham, Nottingham, 1998.

Easterly, W., Levine, R., and Roodman, D., New data, new doubts: a comment on Burnside and Dollar's "Aid, policies and growth (2000)", *Am. Econ. Rev.*, 94 (3), 774–780, 2004.

Feeny, S., Foreign aid to Papua New Guinea: causes and consequences, Ph.D. dissertation, RMIT University, Melbourne, 2003.

Fry, M.J., *Money, Interest and Banking in Economic Development*, 2nd ed., Johns Hopkins University Press, Baltimore, 1995.

Gallup, J.L., Sachs, J.D., and Mellinger, A., Geography and economic development, in *Annual World Bank Conference on Development Economics 1998 Proceedings*, Pleskovic, B. and Stiglitz, J.E., Eds., The World Bank, Washington, DC, 1999, pp. 127–178.

Gemmell, N., Fiscal policy in a growth framework, in *Fiscal Policy for Development: Poverty, Reconstruction and Growth*, Addison, T. and Roe, A., Eds., Palgrave/McMillan, Basingstoke, 2004, pp. 149–176.

Gomanee, K., Girma, S., and Morrissey, O., Searching for aid threshold effects: aid, growth and the welfare of the poor, in paper presented at a Seminar at the Centre for the Study of African Economies, Oxford, January 28, 2003.

Guilleaumont, P. and Chauvet, L., Aid and performance: a reassessment, *J. Dev. Stud.*, 37 (6), 66–87, 2001.

Hansen, H. and Tarp, F., Aid effectiveness disputed, *J. Int. Dev.*, 12 (3), 375–398, 2000.

Hansen, H. and Tarp, F., Aid and growth regressions, *J. Dev. Econ.*, 64 (2), 547–570, 2001.

Hermes, N. and Lensink, R., Changing the conditions for development aid: a new paradigm? *J. Dev. Stud.*, 37 (6), 1–16, 2001.

Hermes, N. and Lensink, R., Fiscal policy and private investment in less developed countries, in *Fiscal Policy for Development: Poverty, Reconstruction and Growth*, Addison, T. and Roe, A., Eds., Palgrave/McMillan, Basingstoke, 2004, pp. 177–198.

Hudson, J. and Mosley, P., Aid, policies and growth: in search of the holy grail? *J. Int. Dev.*, 13 (7), 1023–1038, 2001.

Islam, N., Regime changes, economic policies and the effects of aid on growth, in paper presented at the Conference "Exchange Rates, Economic Integration and the International Economy", Ryerson University, Canada, May 17–19, 2002.

Jensen, P.S. and Paldam, M., Can the new aid–growth models be replicated? Working Paper 2003-17, Institute for Economics, Aarhus, 2003.

Kaufman, D., Kraay, D., and Zoido-Lobaton, P., Aggregating governance indicators, World Bank Policy Research Working Paper 2195, The World Bank, Washington, DC, 1999.

Kosack, S., Effective aid: how democracy allows development aid to improve the quality of life, *World Dev.*, 31 (1), 1–22, 2003.

Lensink, R. and Morrissey, O., Aid instability as a measure of uncertainty and the positive impact of aid on growth, *J. Dev. Stud.*, 36 (3), 31–49, 2000.

Lensink, R. and White, H., *Assessing Aid*: A manifesto for aid in the 21st century? *Oxford Dev. Stud.*, 28 (1), 5–17, 2000.

Lensink, R. and White, H., Are there negative returns to aid? *J. Dev. Stud.*, 37 (6), 42–65, 2001.

Levine, R. and Renelt, D., A sensitivity analysis of cross-country growth regressions, *Am. Econ. Rev.*, 82 (4), 942–963, 1992.

Lu, S. and Ram, R., Foreign aid, government policies and economic growth: further evidence from cross-country panel data for 1970 to 1993, *Econ. Int.*, 54 (1), 14–29, 2001.

Marshall, M.G. and Jaggers, K., Polity IV Project: Political Regime Characteristics and Transitions, 1800–1999, Integrated Network for Societal Conflict Research (INSCR), Center for International Development and Conflict Management (CIDCM), University of Maryland, 2000.

Mosley, P., *Overseas Development Aid: Its Defence and Reform*, Wheatsheaf, Brighton, 1987.

Pritchett, L., Measuring outward orientation in LDCs: can it be done? *J. Dev. Econ.*, 49 (2), 307–335, 1996.

Sachs, J.D. and Warner, A., Economic reform and the process of global integration, *Brookings Pap. Econ. Activity*, 1, 1–18, 1995.

Sala-i-Martin, X., I just ran two million regressions, *Am. Econ. Rev.*, 87 (2), 178–183, 1997.

White, H., The macroeconomic impact of development aid: a critical survey, *J. Dev. Stud.*, 28 (2), 163–240, 1992.

World Bank, *Assessing Aid: What Works, What Doesn't, and Why*, The World Bank, Washington, DC, 1998.

Chapter 10

Governance for Sustainable Development in Southeast Asia: Means, Concerns, and Dilemmas

M. Shamsul Haque

CONTENTS

I. Introduction

Nowadays, there is an increasing proliferation of policies, institutions, debates, and publications related to the so-called "sustainable development" with the field of state-centric development studies or development economics being under challenge in an anti-state global atmosphere. Owing to its integral linkage with the environment, the idea of sustainable development has gained, to a great extent, worldwide recognition with the growing concern for natural disasters, nonrenewable resources, ecological dangers, and unpredictable environmental catastrophes (Brown et al., 1990; Hempel, 1996; Haque, 1999). In fact, the principle of sustainable development has gradually become so widely accepted, legitimized, and entrenched that its conceptual controversies and theoretical debates seem to have become less significant than the concerns for its actualization or implementation through appropriate modes of governance at the international, national, and local levels. Due to the borderless nature of environmental sustainability, almost all nations are required to adopt appropriate policies, programs, and institutions in compliance with various international agreements, conventions, and protocols. There is a growing emphasis on pursuing a mode of governance that is conducive to sustainable development. In examining this issue, it is necessary to illustrate the connotations of sustainable development and governance, and explain the nature of relationship between them.

Sustainable development is defined as "development that meets the needs of the present generation without compromising the ability of future generation to meet their own needs" (WCED, 1987: 8). Apart from this, the existing literature interprets sustainable development as follows: as economic development that is conducive to environment and society; as improvement in present living standards without constraining future living conditions; as optimization of current socioeconomic benefits without jeopardizing similar benefits in the future; and as development that emphasizes inter-generational and inter-group equity (Barrow, 1995; Noman, 1996; Haque, 1999). However, various environmental or ecological concerns including rapid resource depletion, excessive waste accumulation, and fast decline in biological diversity remain central to the sustainability debate (Dovers, 1989: 33). According to the *Rio Declaration on Environment and Development* emerging from the Earth Summit (1992), "In order to achieve sustainable development, environmental protection shall constitute an integral part of the development process and cannot be considered in isolation from it" (Lebel and Steffen, 1998: 99).

Governance is the exercise of a nation's political, economic, and administrative powers or authorities at various levels, and it covers the institutional and procedural mechanisms for citizens to realize their interests and rights, carry out their obligations, and negotiate their mutual differences (UNDP, 1997). When such governance is based on major features such as participation, accountability, transparency, equity, rule of law, and partnership, it can be portrayed as "good governance," which is considered essential for environmental protection and sustainable development (UNDP, 1997). In fact, these major features are emphasized in Chapter 10 ("Institutional Frameworks for Sustainable Development") of *Plan of Implementation*, which is a multilaterally agreed document emerging from the World Summit on Sustainable Development, held at Johannesburg, 2002 (Gardiner, 2002).

It should be mentioned, however, that governance for sustainable development affects diverse stakeholders, involves multiple actors, and operates at all levels. As Carley and Christie (2000: 12) mentioned, "Sustaining the common resources for the benefit of present and future generations will depend very much on how governments, in partnership with all sectors of civil society, organize, coordinate and implement policy at all levels of action: the international, national, ecosystem, and town and village levels." The state still plays a crucial role in creating an "enabling environment for sustainable human development" between the stakeholders and actors of governance. However, recently there has been greater recognition of the role played by nonstate actors, especially private firms, nonprofit institutions, and community-based grassroots organizations, in this endeavor (UNDP, 1997).

Keeping this in mind, the recent two decades have witnessed a mushroom growth of international institutions, regional associations, national agencies, and local organizations created for making policies, implementing programs, and enforcing conventions related to environmental sustainability. It was concluded by the World Summit on Sustainable Development (2002) that despite all the measures adopted for sustainability, there was no significant progress in environmental conditions, instead there was continuing loss of biodiversity, depletion of fish stocks, desertification of land, pollution of air and water, and greater frequency of severe natural disasters (WSSD, 2002). This inconsistency between the mission of new governance for sustainable development, on one hand, and the worsening indicators of environmental sustainability, on the other hand, implies the need for more critical studies on the issue.

On the basis of this context, this chapter attempts to examine the systems of governance for sustainable development in Southeast Asia. The region is important to explore the issue for various reasons. First, the region has global ecological significance, because its humid tropics may have considerable impact on land-use changes, climate variations, biogeochemical cycles, and nutrient and water cycles with worldwide consequences (Lebel and Steffen, 1998). It is estimated that about two thirds of the world's tropical rain forests are in Southeast Asia (Lim and Valencia, 1990). Second, most countries in the region have adopted considerable local, national, and regional measures of governance for environmental sustainability (Dupar and Badenoch, 2002), but continue to suffer certain severe forms of environmental disorders. According to one estimate, the cost of environmental remedies in Southeast Asia may amount to nearly 5% of its gross domestic product or GDP (UNESCAP, 2003: 21).

Third, the region is internationally known for its economic success based on the economic growth principle, export-led production, intensive industrialization, and rapid urbanization. In terms of its adverse implications for long-term sustainability (Angel, 1998: 2) such a successful model itself requires critical study. Finally, the credibility of the region's economic success is under challenge due to its recent financial crisis, and this crisis has implications for worsening unemployment, increasing people's dependence on environmental resources, and thus undermining sustainable development (Cylke, 1998: 3–5). The chapter begins with an overview of the system of governance for sustainable development in Southeast Asia. It then explains how the relative failure of such governance continues to be evident in the region's experience with various environmental predicaments, and how this lack of success in environmental governance may have been caused by other dimensions of governance, including the region's excessive concern for economic growth, urban and industrial expansion, lifestyle based on consumerism, and so on. It concludes by suggesting some policy alternatives with a view to achieve a more effective mode of governance for sustainable development.

II. Levels and Measures of Governance for Sustainable Development in Southeast Asia

Southeast Asia consists of countries such as Brunei, Cambodia, Indonesia, Laos, Malaysia, Myanmar, the Philippines, Singapore, Thailand and Vietnam, which are extremely diverse in terms of territorial size, demographic composition, economic development, political system, and cultural and religious identity (Soegiarto, 1994). However, they share some common interests and face similar challenges with regard to environmental sustainability. In terms of governance for sustainability, although each country in the region has its own national and local sets of policies, rules, and institutions, they often exchange experiences, share information, and pursue collective initiatives at the regional and international levels. In discussing the major means and dimensions of governance for sustainability in Southeast Asia, it is crucial to adopt a multi-level approach involving various initiatives undertaken at the international, regional, national, and local levels (see Carley and Christie, 2000: 18).

First, at the international level, there have emerged various conventions, protocols, and agreements related to environmental sustainability, which are to be followed by most countries, including those in Southeast Asia. The examples of such international measures include the Vienna Convention for the Protection of the Ozone Layer (1985), the Montreal Protocol on Substances that Deplete the Ozone Layer (1987), the Agenda 21 (1992), the UN Framework Convention on Climate Change (1992), the Convention on Biological Diversity (1992), the Convention to Combat Desertification (1994), the UN Framework Convention on Climate Change or the Kyoto Protocol (1997), and so on. In enforcing these measures, there are well-established international bodies such as the United Nations Environment Programme, the United Nations Commission on Sustainable Development, the Climate Change Secretariat, the Secretariat of the Convention on Biological Diversity, and the Secretariat of the Convention to Combat Desertification. Among the ten countries in Southeast Asia, the Convention on the Law of the Sea has been signed or ratified by all, the Convention for the Protection of the Ozone Layer has been signed or ratified by all except Cambodia, and the Convention on Climate Change and the Convention on Biological Diversity signed or ratified by all except Brunei (Earth Council, 1997; Task Force, 2001). In addition, the Agenda 21 has been followed in cases like the Philippines, Indonesia, and Thailand (Earth Council, 1997); and some national biodiversity action plans and strategies have been formulated and adopted by Indonesia, Malaysia, the Philippines, Singapore, Thailand, and Vietnam (UNESCAP, 2000b).

On the other hand, there are many international sources providing financial and technical assistance to Southeast Asian countries in order to enable these countries to develop environmental management and practice a sustainable mode of development. For instance, the U.S. Agency for International Development has assisted the Clean Industrial Production Program in Indonesia; the Industrial Environmental Management Project and the Environment and Natural Resources Accounting Project in the Philippines; and various projects related to biodiversity, coastal resource management, toxic waste, and air pollution in Thailand (US-AEP, 1997d). The United States-Asia Environmental Partnership (US-AEP) has provided financial support to environmental exchanges, clean technologies, and training programs in cases like Indonesia, Singapore, Thailand, and the Philippines (US-AEP, 1997a–c). Similar environment-related assistance is also received by most Southeast Asian countries from the governments of developed nations (e.g., Australia, Canada, Japan, Germany, and the Netherlands) and donor agencies like the Japanese International Cooperation Agency, the German Agency for Technical Cooperation, the Danish International

Development Agency, and so on (US-AEP, 1997a,d). These are some examples of many such external sources of financial and technical supports that constitute a part of the international dimension of governance for sustainable development in the region.

Second, at the regional level, it is possible to identify some major initiatives and institutions introduced by Southeast Asian countries in pursuing developments based on environmental sustainability. The areas of inter-state cooperation in the region include sustainable forest management, freshwater resources, land and forest fires, transboundary haze pollution, coastal and marine environment, environment-friendly technology, environmental education, and so on (UNESCAP, 2003: 26). One major approach for pursuing discussion and collaboration in this regard is the regular use of ministerial conferences. The major outcomes of the 1995 Ministerial Conference on Environment and Development in Asia and the Pacific were "the Ministerial Declaration on Environmentally Sound and Sustainable Development in Asia and the Pacific and the Regional Action Programme for Environmentally Sound and Sustainable Development, 1996–2000" (UNESCAP, 2001: 1). The main objective of the 2000 Ministerial Conference on Environment and Development in Asia and the Pacific, on the other hand, was to review the findings about the trends of environment and development in the Asia-Pacific region emerging after the Regional Action Programme (1996–2000), and to develop the new "Regional Action Programme for Environmentally Sound and Sustainable Development, 2001–2005" (UNESCAP, 2001: 1).

The Association of Southeast Asian Nations (ASEAN) is one of the most active entity to foster regional cooperation for the environment and sustainable development (Task Force, 2001). In this regard, there are institutional means such as the ASEAN Committee on Science and Technology (especially its Sub-Committee in Marine Science), the ASEAN Senior Officials on Environment (ASOEN), and the ASEAN Fisheries Forum (Soegiarto, 1994). Under the ASOEN, there are three working groups dealing with three major dimensions of environmental sustainability — including Working Groups on Nature Conservation and Biodiversity, Coastal and Marine Environment, and Multilateral Environmental Agreement — as well as the Haze Technical Task Force (UNESCAP, 2003: 27). Among the more recent ASEAN initiatives are the Cooperation Plan on Transboundary Pollution (1995) and the Action Plan on the Haze (1997), which prescribe greater cooperation among Southeast Asian countries for the prevention, firefighting, and monitoring (Tay, 1998). In response to severe haze pollution in 1997, the ASEAN introduced the Hanoi Plan of Action (1999–2004), which reinforced the commitment of its member states to implement the above Cooperation Plan on Transboundary Pollution and the Action Plan on the Haze (UNESCAP, 2001: 5). Moreover, the ASEAN Regional

Centre for Biodiversity Conservation attempts to generate awareness and develop networks related to biodiversity conservation in the region (UNESCAP, 2000b). One of the main objective of the recently launched ASEAN Vision 2020 is to achieve "a clean and green ASEAN with fully established mechanisms for sustainable development to ensure the protection of the region's environment, the sustainability of its natural resources, and the high quality of life of its peoples" (Task Force, 2001: 224).

Another source of regional cooperation for environmental sustainability is the Asia-Pacific Economic Cooperation (APEC), which is basically an economic bloc, but has two Working Groups (out of ten) dealing with the Conservation of Marine Resources as well as Fisheries (Soegiarto, 1994). As most Southeast Asian countries (except Myanmar, Laos, and Cambodia) are APEC members, they are partners in its "Action Plan for Sustainability of the Marine Environment" (which aims to prevent and control marine pollution) and "Cleaner Production Strategy" (which promotes more environment-friendly policies and technologies) (Lebel and Steffen, 1998). Another regional institution is the Mekong River Commission (comprised of Cambodia, Laos, Thailand, and Vietnam), which plays a role in water allocation and flood control, and deals with environmental issues associated with water management (Badenoch, 2002: 8). Some other organizations associated with the regional-level governance for environment and sustainable development include the Southeast Asian Fisheries Development Center which is involved in research and training in fisheries; the Acid Deposition Monitoring Network in East Asia which helps monitor the acidification of the environment caused by sulfur dioxide emissions in East and Southeast Asia; and the network for the transfer of environmentally sound technologies which facilitates sharing of information (about the environmental impacts of certain technologies) among Asian nations, including Southeast Asian countries such as Indonesia, Malaysia, the Philippines, Thailand, and Vietnam (Soegiarto, 1994; UNESCAP, 2000a,b).

Third, at the national level, governments in Southeast Asia have adopted various policies and established institutions to manage growing environmental problems and achieve development based on sustainability. In Brunei, the environment or sustainable development has gained increasing significance in its National Development Plans. For instance, the Fifth National Development Plan (1986–1990) set certain environmental objectives like forest conservation, biodiversity, and wasteland protection; the Sixth National Development Plan (1991–1995) adopted the principle of sustainable development as a part of overall national development; and Seventh National Development Plan (1996–2000) stressed the sustainable use of natural resources, reduction in population pressure on the environment, and balanced economic development in favor of environmental quality (Environment Unit, 2004). The state institutions to carry out these policies and programs include the Environment Unit (Ministry of Development) and the National Committee on Environment chaired by the Minister of Development.

Similarly, in the case of Malaysia, government adopted long-term Outline Perspective Plan (1991–2000) as well as few medium-term (5-yr) Malaysia Plans, which increasingly recognized the importance of environmental sustainability. For example, the Sixth Malaysia Plan (1991–1995) incorporated some principles of the Earth Summit's Agenda 21; and the Seventh Malaysia Plan (1996–2000) laid greater emphasis on sustainable development and environmental management, especially under the overall guidance of the country's National Policy on Environment (Government of Malaysia, 1997). Realizing the increasing environmental dangers, the Malaysian government made some amendments to the Environmental Quality Act adopted in 1974 (US-AEP, 1997b). The main organizations responsible for such environmental policies and programs are the Economic Planning Unit, Prime Minister's Department; Ministry of Science, Technology and Environment; and the National Development Council.

In Indonesia, the government developed the Forestry Action Plan in 1992, the National Biodiversity Action Plan in 1993, and the environment issues became a major component of the country's 25-yr National Development Plan (1991–2015) (Task Force, 2001). The government also adopted a series of programs and strategies in favor of environmental sustainability, including the Blue Sky Program, the Prokasih (Clean Rivers) Program, the Cleaner Production Program, Environmental Impact Assessment, the Clean City Award, and so on. The main institutions that are directly or indirectly involved in formulating, implementing, and assessing such environmental policies and programs in Indonesia include the Environmental Impact Management Agency (BAPEDAL) under the Ministry of Environment, Ministry of Industry and Trade, Ministry of Public Works, Agency for the Assessment and Application of Technology, and so on (US-AEP, 1997a). However, it is BAPEDAL that plays the most crucial role in environmental management in Indonesia.

In the case of the Philippines, the government has adopted the Philippine Agenda 21 with a view to achieve sustainable development by integrating it into socioeconomic planning, allowing participation of all stakeholders, and adopting a comprehensive system of evaluation and monitoring (GOP, 1997). In fact, the government introduced the Philippine Strategy for Sustainable Development quite early in 1989, and it became a major part in the country's overall National Environmental Action Plan ratified in 1990 (US-AEP, 1997b). In line with the Clean Air Act (1999) requiring industries to decrease emissions, the Clean Air 2000 Program was introduced by the government to reduce the worsening vehicular air pollution (US-AEP, 2002). The state institutions dealing with such environment-related provisions and programs in the Philippines include the Department of Environment and Natural Resources, the Environmental Management Bureau, the Pollution Adjudication Board, and so on.

In Singapore, the government launched the Singapore Green Plan (SGP), which is considered the "environmental master plan" indicating government achievements related to environment and mapping out government policies and programs for future environmental concerns and issues (Government of Singapore, 1997). The purpose is to transform Singapore into a "model green city." There are various laws in Singapore with regard to any form of pollution (air, water, noise, etc.), and there are heavy penalties for violating these environmental rules (US-AEP, 1997c). The institutional responsibilities for the environment lie with the Ministry of Environment, including environmental regulation, enforcement of emission standards, environmental monitoring, and public awareness campaigns.

In the case of Thailand, the environmental regulations are included even in its new constitution introduced in 1997, which is supposed to make such regulations more effective (UNESCAP, 2000b). The Thai government adopted the National Environmental Quality Act, the Hazardous Substances Act, and the Enhancement and Conservation of Environmental Quality Act in 1992 for enhancing environmental sustainability. It also introduced new plans and strategies for environmental management and sustainability, especially under its "Environmental Management Master Plan 1999–2006" (Bateman, 1999a). There are more specific environmental programs in Thailand, including Industry and Environment Program (for waste minimization, improvement in environmental quality, and clean technology), National Resources and Management Program (for exploring problems and policies related to natural resources management), and so on (Earth Council, 1997). The most important government organization dealing with all these environmental provisions, programs, and concerns is the Ministry of Science, Technology, and Environment under which there are more specialized units like the Office of Environment Policy and Planning, the Pollution Control Department, and the Environmental Quality Promotion Department (US-AEP, 1997d). In addition, there is an inter-ministerial body like the National Environmental Board headed by the Prime Minister, which approves environmental action plans and quality standards, recommends policy measures, and supervises environmental funds (US-AEP, 1997d).

Other Southeast Asian cases have also developed considerable policy initiatives and institutional mechanisms for environment and sustainable development. For example, Cambodia introduced the Environmental Action Plan, and was considering other plans such as the Regional Biodiversity Action Plan, National Wetlands Action Plan, and so on (Task Force, 2001). It also adopted the Law on Environment Protection and Natural Resources Management in 1996, which now defines the government's

obligation for ensuring environmental protection and sustainable development. The Ministry of Environment is the main institution in this regard. In
Vietnam, the government launched the National Plan on Environment and
Sustainable Development, introduced the Law on Environmental Protection,
and assigned the Ministry for Science, Technology and Environment with
responsibility for managing environmental protection (Task Force, 2001).

In addition to all the above-mentioned national plans, programs, laws,
and institutions, there are many strategic instruments and measurement
criteria adopted by various countries in Southeast Asia. These include
the pollution charges in the Philippines, environmental quality standards
in Vietnam, environmental impact assessment in Indonesia and the
Philippines, means for regulating mining wastes in Laos and Malaysia, and
cleaner production centers in Indonesia and Thailand (UNESCAP, 2000b).
However, there is a growing trend towards the use of market-based instruments (MBIs) in terms of imposing charges for wastewater, emission
charges, and differential pricing systems, and these MBIs have already
been tested in some Southeast Asian countries like Indonesia, Malaysia,
the Philippines, Singapore, and Thailand (ADB, 2001: 6).

Finally, at the local level, there is an increasing preference for non-
government organizations (NGOs), grassroots institutions, and decentralized local governments in the overall governance for sustainable
development (UNDP, 1997). Based on an assumption that such governance
requires greater organizational flexibility, people's participation, and community involvement, there emerged many NGOs dealing with issues
related to environmental sustainability (Zarsky, 1999). Among Southeast
Asian countries, in Indonesia, there are nearly 270 NGOs dealing with
environmental matters — including the Indonesian Forum for the Environment (working as an umbrella organization for many environmental
NGOs), Indonesian Legal Aid Foundation (representing human rights
and environmental lawyers), Indonesian Center for Environmental Law
(providing policy inputs to the government and legal assistance to various
advocacy groups), and Friends of the Environment Fund (providing fund
for the recycling purpose and addressing industry-related environmental
concern) (US-AEP, 1997a).

In Malaysia, there are NGOs like the World Wide Fund for Nature
(Malaysia), the Malaysian Nature Society, and Environmental Protection
Society of Malaysia, which are often engaged in dialogues with the government regarding environmental concerns (Task Force, 2001). Other environmental NGOs in Malaysia include Sahabat Alam Malaysia, Friends of the
Earth-Malaysia, and the Consumers' Association of Penang. In the Philippines, some of the major environmental NGOs are the Philippine Businesses
for the Environment (facilitating public–private partnerships for managing
environmental issues), the Water Environmental Association of the

Philippines (providing an avenue for networking by environmental professionals), and so on (US-AEP, 1997b). Among the Singaporean environmental NGOs, most well-known cases are the Nature Society (focusing on natural conservation and impact assessment), the Singapore Council for the Environment (fostering environmental awareness and organizing various workshops and seminars on environment), Singapore Association of Environmental Companies (dealing with technology transfer and environmental business), and so on (US-AEP, 1997c; Tay, 1998). Similar examples of environmental NGOs can be found in Thailand where NGOs have increasingly greater role in environmental management. In recent years, such NGOs have also emerged in Cambodia and Vietnam, and these NGOs are largely involved in environmental matters and natural resources management (Pednekar, 1995).

III. Growing Threats to Sustainability Despite Its Multifaceted Governance

It is evident from the previous description that almost all countries in Southeast Asia have a significant proliferation of policy-, program-, law-, and institution-related environmental issues and concerns, which represent a considerable expansion of governance for sustainable development at the international, regional, national, and local levels. However, the effectiveness of such multilayered governance is questionable, because according to existing studies, the region continues to face some serious forms of sustainability challenges, including atmospheric pollution, land degradation, pollution of marine ecosystems, deforestation, decline in biodiversity, hazardous wastes, and so on (Lebel and Steffen, 1998; UNESCAP, 2003). To comprehend this relative failure of governance, this section examines some of these major challenges to environmental sustainability in Southeast Asia.

First, in terms of air pollution, the condition in Asia as a whole is worse than many other regions. It has been observed that during 1991–1995, the average levels of air particulates in Asia were five times higher than that of the OECD countries and two times higher than that of the world average (Angel et al., 1999). In Southeast Asia, the emissions of CO_2 (the most critical greenhouse gas) have grown fast due to increasing use of energy—between 1980 and 1995, the volume of CO_2 emissions increased from 25,825,000 to 80,821,000 metric tons in Indonesia, from 7,838,000 to 28,095,000 metric tons in Malaysia, and from 10,921,000 to 47,773,000 metric tons in Thailand (Lebel and Steffen, 1998). It is observed that the industrial sector accounts for 15% of emissions of suspended particulates, 63% of sulfur oxide, and 16% of nitrous oxide in Indonesia (Jakarta); and 56% of suspended particulates and 22% of sulfur dioxide in Thailand

(Sachasinh et al., 1992; World Bank, 1994). Due to rapid industrialization, between 1975 and 1988, the pollution caused by the emissions of sulfur oxide, nitrous oxide, and suspended particulates increased five times (US-AEP, 1997a).

The transboundary nature of the region's air pollution can be seen from the fact that in the case of Vietnam, about 39% of the total annual sulfur deposition in the air comes from China and 19% from Thailand; and in the case of Malaysia about 30% of such sulfur deposition comes from Singapore (Lebel and Steffen, 1998). However, one of the most widely known examples is transboundary haze in Southeast Asia caused by slash-and-burn agriculture, large-scale clearing of forests for plantations, and so on (especially in Sumatra and Kalimantan, Indonesia), which eventually led to the formation of the ASEAN Cooperation Plan on Transboundary Pollution (Lebel and Steffen, 1998). The adverse impacts of such fire and haze, especially on human health and tourism industry, were most severely felt in Malaysia, Thailand, and Singapore (Lebel and Steffen, 1998; Murdiyarso, 1998).

There are also serious problems of water and marine pollution in some Southeast Asian countries. It is estimated that in the region, in 1999, diarrheal diseases killed more than one million people, and most of these cases were caused by contaminated water and poor sanitation (ADB, 2001). On the other hand, oil and cargo shipping and offshore oil and gas production in Southeast Asia are responsible for oil slicks and tar residues affecting the Straits of Malacca and Johor and the South China Sea (Lebel and Steffen, 1998). In most countries in the region except Singapore, the declining water quality in major rivers is caused by resource-based industries like food and beverages, rubber, textiles, and palm oil (Lebel and Steffen, 1998). In the case of Indonesia, industrial water pollution accounts for 25–50% pollution of some rivers in Java (US-AEP, 1997a).

Second, there are serious problems of land degradation in Southeast Asia (especially Thailand) caused by deforestation, soil erosion, salinization, soil acidification, and waterlogging (ADB, 2001). Salinization of soil caused by excessive use of groundwater is quite serious in some areas in Indonesia, the Philippines, and Thailand; and land desertification caused by deforestation remains a critical concern in agricultural countries like Cambodia, Indonesia, Laos, Malaysia and Vietnam (ADB, 2001). The process of soil erosion and degradation is considered an environmental problem by governments in some Southeast Asian countries (UNDP, 1997; ADB, 2001). According to Lebel and Steffen (1998), as long as Southeast Asian countries continue to expand and intensify cultivation to increase the production of food, fiber, and energy, it will be difficult to reduce environmental costs such as land or soil degradation.

Land scarcity resulting from land degradation is becoming even worse in Southeast Asia due to the growing need for using land to dump hazardous waste. In the case of Thailand, according to the US-AEP (1997d), the number of industries generating hazardous waste increased from only 631 in 1969 to 51,500 in 1990, and between 1979 and 1989, the number of hazardous waste generators doubled. In Indonesia, it is estimated that about 2.2 million tons of hazardous wastes per year are being generated in West Java and metropolitan Jakarta (US-AEP, 1997a). Such a colossal amount of wastes creates additional pressure on land.

Third, in Southeast Asia, the rapid depletion of nonrenewable resources like fuel oil and ecological resources like mangroves poses a considerable challenge to sustainability. Since the 1980s, oil has been the primary source (over 70%) of energy in ASEAN countries (Lebel and Steffen, 1998). In the region, most electricity is generated from fuel oil, and there is increasing demand for such energy due to expansive industrialization and urbanization.

Among ecological resources, most Southeast Asian countries lost about 50% of their mangroves between 1980 and 1994 in the process of expanding urban settlements, developing agriculture, harmful fishing practices, and building shrimp ponds (Lebel and Steffen, 1998; ADB, 2001). Since 1980, the percentage of mangroves lost has been 17% in Brunei, 32% in Malaysia, 48% in Thailand, 62% in Vietnam, 45% in Indonesia, and 76% in Singapore, (Lebel and Steffen, 1998). According to von Post and Ahman (1997), the overexploitation of fisheries and the expansion of shrimp aquaculture have adverse impacts on mangroves in ASEAN countries. Another ecological resource under serious threat in Southeast Asia is the region's coral reefs. According to some estimates, Southeast Asia holds one third of the world's coral reefs of which more than 80% are at risk due to overfishing, sedimentation, coastal development, and so on (Lebel and Steffen, 1998).

Finally, another major form of challenge to sustainable development in Southeast Asia is the process of deforestation and biodiversity loss in the region. In the whole Asia-Pacific region, the annual rate of deforestation increased from 2 million hectares during 1976–1981 to 3.9 million hectares in 1981–1990 (UNESCAP, 2000a). Some of the Southeast Asian countries had the fastest rates of deforestation during 1981–1990 — about 1.0% in Indonesia, 1.8% in Malaysia, 2.9% in Philippines, 2.9% in Thailand, and 1.4% in Vietnam (Lebel and Steffen, 1998). Such a rapid rate of deforestation began in the 1950s — for example, between 1952 and 1977, the Philippines lost 61% of its forest reserves with rapid destruction of their trees. Between 1966 and 1971, the rate of deforestation accelerated in Indonesia as its timber exports increased by 1500% (Lim and Valencia, 1990). The main causes of deforestation in the region are commercial logging and land-clearing for commercial agriculture and plantation crops (ADB, 2001).

This process of deforestation — together with factors such as pollution, hazardous wastes, and habitat modification — is also responsible for losses in biodiversity in Southeast Asia. According to ADB (2001), in the region, most severe biodiversity losses have been experienced by Vietnam and the Philippines. On the other hand, the conversion of natural habitats, which threatens biodiversity by endangering various animal and plant specifies, has been quite significant in Thailand, Indonesia (Java), and the Philippines (UNESCAP, 2001: 16). It has been pointed out that the loss of biodiversity — caused by damages done to forests, watershed areas, and wildlife habitat — has continued in Southeast Asia even after the adoption of the Convention on Biological Diversity, the Convention on International Trade in Endangered Species of Wild Fauna and Flora, and the ASEAN Agreement in this regard (UNESCAP, 2001: 16).

IV. Inherent Dilemmas in Governance for Sustainable Development in Southeast Asia

It is clear from the previous analysis that in Southeast Asia, despite the unprecedented expansion of governance for environmental sustainability, the region has not been able to make much progress in terms of overcoming environmental predicaments (e.g., air and water pollution, land degradation, deforestation, resource depletion, and biodiversity loss), which represents a major challenge to sustainable development in the region. The contention of this chapter is that in Southeast Asia, the expansion of environmental governance has not often been complementary or consistent with the region's economic governance dominated by the mission of economic growth, industrial and urban expansion, utilitarian consumerism, and market-driven policy agenda. This section attempts to explain how this anti-environmental mode of economic development may worsen environmental problems and jeopardize governance for sustainable development in Southeast Asia.

First, almost all Southeast Asian countries (except latecomers like Myanmar, Vietnam, and Cambodia) have single-mindedly pursued the mission or ideology of "economic growth" through rapid and intensive industrialization process. But some scholars mention that market-led economic growth is "ecologically expansionist" and the "root cause" of ecological crisis; that unsustainable development is the direct result of growth; and that the unsustainable nature of growth has made it urgent to initiate sustainable development (Redclift, 1987; Stokke, 1991; Wee, 1995). In developed countries, in the past, the growth-led and profit-driven industrialization created havoc on the environment in terms of intensive exploitation of natural resources (e.g., croplands, forests, minerals, water resources) (Haque, 1999). During the recent decades, the newly industrialized countries

(NICs) in Southeast Asia have followed similar route to economic growth often at the expense of environmental degradation (Rock, 1998; UNESCAP, 2000a). It has been pointed out that the principle of "grow now and clean up later" has led to energy-intensive production, natural resource depletion, unhealthy air, and polluted rivers (Angel et al., 1999).

In Southeast Asia, following the first-tier NICs (Singapore, Malaysia), the second-tier NICs (Indonesia, Malaysia, the Philippines, Thailand) and latecomers (Myanmar, Vietnam, Cambodia, Laos) have expanded their efforts to accelerate growth through rapid industrial and urban expansion, which have intensified energy consumption and environmental degradation (Angel et al., 1999). Even in the agriculture sector, there have emerged large-scale agribusinesses in the name of higher growth, in Indonesia, Malaysia, and Thailand where native forests and smallholder agricultural areas have been converted into large-scale plantations (Lebel and Steffen, 1998). There is no doubt that some of these Southeast Asian countries have performed "economic miracle" by achieving an average growth rate of 7–8% (Esty and Pangestu, 1999). But these impressive figures of economic growth do not often reflect the environmental costs of such growth. It has been calculated that the toxic intensity of GDP growth increased during 1976–1984: about 5.4 times in Indonesia, 3.05 times in Malaysia, and 2.48 times in Thailand (Angel et al., 1999). According to Pednekar (1995), since the late-1980s, the rapid economic growth in Southeast Asia has coincided with increasing degradation of natural resources. It is largely due to this environmental cost of economic miracle in Southeast Asia that some observers consider this model flawed and unsustainable (Cylke, 1998: 3–5).

Second, the narrow concern for economic growth often worsens the condition of poverty and inequality — in the process of pursuing economic growth, often the rich get richer while the poor suffer from worsening poverty. In the case of Southeast Asia, according to Zarsky (2001), the Asian Miracle often produced adverse social outcomes like the worsening disparity in income distribution. A noted example of the situation is when the rich began to earn 8–10 times higher than the poor in Indonesia, and only 5% of farming households owned nearly 80% of the land (Wee, 1995). In this context, both the worsening poverty and the growing affluence may endanger environmental sustainability, because the poor increasingly rely on environmental resources and the rich consume more luxurious industrial products that are hazardous to the environment. Thus, a country with high-income inequality is likely to have more harmful effect on the environment as compared with a country with less-income inequality. In particular, the growing consumption of hazardous industrial products by the affluent class, often facilitated by the globalization of consumerism, may pose a challenge to sustainability. This involves the increasing

consumption of environmentally harmful goods like private cars, air condi-
tioners, washing machines, televisions, and so on (ADB, 2001). In Southeast
Asia, this luxurious lifestyle has rapidly expanded, and is becoming a
common norm for the younger generation.

With regard to the poverty–environment linkage, ADB (2001: 3) mentions
that, "environmental degradation reinforces poverty, which in turn reinforces
environmental degradation, and so on." Although, Southeast Asia as a region
has been able to substantially reduce the overall percentage of people living
below the poverty line, the situation did not improve drastically in cases such
as Indonesia, the Philippines, Laos, and Cambodia where poverty still continues to create pressure on the environment. According to Lim and Valencia
(1990), the rural poverty of the Philippines, continuously increased with
almost 80% of rural households falling below the poverty line in the late
1980s. It is this poverty, which usually pushes the low-income households
to overexploit forest resources, use fire to clear land for cultivation, and so
on (Zarsky, 2001). However, the poverty situation has worsened in most
cases after the severe economic crisis in 1997 — all countries in the region
except Singapore and the Philippines, experienced negative economic
growth (Bateman, 1999b). The hardest hit was Indonesia where per capita
income fell from US $1100 in 1996 to US $460 in 1998 and the average rate
of GDP growth declined from 7.3% during 1991–1997 to 4.6% in 1997 to
− 15.3% in 1998 (Angel et al., 1999; Esty and Pangestu, 1999). This worsening
economic condition not only pushed low-income households to intensify the
use of environmental resources, but also led to government cutbacks in
environmental regulatory activities (Angel et al., 1999).

Third, another underlying causal factor challenging sustainable development in Southeast Asia is the region's rapid pace of industrialization
and urbanization in the process of economic growth or development. It
is not necessary to explain the obvious fact that industrial expansion
means more depletion of nonrenewable resources, pollution of air and
water, accumulation of hazardous wastes, and emissions of environmentally harmful gases. Despite this adverse effect, in most Southeast Asian
countries, the rapid pace of economic success has been realized through
a high rate of industrial growth. Between 1970 and 1993, Southeast Asia's
industrial output increased by 25 times, and the contribution of industries
to the region's GDP increased from 25 to 40% (Lebel and Steffen, 1998). In
the case of Indonesia, its Environmental Impact Management Agency
(BAPEDAL) reports that in Jakarta, the industrial sector was responsible
for emitting 15% of total suspended particulates, 16% of nitrous oxide,
and 63% of sulfur oxide; and in Surabaya, the industrial sector accounted
for 28, 43, and 88% of such emissions, respectively (US-AEP, 1997a). In
Malaysia, the major industrial polluters were food processing, chemicals
and electronics, rubber and palm oil, and textiles (US-AEP, 1997b). It is

predicted that with the process of expansive industrialization, the pollution problem is likely to worsen (Lebel and Steffen, 1998).

Another integral facet of rapid industrial expansion is the intensive urbanization process since cities are the centers of trade and industry in Southeast Asia. During the period 1980–1995, the average annual growth rate of urban population was 2.1% in Singapore, 2.3% in Myanmar, 3.4% in Vietnam, 4.3% in Thailand, 4.5% in the Philippines, 6.9% in Indonesia, 7.5% in Malaysia, 9.3% in Laos, and 13.9% in Cambodia (Lebel and Steffen, 1998). Between 1970 and 1996, the number of urban population, as a percentage of total population, increased from 34 to 54% in Malaysia, 17 to 36% in Indonesia, 33–55% in Philippines, and 13–20% in Thailand (Esty and Pangestu, 1999). This expansion of urbanization and urban population may imply more vehicle emissions and more pollution problems (Lebel and Steffen, 1998). Expansion of cities in Southeast Asia also represents a threat to environmental sustainability.

Fourth, in line with the global trend, Southeast Asian countries have adopted various market-led neoliberal economic policies such as privatization, trade liberalization, welfare cut, deregulation, and so on. Although, such market-oriented policies have been embraced extensively by Malaysia, Indonesia, Singapore, Thailand, and the Philippines, for some critics, these policies are inappropriate for sustainable environment and may lead to environmental degradation (see Stokke, 1991: 17; Hempel, 1996: 83). Although, the advocates of free trade emphasize its positive benefits in terms of gaining from cleaner technologies and technical innovations, the critics argue that liberalization may lead to worsening pollution and abuse of natural resources (Lebel and Steffen, 1998). For instance, the expansion of export-led textile production in Indonesia and Thailand worsened the pollution of rivers by the textile industry that accounts for nearly 70% of total pollution (UNESCAP, 2000c).

In terms of foreign direct investment (FDI), Southeast Asia has been an attractive region for foreign investors. Between 1988–1991 and 1997, the average FDI flow increased from $746 million to $5.4 billion in Indonesia, $1.6 billion to $3.8 billion in Malaysia, $501 million to $1.3 billion in Philippine, and $3.6 billion to $10 billion in Singapore (Esty and Pangestu, 1999). There are numerous studies showing that foreign investment is often encouraged by factors such as chief labor, available raw materials, expansive market, good infrastructure, and lack of environmental regulations. It has been pointed out that in the case of the Philippines, the liberalization of mining industry and increasing foreign investment in the sector was not environmentally sustainable (Earth Council, 1997). The adverse implications of contemporary promarket policies for the environment have to be seriously taken into account in exploring governance for sustainable development in Southeast Asia.

V. Concluding Remarks

In this chapter, it has been emphasized that although considerable efforts have been made by most countries in Southeast Asia to expand the scope of governance for sustainable development in terms of policies, programs, and institutions, there are still serious threats to sustainability, including the worsening conditions of pollution, land degradation, loss of biodiversity, and other environmental disorders. It is argued that this relative failure to attain environmental sustainability is largely due to the dilemma between excessive concern for economic growth and need for sustainable development, between industrial expansion and environmental protection, between market-led policy and environmental agenda, and so on. In this regard, the policymakers in Southeast Asia have to explore alternative development perspectives and policy priorities, especially since they appear to be strongly committed to the cause of sustainable development (IISD, 1997).

In particular, it is crucial to reexamine the single-minded mission of economic growth based on industrial and urban expansion, which is widely known to be detrimental to the environment. It is necessary to redress the problem of income disparity through appropriate measures of income redistribution, because as discussed in this chapter, such disparity in income has serious implications for environmental sustainability. Finally, although adopting promarket neoliberal policies has become a common global trend, such policies need serious reconsideration in terms of their adverse consequences for the environment. There is no doubt that the realization of sustainable development requires relevant state policies and institutions, but the construction of this sustainability-driven governance alone may eventually become futile if it is not complemented by appropriate structures and priorities in other domains of governance related to overall socioeconomic development. More specifically, it may be necessary to reexamine, and even reverse, the primacy of economic growth, industrialization, consumerism, and overall market ideology (Haque, 1999) in order to achieve the success of much-debated governance for sustainable development, especially in Southeast Asia where economic growth seems to be considered the ultimate measure of legitimation for most policy decisions.

References

ADB, *Asian Environment Outlook 2001*, Asian Development Bank, Manila, 2001.

Angel, D., Will industry lead to a sustainability transition? in *Background Papers*, US-AEP, Ed., United States-Asia Environmental Partnership, Washington, DC, July 1998, pp. 1–3.

Angel, D.P., Feridhanusetyawan, T., and Rock, M., *Toward Clean Shared Growth in Asia*, United States-Asia Environmental Partnership, Washington, DC, 1999.

Badenoch, N., *Transboundary Environmental Governance: Principles and Practice in Mainland Southeast Asia*, World Resources Institute, 2002.

Barrow, C.J., Sustainable development: concept, value and practice, *Third World Plann. Rev.*, 17 (4), 369–386, 1995.

Bateman, B.O., *Sector-Based Public Policy in the Asia-Pacific Region: Planning, Regulating, and Innovating for Sustainability*, US-AEP, Washington, DC, 1999a.

Bateman, B.O., *Place-Based Public Policy in Southeast Asia: Developing, Managing, and Innovating for Sustainability*, United States-Asia Environmental Partnership, Washington, DC, 1999b.

Brown, L.R., Flavin, C., and Postel, S., Picturing a sustainable society, in *State of the World, 1990*, Worldwatch Institute, Ed., W.W. Norton and Company, New York, 1990, pp. 173–241.

Carley, M. and Christie, I., The world's commons: the challenge of governance, in *Governance for a Sustainable Future*, The World Humanity Action Trust, Ed., Russell Press Ltd., Nottingham, UK, 2000, pp. 9–36.

Cylke, O., Asia, environment, and the future of development, in *Background Papers*, US-AEP, Ed., United States-Asia Environmental Partnership, Washington, DC, July 1998, pp. 3–5.

Dovers, S., Sustainability: definitions, clarifications and contexts, *Development*, 2–3, 33–36, 1989.

Dupar, M. and Badenoch, N., *Environment, Livelihoods, and Local Institutions: Decentralization in Mainland Southeast Asia*, World Resources Institute, Washington, DC, 2002.

Earth Council, *Rio+5 Regional Consultation Synthesis Report: Asia-Pacific*, Rio+5 Secretariat, The Earth Council, San Jose, Costa Rica, 1997.

Environment Unit, *Brunei Darussalam environmental policies*, 2004. http://www.brunet.bn/gov/modev/environment/512.html.

Esty, D. and Pangestu, M., *Globalization and the Environment in Asia*, United States-Asia Environmental Partnership, Washington, DC, 1999.

Gardiner, R., Governance for sustainable development: outcomes from Johannesburg, in *Proceedings of the Presentation at Global Governance 2002: Redefining Global Democracy*, Montreal, Canada, October 2002.

GOP (Government of Philippines), *Philippines: Country Profile*, Information Provided to the United Nations Commission on Sustainable Development, Fifth Session, United Nations Commission on Sustainable Development, New York, April 7–25, 1997.

Government of Malaysia, *Malaysia: Country Profile*, Information Provided to the United Nations Commission on Sustainable Development, Fifth Session, United Nations Commission on Sustainable Development, New York, April 7–25, 1997.

Government of Singapore, *Singapore: Country Profile*, Information Provided to the United Nations Commission on Sustainable Development, Fifth Session, United Nations Commission on Sustainable Development, New York, April 7–25, 1997.

Haque, M.S., The fate of sustainable development under the neoliberal regimes in developing countries, *Int. Pol. Sci. Rev.*, 20 (2), 199–222, 1999.

Hempel, L.C., *Environmental Governance: The Global Challenge*, Island Press, Washington, DC, 1996.

IISD (International Institute of Sustainable Development), A Summary Report on the APEC Environment Ministerial Conference, *Sustainable De.*, 6 (3), 1–9, 1997.

Lebel, L. and Steffen, W., Eds., *Global Environmental Change and Sustainable Development in Southeast Asia*, Southeast Asian Regional Committee, Taiwan, 1998.

Lim, T.G. and Valencia, M.J., Eds., *Conflict over Natural Resources in South-East Asia and the Pacific*, United Nations University Press, Singapore, 1990.

Murdiyarso, D., Transboundary haze pollution in Southeast Asia, *Int. For. Fire News* (Germany), September 19, 1998.

Noman, O., *Economic Development and Environmental Policy*, Kegan Paul International, London, 1996.

Pednekar, S.S., NGOs and natural resource management in mainland Southeast Asia, *TDRI Quart. Rev.*, 10 (3), 21–27, 1995.

Redclift, M., *Sustainable Development: Exploring the Contradictions*, Methuen and Co., London, 1987.

Rock, M.T., *A Policy Menu for Cleaner Production*, US-AEP Partnership, Washington, DC, 1998. http://www.usaep.org/programs/policy/pol_paper_polmencle.html.

Sachasinh, R., Phantumvanit, D., and Tridech, S., Thailand: challenges and responses in environmental management, in *Paper Presented to the Workshop on Environmental Management in East Asia: Challenges and Responses*, OECD Development Centre, Paris, August 6–7, 1992.

Soegiarto, A., Sustainable fisheries, environment and the prospects of regional cooperation in Southeast Asia, in *Paper Presented at the Nautilus Institute Workshop on Trade and Environment in Asia-Pacific: Prospects for Regional Cooperation*, Honolulu, East-West Center, September 23–25, 1994.

Stokke, O., Sustainable development: a multi-faceted challenge, *Eur. J. Dev. Res.*, 3 (1), 8–31, 1991.

Task Force for the Preparations of WSSD, *Synthesis Report for Asia and the Pacific*, UN Economic and Social Commission for Asia and the Pacific, Bangkok, 2001.

Tay, S.C., Singapore Environment Council: International policy dialogue on the Southeast Asian fires, *Int. For. Fire News* (Germany), September 19, 1998.

UNDP, *Governance for Sustainable Human Development: A UNDP Policy Document*, United Nations Development Programme, New York, 1997.

UNESCAP, *Review of the State of the Environment in Asia and the Pacific*, United Nations Economic and Social Commission for Asia and the Pacific, Bangkok, Thailand, 2000a. http://www.unescap.org/mced2000/so1.htm.

UNESCAP, *Review of the Implementation of Agenda 21, International Environmental Conventions, and Regional Action Programme for Environmentally*

Sound and Sustainable Development 1996–2000, United Nations Economic and Social Commission for Asia and the Pacific, Bangkok, Thailand, 2000b. http://www.unescap.org/mced2000/so3.htm.

UNESCAP, *Critical Environment and Sustainable Development Issues of the Region and Measures for Promoting Sustainable Development*, United Nations Economic and Social Commission for Asia and the Pacific, Bangkok, Thailand, 2000c. http://www.unescap.org/mced2000/so5.htm.

UNESCAP, *Regional Action Programme for Environmentally Sound and Sustainable Development, 2001–2005*, United Nations Economic and Social Commission for Asia and the Pacific, Bangkok, Thailand, 2001. http://www.unescap.org/mced2000/rap2001-2005.pdf.

UNESCAP, *Regional Follow-up to the World Summit on Sustainable Development in Asia and the Pacific*, UN Economic and Social Commission for Asia and the Pacific, Bangkok, 2003.

US-AEP, *Industry and Environment in Asia: Indonesia*, United States-Asia Environmental Partnership, Washington, DC, 1997a. http://www.usaep.org/fy2002/index.htm.

US-AEP, *Industry and Environment in Asia: Malaysia*, United States-Asia Environmental Partnership, Washington, DC, 1997b. http://www.usaep.org/country/malaysia.htm#1.

US-AEP, *Industry and Environment in Asia: Singapore*, United States-Asia Environmental Partnership, Washington, DC, 1997c. http://www.usaep.org/country/singpore.htm#1.

US-AEP, *Industry and Environment in Asia: Thailand*, United States-Asia Environmental Partnership, Washington, DC, 1997d. http://www.usaep.org/country/thailand.htm#1.

US-AEP, *United States–Asia Environmental Partnership Work Plan 2002*, United States-Asia Environmental Partnership, Washington, DC, 2002. http://www.usaep.org/fy2002/index.htm.

von Post, C. and Ahman, U., The dependency of commercial fisheries and aquaculture on the mangrove forests in Thailand, Swedish University of Agricultural Sciences, *Minor Field Studies*, 8, Uppsala, Sweden, 1997.

WCED (World Commission on Environment and Development), *Our Common Future*, Oxford University Press, Oxford and New York, 1987.

Wee, V., The gender dimension in environment and development policy: the Southeast Asian experience, in *Paper Prepared for the Northeast Asia–Southeast Asia Consultation on Development and Environment*, Bangkok, October 20–22, 1995.

World Bank, *Indonesia: Environment and Development*, World Bank, Washington, DC, 1994.

WSSD, *The Johannesburg Declaration on Sustainable Development*, World Summit on Sustainable Development, Johannesburg, South Africa, August 26–September 4, 2002. http://www.johannesburgsummit.org/html/documents/summit_docs/1009wssd_pol_declaration.htm.

Zarsky, L., Civil Society and clean shared growth in Asia: towards a stakeholder model of environmental governance, in *Presented at the Outlook for*

Environmentally Sound Development Policies Workshop, Manila, Philippines, August 2–3, 1999.

Zarsky, L., Civil society and the future of environmental governance in Asia, in *Asia's Clean Revolution: Industry, Growth and the Environment*, Angel, D. and Rock, M., Eds., Greenleaf Publishing, Sheffield, UK, 2001, pp. 128–154.

Chapter 11

The Developmental State: The East Asian Perspective

Kristen Nordhaug

CONTENTS

I. Introduction

This chapter gives an overview of theories and approaches to East Asian developmental states. Section 1 briefly outlines the intellectual context of these theories. Section 2 presents the findings of developmental state approaches regarding East Asian economic policies. Section 3 addresses the issue of the political-institutional foundation of developmental states, in terms of state–society relations and bureaucratic organization. Section 4 discusses the historical conditions that led to the emergence of developmental states. Section 5 examines the discussion on the decline of the developmental state. In Section 6 this "decline thesis" is related to the East Asian financial crisis of 1997–1998. Finally, the conclusion addresses the issue of whether East Asian developmental performances can be replicated by other developing countries.

The prevalent mainstream view, within postwar development economics and modernization theory, was that an active state was necessary to correct, "market failure" in developing countries. From the 1970s these arguments were challenged by the "counter-revolution" within development economics, which contended that market failure was negligible as compared with state failure (Toye, 1993). Policy recommendations based on the new framework played an important role in the structural adjustment programs for indebted developing countries in the 1980s. By then the "counter-revolutionaries" were criticized by institutional economists and political economists, who revived the argument that a high degree of nonliberal forms of state intervention was needed for successful late industrialization. It was claimed that the development of new East Asian industrializing countries, especially South Korea and Taiwan, vindicated these arguments.

The term "developmental state" was coined by Johnson (1982) to characterize the role of the state in promoting Japan's postwar development. A group of scholars associated with the Institute of Development Studies in Sussex applied the concept in case studies of Taiwan, South Korea, and China (White and Wade, 1985), while Johnson was extending his Japan-based model to Taiwan and South Korea (Johnson, 1987). Currently, most studies reserve the concept for Japan, South Korea, Taiwan, and Singapore. The following discussion will draw on examples from South Korea and Taiwan.

II. Policies of Developmental States

According to the neoclassical approach, state intervention will have a detrimental effect if it disturbs the relative ("right") prices that would have occurred under a freely working market economy, approximated by the relative prices in the world market. Against these views, Robert Wade argued that the problem of late economic development was to promote capital accumulation based on a large amount of investment in strategic economic sectors with spin-offs to the rest of the economy. In order to accomplish that, East Asian "[g]overnment policies deliberately got some prices 'wrong,' so as to change the signals to which decentralized market agents responded, and also used nonprice means to alter the behavior of market agents" (Wade, 1990: 29). Similarly, Amsden (1989: 39 ff.) coined the polemic notion of "getting relative prices wrong." It was argued that these policies resulted in a higher level of productive economic investments, which were more concentrated in certain key economic sectors with greater spin-offs to the overall economy than that would have taken place without government intervention.

The policies were oriented to industrial policy priorities and the promotion of production and investment, rather than consumption. For instance, customs and other trade barriers tended to be lower for industrial inputs and raw materials that were needed in production than for consumer goods; and the fiscal system was used to encourage investment.

It was argued that subsidies like cheap credits from state-controlled banks targeted at specific industries or even specific producers in South Korea had promoted South Korea's strong industrial performances (Amsden, 1989: 14–18, 72–76, 145–147). Fiscal benefits were used to reward high performances by a few outstanding firms in a wide range of industries in Taiwan, but also — and more controversially from the neoclassical point of view — to reward firms within targeted strategic industries (Wade, 1990: 182–185). Taiwan's public enterprises were used to pioneer new strategic products and new lines of production, paving the way for private investors in the next round (Wade, 1990: 110–111).

The developmental state approach not only emphasizes the *quantity* of nonliberal state intervention in East Asia, but also its *quality*. It is claimed that East Asian economic policies had a longer time horizon, were better designed, more coherent, more oriented to economic upgrading, and implemented more fully than policies in other developing countries. Support to the private sector went along with disciplining measures and demands for performance that were strictly enforced. Government support was concentrated to strategic sectors with potentials of technological upgrading and linkages to other economic activities that created new comparative advantages (Weiss and Hobson, 1995: 150–156).

The policies required extensive information, co-ordination of numerous government and business sectors, well-working arrangements to transmit information, and institutional mechanisms to resolve distributional conflicts that emerged in the process. For instance, Taiwan's trade control that was used to protect upstream industry from foreign competition was potentially harmful to downstream producers. It was accompanied by elaborate schemes to compensate downstream producers, who had to pay prices above world market levels, while imports were allowed if a producer could document that locally produced inputs were of inferior quality (Wade, 1990: 129–132). The high performances of East Asian states are explained in terms of institutional, political and social power relations, and forms of government organization.

III. Structures and Organization

Early arguments on the developmental state tended to stress that successful economic policies in East Asia benefited from a high degree of state autonomy from domestic and foreign class interests (Amsden, 1989; Haggard, 1990; Wade, 1990; Jenkins, 1991). It was argued that state autonomy sustained consistent long-term strategic government policies unrestrained by interest groups pressure. For instance, in Chalmer Johnson's model of "soft authoritarianism" a dominant political leadership with (parliamentary or nonparliamentary) government power for long duration provides the necessary political stability and protection so that the bureaucracy can plan long-term economic transformation without being "disturbed" by popular groups, economic lobbyists, or interest groups within the state (Johnson, 1982: 316, 1987: 152).

It was also argued that state autonomy allowed the government to discipline business. According to Amsden, the government in South Korea and other successful late industrializing countries applied their control of subsidy in the form of cheap credits from the public banking system, production licenses, foreign trade regulations, foreign exchange, aid deliveries, tax benefits, and crucial intermediate goods to discipline private business, and obtained high performances in return. In contrast, in states with limited autonomy, "rent-seeking coalitions" emerged between nonstate elites and government officials, and business elites got access to unconditional support (Amsden, 1989: 14–18, 145–147).

Later varieties of the developmental state approach have challenged or modified this favorable view on state autonomy. Evans (1995) and Weiss (1998: Chapter 3) claim that institutionalized co-operative relations between government and business have prevailed in Japan, South Korea, and Taiwan, and explain the high quality of government action in these countries. State power or state capability is viewed as an outcome of state–society linkages, rather than government control over society.[1]

Strong state autonomy from business is seen as a drawback, as policymakers then are deprived of important sources of information and feedback and lack the local networks to implement their policies. The East Asian "take off" started from a situation of high state autonomy *vis-à-vis* business, but success in the long term relied on the states' ability to transform exercise of power "over society" into exercise of power "through society" by means of institutionalized co-operation, negotiation, and competition within government–business networks (Weiss, 1998).

Evans has coined the term "embedded autonomy" to describe the institutions of intra-state and state–business relations in East Asia. The "autonomy-side" of this term refers to effective, insulated bureaucracies, which provide protection against uncontrolled influence by particularist societal groups on the states' decisions. Embeddedness is based on "connections that link the state intimately and aggressively to particular social groups with whom the state shares a joint project of transformation," that is, the business class (Evans, 1995: 59).

This approach is taken further by Weiss under the heading "governed interdependence." Weiss focuses on the formal corporate channels of government–business interaction as she argues that co-operation between government and business requires well-developed collective representation by business through industry and trade organizations that serve as the main vehicles of business influence on government decisions. Government–business relations have evolved from being strictly top-down to become more genuinely co-operative and motivated by utility. State autonomy was converted into increased state capacities through increasingly institutionalized government–business co-operation (Weiss and Hobson, 1995: 179–183).

Weiss (1998: 73–79) identifies four varieties of government–business interaction that have been important in East Asia. "Disciplined support" entails the exchange of business performance for government support as emphasized by Amsden, but Weiss departs from Amsden by arguing that this asymmetric power relation between state and business mainly prevailed during the early phase of East Asian industrialization, while more co-operative forms of government–business interaction became more important at later stages. A second type is public risk absorption. These are public initiatives to encourage the establishment of new industries or the expansion of recently established industries through government guarantees that reduce the risks associated with private investment. While the government initiates the process, the success of these initiatives will depend on the private sector's response and co-operative relations to develop the correct kinds of incentives. A third type is "private-sector initiative in public policies," where the initiative for new policies comes from the private sector, typically from industrial sectors that are in a state of depression or decline. Well-working government–business ties provide the government with information and suggestions, which, then, are evaluated. A fourth type is public–private innovation alliances "for acquiring, developing, upgrading, and diffusing technology." These policies have become increasingly important as East Asian producers developed into high-tech producers, with innovation through R&D capabilities.

Most theories on the developmental state contend that public bureaucracies and in particular key agencies of economic planning are bureaucratically organized. This includes recruitment by competitive exams, promotion by merit, remuneration that is competitive with the private sector, and effective supervision and control against corruption (Doner et al., 2005).

The liberal Anglo-American type of regulatory state is mainly concerned with setting the rules of market economies. In contrast, the developmental state gives highest priority to industrial policies that promote economic sectors, whole industries, or individual enterprises discriminately (Johnson, 1982: 19–20). Its organization prioritizes industrial policy planning to a greater extent than the liberal Western model where responsibility for industrial policies tends to be located to relatively weak government agencies, while the stronger agencies are concerned with macroeconomic management and the budget. Industrial policy making includes both domestic industrial policy and trade policy, while these two areas normally are separated in the regulatory state (Wade, 1990: 224–225).

In Johnson's model, the economic bureaucracy is led by a pilot agency with a supra-ministerial position that plans and co-ordinates economic policy decision-making. Johnson claimed that Japan's Ministry of International Trade and Industry, South Korea's Economic Planning Board, and Taiwan's Council of International Economic Cooperation and Development all fitted into this model (Johnson, 1982, 1987). Alternatively, Robert Wade has argued with reference to Taiwan that the power concentration that facilitates a coherent economic decision-making may be personalized, rather than institutionalized through leaders who occupy several top positions within the economic bureaucracy and horizontal contact, which results from circulation between government positions and overlapping membership (Wade, 1990: 225). Centralization of economic policy-making is promoted by a distinctive sense of corporate identity, which frequently has been based on common recruitment from elite universities (Rueschemeyer and Evans, 1985: 55–56; Evans, 1995: 59).

IV. Developmental Orientation and the Origins of Developmental States

A development-oriented political leadership is normally seen as a defining feature of the developmental state. However, many accounts fail to explain how this developmental orientation emerged. Promotion of long-term economic transformation with industrial upgrading is a difficult process. Scarce government resources are needed, there are many potential pitfalls and the benefits from these policies will only appear in the long run. Alternatively, economic policies might have been used to pursue objectives with more immediate benefits, such as coalition building through unconditional subsidies and other favors to political partners. So, why would the political rulers go for the uncertain long-term benefits of development promotion?

Some varieties of the developmental state approach explain the developmental orientation of the political rulers in terms of national security policies. It is argued that durable geopolitical threats in Meiji, Japan as well as in postwar South Korea and Taiwan induced political rulers to initiate mercantilist developmental policies as part of their state-centralizing reforms in response to serious external threats that jeopardized the very existence of the state. The result was state-led promotion of capitalist development to muster economic resources to finance warfare and develop military production capabilities (Lewis, 1993; Weiss and Hobson, 1995: 84–85, 96, 98–99, 179–180; Nordhaug, 1997, 1998; Woo-Cumings, 1998; Zhu, 2001).

This argument is developed further by Doner et al. (2005). It is argued that East Asian developmental states emerged in response to external geopolitical threats, which forced the governments to attempt to boost revenue. The response to these threats took place under hard budget constraints due to the absence of abundant primary commodities and other easily accessible revenue sources. Major social conflicts forced the ruling elites to combine repression with efforts to build broad social coalitions through "wealth-sharing" social reforms such as egalitarian land reforms, subsidized public housing programs, and provision of cheap public education and high salaries.

Problems of foreign trade balance and shortage of government revenue forced the governments to embark on export-oriented industrialization programs. Industrial deepening into higher-value activities was stimulated by security concerns to build defense industries and by the coalition-building strategy, which restricted opportunities for real wage cuts in response to competition from low-wage exporters.

V. Decline of the Developmental State?

It is frequently argued that developmental states are undermined by changes in their domestic and international environment. A general theoretical framework for this hypothesis was developed by Dietrich Rueschemeyer and Evans (1985: 68–70). Capitalists and other social groups and classes that have been strengthened by the interventionist state mobilize to control it and to reduce its interference in their activities. As a result, the autonomy and coherence of the state as an institution is enfeebled. This argument has been applied to Taiwan (Gold, 1986: 128–132; Pang, 1992: 240–253) as well as to South Korea (Evans, 1995: Chapter 8; Kim,

1997: Chapter 6). Other authors focus on external dynamics. Moon (1988) argued that the Korean economic crisis of 1979–1980 and the subsequent structural adjustments weakened the previous policy instruments and the legitimacy of the government, while Woo (1991: Chapter 7) related the weakening of the Korean developmental state to pressure by the United States for liberalization of trade and foreign investment.

In some of these accounts, the developmental state is identified with strongly "statist" policies, so that foreign trade liberalization, financial deregulation, and privatization necessarily imply the end of the developmental state. Liberalization and privatization may however, be less relevant to a "mature" developmental state, where the main issue is public support of research and development. Thus, Weiss is contending that the developmental states[2] have changed their policy instruments, but not their developmental orientation and basic institutions, while new developmental government policies are focusing on industrial restructuring and economic upgrading through support of research and development (Weiss, 1998: 47). The argument that the developmental state is undermined by the business class is criticized for taking a zero-sum view of state–society relations, and failing to consider that state–business co-operation have been strengthened through new measures such as "public–private innovation alliances" (Weiss, 1998: 65).[3] Similarly, the relationship between the state and the global economy should not be seen as a zero-sum power relationship. Rather, the developmental states were promoting and taking advantage of the globalization of their companies (Weiss, 1998: 204 ff.).

VI. The East Asian Financial Crisis and the Developmental State Approach

Weiss' thesis on the resilience and renewal of developmental states was challenged by real-world events as the East Asian regional financial crisis coincided with the completion of her book. The crisis was creating great economic harm to South Korea, while Taiwan and Singapore managed to escape from it. In response, scholars associated with the developmental state approach developed explanations of the weakening of the Korean developmental state.

Ha-Joon Chang analyzed the South Korean crisis as a crisis of under-regulation that resulted from policy shifts in the 1990s, including domestic financial deregulation, liberalization of foreign borrowing, neglect to hold down the won exchange rate, and abandonment of government industrial policies and investment co-ordination. These policy changes went along with the dismantling of the pilot agency of the Korean development state, the Economic Planning Board (EPB), which was merged with the

Ministry of Finance. These changes led to excessive short-term foreign borrowing, declining competitiveness, and over-investment in key industrial sectors (Chang, 1998: 1557–1559).

Weiss (2000) differed slightly from Chang as she explained the Korean crisis as an outcome of declining state capability, which also implied imprudent financial liberalization. The main foundation of the Korean developmental state had been the provision of preferential credits from state-controlled banks to the large Korean business groups (chaebol). Preferential credits were scaled down in the 1980s and abandoned in the early 1990s in an attempt to distance the regime from the unpopular big business. These moves were sustained by changes within the state itself as a new generation of US-trained neoclassical economists replaced the former state-interventionist generation. The EPB was marginalized and liberal technocrats joined forces with the foreign ministry and the presidential office to promote fast-track capital liberalization (Weiss, 2000: 34–35). Liberalization of short-term foreign borrowing was an attempt to support the chaebol sector, which faced problems of declining competitiveness by giving them access to cheap credit in international markets (Weiss, 2000: 31–32). A weakening of the institutions and practices on which Korean transformative capacity was based translated into capital account liberalization in an attempt to sustain economic performance. The resulting inflow of volatile short-term capital opened up for the financial crisis of 1997–1998. Weiss emphasizes that South Korea should be seen as a special case. Taiwan and Singapore maintained their developmental capabilities.

The Taiwan government was also undertaking financial liberalization in the 1990s, but in a more prudent way than in South Korea. Taiwan's transformative capabilities and developmental orientation was maintained and renewed, as seen by the new government policies to promote industrial upgrading through innovation alliances with the private sector. In South Korea, financial deregulation was part of the process of dismantling previous developmental institutional arrangements and withdrawing the state from business financing. In contrast, Taiwan's financial liberalization was accompanied by re-regulation to ensure that inbound portfolio capital flows were invested in production, not in asset markets (Weiss, 2000: 28, 31–32).

Weiss was noting briefly that the emphasis on financial stability in Taiwan was reinforced by security concerns. This relationship has been discussed in greater detail by Yun-Han Chu who argues that the historical experiences of hyperinflation from the mainland Republic of China led to a strong commitment to monetary and financial stability within the Nationalist refugee government in Taiwan. This commitment was institutionalized in the form of a powerful central bank in control of a network of state-owned banks. It was reinforced by Taiwan's continuously fragile security situation *vis-à-vis* mainland China, including the 1996 Taiwan Strait crisis. The loss of international diplomatic status after 1979 made it urgent to maintain financial stability, as Taiwan could not rely on assistance from the IMF and the World Bank (Chu, 1999: 189–193). These external conditions were quite similar to those that promoted the rise of the developmental state, and it may also be argued that structural and institutional conditions are relatively similar. A strong, competent bureaucratically organized regulatory agency serves as a pilot agency with regard to monetary and financial policies and enjoys a high degree of autonomy (rather than embedded autonomy) *vis-à-vis* business and financial institutions, as it is protected by a security-oriented executive (Nordhaug, 2005). Correspondingly, a weaker commitment to financial stability in South Korea, also during its developmental period, can be explained in terms of the absence of historical experiences with hyper-inflation, a secure diplomatic status, and the decline of the North-Korean threat.

VII. Concluding Remarks: Can the East Asian Developmental State be Emulated?

The short answer to the aforementioned question is "no." According to the claim in Section 4, the developmental states emerged from a very specific context of fiscal resource scarcity, persistent security threats, and domestic social conflict with ensuing legitimacy pressure. This setting is unlikely to occur elsewhere, government policies and their institutional setting will be less developmental.

One possible exception would be the People's Republic of China. While China's fast economic transformation over the past two decades mainly has been based on unskilled, low-quality industrial development, and the technological upgrading is proceeding at a fast pace with support from government policies that resemble those of China's East Asian neighbors. The initial state building of the People's Republic took place under conditions of strong social conflicts and external geopolitical pressure. The economic reforms after 1979 that initiated China's strong growth were in part a response to problems of weakening of the central government's control. New reforms followed as the government faced problems of dwindling tax revenue by the late 1980s and early 1990s.

One should however, be careful to characterize China as a full-fledged developmental state. Its industrialization has benefited from large and relatively homogeneous domestic markets with ensuing economy-of-scale advantages. Large domestic markets have also given the government strong leverage *vis-à-vis* foreign investors, which has been helpful to promote economic upgrading through joint ventures. In the continental-size Chinese economy, competition among provinces has provided a certain degree of disciplining. At the local level, township-village enterprises with roots back to previous Maoist institutions compete with one another. In these processes developmentalism and unproductive rent seeking coincide.

China may be viewed as an "intermediary state." This is a concept developed by Peter Evan to characterize the blend of developmentalism and unproductive rent seeking in a number of developing countries. In Brazil this took the form of executive support and protection of economic–bureaucratic elite agencies that were added on to the existing clientelist state structure, rather than supplanting it. These agencies therefore remained "pockets of efficiency surrounded by a sea of traditional clientelist norms." These arrangements were fragile since the "developmental factions" of the bureaucracy depended on political protection, which periodically declined (Evans, 1995: 60–66). Still, this kind of institutional setting may be the best to hope for in most developing countries.

The most hotly debated issue is, however, about obstacles to the kind of economic policies applied in East Asian industrialization, irrespective of the quality of states and their policies due to economic globalization and political regulation through "global governance institutions" (IMF, World Bank, WTO) and powerful states (USA, EU). Here, I will restrict my discussion to the WTO.

Trade liberalization has complicated the use of selective protection as seen in East Asia. In addition, the trade issues within the WTO framework are likely to have a strong impact. Robert Wade talks about "shrinking of development space." A strong patent and property protection regime (Trade-Related Intellectual Property Rights, TRIPS) outlaws or complicates the catch-up strategies used in East Asia, such as reverse engineering and imitation. The Agreement on Trade-Related Investment Measures (TRIMs) restricts host country regulations of TNCs through requirements and incentives (i.e., tax benefits) regarding local content and export share. These measures were widely used in Taiwan. TRIMs do also rule against requirements that public agencies procure goods from local suppliers. The general Agreement on Trade in Services (GATS) restrain protection of local service industries against transnational companies, for instance local banks which played a strong role in financing East Asian industrialization (Wade, 2003: 626–629).

In contrast, Alice Amsden and Takashi Hikino contend that the impacts of the WTO on late-developer strategies are limited. There is leeway for protection against aggregate imports that destabilizes the balance of payments and against imports, which threaten individual industries. There are also loopholes in the TRIM regulations that allow for trade-balancing demands on foreign investors. Brazil has succeeded in demanding that the imports by foreign automobile assemblers should be matched by exports. Furthermore, subsidies to promote R&D are permissible under the WTO framework (Amsden and Hikino, 2000: 108–110).

This would indicate that there still is some "development space" left for selective support to national upgrading and disciplining of foreign investors under the WTO framework. However, a question left unanswered by Amsden and Hikino is, whether these options are restricted to the few powerful developing countries with economic leverage in trade negotiations, such as China, India, Brazil, Mexico, and Argentina. There may not be much development space left to the small least developed countries.

Notes

1. The distinction by Mann (1988) between "despotic" and "infrastructural" state power, and the elaboration of this framework in Mann (1993) has been important for this re-conceptualization of state power.
2. Weiss prefers the notion "catalytic states."
3. Weiss had some reservation regarding government–business co-operation in South Korea (see Weiss, 1998: 61).

References

Amsden, A.H., *Asia's Next Giant: South Korea and Late Industrialization*, Oxford University Press, New York, 1989.

Amsden, A.H. and Hikino, T., The bark is worse than the bite: new WTO law and late industrialization, *Ann. AAPSS*, 570, 104–114, 2000.

Chang, H.-J., Korea: the misunderstood crisis, *World Develop.*, 26 (8), 1555–1561, 1998.

Chu, Y., Surviving the East Asian financial storm: the political foundation of Taiwan's economic resilience, in *The Politics of the Asian Economic Crisis*, Pempel, T.J., Ed., Cornell, Itacha/London, 1999.

Doner, R.F., Ritchie, B., and Slater, D., Systemic vulnerability and the origins of the developmental states: Northeast and Southeast Asia in comparative perspective, *International Organization*, 59 (2), 327–361, 2005.

Evans, P.B., *Embedded Autonomy: States and Industrial Transformation*, Princeton University Press, Princeton, NJ, 1995.

Gold, T.B., *State and Society in the Taiwan Miracle*, M.E. Sharpe, Armonk, NY, 1986.

Haggard, S., *Pathways from the Periphery: The Politics of Growth in the Newly Industrializing Countries*, Cornell University Press, Itacha/London, 1990.

Jenkins, R., The political economy of industrialization: a comparison of Latin American and East Asian newly industrializing countries, *Develop. Change*, 22, 197–231, 1991.

Johnson, C., *MITI and the Japanese Miracle: The Growth of Industrial Policy, 1925–1975*, Stanford University Press, Stanford, 1982.

Johnson, C., Political institutions and economic performance: the government–business relationship in Japan, South Korea, and Taiwan, in *The Political*

Economy of the New Asian Industrialism, Frederic, C. and Deyo, F.C., Eds., Cornell University Press, Itacha/London, 1987, pp. 136–164.

Kim, E.M., *Big Business, Strong State: Collusion and Conflict in South Korean Development, 1960–1990*, State University of New York Press, Albany, 1997.

Lewis, R.P., The origins of Taiwan's trade and industrial policies, Unpublished Ph.D. Dissertation, Graduate School of Arts and Sciences, Columbia University, 1993.

Mann, M., The autonomous power of the state: its origins, mechanisms and results, in *States, War and Capitalism. Studies in Political Sociology*, Mann, M., Ed., Basil Blackwell, Oxford, 1988, pp. 1–32.

Mann, M., *The Sources of Social Power: Volume II. The Rise of Classes and Nation–States, 1760–1914*, Cambridge University Press, Cambridge, 1993.

Moon, C., The demise of a developmentalist state? Neoconservative reforms and political consequences in South Korea, *J. Develop. Soc.*, 4 (1), 67–84, 1988.

Nordhaug, K., State and U.S. Hegemony in Taiwan's Economic Transformation, Centre for Development and the Environment, University of Oslo, Dissertations and Theses no. 3/97, 1997.

Nordhaug, K., Development through want of security: the case of Taiwan, *Forum Develop. Stud.*, 1, 129–161, 1998.

Nordhaug, K., Global finance and financial regulation in Malaysia and Taiwan, in *Global Challenges–Local Responses: An Institutional Perspective on Economic Transformation in Asia*, unpublished manuscript, Roskilde University, 2005.

Pang, C., *The State and Economic Transformation: The Taiwan Case*, Garland Publishing Inc., New York, 1992.

Rueschemeyer, D. and Evans, P.B., The state and economic transformation: towards an analysis of the conditions underlying effective intervention, in *Bringing the State Back*, Evans, P., Rueschemeyer, D., and Skocpol, T., Eds., Cambridge University Press, 1985, pp. 45–77.

Toye, J., *Dilemmas of Development: Reflections on the Counter-Revolution in Development Economics*, 2nd ed., Blackwell, Oxford, UK, 1993.

Wade, R., *Governing the Market: Economic Theory and the Role of Government in East Asian Industrialization*, Princeton University Press, Princeton, NJ, 1990.

Wade, R.H., What strategies are viable for developing countries today? the World Trade Organization and the shrinking of development space, *Rev. Int. Pol. Econ.*, 10 (4), 621–644, 2003.

Weiss, L., *The Myth of the Powerless State: Governing the Economy in a Global Era*, Polity Press, Cambridge, 1998.

Weiss, L., Developmental states in transition: adapting, dismantling, innovating, not "normalizing", *Pacific Rev.*, 13 (1), 21–55, 2000.

Weiss, L. and Hobson, J.M., *States and Economic Development: A Comparative Historical Analysis*, Polity Press, Cambridge, UK, 1995.

White, G. and Wade, R., Eds., *Developmental States in East Asia: A Research Report to the Gatsby Charitable Foundation*, IDS Research Report: No. 16, IDS University of Sussex, Brighton, 1985.

Woo, J., *Race to the Swift: State and Finance in Korean Industrialization*, Columbia University Press, New York, 1991.

Woo-Cumings, M., National security and the rise of the developmental state in South Korea and Taiwan, in *Behind East Asian Growth: The Political and Social Foundations of Prosperity*, Rowen, H., Ed., Routledge, London, 1998, pp. 319–337.

Zhu, T., *Threat Perception and Developmental States in Northeast Asia*, Working Paper 2001/3, Research School of Pacific and Asian Studies, The Australian National University, Canberra, Australia, 2001.

ISSUES AND PROBLEMS IN DEVELOPMENT GOVERNANCE

Chapter 12

Poverty Reduction and Development Governance

Isabel Ortiz

CONTENTS

I. Introduction

Poverty is a central issue in development governance as its existence questions the commitment of a government to the public interest. When poverty exists in a country, it evidences the government's lack of public accountability and the government's failure to provide opportunities and services to its citizens, allowing public policies to explicitly benefit some social groups more than others. Weak governance, biased policies in favor of powerful interest groups, nepotism, or corruption affect mostly those with least power — the poor.

Because the poor have less voice, they are often under-represented in people's minds. However, more than 2.8 billion people, or around half the world's population, live below the international poverty line of US $2 a day. Of those, 1.2 billion people live in extreme poverty, with consumption levels below $1 a day. Given that population growth remains high in developing countries, many are born in poverty and destitution. Using World Bank's data, the number of poor people has actually increased since the late 1980s.[1] Further, many argue that poverty is not only income poverty. Poverty also has noneconomic dimensions such as lack of control of resources, vulnerability to shocks, helplessness to violence and corruption, lack of voice in decision-making, exploitation, and social exclusion. As we expand the definition of poverty, the number of people affected by it increase. This shows the magnitude of the problem and the urgent need for public action. Poverty reduction should be a central priority of development governance.

This chapter will discuss issues related to poverty reduction and governance under five main topics: poverty measurements, national policies, translating policies into budgets, international policies for poverty reduction, and the need for global governance in the 21st century.

II. The Basics: Towards Good Governance in Measuring Poverty and Income Inequalities

The definition and measurement of poverty is a highly political issue. Countries tend to hide the existence of large pockets of poverty as this makes them look underdeveloped and point evident public policy failures. Currently, national poverty lines use different methodologies and are not comparable — often they are based on the per capita expenditure necessary to attain 2000–2500 calories per day, plus a small allowance for nonfood consumption. However, these reflect inadequately other expenses necessary to cover basic needs — clothing, drinking water, housing, access to basic education and health, among others. These were the reasons why United Nations institutions started using the one- and two-dollar-a-day poverty lines; but these also have obvious flaws. If adequate money-metric poverty lines were developed, based on a real minimum consumption basket, the amount of people living in poverty would soar.

The World Bank has been developing Living Standards Measurement Surveys in many countries, and by now they are the best source of information for national poverty profiles. In parallel, the United Nations Development Program has consolidated different poverty proxies at the national level (life expectancy, adult literacy), and created a composite, the Human Development Index, which serves for basic international comparisons.

National estimations on inequality are even less reliable than those on poverty. Inequality shows the distribution of income, consumption, and other welfare indicators in society; as an aggregate, it is estimated that the richest 20% of the world have 89% of world income while the poorest 20% share is only 1.2%. The comparison between what the rich and the poor possess raises serious questions on the adequacy of current development models (development for whom?).

Income disparities are not at the core of national statistical data, they lack rigor and if available often seem "Mickey Mouse numbers" (Colman and Nixson, 1994) (for instance, Egypt and Indonesia are "officially" more equal societies than Australia or France).[2] After World War II, international organizations are focused on harmonizing growth-oriented measurements (i.e., gross domestic product, input–output tables, etc). Harmonizing cross-country poverty and inequality measurements is a main development governance issue of the 21st century.

III. How Is Poverty Reduced? The National Policies

Many, particularly those who have a vested interest in maintaining the *status quo*, pretend this is a too difficult question to be answered. The fact is that we have clear and compelling historical evidence that poverty reduction can be achieved — and it can be achieved fast.

Poverty was widespread in Europe, Japan, the US, or Australia during the 19th century and during the interwar period, particularly after the 1929 depression. From Dickens to Steinbeck, there are many descriptions of children working in bad conditions, people migrating with little more to sell than their own labor, mafias extorting people, shanty-towns and squats around cities, very common situations to today's developing world. What happened in developed countries, the progressive development of citizen rights and welfare, can also happen in developing countries.

Precisely, social development policies were an essential part of the modernization programs of these wealthier societies at the early stages of their development. Their governments became increasingly convinced that full employment should be a primary national policy objective, and expanded public interventions in education, medical care, social and housing assistance, minimum retirement levels, unemployment insurance, employment policies, and enforcement of labor laws and regulations. These policies allowed high-productivity gains in the workforce, expanded domestic demand, and increased economic growth. The population of North America, Europe, Japan, Australia, and New Zealand experienced prosperity unseen in history.

Which are then the poverty reducing policies? There has been a substantive debate and, based on extensive literature, major international organizations such as the World Bank, United Nations, or OECD, currently endorse that reducing poverty involves fighting its multidimensional aspects. This is an agenda for poverty reduction, which will focus on the country-specific obstacles for poverty reduction at its different dimensions (Figure 12.1).

Poverty reduction is not achieved by charity-type safety nets. Poverty reduction requires structural changes at the economic, political, and social levels through policies[3] that:

A. *Create opportunities for the poor* by promoting employment under good working conditions (ILO, 1999), supporting and regulating

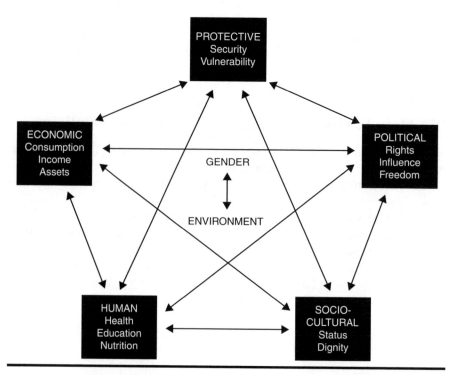

Figure 12.1   Dimensions of Poverty. (From *Development Assistance Committee (DAC) Guidelines for Poverty Reduction*, OECD, Paris, 2001, pp. 39.)

adequate private-sector activity. Not all economic growth is employment-generating, developing the so-called "pro-poor growth" implies the promotion of quality, nonvolatile growth that supports employment and well-being, with attention to distributive aspects and good governance (Thomas et al., 2000). Small and medium enterprises are particularly labor absorbing. For the private sector to contribute to poverty reduction, an enabling environment and effective regulatory framework should be enforced to promote competition, enforce fair practices and standards, and ensure that essential goods and services are affordable and reach the poor.

Opportunities should also be addressed by tackling asset inequalities and reducing barriers to entry, using distribution or re-distribution policies to assist the poor to access:

- Physical assets — infrastructure from which the poor benefit directly, such as water and sanitation,
- Natural assets — through policies such as land reform,
- Financial assets — access to credit,
- Human assets — investing in social sectors to ensure access to health and education, skills and training.

B. *Empower the poor and excluded groups* to influence the institutions that affect their lives, and strengthen their participation in political and economic processes. Organizing the poor and excluded groups to fight for their rights was a critical factor to promote social progress in developed countries — social development would have not happened without the fight of unions and civil rights groups. This includes fighting gender discrimination against women's basic rights, for example, education, employment, property, etc. This should result in reforming institutions and laws to ensure equality. Empowerment and social mobilization are intrinsically linked to the broader agenda of good governance, transparency, and accountability of the government to its citizens.

C. *Reduce vulnerability and risks to the poor*, many households with incomes near the poverty line face various risks that can plunge them into poverty. Risks may include covariant risks such as natural disasters; civil conflicts; economic downturns, financial crisis, or idiosyncratic household reversals such as crop failures, unemployment, illness, work injury, disability, death, and old age, threatening the future of the household and its members. A combination of public investments in social insurance, safety nets, disaster prevention or mitigation programs, and emergency relief are essential to provide security to the poor and vulnerable groups.

If good governance was enforced in public administrations and governments were accountable, transparent, and responsive, they would have a mandate and capacity for pro-poor interventions, and the policies described earlier may not be necessary. Well-governed public administrations would ensure that both their policies and legal systems are equitable and accessible to the poor and excluded groups. They would build public management systems free of political distortions, with decentralized mechanisms for broad-based participation in the delivery of public services; they would promote progressive tax systems and adequate allocations for social services, and would fight nepotism and corruption, minimizing the likelihood of public services being captured by local elites (DFID, 2000). However, given the large amount of poor in the world, good governance is not the norm.

IV. From Rhetoric to Reality: Translating Poverty Priorities into Budgets

All governments are doing something for the poor — the issue is *how much*. Around three-quarters of countries in the developing world have anti-poverty plans incorporated in their national planning, and virtually all governments have some programs targeted to the poor. These, plans and programs, however, are often under budgeted and have no target objectives or deadlines (McInley et al., 2000).

Let us see, for instance, the case of social sectors investments. If well planned, social services have large impacts on the poor. All developing countries have developed social policies over the last decades, and Ministries of Education, Health and Social Security or Welfare exists in most countries. However, they often fail to ensure services to the poor (Ortiz, 2002). This lack of effectiveness is normally due to:

(1) Limited coverage, serving only a portion of the population, often serving the wealthiest segments of society instead of the poor (health and pensions being recurrent cases), and more males than females (i.e., education).

(2) Insufficient funds, incorrectly distributed among programs — typical examples are national programs subsidizing universities that benefit upper urban income groups instead of basic education for the poor, or large cardiology hospitals in the capital instead of health clinics in villages.

When analyzing public policies, it is essential to distinguish between rhetoric and reality. Most governments and public institutions claim they do a lot for the poor: their real priorities are reflected in the budgets. Who benefits most from public expenditures? Is spending pro-poor? Or is spending centered on sustaining administrative structures or vested interests? Are key sectoral programs (agriculture, infrastructure, education, health, pensions, etc.) working to reduce poverty? Who or which subprograms receive the largest funding? Is this at national or decentralized level? Are expenditures reaching the poorest regions? How are government revenues collected? Is there a progressive tax system enforced?

There are several instruments that measure the adequacy of programs to serve the poor, most significantly:

(a) Public policy analysis, attending to issues of coverage and distribution, adequacy of benefits or services, adequacy of priorities, sustainability and efficiency, management, transparency, and auditing of public expenditures.

(b) Incidence benefit analysis, focusing on equity issues (*who receives how much?*), presenting the distribution of expenditures by socio-economic group (quintiles — 20% richest to 20% poorest), by geographical area (X–Z region), etc.

Pro-poor budgets are those that benefit the population near or below the poverty line, proportionally to other nonpoor socio-economic groups. Public policy and incidence benefit analyses developed around the world for a variety of public services[4] evidence that, generally, the following are pro-poor expenditures:

•   Education: primary education and, to a lesser degree, secondary education.
•   Health: preventive, primary health; child and mother care.
•   Infrastructure: rural electrification, water and sanitation, rural roads.
•   Social protection: if correctly designed, all social security or welfare programs except private pensions.
•   Decentralization: if good governance at the local level, and if proper equalization formulas exist between regions.
•   Rural development programs targeted to the poor.
•   Urban development focused on marginal areas (shanty towns).

Alter alia, the following expenditures do not benefit the poor:

•   Education: university or tertiary education.
•   Health: urban hospitals far from urban marginal areas (i.e., serving the wealthy), specialized clinics (cardiology, etc.).
•   Infrastructure: large infrastructure projects — dams, motorways, and airports.

- Social protection: private pensions; public pensions where the informal sector is large.
- Subsidies to public and private enterprises (except small and microenterprises); untargeted consumption subsidies.
- Financial sector reform or rescue transfers to banks.
- Defense or military expenditures.

V. International Policies for Poverty Reduction

Given slow progress in reducing poverty, in 1995 the international community committed to a set of time-bound targets at the World Summit for Social Development, the Millennium Development Goals (MDGs), later endorsed by all countries at the United Nations 55th General Assembly (2000). The MDGs include halving hunger and extreme poverty by 2015, and improving a basic set of development policies: achieve universal primary education, reduce infant mortality rates, improve maternal health, promote gender equality and empower women, combat HIV/AIDS and malaria, support environmental sustainability, and consolidate development partnerships (Table 12.1).

The MDGs are ambitious but achievable, provided governments' and international organizations commitment. United Nations institutions, the OECD, bilateral donors, and international NGOs, all support developing countries to reach the MDGs targets. In this context, the multilateral financial institutions (World Bank, ADB, AfDB, and IADB, with the support of the IMF) changed their operational objectives from economic growth to poverty reduction — at least rhetorically. From a poverty reduction viewpoint, no matter the institutional transformation may be far from perfect, it is a very positive step towards achieving social progress.

Three main instruments have been agreed by the international community to foster poverty reduction and to achieve the MDGs:

A. Poverty Reduction Strategy Papers (PRSPs)

PRSPs are country-specific documents that present a diagnosis of poverty and the agreed strategies to overcome it. PRSPs are prepared by governments through a participatory process involving civil society and development partners, every 3 yr. The first stage consists on understanding why poverty exists in a determined country, agreeing on a poverty line, reviewing which may be the obstacles to reduce poverty in order to establish successful and feasible strategies. On a second stage, PRSPs identify medium-term targets for the country's poverty reduction strategy and set out the macroeconomic, sectoral, and social policies to achieve them.

Table 12.1　The MDGs and their Targets

Goals	Targets
Eradicate extreme poverty and hunger	Reduce by half the proportion of people living on less than a dollar a day
	Reduce by half the proportion of people who suffer from hunger
Achieve universal primary education	Ensure that all boys and girls complete a full course of primary schooling
Promote gender equality and empower women	Eliminate gender disparity in primary and secondary education preferably by 2005, and at all levels by 2015
Reduce child mortality	Reduce by two thirds the mortality rate among children under five
Improve maternal health	Reduce by three quarters the maternal mortality ratio
Combat HIV/AIDS, malaria, and other diseases	Halt and begin to reverse the spread of HIV/AIDS
	Halt and begin to reverse the incidence of malaria and other major diseases
Ensure environmental sustainability	Integrate the principles of sustainable development into country policies and programs; reverse loss of environmental resources
	Reduce by half the proportion of people without sustainable access to safe drinking water
	Achieve significant improvement in lives of at least 100 million slum dwellers, by 2020
Develop a global partnership for development	Develop further an open trading and financial system that is rule-based, predictable, and nondiscriminatory. Includes a commitment to good governance, development and poverty reduction — nationally and internationally
	Address the least developed countries' special needs. This includes tariff- and quota-free access for their exports; enhanced debt relief for HIPC; cancellation of official bilateral debt; and more generous official development assistance for countries committed to poverty reduction
	Address the special needs of landlocked and small island developing states
	Deal comprehensively with developing countries' debt problems through national and international measures to make debt sustainable in the long term

(Continued)

Table 12.1   (*Continued*)

Goals	Targets
	In cooperation with the developing countries, develop decent and productive work for youth
	In cooperation with pharmaceutical companies, provide access to affordable essential drugs in developing countries
	In cooperation with the private sector, make available the benefits of new technologies — especially information and communications technologies

Source: Millennium Development Goals (http://www.developmentgoals.org).

There are five core principles underlying the development and implementation of the PRSPs; these should be country-driven, results-oriented towards the poor, participatory and resulting in lasting development partnerships, comprehensive and based on a long-term perspective for poverty reduction.

PRSPs guide World Bank, IMF, and other donor activities in poor countries. As of early 2004, 17 countries in Africa, 4 in Latin America, 6 in Europe and Central Asia, 6 in Asia, and 1 in the Middle East have presented their PRSPs to the World Bank or IMF Boards.[5] Many more are forthcoming.

B. Medium-Term Expenditure Frameworks (MTEFs)

Earlier we discussed about the need to differentiate rhetoric from reality, and the importance of translating poverty reduction priorities in the national budget. In the context of a PRSP, an MTEF is a medium-term instrument (3–5 yr) that combines strategic poverty reducing priorities with a bottom-up estimation of their current and medium-term costs and, ultimately, matches these costs with available resources in a multi-annual budget process.

The majority of OECD countries use MTEFs as a planning and budgeting tool; in developing countries, international organizations and donors are strongly supporting MTEFs as a tool to bring transparency and rationality in public expenditure allocation. A MTEF involves a radical change in the business of budgeting; consequently, without political commitment, it has little chance of succeeding. MTEFs should ensure that poverty-reducing priorities are effectively translated into multi-annual budgets and thus public expenditures are pro-poor (Norton et al., 2000).

C. New Financial Instruments for Poverty Reduction

To further ensure that poverty is addressed in a country, international organizations and donors are aligning their efforts, providing budgetary support to a country (often focused on social sector expenditures), conditional to having a good PRSP and MTEF. This is a complete reversal from the neoliberal development strategies of the 1980–1990s, when social sector expenditures were often curtailed due to anti-inflationary austerity programs and the debt crisis. This budgetary support to poverty reducing expenditures has different forms:

- The poverty reduction growth facility (PRGF) is an IMF program for the poorest countries, replacing ESAF, and must be based on a country's PRSP.
- Direct budgetary support (DBS) consists on direct transfers from international donors or organizations to a developing country's general budget; for example, the poverty reduction support credits (PRSC) provided by the World Bank to support implementation of a PRSP in a country, or a multi-donor DBS provided donors agree with the quality of a country's PRSP and MTEF.
- Sector wide approaches (SWAps) are based on multi-donor support to a government sector strategy and budget; once there is an agreement or partnership between government and major donors or institutions, donors release funds to the government's budget, relying on government procedures to disburse and account for all funds. In early 2004 there are about 100 SWAps in the developing world, 85% of them in Africa, mostly on health and education but increasingly in areas such as agriculture, water supply, environment, energy, and others.

The importance of these new mechanisms comes in the harmonization of objectives between donors, international organizations, and a developing country governments — all focused on poverty reduction. Before, each donor would develop little projects to assist the country (i.e., support a number of heath centers, the local administration in some regions, train or advise a ministry, etc.), while the government would have to carry the weight of overall public administration, plus coordinating different donors (all of which have different administrative and reporting systems — a lot of paperwork — therefore high transactions costs). By harmonizing policy objectives and providing direct support to the government, donors ensure that poverty-reducing priorities are addressed in a transparent manner and their funds are well utilized, otherwise they could withdraw support. On the other hand, governments from developing countries find strong support to fight the internal obstacles to poverty reduction (often the hardest, political resistance), minimize the transaction costs of development aid, and strengthen their capacity to develop a modern administration.[6]

VI. Is this Sufficient to Reduce Poverty? The Future Agenda: Global Governance in the 21st Century

In earlier pages, an agreed national and international agenda for poverty reduction has been presented. These policies and instruments will certainly reduce poverty and promote social progress — but will not likely eradicate it. These are some of the outstanding points, which may become part of the future poverty reducing agenda:

- *Bringing politics back in*: given that most international development organizations were established after the World War II, these Bretton Woods Institutions left politics officially outside the development arena. The reality is that politicians and parties make huge difference to national policies and priorities, as unofficially all international organizations recognize when talking about "the lack of political will for reform." Bringing politics back in is essential to understand how change may occur in a country to reduce poverty. Development agencies like DFID are engaging more effectively in bringing politics to development in order to support pro-poor change (DFID, 2004).
- *Canceling Third World debt*: despite debt reduction attempts by IMF or World Bank through the heavily indebted poor countries (HIPC) initiative, many developing countries remain highly indebted and their scarce funds have to be used for debt repayment instead than for poverty reduction — NGOs like Jubilee 2000 or Oxfam[7] have been fighting for a cancellation of all debt in the poorest nations.
- *Building a new financial architecture to reduce poverty*: continual shocks and instabilities in today's financial markets have led critics to talk about a "global casino" and the need to regulate it through a new financial architecture that supports development, fights short-term speculative capital flows, tax evasion, and money laundering.[8]
- *Removing intellectual barriers for poverty reduction*: despite there have been major changes in development moving away from the 1980–1990s so-called "Washington Consensus,"[9] still neoliberal thinking impregnates a lot of the development discourse, often not reflecting real policy-making in developed countries as explained below.

- *Reforming international trade including the World Trade Organization* (WTO): abandoning the present model based on supposedly free, nondiscriminatory competition among countries. The model is a fallacy given that the EU, US, and Japan subsidize their own producers, including the agricultural sector — agriculture is one of the few economic activities that poor countries can develop to reduce poverty. Instead, in the name of "efficiency" and "free markets," developing countries are told to open-up and liberalize their economies — as a result, domestic producers cannot compete with the subsidized, higher quality products from developed countries and close down, generating further unemployment and poverty. Abandoning this double moral ("Do as I tell you, not as I do") and acritical implementation of markct-fundamentalist policies is essential to reduce poverty. Current trade policies should be replaced for a system of "fair" trade discriminating in favor of the poorer regions, ensuring that developing countries arc given a role in the world economy.[10]

Several of these issues were already foreseen in the MDGs presented earlier in this paper. The eight MDG, *Developing a Global Partnership for Development*, involves structural changes in development flows between developed and developing countries, like the ones mentioned in this section. However, while the first seven MDGs have very specific quantifiable targets, the eight MDG — a long list of important development topics — was left without specific targets. Getting serious about the eighth MDG is a matter of good international development governance.

Notes

1. See the absolute numbers at http://www.worldbank.org/poverty/data/trends/income.htm.
2. For inequality data, see the UNDP/UNUWIDER database: http://www.undp.org/poverty/initiatives/wider/wiid.htm and latest update of UNDP's Human Development Report available online at http://hdr.undp.org/reports/default.cfm (see also Cornia, 2004).
3. See World Bank (2001), OECD (2001), Utting et al. (2000).
4. See, among others, World Bank, Poverty Reduction Sourcebook (http://www.worldbank.org/poverty/strategies/sourctoc.htm).
5. Africa (Benin, Burkina Faso, Cameroon, Chad, Ethiopia, Ghana, Guinea, Madagascar, Malawi, Mali, Mauritania, Mozambique, Niger, Rwanda, Senegal, Tanzania, and Zambia), Asia (Cambodia, Laos, Mongolia, Pakistan, Sri Lanka, and Vietnam), Europe and Central Asia (Albania, Armenia, Azerbaijan, Georgia, Kyrgyz Republic, Tajikistan), Latin America (Bolivia, Guyana, Honduras, Nicaragua), Middle East and North Africa (Yemen).

6. There are risks to these new financial instruments. They could become technically correct tools but loose the impetus to reduce poverty. Governments in
developing countries could become used to transfers from developed countries,
and use the savings for nonpoverty reducing activities (i.e., defense). Donors
could use it as a conditionality instead of a partnership. Further, donors could
use social sector transfers as a pay-off for not doing more significant economic
reforms in their own countries to allow development to happen (i.e., agricultural reforms). But these risks can be avoided if the instruments are properly
used (Maxwell, 2003).

7. See http://www.jubilee2000uk.org and htttp://www.oxfam.org.

8. See Association for the Taxation of International Transactions for the Aid of
Citizens (ATTAC), http://www.attac.org; Shutt (2001).

9. A set of policies focused on structural adjustments, reducing controls on capital
and trade, curving public expenditures, privatization (instead of investing in
human capital) instead of promoting investments in human development
(Stiglitz, 2002), to the point that the 1980–1990s have been called "the lost
decades."

10. See the work of think-tanks such as The Third World Network (http://
www.twnside.org) and Focus on the Global South (www.focusweb.org).

References

Colman, D. and Nixson, F., *Economics of Change in Less Developed Countries*,
Harvester Wheatsheaf, New York, 1994.

Cornia, A., Ed., *Inequality, Growth, and Poverty in an Era of Liberalization and
Globalization*, Oxford University Press, New York, 2004.

DFID, *Making Governments Work for Poor People*, Department for International
Development, London, 2000.

DFID, *Drivers of Change*, Department for International Development, London,
2004.

ILO (International Labour Organization), *Report of the Director General: Decent
Work*, ILO, Geneva, 1999.

Maxwell, S., Heaven or hubris: reflections on the New Poverty Agenda, *Develop.
Policy Rev.*, 21 (1), 5–25, 2003.

McInley, T., et al., *Overcoming Human Poverty*, United Nations Development
Program (UNDP), New York, 2000.

Millennium Development Goals (http://www.developmentgoals.org).

Norton, A., Fozzard, A., and Foster, M., *Budgets, Donors and Poverty*, Overseas
Development Institute, London, 2000.

OECD, *Development Assistance Committee (DAC) Guidelines for Poverty Reduction*,
OECD, Paris, 2001.

Ortiz, I., Social policies for the 21st century, in *Defining an Agenda for Poverty
Reduction*, vol. 2., Ortiz, I., Ed., Asian Development Bank (ADB), Manila,
2002, pp. 47–72.

Shutt, H., *A New Democracy*, Zed, London, 2001.

Stiglitz, J., *Globalization and Its Discontents*, W.W. Norton, New York, 2002.

Thomas, V., Dailami, M., Dhareshwar, A., Kaufmann, D., Kishor, N., Lopez, R. E., and Wang, Y., *The Quality of Growth*, Oxford University Press, New York, 2000.

Utting, P., de Alcantara, C.H., and Stalker, P., Eds., *Visible Hands: Taking Responsibility for Social Development*, United Nations Research Institute for Social Development (UNRISD), Geneva, 2000.

World Bank, *World Development Report: Attacking Poverty*, Oxford University Press, New York, 2001.

World Bank, *Poverty Reduction Sourcebook*, The World Bank, Washington, DC, 2001. (available at: http://www.worldbank.org/poverty/strategies/sourctoc.htm).

Chapter 13

Civil Society and Development: Normative, Theoretical, and Practical Considerations

Terrance Carroll

CONTENTS

> Among laws that rule human societies there is one which seems
> to be more precise and clear than all others. If men are to remain
> civilized or to become so, the art of associating together must
> grow and improve in the same ratio in which equality of
> conditions is increased (Tocqueville, 1990[1840]: 110).

As Tocqueville suggests, the civil society concept has a lengthy intellectual
history. However, its utility in developmental studies began to be recognized
only during the 1980s when the concept was rediscovered by social scientists
studying Latin America and Eastern Europe (Hagopian, 2000: 897). It has
since been applied in studies of development throughout the world.
The strength of civil society is thought to be important in several ways,
including encouraging greater civility in public life, increasing the accountability of governments to their peoples, and as a force for democratization.

I. Defining Civil Society

There is a general agreement in the literature that civil society is an area of
social life bounded on one side by the state and on the other by families and
kinship networks (Kasfir, 1998a: 4). However, that consensus yields quickly
to ambiguities, differences of emphasis, and areas of disagreement.

Scholars who write about civil society differ immensely about what they
wish to include within the concept, and what they wish to exclude. As
Fierlbeck (1998) has demonstrated, some authors emphasize associational
life, and others formal organizations. Some authors wish to exclude organizations that participate in the economy or the market, while others would
include at least some of such bodies. No author appears to have developed
a usable operational definition of civil society, and it seems unlikely that
any operational definition can be developed that would incorporate more
than a very narrow sub-set of the activities generally considered to be part
of civil society.

To outline just one of the many problems that Fierlbeck (1998: 155) analyzed, the almost universal distinction that is made between civil society and
the state is difficult, perhaps impossible, to operationalize. Are self-
regulating professional associations part of the state or civil society? Are
publicly funded universities part of the state apparatus? Are they part of
the state apparatus if they receive significant funding from the state, but
more of their revenue comes from other sources? Are state employees
who participate in evenings or on weekends in human rights organizations,
women's groups, or environmental NGOs part of the state or civil society?

In fact, it appears that any sensible and potentially operational definition
of the distinction between state and civil society would need to focus not on

groups or individuals, but on activities. A person who is a state employee may function as a member of civil society in some of his or her activities (Hutchful, 1995: 71). An individual who is employed by a nonprofit, public interest NGO may function as part of the state apparatus if the NGO has signed a contract to implement certain government policies or programs. An organization may similarly function as an organ of civil society in some of its activities, and as an agent of the state in others. Indeed, there may be situations in which a single set of organizational activities would best be seen as constituting parts of *both* civil society and the state. If, for instance, a women's organization is contracted by the state to help to educate rural women about elections and their right to vote, we would seem to have a situation in which the goals of both civil society and the state are being advanced simultaneously.

Fierlbeck (1998: 172) concluded that, "the concept of 'civil society' is overused, over-rated, and analytically insubstantial." So, should we abandon it altogether? I think not. Despite its shortcomings as an operational concept, it remains useful as a sort of *meta*-concept, or what Kaplan (1964: 55–56) has termed a "construct." That is, civil society is a concept that itself cannot be observed, directly or indirectly, in its entirety. In this respect, it is similar to many key concepts in the social sciences, including the "state," "democracy," and "power." As is true of these and many other constructs, they can guide our research at a theoretical level, but when we wish to turn to empirical research, we need to develop operational definitions for narrower parts or sub-sets of the construct itself.

While I believe that civil society remains a useful social science concept at this level, it is important for us to be aware of the fact that it is not a value neutral idea. Civil society is positively valued by virtually every scholar who writes about it, and by all of the civic activists who feel themselves to be participants in it. While Tocqueville was aware that civil society could be as tyrannical as any state, this insight is largely absent from the contemporary literature of comparative politics (Fierlbeck, 1998: 149–165). Nor does the literature on civil society and development pay sufficient attention to the fact that participants in civil society in poorer countries tend to come from the middle and upper-middle classes, which creates at least a potential for the influence of civil society on public policy to contribute to an increase in inequalities among different social strata (Clarke, 1998: 50–52).

Fierlbeck (1998: 159) also has noted that the idea of civil society is firmly rooted in liberal political thought. By emphasizing the supposed benefits of civil society, international institutions like the World Bank and western donor governments, have been able to use widespread popular enthusiasm for strengthening civil society as a means of encouraging such fundamentally liberal values as the accountability of the state to the public, due process, and transparency in public life, without calling this "liberalism."

They also have been able to associate contested elements of liberalism or neoliberalism, such as a preference for a small state sector, with the development of civil society (Fierlbeck, 1998: 170–171). In the short run, it is much easier to gain public acceptance for contracting out state activities if they are, or may be, contracted to organs of civil society, than it is when they are contracted to private corporations. However, Pearce (2000: 19–21) notes that NGOs that cooperate in implementing neoliberal policies frequently lose legitimacy with their public.

Given the liberal intellectual roots of the civil society concept, Fierlbeck (1998: 159) asks, "to what extent can it or ought it to be applied to manifestly non-liberal states?" I think that the concept can be usefully applied in non-liberal states because both liberal values and civil society itself come in varying degrees. Both may be virtually nonexistent, or both may exist to some limited degrees. Changes in the strength of civil society, and in the liberal values associated with it, can be interesting and important, even in states that are fundamentally nonliberal. The growing literature on civil society in Arab or Islamic states is evidence of the utility of the concept in nonliberal settings (Norton, 1993; Mardin, 1995; Kubba, 2000). Indeed, the very contradictions between an older and still dominant set of nonliberal values and those associated with civil society can be central to a valid understanding of many societies. For example, Hall (1995: 25) has pointed out that, "[a]dherence to the ideal of civil society in modern India, amongst popular sectors as well as within the elite, is very remarkable; but this exists within the social context of caste, which still cages huge numbers with awful efficiency."

Three important points do follow from the recognition of the ideological biases that are inherent in the civil society concept. One is that, those of us who study civil society and development ought to explicitly acknowledge the ideological baggage that accompanies the concept. Second, we need to develop standards for determining whether a particular organization truly is "civil" in its activities. If we blindly accept that any and every nongovernmental organization is a part of civil society, we may find that we are including groups such as the Ku Klux Klan and Al Qaeda. Finally, when we analyze the views of civil society offered by other writers and institutions, we need to ask what values they build into their understanding of the concept.

II. Two Approaches to Civil Society

Two different emphases can be detected in various authors' conceptions of civil society. One conception focuses on its associational character. This approach, found in the works of such writers as Habermas (1987: 119–152) and Putnam (1994, 1995), sees the web of associations among individuals as the key characteristic of civil society. It is this web of associations that builds tolerance of diversity and a shared sense of a public sphere of life. Several proponents of this approach would include all types of associations, whether formal or informal, and whether political or apolitical. Others see the organizational aspect of civil society as consisting at most of spontaneous, unstructured social formations (Isaac, 1993; Lin, 2001: 19–28). This emphasis on the associational character of civil society is found most frequently in theoretical analyses of the concept, and occasionally in empirical research in developed countries. It is less common, but not unknown, in empirical studies of less developed countries. Widner and Mundt (2000) provide one example of this general approach to civil society in research on developing countries. Using survey research data from selected districts in Botswana and Uganda, they explore the relationships among such factors as citizens' number of memberships in associations, frequency of attendance, voluntarism, frequency of conversations with people of different ethnic or religious backgrounds, and social trust.

The second emphasis is on formal organizations, especially nongovernmental organizations (NGOs) that take positions on issues of public policy. This is the most frequent approach in studies of civil society in developing countries. Researchers count the number and type of civil society organizations in a country (Holm et al., 1996). They sometimes estimate the number of active members of such groups (Seligson, 1999). In some studies state officials and group leaders are interviewed about their activities, and perceived successes and failures (Carroll and Carroll, 1999).

There are, however, at least two important conceptual differences among authors who focus on the organizational make-up of civil society. One such issue is the role of ethnic or tribal organizations in civil society. The second question is whether the business community can properly be considered to be a part of civil society.

III. Organizations Rooted in an Ethnic or Tribal Community

For most scholars, civil society consists of all politically active voluntary organizations that are broader in scope than the family and narrower than the state, and that base membership on universalistic criteria (Kasfir, 1998a: 4). Because civil society is supposed to help to overcome social divisions based on ethnic, tribal, or religious identities, organizations rooted in specific identity groups are explicitly excluded from civil society. They are the "old" associations that should gradually give way to "new" formal organizations based upon shared interests rather than on ascribed characteristics (Kasfir, 1998b: 136–138). This conventional wisdom holds that a group life that is based on ethnic, religious, or tribal identities undermines democratic processes and institutions by turning politics into a battle to maximize the interests of each group, no matter what the consequences for others (Holm and Molutsi, 1992: 87–89; Hyden, 1992: 10–12; Fierlbeck, 1998: 190–200).

A well-developed civil society provides the foundation for stable and effective democratic politics, on the other hand, and according to this view, such a civil society consists of strong and autonomous secondary organizations based upon universalistic membership criteria (Shils, 1991; Hall, 1995: 15–17; Leftwich, 1997: 531; Mohamedou, 1998: 74–76). As Saxton (1997: 16) has pointed out, many of the authors who insist on universalistic membership criteria for the organs of civil society would consider a civil society that incorporates ethnically based organizations to be a civil society that is "stunted" or "incomplete."

Kasfir (1998a, b) has objected to the exclusion of ethnic groups from civil society on several grounds. One is that, by insisting upon formal organizations rather than the often informal associations associated with tribal identities in Africa, we would exclude the poor. Because the poor are disadvantaged at forming formal organizations, and because those organizations that are established have less access to state elites than those based within the modern middle class, "it is a relatively safe assumption that if civil society is defined as the activities of formal organizations, it will reflect the interests and ideas of elites or dominant classes" (Kasfir, 1998a: 5). A second objection is that, in societies in which ethnic identities are strong and politicized, "[i]f ethnic demands are excluded from civil society, it will be difficult to expect civil society organizations to represent anything close to the full agenda of citizens' demands" (Kasfir, 1998a: 7). He points out that it is difficult to argue that the ends of democracy are furthered by excluding from democratic processes the issues and organizations that are most salient for the majority of the population (Kasfir, 1998b: 136–138).

A number of studies of civil society in an African context have similarly concluded that groups based in particular ethnic, tribal, or religious communities need to be included. Karlström (1999: 111) argues that "traditional, ethnically-based political organizations provide at least the potential for a positive articulation between state and society," and that they therefore should be included. According to Olowu (2002: 64), in many parts of Africa, religious institutions are the best-developed civil society organizations. Comaroff and Comaroff (1999: 20) suggest that, rather than simply transposing a model of civil society derived from European experience on African societies, we need to "identify what African hybrids, Africanized modes of civil society, might actually look like. Or how they might resonate with ideals of society and accountability that differ from those found in the West." After reviewing the arguments for and against including ethnically based groups within civil society in an African context, Osaghae (1997: 19) concluded, "[t]heir inclusion is perhaps the distinctive mark of civil society in Africa."

In fact, some societies in which ethnic identities are powerful do display a group life that appears indistinguishable from that of conventional civil societies, except that many of the component organs are groups based within particular ethnic, religious, linguistic, or tribal communities. In at least a few such cases, this type of *ethnicized* civil society also seems to provide precisely the type of support for democratic institutions and processes that is associated with the conventional version. Mauritius may be the clearest example of a state with "a vibrant civil society" (Srebrnik, 2000: 17), in which the majority of the component organizations have their roots in one of the country's ethnic communities, and in which some of these organizations are tied specifically to the interests of members of a particular ethnic group (Carroll and Carroll, 1999, 2000).

We should also note that the distinction between groups based on ascriptive or universalistic criteria is not always clear. In many cases formal organizations exist to pursue nonethnic goals such as human rights, aspects of social welfare, or workers rights, with no restrictions on the ethnic identities of members, but draw their membership largely or entirely from a particular ethnic community for such reasons as geographical segregation, or the ethnic composition of the personal networks of group founders or leaders.

For these reasons, I believe that studies of civil society and development will be richer and more fully informed if they include groups whose members come largely or entirely from a single ethic or tribal community as potential components of civil society in conceptual terms, and as actual members if, and to the extent that, they attempt to influence questions of public policy in a peaceful and relatively civil manner.

IV. Business Organizations

The second theoretical dispute is between those who would exclude all business organizations and those who would include them. The definition offered by the United Nations Development Programme (UNDP, 1993: 1) is quite typical: "civil society is, together with state and market, one of three 'spheres' that interface in the making of democratic societies." Swift (1999: 4–5, emphasis in the original) defines civil society as "the *activity of citizens in free association who lack the authority of the state...Such activities are motivated by objectives other than profit-making...*" Stanton (1999: 243) has noted that most definitions of civil society exclude business firms, but that there is disagreement about whether organizations like chambers of commerce or unions should be included. Van Rooy (2002: 490) similarly observes that most conceptions of civil society do not include "groups belonging to the market place." Cox (1999: 10) claims that the "current widely understood usage" of the term "civil society" is one that places it in opposition to the power of both the state and corporations. This position also is commonly held among writers who are associated with the nonprofit NGO sector.

Kasfir (1998a: 16) suggests, on the other hand, that the reason that African civil societies are weak is because the "business sector is often expected to play a leading role in civil society [but] the business sector in Africa cannot play this role, because it is too weak and too politically acquiescent." Lawson (1999) similarly attributes the frequent failure of democracy in Africa in part to the weakness of the private sector and its resulting inability to play a central role in civil society. In the case of such African countries as Botswana, Ghana, Nigeria, and South Africa, however, this question is of considerable significance because there is now an independent private sector of reasonable size that does attempt to act collectively to influence government policy. For example, the successful public protest against the sudden imposition of a 17.5% value-added tax in Ghana in 1995 was led by such organizations as the Association of Ghana Industries, the Chamber of Commerce, the Employers Association, and the Trades Union Congress (Ayee, 2002: 188–189). In other regions, such as Latin America and much of Asia, the private sector often is very significant in size and influence, and it interacts regularly with the state.

The debate about the inclusion or exclusion of the private sector seems to revolve around the issue of actors' motivations or intentions. Those who would exclude the private sector do so because private sector organizations are motivated by the desire for profit, and their intention in participating in civil society is to further that private and selfish goal. In this view, only groups motivated by a concern for the public good should be considered to be organs of civil society.

In fact, motives are usually mixed. Business people also may be residents of a particular town, parents of young children, sports fans, and so on. In trying to influence governments, their positions may be influenced by several of their roles, in addition to their profit-seeking role as members of the business sector. And leaders of nonprofit NGOs often are concerned about their own careers and incomes and families, as well as pursuing the stated goals of their organizations.

If we focus on the potential effects of organizations on the emergence and endurance of democracy, rather than on their leaders' motives and intentions, treating for profit organizations (and unions) as components of civil society seems logical. A strong civil society contributes to democracy in at least five ways. First, it embodies the value of civility, permitting political debate and disagreement without resorting to coercion or violence. Second, it provides a zone of at least partial autonomy from the state within which individuals and groups can pursue personal and collective interests. Third, it helps to make the state accountable to the people. Fourth, it provides a forum for input into policy issues by the public. And finally, it adds to the policy implementation capacity of the state. Together, these contributions help to make the state–society relationship more balanced and reciprocal, rather than being unidirectionally top-down (Hyden, 1992).

Business organizations can contribute to each of these outcomes. As Moore (1966) has argued, it was the emergence of an industrial bourgeoisie in Britain, France, and the United States that set those countries on the path toward liberal democracy. Private sector organizations will be interested in the profitability of their members, but they nonetheless can pursue their goals with civility; they can help to foster a degree of autonomy from the state; they can help to make the state accountable for its actions; they can add to the diversity of voices in the policy process; and they can assist the state in the implementation of some of its policies.

In summary, then, the conception of civil society that I find most useful includes all voluntary associations that attempt, at least periodically, to influence public life, without trying to take direct control of the state. These include both business organizations and groups that draw their members from a particular ethnic or tribal community, as well as nonprofit NGOs with memberships based entirely on universalistic criteria.

V. Civil Society and Development

Earlier chapters in this volume have explored the meaning of development. For our purposes, it is sufficient to note that development includes at least three sectors of society: the economy, of course; the political system itself; but also the society in senses ranging from health and education to the role of women to interpersonal and inter-community relations.

We can note a number of characteristics of the relationships among civil society, political development, economic development, and social development. First, the relationship between civil society and each aspect of development is *reciprocal*. The strength and composition of civil society have consequences for each aspect of development, and changes in each aspect of development are likely to have consequences for the strength and composition of civil society.

Second, the nature of these relationships is *contingent* upon the circumstances of each country. The enthusiasm for civil society in recent years has been so great that the literature on civil society deals almost exclusively with its positive consequences, especially in the realm of political development. The evidence for these positive links is largely logical. What empirical evidence is provided often is impressionistic rather than systematic. Nevertheless, a plausible logical connection has been drawn between the strength of civil society and the character of state–society relations. A strong civil society provides support for the rule of law and observance of human rights. It helps to make the government accountable to the public. It educates the public and state actors about issues. It can provide expertise to complement or challenge that of the state. While civil society organizations sometimes can be surprisingly active and effective under authoritarian regimes (Otobo, 2002: 160), a strong civil society ultimately is a force for democratization, and a powerful supporting institution for democratic institutions when they come into existence (Morales et al., 1999). A stronger civil society also increases the capacity of the state to develop and implement policies, and thereby can contribute to economic and social development (Carroll and Carroll, 1999).

All of these propositions seem likely to be true with some frequency. However, we should not neglect much more negative possibilities. No actual civil society is likely to incorporate and represent all social groups equally (Sandbrook, 1993: 4; White, 1994: 385–386). Given inequality in the composition of civil society, and in the influence of different component organizations, civil society may sometimes provide support for maintaining or increasing inequalities, and for political domination by one social sector over others (Buchman, 1996: 96). Even if we exclude groups that pursue their goals by uncivil means from our understanding of civil society, South Africa under *apartheid* may have had the strongest civil society in sub-Saharan Africa. Some parts of that civil society struggled heroically to overcome *apartheid*, but, on balance, the net effect of South African civil society in that era probably was to reinforce *apartheid*, and to resist democratization.

A third characteristic of these relationships between civil society and economic, political and social development is that they are likely to be *contributory* or probabilistic rather than necessary or sufficient. Newton (2001: 211–212) seems to expect something very close to a necessary relationship between civil society and democracy:

> It is difficult to imagine good government without a solid foundation of effective institutions, both public and private, for it is virtually impossible to create good government out of the poorly developed civil societies of banana republics... Poorly developed civil societies are unlikely to sustain developed democracies.

Lawson (1999) also doubts that democracy can be established in a country with a weak civil society. However, Botswana stands as a counter example, having remained democratic for almost four decades since independence despite having a very weak civil society for much of that time (Molutsi and Holm, 1990; Holm et al., 1996).

In many circumstances, then, a strengthening of civil society may make positive contribution to political, economic, and social development, but we should be alert to exceptions to this pattern. It is also true that, in states that manage to achieve unusual degrees of political, economic, and social development in the absence of a strong civil society, we are likely to find that development in those areas contributes positively to the strengthening of civil society. Again, however, there are likely to be exceptions. If, for example, development occurs under an authoritarian regime, as in Cuba after the revolution, relative success in improving upon the previous circumstances in the realms of politics, economics, and social services may make little contribution to the development of civil society.

VI. Conclusion: Civil Society and Development Governance

In Section 5, I cautioned that the effects of civil society may not always be in the direction of greater equality, more accountability, or a more democratic system. Nevertheless, it is clear that most frequently the net consequences of the influence and activities of civil society are, in fact, in these widely desired directions. A stronger civil society generally will help to produce more effective development governance. That raises the question of how civil society can be strengthened. There are three general approaches that may be helpful.

One is to assist those organizations that do exist in a fledgling civil society in their own efforts to become stronger. International institutions play a very important role when they bring together representatives of civil society organizations in international conferences. In research by the author on state–civil society relations in Botswana and Mauritius, for example, leaders of women's organizations, and of trade unions, repeatedly reported that the experience and contacts they gained through such conferences had been vital to the subsequent development of their organizations (Carroll and Carroll, 1997). Donors often insist that recipient states channel some or all of their assistance through NGOs, and this can provide a base of funding that would otherwise not be available (Fisher, 1998: 181–184). Civil society organizations in more developed countries can seek out partners in developing countries to whom they can provide expertise and assistance. Even when civil society is least developed, assistance can be provided to community-based organizations to work cooperatively to resolve some of the most pressing local problems.

When foreign governments provide assistance to indigenous organizations, however, it is important to avoid the appearance of supporting enemies of the existing regime. Stanton (1999: 247–248) reports that efforts by the US government to strengthen civil society in Cuba were tied explicitly to the goal of toppling the regime of Fidel Castro. During the late 1990s, this produced a crackdown on the quasi-independent organizations that then existed, effectively narrowing the room available for political thought, discussion, and activity. A related danger is that if domestic NGOs rely too heavily on foreign supporters, they may lose credibility with both the government and the people of their country (Nyerere, 1993: 21).

A second, complimentary approach to strengthen civil society is to try to convince governing elites in less developed countries of the advantages, *from their own perspective*, of an active and effective civil society. This probably is an impossibility in the case of gangster regimes that exist entirely to enrich the rulers. However, even authoritarian governors who maintain some desire for real development may be convinced that civil society can add to their capacity for policy implementation. Almost all less developed countries lack the trained, experienced personnel required in order to implement their own policies. International institutions and donors may organize conferences on the possibilities of using civil society organizations to carry out some aspects of policy implementation, and they can fund pilot projects. As civil society itself begins to develop greater knowledge and expertise, and as the state gains experience in working cooperatively with civil society, it may begin to turn to civil society organizations for policy advice, at least in areas that do not reflect core values or interests of the state elite.

Finally, the international community can encourage the governments of developing countries to move toward the conditions under which civil society is best able to develop naturally. These include rule of law, respect for human rights, and regulations that facilitate the formation of organizations. Considerable progress has sometimes been possible under even authoritarian governments when they have committed themselves to international standards in areas such as these. When this occurs, domestic supporters of such goals are able to pursue their ends by urging the government to abide by its own declared principles, rather than being in direct opposition to its rule.

Where civil society is weak, its development may require a considerable period of time. However, even modest improvements in the size and activities of civil society can make a difference. Civil society can play an important role in development governance. This chapter has attempted to demonstrate that its role is somewhat more complex and multifaceted than some of the recent literature suggests. Nevertheless, to the extent that domestic and international actors can encourage or assist the growth of civil society in less developed countries, the prospects for good, effective and accountable development governance will be increased.

References

Ayee, J., Governance, institutional reforms, and policy outcomes in Ghana, in *Better Governance and Public Policy: Capacity Building for Democratic Renewal in Africa*, Olowu, D. and Sako, S., Eds., Kumarian Press, Bloomfield, CT, 2002, pp. 173 193.

Buchman, C., The state and schooling in Kenya: historical developments and current challenges, *Afr. Today*, 46 (1), 93–117, 1996.

Carroll, B.W. and Carroll, T., State and ethnicity in Botswana and Mauritius: a democratic route to development? *J. Develop. Stud.*, 33 (4), 464–486, 1997.

Carroll, B.W. and Carroll, T., Civic networks, legitimacy and the policy process, *Governance: An International Journal of Policy and Administration*, 12 (1), 1–28, 1999.

Carroll, B.W. and Carroll, T., Accommodating ethnic diversity in a modernizing democratic state: theory and practice in the case of Mauritius, *Ethnic Racial Stud.*, 23 (1), 120–142, 2000.

Clarke, G., Non-governmental organizations (NGOs) and politics in the developing world, *Polit. Stud.*, 66, 36–52, 1998.

Comaroff, J.L. and Comaroff, J., Introduction, in *Civil Society and the Political Imagination in Africa*, Comaroff, J.L. and Comaroff, J., Eds., University of Chicago Press, Chicago, 1999, pp. 1–34.

Cox, R.W., Civil society at the turn of the millennium: prospects for an alternative world order, *Rev. Int. Stud.*, 25 (1), 3–28, 1999.

Fierlbeck, K., *Globalizing Democracy: Power, Legitimacy and the Interpretation of Democratic Ideas*, Manchester University Press, Manchester, 1998.

Fisher, J., *Nongovernments: NGOs and the Political Development of the Third World*, Kumarian Press, West Hartford, CT, 1998.

Habermas, J., *Theory of Communicative Action*, vol. II, *Lifeworld and System: A Critique of Functionalist Reason*, Beacon Press, Boston, 1987.

Hagopian, F., Political development, revisited, *Comp. Polit. Stud.*, 33 (6–7), 880–911, 2000.

Hall, J.A., In search of civil society, in *Civil Society: Theory, History, Comparison*, Hall, J.A., Ed., Polity Press, Cambridge, UK, 1995, pp. 1–31.

Holm, J.D. and Molutsi, P.P., State–society relations in Botswana: beginning liberalization, in *Governance and Politics in Africa*, Hyden, G. and Bratton, M., Eds., Lynne Rienner, Boulder, CO, 1992, pp. 75–95.

Holm, J.D., Molutsi, P.P., and Somolekae, G., The development of civil society in a democratic state: the Botswana model, *Afr. Stud. Rev.*, 39 (2), 43–69, 1996.

Hutchful, E., The civil society debate in Africa, *Int. J.*, 51 (1), 54–77, 1995.

Hyden, G., Governance and the study of politics, in *Governance and Politics in Africa*, Hyden, G. and Bratton, M., Eds., Lynne Rienner, Boulder, CO, 1992, pp. 1–26.

Issac, J., Civil society and the spirit of revolt, *Dissent*, 29 (1), 356–361, 1993.

Kaplan, A., *The Conduct of Inquiry: Methodology for Behavioral Science*, Chandler, San Francisco, 1964.

Karlström, M., Civil Society and its presuppositions: lessons from Uganda, in *Civil Society and the Political Imagination in Africa*, Comaroff, J.L. and Comaroff, J., Eds., University of Chicago Press, Chicago, 1999, pp. 104–123.

Kasfir, N., Introduction — the conventional notion of civil society: a critique, *J. Commonw. Comp. Polit.*, 36 (2), 1–20, 1998a.

Kasfir, N., Civil society, the state and democracy in Africa, *J. Commonw. Comp. Polit.*, 36 (2), 123–149, 1998b.

Kubba, L., Arabs and democracy: the awakening of civil society, *J. Democr.*, 11 (3), 84–90, 2000.

Lawson, L., External democracy promotion in Africa: another false start? *Commonw. Comp. Polit.*, 37 (1), 1–30, 1999.

Leftwich, A., From democratization to democratic consolidation, in *Democratization*, Potter, D., Goldblatt, D., Kiloh, M., and Lewis, P., Eds., Polity Press, Cambridge, UK, 1997, pp. 517–536.

Lin, N., *Social Capital: A Theory of Social Structure and Action*, Cambridge University Press, Cambridge, 2001.

Mardin, Ş., Civil society and Islam, in *Civil Society: Theory, History, Comparison*, Hall, J.A., Ed., Polity Press, Cambridge, UK, 1995, pp. 278–300.

Mohamedou, M.-M., Political transformation and democratization: new patterns of interaction between public administration and civil society in North Africa, *Int. Rev. Adm. Sci.*, 64 (1), 73–82, 1998.

Molutsi, P.P. and Holm, J.D., Developing democracy when civil society is weak: the case of Botswana, *Afr. Affairs*, 89 (356), 323–340, 1990.

Moore, B., Jr., *Social Origins of Dictatorship and Democracy: Lord and Peasant in the Making of the Modern World*, Beacon Press, Boston, 1966.

Morales, I., De Los Reyes, G., and Rich, P., Preface — civil society and democratization, *Ann. Am. Acad. Polit. Social Sci.*, 565, 7–14, 1999.

Newton, K., Trust, social capital, civil society, and democracy, *Int. Polit. Sci. Rev.*, 22 (2), 2001–2014, 2001.

Norton, A., The future of civil society in the Middle East, *Middle East J.*, 47 (2), 205–216, 1993.

Nyerere, J.K., Reflections on empowerment, in *Empowering People: Building Community, Civil Associations and Legality in Africa*, Sandbrook, R. and Halfani, M., Eds., Centre for Urban and Community Studies, University of Toronto, Toronto, 1993, pp. 15–22.

Olowu, D., Governance, institutional reforms, and policy processes in Africa: research and capacity-building implications, in *Better Governance and Public Policy: Capacity Building for Democratic Renewal in Africa*, Olowu, D. and Sako, S., Eds., Kumarian Press, Bloomfield, CT, 2002, pp. 53–71.

Osaghae, E.E., The role of civil society in consolidating democracy: an African perspective, *Afr. Insight*, 27 (1), 15–23, 1997.

Otobo, E.E., Policy process in a democratic context: a glimpse at Nigeria's privatization program, in *Better Governance and Public Policy: Capacity Building for Democratic Renewal in Africa*, Olowu, D. and Sako, S., Eds., Kumarian Press, Bloomfield, CT, 2002, pp. 159–172.

Pearce, J., Development, NGOs, and civil society: the debate and its future, in *Development, NGOs, and Civil Society*, Pearce, J., Ed., Oxfam GB, Oxford, 2000, pp. 15–43.

Putnam, R.D., *Civic Traditions in Modern Italy*, Princeton University Press, Princeton, NJ, 1994.

Putnam, R.D., Bowling alone: America's declining social capital, *Democracy*, 6 (1), 65–78, 1995.

Sandbrook, R., Introduction, in *Empowering People: Building Community, Civil Associations and Legality in Africa*, Sandbrook, R. and Halfani, M., Eds., Centre for Urban and Community Studies, University of Toronto, Toronto, 1993, pp. 1–12.

Saxton, G.D., Identity group formation, ethnic group demands, and subsequent integrative response: a model of Malaysia's paradoxical national integration strategy, A paper presented at the Annual Meeting of the Canadian Political Science Association, St. John's, NF, 1997.

Seligson, A.L., Civic association and democratic participation in Central America, *Comp. Polit. Stud.*, 32 (3), 342–362, 1999.

Shils, E., The virtue of civil society, *Gov. Oppos.*, 26 (2), 3–20, 1991.

Srebrnik, H., Can an ethnically-based civil society succeed? The case of Mauritius, *J. Contemp. Afr. Stud.*, 18 (1), 7–20, 2000.

Stanton, K., Promoting civil society: reflections on concepts and practice, in *The Revival of Civil Society: Global and Comparative Perspectives*, Schechter, M.G., Ed., Macmillan Press, London, 1999, pp. 243–251.

Swift, J., *Civil Society in Question*, Between the Lines, Toronto, 1999.

Tocqueville, A.de., *Democracy in America*, vol. 2, Vintage Books, New York, 1990 [1840] (the Henry Reeve text, as revised by Francis Bowen, and corrected and edited by Philips Bradley).

UNDP (United Nations Development Programme), *UNDP and Organizations of Civil Society*, UNDP, New York, 1993.

Van Rooy, A., Strengthening civil society in developing countries, in *The Companion to Development Studies*, Desai, V. and Potter, R.B., Eds., Arnold, London, 2002, pp. 489–495.

White, G., Civil society, democratization and development (I): clearing the analytical ground, *Democratization*, 1 (3), 375–390, 1994.

Widner, J. and Mundt, A., Researching social capital in Africa, *Africa* 68 (1), 1–24, 2000.

Chapter 14

Macroeconomic Management and Economic Development

Anis Chowdhury

CONTENTS

I. Introduction

As part of paradigm shifts in development economics in the 1980s and 1990s, the role of macroeconomic management in economic development has swung from one extreme to the other. This paradigm shift was driven by the experience of the 1970s. In the wake of two oil price shocks in the 1970s, most developing countries struggled to grow under the weight of high inflation, large budget deficits, and chronic imbalance in the balance of payments. Yet a small band of countries in East Asia and Southeast Asia experienced rapid economic growth and remarkable macroeconomic stability. For the orthodox neoclassical economists this provided a *prima facie* case in favor of a conservative macroeconomic policy stance, which is supported by the World Bank and the International Monetary Fund (IMF). It is argued that development economists, influenced by Keynes' idea, prescribed policies that relied heavily on large budget deficits financed through monetary expansion, which ultimately cause inflation and balance of payments problem. Therefore, achieving macroeconomic stability occupies a center stage in the IMF or World Bank policy package.

However, two decades of IMF or World Bank programs have failed to reignite the economic growth necessary to reduce poverty and improve quality of life in most countries. This has led to an intense debate about conservative macroeconomic policies. While there is a consensus about the importance of macroeconomic stability for economic growth, economists and policy makers are increasingly asking questions about the specific way of defining macroeconomic stability. It seems that strict adherence to a rigid inflation target of less than 5% and fiscal balance will drive the countries to a situation that can be described as a "stabilization trap." This chapter aims to review the theoretical underpinning of the debate in light of historical evidence, and is organized as follows: Section II reviews the theoretical debate on the role of fiscal and monetary policies and empirical evidences on the relationship between inflation and growth. Section III reviews the role of exchange rate in stabilization and growth. Section III contains concluding remarks.

II. The Role of Fiscal and Monetary Policies — Theory and Evidence

The three main macroeconomic instruments — budget, money, and exchange rate — are interlinked. This can be seen from the following simple relationships:

The stock of money supply (M) can be written as:

$$M = \text{domestic credit (DC)} + \text{net foreign assets (NFA)} \qquad (14.1)$$

where DC = central bank's credit to government (CG) + bank credit to public (CP).

This shows that the money supply is directly related to government's borrowing from the central bank to finance budget deficits. It becomes clearer from the "public financing identity" (Easterly and Schmidt-Hebbel, 1993: 213):

Fiscal deficit financing (FDF) = money financing (MF)

+ domestic debt financing (DDF)

+ external debt financing (EDF)   (14.2)

The relationship (2) shows that the government can finance deficits by seigniorage (printing money — MF above), borrowing at home (DDF), or borrowing from abroad (DDF). Easterly and Schmidt-Hebbel (1993: 213) highlight the macroeconomic implications that follow from the above identity:

> [E]ach type of financing, if used excessively, results in a specific macroeconomic imbalance. Money creation leads to inflation. Domestic borrowing leads to a credit squeeze... and the crowding out of private investment and consumption. External borrowing leads to current account deficit and the appreciation of the real exchange rate and sometimes to a balance of payments crisis ... or an external debt crisis.

Given the underdeveloped nature of bond and financial markets, borrowing from the central bank (printing money) is the dominant mode of financing budget deficits in developing countries.[1] Therefore, this chapter will focus on the budget deficit–money-inflation and economic growth only.[2]

The early development economists identified lack of capital needed to give a big push to the economy as the fundamental problem of development. They characterized the poor countries as trapped in a vicious circle of low income–low savings–low investment–low productivity and low income. They also saw underdevelopment as a market failure where either the private sector was very rudimentary (i.e., market did not exist) or the market produced undesirable outcomes (e.g., inequality). In such a situation, the public sector needed to play a larger role, and the only course that the governments could take was deficit financing through borrowing from the central banks. This is known as inflationary financing, as borrowing from the central bank to finance budget deficit means growth of money supply in excess of real economic growth.

According to the early development economists, inflation contributes to economic growth through a number of channels:

(a)   Redistribution of income in favor of profit earners with high savings propensity (Keynes–Kaldor effect).

(b)   Changes in the portfolio of investment from the financial sector to the real sector as the real returns from financial investment decline. This raises capital intensity (Tobin effect).

(c)   Forces people to hold more money to maintain the real value of their savings. This is known as inflation tax. As people hold more money, government profits since the cost of printing money is a tiny fraction of their nominal (face) value. This is known as seigniorage.

(d)   As nominal income rises with inflation, people move to higher income tax bracket and pay more taxes although their real income does not rise. This is known as bracket creeping.

Both (c) and (d) transfer resources to the government to be used for investment (Kalecki effect). In short, inflation creates a situation where people are forced to save more, so that investment requirement determines savings, rather than savings constraining investment. The policy prescription that follows the above argument has two main features — (a) high inflation and (b) control of interest rate. The combination of them produces a very low (or at the extreme, a negative) real interest rate, known as financial repression. This is expected to encourage investment, and at the same time forces people to save more, as the income effect dominates the substitution effect.[3]

Other economists, mainly of the neo-classical school, believe that inflation affects economic growth negatively, for the following reasons:

(a)   Inflation causes uncertainty about the future earning stream and hence adversely affects investment.

(b)   A high rate of inflation leads to high variability of inflation that gives confusing signals to economic agents. This, in turn, leads to lower investment and hence lower growth.

(c)   Since different sectoral prices rise at different rates, inflation causes distortion in investment decisions, and hence misallocation of resources.

(d)   Since inflation reduces the real value of financial assets, it encourages people to save in real assets such as precious metals or real estate. This adversely affects financial deepening.

(e)   Inflation causes real appreciation of domestic currency and hence adversely affects exports.

The opposing school, therefore, prescribes control of inflation and deregulation of interest rates, known as financial liberalization. They see money's role in stabilizing price rather than output. In other words, they hold the view that money by stabilizing the price level and maintaining the inflation rate at a low level generates certainty of returns that creates investor confidence. Financial liberalization at the same time encourages the act of savings, as the real rate of interest turns positive.

What is the evidence for either side of the inflation debate? We begin with the following observation by Friedman (1973: 41): "Historically, all possible combinations have occurred: inflation with and without [economic] development, no inflation with and without [economic] development." Thus, there are two aspects to this debate: (a) the nature of the relationship, if one exists; and (b) the direction of causality.

Earlier works (e.g., Tun Wai, 1959; Bhatia, 1960–1961) failed to establish any meaningful relationship between inflation and economic growth. Examination by Paul et al. (1997) involving 70 countries (of which 48 are developing economies) for the period 1960–1989 found no causal relation between inflation and economic growth in 40% of countries; the authors reported bidirectional causality in about 20% of countries and unidirectional (either inflation to growth or vice versa) relationship in the rest. Of greater interest, the relationship was found to be positive in some cases, but negative in others.

More recent cross-country studies that found inflation negatively affecting economic growth include Fischer (1993) and Barro (1996). The studies by Fischer and by Barro found inflation had a very small negative impact on growth. Fischer (1993) found that a 10 percentage point rise in inflation (from 5 to 15%) is correlated with a decline in output growth of only 0.4% per annum. Similarly, Barro (1996) estimated that 1% extra inflation reduces economic growth by between 0.02 and 0.03% per annum.[4]

Bruno and Easterly's (1998) work should perhaps end the debate. As Bruno and Easterly (1998) observed, there are more passions than facts in this debate.[5] They found that the negative correlation between inflation and economic growth "loses significance with the omission of single observation — Nicaragua, which had hyper-inflation and negative growth in the 1980s ... More generally, significance and sign of the cross-section correlation depends on the inclusion of the countries with high inflation crises — the above 40% episodes ...". They also observed, "the significance of the negative growth during 20–40% inflation vanishes if a *single* extreme annual observation is omitted — Iran in 1980." Easterly (2003) reported similar findings and regarded inflation rates below 35% as "moderate."[6]

III. The Role of Exchange Rate Policy

Exchange rates have both microeconomic and macroeconomic roles. As a relative price,[7] exchange rates play an important microeconomic function of structural change between tradable and nontradable sectors of an economy, and maintaining international competitiveness. Due to a close association of balance of payments outcomes with budget deficits and monetary policy stance, exchange rates can also function as an important macroeconomic policy tool. It is believed that exchange rate regimes can impose discipline on macroeconomic policy mix, especially by constraining government's ability to pursue unsustainable budget deficits through printing money.

Because of its multi-faceted roles, the choice of an exchange rate regime and its use as a policy tool has always generated debates. The exchange rate has historically been seen as an important policy instrument for promoting economic growth and prosperity through international trade. Thus, its stability is regarded as vital for economic progress. Adjustments to the exchange rates are made in response to severe imbalances in the balance of payments in order to restore international competitiveness. The earlier debate on exchange rates revolved around the impact of devaluation in improving balance of payments.[8] In recent times, however, the exchange rate has been used as a tool for macroeconomic stabilization. For example, firmly pegging the value of domestic currency to the currency of a country with low inflation, known as a nominal anchor, is suggested for bringing hyper-inflation under control. Adjustment to exchange rates (mainly devaluation) is a common element of the rescue package of the IMF.

Although, historically one or other role received more attention, both microeconomic and macroeconomic roles are interdependent. For example, if the exchange rate policy is used to lower inflation (a macroeconomic function), it should also improve international competitiveness and induce structural change in favor of the tradable sector (a microeconomic function). To the extent that macroeconomic stability and international competitiveness contribute to economic growth, exchange rate policies have important bearings for poverty reduction. Furthermore, the overall macroeconomic policy stance (fiscal, monetary, and exchange rates) must be consistent with the trade policy stance for maximizing the impact of poverty reduction efforts.

In the last two decades, most developing countries experienced major changes in their exchange rate regimes. There are several reasons for this policy shift but most obvious reasons are: (i) loan conditions from the IMF and the World Bank and (ii) implementing open economy policies. For example, 87% of developing countries had some type of pegged exchange rate policy in 1975 but by 1996 this had fallen to well below 50%.[9] Although these countries moved *officially* away from a fixed exchange rate regime, they were not fully flexible in *practice*. Their exchange rate regime can be characterized as "fixed-but-adjustable" (FBAR). But many observers have been quick to attribute the economic crises of Southeast Asia and other emerging economies to their pegged exchange rates (*in practice*) or FBAR.[10] The currency crises have prompted international financial institutions such as the IMF and the World Bank to argue the need for a more flexible exchange rate regime. But greater flexible exchange rate is not always an optimum policy for the developing world. Eichengreen (1999) found that out of 29 cases, for example, 23 countries abandoned fixed exchange rate regimes in favor of a more flexible one, and the change was accompanied by a financial crisis.[11] Corden (2002) has convincingly argued that the exchange rate regimes are not the root cause of economic crises, but they can either mitigate or militate the crisis once it sets off. So regardless of the exchange rate regimes, developing countries may experience financial crises. Most observers believe that the exchange rate is not a panacea for all problems and the choice of a regime must be based on the specific characteristics of a country.

A. Pros and Cons of Different Exchange Rate Regimes

The discussion on exchange rates focuses mainly on two polar versions — absolutely fixed (AFER) versus purely flexible (PFER). But in between them lies a whole range of intermediate regimes with varying degrees of flexibility or fixity. Corden (2002) regards FBAR as a third polar regime because of its own specific problems to do with speculation. AFER is a version of the gold or silver standard where the currency of a country is fixed to a specified value of these precious metals. In its modern version, the currency of a country is tightly fixed to the currency of another country (regarded as a strong currency). At the extreme, under AFER, a country uses the currency of another country — an arrangement known as "dollarization." On the other hand, the absence of commitment to any particular rate is crucial in a PFER regime. The exchange rate is determined by the interplay of market forces (especially expectations) without any intervention by the central bank, although the exchange rate responds to monetary policy acting on the difference between the domestic and international interest rates. The pros and cons of these two polar regimes are summarized below under two headings — stability versus flexibility and credibility versus independence.

1. Stability versus Flexibility

   (a)   AFER reduces potential transaction costs of engaging in international transactions that results from frequent exchange rate adjustments.[12] Frequent ups and downs in the value of a currency are harmful for trade and foreign direct investment (Mckinnon, 1963). They also cause domestic income redistribution between people engaged in tradable and nontradable sectors. The exchange instability can create balance sheet problems for firms that borrow in foreign currencies, and cause debt crisis (see Jahajah and Montiel, 2003).

(b) On the other hand, if the shocks to the goods market are more prevalent than shocks to the money market, a PFER allows countries to maintain their competitiveness as the exchange rate depreciates in response to a fall in export demand. Under an AFER a country can lose its international competitiveness when its currency appreciates along with the currency to which it is tied if they have different trade patterns. This was what happened to Hong Kong during the mid-1980s when the US dollar appreciated against major currencies, and recently to Argentina when its major competitor Brazil allowed its currency to depreciate and Argentina's currency remained tied to the US dollar. To some extent the same can be said of Southeast Asian countries that pegged their currencies to the US dollar but China devalued its currency causing loss of Southeast Asia's competitiveness leading to the crisis.

(c) Since AFER encourages capital flows, a large inflow of foreign exchange or a balance of payments surplus will cause inflation to rise unless its impact on money supply is sterilized. This will eventually lead to real appreciation and hence a decline in competitiveness. On the other hand, sterilization is not completely costless as the central bank will be forced to offer higher interest on government bonds or will have to raise reserve requirements for commercial banks. Higher interest rate will encourage more capital inflows, the very cause of the problem, making the sterilization increasingly difficult. In the end, the economy will contract either due to loss of competitiveness (higher inflation) or higher interest rate. If sterilization is not effective, commercial banks may end up with excess liquidity. This may create pressure on them to expand credit without applying strict financial analysis and probity check, thus increasing the risk of a banking crisis.[13]

(d) Foreign exchange market in the developing countries is often characterized by herd behavior that does not always reflect economic fundamentals. So the adoption of a fixed exchange rate rules out the possibilities of internal fluctuations among participating currencies and could have beneficial impacts on the economy. On the other hand, countries with a fixed exchange rate regime will have a high possibility of speculation against their currencies, forcing the central bank to raise the domestic interest rate significantly in order to defend the fixed rate. This can be very expensive and the economy will be in a turmoil as is evident from the Asian crisis. Managing large capital flows and preventing their reversals are very difficult tasks.

2. Credibility versus Independence

(a) A country with an AFER loses its monetary policy independence. Thus, it is unable to respond to domestic idiosyncratic shocks, as its monetary policy is determined by the central bank of the country to whose currency its own currency is fixed. This also means that domestic disturbances of the other country will be transmitted to this country. Therefore, if the two countries have different characteristics, an AFER will have undesirable consequences.

(b) An AFER also has implications for fiscal policy. By effectively abandoning its own currency, the country has to sacrifice real resources to obtain currency of another country. This means loss of seigniorage. For a country with a very low tax and revenue base, this can be a substantial constraint on the government's fiscal capacity.

(c) An AFER by removing monetary independence and imposing restriction on government's ability to finance budget deficits by borrowing from the central bank enhances credibility and macroeconomic discipline. This helps bring inflation down and maintain it at a low level and improves the balance of payments position.[14]

(d) On the other hand, both (a) and (b) mean that a country following an AFER will be severely restricted from pursuing any stabilization measure. Whereas a PFER allows countries to have its own inflation and output targets. However, this independence may be "abused" leading to unsustainable budget deficits, accelerating inflation, and destabilizing balance of payments problems.

B. The Fixed but Adjustable Exchange Rate Regime

This regime is in between fixed and flexible regimes and one can interpret it as the Bretton Woods regime.[15] Many developing countries maintained (officially or unofficially) this regime until the late 1990s. The key feature of this regime is that the exchange rate is determined by policy and maintained by central bank's direct or indirect intervention in the foreign exchange market, offering to buy and sell foreign currencies at a fixed price. Normally changes in this market come from either government's perceptions of changes in "economic fundamentals" that require an exchange rate adjustment, or strong market pressures affecting the foreign exchange reserves that lead to an adjustment.[16]

The driving force behind FBAR is a desire to minimize the cons of both AFER and PFER, and to maximize advantages of them. However, FBAR has its own problems, especially arising from the risks associated with high capital mobility and associated problems of speculation. A country trying to attract capital flows usually hesitates to frequently adjust its exchange rate, tending the rate more towards a fixed or pegged regime. Thus, it becomes vulnerable to loss of competitiveness, banking crisis, and speculative attacks, while its ability to pursue fiscal and monetary policy becomes restricted. This phenomenon is described as "open economy trilemma."[17] That is, a country cannot simultaneously pursue the goals of international financial integration, monetary independence, and an independent exchange rate policy — it has to give up at least one. Thus, it can have one of the three following options:

(i)   Simultaneous pursuit of exchange rate stability and monetary independence, but no financial integration, known as the exchange rate stability approach.

(ii) Financial integration and monetary independence, but no independent or pegged exchange rate policy, known as the real targets approach.

(iii) A pegged exchange rate policy and financial integration, but no monetary independence, known as the nominal anchor approach.

C. Implications for the Choice of Exchange Rate Regimes for Developing Countries

Which option should a developing country choose? The answer depends on its economic characteristics. If a country is characterized by high inflation and macroeconomic instability, then the obvious choice is option (iii). This option is known as "nominal targeting" as the domestic currency is tied to an anchor currency with a view to achieve a low inflation target. In this case, the commitment to a currency board system or dollarization will enhance credibility of inflation targeting and hence establish macroeconomic stability. However, the advantages of a hard-peg should be weighed against the costs associated with that, especially when such a regime is found to end invariably in crisis. Thus there should be a clear exit strategy once the stabilization is achieved. The exit strategy, of course, runs the risk of giving a signal that the country is not firmly committed to low inflation.[18] Perhaps a better alternative could be to tackle the problem of macroeconomic instability directly by fiscal reforms and removing the government's access to borrowing from the central bank.

Fortunately, there are not many developing countries with hyper-inflation. Most developing country policy makers understand the danger of macroeconomic instability caused by unsustainable fiscal deficits financed through borrowing from the central bank. For example, based on the World Development Report data, we find that out of 180 countries, 100 countries had inflation rates less than 10% during the period 1960–2000. Only 35 countries had inflation rates over 40% beyond which inflation is found to be harmful for growth. During the same period 82 countries had budget deficits less than 5%, and a small number of countries (about 5) had budget deficits above 10%. This means, for majority of developing countries the relevant options are (i) and (ii) that do not require them to give up monetary independence. This is good news for poverty reduction as governments can retain output or employment stabilization role in the face of adverse demand and supply shocks. As documented in Blank and Blinder (1986) and Blank and Card (1993), economic cycles have asymmetric effects on the poor. That is, poverty increases more rapidly during a downturn than it falls during a boom. The most recent and clear evidence of this asymmetry is the rapid and sharp rise in poverty during the Asian crisis. For example, it took nearly three decades for Indonesia to reduce poverty from over 60% to <15%, but the poverty rate went beyond 30% in less than a year immediately following the crisis.

Critics often point out that the ability to maintain a pegged rate depends on a country having a large foreign exchange reserve. As a matter of fact, the same could also be required of a flexible regime. This arises from the fact that most developing countries do not have well developed financial and exchange markets. As a result, their exchange rates are likely to be influenced by herd behavior and experience wild fluctuations. The central banks cannot ignore these fluctuations and need to intervene regardless whether the official regime is a flexible one.

IV. Concluding Remarks

Empirical evidence shows that very low and high inflation is harmful for economic growth, but moderate inflation positively correlates with respectable growth rates. What constitutes "moderate" inflation can vary across time and countries. Cross-country studies indicate that moderate inflation lies in the range of 10–30%. Thus, conservative fiscal and monetary policies aimed at an inflation rate between 3 and 5% may run the danger of deflation leading to a situation that can be described as a "stabilization trap." On the other hand, too lax expansionary macroeconomic policies may cause inflation to accelerate and harm economic growth. Fortunately, however, the upper range of "moderate" inflation and the threshold inflation rate beyond which it can become harmful is quite high, 35–40%.

The survey of theoretical and empirical literature overwhelmingly supports an intermediate exchange rate regime for developing countries. It is also important to bear in mind Frankel's (1999) observation that "no single currency regime is best for all countries, and that even for a given country it may be that no single currency regime is best all time." Thus, simplistic recommendations for exchange rate regimes based on macroeconomic performance can be extremely hazardous.

Thus, a number of factors should be considered when choosing an exchange rate regime. They are:

(a) The need for ensuring economic growth, and the role exports and foreign direct investment (FDI) play. The empirical evidence shows that exchange rate volatility adversely affects both exports and FDI.

(b) The need to stabilize output or employment in the light of empirical evidence that a downturn affects poverty more adversely than a boom reduces poverty.

(c) Given the condition of financial market, the possibility of banking and financial crisis in the face of increased short-term capital flows.

These considerations indicate that a developing country should follow an exchange rate stability approach. This may mean some loss of monetary independence. This will not matter when the economy is doing well as export grows and FDI flows in. Furthermore, a country following this approach does not necessarily lose monetary independence. It can retain monetary independence with some control on short-term capital mobility or if capital mobility is not significant. The important point here is to make sure that this nominal stability does not end up in real appreciation.

When there is a negative shock or boom ends, the country should have the ability to adjust its exchange rate downward. That is, it should adopt the real target approach. When the exchange rate is allowed to depreciate, a country also gains the ability to use fiscal-monetary policy to stabilize employment and minimize the adverse effects on poverty. The cautionary note here is that governments may delay depreciation for political reasons, which can throw the economy into a deeper recession.

Finally, countries which have lost fiscal and monetary control and are in the midst of hyperinflation, may consider a hard peg (complete dollarization) or a currency board arrangement. This is the last option when no other action could restore credibility of stabilization programs. But actions should be taken to de-dollarize as soon as credibility is restored and inflation is brought under control. It is a difficult task, but failure to do so may be very costly.

Notes

1. A typical developing country finances approximately 50% of budget deficits through the banking system (Little et al., 1993). Easterly and Schmidt-Hebbel (1993: 221) estimated a seigniorage of about 2% of GNP for a sample of 35 developing countries as opposed to 1% for a sample of 15 developed countries. Thus, in developing countries, monetary policy becomes subservient to fiscal authorities. Taylor (1979: 27) puts it succinctly: "The Bank has to 'print' money by absorbing government obligations if the Finance Minister orders it to do so...." For more details on the link between budget deficits and money supply in developing countries, see Hossain and Chowdhury (1996).
2. For a survey of literature on budget deficit-domestic borrowing and crowding out, see Hemming et al. (2002). Based on their extensive survey, Hemming et al. (2002, p. 36) conclude that, "There is little evidence of direct crowding out or crowding out through interest rates and the exchange rate. Nor does full Ricardian equivalence or a significant partial Ricardian offset get support much support from the evidence."
3. When real interest rate falls, people substitute future consumption with current consumption (the substitution effect). However, as the income from interest income declines, people should save more to maintain their future living standard (the income effect). The overall volume of savings will rise if the substitution effect is smaller than the income effect.
4. Yet Fischer (1993:281) concluded, "...however weak the evidence, one strong conclusion can be drawn: inflation is not good for longer-term growth." Similarly, Barro (1996: 159) asserted, "...the magnitude of effects are not that large, but are more than enough to justify a keen interest in price stability."
5. "Is inflation harmful to growth? The ratio of fervent beliefs to tangible evidence seems unusually high on this topic." Bruno and Easterly (1998: 3)
6. These findings confirm the observations of Dornbusch (1993), Dornbusch and Reynoso (1989), Levine and Renelt (1992) and Levine and Zervos (1993), that the inflation–economic growth relationship is influenced by countries with extreme values (either very high or very low inflation). Thus, Bruno and Easterly (1998) examined only cases of discrete high inflation (40 per cent and above) crises. The authors found a robust empirical result that growth falls sharply during high inflation crises, then recovers rapidly and strongly after inflation falls.
7. Between the tradable and nontradable products or between the domestic and foreign goods.
8. This debate produced the famous Marshall–Lerner conditions and highlighted the possibility of counter productive competitive devaluation, popularly known as "beggar-thy-neighbour."

9. Caramazza and Aziz (1998: 2).
10. According to Fischer (2001), each of the major international capital market related crises since 1994 had in some way involved a pegged exchange rate regime.
11. Eichengreen (1999).
12. Using panel data covering the period 1973–1993 for 69 developing countries, Sauer and Bohara (2001) have found that exchange rate volatility are harmful for developing countries. Based on an econometric study of 22 countries, Kandil (2000) has concluded that exchange rate variations cause significant output contraction and price inflation.
13. Capital inflows to the developing countries have risen considerably as a share of GDP since the early 1980s. Net private flows to the developing countries, after staying 0.05% of GDP during the 1970s and the 1980s, rose sharply to 3% in the mid-1990s and dropped back to 1.5% 1998 (Mussa et al., 2000). Since before the mid-1990s, most developing countries were pursuing some kind of fixed exchange rate (or some kind of managed float) regimes, it is possible that the reduction in capital flows in the 1990s is due to the movement of exchange rate regimes toward floating. Higher gross flows have created the potential for large and sudden reversals in net flows, particularly in the case of private flows.
14. Edwards (1993) considered 52 developing countries for the period 1980–1989 to see the relationship between exchange rate regimes and inflation performance by introducing financial discipline. His results suggest that countries that had a fixed exchange rate during the 1980s experienced lower inflation rates than did countries that had flexible arrangements. Ghosh et al. (1995) also found similar results for 136 countries using data for 1960–1989. The results show that after controlling for money growth rates, fixed exchange rate regimes experience lower and less volatile inflation than do most flexible exchange rate regimes. IMF (1997) study also found similar results for 123 developing countries for the period 1975–1996. These results are not free from "interpretation problems," as these studies are based on official classification of exchange rate regimes. Many countries, in practice, follow some kind of an adjustable pegged regime even though they report to the IMF as having a flexible regime. Edwards and Savastano (1999) have provided an excellent review of empirical literature on the link between exchange rate regimes and economic performance (also see Larrain and Velasco, 2001). More disturbingly, most exchange rate based stabilization programs ended up in major devaluation crisis (see Edwards, 1993; Corden, 2002).
15. In the sense that it has most characteristics of the Bretton Woods System that was essentially a fixed rate system, but allowed countries to adjust the par value of their currencies in response to changes in fundamentals.
16. Cordon (2002: 41).
17. This is also known as "impossible trinity" (see Frankel, 1999).
18. The Turkish program had an exit plan. This made the speculator doubt the commitment of the government to fiscal and other reforms, and anticipate the exit. At the end Turkey crushed in 2001. Obstfeld (1997) has raised the

issue against escape clauses in fixed exchange rates; they can open the door to multiple equilibria. Under fixed exchange rate regime, government force to devalue if situation arise (for example if currency is overvalued or economy is loosing competitiveness). But the expectation that the government might devalue could lead the private sector to take actions (for example by demanding large wage increases and high nominal interest rates) that could make the situation unpleasant to begin with. If the government does not devalue, it has to live with costly high real wages and real interest rates.

References

Barro, R., Inflation and growth, *Fed. Reserve Bank St. Louis Rev.*, 78, 153–169, 1996.

Bhatia, R., Inflation, deflation and economic development, *IMF Staff Papers*, 8, 101–114, 1960–1961.

Blank, R.M. and Blinder, A.S., Macroeconomics, income distribution, and poverty, in Sheldon, H.D. and Weinberg, D.H., Eds, *Fighting Poverty: What Works and What Doesn't*, Harvard University Press, Cambridge, 1986, pp. 180–208.

Blank, R.M. and Card, D., Poverty, income distribution, and growth: are they still connected?, *Brookings Papers on Economic Activity*, 2, 285–229.

Bruno, M., Does high inflation really lower growth? *Finance Develop.*, 32, 35–38, 1995.

Bruno, M. and Easterly, W., Inflation crises and long-run growth, *J. Monetary Econ.*, 41, 3–26, 1998.

Caramazza, F. and Aziz, J., Fixed or flexible? Getting the exchange rate right in the 1990s, *Econ. Issues*, 13, 1998 (International Monetary Fund, Washington, DC).

Corden, W.M., *Too Sensational: On the Choice of Exchange Rate Regimes*, The MIT Press, London, 2002.

Dornbusch, R., *Stabilization, Debt, and Reform; Policy Analysis for Developing Countries*, Harvester Wheatshef, New York, 1993.

Dornbusch, R. and Reynoso, A., Financial factors in economic development, *Am. Econ. Rev. Papers Proc.*, 79 (2), 204–209, 1989.

Easterly, W., National policies and economic growth: a reappraisal, *Working Paper*, vol. 27, Center for Global Development, New York University, 2003.

Easterly, W. and Schmidt-Hebbel, K., Fiscal deficits and macroeconomic performance in developing countries, *World Bank Res. Obser.*, 8 (2), 211–239, 1993.

Edwards, S., Exchange rates as nominal anchors, *Weltwirtschaftliches Arch.*, 129, 1–32, 1993.

Edwards, S. and Savastano, M., Exchange rates in emerging economies: what do we know? WHAT do we don't know? *Natl. Bureau Econ. Res. Working Paper*, 7228, 1999.

Eichengreen, B., Kicking the habit: moving from pegged rates to greater exchange rate flexibility, *Econ. J.*, 109, C1–14, 1999.

Fischer, S., The role of macroeconomic factors in economic growth, *J. Monetary Econ.* 32, 485–512, 1993.

Fischer, S., Exchange rate regimes: is the bipolar view correct? *J. Econ. Perspect.* 50 (2), 3–24, 2001.

Frankel, J., No single currency is right for all countries or at all times. *Princeton Essays in International Finance*, vol. 215, International Finance Section, Department of Economics, Princeton University, Princeton, NJ, 1999.

Friedman, M., *Money and Economic Development*, Lexington Books, Toronto, 1973.

Ghosh, A., Gulde, A.M., Ostry, J., and Wolf, H., Does the nominal exchange rate regime matter? *IMF Working Paper* 95/121, Washington, DC, November, 1995.

Hemming, R., Kell, M., and Mahfouz, S., The effectiveness of fiscal policy in stimulating economic activity – a review of the literature, *IMF Working Paper* WP/02/208, 2002.

Hossain, A. and Chowdhury, A., *Monetary and Financial Policies in Developing Countries: Growth and Stabilisation*, Routledge, London, 1996.

IMF, *Exchange Rate Arrangements and Exchange Restrictions*, IMF, Washington, DC, 1997.

Jahajah, S. and Montiel, P., Exchange rate policy and debt crises in emerging economies, *IMF Working Paper* WP/03/60, 2003.

Kandil, M., The asymmetric effects of exchange rate fluctuations: theory and evidence from developing countries, *IMF Working Paper* WP/00/184, 2000.

Levine, R. and Renelt, D., A sensitivity analysis of cross-country growth regressions, *Am. Econ. Rev.* 82, 942–963, 1992.

Levine, R. and Zervos, S., What have we learned about policy and growth from cross-country regressions? *Am. Econ. Rev.*, 82, 426–430, 1993.

Little, I.M.D., Cooper, R.N., Corden, W.M. and Rajapatirana, S., *Boom, Crisis and Adjustment: The Macroeconomic Experience of Developing Countries*, Oxford University Press, New York, 1993.

McKinnon, R., Optimal currency areas, *Am. Econ. Rev.*, 53 (4), 717–725, 1963.

Mussa, M., Masson, P., Swoboda, A., Jaresic, E., Mauro, P., and Berg, A., *Exchange Rate Regimes in an Increasingly Integrated World Economy*, International Monetary Fund, 2000 (available at: http://www.imf.org./external/pubs).

Obstfeld, M., Destabilizing effects of exchange-rate escape clauses, *J. Int. Econ.*, 43, 61–77, 1997.

Paul, S., Kearney, C., and Chowdhury, K., Inflation and economic growth: a multicountry empirical analysis, *Appl. Econ.*, 29, 1387–1301, 1997.

Sauer, C. and Bohara, A., Exchange rate volatility and exports: regional differences between developing and industrialized countries, *Rev. Int. Econ.*, 9 (1), 133–152, 2001.

Taylor, L., *Macro-Models for Developing Countries*, McGraw-Hill, New York, 1979.

Tun Wai, U., The relation between inflation and economic development: a statistical inductive study, *IMF Staff Papers*, 7, 302–317, 1959.

Chapter 15

Accountability and Good Governance: Concepts and Issues

Derick W. Brinkerhoff

CONTENTS

I. Introduction

Along with transparency and responsiveness, accountability constitutes one of the core components of the definition of good governance (March and Olsen, 1995; World Bank, 1997; Behn, 2001; UNDP, 2002). These terms are firmly entrenched in the good governance landscape, yet their co-ordinates and connections are difficult to locate precisely. Transparency and the availability of information are posited as necessary elements of accountability, but are insufficient without appropriate institutional structures and rules that support accountability outcomes. Responsive governance is, in turn, often cited as an outcome of increased accountability. In democracies, accountability institutions and actors function in a dense web of relationships of checks and balances that allocate power and authority (e.g., Behn, 1998; Aucoin and Heintzman, 2000). These need to be unpacked in order to sort out: the relational aspects of accountability, that is, identifying who is accountable to whom; and the conditions under which accountability can be increased. Such analysis will inform the design and implementation of systems, procedures, and mechanisms that impose restraints on power and authority and that create incentives for accountable behaviors and responsiveness by governance actors. This chapter clarifies the meaning of accountability, elaborates its basic elements, and offers some options for strengthening accountability within the context of democratic governance.

II. Defining Accountability

Despite its popularity, accountability is often ill-defined. For example, Mulgan (2000: 555) calls accountability a "complex and chameleon-like term." In general, accountability involves the power of one actor to make demands upon another to provide information about, or justification for, his/her actions; and the compulsion of the actor subject to those demands to respond.

A. Answerability and Sanctions

The essence of accountability is answerability; being accountable means having the obligation to answer questions regarding decisions or actions (see Schedler, 1999; Uhr, 2001). There are two types of accountability questions. The first asks simply to be informed. This type of question characterizes basic monitoring and implies a one-way transmission of information from the accountable actor(s) to the overseeing actor(s). In democratic governance terms, the informing aspect of answerability relates to transparency. The second type of question asks for explanations and justifications.

It inquires not just about what was done but why. This scrutiny can take place in a range of venues, from internal to a particular agency (e.g., personnel answering to their hierarchical superiors), among agencies (e.g., local service provider facilities reporting to their funders at the center), to more public arenas (e.g., parliamentary hearings where ministers answer to legislators, or community meetings where local officials answer to residents).

The availability and application of sanctions for illegal or inappropriate actions constitute the other defining element of accountability. Punishment for failures and transgressions gives "teeth" to accountability, and in the popular view this is what increasing accountability is all about. Most people equate sanctions with requirements, standards, and penalties embodied in laws, statutes, and regulations. However, sanctions can be thought of more broadly. They include, for example, professional codes of conduct, which do not have the status of law. They also include an array of incentives that are intended to reward good behavior and action, and deter bad behavior and action without necessarily involving recourse to legal enforcement. One category of such incentives relates to the use of market mechanisms for performance accountability. For example, if public service providers are required to compete for clients on the basis of publicly available information on quality and performance, accountability is enforced through the ability of clients to switch from low quality/performing providers to high quality/performing ones. The ability of service users to hold providers accountable by exercising their exit option creates incentives for responsiveness and service quality improvement (e.g., see Paul, 1992). Another category of "softer" sanctions concerns public exposure or negative publicity. This creates incentives to avoid damage to the accountable actor's reputation or status. For example, investigative panels, the media, and civil society watchdog organizations use these sanctions to hold government officials accountable for upholding ethical and human rights standards. Self-policing among service providers is another example of the application of this type of sanction, where professional codes of conduct are used as the standard.

B. Where Does the Exercise of Accountability Happen?

Within a particular governance system, the constitutional framework and administrative institutions determine where the accountable and overseeing actors are located — either inside or outside the state — and what their relationships with each other are. Accountability within the state refers to state institutions that curb abuses by other public agencies and branches of government, so-called "agencies of restraint." O'Donnell (1999: 38) terms this category, horizontal accountability, which he defines as, "the existence of state agencies that are legally enabled and empowered...to take actions that span from routine oversight to criminal sanctions or impeachment in relation to actions or omissions by other agents or agencies of the state that may be qualified as unlawful."

These state agencies comprise the classic separation of powers, but also include a variety of oversight entities, such as audit offices, ombudsmen, courts of accounts, electoral commissions, and so on. The effectiveness of these entities depends both on their autonomy, which is required to effectively pursue their control and sanctioning functions, and on their links to other institutions within the government. An important link is to the judicial system, which has the authority to pursue prosecution if needed. In addition, these agencies link to accountability actors outside the state in that they derive some of their power from the weight of public opinion; and the outcomes of their inquiries, investigations, or prosecutions can influence voting, assuming citizens make retrospective assessments of government performance part of their voting criteria.

The other category concerns accountability from outside of the state. This refers to overseeing actors located outside the state that play a role in holding state actors accountable. A number of analysts call this category, vertical accountability (see O'Donnell, 1999; Schedler, 1999). The classic expression of vertical accountability is through periodic elections, which is an imperfect instrument for punishing or rewarding governments. Besides elections, this category involves citizens, media, civil society organizations (CSOs), and the private sector in various activities that seek to articulate demands, investigate and denounce wrongdoing, enforce standards of conduct, and provide commentary on the behavior and actions of public officials and agencies.

The ability of these actors to play an effective role in accountability is influenced by three factors. First, they need to be connected to some degree to the accountability agents within the state. For example, if journalists expose corruption via the press, they will have little impact unless the judicial system follows through with investigations and prosecutions. Second, the quality of democracy in the country influences what they are able to accomplish. If basic freedoms, such as access to information, freedom of expression and of association, are absent or circumscribed, or if criticism of government actions is treated as grounds for harassment or physical violence, then accountability from outside the state will be severely constrained. Third, the capacities of these actors must be sufficient to allow them to engage in accountability activities. For example, the media need basic investigation and reporting skills, as well as agreed-upon reporting standards so as to be credible (see Waisbord, 1996). Civil society needs to be sufficiently developed in order to aggregate demands, exercise voice, take advantage of freedom-of-information and sunshine laws, and be taken seriously by public officials.

Table 15.1   Typology of Accountability with Illustrative Examples

	Accountability Within Government (Horizontal)	*Accountability Outside Government (Vertical)*
High enforcement/ sanctions capacity	Supreme audit institutions Courts Comptrollers general Law enforcement agencies Parliamentary hearings Legislative committees Administrative review councils Anti-corruption agencies	Elections Professional codes of conduct National/international standard-setting bodies Accreditation agencies Referenda Public interest law
Low enforcement/ sanctions capacity	Advisory boards Interministerial committees Ombudsman offices Blue ribbon panels Citizens' charters "Sunshine" laws Freedom of information laws	Citizen oversight committees Service delivery surveys Civil society watchdog organizations Policy research (e.g., by think tanks or universities) Investigative journalism (media)

These defining elements of accountability can be combined into a matrix, presented in Table 15.1 with an illustrative, not exhaustive, set of examples. A couple of preliminary observations emerge. First, it is apparent that accountability that is initiated by civil society has, for the most part, limited enforcement and sanctions capacity. This reinforces the point mentioned earlier about the need for linkages with state accountability actors. Second, the strongest accountability institutions and mechanisms lie within the state. This suggests the importance of capacity and political will on the part of public officials to use these institutions and mechanisms for the enforcement of sanctions. It also suggests the importance of having in place a supportive legal and institutional framework that CSOs and private sector actors can utilize to exercise accountability functions successfully.

III. Accountability for What?

Three general categories emerge from answering this question. The first addresses the most commonly understood notion of accountability, financial accountability. This deals with compliance with laws, rules, and regulations regarding financial control and management. The second type of accountability is for performance; that is, for the consequences of government policies, programs, and actions. Do they lead to the intended results, produce the desired benefits and results? The third category focuses on democratic/political accountability. This consists of holding leaders accountable through elections, and touches upon the administrative machinery of government that elected leaders direct to achieve public purposes. It deals with the relationship between the state and the citizen, citizen participation, equity issues, transparency and openness, responsiveness, and trust-building.

A. Financial Accountability

Financial accountability concerns tracking and reporting on allocation, disbursement, and utilization of financial resources, using the tools of auditing, budgeting, and accounting. The operational basis for financial accountability begins with internal agency financial systems that follow uniform accounting rules and standards. Beyond individual agency boundaries, finance ministries, and in some situations planning ministries, exercise oversight and control functions regarding line ministries and other executing agencies. As many executing agencies contract with the private sector or with nonprofit organizations, these oversight and control functions extend to cover public procurement and contracting. Legislatures pass the budget law that becomes the basis for ministry spending targets, for which they are held accountable. Obviously, a critical issue for the viable functioning of financial accountability is the institutional capacity of the various public and private entities involved. For example, municipal governments need to install and employ accurate and transparent budget systems that can produce usable data for monitoring and planning purposes by both budget officials and external overseers (Thurmaier 2003).

B. Performance Accountability

Performance accountability refers to demonstrating and accounting for performance in light of agreed-upon performance targets. Its focus is on the services, outputs, and results of public agencies and programs. Performance accountability is linked to financial accountability in which the financial resources to be accounted for are intended to produce goods, services, and benefits for citizens, but it is distinct in that financial accountability's emphasis is on procedural compliance whereas performance accountability concentrates on results. For example, health care provider payment schemes that maximize efficiency, quality of care, equity, and consumer satisfaction demand strong financial and management information systems that can produce both financial and performance information. Performance accountability is connected to democratic/political accountability in that among the criteria for performance are responsiveness to citizens and achievement of service delivery targets that meet their needs and demands.

C. *Democratic/Political Accountability*

In essence, democratic/political accountability has to do with the institutions and mechanisms that seek to ensure that government delivers on electoral promises, fulfills the public trust, aggregates and represents citizens' interests, and responds to ongoing and emerging societal needs and concerns. Beyond elections, however, democratic/political accountability encompasses citizen expectations for how public officials act to formulate and implement policies, provide public goods and services, fulfill the public trust, and implement the social contract. Policy-making and service delivery relate to aggregating and representing citizens' interests, and responding to ongoing and emerging societal needs and concerns. A central concern here is the issue of equity. An important government responsibility is to remedy service provision market failures both through regulation and resource allocation. Poor communities, rural and urban, often suffer from lack of resources; even if government provides fiscal subsidies, facilities and service providers are frequently scarce or nonexistent.

Table 15.2 presents these three accountability types and notes the links among them. The table demonstrates that democratic/political accountability in a sense defines the broader governance context in which the other two types of accountability are nested.

IV. **What Can Be Done to Increase Accountability?**

This section offers some suggestions for accountability improvement, building upon the typology summarized in Table 15.1. Several strategic choices are involved. The first is a choice among focusing on increasing answerability, increasing enforcement, or both. Second, for answerability or enforcement, there is a choice of targeting: the supply-side of accountability, that is, either internal to a particular agency of restraint or — more broadly — internal to government (horizontal accountability); or the demand side, that is, external to government, namely civil society and the private sector (vertical accountability). This choice is not either-or, but rather a question of relative emphasis.

Table 15.2   Accountability Types, Definitions, and Links

Accountability Type	Definition	Links to Other Types
Democratic/ political	Oversight of public officials and agencies in terms of their responsiveness to political leaders and to citizens, and of fulfillment of the public trust.	To financial: officials and agencies budget and spend resources to discharge their public mandates, dialogue and deliberation on budgets are a core feature of democratic discourse and policy-making. To performance: delivering services and results is a concrete manifestation of responsiveness to citizens' interests and societal needs; judgments about performance influence voter behavior
Financial	Examination of compliance of officials and agencies with laws, regulations, and procedures for the transparent allocation, expenditure, and reporting of financial resources.	To democratic/political: financial accountability assures that resources are used for agreed-upon public purposes transparency in financial accountability enhances citizens' ability to participate in oversight. To performance: goods and services cannot be produced without financial resources; many accountability systems join financial and performance accountability
Performance	Scrutiny of the actions of officials and agencies related to the production of outputs, delivery of services, accomplishment of objectives, and achievement of results and impacts.	To democratic/political: politicians and citizens look at performance to determine whether government is responsive, trustworthy, effective, and democratic. These determinations can affect citizen satisfaction with government and the outcome of elections. To financial: performance links allocation and spending of financial resources to achieving desired results.

Experience indicates that successful interventions must consider both the supply and demand sides. Table 15.3 illustrates these strategic options, which are then discussed in more detail, along with some examples.

A. *Increase Answerability*

As noted earlier, answerability has two facets: reporting on plans and actions, and justifying those plans and actions. For horizontal accountability (internal to government), routine answerability takes place both within individual agencies through hierarchical reporting relationships, and through interactions among the legislative, executive, and judicial branches. Most legislatures, through committees, hold hearings where agencies are required to report on the uses of their resources. For example, in parliamentary democracies, Public Accounts Committees, often chaired by members of the opposition party, exercise ex post review of agency spending to assure conformity with intended uses of funds. Constitutionally mandated audit and review entities, reporting either to the legislature or the head of state, comprise the Office of the Auditor General, and of the Comptroller General.

For external accountability (vertical) between government and citizens, answerability relates directly to transparency. In mature democracies, information about available services, eligibility, service delivery procedures, and standards is publicly available (e.g., most government ministries and departments have websites). New policies, changes in existing policies and procedures, and plans for the future undergo public comment and discussion, with citizen participation actively sought out. The media and CSOs (think tanks and interest groups) provide independent analysis and commentary on these policies and plans, and help interpret government actions and decisions to citizens (McGann and Weaver, 2001).

Table 15.3 Accountability Improvement Options

Increase Answerability	Increase Enforcement
Make existing answerability structures or procedures functional	Strengthen key agencies of restraint
Establish new structures and procedures	Strengthen or revise rules and regulations that agencies of restraint apply
Strengthen civil society's role in answerability	Build or strengthen links between external stakeholders and agencies of restraint
	Develop positive accountability sanctions

New information technology figures prominently in expanding the frontiers of transparency and answerability (e.g., see PUMA, 1998). It can enhance government's ability to communicate with citizens. For example, the Bulgarian parliament created an e-mail distribution network where draft legislation is circulated for comment to associations and businesses. The network has approximately 180 addresses, about 60% are business associations, slightly over 30% are research institutes and think tanks, and the rest are government officials and individual entrepreneurs. Information technology also helps civil society and individual citizens to exchange information, build constituencies, and support advocacy campaigns.

Despite the promising inroads of information technology, however, as has been frequently documented, transparency in many developing countries is weak or nonexistent. Budgets and sectoral plans are treated as secret documents. Citizens, both as individuals and in CSOs, have difficulty getting access to basic information. Open meetings or hearings are rare, unannounced, and scheduled to minimize participation. However, in some democratizing and transitioning countries, governments have made changes in the direction of increased transparency and participation. The Porto Alegre municipal budgeting case is one example. In this Brazilian city, a participatory budgeting process that involved citizens in establishing spending priorities, choosing investments and monitoring results led to better accountability, increased citizen motivation to pay taxes, and a nearly 50% rise in municipal revenue. A notable change in attitudes of public officials, well-versed in the technical aspects of budgeting and engineering, has also been observed as a result of their increasing interaction with citizens through the participatory process (de Sousa Santos, 1998).

The establishment of ombudsmen is a common government response to the need to increase answerability by creating a point of contact between government agencies and citizens with complaints or problems requiring investigation. Ombudsman offices have been created in most industrialized countries and are becoming more prevalent in developing and transitioning ones too (Giddings and Gregory, 2000).

Involving CSOs in monitoring performance is a potentially high-payoff approach to increasing answerability through the demand side. Service delivery surveys are an increasingly widespread mechanism that CSOs are employing, often with assistance from donors (see Uruena, 1996; Paul and Sekhar, 2000). Some countries have initiated court watch programs, where CSOs monitor and report on the actions of the judiciary, tracking basic indicators of due process and judicial efficiency. In countries where governments are shifting to private provision of public services, there is experimentation with delegating service quality monitoring to associations. For example, in Kazakhstan and Kyrgyzstan, among the functions of Family

Group Practice Associations is the monitoring of primary health care services provided by newly privatized health care providers (Brinkerhoff, 2002).

In short, within this option, there are three possibilities:

1. *Make existing answerability structures and procedures functional.* Many countries have the structures, particularly in the judiciary and the executive, but they are moribund and feeble. Legislative committees and audit entities are weak and unable to perform their answerability functions. Improving effectiveness can be addressed through systems improvements, training, and technical assistance. Sometimes, small interventions can have solid impacts. For example, in Nepal, the U.S. Agency for International Development noted that the parliament's Public Accounts Committee was inactive, and funded the Asia Foundation to take the committee members on a study tour of parliaments in the region. Upon the members' return to Nepal, the committee almost immediately began holding hearings. Assistance to ombudsman offices is another appropriate target for increasing answerability.

2. *Establish new procedures and new structures.* New procedures are particularly useful for weak legislatures, where often legislators have a poor understanding of how to fulfill their functions, little knowledge of appropriate procedures and behaviors, and an absence of committee structures and analytic support. At the municipal level, increasing budgetary transparency and reporting to citizens on expenditures and programs are effective mechanisms for enhancing answerability. For example, the Porto Alegre participatory budgeting process illustrates the powerful impact of creating government–citizen forums and committees for budget review and oversight (new structures) and soliciting community proposals for service delivery improvements (new procedures). As noted, such practices have resulted in documented increases in citizen satisfaction, government responsiveness, and taxpayer compliance.

3. *Strengthen civil society's role in answerability.* As noted, CSOs can be effective monitors of all three branches of government, for example, by conducting service delivery surveys, serving as election monitors, conducting voter exit polls and civic education, and so on. When combined with professionalization of the media, these efforts can go a long way to increasing the availability of information and educating citizens, both as voters and as users of government services. Efforts to increase advocacy and lobbying capacity can also be helpful.

From the Indian state of Gujarat, the case of DISHA, a nongovernmental organization that focuses on helping disadvantaged groups to influence public officials through budget analysis, illustrates the power of CSOs to increase answerability and the positive results that can be achieved. The budget analysis briefs DISHA prepares have put pressure on public officials to report more transparently regarding government plans and expenditures. Allocations for tribal development projects have moved from rhetoric to reality. The media use DISHA's analyses in their reporting, which has led to more informed public debates on spending priorities. As part of its budget monitoring, DISHA writes to village authorities in tribal areas about the status of construction projects and publicizes them. Budget data have also been used to advocate for policy change in areas such as forestry. Through comparative analysis of promised versus actual public expenditures for disadvantaged groups, DISHA has created an information network to assist local communities to articulate demands and create pressure for answerability. The Gujarat experiment has been replicated in 12 other states of India. In February 2000, these CSOs formed an umbrella organization called People's BIAS (Budget Information and Analysis Service) to analyze the national budget of India. DISHA has been a central influence and an important driving force behind the coalition.

B. Increase Enforcement

The application of sanctions predominates in both the practice and theory of increasing accountability. It is reflected, for example, in the "fry the big fish" approach to fighting corruption where prosecution of prominent lawbreakers is intended to convey the message that accountability applies to everyone. Enforcement looms large in efforts to increase the effectiveness of financial and performance accountability actors and mechanisms. Enforcement measures include, for example, increases in penalties for noncompliance or malfeasance; and reductions in administrative discretion, for instance, more reporting, and lowered ceilings for approvals to spend funds or take actions.

As Table 15.1 shows, the majority of enforcement mechanisms lie within government. However, external actors can play a role in accountability that moves beyond answerability. This highlights the connections between civil society actors and the agencies of restraint. As various observers have pointed out, the exposure and denouncing of wrongdoing, inequities, or inefficiencies by citizen review committees, watchdog CSOs, or the media will not have much impact on increasing accountability unless these actions trigger some sort of sanctions (e.g., see Smulovitz and Peruzotti, 2000).

Increasing enforcement does not deal only with negative sanctions imposed by formal agencies of restraint. Another, more positive, type of sanction is referred to as incentives-based enforcement. These sanctions set expectations for behavior, and provide various incentives for meeting the expectations. Implementation takes place largely through self-policing by public sector actors. Examples include codes of conduct, internal agency review boards, employee whistleblowing programs, professional associations, and accreditation agencies. An example of codes of conduct comes from the United Kingdom where the Committee on Standards in Public Life set out seven core principles:

1. Selflessness
2. Integrity
3. Objectivity
4. Accountability
5. Openness
6. Honesty
7. Leadership

These principles have been incorporated into the codes of conduct of numerous government institutions, including the parliament (Nolan, 1998). In Madagascar in 1997, the Ministry of Justice issued a circular elaborating a code of conduct for judges in an effort to increase the credibility of the judiciary (Brinkerhoff and Fox, 1999). An example from Tanzania is the integrity pledges to avoid corrupt practices that civil servants have made publicly (Langan and Cooksey, 1995). These self-policing mechanisms are reinforced by laws, sanctions, and oversight bodies, both government agencies and CSOs. Besides accountability, an important adjunct to self-policing mechanisms is their contribution to building citizens' trust in government and to changing their perceptions of acceptable versus unacceptable (e.g., corrupt) practices and behaviors.

A thread running through the enforcement dimension of accountability concerns the issue of standards. What are appropriate standards to enforce for accountability? How are "good" and "bad" defined? How are they measured? Are these formal or informal, explicit or implicit, technical or political, etc.? Of course, a country's constitutional and legal framework, the legislative process, and the political structure determine many accountability standards. These standards are further specified within the public administration framework in terms of allocation of functions across agencies and to different levels of government (decentralization), and through their elaboration in administrative rules and regulations.

International standards play a role in setting rules and regulations within a particular country. For example, the rules and procedures of the International Accounting Standards Committee govern financial accountability. CSOs can play a role in standard-setting too. For example, Transparency

International (TI) has been influential in establishing widely accepted standards for probity and ethical behavior related to corruption, and TI's Corruption Perception Index has served as an internationally available outcome measure for application of the standards.

Citizens can have a role in determining standards. One method for such input is through service delivery surveys, which collect and report on citizens' views of service quality, availability, cost, and impacts. These surveys use a combination of focus groups, household questionnaires, key informant interviews, and community surveillance committees to gather information. The surveys provide feedback to service delivery providers and public policy makers, and constitute an accountability mechanism. The link to standard-setting comes from the use of the surveys in contributing to determinations of appropriate and desirable levels and quality of service, so-called benchmarking (e.g., see Paul and Sekhar, 2000). These surveys are often used in combination with government oversight and audit to set performance goals and standards (PUMA, 1996).

Four choices can be identified for increasing enforcement:

1. *Strengthen key agencies of restraint.* Without functioning agencies of restraint, enforcement will be weak, selective, and partial. Credibility and effectiveness suffer as a result. In many countries, investigative agencies are starved for resources. In Madagascar, for example, field audit teams must rely upon the hospitality of the institutions they are auditing for transportation and lodging, which raises issues about impartiality and corruption (Brinkerhoff and Fox, 1999). An important issue for institutional strengthening is insulating agencies from inappropriate influences. The argument for insulation is based on the assumption that often the most pressing accountability problem is too much access by outsiders, with the result being undermining of due process, undemocratic outcomes, and corruption. Clearly, some degree of autonomy and insulation is necessary for effective enforcement, but the question remains, who watches the watchdogs? For horizontal accountability, this enforcement issue is addressed within the framework of the state's institutional and procedural checks and balances.

2. *Strengthen/revise the rules and regulations that agencies of restraint apply.* This option zeroes in on the laws, statutes, and regulations that a particular agency of restraint is supposed to apply. In some cases these rules are too weak, and need to be strengthened; this is a situation frequently found in public procurement and contracting practices in developing and transitioning countries. For example, in the municipality of Campo Elias in Venezuela, the rules governing procurements for public services were full of

loopholes that gave local officials wide administrative discretion, and had few accountability or transparency provisions (AAA, 2000). Reformers wanted to strengthen the laws and regulations for contracting for public services. In 1998, the Campo Elias municipal government in collaboration with community groups, and supported by the World Bank, simplified administrative procedures, closed loopholes, eliminated duplicative and unnecessary steps, and devised new rules for government and citizen oversight. A study conducted a year later showed approximately a 50% improvement in a number of indicators of service delivery efficiency, accessibility, and transparency. The model has spread to 400 other Venezuelan municipalities.

In other cases, the rules are too strong, creating distortions and perverse outcomes, and need to be revised. An example comes from Bolivia, where prior to 1985, the Office of the Comptroller General exercised pre-review authority for all government contracts and payment orders, undertook ex post audits, judged whether any regulations or standards had been deviated from, and imposed sanctions (Sanchez de Lozada, 1999). These rules led to paralysis of government actions, serious corruption, conflict of interest, lack of internal controls, and political manipulation. Beginning in the mid-80s, with donor support, Bolivia began to reform the legal framework for financial accountability and its agencies of restraint. For the Office of the Comptroller General, an important change came with the passage of Law 1178. This law increased the Office's operational and technical autonomy, but at the same time narrowed its mandate, and eliminated the conflict of interest. Its jurisdiction over financial administration in public agencies and appeals of audits was transferred to the judiciary, and its financial pre-review functions were eliminated. Implementation of these changes has been difficult, with some setbacks encountered, but reductions in corruption and increases in effective financial accountability have been achieved.

3. *Build or strengthen links between external stakeholders and agencies of restraint.* For democratic governance, the enforcement dimension of accountability ultimately needs to connect to citizens. Thus, creating and reinforcing links between external actors and agencies of restraint is important for effective enforcement. Ombudsman offices, noted previously in relation to answerability, can be a conduit for these connections. In some countries, ombudsmen have both investigative and prosecutory powers, which increases their relevance for enforcement. For example, the Philippines 1987 constitution gives the Ombudsman a mandate to investigate and prosecute

public officials or agencies for "any act or omission which appears illegal, unjust, improper, or inefficient." It should be noted that such broad powers, depending upon how they are interpreted and applied, can give rise to administrative gridlock and over-accountability. Finding the right balance is important.

Anti-corruption agencies are another target for strengthening connections to external actors. Some agencies have set up volunteer watchdog programs and telephone hotlines. Others have conducted publicity campaigns to publicize the problem of corruption. On the demand-side, CSOs have undertaken similar sensitization campaigns and watchdog efforts.

A related strategy for performance accountability is to involve citizens in evaluating service quality and staff performance in service delivery agencies. Tendler (1997) provides an example from the health sector in Brazil. The state of Ceara's health department designed a decentralized primary health care program for municipalities that created strong links between health care providers (community health workers) and citizens. The state health department served the function of an agency of restraint, exercising tight control over the hiring, and payment of the large labor force of health agents, who worked under the direction of nurse-supervisors hired by the municipality. This oversight led to increased objectivity in hiring, a professional esprit de corps, and local accountability for performance. At the municipal level, the program established community monitoring of the workers and encouraged client–worker interchange regarding health problems and needs. As a result, over time the health workers voluntarily took on more tasks in response to their clients' needs, clients came to trust the workers and their commitment, leading to further increases in program performance. The reasons for the program's success stemmed from practices that reinforced accountability to clients, community participation in performance monitoring, commitment to service delivery, and transparency. This process of embedding public agencies in their local environments is recognized as encouraging responsiveness to citizens and providing incentives for positive behaviors (e.g., see Evans, 1996).

4. *Develop positive accountability sanctions.* In many developing and transitioning countries, institutional weaknesses in agencies of restraint and the high costs of enforcement can impose constraints on increasing accountability. As a supplementary strategy, the use of incentives-based enforcement is an option worthy of further exploration. The World Bank's support of civil servants making public integrity pledges, already noted earlier, is an example (see Langseth et al., 1999). The International Development Law

Institute's (IDLI's) work on judicial codes of conduct is another. IDLI also supports the formation of professional associations of lawyers and judges in developing countries, using as a nucleus participants in IDLI seminars and training courses. The Brazilian primary health care case also illustrates how positive sanctions, such as the affirmative feedback clients give to health care workers, can support increased accountability.

External to government, professionalization of the media is an intervention option that can create positive sanctions for accountability. For example, USAID has supported a program for increased media independence and quality of reporting in Central and Eastern Europe, in co-operation with the U.S. Information Agency (Biddle et al., 1998). CSO watchdog support programs can also fall into the category of providing positive sanctions because they sometimes include efforts to establish standards of ethics and equity as part of their performance monitoring of government actors.

References

AAA (Americas' Accountability Anti-Corruption Project), World Bank Institute successfully integrates civil society input with municipal governance to thwart corruption at local level. *Accountability/Anti-Corruption* 21 (January), 1, 12–13, 2000.

Aucoin, P. and Heintzman, R., The dialectics of accountability for performance in public management reform. *Int. Rev. Adm. Sci.*, 66 (1), 45–55, 2000.

Behn, R.D., The new public management paradigm and the search for democratic accountability, *IPMJ*, 1 (2), 1331–1164, 1998.

Behn, R.D., *Rethinking Democratic Accountability*, Brookings Institution Press, Washington, DC, 2001.

Biddle, C.S., Hopkins, M., and Harencar, O., *Evaluation of the USAID Professional Media Program in Central and Eastern Europe.* Arlington, VA: Development Associates, for the U.S. Agency for International Development, 1998.

Brinkerhoff, D.W., Government-nonprofit partners for health sector reform in Central Asia: family group practice associations in Kazakhstan and Kyrgyzstan. *Pub. Adm. Dev.*, 22 (1), 51–63, 2002.

Brinkerhoff, D.W. and Fox, L.M., *Combating Corruption in Madagascar: An Analysis and Assessment.* Washington, DC: U.S. Agency for International Development, Center for Democracy and Governance, Implementing Policy Change Project, Phase II, July, 1999.

de Sousa Santos, B., Participatory budgeting in Porto Alegre: towards a redistributive democracy, *Politics Soc.*, 26 (4), 461–510, 1998.

Evans, P., Government action, social capital and development: reviewing the evidence on synergy, *World Dev.*, 24 (6), 1119–1132, 1996.

Giddings, P. and Gregory, R., Eds., *Righting Wrongs: The Ombudsman in Six Continents*, IOS Press, Amsterdam, 2000.

Langan, P. and Cooksey, B., Eds., The National Integrity System in Tanzania: Proceedings of a Workshop Convened by the Prevention of Corruption Bureau, Tanzania, Mount Meru Hotel, Arusha, Tanzania, 10–12 August 1995. Washington, DC and Dar es Salaam: World Bank, Economic Development Institute and Prevention of Corruption Bureau of Tanzania, 1995.

Langseth, P., Stapenhurst, R., and Pope, J., National integrity systems, in *Curbing Corruption: Toward a Model for Building National Integrity*, Rick Stapenhurst, R. and Kpundeh, S.J., Eds., World Bank, Economic Development Institute, Washington, DC, 1999, pp. 127–149.

March, J.G. and Olsen, J.P., *Democratic Governance*, Free Press, New York, 1995.

McGann, J.G. and Weaver, R.K., Eds., *Think Tanks and Civil Societies: Catalysts for Ideas and Actions*, Transaction Publishers, Piscataway, NJ, 2001.

Mulgan, R., Accountability: an ever-expanding concept? *Pub. Adm.*, 78 (3), 555–573, 2000.

Nolan, L.M,. Just and honest government. *Pub. Adm. Dev.*, 8 (5), 447–457, 1998.

O'Donnell, G., Horizontal accountability in new democracies, in *The Self-Restraining State: Power and Accountability in New Democracies*, Schedler, A., Diamond, L., and Plattner, M.F., Eds., Lynne Rienner Publishers, Boulder, CO, 1999, pp. 29–53.

Paul, S., Accountability in public services: exit, voice and control, *World Dev.*, 20 (7), 1047–1060, 1992.

Paul, S. and Sekhar, S., *Benchmarking Urban Services: The Second Report Card on Bangalore*, Public Affairs Centre, Bangalore, June, 2000.

PUMA (Public Management Service), *Performance Auditing and the Modernisation of Government*, Organisation for Economic Co-operation and Development, Paris, 1996.

PUMA, Impact of the emerging information society on the policy development process and democratic quality. *PUMA Report* No. 98, Organisation for Economic Co-operation and Development, Paris, 1998.

Sanchez de Lozada, A., In pursuit of public accountability in Bolivia, in *Curbing Corruption: Toward a Model for Building National Integrity*, Stapenhurst, R., and Kpundeh, S.J., Eds., World Bank, Economic Development Institute, Washington, DC, 1999, pp. 67–87.

Schedler, A., Conceptualizing accountability, in *The Self-Restraining State: Power and Accountability in New Democracies*, Schedler, A., Diamond, L., and Plattner, M.F., Eds., Lynne Rienner Publishers, Boulder, CO, 1999, pp. 13–29.

Smulovitz, C. and Peruzzotti, E., Societal accountability in Latin America. *J. Democracy*, 11 (4), 147–158, 2000.

Tendler, J., *Good Government in the Tropics*, Johns Hopkins University Press, Baltimore, 1997.

Thurmaier, K., The role of budget reform in the accountability of Polish and Ukrainian local governments, *IPMJ*, 6 (1), 17–43, 2003.

Uhr, J., *Accountability, Scrutiny, and Oversight*. Canberra: Australian National University, Center for Democratic Institutions and Commonwealth

Secretariat. Workshop on Accountability, Scrutiny, and Oversight, Background Paper, May, 2001.

UNDP (United Nations Development Program), *Deepening Democracy in a Fragmented World: Human Development Report*, Oxford University Press, for UNDP, New York, 2002.

Uruena, M., Service delivery surveys and performance measurement. Washington DC: World Bank, Economic Development Institute. Summary Proceedings of a Workshop for El Salvador, Guatemala, and Nicaragua, April 22–26, 1996.

Waisbord, S.R., Investigative journalism and political accountability in South American democracies, *Crit. Stud. Mass Commun.*, 13 (4), 343–363, 1996.

World Bank, *World Development Report 1997: The State in a Changing World*, Washington, DC, Author, 1997.

Chapter 16

Corruption and Development

Susan Rose-Ackerman

CONTENTS

I. Introduction

All political systems need to mediate the relationship between private wealth and public power. Those that fail risk a dysfunctional government captured by wealthy interests. Corruption is one symptom of such failure with private willingness-to-pay trumping public goals. If corruption is endemic, public officials, both bureaucrats and elected officials, may redesign programs and propose public projects with few public benefits and many opportunities for private profit.

This chapter uses the common definition of corruption as the "misuse of public power for private or political gain," recognizing that "misuse" must be defined in terms of some standard. Many corrupt activities under this definition are illegal in most countries. However, part of the policy debate turns on where to draw the legal line and how to regulate borderline phenomena, such as conflicts of interest, which many political systems fail to regulate. One of the most important debates turns on the issue of "state capture" or the problem of creating open democratic and market societies in states where a narrow elite has a disproportionate influence on state policy.

Data on corruption and poor governance are difficult to obtain both because there is no agreement on how to measure these phenomena and because corruption and many aspects of poor governance are not widely publicized. Thus, their impact on economic growth, human well being, and government legitimacy is also difficult to assess. Because corrupt payments are made in a wide range of different contexts, their impact will depend upon what is being purchased and who benefits. Nevertheless, in practice, there seems to be a correlation between corruption in one area (e.g., contracting), and in others (e.g., customs).

This chapter provides an overview of the empirical evidence. It does not discuss theoretical work on the causes and consequences of corruption and poor governance. Those who want to pursue these issues further should refer to my two books — Rose-Ackerman (1978, 1999) which includes extensive references to the literature. To access current work, the World Bank Institute maintains a website [http://www.worldbank.org/wbi/governance] as does Transparency International (TI), an international nongovernmental organization committed to fighting corruption [http://www.transparency.org]. Several recent literature reviews are at the website of U4 Utstein Anti-Corruption Resource Centre [http://www.u4.no].

I begin with cross-country studies that explain the consequences of corruption and poor governance for economic growth and well being. The second section considers firm level surveys that explore the consequences of corruption for firm behavior. Next, I summarize surveys that provide a window onto individual attitudes toward and experiences with corruption and dysfunctional government. Then, I turn the causal link around and review studies that seek to determine the causes of poor government and corruption. Finally, I introduce distinctions between administrative corruption and "state capture." I conclude with some thoughts on promising reform strategies.

II. The Consequences of Corruption and Poor Governance: Cross-Country Research

Measures of corruption and poor governance are correlated with per capita income and with the United Nations Human Development Index (HDI). Richer countries, on average, have less reported corruption and better functioning governments.[1] The same holds true for countries with high levels of the HDI, a measure that includes estimates of health and educational attainment as well as a logarithmic estimates of income. However, the direction of causation is not clear. To some, marginal improvements in governance are of questionable benefit to poor and corrupt countries, and good governance is a "luxury good" that citizens will demand once they are rich enough to care. However, the available statistical evidence demonstrates that, correcting for other factors, poor governance is itself one of the reasons why some countries are poor and have low or negative growth rates (Kaufmann and Kraay, 2002). Most likely, both directions of causation hold. Demands for greater democracy, transparency, and integrity in government often become more insistent as per capita income rises. However, to the extent that corrupt rulers recognize this possibility, they have an incentive to limit prosperity to constrain such demands. Those who benefit from a corrupt status quo will try to impede reform. Improvements in human well being seldom occur spontaneously but, instead, require government actions to complement private efforts. Governments that waste resources through malfeasance or inadvertence are a drag on growth and undermine the achievement of other goals.

Numerous studies use indices for measuring perceptions of corruption at the country level.[2] They find that high levels of corruption are associated with lower levels of investment and growth, and that corruption discourages both capital inflows and foreign direct investment (Mauro, 1995; Wei, 2000; Graf Lambsdorff, 2003a). Countries perceived as more corrupt pay a higher risk premium when issuing bonds (Ciocchini et al., 2003). Corruption lowers productivity, reduces the effectiveness of industrial policies, and encourages business to operate in the unofficial sector in violation of tax and regulatory laws (Ades and Di Tella, 1997; Kaufmann, 1997; Graf Lambsdorff, 2003b).

Highly corrupt countries tend to under-invest in human capital by spending less on education, to over-invest in public infrastructure relative to private investment, and to have lower levels of environmental quality (Mauro, 1997; Esty and Porter, 2002; Tanzi and Davoodi, 2002). High levels of corruption produce a more unequal distribution of income under some conditions, but the mechanism may be complex—operating through lower investments in education and lower per capita incomes (Gupta et al., 2001, 2002; Li et al., 2000).

Corrupt governments lack political legitimacy (Anderson and Tverdova, 2003). However, political supporters of corrupt incumbent governments express more positive views. Surveys carried out in Latin America in 1998 and 1999 showed that those exposed to corruption had both lower levels of belief in the political system and lower interpersonal trust (Seligman, 2002). In Nicaragua, respondents were asked if the payment of bribes "facilitates getting things done in the bureaucracy." Those who agreed that corruption gets things done were *less* likely to believe in the legitimacy of the political system (Seligman, 2002: 429). Surveys of firms in countries making a transition from socialism provide complementary findings. Firms with close connections with the government did better than other firms, but countries where such connections were seen as important for business success did worse overall than those where political influence was less closely tied to economic success (Fries et al., 2003).

In circumstances of low government legitimacy, citizens try to avoid paying taxes, and firms go underground to escape the burden of bureaucracy, including attempts to solicit bribes. Uslaner (2003) shows that high levels of perceived corruption are associated with high levels of tax evasion. Torgler's (2003) study of attitudes toward tax evasion in Central and Eastern Europe shows that when individuals perceived that corruption was high, they were less likely to say that people have an obligation to pay taxes. Corrupt governments tend to be smaller than more honest governments, everything else equal (Friedman et al., 2000; Johnson et al., 2000). Thus in corrupt governments, the individual projects are excessively expensive and unproductive, but the overall size of the government is relatively small.

III. Business Surveys on the Consequences of Corruption

More nuance comes from surveys that questioned businesses about the costs of corruption, red tape, and other constraints on doing business. The World Business Environment Survey (WBES), carried out between the end of 1998 and the middle of 2000 under World Bank auspices, questioned several thousand enterprises in 80 countries (Batra et al., 2003). A high frequency of corruption had a significant negative impact on firms' sales and investment growth over 1997–1999. As the authors conclude, "While it may be difficult and take years to reform taxes, financing, corruption, and policy predictability, the evidence suggests that higher growth and investment are associated with such improvements" (Batra et al., 2003: 14).

Other research studied countries as diverse as those in Asia, sub-Saharan Africa, and Central and Eastern Europe. Most results are broadly consistent with the WBES survey (Hellman et al., 2000; Johnson et al., 2000; Dollar et al., 2003: 7; Hellman and Kaufmann, 2004). Surveys demonstrate how firms manage to cope when the legal system is weak. Informal relationships built on trust and private sanctions exist but cannot easily bear the entire burden of maintaining business deals. Weak states produce widespread corruption, private protection rackets, and the flouting of regulatory and tax laws. The countries of Eastern and Central Europe vary in the security of property rights, and countries with more secure property rights have higher levels of new investment by established firms (Johnson et al., 2000, 2002). Property rights are less secure if bribery and protection payments are common and if the courts do not enforce contracts (Johnson et al., 2002). Trust in the state, as a reliable actor seems important. Firms appear willing to substitute legal and impartially administered taxes for the uncertainties of bribe payments and the dangers of relying on private protection services (Friedman et al., 2000; Graf Lambsdorff, 2003a).

IV. Household Surveys

Surveys of individuals provide a counterweight to those who claim that corruption is acceptable to ordinary citizens. Surveys in a range of countries have found widespread popular disapproval of entrenched corruption (e.g., Pasuk and Piriyarangsan, 1994; Anderson et al., 2003).

A study of four countries in Central and Eastern Europe revealed that people disapprove of corruption even if they report engaging in it themselves (Miller et al., 2001, 2002). Although, experience with corruption varied markedly, the public's underlying values and norms did not differ greatly. A majority in each country expressed strong moral disapproval of payoffs, but, at the same time, a plurality of citizens said they would pay a bribe if asked. The basic problem is not a weakness in the underlying values of citizens and public officials but an excess of corrupt opportunities. The officials most likely to receive gifts or bribes are hospital doctors, traffic police, and customs officials. One hopeful finding was that people's attitudes toward bribery were affected by their perceptions of others' actions. Attitudes are not deeply entrenched but depend on situation-specific variables, such as one's perception about whether or not others are paying.

V. Causes of Corruption and Poor Governance

Cross-country data permit one to obtain a broad overview of the underlying causes of corruption and weak governance. I have already mentioned the role of income and wealth as both a cause and a consequence of corruption. Poor governance contributes to low growth and to the other harmful outcomes noted earlier, and weak underlying economic conditions facilitate corruption.

Some studies find that trade openness and other measures of competitiveness reduce corruption (Ades and Di Tella, 1999; Sandholtz and Keotzle, 2000; Blake and Martin, 2002), suggesting that societies with fewer rents to share are less corrupt. However, once again the causation is unclear; countries that do not favor corrupt firms may be able to establish a policy of open and competitive markets. Graf Lambsdorff (2003a), for example, finds that weak law and order and insecure property rights encourage corruption, which in turn discourages foreign capital inflows. Inequality can contribute to high levels of corruption. In democracies in particular, inequality facilitates corruption, a result consistent with the state capture variant of corruption. The negative effect of inequality on growth may be the result of its impact on corruption taken as a proxy for government weakness (You and Khagram, 2005).

Historical and social factors help to explain cross-country differences. For example, Acemoglu et al. (2001) use the mortality rates of European settlers as an instrument for the type of colonial regime put in place by the imperial power, and find that it does a good job of predicting expropriation risk (and corruption levels) at the end of the 20th century. La Porta et al. (1999) consider legal origin, religion, ethnolinguistic fractionalization, latitude, and per capita income as determinants of a range of features of economic, social, and political life. Corruption, as well as other measures of institutional weakness, is worse in countries with higher ethnolinguistic fragmentation, few Protestants, and Socialist or French legal origins (see also Sandholtz and Keotzle, 2000; Treisman, 2000).

Colonial heritage, legal traditions, religion, and geographical factors seem associated with corruption and other measures of government dysfunction, but they are not policy variables that present day reformers can influence. The key issue is whether these historical regularities directly affect government quality or whether they help to determine intermediate institutions and attitudes that present day policies can affect. In La Porta et al. (1999), the historical variables are not always significant and become entirely insignificant when they add income and latitude. Thus, these historical patterns may operate through their impact on underlying institutional structures, not as direct determinants of corruption. Latitude and history need not be destiny.

A number of studies examine the impact of democracy on corruption. High levels of economic freedom are associated with lower levels of corruption as is an index of democratization (e.g., Sandholtz and Koetzle, 2000; Blake and Martin, 2002; Kunicová and Rose-Ackerman, 2005). Governments with more female participation in politics are less corrupt, and this is consistent with survey evidence suggesting that women are more disapproving of corruption than men (Crook and Manor, 1998: 42; Swamy et al., 2001). Within the universe of democracies, features of government structure, such as presidentialism, closed-list proportional representation (PR), and federalism, facilitate corruption (Treisman, 2000; Kunicová, 2002; Kunicová and Rose-Ackerman, 2005; see Fjeldstad, 2003 for contrasting results for federalism). Presidential systems that use PR to elect their legislature are more corrupt than other types of democracies.

A World Bank survey of business permits cross-country comparisons (Kaufmann et al., 2003: 363–364). Although broad measures of corruption, government quality, and informal sector activity are strongly correlated, more fine-grained analysis often shows pockets of strength and weakness. For example, a study of Bolivia, using this survey, showed that it ranks poorly on several measures of corruption, judicial quality, and property rights, but rather well on standard macro-economic variables such as inflation, the exchange rate, and the quality of the central bank. Because Bolivia has had a low growth rate, the results suggest that getting the macro-economics fundamentals right is not sufficient. Institutional reforms are needed, and within Bolivia itself some public institutions score better than others and may provide reform models (Kaufmann et al., 2003: 364–365).

VI. Crony Capitalism and the Links between Political and Economic Power

World Bank researchers distinguish between administrative corruption and what they call "crony capitalism" or "state capture." Country-specific research on countries such as Russia, Albania, Indonesia, and Malaysia confirms the importance of the distinction. Administrative corruption includes the use of bribery and favoritism to lower taxes, escape regulations, and win low-level procurement contracts. "State capture" implies that the state itself can be characterized as largely serving the interests of a narrow group of business people and politicians, sometimes with criminal elements mixed in. Even if the group with influence changes when the government changes, most of the citizens are left out. Johnston (2004) proposes a richer taxonomy that includes political systems that manipulate private firms for personal gain. He calls this "power chasing wealth" as opposed to "wealth chasing power."

Favored firms may not have secure property rights in the legal sense but may be able to obtain favored treatment because of their insider status (Hellman et al., 2000). The main risk facing such firms is the risk of a change in the political leadership. For example, in a study of Indonesia under President Suharto, Fisman (2001) used an index of the political connectedness of firms listed on the Jakarta Stock Exchange and dubbed it the Suharto Dependency Index. He demonstrates that rumors about Suharto's health problems between 1995 and 1997 had a more negative impact on the share prices of firms with high levels of this index, and that the differential impact was greater as the rumors become worse.

If top political figures themselves exploit their position for private gain, the effectiveness of government programs and the impact of foreign aid and lending suffer. Even if those with good political connections are also good economic managers, there is a long-term risk that they will exploit their dominant positions to squeeze out potential competitors (Acemoglu, 2003). This inequality of influence can extend beyond special treatment by the executive and the legislature to include the courts as well.

VII. Reform Proposals

This research suggests ways to think about reform. First, the simultaneity between income and poor governance implies that purely economic prescriptions, taken alone, will not succeed either in promoting growth or in improving government performance. These policies presuppose a well-functioning government, which is just what is lacking in corrupt countries. Similar problems of simultaneity exist for trade openness and inequality. Thus proposals to improve governance by concentrating on economic growth, trade openness, and reductions in inequality beg the question of how weak states could accomplish such fundamental changes. Second, history and latitude may be important, but they are givens, not policy tools. Third, some features of political systems seem to promote honest and effective government: high levels of economic freedom, parliamentary structure, certain types of electoral institutions, and avoidance of private capture of the state and of state capture of the economy. Some of these statistical associations could be translated into particular policy proposals, but most of them are not easy to operationalize. My own emphasis is on middle-range proposals that concentrate on particular sectors and deal with government accountability from the bottom up. They are consistent with the broad empirical regularities outlined previously, but they have a more selective focus.

My proposals are grounded in the following: (1) To the extent that low corruption is associated with beneficial outcomes — stronger growth, higher incomes, and more equal income distribution — the explanation is not corruption taken in isolation but, rather, the close correlation between corruption and other measures of the way government functions. (2) From this, it follows that policies to improve government functioning should not primarily focus on enforcing criminal laws against corrupt dealings. These laws are a necessary background condition but will mean little unless accompanied by more systemic reforms. (3) Instead, one must consider the underlying institutions and habits of behavior that make corruption endemic in some countries and sectors but not in others. (4) Although norms of behavior with historical and social roots influence the level of corruption, corruption is also a crime of opportunity that requires willing participants on both sides of the transaction. Variations in corruption within a country suggest that this is so. Thus, a country's legacy of corruption and poor governance need not be accepted as somehow determined for all time. The situation can be improved on a case-by-case basis. (5) Political and bureaucratic corruption can be traced to the interaction of greed and self-interest with government institutions. However, different factors create corrupt incentives in each case, and hence they need different policy responses.

Based on existing research and my own view of the way the parts of the good government puzzle fit together, the following policies seem worthy of further analysis. This is not meant to be an exhaustive list, but only a set of suggestions. In this short paper, I am not able to assess these proposals in detail, but readers interested in these issues should refer to my paper for the Copenhagen Consensus project.[3] Here, I mention the main outlines of possible policy responses.

(1) *Accountability*: There are many successful examples of programs that improve accountability at the grass roots, and these cases provide lessons that can be applied elsewhere. Some cases, such as school financing in Uganda and public works construction in Nepal, suggest that relatively simple, inexpensive reforms can have large benefits if the political will exists (Meagher et al., 2000; Reinikka and Svensson, 2002, 2004a, 2004b).

(2) *Procurement*: Efforts to develop benchmark cost estimates that can help constrain procurement fraud and corruption appear promising. This would require a fairly costly data gathering efforts, but

given the large cost distortions in contracting, the gains could be large. Research in Italy suggests the feasibility of such efforts (Golden and Picci, 2005).

(3) *Revenue collection*: Corruption in revenue collection can be contained through tax simplification and incentive-based reforms (Das Gupta and Mookerjee, 1998; Chand and Moene, 1999; Devas et al., 2001). Once again, the net benefits of a well-designed program can be large, but the mixed record of past efforts suggests caution. See, for example, the instructive study of a failed reform in Fjeldsted (2003).

(4) *Business regulation*: Streamlining business regulations can limit corruption (Fries et al., 2003). However, past work has only looked at the gains to business and had failed to consider the costs to society of eliminating regulations that provide social benefits. Thus policy must balance the benefits and costs of regulations.

(5) *International initiatives*: Several initiatives are underway to increase transparency in international concession contracts for natural resources. (See http://www.dfid.gov.uk for more details.) The World Bank has set up monitoring institutions to increase transparency in a major infrastructure project in Africa (http://www.gic-iag.org). These options appear promising and should be watched closely for the lessons they can provide.

The operation of the state and its interaction with the public are key challenges facing the world. If government performance does not improve in many states, programs designed to help the poor, improve the natural environment, and stimulate economic growth will have little impact and risk inflicting harm. The reform options outlined above all seem to have some promise and deserve more careful development and testing in pilot programs.

Discussions of how to allocate foreign assistance to developing countries sometimes conclude that some countries have such poorly functioning institutions that no external aid should be provided because so much of it will be lost. This represents not, as some say, an end to conditionality but is instead conditionality writ large — at the level of the country as a whole, rather than at the level of the program. The best mixture seems to be broad-based decisions about which countries to support with some share of aid taking the form of grants to improve government performance. Outsiders would not micro-manage individual projects, for example, to build roads, support education, and provide health care. Instead they would supply technical assistance that sometimes might lead to a quite deep involvement with the details of government operations. In contrast, policies which try to isolate corrupt countries and individuals from the international community encourage their rulers to descend into paranoia and isolation and are ineffective ways to help the citizens of these countries who are the real victims of corruption. Corruption is a problem of institutional failure. A "clean hands" policy in which wealthy countries hold themselves aloof from tainted countries and individuals without doing anything actually to address the underlying problems will simply further divide the world into rich and poor blocs.

Acknowledgments

This paper is derived from Rose-Ackerman (2004b), a longer paper prepared for the Copenhagen Consensus Project of the Environmental Assessment Institute, Copenhagen. I also draw on Rose-Ackerman (1999). I am grateful to Madiha Afzal and Dionysia-Theodora Avgerinopoulou for very useful research help.

Notes

1. Kaufman (2003, Annex 2, Figures 1A, 1B, IC) presents three figures showing the positive correlations between the log of read GDP per capita and corruption, the rule of law, and voice and accountability, respectively. The governance measures are derived from survey evidence mostly based on the perceptions of business people.
2. The original Corruption Perceptions Index was developed by TI as a compilation of various surveys. The World Bank has made use of similar data to produce its own index. The indices are highly correlated.
3. Rose-Ackerman (2004b). For more on the establishment of the rule of law in weak states see Rose-Ackerman (2004a).

References

Acemoglu, D., The form of property rights: oligarchic vs. democratic societies, NBER Working Paper No. 10037, Cambridge MA, 2003.
Acemoglu, D., Johnson, S., and Robinson, J.A., The colonial origins of comparative development: an empirical investigation, *Am. Econ. Rev.*, 91, 1369–1401, 2001.
Ades, A. and Di Tella, R., National champions and corruption: some unpleasant interventionist arithmetic, *Econ. J.*, 107, 1023–1042, 1997.
Ades, A. and Di Tella, R., Rents, competition, and corruption, *Am. Econ. Rev.*, 89, 982–993, 1999.

Anderson, C.J. and Tverdova, Y.V., Corruption, political allegiances, and attitudes toward government in contemporary democracies, *Am. J. Polit. Sci.*, 47, 91–109, 2003.

Anderson, J., Kaufmann, D., and Recanatini, F., Service delivery, poverty and corruption — common threads from diagnostic surveys, Background paper for 2004, *World Development Report*, World Bank, Washington, DC, June 27, 2003 (www.worldbank.org/wbi/governance/capacitybuild/d-surveys.html).

Batra, G., Kaufmann, D., and Stone, A.H.W., The firms speak: what the world business environment survey tells us about constraints on private sector development, in *Pathways Out of Poverty: Private Firms and Economic Mobility in Developing Countries*, Fields, G. and Pfefferman, G., Eds., Kluwer Academic Publishers, Amsterdam, 2003 (Chapter 9, http://www.worldbank.org/wbi/governance/pubs/firmsspeak.html).

Blake, C.H. and Martin, C.G., Combating corruption: reexamining the role of democracy, Paper presented at the Annual Meeting of the Midwest Political Science Association, Chicago, April 25–28, 2002.

Brown, T., Contracting out by local governments in transitioning nations: the role of technical assistance in Ukraine, *Admin. Soc.*, 32, 728–755, 2001.

Chand, S.K. and Moene, K.O., Controlling fiscal corruption, *World Dev.*, 27, 1129–1140, 1999.

Ciocchini, F., Durbin, E., and Ng, D.T.C., Does corruption increase emerging market bond spreads? *J. Econ. Bus.*, 55, 503–528, 2003.

Crook, R.C. and Manor, J., *Democracy and Decentralization in South Asia and West Africa: Participation, Accountability and Performance*, Cambridge University Press, Cambridge, UK, 1998.

Das Gupta, A. and Mookerjee, D., *Incentives and Institutional Reform in Tax Enforcement: An Analysis of Developing Country Experience*, Oxford University Press, Delhi, 1998.

De Soto, H., *The Other Path: The Invisible Revolution in the Third World*, Harper and Row, New York, 1989.

Devas, N., Delay, S., and Hubbard, M., Revenue authorities: are they the right vehicle for improving tax administration? *Public Admin. Dev.*, 21, 211–222, 2001.

Dia, M., *Africa's Management in the 1990s and Beyond: Reconciling Indigenous and Transplanted Institutions*, The World Bank, Washington, DC, 1996.

Dollar, D., Hallward-Driemeier, M., and Mengiste, T., Investment climate and international integration, Draft paper prepared for Conference on the Future of Globalization, Yale Center for the Study of Globalization, October 11, World Bank, Washington, DC, 2003.

Esty, D. and Porter, M., National environmental performance measurement and determinants, in *Environmental Performance Measurement: The Global Report 2001–2002*, Esty, D. and Cornelius, P.K., Eds., Oxford University Press, New York, 2002, pp. 24–43.

Fisman, R., Estimating the value of political connections, *Am. Econ. Rev.*, 91, 1095–1102, 2001.

Fjeldsted, O.-H., Fighting fiscal corruption: Lessons from the Tanzania Revenue Authority, *Public Administration and Development*, 23, 165–175, 2003.

Fjeldsted, O.-H., *Decentralisation and Corruption: A Review of the Literature*, U4 Report, Chr. Michelsen Institute, Bergen, Norway, 2003.

Friedman, E., Johnson, S., Kaufmann, D., and Zoido-Lobaton, P., Dodging the grabbing hand: the determinant of unofficial activity in 69 countries, *J. Public Econ.*, 76, 459–493, 2000.

Fries, S., Lysenko, T., and Polanec, S., The 2002 Business Environment and Enterprise Performance Survey: Results from a Survey of 6,100 Firms, *Working Paper* No. 84, European Bank for Reconstructions and Development, London, November, 2003.

Golden, M. and Picci, L., Proposal for a new measure of corruption, illustrated with Italian data, *Economics and Politics*, 17, 37–75, 2004.

Graf Lambsdorff, J., How corruption affects persistent capital flows, *Econ. Govern.*, 4, 229–243, 2003a.

Graf Lambsdorff, J., How corruption affects productivity, *Kyklos*, 56, 457–474, 2003b.

Gupta, S., Davoodi, H.R., and Alonso-Terme, R., Does corruption affect income inequality and poverty, *Econ. Governance*, 3, 23–45, 2002.

Gupta, S., Davoodi, H.R., and Tiongson, E., Corruption and the provision of health care and education services, in *The Political Economy of Corruption*, Jain, A.K., Ed., Routledge, London, 2000, pp. 111–141.

Hellman, J.S., Jones, G., and Kaufmann, D., *Seize the State, Seize the Day: State Capture, Corruption, and Influence in Transition*, Policy Research Working Paper 2444, World Bank, Washington, DC, 2000.

Hellman, J.S. and Kaufmann, D., The inequality of influence, in *Building a Trustworthy State in Post-Socialist Transition*, Kornai, J. and Rose-Ackerman, S., Eds., Palgrave, New York, 2004, pp. 100–118.

Hubbard, M.E.V., Delay, S., and Devas, C.N., Revenue authorities: are they the right vehicle for improving tax administration? *Public Admin. Dev.*, 21, 211–222, 2001.

Johnson, S., Kaufmann, D., McMillan, J., and Woodruff, C., Why do firms hide? Bribes and unofficial activity after communism, *J. Public Econ.*, 76, 495–520, 2000.

Johnson, S., McMillan, J., and Woodruff, C., Entrepreneurs and the ordering of institutional reform: Poland, Slovakia, Russia and Ukraine compared, *Econ. Transition*, 8, 1–36, 2000.

Johnson, S., McMillan, J., and Woodruff, C., Property rights and finance, *Am. Econ. Rev.*, 92, 1335–1357, 2002.

Johnston, M., Comparing corruption: participation, institutions, and development, in *Private and Public Corruption*, Heffernan, W.C., and Kleinig, J., Eds., Rowman and Little Field, Lanham MD, 2004, 275–322.

Kaufmann, D., The missing pillar of growth strategy for Ukraine: institutional and policy reforms for private sector development, in *Ukraine: Accelerating the Transition to Market*, Cornelius, P.K. and Lenain, P., Eds., IMF, Washington, 1997, pp. 234–275.

Kaufmann, D., Rethinking governance: empirical lessons challenge orthodoxy, Discussion draft, World Bank, Washington, DC, 2003.

Kaufmann, D. and Kraay, A., Growth without governance, *Economica*, 3, 169–229, 2002.

Kaufmann, D., Mastruzzi, M., and Zaveleta, D., Sustained macroeconomic reforms, tepid growth: a governance puzzle in Bolivia, in *In Search of Prosperity: Analytic Narratives on Economic Growth*, Rodrik, D., Ed., Princeton University Press, Princeton, 2003, pp. 334–398.

Kunicová, J., Are presidential systems more susceptible to political corruption? Draft, California Institute of Technology, Pasadena, CA, 2002.

Kunicová, J. and Rose-Ackerman, S., Electoral rules and constitutional structures as constraints on corruption *British J. Pol. Sci.*, 35, forthcoming 2005.

La Porta, R., Lopez-de-Silanes, F., Shleifer, A., and Vishny, R., The quality of government, *J. Law Econ. Organization*, 15, 222–279, 1999.

Li, H., Xu, L.C., and Zou, H.F., Corruption, income distribution, and growth, *Econ. Polit.* 12, 155–182, 2000.

Mauro, P., Corruption and growth, *Quart. J. Econ.*, 110, 681–712, 1995.

Mauro, P., The effects of corruption on growth, investment, and government expenditure: a cross-country analysis, in *Corruption and the Global Economy*, Elliott, K.A., Ed., Institute for International Economics, Washington, DC, 1997, pp. 83–108.

Meagher, P., Upadhyaya, K., and Wilkinson, B., *Combating Rural Public Works Corruption: Food-for-Work Programs in Nepal*, IRIS Center Working Paper No. 239, University of Maryland, College Park, MD, February, 2000 (available at http://www.iris.umd.edu/publications.asp).

Miller, W.L., Grødeland, A., and Koshechkina, T.Y., *A Culture of Corruption: Coping with Government in Post-Communist Europe*, Central European University Press, Budapest, 2001.

Miller, W.L., Grødeland, A., and Koshechkina, T.Y., Values and norms *versus* extortion and temptation, in *Corrupt Exchanges: Empirical Themes in the Politics and Political Economy of Corruption*, della Porta, D. and Rose-Ackerman, S., Eds., Nomos Verlag, Frankfurt, 2002, pp. 135–146.

Pasuk P. and Piriyarangsan, S., *Corruption and Democracy in Thailand*, The Political Economy Centre, Faculty of Economics, Chulalongkorn Univerisity, Bangkok, 1994.

Reinikka, R. and Svensson, J., Measuring and understanding corruption at the micro level, in *Corrupt Exchanges: Empirical Themes in the Politics and Political Economy of Corruption*, della Porta, D. and Rose-Ackerman, S., Eds., Nomos Verlag, Frankfurt, 2002, pp. 134–146.

Reinikka, R. and Svensson, J., Local capture: evidence from a central government transfer program in Uganda, *Quart. J. Econ.*, 119 (2), 678–704, 2004a.

Reinikka, R. and Svensson, J., The power of information: evidence from a newspaper campaign to reduce corruption, Policy Research Working Paper Series, World Bank, Washington, DC, 2004b.

Rose-Ackerman, S., *Corruption: A Study in Political Economy*, Academic Press, New York, 1978.

Rose-Ackerman, S., *Corruption and Government: Causes, Consequences and Reform*, Cambridge University Press, Cambridge, England, 1999.

Rose-Ackerman, S., Establishing the rule of law, in Rotberg, R., Ed., *When States Fail: Causes and Consequences*, Princeton University Press, Princeton, NJ, 2004a, pp. 182–221.

Rose-Ackerman, S., Governance and corruption, Global Crises, Global Solutions, in Lomborg, B., Ed., Cambridge University Press, Cambridge, UK, 2004b, pp. 301–362.

Sandholtz, W. and Keotzle, W., Accounting for corruption: economic structure, democracy, and trade, *Int. Stud. Quart.*, 44, 31–50, 2000.

Seligman, M., The impact of corruption on regime legitimacy: a comparative study of four Latin American countries, *J. Polit.*, 64, 408–433, 2002.

Swamy, A., Knack, S., Lee, Y., and Azfar, O., Gender and corruption, *J. Dev. Econ.*, 64, 25–55, 2001.

Tanzi, V. and Davoodi, H., (2002). Corruption, public investment and growth, in *Governance, Corruption, and Economic Performance*, Abed, G.T. and Khagram, S., Eds., International Monetary Fund, Washington, DC, 2002, pp. 280–299.

Torgler, B., Tax morale in Central and Eastern European Countries, Prepared for the Conference on Tax Evasion, Trust, and State Capacity, University of St. Gallen, St. Gallen, Switzerland, October, 2003.

Treisman, D., The causes of corruption: a cross-national study, *J. Public Econ.*, 76, 399–457, 2000.

Uslaner, E.M., Tax evasion, trust, and the strong arm of the law, Prepared for the Conference on Tax Evasion, Trust, and State Capacity, University of St. Gallen, St. Gallen, Switzerland, October, 2003.

Webster, L.M. and Charap, J., *The Emergence of Private Sector Manufacturing in St. Petersburg*, World Bank Technical Paper 228, World Bank, Washington, DC, 1993.

Wei, S.-J., How taxing is corruption on international investors? *Rev. Econ. Statist.*, 82, 1–11, 2000.

You, J.-S. and Khagram, S., A comparative study of inequality and corruption, *Amer. Soc. Rev.*, 70, 136–157, 2005.

Chapter 17

Ten Major Flaws in Combating Corruption: A Cautionary Note

Gerald E. Caiden

CONTENTS

305

I. Introduction

In December 2003, the United Nations General Assembly passed its first major sweeping resolution on corruption after several years of drafting, during which it was watered down from its original formulation. This was the culmination of a decade-long pressure by international agencies to put the issue in the forefront of world attention (International Monetary Fund, 1997; Council of Europe, 1998; Organization for Economic Cooperation and Development, 1999; United Nations Development Program, 1999; World Bank, 1997, 2000, 2004). Many of them had previously shied away from the whole topic, but with time it became more and more obvious that corruption was an impediment to world development. They took the initiative to organize conferences and programs to educate the world leaders about the menace of corruption and ways by which it could be combated (Leiken, 1996; Kauffman et al., 1999, 2002; Caiden, 2000; Sheptycki, 2000). Enthused, they expected dramatic results. Despite their fruitful efforts and the progress observed, more than in the previous decades, they have been somewhat disappointed, probably because of their high expectations. The major reason for the setback is that they overlooked the flaws and the difficulties involved in the anticorruption campaigns. This chapter examines ten such flaws in light of recent history. The aim is to be more realistic. It is not intended to disparage any attempt to reduce corruption, for any progress in doing so is a blessing for civilization and a relief for the world's poor.

Almost all great books of the civilized literature dwell on the imperfections of human-kind and they go beyond mere description to prescribing better behavior, improved arrangements, and guidelines towards some better utopia. They condemn harmful behavior such as murder and rape; foul motivations such as lust and greed; horrifying outcomes such as genocide and other crimes against humanity. Religious tend to lump all these together as "sin," whereas the nonreligious tend to use "corruption" to describe a conduct unbecoming, a conduct that deviated from expected social norms, grace, and models for the innocent young. In any event, both recognize that flawed human beings are susceptible to corruption, to disrespectful social behavior, irrespective of circumstances, and that they should be held personally responsible for their antisocial acts.

Optimists are forever hopeful that in time human beings can improve their behavior, master their basic instincts, and adopt more civilized social arrangements, thereby diminishing corrupt conduct (Caiden et al., 2001). Looking back over thousands of years of emerging civilization, they can point to many successes such as overcoming habitual cannibalism and incest, even if they have been disappointed when it comes to warfare, violence, exploitation, and discrimination (Woodworth, 2001). Their idealism leads them to believe that one day, good will eventually triumph over evil, although the going will be tough. For instance, political economist Adam Smith in his classic *The Wealth of Nations* (1776) pointed out that although the hidden hand of the market and perfect competition would transform individual self-interest into collective good, the natural instinct of producers was to combine, restrict competition, and ignore the social obligations of business. Almost a century later, another political economist, Karl Marx in *Das Kapital* (1867) predicted that this greed of capitalists would eventually result in class warfare, wherein an alternative socialist economy would emerge based on the essential goodness of the laboring classes and people's willingness to share and share alike. But realist Lord Acton cautioned that "power corrupts; absolute power corrupts absolutely," whether capitalist or socialist, as subsequent history has shown.

At this metaphysical level, attempts to combat corruption seem to be doomed as long as human nature is flawed. Progress may be made occasionally, but the bad will eventually reappear just like the plague unless vigilance is maintained. Even then, corruption forever lurks in the background, and if it is not combated will eventually undermine whatever progress has been achieved and will destroy civilization itself (Bayat et al., 1999). However, such pessimism is probably unfounded as clearly there is much difference between societies where corruption has become an isolated fact of society and societies where it is a way of life (Gray and Kauffman, 1998). Nevertheless, even modernized societies like Italy, Russia, and South Korea ponder why they have yet to curb traditional patterns of corruption that include pervasive bribery, inappropriate gift giving, and under-the-table payments (Demick, 2004).

This is made abundantly clear in all the current attempts, however crude, to measure it by the *Global Corruption Report* and the Bribe Payers Index of Transparency International (TI); the Civil Society Index of CIVICUS (2000); the Index of Budget Transparency, which is a five country study in Latin America; the Post Communist (New Europe) Barometer, which is a mass public opinion survey assessing changes in the countries of the former Soviet Union; the *Latinobarometro* (1995) and confidential studies conducted by the World Bank and the regional development banks, the International Monetary Fund, and the United Nations Organization; as well as the studies undertaken by nongovernmental organizations and academic researchers (Tanzi, 1998; Hellman et al., 2000; Lambsdorff, 2000; Court and Hyden, 2003; Transparency International, 2003). They all confirm that the quality of life is so different where people respect one another, trust each other, cooperate for the common good, invest without fear and behave with integrity, as contrasted with where people are forever at one another's throats, suspicious, fractious, threatening, and untrustworthy. The former build on solid foundations and progress, whereas the latter get stuck in shifting sand and barely move (Mauro, 1995; Williams, 2000; Williams and Theobald, 2000). For example, the current plight of China's north-east rust belt, plagued by bribery, favoritism, mafia influence, and other widespread criminal activities, which will be impossible, says Governor Bo Xilai, to reinvigorate if "we cannot create a clean and honest government and a law abiding society" (Kynge, 2004).

Once such global comparisons are made, the reasons for the contrast between extremes become readily apparent. They involve a whole host of factors, including religion, culture, demography, human rights, socialization, governance, rule of law, social dynamics, economy, literacy, and so forth, all of which make for complex analysis of why corruption persists and what dominant forms it takes in any given society (Tiffen, 1999; Williams, 2000). While no society is absolutely free of corruption, there are some that are so corrupt that one does not know where to start and whether there is any point in trying. This is best seen in the current frustration experienced in Iraq where the foreign governing forces have rarely, if ever, come across such a culture of corruption that seemingly pervades every aspect of Iraqi society while Iraqis blame their ignorance for their inability to maintain control. Corruption is seen as a basic reason for insecurity and doubt, whether the new National Commission on Public Integrity will make that much difference as it will take many years to make any impact on this culture of corruption (Riccardi, 2004). But as with any missionaries, corruption fighters have to believe that the effort in itself is noble and redeeming, that any result is better than none (Frederickson, 1993; Siddiqui, 2001), and that small victories will eventually pay off and mount one day into a bigger victory that would have been worth all the effort (Tanzania Presidential Commission of Inquiry Against Corruption, 1996; Volkov, 2002). By reducing corruption, the quality of life for every man would have improved, the society put on a firmer footing for real development, and social arrangements so altered to prevent any serious reversal.

The task of combating corruption is never easy (Cusimano, 2000). Very often, it is underestimated. Initial successes may blind corruption fighters to their superficial (and easily reversible) results, to the fact that they replace the actors while the play continues virtually unchanged, when it is the play that needs to be radically altered or to the fact that they succeed in actually changing the play but as soon as they have left the scene, the play is restored to what it was previously. They never get to the heart of why corruption exists, why it persists, and why the corrupt outwit them. Despite their good intentions, hard work, and talent, their attempts to combat corruption are flawed (Klitgaard, 1988; Klitgaard et al., 2000; Quah, 2003). Here, ten all too common flaws are considered but they are only samples.

These flaws are generalized in this chapter to avoid giving exact identification of detailed examples, as the legal grounds in doing so are treacherous. The Bank of England (BoE) is finding this out when it now finds itself being sued by the liquidators of the notorious Bank of Credit and Commerce International (BCCI), once a depository for the ill-gotten money of many of the world's corrupt rulers (Adams and Frantz, 1992). Deloitte & Touche are alleging that the supervisory officials of BoE were so reckless in their oversight that they unwittingly put depositors at risk. Although the BoE has statutory immunity against charges of negligence, the case is being brought under the more demanding "malfeasance in public office" requiring the claimants to prove bad faith (dishonesty) by the BoE back to the first licensing of BCCI in 1980s. Regardless of how the BCCI operated, it is the BoE that is at fault for licensing it to operate. The potential damages could amount to well over $1 billion in addition to the tens of millions that will be spent on the case before judgment is reached (Tait, 2004).

Although the facts behind the examples are in the public domain, the risk of being sued by any party is just too high, yet another flaw in fighting corruption (Sunstein, 1998). Suffice to say that the details have been gleaned over many decades of research from newspaper clippings (especially *The Economist, The Wall Street Journal*, and *The Financial Times*), court hearings, interviews, official documents, conferences, whistle-blowers (van Buitenen, 2000; Skapinker, 2004), and exchanges with academics and practitioners who have taken on the corrupt and survived to tell their tales.

II. The Ten Flaws

A. Flaw 1: Tunnel Vision

Corruption, like sin, covers a wide variety of human misconduct, deception, and cheating, any form of which deserves a study in itself. Espionage is quite different from influence-peddling, just as illicit trade is different from money laundering (Naylor, 1999) or fraud. There may or may not be any connection between them but to focus on just one aspect is to ignore the actual dimensions of the subject and the actual extent to which corruption exists in any community. Too many definitions of corruption are unwieldy, confusing, and narrow, concentrating on bribery and graft and associated cover-ups of extra-legal emoluments and overpayments, which all add to costs and penalize purchasers of goods and services (Alatas, 1990; Tiihonen, 2001; Heidenheimer and Johnston, 2002; Harris, 2003). This is a form of extortion, whenever demand exceeds supply, and it can be extracted wherever the goods and services in question are basic to survival and the purchasers are desperate to obtain them, as is often the case in disasters and emergencies.

Extortion is a serious form of corruption that deserves prior attention and it is likely to be associated with other serious forms that accompany bribery and graft (Noonan, 1984). But it is not the only form that merits priority. Scarcity is handicapping enough to those without any means to pay or access bribe takers, but the deliberate or false creation of scarcity by hiding or otherwise withdrawing goods and services in order to exploit people's plight is worse. So too is the masking of bribes and graft by so-called voluntary gift-giving and other ingenious disguises. For instance, an agreed upon bribe of $100,000 can be arranged simply by betting on a golf match in which the price of $10,000 is bet on each hole. The bribed wins 14 holes and the briber wins the other 4 holes, all legitimate, open, above board, but part of a wider scheme to amass ill-gotten gains.

Corruption should include all misconduct that harms the public and that works to the unfair advantage of the perpetrators. This grand concept has obvious difficulties. First, what exactly constitutes "harm?" All professionals are forbidden from doing harm, not just to their clients but generally. How is harm to be established and proved beyond doubt? Second, what time limits should apply? Should the perpetrators be liable for life and even beyond to claims against their estates? Third, what compensation should be awarded for being harmed and from whom should it be claimed; fourth, to what extent should ignorance be a defense? Or should the Nuremberg doctrine apply (Davidson, 1966), that is, the leaders should have made it their business to know what was being done in their name? Fifth, what exactly constitutes "unfair advantage?" It maybe that this grand concept is too broad and needs to be reduced, but at least it has more content to it than most restricted definitions currently used. In any event, the complex and complicated nature of corruption means that there is unlikely to be a simple solution, that there are very few universal prescriptions, and that there is no one best way to deal with its ubiquity. Every solution probably needs a properly tailored fit and intimate knowledge of the corrupt and the ways they operate in the specific circumstances (Clark and Jos, 2000).

B. Flaw 2: Partial Vision

For reasons unknown, most studies of corruption concentrate predominately on corruption in government, corruption in the public sector, corruption in public organizations, corrupt behavior among public officials, public employees, and government representatives as if corruption did not occur anywhere else, or if it did, it was much less important or was the result of public sector corruption (Anechiarico and Jacobs, 1996). Clearly, people do expect more of government and public organizations and probably do hold them to a higher standard of conduct. What people in private do with their own money is considered to be their own business but they are warned to be on their guard against villains and to be careful but otherwise left to their own responsibility and judgment (Larson, 1997). In public business, other values intrude. It is not expected that government and public organizations will play with other people's money, with public and collective property, and with public power and position. Public representatives, officials, and employees are expected to be guardians acting on behalf of the public; they are caretakers of the public interest, expected to be above reproach and suspicion, models of integrity and trustworthiness, fair dealing, exemplars of the highest morality (Kernaghan and Langford, 1990; Frederickson, 1993; Commonwealth of Australia, 1995; Institute of Public Administration, 1996). Any scandal is to be treated seriously, investigated and revealed. Any guilty party has to be driven out of public office in disgrace as a warning to others not to follow suit, not even to think of following suit (Coronel, 1997).

This double standard is far too one-sided and makes it appear that corruption occurs predominantly in the public sector or only counts when it occurs there. The result is that corruption in the public sector tends to be exaggerated, often taken out of context, and generalized as if the specific were true of all government, which is far from the case. Meantime, despite some notorious corporation scandals, corruption in the private sector is overall down-played and tends to be better tolerated although it may be more scandal-ridden, more widespread, and of greater public harm (Kang, 2002). Private business is fortunate that in many countries, especially in underdeveloped countries, it does not have to operate in such a visible fashion as does the conduct of public business and its privacy is legally protected. It can hide more and whistleblowers have fewer protections and can be victimized into silence. It can pay off victims and witnesses behind closed doors and swear them to secrecy. Add to this, lax record keeping, more so than probably in the public sector, to say nothing of destroying evidence, and the falsification of records by compliant employees and contractors. The conclusion must be that if it is difficult enough to uncover corruption in the public sector, it is even more so when it comes to private business.

Common sense suggests that in any given population, where people grow up together, study together, live together, mix together, there cannot be that much difference in how they conduct themselves, irrespective of where they work because people are much alike and probably much the same. Therefore, public and private ethics cannot be that much different. With increasing inter-connectedness in the modern state and in the global society, corruption in one area is likely to spread to others, with few able to isolate themselves and keep themselves apart. Corruption in the private sector seeks to penetrate the public sector and likewise corruption in the public sector induces corruption in the private sector, just as corruption at different levels of society seeks outlets elsewhere. Thus, corrupt international business seeks out corrupt governments and vice versa. Corrupt international agencies provide a haven for corrupt businesses, including international organized crime, and corrupt governments, all preying on public money (Williams and Godson, 2002). Hence, the one-sided picture of corruption as occurring mostly in the public sector distorts and is most unfair to public officials and employees.

C. Flaw 3: Undifferentiated Vision

In the conduct of public business, although the political merges into the administrative, political and administrative careers are usually separated and take different paths. All too often, they are grouped together by corruption fighters (Levi and Nelken, 1996). Political corruption probably cannot occur without administrative corruption, that is, without someone in the machinery of government knowing about it, aiding and abetting in it, and shielding it from public discovery (Heywood, 1997; Bozkurt and Vargas, 1999). The same is not true of administrative corruption, which can occur without the knowledge of political careerists just as one level of administration can hide its corruption from other levels, given the sheer size and complexity of the machinery of government. Distinctly political corruption, that solely within the province of career politicians, should be differentiated from administrative corruption, that within the province of administrative careerists, even though the line is blurred and there is much overlapping when no distinction at all is made in spoils systems (Catanzaro, 1992; Bhagava, 1999; Chan, 2000; Das, 2001).

Politics has an unsavory reputation the world over because it often involves playing dirty tricks on rivals, the rewarding of friends, and access to public resources. Indeed, in many countries, government (and public office) is just seen as another business to be exploited for personal enrichment and for consolidating one's personal power (Clark, 1993; Della Porta and Pizzorno, 1996). It is fully expected that political careerists will enjoy all the trappings of public office and will see to it that their entourage and supporters will also enjoy the spoils of office. This is especially true where those attaining office have never before experienced such access, such fawning, such privilege, such luxury (being whisked around in expensive limousines, traveling first class all the way, staying at the most fashionable hotels, and inhabiting splendid buildings with exquisite furnishings and service), such convenience, such obedience, all of which can quickly go to one's head. Government is partisan in rewarding loyalty and punishing disloyalty and anyone who acts otherwise is seen as naïve or stupid or incompetent at politics (Levi and Nelken, 1996). In such circumstances, all who do go along may well advance their careers, political and administrative, whereas those who object may well find themselves bypassed, overlooked, demoted, and released or dismissed in an undignified manner.

In contrast, administrative corruption is usually more confined and limited by specialization and fragmentation and by administrative systems which are supposed to catch possible massive swindles and gross abuses of power and position unless condoned by political careerists (Zafarullah and Siddiquee, 2001). Such collusion does occur and whether it is considered political or administrative corruption depends on who was the instigator, who participated, and who else knew but remained silent (Harris, 2003). But most administrative corruption is on a smaller scale with exceptions when it comes to major centers of independent bureaucratic power such as the military, intelligence agencies, police, courts, and profitable public enterprises. Here, it is rare for political careerists to be involved. Rather, it is the domain of the so-called public service professionals and administrative careerists who seize (and may even create) opportunities to exploit office and position to harm the public by killing and torturing innocent victims at one extreme to demanding petty, illegal fees for services rendered at the other. In the worst cases, arbitrary and discretionary actions replace the rule of law and disregard human rights, plunder is regularized, access is denied, and people are victimized without any means of complaint or redress (Doig, 1999).

Should such administrative corruption exist on an extensive scale, political careerists must know about it and they are just as guilty for failing to act. But this assumes that they can do something effective to combat administrative corruption whereas real power may not be in their hands at all (Jamieson, 2000). Real power may be in the hands of the administrative perpetrators who really run things and keep the politicians subordinated rather than the other way around (Mbaku, 1999). In some countries, the military is in charge, out of control, and rides roughshod over the political leaders. In others, besides imperious bureaucrats, it is the police or foreign intruders or organized crime or war lords, religious fundamentalists, and terrorist groups who hold everyone else hostage (Buscaglia, 1997; Asad and Harris, 2003). However difficult, political corruption has to be separated from administrative corruption and their different forms differentiated as clearly and electoral fraud has to be handled quite differently from the street level bribery of government inspectors (Doig and Theobald, 2000).

D. Flaw 4: Undistinguished Vision

Just as there is small-scale petty corruption and large-scale imperious corruption, so there is individual corruption confined to relatively few people and there is the systemic corruption of whole organizations. Too many corruption fighters believe that they can be tackled in much the same way. All that has to be done is to stop individual acts of corruption and institutionalized corruption will automatically disappear. If only things were that simple. Of course, institutionalized corruption can only exist with the participation of individuals, where they collude, where they cover up for one another, where they silence potential whistleblowers (van Buitenen, 2000), where they convince themselves that what they do is right and beneficial or at least they delude themselves that nobody is being harmed. So by getting individuals to cease, the whole system will collapse. Unfortunately, in systemic corruption, there are always other individuals prepared to replace them and the system continues virtually without interruption.

In systemic corruption, the whole organization pursues a corrupt or corrupted path. The organization, its policies, its management, the laws under which it operates, may have been set up that way quite deliberately as part of political corruption, patronage, dirty tricks, cronyism, political financing, and espionage (LaPalombara, 1994). People demand things and the task of the organization is to see that they are satisfied without too many questions being asked. People want less violence or illegal goods and services or money and the organizational objective is to help them, not to make matters difficult for them (Caiden and Caiden, 1977). And within such organizations, employees from top to bottom see a way of making good for themselves as long as they keep quiet about what is really going on and know they can rely on their fellow employees not to say anything. It is a cozy arrangement for everyone except for their victims whom they cannot identify or whom they do not care to identify. Hence, it is so easy to believe what they do is victimless crime although the whole society is being victimized (Mbaku, 1998).

The snag with systemic corruption is that any participant may blow the whistle at any time. Actually, what tends to happen instead is that once employees find out that they are unwitting partners in corruption, they leave in disgust without doing anything further. In response, the corrupt organization blackballs them for not being good team players or for not fitting in or for not being suitable anyway, and it is glad that they leave. Troubled participants just shrug their shoulders and comply, uneasy but unwilling to buck the system for fear of retaliation and unwilling to break the code of silence that is all too often present in several public service occupations, particularly law enforcement. They know what befalls potential whistleblowers, never mind actual whistleblowers who find nobody will listen to them or cares, who cannot obtain substantial evidence to prove what they say, who face being discredited by the much superior organization and its employees in self-protection, and who if they persist, often end up disillusioned, dispirited and wonder why they ever started in the first place because they usually end up worse off for all their public spiritedness.

Damaged whistleblowers contrast with successful corrupt individuals. Acting on their own, the corrupt are often smart enough in their own interest to evade detection until after they have left the scene or they are clever enough to cover their tracks to allay any suspicions that they may be up to no good. The clumsy get caught but the shrewd and ingenious keep one step ahead of corruption fighters. Some individuals are so devious and criminally minded that they create opportunities that nobody else would dream exist. For this reason, individual corruption never ceases and may be impossible to forestall. This is not the case when it comes to systemic corruption which can be penetrated and infiltrated by undercover agents, where uneasy participants with a conscience and a moral sense of wrong can be turned into honest witnesses and give reliable testimony, and where dedicated reformers can replace deficient systems with something better and less susceptible to corruption. The prospects are brighter when the system is tackled first, not the individuals in it who may be unaware of how they are participating in regularized corruption and personally quite innocent.

E. Flaw 5: Unrealistic Vision

Irrespective of the forms corruption takes, it is unlikely to be eliminated altogether (Commonwealth of Australia, 1995; Institute of Public Administration, 1996). The best that can be done is to reduce it, to transform it from being a regular way of life into an occasional fact of life, and to shift it from harmful and intolerable forms into less harmful and tolerable incidents. This is not to settle for what corruption fighters can get but to aim at minimizing corruption so that people are hardly aware of it, can live with it, and can tolerate its presence. To achieve this state, as countries in Scandinavia and some in the Commonwealth have done, is taxing enough, and it requires the strictest vigilance, whole-hearted public support, honest governance, and artful preventative measures. It has taken those countries several generations and much investment. Even so they find themselves running in the same place just to keep abreast with the increasing opportunities for corruption created by technology and the increasing inventiveness of the corrupt. Globalization has increased the scope for illicit international trade in all manners of harmful products from weapons of mass destruction and the transport of slaves to the disposal of scarce and imperiled species, from the spread of deadly diseases to the looting of public treasures. Computer technology has opened up new avenues for corrupt activities that prey on unsuspecting victims (Williams et al., 2000).

Ongoing scandals blazed across global mass media and spread on the Internet reveal how unprepared most countries are in curbing, whatever corruption has existed for decades let alone novel forms that appear over-night. Privatization and outsourcing have merely transformed the pro-duction and supply of essential goods and services from regulated public monopolies to unregulated private monopolies and combines. Divestment has gifted heavy public investments to private exploiters with little social conscience. Contracting out government functions has diminished public accountability and complicated public accounting. Business deception has revealed how out of date are laws, how ill-equipped is law enforcement, and how the unscrupulous can escape scot-free much to the astonishment and outrage of the general public. Has the term "business ethics" any meaning left? What about the concept of "professional ethics" in the practice of law, medicine, accountancy, auditing, banking, even religion? All are suspect with their protection of professional villains who get off with mere reprimands, although they are guilty of intolerable public harm and skullduggery and with their defense of blatant systemic corruption (Chapman, 2000). How far is the rot among the reputed most civilized cul-tures is now anyone's guess but the victimized public and responsible public leaders are alarmed because so little has yet to be done to rectify gross misuse and abuse of public trust and the corrupt have been spared to enjoy their ill-gotten gains. Finally, in December 2003, after several years of drafting, the United Nations General Assembly passed a wide-sweeping measure to tackle international corruption but it was a much watered down version of the original proposal and there is skepticism that it will probably go the way of so many other pious international declarations. As with so much else, there may well be lip service in abundance but action on the ground may lag quite far behind requirements.

F. Flaw 6: Lack of Political Will

How many countries publicized the 2003 UN resolution on corruption; how many of their citizens know about it; probably, as with previous resolutions on the subject and the declared intentions of major international agencies to take effective action against corruption, the latest resolution will pass them by. Much the same thing has already occurred at national and local levels.

The intention is there but there is precious little follow up action. Yet, to contain and reduce corruption, as so many public (and private) authorities promise (Kakabadse et al., 2003), needs strong political will to act, to strengthen preventive measures, and to support corruption fighters. The cynical claim that the political will is weak because too many politicians profit from corruption or they fear that they have too much to lose should they balk the corrupt (Jamieson, 2000; Volkov, 2002).

Too many politicians are unscrupulous, untrustworthy, and dishonest to the point of sheer hypocrisy. They all make promises but few keep them (Harris, 2003). They all promise to tackle corruption, which is invariably the fault of their predecessors, but when in a position to do something about it, somehow they fall strangely quiet and perpetuate the very corrupt practices they once condemned. They find corrupt practices too much to their advantage (Della Porta and Vannucci, 1999). Even if they are not personally corrupt, they are advanced and preserved by powerful corrupt interests who find politicians all too easy to manipulate. The corrupt are independently powerful and their corruption empowers them even more. They are not to be taken on lightly or underestimated. They can switch at will, whenever it suits their purpose (Kang, 2002). They can reward or punish and they are not exactly beholden to anybody. Even if politicians and other public leaders want no part of them, they have to be handled with care, especially where they contribute to political campaigns, control political parties and pressure groups, influence mass media, and head organized crime (Fiorentini and Peltzman, 1995).

In contrast, the unorganized public carries little weight. They may dislike corruption but they do not know what to do about it except demonstrate and protest usually to little avail because they can be so easily distracted and if need be quieted, bought off, and diverted by gimmicks. People have short memories and in time forget or become complacent while all the time they are being socialized to accept the corruption around them. On the other hand, an organized public, triggered by outrageous scandal or prompted by unimpeachable leaders and other impeccable sources, are a force to be reckoned with for they are not so compliant (Dobel, 1999). Disciplined and organized public can refuse to go along with corrupt practices (Gregory, 1999). Collectively, it has access to resources and can employ experts to give advice on how to fight corruption and the corrupt. Organized public constitutes the backbone of political will and it has brought down corrupt regimes without violence as happened during the 1990s in the former Soviet sphere of influence (Clark, 1993). Indeed, this is the virtue of civic culture which all too often is ignored by corruption fighters who believe they can proceed alone which is a bad mistake because the civic culture has to be stirred first for without its support corruption fighters will not get far (Della Porta, 2001). All politicians heed the civic culture and with its backing their political will is strengthened to combat the corrupt.

The drawback is that the civic culture itself can be corrupted. In poor countries where democracy is unversed, corruption can be so penetrating, so much a part of everyday living, that few people trust each other and most remain highly suspicious of any person they consider to be a stranger. In them, people trust only their immediate friends and family and not always these. Their major concern is for a small circle, its defense and its advancement, and they are prepared to take advantage of anybody outside their select band. Self-interest and opportunism remain high in priority, possibly more than anything else other than sheer survival for which some minimal cooperation with others is required (Mitra, 1998). Unless these circumstances are changed, as they have been in many prosperous democracies, the prospects for mounting political will against corruption are slim.

G. Flaw 7: Sabotage

As the lack of political will is passive, the sabotage of anticorruption campaigns is active, deliberate, and contrived. Politicians and their helpmates are not just indifferent but they seek to nullify efforts to contain and reduce corruption. Many stand to lose with the lessening of corruption and the abandonment of dirty tricks. It is worthwhile for the corrupt to share their ill-gotten gains with amenable politicians who are in a position to favor and protect them, give them access to sizeable public resources, and curtail official investigations. Few politicians are likely to endure the wrath of their comrades by putting an end to the means of their self-promotion, re-election and reappointment, electoral advantage, and possible guaranteed tenure. The better course is to appear to the uninitiated to be doing something about the scourge of corruption while actually doing very little or blocking effective action.

It looks good to promise to take on the corrupt and to abolish corrupt practices, and almost everyone running for public office does this until they actually get there when they forget what they once said, or, worse still, they put on a virtually meaningless show by appointing investigators who cannot investigate, draft laws that never get implemented, establish anticorruption commissions without teeth, and publicize past but never current scandals. Investigators are handicapped by lack of jurisdiction, funding, staff, and official cooperation. The draft laws never get passed or enforced. The anticorruption agencies suffer the same fate as the crippled investigators. The publicity of wrongdoing is replaced by the strictest secrecy of current operations. Even cruder tactics are employed. The so-called corruption chasers (they cannot be called real corruption fighters because their hearts are not in it) are headed by loyalists who can be trusted to confine themselves to fingering only small fish (the bigger fish having been forewarned). The corrupt can be employed, just to see that the investigators do not get too close to the big fish or have themselves exposed as being guilty, thereby discrediting all the investigation although the named villains somehow escape in all the hubbub with little penalty (or later secretly compensated for their trouble).

Investigators who show themselves to be too independent are warned that they are putting their appointment or re-appointment in jeopardy unless they cease embarrassing public leaders and follow the government's line and protect officialdom generally. If this does not work, then they are further warned that their organization will lose any influence it may have with the authorities. Given this message, the anticorruption chasers voluntarily curb themselves by adopting restricted techniques that limit the scope of their inquiries and refrain from requesting additional resources essential to their investigations with the result that they overburden themselves and cannot complete their work. Take, for example, the Economic and Financial Crimes Commission of Nigeria, set up in 2003 because of criticism of the government's lack of progress in combating corruption, which has made scores of well publicized arrests but has yet to secure any big convictions in admitted bribery and kickbacks by foreign oil companies and the looting of the public treasury by local officials (Peel, 2004).

Yet, success can be as handicapping as failure. Success gives the anticorruption campaigners publicity and credibility, thereby giving rise to jealousy and fear within the establishment. They then get accused of being just publicity seekers, glowing in the sensationalism generated by public service bashing and taking advantage of the inability of the establishment to defend itself properly against malicious and exaggerated charges taken out of context because of the very nature of government not to spread unnecessary alarm. This provides the excuse to question the whole mission of the investigators and to clip their wings for being too bold or too revealing or too unreliable for comfort. It goes without saying that should they make mistakes or questionable judgments (as can be the case as they often operate without well established guidelines and procedures), they are in deep trouble. It must be remembered that they are often armed with unusual coercive powers to hold public hearings, summon unwilling witnesses, take public testimony, and compel documentation, all of which can damage political and administrative reputations, giving further incentive to governments to undermine their credibility, shorten their lives, and restrict their operations, stopping just short of complete sabotage (Heyman, 1999; Johnston, 1999). The investigators find themselves being investigated, being accused of carrying on personal vendettas or conducting a nasty campaign on behalf of the government's opponents or just being unethical, unprofessional, demeaning, fabricating prosecutors. They cannot do, let alone finish, the job (Sunstein, 1998).

H. Flaw 8: Having to Become Corrupt to Catch the Corrupt

Some forms of corruption are so well organized and hidden that the only way to penetrate corrupt activities and find the really corrupt big fish is to employ undercover agents who in order to preserve their cover have to participate and pretend themselves as corrupt. The motives are pure and the intention is eventually to put a complete stop to the harm caused by the really corrupt. The *modus operandi* is to accumulate unfailing evidence of wrongdoing. But the undercover agents compromise themselves, indulge in corruption, and may plant (and even invent) evidence on unwitting bystanders. Do the ends always justify the means? If so, those who undertake such missions can be counted as heroes, not villains, for the perils they endure. If prematurely discovered, they are treated harshly by the corrupt to deter anyone who might think of emulating them. Organized crime is particularly cruel but other corrupt groups can be equally merciless when it serves their purpose.

Sting operations raise similar questions, especially about entrapment (Roser, 1992). But there may be no other way to catch the corrupt at work. The danger is that once someone has joined the other side for whatever reason, he may get to like being corrupt, forget any qualms, and switch altogether, which is always a risk. Another problem is blackmailing small fish to lead to bigger fish within safeguards if only safeguards could be devised. The current issue of international terrorism highlights all the traps. When are corrupt acts justifiable, useful, and essential, by whom, for what social ends, at what risks? None of these fits with the notion of too many corruption fighters that all corruption by definition is wrong, dysfunctional, and immoral, and all forms should be condemned out of hand (Stapenhurst and Kpundeh, 1999).

I. Flaw 9: The Corrupt Can Be Perfectly Normal

Many of the corrupt are not abnormal or exceptional. They behave much the same as everybody else and they use perfectly normal channels. They have no distinguishing characteristics. This is obviously true of corrupt societies where corruption is a way of life, even *the* way of life where one of the few possibilities to contract out is just to emigrate. The corrupt are otherwise normal (Catanzaro, 1992; Gupta et al., 2000), but just seize whatever opportunities come their way and succumb to temptation in the hope that no one else will suspect them (Findlay, 1999). They may lack personal integrity but they do not have to create anything; the avenues already exist and others use them. There are buyers for their products and services. There are ready means for money laundering. Money is money and no one questions its source as long as it is legal tender. Couriers carry things and they find space for whatever needs to be transported without too many questions being asked (Somerset 2001; Asad and Harris, 2003). If one cannot earn legally what they require to keep their immediate dependents alive, none can be blamed for trying to make it up. The means for perpetrating corruption are present and merely have to be taken advantage of: they rarely have to be invented (Heyman, 1999).

This is what is so difficult about corruption and fighting corruption. On the surface, everything looks so normal. So, how can the abnormal be distinguished from the normal? How can the normal be disturbed and interrupted at great inconvenience to discover the abnormal? What is the justification for suspicion? Is this or that mistake intentional or unintentional, a blind for something less innocent? Who can be blamed for being fooled or for failing to question anything out of normal and routine? Many things would be slowed down if this were the case. So despite the best of intentions, a certain amount of corruption is likely to go undetected and another amount might better be ignored because interference would be just too costly and scarcely worth the effort of hunting down.

J. Flaw 10: The Corrupt Can Usually Justify Themselves

The last, by no means final, flaw to be considered here is that people can usually find excuses for whatever they do. The corrupt are no different. To hear them, they are all sweetness and light; they are honest, straight, and fair dealing. They would not dream of doing wrong or hurting anybody. Indeed, they perform useful services and provide goods much in demand. They fill vacuums, make up shortages, and generally help those in need. In support, there are many who justify what the corrupt do and describe their activities nonchalantly as rent seeking, entrepreneurial, enterprising, innovating, and investing: the so-called corrupt are just functional middlemen (Cadot, 1987; Tullock, 1989; Rose-Ackerman, 1999). And a very good case can be made out for the corrupt in the absence of definitive proof either way simply because the circumstances are so confusing and complicated and the corrupt can be very convincing in their own defense. On the other hand, the mere suspicion of corruption and certainly public investigation of such mere suspicion can never completely eradicate all doubt even when the suspected are exonerated. For this reason, each situation has to be studied carefully. What appears on the surface to be identical to another situation may turn out to be radically different and require quite different treatment. There must always be room for doubt, for corruption may indeed turn out to be nothing of the kind, just a misreading by outsiders who are prevented from knowing how things really work.

III. The Bottom Line

Just because flaws exist in everything that human beings undertake does not mean that they should stop trying to do better. Knowing that they are unlikely to attain perfection should make them realize that there is always room for improvement no matter how proud they may be of their achievements. When it comes to combating corruption, much progress has been made compared with yesteryear when the whole topic was largely taboo. The countries that are reputed to be the most clean probably are largely because of their underlying democratic ethos which supports strong civic cultures, many institutional safeguards, widespread transparency, good governance, vigilant watchdogs, and wary public guardians. Even so, some bad spots exist in political campaigning, business practices, professional self-indulgence, contracting, and fraud (Niland and Satkunandan, 1999). To escape detection in the open society, corruption has to be quite sophisticated and well hidden so that most folks are unaware of it as they go about their daily routines. They cannot substantiate the corruption they suspect. But when they are stung by scandals, offended by brazen wrongdoing, and believe that they have been shabbily treated, they quickly strike back and demand a cleansing blood letting, whereby the guilty rascals are thrown out of office until rehabilitated.

Other countries pine to join them. They have been told repeatedly by global authorities that one reason why their development has been held back is that their corruption holds them back, and the sooner they combat corruption, the sooner prosperity and better times will arrive. Most international agencies involved in world development offer aid to them in the form of prescriptions, advisors, grants, and backing (Mauro, 1995; International Monetary Fund, 1997). Indeed, anticorruption efforts are fast becoming a business of their own with reputable organizations, special web sites, regular meetings and conferences around the globe, an expanding list of publications, and annual outpourings of measures whose release causes embarrassment to fingered governments and goads concerned citizens into demanding remedial action. Unfortunately, they expect too much too quickly. Their enthusiasts tend to overestimate what can be done and underestimate the obstacles that confront even the most expert corruption fighters. Explaining possible flaws in the process is just a cautionary note. It is not intended to dampen the idealism that is a crucial component of all anticorruption campaigns.

References

Adams, J. and Frantz, D., *A Full Service Bank: How BCCI Stole Billions Around the World*, Pocket Books, New York, 1992.

Alatas, S., *Corruption: Its Nature, Causes and Functions*, Aldershot, Avebury, 1990.

Anechiarico, F. and Jacobs, J., *The Pursuit of Absolute Integrity: How Corruption Control makes Government Ineffective*, University of Chicago Press, Chicago, 1996.

Asad, A. and Harris, R., *The Politics and Economics of Drug Production on the Pakistan–Afganistan Border*, Aldershot, Ashgate, 2003.

Bayat, J.F., Ellis, S., and Hibou, B., Eds., *The Criminalization of the State in Africa*, James Currey, Oxford, 1999.

Bhagava, V., *Combating Corruption in the Philippines*, World Bank, Washington, DC, 1999.

Bozkurt, O. and Vargas, J., Eds., *Political and Administrative Corruption*, International Institute of Administrative Sciences, Brussels, 1999.

van Buitenen, P., *Blowing the Whistle*, London, Politicos, 2000.

Buscaglia, E., Corruption and judicial reform in Latin America, *Pol. Sci. J.*, 17, 273–295, 1997.

Cadot, O., Corruption as a gamble, *J. Public Econ.*, 33, 223–244, 1987.

Caiden, G., Dealing with administrative corruption, in *Handbook on Administrative Ethics*, Cooper, T., Ed., Marcel Dekker, New York, 2000, pp. 429–455.

Caiden, G. and Caiden, N., Administrative corruption, *Public Admin. Rev.*, 37, 301–309, 1977.

Caiden, G., Dwivedi, O.P., and Jabbra, J., *Where Corruption Lives*, Kumarian Press, Bloomfield, CT, 2001.

Catanzaro, R., *Men of Respect: A Social History of the Sicilian Mafia*, The Free Press, New York, 1992.

Chan, K., Towards an integrated model of corruption: opportunities and control in China, *Int. J. Public Admin.*, 23, 507–551, 2000.

Chapman, R., Ed., *Ethics in Public Service for the New Millenium*, Aldershot, Ashgate, 2000.

CIVICUS, *Annual Reports*, Washington, DC, 2000.

Clark, W., *Crime and Punishment in the Soviet Officialdom: Combating Corruption in the Political Elite 1965–1990*, M.E. Sharpe, Armonk, NY, 1993.

Clark, W. and Jos, P., Comparative anti-corruption policy: the American, Soviet and Russian cases, *Int. J. Public Admin.*, 23, 101–148, 2000.

Commonwealth of Australia, *Guidelines on Official Conduct for Commonwealth Public Servants*, Public Service Commission, Canberra, ACT, 1995.

Coronel, S., Ed., *Pork and Other Perks: Corruption and Governance in the Philippines*, Philippine Center for Investigative Journalism, Metro Manila, 1997.

Council of Europe, Working Group on Civil Law Matters of the Multidisciplinary Group on Corruption, 1998 (http:www.coe.fr/corruption/etudeb.htm).

Court, J. and Hyden, G., World governance survey: a new approach to assessing governance, *Global Corruption Report*, Transparency International, Berlin, 2003.

Cusimano, M., *Beyond Sovereignty: Issues for a Global Agenda*, St. Martin's Press, Boston, 2000.

Das, S., *Public Office, Private Interest: Bureaucracy and Corruption in India*, Oxford University Press, New Delhi, 2001.

Davidson, E., *The Trial of the Germans: Nuremberg 1945–1946*, Macmillan, New York, 1966.

Della Porta, D., A judges' revolution; Political corruption and the judiciary in Italy, *Eur. J. Pol. Res.*, 39, 1–21, 2001.

Della Porta, D. and Pizzorno, A., The business politicians: reflections from a study of political corruption, *J. Law Soc.*, 23, 73–94, 1996.

Della Porta, D. and Vannucci, A., *Corrupt Exchanges: Actors, Resources and Mechanisms of Political Corruption*, Aldine de Gruyter, New York, 1999.

Demick, B., South Koreans ponder just how far corruption reaches, *Los Angeles Times*, A1, p. 6, January 27, 2004.

Dobel, P., *Public Integrity*, The Johns Hopkins University Press, Baltimore, 1999.

Doig, A., In the state we trust; democratisation, corruption and development, *J. Commonwealth Comp. Politics*, 37, 13–36, 1999.

Doig, A. and Theobald, R., Eds., *Corruption and Democratization*, Frank Cass, London, 2000.

Findlay, M., *The Globalisation of Crime*, Cambridge University Press, Cambridge, 1999.

Fiorentini, G. and Peltzman, S., Eds., *The Economics of Organized Crime*, Cambridge University Press, Cambridge, 1995.

Frederickson, G., Ed., *Ethics and Public Administration*, M.E. Sharpe, Armonk, NY, 1993.

Gray, C. and Kauffman, D., Corruption and development, *Finance Develop.*, 35, 7–10, 1998.

Gregory, R., Social capital theory and administrative reform: maintaining ethical probity in public service, *Public Admin. Rev.*, 59, 63–75, 1999.

Gupta, S., de Mello, L., and Sharan, R., *Corruption and Military Spending*, International Monetary Fund, Washington, DC, 2000.

Harris, R., *Political Corruption: In and Beyond the Nation State*, Routledge, London, 2003.

Heidenheimer, A. and Johnston, M., Eds., *Political Corruption: Concepts and Contexts*, Transaction Press, New Brunswick, NJ, 2002.

Hellman, J., Jones G., and Kauffman, D., *Seize the State*, World Bank Research Working Paper 2444, World Bank, Washington, DC, 2000.

Heyman, J., Ed., *States and Illegal Practices*, Oxford, Berg, 1999.

Heywood, P., Ed., *Political Corruption*, Blackwell, Oxford, 1997.

Institute of Public Administration, *Statement of Principles Regarding the Conduct of Public Employees*, Toronto, Canada, 1996.

International Monetary Fund, *Good Governance: The IMF's Role*, Washington, DC, 1997.

Jamieson, A., *The Antimafia: Italy's Fight Against Organized Crime*, Macmillan, Basingstoke, 2000.

Johnston, M., A brief history of anticorruption agencies, in *The Self-Restraining State: Power and Accountability in New Democracies*, Shedler, A., Diamond, L., and Plattner, M., Eds., Lynne Rienner Publishers, Boulder, CO, 1999.

Kakabadse, A., Korac-Kakabadse, N., and Kouzmin, A., Ethics, values and behaviours: comparison of three case studies examining the paucity of leadership in government, *Public Admin.*, 81, 477–508, 2003.

Kang, D., *Crony Capitalism: Corruption and Development in South Korea and the Philippines*, Cambridge University Press, Cambridge, 2002.

Kauffman, D., Kraay, A., and Zoido-Lobaton, P., *Governance Matters*, World Bank Policy Research Working Papers 2196 and 2772, World Bank, Washington, DC, 1999, 2002.

Kernaghan, K. and Langford, J., *The Responsible Public Servant*, Institute of Public Administration, Toronto, 1990.

Klitgaard, R., *Controlling Corruption*, University of California Press, Berkeley, 1988.

Klitgaard, R., MacLean-Abarao, R., and Parris, H., *Corrupt Cities: A Practical Guide to Cure and Prevention*, ICS Press, Oakland, CA, 2000.

Kynge, J., Curbing corruption vital; for China's north-east rustbelt, *The Financial Times*, p. 4, January 9, 2004.

Lambsdorff, J., *The Precision and Regional Comparison of Perceived Levels of Corruption: Interpreting the Results*, Transparency International, Berlin, 2000.

LaPalombara, J., Structural and institutional aspects of corruption, *Soc. Res.*, 61, 325–351, 1994.

Larson, P., Public and private values at odds: can private sector values be transplanted into public sector institutions; *Public Admin. Develop.*, 17, 131–139, 1997.

Latinobarometro Survey, Santiago, 1995 (http://www.latinobarometro.org).

Leiken, R., Controlling the global corruption epidemic, *Foreign Policy*, 5, 55–73, 1996.

Levi, M. and Nelken, D., Eds., The corruption of politics and the politics of corruption, Special issue of *J. Law Soc.*, 23, 1, 1996.

Marx, K., *Das Kapital: A Critique of Political Economy*, Hamburg, 1867.

Mauro, P., Corruption and growth, *Quart. J. Econ.*, 110, 681–711, 1995.

Mbaku, J., Ed., *Corruption and the Crisis of Institutional Reforms in Africa*, The Edwin Mellen Press, Lewiston, NY, 1998.

Mbaku, J., Corruption cleanups in developing societies: the public choice perspective, *Int. J. Public Admin.*, 22, 309–345, 1999.

Mitra, C., *The Corrupt Society: The Criminalization of India from Independence to the 1990s*, Penguin Books India, New Delhi, 1998.

Naylor, R., *Follow-the-money Methods in Crime Control Policy*, York University, Toronto, 1999 (http://www.yorku.ca//nathanson/nathanso.htm).

Niland, C. and Satkunandan, S., The ethical value of red tape! specialized institutions in ensuring accountability (the NSW experience), *Aust. J. Public Admin.*, 58, 80–86, 1999.

Noonan, J., *Bribes*, Macmillan, New York, 1984.

Organization for Economic Cooperation and Development, *Countering Public Sector Corruption: An Overview of Corruption Prevention Measures in OECD Countries*, OECD, Paris, 1999.

Peel, M., Nigerian anti-graft body plans to investigate oil companies; tax affairs, *The Financial Times*, p. 2, January 17, 2004.

PROBIDAD, 2004 (http://www.probidad.org and 1_amlat@probidad.org).

Quah, J., *Curbing Corruption in Asia: A Comparative Study of Six Countries*, Times Academic Press, Singapore, 2003.

Riccardi, N., A culture of corruption, *Los Angeles Times*, A1 (February 1), 12, 2004.

Rose-Ackerman, S., *Corruption and Governance: Causes, Consequences, and Reform*, Cambridge University Press, Cambridge, 1999.

Roser, W., The Independent Commission Against Corruption: The New Star Chamber, *Crim. Law J.*, 16, 225–245, 1992.

Sheptycki, J., Ed., *Issues in Transnational Policing*, Routledge, London, 2000.

Siddiqui, T., *Towards Good Governance*, Oxford University Press, Oxford, 2001.

Skapinker, M., Whistle while you work-not after you have left, *The Financial Times*, p. 8, January 21, 2004.

Smith, A., *An Inquiry into the Nature and Causes of the Wealth of Nations*, 4 volumes, Edinburgh, 1776.

Somerset, K., *What the Professionals Know: The Trafficking of Children into and through the United Kingdom for Sexual Purposes*, 2001 (http://www.antislavery.org/homepage/resources/Children.PDF).

Stapenhurst, R. and Kpundeh, S., Eds., *Curbing Corruption: Toward a Model for Building National Integrity*, World Bank, Washington, DC, 1999.

Sunstein, C., Lessons from a debacle: from impeachment to reform, *Florida Law Rev.*, 51, 599–614, 1998.

Tait, N., BCCI tragedy; awaits long run, *The Financial Times*, p. 2, January 12, 2004.

Tanzania Presidential Commission of Inquiry Against Corruption, *The Warioba Report*, Dar Es Salaam, Government of Tanzania, 1996.

Tanzi, V., Corruption around the world, *IMF Working Paper* WP/98/63, International Monetary Fund, Washington, DC, 1998.

Tiffen, R., *Scandals: Media, Politics and Corruption in Contemporary Australia*, University of Sydney Press, Sydney, 1999.

Tiihonen, S., *The History of Corruption in Central Government*, IOS Press, Amsterdam, 2001.

Transparency International, *National Integrity Systems: The TI Source Book*, 2003 (http://www.Transparency.de/document/source-book/summary.htmls).

Tullock, G., *The Economics of Special Privilege and Rent Seeking*, Kluwer Academic, Boston, 1989.

United Nations Development Program, *Fighting Corruption to Improve Governance*, Management and Governance Division, New York, 1999.

Volkov, V., *Violent Entrepreneurs: The Use of Force in the Making of Russian Capitalism*, Cornell University Press, Ithaca, NY, 2002.

Williams, R., Ed., *Explaining Corruption: The Politics of Corruption 1*, Edward Elgar, Cheltenham, 2000.

Williams, P. and Godson, R., Anticipating organized and transnational crime, *Crime, Law Soc. Change*, 37, 311, 2002.

Williams, R., Moran, J., and Flanary, R., Eds., *Corruption in the Developed World: The Politics of Corruption 3*, Edward Elgar, Cheltenham, 2000.

Williams, R. and Theobald, R., Eds., *Corruption in the Developing World: The Politics of Corruption 2*, Edward Elgar, Cheltenham, 2000.

Woodworth, P., *Dirty War, Clean Hands: ETA, the GAL, and Spanish Democracy*, Cork University Press, Cork, 2001.

World Bank, *Helping Countries Combat Corruption*, World Bank, Washington, DC, 1997.

World Bank, *Anticorruption in Transition: A Contribution to the Policy Debate*, World Bank, Washington, DC, 2000.

World Bank, 2004 (http://www.worldbank.org/wbi/governance/).

Zafarullah, H. and Siddiquee, N., Dissecting public sector corruption in Bangladesh: issues and problems of control, *Public Org. Rev.*, 1, 465, 2001.

Chapter 18

Sound Governance and Administrative Ethics in the Former East Germany: The Dilemmas of a Transition

Jean-Claude Garcia-Zamor

CONTENTS

I. Introduction

This chapter reviews the concept of sound governance and discusses how it intertwines with administrative ethics in the former East Germany during the transition from communism to democracy. The issue of sound governance is a complex one. To what exactly this ambiguous term refer? An examination of the two words in the term sound governance provides a good starting point to analyze its meaning. As the word sound is modifying governance, the adjective form of the word must be defined. According to the *Oxford English Dictionary*, it means "showing good judgment and high morality." Governance is referred to as "the act or process of exercising power, or functioning control of government." Far from clearing up the ambiguity, these definitions seem to give to the term sound governance a different meaning to each reader. Although it is simple in today's terms, it is quite complicated in a historic perspective. What contemporary readers deem to be sound, most certainly has undergone a metamorphosis over time. The answer to the question "What is Sound Governance?" is based upon innumerable cultural and social expectations. The academic literature has literally hundreds of definitions of what constitutes sound governance in today's society.

II. What Is Sound Governance?

Thompson (1992: 523) argues that moral principles specify the rights and duties that individuals should respect when they act in ways that seriously affect the well-being of other individuals and society, and also define the conditions that collective practices and policies should satisfy when they similarly affect the well-being of individuals and society. Another scholar states that "Governance would be at his best in society when there are effective production and services in an efficient way in legitimate conditions taking into account the degree of dynamics, complexity, diversity, and risk" (Kooiman, 1993: 146). However, public administrators, as individuals, are also responsible for any government's success. The action or lack of action by public officials and employees of a government agency determine whether the agency operates in the most efficient and effective manner possible. "Corruption, laziness, and ignorance ultimately destroy any dominant bureaucracy" (Riggs, 1998: 27).

Many people believe that a democracy, or a democratic state would necessarily have a sound government. One reason for that view is that the features of a democracy include freedom of expression, free elections, majority rule and minority rights, political parties, division of power, constitutional government, and private organizations. Thus, a democracy seems to ensure a society with a complete, firm and stable form of government. Recent literature emphasizes the importance of electoral governance (Eisenstadt, 2002; Lehoucq, 2002; Mozzafar and Schedler, 2002; Schedler, 2002, Mozzafar, 2002). But one scholar argues that cleaning up the elections might keep people away from the polls. In examining both historical and contemporary cases, his article identifies three mechanisms by which clean election reform today might actually keep potential voters away from the polls: legal disfranchisement, cutting out the go-between, and buying abstention (Schaffer, 2002). Such arguments might tend to confirm that sound governance is not necessarily associated with electoral democracy. Some people think that communism could also be a good example of sound governance. For communists, control is an important factor for a stable and firm government. According to communists, who base their views on the ideologies of Marx and Lenin, their goal is a society that provides equality and economic security for all. Still others view a monarchy as sound government. Although the old traditional monarchies were not very good illustrations of sound governance, some of the contemporary ones have establish parliaments and strong constitutions, and have limited the power of the monarch. In reality, a sound government could exist in any form of political regimes. Therefore, the ideology of a government does not necessarily determine sound governance. Corruption exists within the spheres of all types of governments.[1] Morality, virtue, fairness, honesty, and consistency are necessary for sound governance. All five are at the roots of any system that can create a climate of trust and cooperation between the government and the citizenry.

In recent years, the ideologies and strategies behind sound government have shifted from a methodological approach to a results-oriented approach. Bowman and Williams (1998) examined changing attitudes about ethics in government comparing the perceptions of public managers in 1989 with those in 1996, a time according to the authors that saw the passing of the Decade of Greed and the coming of the Decade of Reinventing Government. Their findings from a national survey explored attitudes toward ethics in society and concluded that individuals are increasingly empowered, agencies are effecting change, and that the Code of Ethics of the American Society for Public Administration may be impacting management practices. Similarly, a book advocating this new approach addresses some fundamental issues in governance and describes ten principles of entrepreneurial governance. According to the two authors, there is a third choice in addition to raising taxes and cutting essential services to develop a sound and less bureaucratic government (Osborne and Gaebler, 1993: 22–24). Their book has influenced the strategies of the administrative reform presently being pursued by the United States Government.

After the Watergate scandal in the United States, Frederick C. Mosher and several others who were members of a panel of the National Academy of Public Administration were invited to present their views to the Senate Select Committee on Presidential Campaign Activities. Most of the report has concerned, directly or indirectly, the subject of ethics in the public service. They stated that "those who have committed most of their lives to public service ... feel a special obligation to preserve the values that have so long contributed to an effective and progressive social order" (Mosher, 1992: 411). The framework of government is very diversified and complex. It begins at the initial level of public input through voting, public meetings and other input avenues. At this level, one important element to ensure a sound government is accessibility and responsiveness to the public. Ideals such as trustworthiness, dependability, stability, honesty, rationality, justice, and prudence are also associated with the word "sound" as it applies to sound governance. The public officials, whose job is to provide services in any given governmental agency, must adhere to those ideals to successfully provide sound governance.

In the international arena, the term "sound governance" is now linked to most of the international agencies and the United Government's efforts to foment economic development in the developing countries. They all recognize that an effective state apparatus is indispensable for their programs and projects to be successful. However, despite the accepted notion that administrative capability and efficiency are crucial, there is no real consensus on how sound governance can be achieved. The following paragraphs review briefly how three major international donors view the concept of sound governance.

According to the United Nations Development Programme (UNDP), sound governance can be seen as the exercise of economic, political and administrative authority to manage a country's cities or counties affairs throughout all different levels. UNDP also views human rights as an important ingredient for the progress of every society. The Universal Declaration of Human Rights recognizes several dimensions of human rights for all people. Some are tangible and quantifiable, such as access to education, health and a decent standard of living and ability to take part in the government of the country. Others are intangible, such as freedom, dignity, security of person and participation in the cultural life of the community (UNDP, 1995: 99).

The United States Agency for International Development (USAID) places the emphasis on democratization and free elections. A new Center for Democracy and Governance was created within USAID in 1994 to oversee the promotion of political reform in the developing countries. USAID's Democracy Initiative embraces new programs in four different areas:

1. The fostering of genuine and competitive political systems.
2. The strengthening of the rule of law and respect for human rights.

3. The strengthening of civil societies.
4. The promotion of greater accountability of political institutions and ethical standards in government (Adams, 1998: 9–10).

However, the most contentious aspect of international ethics is in the area of human rights violations and both, political and economic interventions. The current literature on humanitarian intervention is grounded in international law and human rights. After examining this vast literature, two scholars have found several important shortcomings and thought it difficult to develop a framework that is simultaneously both ethical and political for justifying interventions (Fixdal and Smith, 1998: 283–312).

There is little doubt that no other institutions, or countries, possess the combinations of money and expertise controlled by the World Bank and its sister institution the International Monetary Fund. Not surprisingly, the two institutions have a very narrow view of sound governance that is centered in government's capacity to operate a viable, productive economy. To assure the benefits of external assistance, the developing countries are pressured to undertake domestic reforms at very high political costs. Again and again the structural adjustment programs strongly encouraged by the two powerful international economic institutions have proven politically and socially disastrous for numerous Third World countries (Garcia-Zamor, 1994: 110–112). In effect, the structural adjustment programs have accomplished the most undesirable results; the destabilization of several democratic regimes. Thus, from the narrow point of view of achieving "sound governance," the programs have been for the most part a disaster.

III. The East German Civil Service

After the separation of Germany, a wide gap developed between the bureaucracies of the German Democratic Republic (GDR) in the East and the Federal Republic in the West. Although the West German bureaucrats were selected because of their qualifications and continued to form a conservative, honest, and conscientious civil service, the East German bureaucrats were recruited primarily because of their political and ideological loyalty.[2] Magali Gravier has argued that the loyalty factor has offered an important framework for civil service recruitment even after 1990 because it rooted the selection of East Germans in a legal procedure that had been elaborated over the years and could not be considered as an *ad hoc* solution to purge unwelcome personnel (Gravier, 2003a, b). But before 1990, East German bureaucrats had to work according to the principles of socialist morality and ethics. They also had to demonstrate their capacity to transform the general resolutions of the Communist

Party, known as the SED, into concrete administrative actions. One of the main principles of the GDR civil service was the blind observance of a socialist law and order. The disparity between the two bureaucracies added to the socio-economic and political problems that became evident at the time of reunification in 1990. It has been argued that those who steered the processes of reunification failed to design institutions of sound governance that fit the circumstances of the governed.[3]

However, it is important to point out that many of the bureaucrats who served the Western administration after 1950 had a Nazi Past. They were allowed to return to the civil service only after the need for an efficient and effective administration started to threaten the Western (and especially American) efforts to build up a strong Federal Republic as a centerpiece of the Cold War architecture. This is another illustration of the importance administrative "know-how" has in a modern society. Some people were allowed to work for a democratic government often without a thorough investigation of their potentially criminal past. The key for the different situation in the two Germanies was the ideological configuration. In the East, it was impossible to employ former NS-officials because of the role "anti-fascism" played as a legitimizing state doctrine. This enabled the GDR propaganda machine to claim that the East represented the "good Germans," the Communists and Social Democrats, who had fought Fascism. But the West was more interested in establishing itself as a post of the "free world." Starting in the late forties that meant: anti-communism. That made it possible to put criteria like efficiency ahead of questions of guilt. Yet the quick transfer of Western political, judicial and economic institutions to the East without any major modifications turned out to be problematic. It was clear that this radical system change would have a shock-like impact, but the majority of politicians overestimated the capacity of the Western institutions to solve problems under East German circumstances. The sophisticated system elements of the Federal Republic had been developed gradually to meet the specific requirements of its society. Its complexity, over-regulated aspects and its transparency became obstacles to the process of rebuilding in East Germany, especially in light of the fact that in the 1980s the institutions of the West-German welfare state itself were criticized heavily by protagonists of "Reagonomics" and "Thatcherism." Thus, the outdated western laws and rules were used to solve problems in an even more complicated and fundamentally different context. Gert Jooachim Glaessner (1997: 97) wrote "Fundamental differences between the Western and Eastern political cultures are the main obstacles to uniting the two parts of Germany socially and culturally in the foreseeable future." A major problem in the GDR was the overstaffing of the bureaucracy. Since the objective of the Communist government was to have zero unemployment, not only the civil service but also the bureaucracies of all universities and factories were grossly overstaffed.[4] In addition, the federal government of the newly unified country has been demanding from the civil servants of the former East Germany a new adaptability and creativity that was never promoted in the GDR bureaucracy.

The chapter analyzes the state of the bureaucracy in the East prior to reunification and discusses the changes that occurred after 1990 as the country was moving from communism to democracy. It shows that despite some original difficulties in adapting the new Western norms, the Eastern bureaucracy has been able to develop some goal-oriented activities that are typical of good governance in Western bureaucracies. Its recent performance in a variety of public sectors reveals a new efficiency and professionalism. It has developed a sense of the necessities of the time, including globalization. The chapter also is about bureaucratic culture and the influences of external political, economic, legal and social systems upon it and shows the relationship of bureaucratic culture to organizational performance under different conditions. It also reviews two types of bureaucratic cultures over time (GDR and West Germany). In the GDR, there were transitions from "real existing socialism" to democracy to reunification; in West Germany there were transitions from a unified federal democracy to an enlarged geopolitical and bureaucratic structure. Each transition marked a change in laws, norms, structure, etc. In addition, reunification meant that the two separate cultures had to unify, resulting in yet another transition that is still taking place. At each step of the way, culture influences the behavior of individual bureaucrats and the culture of the bureaucratic organization.

In 1946, the Communist and Social Democratic parties merged to form the SED. This became the instrument for Communist rule through the 'block party' system and provided the Communists with legitimacy because of the formally democratic means by which the SED was created (Roberts, 1997). Three years later, the SED created a constitution for the newly founded GDR. Although it appears to be liberal and democratic, in reality it granted to the citizenry very little room for political participation.

A few years after the establishment of communist control in the Soviet zone in Germany, an American scholar wrote that the transformation that East Germany had undergone was, in some ways, more profound than even the one that Nazism wrought on Germany:

> The Nazi regime, while subordinating everything to its power, did not affect certain basic institutions, such as private property in landed estates and industries or the bureaucracy as such. Communism, by contrast, proceeded to transform class lines and society radically... Thus the changes that have occurred resulted not from the free play of social forces but from the policies of the group in political control, the leaders of the

Socialist unity Party (SED), acting under the guidance of Soviet Communists. A new class, which absorbed many formerly independent businessmen, artisans, and members of the professions, performs essential clerical, technical, and administrative functions for the state administration, public enterprises, and the party organizations. In return for these indispensable services, it enjoys social and economic privileges placing it above the other classes (Herz, 1972: 153–154).

Marxism sees bureaucracies as an instrument of oppression used by the ruling economic class in capitalist societies. In this view, it would have been rational to substitute centralized administrational bodies by models of self-government (e.g., workers councils). But instead of giving power to the democratic basis, the *avant-garde* principle used in communist parties was applied also to state and administration. It had quickly become clear (first in the Soviet Union, but also in the GDR) that decentralized forms of government are not suitable tools to organize and rule modern, industrialized nations or empires like the Soviet one, especially not if a single political party is trying to dominate a society. By claiming to have access to privileged knowledge, this *avant-garde* legitimized its power. Thus, only those in power were able to define the "public good." That ideological "twist" — not to refer to models of democratic participation but to promote a communist elite, which would ensure progress — legitimized and strengthened centralized party power. Although Article 3.6 of the GDR basic law guaranteed the independence of civil servants from any party or interest, in practice they were totally dependent on the SED and had to carry out its policies to be able to remain in office. Most staff in the civil service had to be members of the SED (Edwards, 1998).

Unlike many American bureaucrats, most German civil servants both from the East and the West did not derive their job satisfaction from the specialized profession that they practiced in their official position (law, medicine, and engineering) or from the clientele they served. They were more committed to a career in government service, oriented solely to their job, proud of their status in the society, and wed to the authority of the State. As a result, they depended almost entirely on the governmental hierarchy to gain fulfillment of their desire for prestige, security, and life-purpose. Their dependence on the government for these satisfactions made them a relatively pliable instrument for whichever regime held power (Jacob, 1963; Garcia-Zamor, 2003). The American comedian Groucho Marx once boasted to a skeptic "Yes, I have principles, and if you don't like them, I've got others" (Barber, 2001: 95). This could be a sad depiction of the attitude of East German civil servants before the reunification.

An author who had first-hand experience with the East German bureaucracy reached these conclusions:

> Germans apply the random and often illogical practices and rules of bureaucracy in a more exacting way than most of mankind. Rules don't need to make sense, for they are respected as the necessary glue that holds society together; and

> Germans in one realm of bureaucracy will seldom volunteer information about potential problems one might face from a related but different bureaucracy (Kempe, 1999: 268).

Still, a German scholar viewed the GDR bureaucratic administration as a "modern" one even if it was increasingly removed from the classical type of bureaucracy as defined by Max Weber (Kocka, 1999). Bureaucrats in East Germany had to constantly assert their competency when dealing with the members of the ruling elite. The struggle against *bureaucratism* was one of the recurring themes of the socialist ideology. There was great impatience with oppressive bureaucratic requirements, excessive paper work, and with petty regulation from above by administrators of doubtful technical competence. In the 1970s, the GDR ruling elite felt that centralization and the heavy-handedness of the bureaucracy had slowed down economic growth. Several people thought that the bureaucracy had imposed so many directives on the factories that it weakened rather than strengthened effective control. What really was taking place in the GDR was a constant confrontation between a "Weberian" bureaucracy, in its rigid rule implementation and sharp demarcation of responsibilities, and the technocracies, with their more flexible economic and technical approaches to developmental tasks. The GDR called itself a workers' and farmers' state. People identified themselves or were identified by the authorities as laborers. In this vein intellectuals referred to themselves as "mind-laborers." Work was one of the most fundamental themes of self-identification. The workplace was also the center of social and political activities, and it was the distribution channel for some of the most desirable goods, notably vacations and apartments. Thus work was what made somebody a valuable member of society.

In the first two decades of its existence, GDR was urging party members to press the cause of economic rationalization as part of their political duties while failures in economic performance were laid to the "ideological" omissions of state functionaries. Civil servants in the economic sector were also urged to exert "political" leadership and to study the Marxian classics. The idea was to create a new type of bureaucratic leaders both economically skilled and politically faithful to outflank the possible emergence of a self-conscious technocratic elite that might choose to rebel against the status quo (Baylis, 1974). Baylis also remarked that those members of the technical intelligentsia who arrived in positions of political importance were also political conformists; and that the positions that they attained were in the main advisory rather than decisive or genuinely powerful. Political considerations retained their priority over technical or professional considerations (Baylis, 1974). In general, public administration in the GDR followed the Soviet Union's model. Ideologically pitted against the German civil service tradition, the cadre administration rejected the idea of a professional public administration. Instead, it gave priority to ideological indoctrination over professionalism and adequate training. By holding the power to recruit, appoint, move and remove all *nomemklatura* positions, the SED possessed a formidable lever to ensure and enforce ideological and political obedience of the entire administrative elite (Wollmann, 1996).

IV. The Political and Bureaucratic Transition

The GDR's first (and last) freely elected government after the March 1990 election explicitly rejected the idea of a professional civil service and its "traditional principles" that can be found in Article 33 of the Basic Law. However, that decision quickly became meaningless. The overwhelming victory in that election of the *Alliance for Germany* effectively put the German state professional civil service in the GDR's future, regardless of the immediate will of the newly elected East German government (Kvistad, 1999). In June 1990, the last democratic government in the GDR began to restructure state and administration. Reunification was imminent, so creating compatible administrative institutions was the main goal. Work began on the level of the old *Bezirke* (districts), the regional level, on which the reestablishment of the *Länder* would be based. Parallel to that activity local self-government was reintroduced to towns and cities. It was at that time that the first administrative reform aid was provided by the West. Two overlapping phases can be identified: in the beginning acting administrators were sent to the East for a limited period of time. However, it quickly became clear that a "permanent elite-transfer" was necessary since the East German administration would depend on the professional knowledge of Western experts for a very long time (Köning, 1999: 87). Limited time consultants were not seen as a long-term solution, it was necessary to keep them in the East. They were hoping that they could develop more empathy for the people and local conditions. Western personnel went east for a variety of reasons. Some wanted an adventure in the "wild East," while others had ancestral roots there and wanted to rediscover a lost past. For others, monetary rewards certainly played a role. An American expert in East German studies wrote the following:

> Western elites received *Buschgeld*, or bush money to go east, and some also received free weekly flights home. While many of the imported personnel were fully committed to furthering German unity and planned to make the east their home, the behavior of other western imports created resentment among some eastern Germans who perceived they were being colonized by second-rate bureaucrats and carpet-baggers (Yoder, 1999: 92).

For various reasons, the approval of Western civil servants was not unanimous. For some of these expatriates, the East was formerly a distant and unknown world. Problems of integration and little interest in becoming familiar with Eastern problems were common. Andreas Staab mentioned that the mentality and living standards of East and West were too diverse to allow for a smooth integration, and friction was hard to avoid. He added that:

> The persistent post-unification rhetoric of denunciation of the SED regime — not only for its political failures and shortcomings but in general for every aspect of life in the GDR — helped to establish the notion of the victorious West in the fight for systematic supremacy between Capitalism and Communism. As a result, the perception of a political takeover was complemented by notions of an administrative subordination of the East (Staab, 1998: 85).

Yoder also wrote that this development introduced a hierarchy in the new administrative institutions, which instantly put easterners in a subordinate position. Western elites went east with the purpose of retraining indigenous personnel. The existence of a blueprint for administrative institutions, complete with the transfer of West German programs and routines, left little or no room for substantive contributions from the past experiences of eastern Germany (Yoder, 1999). Although the adaptation to the Western system did not seem to present an overwhelming problem for some eastern professionals, on the whole, many of them suffered severe setbacks in their careers. Those who were "taken over" by the West German system (public administrators and teachers) experienced the least disruption. Educational certificates functioned as a safety net for most of them (Kupferberg, 2002). So during 1991, the legal framework was created to transfer these Western *Beamte* to the East (with the new laws protecting their status quo and hierarchical rank). This situation prompted a German scholar to ask if German unification was not a watershed of institutional reform (Helms, 2000). Another European scholar who has published widely on Germany made the point that reform in Germany is typically incremental, painstaking, and legalistic (Flockton, 2001). After reunification, the German public sector seems to have been stabilized by minor adjustments rather than far-reaching reforms. The federalized nature of the institutional system played a decisive role in explaining this outcome. But until today, West-German civil servants hold many leading positions and therefore play a key role in Eastern administrative processes, although they only account for a small percentage of the total staff.

The shortage of trained experts could be bridged that way, but the question whether to keep or to lay off old cadre did not become obsolete. On the one hand, local staff was necessary, on the other hand it was impossible for political reasons to keep the old structures. A quantitative problem added further pressure: overstaffing. Seven percent of the working population in the West were employed in the public sector, twelve percent in the East. Although most of the top positions were cleared of old *nomenklaturists* on October 3rd, 1990, the staff-restructuring was an unsolved question at the time of Reunification and had to be analyzed as an element of the general system transformation. Remaining administrative institutions had to be remodeled, obsolete ones shut down and new ones created. There was one basic principle for remaining institutions: "in the interest both of administrative continuity and the civil service, public employees would not lose their job" (Köning, 1999: 88). In case they worked for a structure no longer necessary, those employees were "placed on hold." Some of them found a new position at a different administration, often they had to accept a lower rank. However, several criteria could be used to lay off staff:

- STASI activities
- Violations of (internationally recognized) human rights and the rule of law
- Lack of qualification
- Overstaffing
- Dissolving of an institution

It was still a tremendous task to move the old socialist administration to the principles of "classical administration" with its specific elements like professionalism, efficiency and effectiveness. The Unification Treaty (*Einigungsvertrag*) specifically demanded public obligations to be performed by *Beamte* (civil servants). The practical solution of the problem consisted to entitle East German civil servants as *Beamte auf Probe* — on probation (Köning, 1999: 89). Furthermore, the specific educational degrees usually necessary to become a civil servant were not required.

Instead, individual performance on the job was evaluated. In addition, while on probation, everybody had to take part in further training classes organized by a network of West-German educational institutions. This way of transforming the East German administration basically accepted a staff continuity and resulted in a longer transitional period.

However, the transition took place within the new legal framework of the 1990 Unification Treaty. Chapter V of the Treaty dealt with public administration and the administration of justice and Article 19 affirmed the validity of decisions taken by GDR administrative bodies. It declared that all the administrative acts of the GDR performed before the accession took effect should remain valid. They could be revoked only if they were incompatible with the principles of the rule of law or with the provisions of the Treaty. In all other respects, the rules on the validity of administrative acts should remained unaffected. But Article 20 on the legal status of persons in the public service merely stated that the exercise of public responsibilities should be entrusted as soon as possible to professional civil servants (Glaessner, 1992). Still, reunification altered significantly the process of policy making. It soon became apparent that policies aiming at equalizing living conditions between East and West could be successful only if these two factors were met: the transformation of the former GDR economy from state socialism to a market economy, and the adaptation of political and administrative structures to the western model.[5] An immediate aim of the decision makers was to institutionalize joint responsibilities between different levels of government. However, after reunification, the new *Länder* placed more emphasis on working together to pursue their specifically East German interests than on trying to work in concert with the western *Länder*. They have in some cases, notably in education policy, pursued a policy agenda clearly different from that of the western *Länder* although they were willing to accept a high degree of federal influence over their affairs in return for extra financial assistance from the Federation (Jeffery, 1995). Policy making in Germany is highly interconnected. In addition to the coordination of decision making between the *Länder*, a wide range of tasks are jointly financed by the *Länder* and the federal government, sometimes with the involvement of European and local actors (Sturm, 1996).

The end of communism in the GDR created a host of new and unexpected challenges for West German government and public administration. As far as the public sector is concerned, stability and continuity seem to have prevailed (Benz and Goetz, 1996). Unlike the other Central and Eastern European countries where the building of new political and administrative institutions evolved in an almost incremental and partly erratic manner, institution building in the former GDR was shaped by a massive institutions transfer in which the entire ready-made legal and administrative model of

West Germany was literally exported overnight and implanted in the new eastern part of the country. This was a unique task: the transformation of the "real-existing socialist" state and its administration was part of a fundamental system change. Since any socialist economy was part of the state administration, one of the main challenges (and transformation starting points) was the necessary "re-differentiation" of state and economy — a crucial aspect to any capitalist, liberal and democratic society. And this process itself was subject to political influence (by the new political power of course), as the different ways to approach that task in Eastern Europe show (with Germany choosing the *Treuhand* model of privatization). The whole process could be analyzed as "re-modernization," after communism had "de-modernized" Central and Eastern European States.

According to Luhmann system theory, modern societies are characterized by "functional differentiation": relatively independent subsystems with specific system rationalities (e.g., the economic sphere with private property, free markets and competition etc.) is separated from the political-administrative sphere featuring democracy, civil liberties, rule of law, separation of powers, etc. The Marxist ideology implemented in the GDR meant a "counter-modernization" because the level of differentiation reached in Eastern Europe was lowered back to "democratic Centralism" as it was called (König, 1999: 74). Holding this perspective, Sigrid Meuschel argues that specific subsystems (especially the economic one) and their system requirements were dominated by the power of the political structure symbolized by the fact that the party always had the last word (Meuschel, 1992), thus, destroying the very conditions of specific system rationalities. A good example is the politically motivated East German welfare program, started in the early 1970s, which was far too generous relative to economic capacity. As a result, foreign debt rose sharply in the 1980s and, among other inefficiencies, infrastructure, equipment and research investments declined, further diminishing the economic capacity. Meuschel pointed out the fact that party power in East Germany was based not only in society's "de-differentiation" but also in specific German traditions of being apolitical as a citizen, an attitude that prevented the development of an opposing civil society. Instead, the people showed a lack of participation or resistance and the majority simply accepted the system in an old authoritarian fashion (Meuschel, 1992). The "re-differentiation" therefore included two major goals: the transformation from a centrally planned economy to a market economy and from an authoritarian to a democratic system.

This was made possible by the political, administrative, financial, and economic might and will of West Germany. In addition, a significant number of West Germans were transferred to the East to occupy high-level political and bureaucratic positions. These factors made the bureaucratic transition in East Germany a unique case in the spectrum of former socialist countries (Wollmann, 1996). The orderly disappearance of the GDR left no institutional void. The dissolution of the East German state and the transfer of West German political institutions were managed with remarkable efficiency as far as the legal groundwork and the merger of organizations were concerned.[6] Some analysts mentioned the crucial role that time played during this period. It would have been impossible, they argued, to design a completely new set of rules quickly. The political pressure of the East's collapse created the need for fast solutions, which was to use Article 23 of the Basic Law to reunite Germany. Article 23 of the Basic Law simply extended the West German constitutional framework to East Germany.

During this period, a political rationality clearly dominated the decision-making process (including some competing economic rationalities). The most controversial one was the introduction of the West Deutsche Mark in the East in July 1990 against the advice of the Bundesbank and many economists. Whether the economic evaluation of the East German transformation process dominated the public discussion relative to questions like *Stasi* past, bureaucracies or general democratic progress depended on whether West Germany or former communist countries were used as a comparison. The problem was twofold: not only did the SED with it's multi-level party organization influenced state and bureaucracy, but there was also a net of party members within the administration or, as König wrote "both a 'party-pyramid' over the 'state-pyramid' and a 'party-pyramid' within the 'state-pyramid' existed" (König, 1999: 82). Thus political transformation had to deal with several problems: potential informal communication networks of the old cadre, the reestablishment of the horizontal separation of power (legislative, executive, and judicial) and the vertical separation of power, which was supposed to create a decentralized administration like the German federalism model, including the principle of local self-government by villages, towns and cities — all in all a sharp contrast to "democratic Centralism." However, as was to be expected, political and administrative integration after reunification have met with a host of obstacles that derive from the legacy of socialism, a lack of resources in the East, and differences in East and West German mentalities. The highly intrusive, demanding political regime of the GDR had forged a very real sense of "GDR identity" among its citizens. The GDR did not collapse because of a nationalist quest for reunification. The quest for reunification arose as a result, not a cause, of the collapse of communist rule in the GDR (Fulbrook, 1999).[7]

One measure of bureaucratic performance is often the administrative capability of the civil servants in the economic sector. In the case of the former East Germany, the slow development of the economy could be traced to several obstacles. However, it has also been proven that when some very efficient technocrats took control of the management of certain economic sectors, they were able to overcome some of these obstacles (Garcia-Zamor, 2002). Among some of the mistakes that were made during the unification period was the Federal government's goal to equalize East and West German wages, even though Eastern workers were only a quarter to a third as productive as their Western counterparts. Robert J. Samuelson (2002: 59) wrote that:

> East Germany's currency (and wages) were converted into West German marks at an unrealistic exchange rate of one to one; then, East German wages were raised more than 50 percent from 1991 to 1995. Instantly, high labor costs made many firms uncompetitive and rendered East Germany unattractive for new factories. Massive unemployment resulted; it still exceeds 18 percent.

In addition, Samuelson also pointed to the fact that huge payments (3 to 4 percent of GDP) from West Germany have been made to the East to pay unemployment and welfare benefits. The cost of unification has had a negative impact on the German economy.[8] Work was what made somebody a valuable member of society in both parts of Germany, but the orientation towards work as the central aspect of life was more pronounced in the East than in the West, a difference that could probably be attributed in part to the threat of unemployment in the East. Unemployment is even more dramatic to Easterners since they were raised in a Communist society where every member of the society had a job (Glaeser, 2000).[9] For them, unification marked the beginning of a transformation that would radically alter their lives. As workers and firms were subjected to the rigors of market forces, the situation that had created the ironic GDR quip, according to which "they pretend to pay us, and we pretend to work," also passed into history (Keithly, 1999: 188). But after reunification, many of the jobs people assumed to be guaranteed for life began to disappear. Professional qualifications were downgraded, and much of previous work experience counted for little. East Germans became disillusioned with the new situation and were shocked by the unexpected burdens and the impact of unification on their personal lives. Many started looking back to the "good old days" of "real existing socialism" in the GDR. Staab (1998: 97) wrote: "Repressing the inhuman aspects of the oppressive regime resulted in a selective memory that disproportionately remembered the positive aspects — for instance, social welfare or job security." This remarkable phenomenon soon earned a name in the media: "GDR nostalgia" (Kapferer, 2000).

Before 1989, many East Germans thought that socialism was a far better system than capitalism despite the fact that they were aware that the West Germans had a higher standard of living. They blamed party officials for the failure to achieve greater economic development, not the system of government. Despite the fact that the policies of *glasnost* or openness begun by Soviet president Mikhail Gorbachev rushed across eastern and central Europe like waters from a burst dam, most East Germans were not really pro-reunification. They had great hope that *perestroika* would only open the system and make it more transparent.[10] It is sometime hard for people who have chosen to leave for the West, or for some Westerners who have always lived in a democratic system, to fully comprehend or to accept this fact (an interesting similarity with the case of Cuba) (Garcia-Zamor, 2001). König wrote a very interesting chapter in his book that might contribute to a greater understanding of this phenomenon. He analyzed the aspect of how to transform the *Kader-Verwaltung*. The specific East-German situation was characterized by the classical question of any regime change: how many of the old faces will remain in power? Is it possible (both by political and professional standards) to keep at least some of them? What about the need to recruit new personnel? This classical situation was further complicated by the "dualism of East- and West-German administrators" (König, 1999: 86). It was clear from the beginning that a transformation to democracy could not work with the old *nomenklaturists* in charge. The consequences of their political incompetence could be observed everywhere (König, 1999: 86). After it became clear, that the system would collapse, they did not put up relevant resistance to the change, but tried to use the time between November 1989 and the Reunification in 1990 to "clean" their personal files or to transfer to a different, potentially safe and un-suspicious position. In any case, they were no longer able to use their former power as administrators.

V. Changes for Integrity in Governance

A new generation of administrators is being educated at new schools for public administration that have been established everywhere on Länder level to gradually replace the old ones. After the Revolution of 1989, there was no relevant (quantitative or qualitative) counter-elite, which could have filled open positions (König, 1999). The reasons for that can be found in the perfect system of oppression, which usually excluded dissidents from higher schools and universities, thus preventing educational careers.[11]

Prof. Dr. Dieter Schimanke who in 2000 was *Staatssekretär* (state secretary, the second highest rank in a ministry, right below the minister) in the Ministry for Work, Social Affairs and Health of Sachsen-Anhalt, Magdeburg wrote an interesting article describing his experience in his ministry. He found that even after thorough further education, Eastern civil servants continued to surprise their Western trainers. When it came to implementing new rules, specific behavior patterns came back to life, based on Eastern experience and socialization. Schimanke especially highlights what he calls "GDR-pragmatism," which meant that each individual case was decided in a discretionary way. If a decision turned out to be a mistake, it was possible to correct it, regardless of what the rule (the abstract norm) demanded. This behavior of course was not compatible with the standards of the rule of law. This pattern corresponds to the informal *Eingaben* (petition system) common in the former GDR. Whenever people had a problem, usually on the local and individual level (need for a new playground, problems with the distribution of consumer products, etc.), they wrote a letter to the administration complaining about what bothered them. Although there was no legal framework for this, these petitions were taken extremely seriously because they were considered to be an indicator of discontent and therefore important with regards to system stability. In a way, this was a method to control the administration, because whenever "Berlin" demanded a report, these letters and petitions usually revealed problems to the disadvantage of the local or district authorities. So the instrument of correcting administrative decisions in order to achieve "individual case justice" was widely used in the GDR (Garcia-Zamor, 2004).

Schimanke (2001: 185) describes his observation of the transformation process' "interim results" as follows:

Professional Quality: Parts of the East German administration meet the requirements, especially if there is a stable authority with skilled civil servants (e.g., infrastructure authorities). A general quality problem is a lack of professionalism when it comes to the legal framework. Very often mistakes are made because authorities exceed their competencies. There are too many incorrect or inadequate decisions that can cause significant damage for administrative authorities.

Independent Work: Very often civil servants wait for orders from a higher level, although they could act independently. And if they do, it is a different way of acting independently ("Eastern behavior patterns") compared to western standards.

Problem-solving capacities: Especially on the level of state ministries there are deficits in this field. Strategic thinking and "intelligent," modern administrative practice are not found often enough. Schimanke stresses the fact that this is a problem also characteristic for West-German *Beamte* who settled in the East.

Budget and overstaffing: Room for personnel policies and promotions is very limited, because of the need to reduce staff. In addition, top positions are filled with a relatively young and homogeneous (with regards to age) Western group, which will block career opportunities for younger Easterners for the next years.

Further education and training: There is a lack of strategies and concepts to deal with the unique situation. In addition, even if they were available, there are motivational problems: if you know that chances for a promotion are very small, the will to obtain more skills might not be very developed.

VI. A Summing-Up: Governance, Ethics, and Bureaucratic Culture

In the transitory period between the opening of the wall in October 1989 and the unification of the two Germanys in October 1990, many people believed in the illusion that only the Wall separated the Germans.

> Initially preoccupied with the enormous legal and financial burdens of Eastern reconstruction, federal officials devoted little energy to the equally formidable task of reforging a sense of national identity from within, beyond a reinvocation of national symbols. United Germany's health as a nation will depend upon the extent to which its predominantly Western leadership succeeds not in "Kohlonizing" but in grafting Eastern political culture on to its own (Mushaben, 1998: 374).

As the disparate citizens' groups that had provided the intellectual and spiritual rationale for the 1989 revolution were unable to present themselves as credible spokesmen for the population of East Germany, political power drained out of the few remaining centers of authority that still existed in the East.[12] A disillusioned one-liner read: "The Revolution had won, the revolutionaries had lost." The mayor of Dresden observed "Power is up for grabs, yet no one picks it up" (Peterson, 2002: 251). The GDR regime had permitted limited protests as long as the system was not generally questioned. The boundaries of criticism allowed by the party sometimes appeared to be far drawn. But the government made sure that the majority of citizens would respect these boundaries. Anyone trying to test the limits of the system by crossing the prescribed lines would incur great personal disadvantages, and most GRD citizens did not take the risk. The dissidents were no exception in this regard. In addition, because they did not truly want a revolution, they never demanded power. They wanted only reforms and focused their entire political energy on defeating the *Stasi*. For them, the *Stasi* was the root evil of GDR socialism. Yet they either did not perceive or did not react to the new tendencies turning up at the demonstrations. They neither expressed opinions on the question of reunification, nor put their objective in concrete terms, nor did they provide any revolutionary program (Voss and Opp, 1995). These two scholars concluded by writing that:

> There were no groups in the GDR that played an outstanding role in the revolution. There was no revolutionary class and no revolutionary party. There was also no charismatic personality who motivated the "masses" to revolutionary actions. One reason for this lack was that the members of opposition groups, who were particularly active in the protests, were also prisoners of the ruling socialist ideology and thus could not offer "the people" any basic alternatives (Voss and Opp, 1995: 165).

The lack of dominant personalities, in the government as well as the opposition, made post-communist East German politics look very different from those of Poland and Czechoslovakia, where personality cults have formed around Lech Walesa and Vaclav Havel, respectively (Darnton, 1992). Contrary to the common view that the dissidents and intellectuals were the leaders of the revolution, at no point did they possess the decisive initiative. They were the reluctant revolutionaries and outsiders in a process that that they neither initiated nor desired. Their prominence was more an effect than a cause of events during the autumn of 1989 (Ross, 2002). They remained a minority not only in Germany as a whole, but also within East Germany. West Germans took little interest in their claims. Moreover, they ended up feeling like the real losers of the democratization process (Müller, 2001).

The burden of GDR's absorption into the Federal Republic practically fell onto the shoulders of West Germany's policymakers. These policymakers were overburdened at the time. Thus, the federal administration had to hand over responsibilities to the *Länder* bureaucracies; in other cases it had to take over responsibilities normally vested in the federal units. But because the *Länder*, in cultural policy for instance, did not want to spend scarce resources on East Germany, the Federation took over. The process became a kind of "Keynesianism of Reunification" — against the will of the actors involved (von Beyme, 1998: 117). Another important reason for West German politicians' early interest and involvement was the fact that the Basic Law required Federal elections in 1990 and the largest political parties in the West were to compete in an all-German vote for the first time. In early 1990, several of these political parties sought to take advantage of their existing or possible counterparts in the East by utilizing them as vehicles for reaching out to new voters (MacAdams, 1993).

After reunification, public administration in the East could not simply be adjusted to accommodate the methods of the West. It had to be significantly modified to eliminate the structural incompatibility that existed between the two models of public administration. The centralized administration of the socialist state, which was subject to strict control by the SED hierarchy, was replaced by a differentiated system in accordance with the tenets of federalism and municipal self-government. An authoritarian and often arbitrary administration lacking many features of efficient bureaucratic and legal organization, such as administrative records, had to be transformed into a service-oriented administration mindful of the protection of citizens' rights, which are provided by administrative courts (Kreile, 1992).

Although in Germany ideas for new policies formally originate from government ministries, parliament or the Chancellor's office, pressure groups, new social movements and even public opinion at home and abroad do have some influence on policy initiation. A very important new source of influence, which has stimulated many policy changes, has been the European Union (EU), especially after the member states agreed on the aim of the post-1992 Single Market with the Single European Act of 1986 (Sturm, 1996). Numerous new German laws are also influenced by the European Union. German unification had presented great challenges for European integration. It bound the larger Germany into a deeper form of EU integration, while providing part of the architecture for a wider Europe, following the end of the Iron Curtain (Flockton, 2000). This factor became an important element in the complexity of the integration of the former GDR bureaucracy into the federal system and relates to patterns of external interaction with regard to Germany's participation in the European Union. Benz and Goetz (1996: 22) describe this as an important new development in the German public sector:

> As regards the contextualization of the German administrative system within the European legal, political and administrative framework, it is becoming increasingly impossible to understand the workings of German public administration without constant and systematic reference to its embeddedness in the European order. The scope and content of administrative action, the national institutional setting, administrative procedures and personnel policy are influenced by European integration to an extent where it is becoming increasingly problematic to conceptualize integration as an external force affecting domestically

defined administrative arrangements. Already the interactive ties between the national administrative system and its European environment are of such variety and intensity that they constitute a decisive new element in Germany's administrative history.

In addition to analyzing the interaction of sound governance and administrative ethics in the former East Germany during the difficult transition of the GDR bureaucracy from communism to democracy, the chapter sought to highlight bureaucratic culture and the influences of external political, economic, legal and social systems on bureaucratic behavior. It illustrated the relationship of bureaucratic culture to organizational performance under different conditions. It also analyzed how two types of bureaucratic cultures (GDR and West Germany) have coped with a series of changes that involved fundamental ideological adjustments in the political systems of the two countries. The bureaucracies of the East and the West had to operate under changing laws, norms, and structures that were designed to maximize the control of the political leaders who were in power at different times. When reunification came in 1990, the two bureaucracies were merged according to plans that were not negotiated between them. West Germany had the sole control over the retention and recruitment of the Eastern civil servants who eventually joined the federal bureaucracy. Although problems still exist in the reunification process, they are not unsurmountable nor are they influencing only the bureaucratic transition. As shown in the chapter, they are also affecting the social, political, and economic integration of the two parts of Germany. It is not easy to determine how long it will take before the former GDR bureaucracy can fully absorb the western norms and values of sound governance and administrative ethics that are being imposed by unification. However, it is safe to say that such integration, even if it takes time, is inevitable.

Notes

1. As a young undergraduate student the author of this chapter attended a summer seminar at Heidelberg University in Germany taught by the late Harvard University professor Carl J. Friedrich. Friedrich, who had helped write the constitution of postwar Germany, liked to say that corruption was like arsenic: every living body needs a small dose to thrive, but more than a little was always fatal (Barber, 2001).

2. Loyalty was also important in the West German civil system but was never a factor in recruitment. A Ministerial Decree was promulgated in 1972 to prevent communists and fascists from entering national, state, and local civil service posts and to dismiss those already in public employment. The decree spawned a massive loyalty check of about 3.5 million persons, including most

applicants for public employment and numerous civil servants (Braunthal, 1990).

3. The main preoccupation in 1990 was to find constitutionally feasible paths to unification. Article 23 of the Basic Law was used. It prescribed that individual states had to apply and that later the Federal Republic had to pass a legal act defining the expansion of the jurisdiction of the Basic Law. Thus when in March 1990 the eastern states held their first free elections since 1933, the victory of the political parties supporting unification legitimized the subsequent decisions by the states to join the Federal Republic in September 1990 (Millett, 1994). Even after reunification, the main concerns remained political and scant attention was given to appropriate institutions design.

4. The East German companies and the universities were never run according to profit or output criteria. The ruling party had consciously shaped the structure and content of East German education to fit the needs and goals set by the economy. The number and specialization of university graduates was determined by the state economic plan, and the character of both teaching curricula and research was shaped in accordance with the specific needs of East German industry (Baylis, 1974). As far as the universities were concerned, overstaffing was quite a problem since it reduced considerably their standards of efficiency. The smaller teams in Western universities, where there was less bureaucracy and more pressure to produce, operated with higher academic results.

5. Philip Zelikow and Condoleezza Rice who were members of the U.S. National Security Council staff of the first Bush presidency participated in some of the negotiations that led to the reunification of Germany. They later told their story from the U.S. perspective, while looking in detail at the other international actors and Washington's efforts to bring them in line with America's priorities (Zelikow and Rice, 1995).

6. It was the opinion of legal experts who examined historical documents that when the GDR polity became unitary in 1952, the five states (Mecklenburg, Brandenburg, Sachsen-Anhalt, Sachsen, and Thüringen), although they disappeared from the map, continued to exist legally; it was necessary only to recognize them once more so that they could apply for admission to the Federal Republic of Germany. Despite some fierce controversy regarding boundaries (which had been altered when the GDR was divided into fourteen districts) and designation of capital cities, a statute for the introduction of the states was enacted in the GDR People's Assembly (Wolfe, 1992).

7. In West Germany, a lone voice spoke against reunification — the voice of the internationally renowned German writer Günter Grass, who for the previous thirty years has argued strenuously against a united Germany (Grass, 1990). An American journalist, Marc Fisher (1995), who was stationed in Germany also voiced later his pessimism about the future of a reunited Germany. He wrote that far from freeing the Germans from the burdens of history, the fall of the Wall has exacerbated the traumas of the past, leaving Germany divided against the continuing legacy of the Nazi and communist eras. He argued that

the readmission of sixteen million East Germans into a reunited Germany uncovered old wounds and lifted half a century of taboos (Grass, 1995).

8. German GDP grew a meager 0.2 percent in 2002. According to Samuelson (2002), since 1991, unemployment in Germany has averaged about 8 percent and the number of jobs in 2002 is roughly what it was a decade ago. Samuelson cited a study by economists Dirk Schumacher and David Walton of Goldman Sachs that concluded that German underperformance could easily persist for another decade or more.

9. In socialist countries, work is a central institution in the technical order of economic production. It is also central to the social structure and to individual motivation, and thus the central point at which the individual relates to society. Lisa Peattie (1981) explored the implications of social planning by looking at the transformation of Cuba in the course of the Revolution. She found that the country was organized around "moral incentives" just as — in the alternative model — around material ones. The Cubans developed a complex system of nonmaterial incentives that resembles in part the former East Germans' one (public praise by the leaders, medals, buttons, diplomas, plaques, certificates of communist work, and honorable mention in factory bulletins etc.). These prizes and honors are the equivalent of the paper currency in the moral-incentive system.

10. Usually in dictatorial systems, the political joke is a sort of safety valve. One that reflected the potential role of *perestroika* in any uprising tells of President Reagan, President Gorbachev, and the then-leader of East Germany, Mr. Honecker, being called by God. God tells all three of them that he does not like what they are doing on Earth and that he is going to send them another biblical flood. Then he sends them back to tell their people. President Reagan goes on TV and says, "My fellow Americans, I have good news and bad news. The good news is that I have talked to God. The bad news is we will have another biblical flood." Gorbachev goes on TV and says to his fellow Russians, "I have two pieces of bad news. First of all, there is a God; second, we will have a biblical flood." The East German leader, Mr. Honecker, goes on TV and says to his people, "Look, there are two pieces of good news. First of all, God has recognized the GDR; second, there won't be *perestroika*, but only a biblical flood" (Pleuger, 1994).

11. The educational system that had developed in pre-war Germany was elitist and provided greater opportunities for intellectual development to children for the upper-middle and upper socio-economic classes. This elitism in education was a reflection of the rigid class structure that existed in German society. Most bureaucrats originated from these upper classes. One of the first acts of the GDR government was the restructuring of East German education. The Law on the Democratization of the German Schools was published and promulgated on June 12, 1946 to give equal rights to education to all children (Klein, 1980).

12. Bertolt Brecht had once declared with memorable irony at the time of the 1953 Workers' uprising that it was time for the East German Communist government "to elect a new people" (Barber, 2001: 287).

References

Adams, F., USAID's Democracy initiative: recipient needs or donor interests? *Int. Stud. Notes*, 23, 9–14, 1998.

Barber, B.R., *The Truth of Power. Intellectual Affairs in the Clinton White House*, W.W. Norton & Company, New York, 2001.

Baylis, T.A., *The Technical Intelligentsia and the East German Elite. Legitimacy and Social Change in Mature Communism*, University of California Press, Berkeley, 1974.

Benz, A. and Goetz, K.H., *A New German Public Sector? Reform, Adaptation and Stability*, Dartmouth Publishing Company, Brookfield, Vermont, 1996.

Bowman, J.B. and Williams, R.L., Ethics in government: from a winter of despair to a spring of hope, *Pub. Adm. Rev.*, 57, 517–526, 1998.

Braunthal, G., *Political Loyalty and Public Service in West Germany. The 1972 Decree against Radicals and Its Consequences*, The University of Massachusetts Press, Amherst, 1990.

Darnton, R., Stasi besieged, in *The Reunification of Germany*, Long, R.E., Ed., The H.W. Wilson Company, New York, 1992, pp. 57–62.

Edwards, G.E., *German Political Parties. A Documentary Guide*, University of Wales Press, Cardiff, 1998.

Eisenstadt, T.A., Measuring electoral court failure in democratizing Mexico, *Int. Political Sci. Rev.*, 23, 47–68, 2002.

Fisher, M., *After the Wall. Germany, the Germans and the Burdens of History*, Simon & Schuster, New York, 1995.

Fixdal, M. and Smith, D., Humanitarian intervention and just war, *Mershon Int. Stud. Rev.*, 42, 283–312, 1998.

Flockton, C., Policy agendas and the economy in Germany and Europe, in *The New Germany in the East. Policy Agendas and Social Developments since Unification*, Flockton, C., Kolinsky, E., and Pritchard, R., Eds., Frank Cass Publishers, London, 2000, pp. 61–83.

Flockton, C., The German economy since 1989/90: problems and prospects, in *Germany Since Unification. The Development of the Berlin Republic*, 2nd ed., Larres, K., Ed., Palgrave, London, 2001, pp. 63–87.

Fulbrook, M., *German National Identity after the Holocaust*, Polity Press, Cambridge, 1999.

Garcia-Zamor, J.C., Neoteric theories for development administration in the new world order, in *Public Administration in the Global Village*, Garcia-Zamor, J.C. and Khator, R., Eds., Praeger Publishers, Westport, Connecticut, 1994, pp. 101–120.

Garcia-Zamor, J.C., Conundrums of urban planning in a global context: the case of the Frankfurt airport, *Pub. Organ. Rev.: A Global J.*, 1, 415–435, 2001.

Garcia-Zamor, J.C., Ethics revisited in a society in transition: the case of the former East Germany, *Pub. Adm. Dev.*, 22, 235–248, 2002.

Garcia-Zamor, J.C., Workplace spirituality in the United States and the former East Germany, in *The Handbook of Workplace Spirituality and Organizational Performance*, Giacalone, R.A. and Jurkiewicz, C.L., Eds., ME Sharpe, Inc., New York, 2003, pp. 314–335.

Garcia-Zamor, J.C., Justice expectations and redress to human rights violations in the former East Germany, in *Bureaucratic, Societal, and Ethical Transformation of the Former East Germany*, Garcia-Zamor, J.C., Ed., University Press of America, New York, 2004, pp. 121–145.

Glaeser, A., *Divided in Unity: Identity, Germany, and the Berlin Police*, The University of Chicago Press, Chicago, 2000.

Glaessner, G.-J., *The Unification Process in Germany. From Dictatorship to Democracy*, Translated from the German by Grant, C.B., St. Martin's Press, New York, 1992.

Glaessner, G.-J., Political culture in Germany and the legacies of the GDR, in *Germany — hoenix in Trouble?* Zimmer, M., Ed., The University of Alberta Press, Edmonton, Canada, 1997, pp. 83–104.

Grass, G., *Two States — One Nation?* Translated from the German by Winston, K. and Wensinger, A.S., Harcourt Brace Jovanovich, Publishers, New York, 1990.

Gravier, M., Entrer dans l'Administration de l'Allemagne Unifiée: Une Approche Anthropologique d'un Rituel d'Intégration (1990–1999), in *Revue Française de Science Politique*, Presses de Sciences Po, Paris, 2003a, pp. 323–350.

Gravier, M., Recruiting East-Germans in the post-unification civil service: the role of political loyalty in a transition towards democracy, paper presented at the 19th World Congress of the International Political Science Association (IPSA) in Durban, South Africa, June 29th to July 4th, 2003b.

Helms, L., *Institutions and Institutional Change in the Federal Republic of Germany*, Macmillan Press Ltd, London, 2000.

Herz, J.H., *The Government of Germany*, 2nd ed., Harcourt Brace Jovanovich, Inc, New York, 1972.

Jacob, H., *German Administration since Bismarck. Central Authority versus Local Authority*, Yale University Press, New Haven, Connecticut, 1963.

Jeffery, C., The changing framework of German politics since unification, in *The New Germany. Social, Political and Cultural Challenges of Unification*, Lewis, D. and Mckenzie, J.R.P., Eds., University of Exeter Press, Exeter, England, 1995, pp. 101–126.

Kapferer, N., 'Nostalgia' in Germany's new federal states as a political and cultural phenomenon of the transformation process, in *Political Thought and German Reunification. The New German Ideology?* Williams, H., Wight, C., and Kapferer, N., Eds., St. Martin's Press, Inc., New York, 2000, pp. 28–40.

Keithly, D.M., The German economy: shocks to the system, in *Between Bonn and Berlin: German Politics Adrift?* Hampton, M.N. and Søe, C., Eds., Rowman & Littlefield Publishers, Inc., Lanham, Maryland, 1999, pp. 171–199.

Kempe, F., *Father/Land: A Personal Search for the New Germany*, G.P. Putnam's Sons, New York, 1999.

Klein, M.S., *The Challenge of Communist Education: A Look at the German Democratic Republic*, Columbia University Press, New York, 1980.

Kocka, J., The GDR: a special kind of modern dictatorship, in *Dictatorship as Experience: Towards a Socio-Cultural History of the GDR*, Jarausch, K.H., Ed., Translated by Duffy, E., Berghan Books, Oxford, 1999, pp. 17–26.

König, K., *Verwaltungsstaat im Übergang. Transformation, Entwicklung, Modernisierung*, Nomos Verlagsgesellschaft, Baden-Baden, 1999.

Kooiman, J., *Modern Governance*, Sage Publications, Newbury Park, California, 1993.

Kreile, M., The political economy of the New Germany, in *The New Germany and the New Europe*, Stares, P.B., Ed., The Brookings Institution, Washington, D.C., 1992, pp. 55–92.

Kupferberg, F., *The Rise and Fall of the German Democratic Republic*, Transaction Publishers, New Brunswick, New Jersey, 2002.

Kvistad, G.O., *The Rise and Demise of German Statism. Loyalty and Political Membership*, Berghahn Books, Oxford, 1999.

Lehoucq, F.E., Can parties police themselves? electoral governance and democratization, *Int. Political Sci. Rev.*, 23, 29–46.

MacAdams, A.J., *Germany Divided. From the Wall to Reunification*, Princeton University Press, Princeton, New Jersey, 1993.

Meuschel, S., *Legitimation und Parteiherrschaft*, Suhrkamp, Frankfurt am Main, 1992.

Millett, A.T., The unification of Germany: problems and consequences, in *Europe and Germany: Unity and Diversity*, Thompson, K.W., Ed., University Press of America, New York, 1994, pp. 129–146.

Mosher, F.C. Watergate: implications for responsible government, in *Classics of Public Administration*, Shafritz, J.M. and Hyde, A.C., Eds., Brooks/Cole Publishing Company, Pacific Grove, California, 1992, pp. 418–441.

Mozzafar, S., Patterns of electoral governance in Africa's emerging democracies. *Int. Political Sci. Rev.*, 23, 85–101, 2002.

Mozzafar, S. and Schedler, A., The comparative study of electoral governance — introduction, *Int. Political Sci. Rev.*, 23, 5–27, 2002.

Müller, J-W., East Germany: incorporation, tainted truth, and the double division, in *The Politics of Memory. Transitional Justice in Democratizing Societies*, de Brito, A.B., González-Enríquez, C., and Aguilar, P., Eds., Oxford University Press, Oxford, 2001, pp. 248–274.

Mushaben, J.M., *From Post-War to Post-Wall Generations. Changing Attitudes Toward the National Question and NATO in the Federal Republic of Germany*, Westview Press, Boulder, Colorado, 1998.

Osborne, D. and Gaebler, T., *Reinventing Government. How the Entreprenarial Spirit is Transforming the Public Sector*, Penguin Books USA Inc., New York, 1993.

Peattie, L., *Thinking about Development*, Plenum Press, London, 1981.

Peterson, E.N., *The Secret Police and the Revolution: The Fall of the German Democratic Republic*, Praeger Publishers, Westport, Connecticut, 2002.

Pleuger, G., German reunification: price and promise, in *Europe and Germany: Unity and Diversity*, Thompson, K.W., Ed., University Press of America, New York, 1994, pp. 147–172.

Riggs, F.W., Public administration in America: why our uniqueness is exceptional and important, *Pub. Adm. Rev.*, 58, 22–31, 1998.

Roberts, G.K., *Party Politics in the New Germany*, Pinter Publishers Ltd, London, 1997.

Ross, C., *The East German Dictatorship. Problems and Perspectives in the Interpretation of the GDR*, Arnold, a member of the Hodder Headline Group, London, 2002.

Samuelson, R.J., The (new) sick man of Europe, *Newsweek*, November 18, 59, 2002.

Schaffer, F.C., Might cleaning up elections keep people away from the polls? historical and comparative perspectives, *Int. Political Sci. Rev.*, 23, 69–84, 2002.

Schedler, A., The nested game of democratization by elections, *Int. Political Sci. Rev.*, 23, 103–122, 2002.

Schimanke, D., Dilemmata der personalpolitik, in *Zehn Jahre Verwaltungsaufbau Ost — eine Evaluation*, Derlien, H., Ed., Nomos Verlagsgesellschaft, Baden-Baden, 2001, pp. 179–187.

Staab, A., *National Identity in Eastern Germany. Inner Unification or Continued Separation?* Praeger Publishers, Westport, Connecticut, 1998.

Sturm, R., Continuity and change in the policy-making process, in *Developments in German Politics 2*, Smith, G., Paterson, W.E., and Padgett, S., Eds., Duke University Press, Durham, North Carolina, 1996, pp. 117–132.

Thompson, D.F., The possibility of administrative ethics, in *Classics of Public Administration*, Shafritz, J.M. and Hyde, A.C., Eds., 3rd ed., Brooks/Cole Publishing Company, Pacific Grove, California, 1992, pp. 523–532.

UNDP (United Nations Development Programme), *Human Development Report*, Oxford University Press, New York, 1995.

von Beyme, K., *The Legislator: German Parliament as a Centre of Political Decision-Making*. Ashgate Publishing Limited, Aldershot Hans, England, 1998.

Voss, P. and Opp, K-D., "We are the people!" a revolution without revolutionaries, in *Origins of a Spontaneous Revolution: East Germany*, Opp, K-D., Voss, P., and Gern, C., Eds., The University of Michigan Press, Ann Arbor, 1989, pp. 155–166.

Wolfe, N.T., *Policing a Socialist Society. The German Democratic Republic*, Greenwood Press, Wesport, Connecticut, 1992.

Wollmann, H., Rupture and transformation: local government in East Germany, in *Strategic Changes and Organizational Reorientations in Local Government. A Cross-National Perspective*, Ben-Elia, N., Ed., St. Martin's Press, Inc., New York, 1996, pp. 109–123.

Yoder, J.A., *From East Germans to Germans? The New Postcommunist Elites*, Duke University Press, Durham, North Carolina, 1999.

Zelikow, P. and Rice, C., *Germany Unified and Europe Transformed: A Study in Statecraft*, Harvard University Press, Cambridge, Massachusetts, 1995.

Chapter 19

Social Capital and Health: A Rural Perspective

Tim Bowyer

CONTENTS

I. Social Capital Inequalities and Health

Explanations for the differences in health status, whether at the level of the individual, household or at the level of the state, have become increasingly linked to social capital rather than any differences in traditional inputs such as drugs, medicines etc.[1] Starting from the idea that societies without social capital are ill and unable to function as effectively as those with ample amounts, the idea of social capital as an effective means of reducing health inequalities has acquired the status of an emerging new paradigm. Through its implications for the well being of households and the level of development of communities, the accumulation of social capital is seen as a necessary pre-condition to any improvement in morbidity levels. In this respect, individuals and groups having little or no social capital are assumed to have a far greater tendency to be ill than those with some or a great deal. This use of social factors to explain ill health is supported by amply documented evidence about the importance of social integration for individual and population health (Berkman and Syme, 1979; Berkman and Breslow, 1984; House and Kahn, 1985). It also reflects evidence from more recent studies that highlight the close relationship between elements of social capital (trust, lack of social support and weak social ties) and mortality rates (Kawachi et al., 1997a, 1999; Putnam, 2000).

However, proof of the positive relationship between health and social capital has so far failed to clarify the precise mechanisms that underlie these links (Leeder and Dominello, 1999; Veenstra, 2000). Instead researchers such as Sampson et al. (1999) and Kawachi (1997a, 1999a), have focused upon the nature of the relationship between the various basic indicators of social capital (civic engagement, trust, social engagement, and reciprocity).

Though these studies demonstrate that direct relationships among the various social variables defined by Coleman (1990) and Putnam (1993) exist, the links among the immediate social environment (family and friends), social networks, mutual trust, civic participation, community engagement and other factors and the health of individuals are not addressed. In developing countries steps have been undertaken to focus research on the link between social capital and general household welfare (expenditure, assets, credit access, savings, and employment) (Grootaert, 1997; Narayan and Pritchett, 1997; Grootaert and Narayan, 1999; Grootaert et al., 1999). However, research into the precise mechanisms underlying the connection between social capital and overall health remains as limited in developing countries as it is elsewhere (Kawachi, 1999b; Fine, 2001; Harpham et al., 2002). In practice this means that the importance of social support as a determinant of longevity and quality of life continues to be predicated around existing epidemiological evidence and little else.

Efforts to identify an underlying link between health and socio-economic inequality have focused around income distribution, on the grounds that income inequality affects mortality both indirectly (e.g., low levels of social capital and limited public investment) and directly (e.g., loss of a job, low social status, lack of respect, feelings of humiliation, inferiority and a sense of shame) (Wilkinson, 1996, 1999b). However, the idea that better health should be automatically associated with higher incomes and social status has been criticized for its over-dependence upon the level of income inequality as a major determinant of mortality rates and existing stocks of social capital (Muntaner and Lynch, 1999: 67; Fine, 2001: 106). In place of any explanation about income inequality and how it is first generated, the starting point for Wilkinson (1996, 1999a) has been the receipt of income.

Not only does this preclude the influence of class relations, powers and conflicts from how greater income equality might lead to less social and political fragmentation and an increase in social capital (Baum, 1999, 2000, Lynch et al., 2000), but also serves to undermine the importance of context (Muntaner and Lynch, 1999). On this basis, illness amongst different individuals or groups is explained by the amount of social capital or income available to them and not through the specific social and historical environment in which social capital is embedded (Bourdieu, 1994; Edwards and Foley, 1997; Berkman and Kawachi 2000).

It also means that the institutions, relationships and norms which shape the quality and quantity of a society's social interactions can be used to explain why one community is healthier than another without reference to any accompanying conditions or circumstances. Although this is consistent with the idea that the incidence of ill health is heavily conditioned by both absolute and relative standards of living, it does not automatically follow that materially disadvantaged conditions constitute a satisfactory basis for understanding social relations and social capital theory. The idea that limited options and poor coping skills for dealing with stress increase vulnerability to a range of diseases is not so much in dispute as the notion that inequalities in health and income can be easily rectified by increases in social capital. Such a restricted interpretation is, however, attractive and advantageous from the perspective of the blueprint approach to development: the definition of social capital is clear and its role fixed; above all, it lends itself to standardized forms of action (Korten, 1980, 1984; Chambers, 1993: 12). Like any concept that has been made independent of its use, the idea that communities supported by a substantial stock of social capital have better economic and social performance (Putnam, 2000) is able to side-step criticism — about the interaction between health and society, and incorporate critics — through neglect of the local action environment such as the poor, remoteness, transport, communication difficulties, women and popular participation etc. However, wide-ranging criticism about Putnam's emphasis on social capital at the expense of neglect and omission of material relating to the role of the state and governance has led to a major re-appraisal of social capital and how it should be defined.

II. Social Interaction and the Importance of Context

Starting with Tarrow (1996) and Grote (1997) and moving on through the commentaries of Jackman and Miller (1998) and Rotberg (1999), the growing scope of social capital and its implications for economic and political efficiency is treated with some alarm on the grounds that evidence about the effects of social capital is so weak. In particular, Jackman and Miller (1998) are concerned that this failure to incorporate evidence about the experience of social capital from the local action environment will have serious implications for both the future of policymaking and its implementation. For example, ignorance about how different rural communities and social groups pursue their interests and grievances translates into a limited understanding of community–state relations and the relevance of joint community–state co-operation to any approach centered on socio-economic inequality, Webster and Engberg-Pedersen (2002).

Such a disassociation from the local action environment in which income inequality and social capital are both created and has its effects is also reflected in the use of social anxiety levels to explain the quality of social interaction and measures of social cohesion. On the basis that insecurity, poor early attachment and lack of confidence effect mental and emotional welfare Wilkinson (1999b) argues that the psychosocial effects of low social status, poverty and neglect are responsive to a more supportive social environment. In this respect improvements in the quality of social interaction through improved social networks will, it is suggested, reduce social anxiety levels and benefit health. However, the failure to engage with the idea that social capital is context contingent implies that social capital will reduce social anxiety levels and improve the quality of social interaction and measures of social cohesion irrespective of the conditions under which it operates. Such apparent disregard for the actual social and historical environment in which social capital may be embedded also suggests that the actual social and historical environment has little or no decisive effect upon how social capital is experienced. Under such conditions demographic factors such as geographic location, level of income, and composition in terms of sex and age are no more relevant to the relationship between social capital and health than the cultural and socio-historical characteristics of the population (Bourdieu, 1993; Falk and Kirkpatrick, 1999; Foley and Edwards, 1999).

Not only does this have profound implications for social capital's capacity to produce a more supportive environment, but also raises serious questions about the influence social capital is likely to have over the psychosocial effects of low social status, poverty and neglect as well.

In spite of an on-going re-assessment of the relationship between civil society and the state (Putnam, 1993; Grootaert, 1998b; Sen, 1999; Grootaert and Van Bastlaer, 2002), this failure to incorporate evidence about the experience of social capital from the local action environment is not encouraging (Marmot and Wilkinson, 1999; Tarlov and St. Peter, 2000). In particular, an emerging argument suggests that ignorance about varying levels of social integration and social support contributes to ineffectual political structures and social fragmentation (Woolcock, 1998; Kawachi and Berkman, 2003). However, studies of social networks and social support have been largely restricted to the interaction between governmental and nongovernmental organizations (NGOs) as part of a strategy to stimulate improved service provision by the government (Riddell and Robinson, 1995; Fox, 1996; Tendler, 1997; Blauert and Zadek, 1998; Fisher, 1998; Narayan, 1999). Much less emphasis has been placed upon the manner in which the strategy and interpretation of interaction evolves, both with respect to contemporary events and in connection with the impact that social networks and social support have upon the level of specific social inequalities in health.

For rural societies where distrust is prevalent and horizontal ties of mutual involvement are replaced by hierarchical politics, the role social networks and social support play in overcoming market failures through collective action and the common pooling of resources is inevitably restricted. Under such conditions, the idea of "an active public-spirited citizenry, egalitarian political relations and a social fabric of trust and co-operation" is simply unrealistic (Putnam, 1993: 15, 170–183). However, although such conditions mean that the legitimacy of civic institutions is fundamentally weakened and the moral community that makes social life coherent is made ineffectual (Wilkinson, 1996), it does not mean that a sense of social justice is absent altogether. It merely means that horizontal and vertical mechanisms of interaction, collaboration and networking will become more variable (Putnam, 1993; Rotberg, 2001).

In this sense, information about the institutions and sets of organizations that describe the operation of social capital from within any specific location is likely to vary from one location-specific set of institutions and organizations to another.[2] This has attracted a great deal of interest from an emerging argument that relates organizational and institutional performance to the unequal distribution of substantive freedoms and basic capabilities (Putnam, 1993; Sen, 1999; Marmot and Wilkinson, 1999; Tarlov and St. Peter, 2000). This literature demonstrates that social opportunities matter for explaining differences in the capabilities of persons to lead the kind of lives they value through public policy and the effective use of participatory capabilities by the public (Sen, 1992; Alsop et al., 2000; Cooke and Kothari, 2001). Such crucial difficulties as geography, poor economic opportunities and systematic social deprivation, discrimination against ethnic or impoverished groups, neglect of public facilities and a top-down approach towards service delivery, encourage the unequal distribution of substantive freedoms and basic capabilities (Berkman and Syme, 1979; Kaplan et al., 1987; Kawachi et al., 1996; Sen, 1999; Alsop et al., 2000). In this sense, it is important to approach the analysis of social factors from a perspective that is not automatically linked to health, but one that is in harmony with the diverse ways in which rural people live their lives (Leach et al., 1998, 1999; Bebbington, 1999a). Such a broad-based approach is vital to any understanding of the variable levels of social integration and social support that help explain what makes social interaction more or less significant in particular rural communities. It therefore follows that any assessment of social capital and social support should start with the nature of the local action environment as it is actually experienced by people and its influence upon social inequalities in health and health related behavior (Kearns and Philo, 1993: 140).

III. Rural Populations, Social Opportunities, and the Quality of Life

In spite of a long standing prejudice against the use of contextual analysis (Hauser, 1974; Piantadosi et al., 1988; Schwartz, 1994), the importance of the physical and social environment for human health and health behavior continues to exert a powerful hold (Macintyre and Ellaway, 2000).

Much of the disdain for this type of approach to analysis derives from the improper use of aggregate data to ascertain individual-level relationships; however our concern here is not with the individualistically oriented epidemiological paradigm that traditionally dominates the sociological study of inequalities in health, but with the influence of socio-economic factors upon the health of rural populations affected by poverty, discrimination or remoteness.

As the rehabilitation of contextual analysis has helped contribute to a resurgence of interest in the effects on health of residence in different types of locations and regions (Kearns and Philo, 1993; Macintyre, 1997; Kawachi and Kennedy, 2002; Kawachi and Berkman, 2003), there has been little research on the relationship between contextual analysis and health in developing countries. This may be because governments think that this diverts attention away from material structural inequalities (Harpham et al., 2002), or that there is disagreement about the definition and measurement of the various types of features of the local action environment. Alternatively, it may be because any investigation into the environmental or cultural effects of the local context upon health is simply beyond the resources of an over-stretched public sector budget. In spite of this neglect issues such as rural migration, rural proletarianization, rural industry and commerce mean that interest in the relationship between different features of the local social and historical context and health is likely to continue (Berry, 1989; Blaikie, 1989; Bebbington, 1999a).

IV. Social Interaction, Social Support, and Human Capability

To understand how the local action environment might impact upon health, it is important that we take into account those factors which affect the unequal distribution of substantive freedoms and basic capabilities. These might derive from demographic, socio-economic and physical features of the environment; in other cases they might be linked to issues surrounding available access to assets and basic services including education, health and welfare services and how these are perceived individually and collectively. Other types of influential factors include the available public and private resources, local public service facilities as well as other aspects of the wider socio-political, socio-cultural environment (Peabody et al., 1999; Macintyre and Ellaway, 2000). How these various types of factors impact upon the health of a population ultimately depends upon the specific features of the local action environment.

In this respect, their influence is likely to derive from a combination of one or more of these different types of factors. For rural societies in particular, this will be reflected in a local environment that is predicated upon variable levels of social co-operation and the promotion of self-interest and cynicism (Wilkinson, 1996).

Such unpredictable levels of social integration and social support have profound implications for local people seeking to build up and draw upon networks and links with state, market or civil society actors (Bebbington, 1999a). It is unlikely, for example, that communities affected by remoteness, conflict or discrimination will be able to organize and apply pressure to government to obtain additional resources such as health and education services. Under such conditions, it is pertinent to ask whether social networks are a valid way to bring about health improvements when citizen capacity for collective action is so limited, and access to and influence over state and markets is ineffectual; as a useful test of the credibility of social networks it should also show us how much social networks have the capacity to transform the rural health sector.

From the perspective of rural people living under the most materially disadvantaged conditions, we know that the longer people have to endure stressful economic and social hardship, the more evident the consequences of prolonged periods of insecurity, anxiety and lack of social integration become (Putnam, 1993; Tarlov and St. Peter, 2000). There is, therefore, a conjunction between place and the reproduction of cultural practices that is strongly manifests in the influence socio-economic factors have upon the emotional environment of life in isolated communities (Putnam, 1993; Bebbington, 1999b). Such conditions suggest that rural health is less to do with physical health hazards than with the social and economic environment and how supportive any social interaction actually is (Marmot et al., 1995; Wilkinson, 1996; Marmot and Wilkinson, 1999; Wilkinson, 1999a). In this context such factors as personal heterogeneities, environmental diversities, variations in social climate, differences in relational perspectives and distribution within the family, social opportunities and the expansion of human capabilities and the quality of life exert a powerful influence (Marmot, 1994; Sen, 1999; Wilkinson, 1999b).

For areas with a strongly vertical social structure based around authority relations, the potential ordinary people have for collective action is limited (Putnam, 1993). Not only does this weaken their access to and influence over state and market but also undermines the operational capacity of social networks and the level of social trust to bring about fundamental changes to the structures of politics and social relations. This means that any future assessment of any given set of institutions and organizations is likely to be determined by information about them in their capacity as interaction mechanisms. This is for several reasons. First, to the extent that the most critical aspect of institutions and organizations is in their poverty alleviation potential, then their capacity to function as a network of interconnectedness which binds people, problems, solutions and contexts for civic engagement is vital (Kawachi et al., 1996; Tarlov and St. Peter, 2000). Second, that although social capital helps us understand how actors engage with other actors in the sphere of market, state and civic society in order to gain access to assets and services, it is relatively intangible and poorly understood (Tendler, 1997; Leach et al., 1998). Third, the processes through which social capital inheres in the interaction mechanisms mean that an understanding of informal mechanisms and relationships within and between institutions and organizations is critical.

V. Social Networks, Social Trust, and the Quality of Relationships

To explain the organizational and institutional issues this involves, the literature looks at how information is pooled, common knowledge created and decision making shared. Starting from the premise that the state, organizations and other institutions share a common commitment to the promotion of horizontal collective action (Wilkinson, 1996; Tarlov and St. Peter, 2000), it is argued that flexibility and openness affect the clarity of interaction (Scoones and Thompson, 1994; Alsop et al., 2000). The literature outlines a number of factors that affect the capacity of social networks to provide ordinary people with the means to defend mutual interests identify priorities and challenge authority:

1. The lack of clarity about the relationship between member organizations inside a social network because interaction is predicated upon a regular exchange of information shared by all the various member organizations (Farrington and Bebbington, 1993; Scoones and Thompson, 1993; Alsop et al., 2000).

2. The physical, social and economic constraints that undermine access to information and the practical difficulties associated with the dissemination of that information (Sen, 1992; Putnam, 1993; Marmot and Wilkinson, 1999; Alsop et al., 2000; Tarlov and St. Peter, 2000).

3. The effect of geography, discrimination against ethnic or impoverished groups, remoteness, location, transport and communication upon the type and quality of information available to member organizations inside a social network (Biggs, 1989; Sen, 1992; Biggs and Smith, 1998; Sen, 1999; Alsop et al., 2000).

In spite of its universal appeal, it is arguable that the single greatest obstacle derives from the political consequences that appear when social networks seek to generate widespread trust, especially if the socio-economic environment is particularly fragmented (Clayton, 1995; Oakley, 1995; Alsop et al., 2000). If greater interaction between the service provider and rural people is to take place, so that social groups or communities that were previously excluded from control over resources have the opportunity to take part in decision making, political action and policy development, a number of changes need to happen. Such a thesis is predicated upon the operation of a local action environment in which the state, organizations and other institutions share a common commitment to the promotion of horizontal collective action. However, the failure to address the problems that prevent any change in the relationship between civil society and the state suggest that the emergence of an alternative conceptualization is less important than the actual influence ordinary people are able to exercise (Putnam, 1993; Tarlov and St. Peter, 2000). Since the function of any network involves pooling information, creating common knowledge and sharing decision making, it is important that the internal and external differences that arise out of any loose configuration of actors with a shared interest and a willingness to act on that interest are established. More often than not, the boundaries that describe the interaction amongst the various participants are unclear, on the grounds that interaction is based around flexibility and openness.[3]

In other words, the actions of one organization and how it influences or is reliant on or linked to the activities of another organization, means that the context in which the interaction takes place is as important as the consequences it has, and the changes that it gives rise to. Because the effectiveness of any social network is also predicated upon a regular exchange of information, its overriding purpose must be one that is shared by all the various member organizations (Biggs, 1989). However, the physical, social and economic constraints that are experienced by organizations associated with rural issues mean that it is impossible to make any normal assumptions about social networks in relation to access and the exchange of information.

VI. Social Networks, Social Organizations, and the Transmission of Information

The problems of location and the positioning of different actors in relation to accessing and using information (Marglin and Marglin, 1990), mean that it is possible that there are problems of creating and ensuring that information is common knowledge as well (Alsop et al., 2000). In these circumstances the type of information available to member organizations inside a social network, is subject to the detrimental influence of remoteness, location, transport and communication. Under such conditions, social trust within the network is not simply governed by the information each member organization has access to, but with the practical difficulties associated with the dissemination of that information as well. This in turn depends on the quality of information available, on the activities in which the social network engages, to whom it is being provided, and the conditions favorable to the development of the social network concerned. Not only are these factors likely to obstruct any spontaneous expansion in the size of a social network, but are also likely to affect any initiative designed to improve the capacity of a social network as well (Bebbington et al., 1992). Under such conditions, many social networks fail because organizations are unable to establish any meaningful relationship beyond that of the structure of their own organization.

To what extent, then, are community organizations capable of providing ordinary people with the capacity to defend mutual interests, identify priorities and challenge authority? Can the emerging ideas about social capital provide a vehicle for building public accountability in the development and implementation of health policies?

If the actual conditions under which people live their lives explain how a given set of institutions and organizations affect civic engagement and trust, how can increased social capital levels be made to impact more effectively upon social anxiety levels and health? Though it is well established that social capital levels have a powerful influence on the quality of people's social relations, it is only possible to assess the actual contribution social interaction makes to the realization of greater equality (and better health), if we examine what we mean by social integration and social support.

To test the impact of social networks upon the level of social inequalities in health, it therefore makes sense to focus on the accumulation of material relating to the arrangements and changes that take place amongst the various group relationships involved. In this context research should look at how organizations work together and under what conditions, the power balance and the contribution each organization makes to the relationship, the effect of the network on both clients and service providers; changes in behavior and attitudes, including health service practices and organizational responses.

Notes

1. Social capital is used here after the definition put forward by Putnam (1993: 664–665): "By social capital I mean features of social life — networks, norms and trust — that enable participants to act together more effectively to pursue shared objectives...To the extent that the norms, networks and trust link substantial sectors of the community and span underlying social cleavages — to the extent that the social capital is of a bridging sort — then the enhanced co-operation is likely to serve broader interests and to be widely welcomed."
2. Institutions are defined as the humanly devised constraints that structure human interaction. They are composed of formal rules, informal constraints and the enforcement characteristics of both. Organizations are defined as a group of individuals bound by a common purpose to achieve objectives. They include political bodies, economic bodies, social bodies and educational bodies (North, 1995: 23).
3. The term interaction is used widely throughout and refers to situations where the actions of one organization, person or group are influenced by, dependent on or oriented towards the actions of another (adapted from Farrington and Bebbington, 1993: 127; Alsop et al., 2000).

References

Alsop, R., Gilbert, E., Farrington, J., and Khandelwal, R., *Coalitions of Interest*. Sage Publications, Overseas Development Institute and New Delhi and London, London, 2000.

Baum, F., Public health and civil society: understanding and valuing the connection, *Aust. N.Z J. Pub. Health*, 21 (7), 673–675, 1999.

Baum, F., Social capital, economic capital and power: further issues for a public health agenda, *J. Epidemiol. Commun. Health*, 53 (4), 195–196, 2000.

Bebbington, A., Capitals and capabilities: a framework for analyzing peasant viability, rural livelihoods and poverty, *World Dev.*, 27 (12), 2021–2044, 1999a.

Bebbington, A., Turning social capital into financial capital: women's village banking in Ayacucho and Norte Potosi. Paper prepared for Andean Studies Group Seminar. Stanford University, CA, May 9, 1999b.

Bebbington, A., Carrasco, H., Peralvo, L., Ramon, G., Torres, V.H., and Trujillo, J., *Los Actores de una decada ganada: tribus, comunidades y campesinos en la modernidad*, Abya Yala, Quito, 1992.

Berkman, L. and Breslow, L., *Health and Ways of Living: The Alameda County Study*. Oxford University Press, New York, 1984.

Berkman, L. and Kawachi, I., *Social Epidemiology*. Oxford University Press, Oxford, 2000.

Berkman, L. and Syme, S., Social networks, host resistance and mortality: a nine year follow-up study of Alameda county residents, *Am. J. Epidemiol.*, 109, 186–203, 1979.

Berry, S., Social institutions and access to resources, *Africa*, 59 (1), 41–55, 1989.

Biggs, S., Resource-poor farmer participation in research: a synthesis of experience from Nine National Agricultural Research Systems, *OFCOR. Project Study* 3. The Hague: ISNAR, 1989.

Biggs, S. and Smith, G., Beyond methodologies: coalition-building for participatory technology development, *World Dev.*, 26 (2), 239–248, 1998.

Blaikie, P., Environment and access to resources in Africa, *Africa*, 59 (1), 18–40, 1989.

Blauert, J. and Zadek, S., *Mediating Sustainability: Growing Policy from the Grassroots*. Kumarian Press, 1998, Kumarian Press Inc, 14 Oakwood Avenue, West Hartford, Connecticut 06119-2127 USA.

Bourdieu, P., Concluding remarks: for a sociogenetic understanding of intellectual works, in *Bourdieu: Critical Perspectives*, Calhoun, C., LiPuma, E., and Postone, M., Eds., Polity Press, Cambridge, 1993, pp. 263–275.

Bourdieu, P., *Towards a Reflexive Sociology*, Polity Press, Cambridge, 1994.

Chambers, R., *Challenging the Professions: Frontiers for Rural Development*, Intermediate Technology, Southampton, 1993.

Clayton, A., *Governance, Democracy and Conditionality*, INTRAC, Oxford, 1995.

Coleman, J., *Foundations of Social Theory*, Harvard University Press, Cambridge, 1990.

Cooke, B. and Kothari, U., *Participation: The New Tyranny*, Zed Books, London, 2001.

Edwards, B. and Foley, M., Social capital and the political economy of our discontent, *Am. Behav. Sci.*, 40 (5), 669–678, 1997.

Falk, I. and Kirkpatrick, S., What is social capital? A study of rural communities Sociologia Ruratis, 40(1) pp. 87–110.

Farrington, J. and Bebbington, A., *Reluctant Partners: NGOs, the State and Sustainable Development*, Routledge, London, 1993.

Fine, B., *Social Capital versus Social Theory: Political Capital and Social Science at the Turn of the Millenium*, Routledge, London, 2001.

Fisher, J., *Non-governments: NGOs and the Political Development of the Third World*, Kumarian Press, West Hartford, CT, 1998.

Foley, M. and Edwards, B., Is it time to disinvest in social capital?, *J. Pub. Policy*, 19 (2), 141–173, 1999.

Fox, J., How does civil society thicken? The political construction of social capital in rural Mexico, *World Dev.*, 24 (6), 1089–1103, 1996.

Grootaert, C., Social capital: the missing link? in *Expanding the Measure of Wealth: Indicators of Environmentally Sustainable Development*, World Bank, Washington, DC, 1997, pp. 77–93.

Grootaert, C., Local institutions and service delivery in Indonesia, Local Level Institutions Study, Social Development Department, Environmentally and Socially Sustainable Development Network, World Bank (mimeo), Washington, DC, 1998a.

Grootaert, C., Social capital, household welfare and poverty in Indonesia, Local Level Institutions Study, Social Development Department, Environmentally and Socially Sustainable Development Network, World Bank (mimeo), Washington, DC, 1998b.

Grootaert, C., Gi-taik, O. and Swamy, A., *Social Capital in Burkina Faso*, Local Levels Institutions Study, Mimeo, World Bank, Washington, DC, 1999.

Grootaert, C. and Narayan, D., *Local Institutions, Poverty and Household Welfare in Bolivia*, Local Level Institutions Study, Mimeo, World Bank, Washington, DC, 1999.

Grootaert, C. and Van Bastelaer, T., *The Role of Social Capital in Development: An Empirical Assessment*, Cambridge University Press, Cambridge, 2002.

Grote, J., Interorganizational networks and social capital in the South of the South. *European Institute Working Papers* 97/38, 1997.

Harpham, T., Grant, E., and Thomas, E., Measuring social capital within health surveys: key issues, *Health Policy Plan.*, 17 (1), 106–111, 2002.

Hauser, R., Contextual analysis revisted, *Sociolog. Methods Res.*, 2, 365–375, 1974.

House, J.S. and Kahn, R., Measures and concepts of social support, in *Social Support and Health*, Cohen, S. and Syme, S.L., Eds., Academic Press, Orlando, 1985, pp. 79–108.

Jackman, R. and Miller, R., Social capital and politics. *Ann. Rev. Polit. Sci.*, 1, 47–73, 1998.

Kaplan, G.A., Haan, M.N., Syme, S.L., Minkler, M., and Winkleby, M., Socioeconomic status and health, in *Closing the Gap: The Burden of Unnecessary Illness*, Amler, R.W. and Dull, H.B., Eds., Oxford University Press, New York, 1987, pp. 125–129.

Kawachi, I. and Berkman, L., *Neighbourhoods and Health*, Oxford University Press, Oxford, 2003.

Kawachi, I. and Kennedy, B., *The Health of Nations: Why Inequality is harmful to your Health?*, The New Press, New York, 2002.

Kawachi, I., Colditz, G.A., Ascherio, A., Rimm, E.B., Giovannucci, E., Stampfer, M.J., and Willett, W.C., A prospective study of social networks in relation to total mortality and cardiovascular disease in men in the USA, *J. Epidemiol. Commun. Health*, 50, 245–251, 1996.

Kawachi, I., Kennedy, B.P., Gupta, V., and Prothrow-Smith, D., Social capital, income inequality and mortality, *Am. J. Pub. Health*, 87, 1491–1498, 1997a.

Kawachi, I., Kennedy, B.P., and Glass, R., Social capital and self-related health: a contextual analysis, *Am. J. Pub. Health*, 89, 1187–1193, 1999a.

Kawachi, I., Kennedy, B., and Wilkinson, R., *The Society and Population Health Reader: Income Inequality and Health*, The New Press, New York, 1999b.

Kearns, G. and Philo, C., Eds., *Selling Places: The City as Cultural Capital*, Pergamon Press, Oxford, 1993.

Korten, D., Community organization and rural development: a learning process approach, *Pub. Adm. Rev.*, 40 (5), 480–511, 1980.

Korten, D.C., People-centered development: towards a framework, in *People Centered Development*, Korten, D.C. and Klauss, R., Eds., Kumarian Press, West Hartford, Connecticut, 1984, pp. 299–309.

Leach, M., Mearns, R., and Scoones, I., Challenges to community based sustainable development: dynamics, entitlements, institutions, *IDS Bulletin*, 28 (4), 4–14, 1998.

Leach, M., Mearns, R., and Scoones, I., Environmental entitlement: dynamics and institutions in community-based natural resource management, *World Dev.*, 27 (2), 225–247, 1999.

Leeder, S. and Dominello, A., Social capital and its relevance to health and family policy, *Aust. N.Z J. Pub. Health*, 23 (4), 424–29, 1999.

Lynch, J., Due, P., Mutaner, C., and Smith, G.D., Social capital: is it good investment strategy for public health?, *J. Epidemiol. Commun. Health*, 54 (6), 404–408, 2000.

Macintyre, S., The Black Report and beyond: what are the issues?, *Soc. Sci. Med.*, 44, 723–746, 1997.

Macintyre, S. and Ellaway, A., Ecological approaches: rediscovering the role of the physical and social environment in social epidemiology, in *Social Epidemiology*, Berkman, L. and Kawachi, I., Eds., Oxford University Press 198 Madison Avenue, New York 10016 2000, pp. 332–348.

Marglin, F. and Marglin, S., *Dominating Knowledge: Development, Culture and Resistance*, Clarendon Press, Oxford, 1990.

Marmot, M. and Wilkinson, R.G., *Social Determinants of Health*, Oxford University Press, Oxford, 1999.

Marmot, M.G., Social Differentials in health within and between populations, *Daedealus*, 123, 197–216, 1994.

Muntaner, C. and Lynch, J., Income inequality, social cohesion and class relations: a critique of Wilkinson's Neo-Durkheimian Research Programme, *Int. J. Health Serv.*, 29 (1), 59–81, 1999.

Narayan, D., *Bonds and Bridges: Social Capital and Poverty*, World Bank, Washington, DC, 1999.

Narayan, D. and Pritchett, L., Cents and sociability: household income and social capital, in *Rural Tanzania, Environment Department and Policy Research Department*, World Bank, Washington, DC, 1997.

North, D., The New Institutional Economics and Third World development, in *The New Institutional Economics and Third World Development*, Harris, J., Hunter, J., and Lewis, C.M., Eds., Routledge, London, 1995, pp. 17–26.

Oakley, P., *People's Participation in Development Projects.* Occasional Papers Series No. 7, INTRAC, 1995.

Peabody, J., Omar, R., Gertler, P.J., Mann, J., Farley, D.O., Luck, J., Robalino, D., and Carter, G., *Policy and Health: Implications for Development in Asia*, Cambridge University Press, Cambridge, 1999.

Piantadosi, S., Byar, D., and Green, S., The ecological fallacy, *Am. J. Epidemiol.*, 127, 893–904, 1988.

Putnam, R.D., *Making Democracy Work: Civic Traditions in Modern Italy*, Princeton University Press, Princeton, NJ, 1993.

Putnam, R.D., *Bowling Alone: The Collapse and Revival of American Community*, Simon and Schuster, New York, 2000.

Riddell, R.C. and Robinson, M., *Developing Country NGOs and Donor Governments*, Overseas Development Institute, London, 1995.

Rotberg, R., Social capital and political culture in Africa, America, Australasia and Europe, *J. Interdiscip. Hist.*, 29 (3), 339–356, 1999.

Rotberg, R., *Patterns of Social Capital: Stability and Change in Historical Perspective*, Cambridge University Press, The Edinburgh Building, Cambridge, UK, 2001.

Sampson, R., Morenoff, J., and Earls, F., Beyond social capital: spatial dynamics of collective efficacy for children, *Am. Sociolog. Rev.*, 64 (5), 633–660, 1999.

Schwartz, S., The fallacy of the ecological fallacy: the potential misuse of a concept and the consequences, *Am. J. Pub. Health*, 84, 819–824, 1994.

Scoones, I. and Thompsen, J., *Beyond Farmer First: Rural People's Knowledge, Agricultural Research and Extension Practice: Towards a Theoretical Framework.* Sustainable Agriculture Programme Research Series 1, International Institute for Environment and Development, London, 1994.

Sen, A., *Inequality Re-examined*, Oxford University Press, Oxford, 1992.

Sen, A., *Development as Freedom*, Oxford University Press, Oxford, 1999.

Tarlov, A. and St. Peter, R., *The Society and Population Reader: State and Community Perspective*, The New Press, New York, 2000.

Tarrow, S., Making social science work across time and space: a critical reflection on Robert Putnam's *Making Democracy Work, Am. Polit. Sci. Rev.*, 90 (2), 773–783, 1996.

Tendler, J., *Good Governance in the Tropics*, Johns Hopkins University Press, Baltimore, 1997.

Veenstra, G., Social capital, SES and health: an individual-level analysis, *Soc. Sci. Med.*, 50 (5), 619–629, 2000.

Webster, N. and Engberg-Pedersen, L., *In the Name of the Poor: Contesting Political Space*, Zed Books, London, 2002.

Wilkinson, R.G., *Unhealthy Societies: The Afflictions of Inequality*, Routledge, London, 1996.

Wilkinson, R.G., Income inequality, social cohesion and health: clarifying the theory: a reply to Muntaner and Lynch, *Int. J. Health Serv.*, 29 (3), 525–543, 1999a.

Wilkinson, R.G., Health, hierarchy and social anxiety. in Adler, N.E., Marmot, M., McEwen, B.S., and Stewart, J., Eds., *Ann. NY. Acad. Sci. 896*, (1), 48–63, 1999b.

Woolcock, M., *Managing Risk, Shocks and Opportunity in Developing Economies: The Role of Social Capital*, World Bank, Washington, DC, 1998.

Chapter 20

New Citizenships: Gender and Governance in Development[1]

Joanna S. Wheeler

CONTENTS

I. Introduction

In a context of a growing crisis of legitimacy of political and economic institutions, and increasing distance between these institutions and the people
whose lives are affected by them, there are also some hopeful signs. Participatory democratic reforms in a variety of contexts, from health councils and
participatory budgeting in Brazil, to the *panchayati raj* system in India,
to South Africa's progressive constitution encoding a broad spectrum of
rights, there are significant attempts being made to make governments
more responsive to marginalized groups. And yet, other research points
to serious questions around representation, voice, inclusiveness, and
accountability even in light of attempts at democratic reform and participatory approaches within development (Cornwall and Coelho, 2004). Citizenship, and particularly notions of active citizenship which is claimed through
struggles for rights, is central to renewed focus on good governance. This is
because active citizenship pressures the state and other institutional actors
to be more responsive to citizens, and also requires that citizens fulfill
certain responsibilities and obligations to engage with political processes.
The underlying assumption is that through this process, marginal groups
will achieve greater voice and inclusion. Yet, even as "good governance"
and participatory reforms are hailed as the newest panacea for global injustice, promoted by the World Bank and range of bilateral donors, a gendered
approach to these mechanisms raises some serious questions about how
effective participatory mechanisms are at representing the voices of marginalized groups, and even how those voices are constituted. A gendered
approach to governance in development widens the scope for what is
understood to be political — to privilege the daily experiences of marginalized groups, and to understand how power dynamics function at the level
of these experiences and their articulation with wider trends such as participatory democratic reforms, neoliberal reforms, globalized flows of
capital, labor, information, ideas, arms, etc.

Engendering development or using a gender lens to inform development is part of a wider trend that recognizes the importance of relationships
among men, women, and other categories of identity as essential for development. In the late 1970s, women's movements and feminist scholars were
able to put women explicitly onto the development agenda. Women in
development (WID) meant looking specifically at how women and women's
interests in particular were excluded from much of development —
focusing on issues like maternal mortality, the poverty rates of female-
headed households, and other statistical indicators (Women's Studies
Quarterly, 2003). As a result of WID, many development actors adopted
programs to mainstream gender by considering the implications for
women in all their work. However, partly in response to criticisms about

the shortfalls of focusing solely on women as a group, this agenda began to evolve into gender and development (GAD), which shifts attention to the dynamics of gender relations *between* men, women, girls, and boys as a way of understanding not only how women are excluded, but also how social exclusion functions in relation to other categories of identity such as sexuality, race, ethnicity, and religion (Kabeer, 1994). So while engendering development has been gaining momentum through the efforts of women's movements, international conventions such as the Convention for the Elimination of All Forms of Discrimination Against Women (CEDAW) and the Beijing Platform for Action adopted after the UN convention on GAD, more recent attempts try to draw together the insights from GAD in relation to the governance agenda.

What are the contributions that a gendered approach can bring to governance in development? First, a gendered approach to citizenship contributes to understanding how formal citizenship can be made substantive. Gender helps to explain why formal political reforms have not been sufficient to address social injustice and lead to deeper democracy. Gender calls for looking beyond the usual suspects of social movements and political parties to family and interpersonal dynamics and how these map onto political community at a variety of levels. A gendered approach to governance and citizenship shifts the focus from looking solely at formal political institutions or organized civil society, to a focus on how the political relates to daily experiences. It is in focusing on these experiences that the exclusions and marginalizations that development is trying to address are most acutely felt, and it is at the level of daily experiences that formal political reforms are most distant (see Clark et al., 2005). A gendered approach to governance in development is not about implementing quotas for women's participation in political or civil society institutions (although these measures may be very useful).

Pro-women political reforms, including quotas for women's participation in political institutions, have been spreading (BRIDGE, 1998; Mukhopadhyay, 2003). However, a gendered analysis of governance and citizenship highlights the divide between formal and substantive citizenship that remains in many contexts despite political reforms aimed at improving equity (Yuval-Davis, 2000). Substantive citizenship is more than political freedom and the right to vote — although these are important. A feminist approach to citizenship moves beyond formal political rights to include entitlements, rights, and agency as central to substantive citizenship (Fraser, 1989; Sen, 2003). Not only does a feminist approach to citizenship expand how citizenship is defined, but it also expands the dimensions of citizenship beyond the public political sphere to include the economic sphere, cultural norms, and the personal level of family, home, relationships, and community. Substantive citizenship must operate in all these realms to be complete (Sen, 2003).

Much analysis of citizenship and governance focuses on the public political realm and on the rights that correspond to that realm. But, while inclusive citizenship has the potential to address gender inequities, exclusionary citizenship can deepen the structural causes of exclusions (Castles and Davidson, 2000). And while attempts at reform may address one dimension of citizenship in reference to a particular level, such reforms will be ultimately undermined by their inability to promote substantive and inclusive citizenship across the multiple dimensions of citizenship and the levels of its experience. This chapter will examine citizenship at the level of entitlements and agency in terms of personal and community relationships in order to understand why formal democratic reforms have not translated into substantive citizenship. In the case of Brazil, there have been a series of democratic of reforms since 1988, and many of the participatory mechanisms for policy-making have been the focus of research (Houtzager et al., 2003).

Hannah Arendt argues that "the fundamental deprivation of human rights [and citizenship] is manifested first and above all *in the deprivation of a place in the world* [a political space] which makes opinions significant, and actions effective (Arendt in Jelin, 1998: 405) (emphasis added). A confluence of different factors in Rio de Janeiro has worked to dislodge the poor from their "place in the world" and increase their distance from the political and economic mechanisms of power. The next section will explore the case of citizenship for marginalized men and women in Rio de Janeiro, Brazil, to explore the implications of a gendered approach to citizenship for governance in development.

II. A Story of Exclusionary Citizenship

Sebastiana "Tiana" Rosaria Jesus Souza, 46, lives in a crumbling and violent housing project in the *Zona Norte* (North Zone) of the Rio de Janeiro that was built in the 1970s to house the dislocated residents of Catacumba — a *favela* (squatter settlement) demolished by Brazil's military dictatorship. She and her second husband (both Afro-brazilians) share their two-bedroom apartment with Tiana's daughter, son, and grand-daughter. She financially supports the household, while taking the responsibility for raising her children and grandchildren, and finding work for her daughter and herself.

In more than 10 years since Tiana migrated to Rio de Janeiro from Brazil's interior, she has worked as a receptionist, a maid, a cook, a hair dresser, a baby sitter, and most recently as a researcher on urban poverty. Since she arrived in Rio de Janeiro, she has managed to establish a moderately successful catering business for wealthy and middle-class clients through her contacts working as a maid.

Tiana attended school intermittently until she was 21, and only completed the first year of high school. She has taken government-sponsored courses in English, information technology, and research training — all to get access to better jobs. Nonetheless, she has been unable to find formal employment in Rio de Janeiro.

While Tiana moves across social and racial boundaries regularly, she does not feel that she is a citizen of Rio de Janeiro. She says that the "lack of dignity" and "the way people treat you — as if you weren't even human," on a daily basis, even more than the deteriorating living conditions in the housing project and her lack of access to better jobs, are the signs that she does not enjoy substantive citizenship.

Formal citizenship has little meaning in terms of Tiana's life. Despite her efforts to engage with the political system, substantive citizenship remains hypothetical. For her, the experiences of her daily life undermine the meaning of formal citizenship. This raises some important questions for governance and development. Why have progressive democratic reforms been unable to change the nature of the relationship between Tiana and that state and economic institutions which affect her life? Brazil's relatively recent democracy, implemented in terms of government institutions, a democratic constitution, and free and fair elections has not translated into substantive, meaningful citizenship for Tiana. The explanation for this alienation lies in the contextualization of her citizenship in her daily life.

Tiana's experiences are emblematic of how formal citizenship can fall short of substantive citizenship. Using a gender lens to examine her story and others from Rio de Janeiro, a narrative emerges which challenges dominant approaches to governance in development. In the context of dramatic changes in formal citizenship and the erosion of effective local governance in poor communities across Rio de Janeiro, the following sections will explore in more depth the privatization of citizenship in Rio de Janeiro, the qualified political and economic participation of the poor, and finally the centrality of dignity (in terms of access to the city's resources) to substantive citizenship.

III. Privatization of Citizenship

Despite a formal transition to democracy in Brazil in 1988, complete with a broad-reaching constitution encoding numerous rights, individual rights-based citizenship as a category for understanding democratic practice has not gained much purchase in Rio de Janeiro's *favelas*. In forty interviews with low-income men and women about citizenship, no participant referred to rights or membership in a Brazilian nation when they defined citizenship. This is an especially interesting result given that in the 1980s Brazil passed through a very public process of debating and ratifying a new constitution encoding extensive individual rights and privileges to its newly democratic citizens. Individual rights and formal democratic practices, such as signing petitions, joining political parties, and participating in commissions, have been heavily promoted by the state and also by organized social and political movements. Further, there is a very high level of awareness about certain rights and entitlements, such as labor protections.

Yet, these features of democracy were almost totally absent from the definitions participants gave for citizenship. Partly because Brazil's history of populist regimes enforcing a national identity, Brazilianness is a strong category of identity (Machado, 1980; Marx, 1998; Davis, 1999) — and yet, in terms of poor men and women it did not enter into their elaborations of citizenship. Instead, they consistently identified their participation in their own communities — not specific rights or Brazilian national identity — as a core feature of citizenship. In terms of the major changes in political regime in the past 20 years, very few could identify any major difference in their lives between dictatorship and democracy. Instead, poor women consistently identified lack of access to urban services, jobs, adequate housing, education, and health care as evidence that they did not in fact live in a democracy — or at least that formal democracy had no meaning for them. They characterized their participation in family, community, and city life as the most meaningful aspect of their political participation. So democracy and democratic impulses are important to poor women and men in Rio de Janeiro's *favelas*, yet they have redefined democratic practice in terms of their own values and beliefs, they have moved away from individual rights-based democratic practices towards a democracy that affects their own families and community. Citizenship has been articulated through family structures in the *favela* — through specific forms of family-based community participation.

Similarly, market logic of efficiency, competitiveness, and individuality has interacted in unexpected ways with notions of citizenship in *favelas*. Market logic in the incarnation of Cardoso's neoliberal reforms has been widely discussed in public discourse and heavily promoted by the state — including Rio de Janeiro's city government in the form of numerous micro credit and funding programs. Residents in Rio de Janeiro's *favelas* face considerable economic exclusion that is exacerbated by extremely poor schools, drug-related violence, and poor infrastructure (Alvito and Zaluar, 1998). Almost every participant considered participation in the market through employment essential. Yet, participants consistently placed their families and community at the center of any market logic.[2] By this I mean that they used their family structures to integrate into the market, and also frequently privileged family and community over the market. In essence, the market and certain aspects of market-driven logic have become prevalent in *favelas*, but *favela* residents have adapted market practices to their own family and community structures.

In spite of the pressure to participate in the formal economy and new democratic structures of the Brazilian state, residents in low-income communities continue to contribute unremunerated labor into projects outside formal channels of political participation — by negotiating directly with those in control of housing projects and *favelas*: residents' associations controlled by drug trafficking mafias. One man living in a housing project ringed by *favelas* with his wife and two small children has committed considerable time and energy to community improvements. Although he has a job at the local university as a security guard, he has negotiated extended leave to carry out community development projects of his own design. Because the drug traffickers have taken control of the community where he lives (i.e., the Quitungo and Guaporé housing projects and surrounding *favelas*) and the local political structure, he has developed a form of community activism that carefully negotiates between the traffickers, other established local activists and his own family's well-being. He has claimed a piece of land in one of the *favelas* to construct a centre to address the problems he recognizes in his community: lack of education, access to the job market and poor infrastructure. Over the past 6 years, friends and family members have contributed labor and money to start construction on the centre — every day he walks through the community to see who has time to help for a few hours. Every day children collect empty plastic bottles for the community center's future recycling program. Hundreds of bottles are stacked in one corner of the construction site — after 6 years, the first floor has yet to be completed. When there is no money or time, the project stops until circumstances improve. He explains that "the community center is being built one bag of cement at a time — but it will be built."

The future center will perform a wealth of functions: it would house a community association board, a recycling center, language and information technology training courses, and a children's choir. He plans to name the center after his daughter because building it has "taken the food out of her mouth, but it will make her life better." Participants from this community identified this community work as their most important form of political participation.[3] Most had little or no interest in citywide or state-wide politics. They consistently identified this community work as important to their own families — and they did not believe that the city government could do much to address the problems in their community. At the community level, democratic impulses[4] in *favelas* are transformed into creative projects to improve specific aspects of the community — the major motivation for these projects according to the participants in the study was to build a better life for their children or their family — citizenship is articulated at the level of the private. Political participation in low-income communities focusing on addressing the serious problems facing residents on a quotidian level: violence, lack of infrastructure, poverty, and inadequate housing and education. National political discourse on democracy and individual rights is very distant by comparison.

IV. Qualified Participation

Various scholars have been critical of the lack of internal democracy in pro-poor social movements (Neuhouser, 1995; Houtzager, 2000). Women participate more frequently than men in social movements; yet hold considerably fewer leadership positions (Neuhouser, 1995). This may have more to do with the way that men and women in *favelas* and other low-income communities understand democracy than inherit patriarchy. In every interview I conducted with men and women in *favelas*, participants believed that their participation in their community and their city was more important than formal political participation such as voting. That is, democracy based on individuality and rights does not fit comfortably with collaborative family and community structures in *favelas*. The people I interviewed, including self-identified community activists, saw democratic practice as participation in a just society rather than open and fair elections and individual rights (Paoli and Telles, 1998).

For the poor, the evidence that society is not just is found in their daily confrontations with the evidence of that injustice — police raids, overcrowded buses, inadequate schools, and crumbling and overcrowded health clinics. In *favelas*, voting and formal political participation in Brazil's institutional democracy was seen as unimportant. Democracy has been reclaimed from this general public meaning and redefined to mean participation and contribution to family, community, and city life. In the words of one veteran community activist in response to a question about his political participation: "I don't feel diminished because I live in a *favela* — each of us has tried to improve our own lives. All the intellectuals who came here, poor things — they never really understood anything because the changes you can make depend on the opportunities you take. [Governments] change and time passes and goes by, but who knows — tomorrow I might manage to do something else [to help the community]."

Several factors have contributed to the shift away from formal political and economic participation towards family and community specific participation. Because the poor have not reaped the rewards of macro-economic reforms and do not have confidence in the effectiveness of formal democratic participation, political participation has moved to new channels. Drug-related violence has further eroded the link between poor communities and formal democratic mechanisms (Holston and Appadurai, 1999).

Over 90% of the participants interviewed reported to have no trust in the national government. This distrust of the formal political structure goes deeper than any particular administration. One poor black woman, who lives in a city housing project, said that "Brazil would be better off with a dictatorship. At least then things were working." Another poor elderly woman from the suburbs identified "more buses" as the major difference in her life between dictatorship and democracy. In a plebiscite held in 1993 mandated by the Constitution established in 1988 at the end of the dictatorship, Brazilians voted to choose a form of government. Only 66% voted to maintain democracy (either as presidential or parliamentary) while 11 percent voted for a monarchy and an additional 33% voted for "other form of government."[5] Several participants in my study voted against democracy for Brazil. One woman explained that she voted for the monarchy because she did not believe that the form of government would make any difference in her life and "a king or queen sounds more interesting than a president." The refusal of several participants to take such a vote seriously, demonstrated by their choice of the highly improbable monarchy, is a symptom of deep mistrust and disinterest in macro-level politics.

Partly because the links between formal political and economic participation as a market citizen have been severed, the participants in this study have qualified their political and economic participation with family and community interests (see Latapi and Roberts, 1991). This qualified participation is an important piece in the narrative of citizenship. The poor have incorporated democracy and market logic into a qualified participation in the city.

A. Recasting Citizenship through the Family

For example, the family has become the point of articulation between the market and individuals. The participants in this study on the whole did not approach the market as an individual, but rather as a member of a family. Getting a job, credit, access to education and health care — all were mediated by the family. The involvement of family in the market means that certain aspects of market logic are promoted while others are rejected. One woman lives with her husband and son in a house built on the family's property with over forty members of her extended family. The land was inherited from her great grandfather who emigrated from Portugal. Although her salary as a housekeeper in the city is essential income for the family, she commutes nearly five hours a day to the city center in order to continue to live with her family. Several employers have offered her accommodation in the city during the week so that she can avoid this lengthy and costly commute but she refuses to move away from her family. She uses her salary to pay for daily household expenses while her husband's salary goes towards bills. When she has extra money, she transfers her son from state funded to private school. She could save a considerable amount by living in Rio and avoiding transportation costs, but she refuses to do this. When she became seriously ill, her mother and sister (also housekeepers in the city center) filled in at her jobs so that she would not lose them. Her other sister stays at home and provides child care for the extended family's children and also does the washing and cleaning. Although she could make more money if she were to get a job outside the home, she and her sisters believe it is more important for her to provide child care and laundry services for the family.

Together these women participate in the market, they use their family ties to secure jobs, health care, childcare, and education for their children. While they participate in the market, they also reject certain market demands. The family works together to responds to crisis and uncertainty — fulfilling market demand for cheap day labor in the city, but using their connections in the city to guarantee other benefits. Yet this integration has affected family structure — increasing numbers of women travel long distances for work, while men are more likely to find work nearer to the home (UNDP, 2000). Because women are still responsible for household tasks, this puts an increasing strain on women to fulfill their work obligations. As a result, men are forced to take a larger role in the home. Women's entry into the labor market has also increased their control over family finances — and women often opt to keep their children in school for longer than would have been possible if they were not working. In *favelas*, the family continues to be the space where integration into the market is negotiated.

B. Dignity

When asked to define citizenship, 74% of the participants in this study identified dignity as citizenship's most important characteristic. Frequently, the lack of dignity was equated with a lack of citizenship. One woman said, "Dignity is everything for a citizen — and we have no dignity. We are treated like cattle in the clinics, on the buses, and in the shops. Only in rich neighborhoods are people treated with dignity." By dignity, the participants in this study most frequently referred to their quotidian experiences in the city — especially in terms of access to public services including health care, education, urban services and public housing. The participants in this study made clear that meaningful citizenship cannot exist without dignity. For the participants in this study, it was not their poverty or lack of rights that meant they had no dignity. Rather, it was the aggregation of everyday interactions and experiences, conflicts and triumphs that meant the difference between dignity and exclusion.

Dignity for the poor, in terms of daily life, is dignified access to public services — the sum of everyday interactions with the health care and education systems, urban services and housing. While access to these public services may be guaranteed by Brazil's constitution as a right, it is the nature of that access that is most important to the poor. The erosion of health, education, housing, and urban services over the past 30 yr has compromised the dignity of the poor in everyday life. The participants in this study identified dignified access to these services as most important characteristics of citizenship and also the biggest lack in terms of their citizenship. For Rio de Janeiro's poor, daily interactions with public services are characterized by corruption, violence, and lack.[6]

C. Public Services in Rio de Janeiro: The Case of Public Health Care

The end of the dictatorship coincided with a marked disintegration of many public services because the new democratic government did not have the funds to make up for 15 yr of under-investment and neglect. The neoliberal reforms of the Cardoso regime over the past 8 yr have further diminished the resources available for the public services. The result is skeletal public education and health care systems that have been abandoned by middle-classes with enough money to afford private education or health services. The participants in this study went to great lengths to gain access to private health care and education — most frequently women (on behalf of their families) working in domestic service jobs for the middle class used their employers to gain access to private health care and better education. The daily struggle of the poor with the public health care system most clearly demonstrates how lack of dignified access to public services affects their lives.

The public health care system (Sistema Único de Saúde Brasiliera), which is supported by a heavy tax paid by employers, is woefully inadequate. Public hospitals do not have the resources to provide basic care. Currently 40% of the total population in Rio de Janeiro has resorted to private health coverage (UNDP, 2001). For poor women, the most readily available form of health services is for pre-natal care. Nonetheless, Brazil has highest mortality rate amongst pregnant women in Latin America. The United Nations estimates that 200 women die in childbirth for every 100,000 children born (UNECLAC, 1997). For all other types of health services, from family planning to hypertension, there are waits varying from months to years for appointments. In order to be seen by a doctor in a public hospital, the line starts to form at three in the morning to get a ticket to enter in the waiting list for an appointment. Several participants travel 3 h across the entire city with their children to go to a public hospital that was rumored to have better pediatric service. But despite the clear problems in getting service in the public health care system, the major complaint of the participants was that at the public hospitals they felt as though they were treated as "cattle" and "not as a real person with dignity." In one interview with a poor black woman who lives in a housing project in the *Zona Norte*, her former employer arranged an appointment for her in a private hospital after she had no success getting treated for her hypertension in the public hospital. She commented that at the private hospital she was treated "like a person" with "politeness and respect", whereas as the public hospital the doctors and nurses were "rude and treated her like an animal." Waiting in lines for inadequate service in public hospitals is tiring and discouraging, and what is most detrimental for the poor is the constant abasement and poor treatment that dealing with the public health care system requires.

It is the challenge of regular access to public services, such as the health care system, that erode the dignity of the poor in Rio de Janeiro, and it is dignity that they place at the center of their conception of citizenship. While access may be limited and services poor, it is the nature of that access that most affects participants' daily lives.

V. Conclusion

In these stories of citizenship, marginalized men and women did not identify themselves as activists in organized social movements nor where they involved in political campaigns. They have recast citizenship in terms of their families and communities in order to contest access to the society's resources, which has the most relevance to their daily lives.[7] This process of addressing their own communities' problems and reinforcing their sense of political community at a local level is the most important form of democratic practice in their view. The women and men I interviewed recast the meaning of citizenship and citizen, and by extension democratic practice, in terms of their communities. They redefined citizenship in their daily lives in three ways:

1. As relating more to the "private" than the public.
2. In terms of a qualified political and economic participation that privileges their own families and communities.
3. As dignity in their quotidian experiences.

The narrative of citizenship for the poor in Rio de Janeiro incorporates aspects of democratic and market logic, but recasts citizenship in terms of family and community structures and participation with dignity in the city's life. In the absence of meaningful discourse of citizenship at the macro-political and economics levels for the participants in this study (the lack "of a place in the world"), the place for the elaboration of citizenship has been in the context of family and community. And this formulation of citizenship situates dignity in daily life at its center.

This examination of substantive citizenship through a gendered analysis raises some important questions for how governance reforms are carried out in development. If formal political reforms are to achieve more substantive citizenship for marginalized groups, they must be able to respond to the personal, family, and community levels described, as well as translate into meaningful access to political and economic structures. While focusing citizenship on daily experiences has its own problems in terms of how these experiences are represented in a meaningful way (Gujit and Shah, 1998), ignoring them condemns governance reforms to providing only partial solutions.

Notes

1. This chapter is based on over forty open-ended interviews conducted between September 2001 and March 2002 in Rio de Janeiro. The primary source of the research is the interviews conducted with women and men in six extended families (e.g., interviews with three to four members of the same family from three generations). These interviews incorporated families from different urban spaces,[2] classes, and races from within Rio de Janeiro: families from *favelas*, families from housing projects, and families from the working-class suburbs. The following analysis also relies on, as a secondary research source, multiple interviews with key community leaders, non-profit workers, and members of the government. This chapter is an amended version of a chapter which appears in Kabeer (2005).
2. For an example of how the family and community responded to market demands in Mexico, see de la Rocha and Latapí (1991) and de la Rocha (1994).
3. Participants were asked: "Do you participate politically? And if so, what is the most important way you participate?"
4. In terms of democratic impulses, the focus here is on forms of political participation that work for the good of some broader collectivity rather than promoting representative governance because that was the notion most commonly elaborated by the study's participants.
5. See http://conhecimentosgerais.hypermart.net. I would also like to acknowledge Carlos Pio of the Federal University of Brasilia for his correspondence regarding the plebiscite on governance.
6. This focus amongst the poor on dignity as the central component of citizenship coincides with Evalina Dagnino's study on conceptions of citizenship in social activists in São Paulo. She asked about fifty social activists which of the following qualities is most important for democracy:

   (a) There are several political parties.
   (b) All have food and housing.
   (c) Whites, blacks, men, women, rich and poor are all treated equally.

(d)   People can participate in unions and associations.

(e)   People can criticize and protest.

Fifty-eight percent of the sample chose the equal treatment of whites, blacks, men, women, rich, and poor as the most important quality (Dagnino, 1998: 53). Dagnino goes on to note that a large majority of the poor and working class activists that she interviewed "mentioned disrespect, discrimination, and prejudice as part of their daily experience in city; referred to their to their status as "second-class citizens"; and complained of mistreatment because of their race or because they were not dressed well enough" (Dagnino, 1998: 55).

7. Ong (1996: 737) makes a similar argument in reference to Asian immigrants to California.

References

Alvito, M. and Zaluar, A., *Um século de Favela*, Fundação GetúlioVargas, Rio de Janeiro, 1998.

BRIDGE, *Gender and Participation Cutting Edge Pack*, Institute of Development Studies, Brighton, 1998, 2004.

Castles, S. and Davidson, A., *Citizenship and Migration: Globalization and the Politics of Belonging*, Routledge, New York, 2000.

Clark, C., Reilly, M., and Wheeler, J.S., 'Living Rights: Reflections from Women's Movement about Gender and Rights in Practice' in Pettit, J. and Wheeler J.S. Eds. IDS Bulletin — Developing Rights, 36(1), 2005.

Cornwall, A. and Coelho, V.S.P., Eds., *IDS Bulletin — New Democratic Spaces?*, 3 (1), 2004.

Davis, D., *Avoiding the Dark: Race and the Forging of National Culture in Modern Brazil*, Ashgate, Brookfield, VT, 1999.

Dagnino, E., Culture, citizenship, and democracy: changing discourses and practices of the Latin American left, in *Cultures of Politics/Politics of Cultures: Re-visioning Latin American Social Movements*, Alvarez, S., Dagnino, E., and Escobar, A, Eds., Westview Press, Boulder, CO, 1998, pp. 33–63.

Fraser, N., *Unruly Practices: Power, Discourse, and Gender in Contemporary Social Theory*, University of Minnesota Press, St. Paul, 1989.

Gujit, I. and Shah, M.K., *The Myth of Community: Gender Issues in Participatory Development*, ITDG Publishing, London, 1998.

Holston, J. and Appadurai, A., Introduction: cities and citizenship, in *Cities and Citizenship*, Holston, J., Ed., Duke University Press, Durham, NC, 1999, pp. 1–20.

Houtzager, P.P., Social movements amidst democratic transitions: lessons from the Brazilian countryside, *J. Dev. Stud.*, 36 (5), 59–88, 2000.

Houtzager, P.P., Lavalle, A.G., and Acharya, A., *Who Participates? Civil Society and the New Democratic Politics in São Paulo, Brazil*, IDS Working Paper 210, Institute of Development Studies, Brighton, 2003.

Jelin, E., Toward a culture of participation and citizenship: challenges for a more equitable world, in *Cultures of Politics/Politics of Cultures: Re-visioning*

Latin American Social Movements, Alvarez, S., Dagnino, E., and Escobar, A., Eds., Westview Press, Boulder, CO, 1998, pp. 405–414.

Kabeer, N., *Reversed Realities: Gender Hierarchies in Development*, Verso, London, 1994.

Kabeer, N., Ed., *Inclusive Citizenship: Meanings and Expressions*, Zed Books, London, 2005.

Latapí, A.E. and Roberts, B.R., Urban stratification, the middle classes, and economic change in Mexico, in *Social Responses to Mexico's Economic Crisis of the 1980s*, de la Rocha, M.G. and Latapí, A.E., Eds., Center for U.S-Mexican Studies, San Diego, 1991, pp. 91–114.

Machado, L.T., *Formação do Brasil e unidade nacional*, Instituto Brasileiro de Difusão Cultural, São Paulo, 1980.

Marx, A., *Making Race and Nation: A comparison of South Africa, the United States, and Brazil*, Cambridge University Press, Cambridge, 1998.

Mukhopadhyay, M., *Governing for Equity: Gender Citizenship and Governance*, KIT Publishers, Amsterdam, 2003.

Ncuhouser, K., "Worse than men": gendered mobilization in an urban Brazilian squatter settlement, 1971–91, *Gender Soc.*, 9 (1), 38–59, 1995.

Ong, A., Cultural citizenship as subject-making: inmigrantes negotiate racial and cultural boundaries in the United States, *Curr. Anthropol.*, 37 (5), 737–762, 1996.

Paoli, M.C. and Telles, V.S., Social rights: conflicts in contemporary Brazil, in *Cultures of Politics/Politics of Cultures: Re-visioning Latin American Social Movements*, Alvarez, S., Dagnino, E., and Escobar, A., Eds., Westview Press, Boulder, CO, 1998, pp. 64–92.

de la Rocha, M.G., *The Resources of Poverty, Women and Survival in a Mexican City*, Blackwell, Oxford, 1994.

de la Rocha, M.G. and Latapí, A.E., *Social Responses to Mexico's Economic Crisis of the 1980s*, Center for U.S-Mexican Studies, San Diego, 1991.

Sen, G., Feminist politics in a fundamentalist world, in *Governing for Equity: Gender Citizenship and Governance*, Mukhopadhyay, M., Ed., KIT Publishers, Amsterdam, 2003, pp. 24–27.

UNDP (United Nations Development Programme), *Relatório de Desenvolvimento Humano do Rio de Janeiro 2001*, United Nations, Rio de Janeiro, 2001.

UNDP, *Poverty Report 2000*, United Nations, New York, 2000.

UNECLAC (United Nations Economic Commission for Latin America and the Caribbean), *Sustainable Development, Poverty and Gender, Latin America and the Caribbean: Working Toward the Year 2000*, United Nations, New York, 1997.

Yuval-Davis, N., Citizenship, territoriality, and the gendered construction of difference, in *Democracy, Cititzenship and the City*, Isen, E., Ed., Routledge, London, 2000, pp. 171–188.

Women's Studies Quarterly, Women and Development: Rethinking policy and reconceptualising practice, 31, 3–4, The Feminist Press at CUNY, New York, 2003.

DEVELOPMENT GOVERNANCE TOOLS

Chapter 21

Decentralization and Development

Dennis A. Rondinelli

CONTENTS

I. Introduction

Governments around the world have used decentralization for more than half a century to democratize their political systems, enhance popular participation in public affairs, and give local administrative units more responsibility for providing public services. Recently, many governments have also decentralized their fiscal systems and political institutions and privatized state-owned enterprises in order to accelerate the growth of market economies. Decentralization — the transfer of responsibilities and authority to lower levels within the central government (deconcentration), or from the center to local government units (devolution) and nongovernmental organizations (delegation), or from government to the private sector (deregulation and privatization) — has a long history (Rondinelli, 1981). Many industrialized nations began to decentralize in the late 1970s after their governments consolidated power and responsibility for nearly two decades. By the early 1990s, all but 12 of the 75 countries with populations of more than five million had undertaken some form of decentralization (Dillinger, 1994). At the end of the 1990s, approximately 95% of the countries with democratic political systems had sub-national units of administration or government (World Bank, 2000).

Why have governments adopted decentralization? What do advocates of decentralization believe it will achieve? How effective has decentralization been in supporting economic and political development? What conditions are necessary to make decentralization successful in developing countries? This chapter addresses these questions by reviewing the theory of decentralization and its experience since the early 1970s.

II. Why Have Governments Decentralized?

National governments centralized the financing and management of public services and infrastructure in both industrialized and developing countries during the 1950s and 1960s for many reasons. In North America and Western Europe, the strength of central government bureaucracies grew from their crucial roles in mobilizing resources during World War II and, afterward, they took on increasing responsibilities for economic and social reconstruction (Sundquist and Davis, 1969). Strong central management in industrialized nations offered convenient models for new governments in developing countries. In the post-colonial period, many newly independent governments in Africa and Asia saw local jurisdictions as colonial institutions or as strongholds of ethnic or religious minorities that could become sources of political opposition. Concentrating resources and authority in the central government was seen as an essential instrument of nation building (Mahwood, 1993).

In developing countries, many political leaders sought to build their new nations through the central government's control of the economy. The dominant development theories of the 1950s and 1960s called for strong central government control over industrial and agricultural sectors as well as the public services and infrastructure needed to accelerate economic growth (Waterston, 1965). The government of Thailand, for example, created more than 50 state-owned industries during the 1950s and 1960s because of the lack of domestic and foreign investment capital and the private sector's weaknesses in mobilizing resources for expansion. As the number of central government agencies in both industrialized and developing countries proliferated, many not only took on commercial functions but also assumed control over expenditures and revenues that had previously been under local control. Many ministries saw their political power and budgets grow from their expanding roles in planning and implementing large-scale, capital-intensive investments and were reluctant to allow private or non-government organizations to participate or compete in many of the service sectors. Service delivery suffered because few central government ministries rewarded civil servants for dealing with citizens as customers and government bureaucracies grew more unresponsive to the needs of their constituents (Rondinelli et al., 1983). Central planning and management brought economic stagnation and increasing poverty in South and Central America, Africa, Eastern Europe, and South Asia.

During the 1970s and 1980s, some governments and most international assistance organizations began to recognize the limitations and constraints of central economic planning and management. A shift in development theories and strategies in international aid agencies during the 1970s and 1980s away from macro-economic planning and toward meeting basic human needs, growth-with-equity, and participatory planning led to increasing calls for decentralizing resources, responsibilities, and control over development activities to local communities and governments (Korten and Alfonso, 1981). International assistance organizations promoted decentralization as an essential part of a "process approach" to economic and social development that depended primarily on self-help by local communities (Rondinelli, 1993).

Heavy borrowing during the 1970s and the economic recessions of the early 1980s left central governments in most countries with little capital for investing in new infrastructure or for expanding public services. The world economic recession of the late 1970s and early 1980s also played an important role in increasing governments' interest in decentralizing services and infrastructure. The recession led many governments in Africa and Latin America to shift responsibilities for revenue generation and service provision to local levels of administration.

The demise of authoritarian regimes in Latin America during the 1980s and in Central and Eastern Europe during the 1990s, along with the spread of market economies and more democratic principles in East Asia a decade ago, led to the current widespread interest in decentralization. In Central Europe, for example, policies promoting transition from socialist to market economies focused on strengthening the private sector, privatizing or liquidating state enterprises, and downsizing large central government bureaucracies. The private sector and local governments had been left weak by many years of socialist central planning (OECD, 1992). Demands for economic, political, and fiscal decentralization spread rapidly among emerging market countries (Bird et al., 1994).

In many poor countries, decentralization was prescribed by international financial and development institutions such as the World Bank and the International Monetary Fund as part of the structural adjustments needed to restore markets, create or strengthen democracy, and promote good governance. The Canadian International Development Agency sought to improve governance in developing countries by assisting projects aimed at strengthening organizations of civil society, democratic political institutions, and human rights groups. Similarly, the Swedish International Development Agency (SIDA, 1991: 11) focused its assistance on "making government work" at both central and local levels. It supported public administration development projects "enabling governments to reform, improve, and perfect their existing systems, instruments, and structures of government in order to execute their policies and programs more democratically and effectively."

Decentralization was closely identified with democratization movements in some Asian countries such as the Philippines, Nepal, and Bangladesh after long periods of authoritarian rule (Aziz and Arnold, 1996). With the passing of authoritarian military regimes in Latin American countries such as Brazil and Argentina, many elected state and local officials and political opposition groups embraced decentralization as a form of democratic institution-building. In much of Africa, calls for decentralization emanated from tribal minorities and economically peripheral ethnic groups. Growing discontent with the inability of central government bureaucracies to deliver effectively almost any types of service to local areas fueled the decentralization movement in Africa (Smoke, 1994). Calls for devolution or autonomous rule also came from ethnic, religious, and political minority groups in Belgium, Quebec, Wales, Scotland, Malaysia, the Baltic countries, Mexico, the Philippines, India, Yugoslavia, and the former Soviet Union that were dissatisfied with their political representation or the allocation of national expenditures.

Continued economic globalization through international trade and investment gave cities and metropolitan regions important new economic roles in the 1990s (Rondinelli, 2001). The world economy was being restructured by technological changes and by the geographic movement of all factors of production — capital, human resources, and technology. This mobility changed the location of production as well as the direction and volume of trade and investment flows among nations and cities. The continuing integration of the world economy also created new opportunities for trade and investment in cities in the formerly socialist countries and in developing nations, requiring municipalities and metropolitan areas to provide new infrastructure and services quickly and effectively (Rondinelli and Vastag, 1998). In China, where growth took place rapidly in coastal cities such as Shanghai and Guangzhou, provincial and metropolitan governments assumed powerful new functions, often *de facto* rather than *de jure*. The opening of the world economy and the expansion of cross-border transactions made cities around the world more interdependent, and sometimes more financially independent of their own central governments (Behrman and Rondinelli, 1995).

In brief, advocates believed that decentralization could help accelerate economic development, increase political accountability, and enhance public participation in governance. They argued that when applied appropriately decentralization policies could help break bottlenecks in decision making that were often caused by highly centralized government planning and management (Rondinelli, 1990). Decentralization could assist local officials to cut through complex central bureaucratic procedures and get decisions made and implemented more quickly. They argued that decentralization could also increase government officials' sensitivity to local conditions and needs; create incentives for government and the private sector to extend services; allow greater political representation for diverse political, ethnic, religious, and cultural groups; and relieve top managers in central ministries of "routine" tasks to concentrate on national policy. More creative, innovative, and responsive programs and more local "experimentation" could accompany decentralization (Rondinelli et al., 1989). It could help governments balance regional development, improve local governance, empower communities, and mobilize private resources for investment in public infrastructure and facilities (Serageldin et al., 2000).

III. How Effective Has Decentralization Been?

More than half a century of experience with decentralization in developing countries has led policy analysts to conclude that the results have been mixed. As Garrett and Rodden (2003) note, there was strong variation in decentralization behavior among countries. Some countries such as Brazil, India, Mexico, and Peru decentralized, whereas others such as Thailand,

Zimbabwe, Malaysia, and Paraguay became more centralized. Decentralization policies have been implemented successfully in some countries but not in others, and in some regions and localities of some countries but not in all. They often worked well for some, but not every government service (Rondinelli and Nellis, 1986).

A. Economic Growth and Development

Although decentralization of decision-making can contribute to economic growth in developing countries, empirical relationships between decentralization and various development variables have more often than not been neutral or negative. Martinez-Vazquez and McNab (2003) found no direct links between fiscal decentralization and economic growth, although they identify several strong potential indirect linkages. Other studies found that fiscal decentralization is associated with lower growth and with fiscal imbalance (Davoodi and Zou, 1998). Ter-Minassian (1997) cautions that decentralization can constrain the central government's ability to stabilize the national economy. Decentralization can also increase business transaction costs. Observers of decentralization policies in Malawi, for example, point out that they are likely to create new barriers to trade and investment by multiplying commodity taxes and the sources of business licensing (Ellis et al., 2003).

Enikopolov and Zhuravskaya (2003) demonstrate, however, that fiscal decentralization can lead to more efficient governance and higher economic growth if the political system is strong. The success of fiscal decentralization in emerging market countries has depended heavily on the quality of national governance (Drummond and Monsoor, 2003). Decentralization resulted in fiscal and economic improvements in middle-income emerging market countries that had strong national budget coordination mechanisms, revenue sharing and tax-effort incentives, effective budget and expenditure controls, and transparent criteria for borrowing.

B. Political Democratization and Public Accountability

The experience in developing countries with achieving increased political accountability and concern for local political preferences through decentralization has also been mixed. Studies of electoral participation and political accountability in 14 major states in India from 1960 to 1992, for example, found that voters were more "vigilant" in the local elections, rewarding incumbents for local income growth in their entire terms in office, while rewarding candidates in national elections for income growth, reductions in income inequality, and inflation only in the previous year (Khemani, 2001).

Research in 59 countries concluded that fiscal decentralization in government expenditure is strongly associated with higher levels of public accountability and lower levels of corruption (Fisman and Gatti, 2002). Decentralization in Colombia during the 1980s led to more competition for political office, the election of more responsible leaders, greater innovation in policies and programs at the local level, and greater ability to build local government capacity (Fizbein, 1997).

C. Efficient and Effective Service Delivery

The evidence is also mixed on decentralization's effect on service delivery. In some countries, decentralization increased public infrastructure expenditure for those services with local benefits but with little or no economies of scale (Estache and Sinha, 1995). Studies of road provision in Nepal, Uganda, and Zambia found that serious implementation problems plagued decentralized service provision (Robinson and Steidl, 2000). Data from Eastern and Central Europe found that local public services often deteriorate quickly (Bird et al., 1995). Some observers concluded that decentralization of public health services in China, for example, led to the weakening of prevention programs in poorer areas, increased costs for medical care, and greater inequity in access to health services (Bloom and Gu, 1997).

Other studies have found that the efficiency of decentralized service delivery depends on its design and institutional arrangements for implementation. Even within the same country, decentralized functions are performed more or less effectively in different localities. In a comprehensive analysis across sectors, Estache's (1995) studies found that at least one performance indicator improved in each sector following decentralization but that some sectors experienced only limited gains. They also found variance across local units in the provision of services reflecting differences in local government capacity, demand, and willingness to pay for infrastructure. In a review of 42 developing countries with decentralized road maintenance, service conditions improved with respect to lower backlogs and better road conditions (World Bank, 1994). Other analyses found that efficiency benefits from decentralization in road provision outweighed the rising costs from losses in economies of scale (Humplick and Moini-Araghi, 1996).

D. Mobilization of Public and Private Resources for Infrastructure and Service Investment

Advocates of decentralization often argue that the public and private provision of services and infrastructure improves when local governments in a politically decentralized system place more weight on infrastructure delivery than does the central government. Studies of decentralization in Bolivia found significant changes in investment patterns in social services and human capital that reflected reallocations of devolved funds by poor municipalities to their highest local priorities (Faguet, 2004). Because of the decentralization of responsibilities, local officials in these municipalities were more sensitive to the needs of the local population. However, the results were not the same throughout the country. In some municipalities decentralization merely strengthened the power of local elites, solidified client-patron relationships, and increased corruption (Kohl, 2003).

Hypothetically, investment in infrastructure and services can either increase if the local governments place infrastructure provision at the top of their economic development agendas and if it is cost effective, or it can decrease if infrastructure is of low priority and less cost-effective. In samples of ten industrialized countries and ten developing countries, Estache and Sinha (1995) found that decentralization increases sub-national infrastructure investment more than the total level and in developing countries the impact is significant on sub-national and total infrastructure investment. The caution that for decentralization to have desired outcomes, however, expenditure and revenue assignments have to be aligned. Despite more than 25 yr of decentralization in Papua-New Guinea, for example, little was accomplished because national political leaders simply off-loaded responsibility for financing and delivering public services on localities without building their administrative capacity or relieving their financial constraints (Edmiston, 2002). Positive impacts of decentralization on infrastructure investment also depend in part on the accuracy of local opinion about needs and priorities (Davis et al., 2001).

E. Political Participation and Social Equity

Advocates of decentralization often urge governments to adopt administrative deconcentration, delegation or devolution in order to increase political participation in decision-making and to achieve greater social equity in the allocation and distribution of public resources. Shankar and Shah (2003) found that countries with federal political systems and decentralized fiscal arrangements generally restrain regional inequalities better than centralized unitary states. The political risks of regional disparities and the incentives to reduce barriers to factor mobility and differences in minimum standards of service among regions are stronger in decentralized governments. In South Korea, devolution of financial resources from the central government to local governments strongly improved the fit between citizens' demands and the provision of public goods (Kwon, 2003). Decentralization of social assistance programs in Albania led to more effective targeting because local officials had better local information about needs and preferences than central government officials could obtain through surveys or by developing uniform allocation formulas (Alderman, 2002).

Yet, North (1990) points out that these benefits may not accrue if policies for decentralization create or strengthen organizations that are not aligned with existing local formal and informal institutions. Conyers (1990) examined the adverse impacts on equity if decentralized political or decision-making powers are captured by local elites. Power plays between the poor and the elite negatively affected the distribution of benefits after decentralization policies were adopted in Bangladesh (Sarker, 2003). In more polarized local societies the poor are often ineffectively targeted for welfare program benefits (Galasso and Ravallion, 2000). Existing institutions that had longed gained from central government decision-making were often locked into suboptimal solutions and government officials frequently stalled or delayed changes from the *status quo*.

IV. Conditions for Successful Implementation of Decentralization Policy

Decentralization is widely perceived as an instrument for promoting democratization, popular participation, more equitable service provision, economic development, and administrative and fiscal efficiency. Experience suggests, however, that decentralization is not a panacea; it can achieve many of the objectives that advocates claim for it only when policies are appropriately designed and effectively implemented, governance systems at all levels are competent, and national political leaders are committed to local participation and shared decision-making.

Even when decentralization policies are effectively designed and implemented, however, shifting administrative and fiscal responsibilities to localities, in some circumstances, has potential disadvantages. Decentralization may not always be efficient, especially for standardized, routine, network-based services requiring economies of scale. It can result in the central government losing control over scarce financial resources or the ability to allocate resources in ways that alleviate regional inequalities. De Mello and Barenstein (2001) found that the relationship between fiscal decentralization and governance depends on how sub-national expenditures are financed. Governance improves if non-tax revenues finance expenditures and sub-national spending is high.

Successful implementation of decentralization policies depends as well on strong and committed political leadership, both at national- and local-government levels. Political leaders must be willing to accept popular participation in planning and management by groups that are outside of the direct control of the central government or the dominant political party (Ascher and Rondinelli, 1999). Support of and commitment to decentralization must also come from line agencies of the central bureaucracy and ministry officials must be willing to transfer those functions that they traditionally performed to local organizations. The failure of Zimbabwe's decentralization policies of the 1980s was clearly due to the lack of political commitment at the center and the failure to develop the administrative and fiscal management capacity of local institutions (Conyers, 2003). In Uganda, the combination of top-down allocation of funds and bottom-up planning for service and infrastructure provision by localities that had no control over financial resources produced ineffective and inefficient resource allocation (Frances and James, 2003). Decentralization was undermined by lack of transparency in the national government, by weak civic engagement at the local level, and by lax public accountability at both levels.

The success of decentralization also depends on effective policy implementation. Ultimately, decentralization — especially delegation, devolution, and privatization — requires extensive institutional development and managerial capacity-building at local levels in both the public and private sectors. The poor results of experiments with deconcentration and weak devolution in Cambodia have been attributed to the cautious and piecemeal implementation of decentralization policies, to the unfamiliarity of local officials with financial management practices, to the limited managerial capacity throughout the country, and to the strong patterns of hierarchy embedded in society and the state (Turner, 2002). The success of decentralization is inextricably tied to strengthening the managerial and political capacity of those organizations to which responsibility and authority are transferred. Ironically, decentralization usually requires strengthening administrative and technical capacity within central government agencies and ministries to carry out national functions and to support — with adequate planning, programming, logistical, personnel, and budgetary resources — their field agencies and lower levels of government. Effective channels of political participation and representation are required to reinforce decentralization by allowing people to express their needs and demands and to press claims for national and local resources (Work, 2003).

The willingness and ability of local officials to implement decentralization policies, depends on laws that clearly define the relationships among different levels of administration, the allocation of functions among organizational units, the roles and duties of officials at each level of government, and their limitations and constraints. Decentralization must be supported by flexible legal arrangements, based on performance criteria, for reallocating functions and resources as the managerial capabilities of local governments change over time. Clearly defined and relatively uncomplicated planning and management procedures for eliciting the participation of local leaders and citizens and for obtaining the cooperation or consent of the beneficiaries of services are also needed.

In essence, decentralization is an exercise in institution building. Its success depends on strengthening the managerial and technical capacities of local administrators, political leaders, and non-government and civic organizations and on granting local government appropriate authority to raise and expend financial resources needed to support decentralized functions. In order to succeed, financial and organizational arrangements for decentralization must be tailored to local conditions and needs, and respect the social practices and political characteristics of the local population.

References

Alderman, H., Do local officials know something we don't? Decentralization of targeted transfers in Albania, *J. Pub. Econ.*, 83, 375–404, 2002.

Ascher, W. and Rondinelli, D.A., Restructuring the administration of service delivery in Vietnam: decentralization as institution-building, in *Market Reform in Vietnam*, Litvack, J.I. and Rondinelli, D.A., Eds., Westport, Quorum Books, CT, 1999, pp. 132–152.

Aziz, A. and Arnold, D., Introduction, in *Decentralized Governance in Asian Countries*, Aziz, A. and Arnold, D., Eds., Sage Publications, New Delhi, 1996, pp. 13–33.

Behrman, J.N. and Rondinelli, D.A., Urban development policies in a globalizing economy: creating competitive advantage in the post-cold war era, in *Post Cold War Policy, Vol. I: the Social and Domestic Contex*, Crotty, W., Ed., Nelson-Hall, Chicago, 1995, pp. 209–230.

Bird, R., Freund, C., and Wallich, C., Decentralization of intergovernmental finance in transition economies, *Comp. Econ. Stud.*, 36, 149–160, 1994.

Bird, R., Ebel, R., and Wallich, C., Decentralization of the socialist state: intergovernmental finance in transition economies, Mimeographed, World Bank, Washington, DC, 1995.

Bloom, G. and Gu, X., Health sector reform: lessons from China, *Soc. Sci. Med.*, 45, 357–360, 1997.

Conyers, D., Centralization and development planning: a comparative perspective, in *Decentralizing for development planning*, de Valk, P. and Wekwete, K., Eds., Avebury, Aldershot, 1990, pp. 15–34.

Conyers, D., Decentralization in Zimbabwe: a local perspective, *Pub. Adm. Dev.*, 23, 115–124, 2003.

Davis, J., Kang, A., Vincent, J., and Whittington, D., How important is improved water infrastructure to microenterprises? Evidence from Uganda, *World Dev.*, 29, 1753–1767, 2001.

Davoodi, H. and Zou, H-F., Fiscal decentralization and economic growth: a cross-country study, *J. Urban Econ.*, 43, 244–257, 1998.

De Mello, L.R. and Barenstein, M., Fiscal decentralization and governance: a cross-country analysis, *IMF Working Paper* WP/01/71, IMF, Washington, DC, 2001.

Dillinger, W., Decentralization and its implications to urban service delivery, *Urban Management Program Paper 16*, World Bank, Washington, DC, 1994.

Drummond, P. and Monsoor, A., Macroeconomic management and the devolution of fiscal powers, *Emerging Markets, Finance and Trade*, 39, 63–82, 2003.

Edmiston, K.D., Fostering subnational autonomy and accountability in decentralizing developing countries: lessons from the Papua-New Guinea experience, *Pub. Adm. Dev.*, 22, 221–234, 2002.

Ellis, F., Kutengule, M., and Nyasulu, A., Livelihoods and rural poverty reduction in Malawi, *World Dev.*, 3, 1495–1510, 2003.

Enikopolov, R. and Zhuravskaya, E., Decentralization and political institutions, *Discussion Paper* DP 3857, Center for Economic Policy Research, London, 2003.

Estache, A., Ed., Decentralizing infrastructure: advantages and limitations, *Discussion Paper 290*, World Bank, Washington, DC, 1995.

Estache, A. and Sinha, S., Does decentralization increase public expenditure in infrastructure? *Policy Research Working Paper* 1457, World Bank, Washington, DC, 1995.

Faguet, J-P., Does decentralization increase government responsiveness to local needs? Evidence from Bolivia, *J. Pub. Econ.*, 88, 867–893, 2004.

Fisman, R. and Gatti, R., Decentralization and corruption: evidence across countries, *J. Pub. Econ.*, 83, 325–345, 2002.

Fizbein, A., The emergence of local capacity: lessons from Colombia, *World Dev.*, 25, 1029–1043, 1997.

Frances, P. and James, R., Balancing rural poverty reduction and citizen participation: the contradictions of Uganda's decentralization program, *World Dev.*, 31, 325–337, 2003.

Galasso, E. and Ravallion, M., Distributional outcomes of a decentralized welfare program, *Policy Research Working Paper* 2136, World Bank, Washington, DC, 2000.

Garrett, G. and Rodden, J., Globalization and fiscal decentralization, in *Governance in a Global Economy*, Kahler, M. and Lake, D., Eds., Princeton University Press, Princeton, 2003, pp. 150–167.

Humplick, F. and Moini-Araghi, A., Decentralized structures for providing roads: a cross-country comparison, *Policy Research Working Paper* 1658, World Bank, Washington, DC, 1996.

Khemani, S., Decentralization and accountability: are voters more vigilant in local than in national elections, *Policy Research Working Paper* 2557, World Bank, Washington, DC, 2001.

Kohl, B., Democratizing decentralization in Bolivia: the law of popular participation, *J. Plan. Educ. Res.*, 23, 153–164, 2003.

Korten, D. and Alfonso, F., Eds., *Bureaucracy and the Poor: Closing the Gap*, McGraw-Hill, Singapore, 1981.

Kwon, O., The effects of fiscal decentralization on public spending: the Korean case, *Pub. Budgeting Finance*, 23, 1–20, 2003.

Martinez-Vazquez, J. and McNab, R.M., Fiscal decentralization and economic growth, *World Dev.*, 31, 1597–1616, 2003.

Mawhood, P., Ed., *Local Government in the Third World: Experience with Decentralization in Tropical Africa*, 2nd ed., Africa Institute of South Africa, Johannesburg, South Africa, 1993.

North, D., *Institutions, Institutional Change and Economic Performance*, Cambridge University Press, Cambridge, UK, 1990.

OECD (Organization for Economic Cooperation and Development), *Reforming the Economies of Central and Eastern Europe*, Paris, 1992.

Robinson, R. and Stiedl, D., Decentralization and road administration in poor countries, *Report* R 7437, United Kingdom Department for International Development, London, 2000

Rondinelli, D.A., Government decentralization in comparative perspective: theory and practice in developing countries, *Int. Rev. Adm. Sci.*, 47, 133–145, 1981.

Rondinelli, D.A., *Decentralizing Urban Development Programs: A Framework for Analyzing Policy*, U.S., Agency for International Development, Washington, DC, 1990.

Rondinelli, D.A., *Development Projects as Policy Experiments: An Adaptive Approach to Development Administration*, 2nd ed., Routledge, London, 1993.

Rondinelli, D.A., Making metropolitan areas competitive and sustainable in the New Economy, *J. Urban Tech.*, 18, 1–21, 2001.

Rondinelli, D.A. and Nellis, J.R., Assessing decentralization policies in developing countries: a case for cautious optimism, *Dev. Policy Rev.*, 4, 3–23, 1986.

Rondinelli, D.A. and Vastag, G., Urban economic growth in the 21st century: assessing the international competitiveness of metropolitan areas, in *Migration, Urbanization and Development: New Directions and Issues*, Billsborrow, R., Ed., Kluwer, Norwell, Mass, 1998, pp. 469–514.

Rondinelli, D.A., Nellis, J.R., and Cheema, G.S., Decentralization in developing countries: a review of recent experience, *World Bank Staff Working Paper* No. 581, World Bank, Washington, DC, 1983.

Rondinelli, D.A., McCullough, J., and Johnson, R.W., Analyzing decentralization policies in developing countries: A political-economy framework, *Dev. Change*, 20, 57–87, 1989.

Sarker, A.E., The illusion of decentralization: evidence from Bangladesh, *Int. J. Pub. Sector Manag.*, 16, 523–548, 2003.

Serageldin, M., Kim, S., and Wahba, S., Decentralization and urban infrastructure management capacity, Background paper for third global report on human settlements, UNCHS/Habitat, Harvard University Graduate School of Design, Cambridge, MA, 2000.

Shankar, R. and Shah, A., Bridging the economic divide within countries: a scoreboard on the performance of regional policies in reducing regional income disparities, *World Dev.*, 31, 1421–1442, 2003.

Smoke, P.J., *Local Government Finance in Developing Countries: The Case of Kenya*, Oxford University Press, Nairobi, 1994.

Sundquist, J.L. and Davis, D.W., *Making Federalism Work*, The Brookings Institution, Washington, DC, 1969.

SIDA (Swedish International Development Agency), *Making Government Work: Guidelines and Framework for SIDA Support to the Development Of Public Administration*, SIDA, Stockholm, 1991.

Ter-Minassian, T., Dentralization and macroeconomic management, *IMF Working Paper* WP/97/155, International Monetary Fund, Washington, DC, 1997.

Turner, M., Whatever happened to deconcentration? recent initiatives in Cambodia, *Pub. Adm. Dev.*, 22, 353–364, 2002.

Waterston, A., *Development Planning: Lessons of Experience*, Johns Hopkins University Press, Baltimore, MD, 1965.

Work, R., Decentralizing governance: participation and partnership in service delivery to the poor, in *Reinventing Government for the 21st Century: State Capacity in a Globalizing Society*, Rondinelli, D.A. and Cheema, G.S., Eds., Kumarian Press, Bloomfield, CT, 2003, pp. 195–218.

World Bank, *World Development Report* 1994, World Bank, Washington, DC, 1994.

World Bank, *World Development Report* 2000, Oxford University Press, New York, 2000.

Chapter 22

Participation in Governance

Andrea Cornwall and John Gaventa

CONTENTS

I. Introduction

In recent years, there has been considerable innovation in governance with the rise of an array of institutions that seek to engage citizens in playing a more active part in decisions which affect their lives. These innovations range from temporally bounded efforts to engage public deliberation — such as citizens' juries — to more durable, regularized spaces into which

405

the state "invites" citizens to contribute to the shaping and implementation of policy. These new institutions offer considerable scope for redefining and deepening the practice of democratic participation in governance. In these new political spaces, questions of how citizens — especially the poor — express voice, who speaks for whom, and how institutional responsiveness and accountability can be ensured have become paramount. In this chapter, we explore some of the challenges associated with extending the scope and reach of participation in governance.

II. Bridging the Gap

In the past, there has been a tendency to respond to the gap that exists between citizens and state institutions in one of the two ways. On the one hand, attention has been paid to strengthening the processes of participation and representation — that is, the ways in which poor people exercise voice through new forms of inclusion, consultation and mobilization designed to inform and to influence larger institutions and policies. On the other hand, growing attention has been paid to how to strengthen the accountability and responsiveness of these institutions and policies through changes in institutional design and a focus on the enabling structures for good governance. Each perspective has often perceived the other as inadequate, with concerns from one side that consultation without attention to power and politics will lead to "voice without influence" and from the other that reform of political institutions without attention to inclusion and consultation will only reinforce the status quo.

As concerns about good governance and state responsiveness grow, questions about the capacity of citizens to engage and make demands on the state come to the fore. In both south and north, there is growing consensus that the way forward is found in a focus on both a more active and engaged civil society which can express demands of the citizenry and a more responsive and effective state which can secure the delivery of needed public services. At the heart of the new consensus of strong state and strong civil society are the need to develop both "participatory democracy and responsive government" as "mutually reinforcing and supportive" (The Commonwealth Foundation, 1999: 76, 82).

III. New Contexts, New Challenges

In many countries, measures to bring government "closer to the people" through decentralization and devolution have prompted shifts in approaches to service delivery. These have created or widened spaces for people to become involved in priority setting, planning, and implementation. However, in many cases, citizens' opportunities for influence have been limited, as potent barriers exist to their active involvement in the decisions that count. Recent research on what we have termed "invited spaces" — that is, opportunities for public engagement that are created by the state or other powerful institutions, into which public are invited to participate — has shown some of the hurdles that need to be crossed if citizens are to gain opportunities for inclusive participation (Brock et al., 2001; Gaventa, 2002; Cornwall, 2004). These include means to amplify voice and turn it into influence, especially on the part of less powerful actors and the significance of political culture, political will and histories of state-civil society engagement.

In many countries, the marketization of service delivery has introduced new roles for those who were formerly the "beneficiaries" of government services. Users have come to be seen as "consumers" or "clients" and civil society organizations have become significant co-producers of what in the past were largely state functions. To some, these new roles are seen as welcome forms of partnership among the state, market and civil society, whereas to others they suggest the danger that the state is off-loading its larger social responsibilities to private or non-governmental actors (Cornwall, 2000; Cornwall and Gaventa, 2000). As Lucy Taylor argues, in the case of Chile, one of the possible consequences of policy shifts towards citizen participation is the diversion of social energy into backwater concerns, whereas bigger decisions continue to be taken behind closed doors. A similar argument has been made in relation to citizen involvement in the Poverty Reduction Strategy Papers (PRSPs), in which certain key economic issues — such as fiscal and monetary policy, privatizations, trade or foreign investments — are declared off limits to citizen engagement, whereas other issues in the poverty and social sphere are opened up for consultation (Brock and McGee, 2004; Rowden and Irama, 2004).

There are, then, potent challenges to the effective engagement of citizens with processes of governance. On the one hand, a series of questions arise about who participates in the name of "civil society," raising questions of representation and representativity that have remained the preoccupation of political theorists and are only now beginning to be explored in any depth in the empirical contexts in which experiments in participatory governance are taking place (Acharya et al., 2004; Coelho, 2004). On the other hand, issues arise around the framing of arenas for public involvement and the extent to which invitations to participate shape opportunities to influence policy debates, whether by circumscribing what is up for discussion or decision and placing other issues out of bounds, or by designating other forms of engagement outside the "invited space" as illegitimate. These, and other challenges, make the prospect of meaningful citizen participation more complicated than it might first appear.

IV. Repositioning Participation

As Gaventa and Valderrama (1999) argue, social participation and political participation have tended to be separate spheres in development policy and practice, each with its own distinctive set of methods or approaches for strengthening or enhancing participation. Traditionally, in the field of political participation, such methods have included voter education, enhancing the awareness of rights and responsibilities of citizens, lobbying and advocacy, often aimed towards developing a more informed citizenry who could hold elected representatives more accountable. In the social and community spheres, we have seen the development of a number of broader participatory methods for appraisal, planning, monitoring large institutions, training and awareness building. The emphasis here has been on the importance of participation not only to hold others accountable, but also as a self-development process, starting with the articulation of grassroots needs and priorities and moving towards the establishment of self-sustaining local organizations.

Engagement in social and community participation has inevitably brought citizens in closer contact with the institutions and processes of governance. Conversely, leaders of projects, programs and policy research initiatives have increasingly sought the voices and versions of poor people themselves. Where citizens have been able to take up and use the spaces that participatory processes can open up, they have been able to use their agency to demand accountability, transparency and responsiveness from government institutions. An informed, mobilized citizenry is clearly in a better position to do so effectively; the capacities built through popular education on rights and responsibilities also extend beyond taking a more active interest in the ballot box. Equally importantly, however, where government agencies have taken an active interest in seeking responsiveness and have not only listened to but also acted on citizens' concerns, otherwise adversarial and distant relationships have been transformed. Clearly, this also holds the promise of electoral advantage. These moves offer new spaces in which the concept of participation can be expanded to one of "citizenship participation" — linking participation in the political, community and social spheres (Gaventa and Valderrama, 1999).

V. New Thinking about Participation

The concept of citizenship has long been a disputed and value-laden one in democratic theory. New approaches to social citizenship aim to bridge the gap between citizen and the state by recasting citizenship as practiced rather than as given. Placing an emphasis on inclusive participation as the very foundation of democratic practice, these approaches suggest a more active notion of citizenship that recognizes the agency of citizens as "makers and shapers" rather than as "users and choosers" of interventions or services designed by others (Cornwall and Gaventa, 2000). As Lister (1998: 228) suggests, "the right of participation in decision-making in social, economic, cultural and political life should be included in the nexus of basic human rights . . . Citizenship as participation can be seen as representing an expression of human agency in the political arena, broadly defined; citizenship as rights enables people to act as agents."

There is a growing recognition that universal conceptions of citizenship rights, met through a uniform set of social policies, fail to recognize diversity and difference, and may in fact serve to strengthen the exclusion of some while seeking inclusion of others (Ellison, 1997). This has come a renewed emphasis on inclusion and on issues of social justice. Greater emphasis is now being placed on the involvement of those with least power and voice, with particular attention being paid to measures to address entrenched gender bias. Such new thinking about citizenship, participation and rights raises the question of how to create new mechanisms, or spaces and places for citizen engagement (Gaventa, 2002). It also requires that greater attention is paid to the interface between citizens and the state, to the intermediaries who play an increasing role in bridging the gap and at processes that can enhance responsibility as well as responsiveness on all sides.

One area of innovation has been to extend the traditional places for citizen engagement from the episodic use of the ballot box to new arenas, whether the multi-stakeholder intermediary institutions created in many contexts as a means for the involvement of the public in holding the state to account or local level sectoral policy (Cornwall and Coelho, 2004). Another area of innovation has been to bring new practices and rules-of-the-game into "old" spaces, transforming their possibilities. Public meetings and committees, for example, can be transformed when lent new powers and responsibilities, as user groups and citizen councils become more actively spaces for deliberation — involving the exchange of information, views and reasoned argument on policy possibilities. Another still has been to reach out into the public spaces in which the majority of citizens spend their everyday lives, through approaches like Participatory Assessments that offer direct democratic interfaces with the general public. The use of Participatory Rural Appraisal (PRA) for wellbeing assessments, for example, offers ways of taking the consultation process to citizens in their own spaces.

Although participatory methodologies have considerable scope for manipulation, serving at times as a form of market research for preferred solutions or legitimation of preferred policy messages, they also open up the possibility of engaging those who lack any connection to policy or political processes in governance. With its emphasis on inclusive processes in which the verbal gives way to collective visual representation, which in turn offers opportunities for those who otherwise remain unrepresented and voiceless to have their say, PRA and other participatory methodologies offer a potentially radical way of engaging less powerful segments of society who might otherwise remain completely outside any possibility of influencing or informing policy (Chambers, 1997). Just as participatory methodologies have been used to rubber stamp Washington-produced policy recipes, there are equally powerful examples where their use has triggered a process through which citizens have mobilized to take action to press for their rights, in the pursuit of social justice.

Another emerging space for the exercise of citizenship has come with the opening up — and indeed the levering open through citizen action — of formerly closed off decision-making processes. In a number of countries, enabling national policy has created a new imperative to consult and involve. In Bolivia, for example, participatory municipal planning is backed by law; in Brazil, the constitution makes public involvement in governance obligatory. In the UK, central government support for public involvement has led to a wave of innovation in consultation over a number of high-profile government schemes. The adoption of participatory mechanisms for project and program planning has extended beyond the bounds of discrete initiatives, in some contexts, to ongoing processes of citizen involvement in monitoring and evaluation through which citizens play a part not only in offering opinions but also in holding agencies to account. Regardless of the methods or strategies used, participatory approaches are more likely to have the greatest potential for influence when they can be strengthened by claims to participation as a legal right. The right to participation is potentially a more empowered form of engagement than participation by invitation of governments, donors, or higher authorities. (For a review of the legal frameworks which support and enable participation in local governance, see McGee et al., 2003)

The increasing use of participatory and deliberative processes have contested and begun to reconfigure the boundaries between "expertise" and "experience" (Gaventa, 1993). Citizens are increasingly considered to have opinions that matter and experience that counts. Government agencies have involved them more in the kinds of decisions that were once presented as technical, rather than acknowledged as value-laden and political. Nowhere is this more the case than in the opening up of public expenditure budgeting to citizen engagement, as has been the case in several municipalities in Brazil — and more recently in other countries, from Peru to the U.K. At the local level, a growing emphasis on the co-production and co-management of services has also served to created new spaces for citizen involvement, as the "owners" — and to some extent the "makers and shapers," rather than simply "users and choosers" — of services.

In some countries, pressure placed on governments by civil society organizations has forced open spaces through demands for responsiveness and accountability. Perhaps the most notable example of this is the work of Mazdoor Kisan Shakti Sangathan (MKSS) in India, whose public hearings on recorded public expenditure have named and shamed officials and exposed graft to audiences of thousands of citizens (Goetz and Jenkins, 1999). Numerous other examples exist where NGOs have sought to intermediate between government and citizens through the use of participatory mechanisms for enhanced service responsiveness and accountability, for example in the growing move for citizen involvement in local health service management.

In areas of policy making characterized by uncertainty, the use of mechanisms such as citizens juries offer an important new dimension: moving beyond eliciting opinions from citizens towards a process in which views are aired and defended, in which contrasting knowledges and versions are weighed up and interrogated, before "judgments" are sought. These processes offer a valuable corrective to the tendency found in some participatory processes of simply gathering people's views, rather than providing opportunities for exploration, analysis and debate.

At the same time, citizen involvement in processes where the emphasis has been on mutual learning and new courses of action has helped mould new forms of consensus, bridging differences of interest and perspective within communities as well as between community members and statutory or non-statutory agencies. This, in turn, has helped create better mutual understanding and with it the prospects for enhancing relationships that were previously characterized by mistrust, suspicion and distance.

VI. Beyond Tokenism: Making Participation in Governance Real

Forms of participation, as Arnstein's (1969) foundational work in the United States in the late 1960s suggested, run across a spectrum from tokenism and manipulation to devolved power and citizen control. As the uses of invited participation to rubber stamp and provide legitimacy for preconceived interventions grows, citizens are becoming increasingly skeptical. A recent report by the Commission on Poverty, Participation and Power in the United Kingdom for instance warns of "phony" participation, in which power relations do not shift, and in which rhetoric is not reflected in reality. As donors and lenders jumped onto an ever more crowded bandwagon in the 1990s, skepticism continued to grow about the extent to which the "development" mainstream would ever be able to genuinely make good its promises to involve the poor and marginalized in the decisions affecting their everyday lives and prospects for the future.

Making participation real raises a set of complex challenges. One of the most important is that those who preach participation actually listen to and take account of what those they seek to involve have to say, rather than simply nodding, cherry-picking the bits they like and then doing what they were going to do in the first place. Where the use of participatory methods for consultation has often been most effective is where institutional willingness to respond is championed by high-level advocates within organizations. Where such "champions" exist and where they can create sufficient momentum within organizations, the processes of invited participation that they help instigate can make a real difference. Recognizing and rewarding changes in practice can have significant ripple effects. By creating spaces within bureaucracies in which responsiveness is valued, wider changes become possible.

Yet, as we suggest earlier, such changes are only one part of the story. The best-laid plans for public involvement can falter where citizens express disinterest and where cynical public officials simply go through the motions with no real commitment to change. Citizen monitoring and other forms of citizen action can help force some measure of accountability (Mott, 2004). To do so effectively, however, requires a level of organization and persistence that is often beyond many communities who are involved in consultation exercises. Building the preconditions for voice and enabling citizens to actively take up and make use of available spaces for engagement calls for new combinations of older approaches to social, community and political participation.

In this, it is that some of the most exciting challenges for a new generation of participatory processes reside: in ways of building more deliberation into consultative processes; in participatory rights assessments that enable people to recognize and articulate their rights; and in moves that turn the tables on processes to gather "voices" to enable poor people to engage in analyzing the policies and institutions that affect their lives, as a starting point for changes that will make a difference.

References

Acharya, A., Lavalle, A.G., and Houtzager, P., Civil society representation in the participatory budget and deliberative councils of São Paulo, Brazil, *IDS Bull.*, 35 (2), 40–48, 2004.

Arnstein, S., A ladder of citizen participation, *AIP J.*, July, 216–224, 1969.

Brock, K. and McGee, R., Mapping trade policy: understanding the challenges of civil society participation, *IDS Working Paper* 225, Institute of Development Studies, Brighton, 2004.

Brock, K., Cornwall, A., and J. Gaventa, Power, knowledge and political spaces in the framing of poverty policy, *IDS Working Paper* 143, Institute of Development Studies, Brighton, 2001.

Chambers, R., *Whose Reality Counts? Putting the First Last*, Intermediate Technology Publications, London, 1997.

Coelho, V.S., Brazil's health councils: the challenge of building participatory political institutions, *IDS Bull.*, 35 (2), 33–39, 2004.

Commonwealth Foundation, *The Way Forward: Citizens, Civil Society and Governance in the New Millennium*, Commonwealth Foundation, London, 1999.

Cornwall, A., Beneficiary, consumer, citizen: perspectives on participation for poverty reduction. *SIDA Studies* 2, SIDA, Stockholm, 2000.

Cornwall, A., New democratic spaces? the politics of institutionalised participation, *IDS Bull.*, 35 (2), 1–10, 2004.

Cornwall, A. and Coelho, V.S., Eds., New democratic spaces? *IDS Bull.*, 35 (2), 2004.

Cornwall, A. and Gaventa, J., From users and choosers to makers and shapers: repositioning participation in social policy, *IDS Bull.*, 31 (4), 50–62, 2000.

Ellison, N., Beyond universalism and particularism: rethinking contemporary welfare theory, *Crit. Soc. Policy*, 19 (1), 57–83, 1997.

Gaventa, J., The powerful, the powerless and the experts: knowledge struggles in a information age, in *Voices of Change*, Park, P., Brydon-Miller, M., Hall, B., and Jackson, T., Eds., Bergin & Garvey, Wesport, Conn, 1993, pp. 21–40.

Gaventa, J., Exploring citizenship, participation and accountability, *IDS Bull.*, 33 (2), 1–11, 2002.

Gaventa, J. and Valderrama, C., Participation, citizenship and local governance. Background note prepared for workshop on "Strengthening Participation in Local Governance". Institute of Development Studies, Brighton, June 21–24, 1999.

Goetz, A.-M. and Jenkins, R., Accounts and accountability: theoretical implications for the right-to-information movement in India. Background note prepared for workshop on "Strengthening Participation in Local Governance". Institute of Development Studies, Brighton, June 21–24, 1999.

Lister, R., Citizen in action: citizenship and community development in Northern Ireland Context, *Commun. Dev. J.*, 33 (3), 226–235, 1998.

McGee, R., Bazaara, N., Gaventa, J., Nierras, R., Rai, M., Rocamora, J., Saule, N., Williams, E., and Zermeno, S., *Legal Frameworks for Citizen Participation*. Logo Link Research Report, Institute of Development Studies, Brighton, 2003.

Mott, A., Increasing space and influence through community organising and citizen monitoring: experiences from the USA, *IDS Bull.*, 35 (2), 91–98, 2004

Rowden, R. and Irama, J., *Rethinking Participation: Questions for Civil Society about the Limits of Participation in PRSPs*, ActionAid International USA and Kampala: ActionAid International Uganda, Washington, 2004.

Chapter 23

Nongovernmental Organizations, Civil Society, and Development Governance

Gerard Clarke and Alan Thomas

CONTENTS

I. Introduction

Since the early 1970s, nongovernmental organizations (NGOs) in the developed and developing worlds alike have gradually become important conduits of development assistance. The volume of aid for development generated by international NGOs (INGOs, normally based in developed countries), for instance, has increased from $3.64 billion in 1970 to $12.4 billion in 1999 (85% of it, in 1999, from private donations), and from 11% of total aid flows in 1970 to 21.6% in 1999 (Clark, 2003: 130).[1] As a result of this dramatic growth in resources, NGOs have become important stakeholders in the management of development at global, national, and sub-national levels. They now complement states, the private sector, and donor organizations (governmental and inter-governmental) in governance arrangements at national and international level, and have become pivotal actors in nascent civil societies.

Many of the NGOs that work with UN agencies and other bodies and thus contribute to global governance, however, are very different both from the INGOs involved in direct delivery of aid and humanitarian assistance and the Southern NGOs with which they often work. Thus NGOs come in a variety of guises and NGO communities are diverse and plural. However, as the amount of aid channeled through NGOs has increased, and as they have become more embedded in governance arrangements at all levels, the strategic challenges facing NGOs of all types have evolved. In this chapter we explore the complex universe of NGOs, the roles they play in international development governance, and the challenges they face in the early years of the new millennium.

II. What Are NGOs?

NGOs are private, nonprofit professional organizations with a legal character concerned with public welfare goals, a broad definition which encompasses a wide range of organizations including philanthropic foundations, faith-based development agencies, academic think-tanks, and other organizations focusing on issues such as rural development, human rights, gender, indigenous peoples, or the environment (Clarke, 1998: 2–3). NGOs are often distinguished from people's organizations (POs – local nonprofit membership-based organizations that organize and mobilize their constituents in support of collective or public welfare goals), such as community associations, cooperatives, or microfinance groups (Clarke, 1998: 3).[2] NGOs often function as intermediary organizations, helping POs to interact with government agencies, donors, or social movements. The PO–NGO distinction is echoed in the distinction between *mutual benefit* and *public benefit* organizations, the latter including most NGOs (Thomas and Allen, 2000). These labels are useful analytically but the distinctions are not always clear-cut in practice; large POs may behave in many ways like NGOs, while an environmental NGO can be both membership-based and committed to securing public benefit.

Another important difference is between INGOs, mostly based in the developed world, and local NGOs, particularly indigenous NGOs in the developing world. Many of the former began as charitable relief or missionary welfare organizations, and they generally work in developing countries through their own branches or with local partner organizations, often NGOs themselves. The majority of the latter are small, employing less than ten staff and operating on budgets of less than $50,000 a year. However, at the other end of the spectrum are organizations such as the Bangladesh Rural Advancement Committee (BRAC), the largest national NGO in the developing world, with over 27,000 staff and anticipated turnover of $174 million in 2003.[3] BRAC and other large NGOs (especially in South Asia) often function as para- or quasi-governmental organizations, operating in parallel with the state and complementing it in the provision of social services.

III. Challenges for Development NGOs: Scaling up Activities and Impact

From the 1980s, as the neo-liberal combination of market economics and liberal democratic politics became dominant, development-focused NGOs became increasingly important. As Edwards and Hulme (1995: 849) explain, NGOs fitted into the "New Policy Agenda" promoted by donors, appearing simultaneously "as market-based actors" and "as components of 'civil society'." Thus on the one hand the increase in provision of services or "gap-filling" (Vivian, 1994) by NGOs was seen as part and parcel of the privatization of state services, despite NGOs' nonprofit basis. On the other hand, NGOs were seen as prime agents of democratization (Clark, 1991), or even as intrinsically democratic simply by virtue of being part of civil society. Thus ROAPE (1992: 3–4) argued that democracy required "a widespread and complex process involving the strengthening of civil society" and that NGOs were "one of the institutional forms that can deepen [civil society]."

Many of those working in NGOs wished to go beyond simply providing relief or other services within the neo-liberal model of market-led development. A symposium on "Development Alternatives: the Challenge for NGOs" held in London in March 1987 explored the suggestion of a distinctive "NGO approach" to development based on empowerment and the idea that poor people could be supported to become the agents of their own development (World Development, 1987; see also Poulton and Harris, 1988; Thomas, 1992). However, despite a number of well-reported success stories at the local level it was unclear whether this "NGO approach" could have a broader impact. In one of the papers from that London conference, Annis (1987) asked: "Can small-scale development be a large-scale policy?" and this question of how to "scale up" from local experience became perhaps the most important of a number of distinct challenges to development NGOs. Although significant progress has been made in addressing these challenges, they remain relevant in many respects today.

A number of writers have seen these challenges in terms of a sequence of strategies. At the same conference, Korten (1990) distinguished between three "generations" of NGO strategies; the first committed to relief and welfare activities, the second promoting small-scale local development that empowered local communities and broke their dependency on humanitarian assistance, and the third involved in a range of activities designed to achieve institutional and policy change. Later, he suggested the need for a "fourth generation" strategy, committed to increasingly complex networks and to advocacy at international as well as national level (Korten, 1990: 123–124). Each level involved a different strategic role for NGOs: doer, mobilizer, catalyst and finally, in the case of fourth-generation NGO strategies, activist and educator (Korten, 1990: 117). Individual NGOs could be involved in various mixes of the strategies. In a similar vein, Fowler (1997: 220–221) characterizes the activities of "nongovernmental development organizations" (NGDOs) as a mixture of three types of effort: "welfare and delivery (the global soup kitchen)," "strengthening people's organizations and movements," and "learning for leverage." He suggests a shift away from the first and towards the third, and that NGDOs should avoid getting "caught in the role of (international) social welfare provider" by adopting one of two strategies: "concentrating on building people's capacities to look after and demand for themselves" and "gaining leverage on structural changes to governments and markets which benefit the poor" (Fowler, 1997: 220–221).

One way of thinking about how NGOs can "scale up" their activities and "make a difference" (Edwards and Hulme, 1992) is that they could shift their strategic focus from one "generation" to the next. However, in practice some NGOs maintain a focus on humanitarian relief (first generation), others emphasize capacity building and facilitating self-reliance (second generation), some focus on advocacy and coalition-building (third generation) while some combine different generational strategies to create a multifaceted yet holistic approach to development.

In turn, "scaling up" of NGO activities and impact can be attempted in a number of ways, for instance, through (1) collaboration with state and

donor agencies in the design, implementation and monitoring of development activities including socio-economic development projects and
legislative or policy reforms; (2) networking with other NGOs and POs to
build issue-based campaigns and generate consensus on key issues such
as NGO relationships with governments and donors; and (3) operational
expansion and greater emphasis on intra-organizational development
(e.g., management practices, financial controls, or staff development)
(Edwards and Hulme, 1992).

The challenge of scaling up can also be viewed in more strategic terms.
Several commentators have used Edwards and Hulme's distinction (1992:
15) between *additive* strategies, where programs or organizations grow in
size, *multiplicative* strategies, where NGOs increase impact through deliberate influence, networking, policy and legal reform, or training and *diffusive*
strategies, where aggregate impact is enhanced through informal and
spontaneous processes across organizations and networks.

Another way of thinking about how to "make a difference" is in terms of
ways of relating to other agencies, and in particular how to influence *their*
policies. Thomas et al. (2001) propose four main ways of trying to
achieve influence: collaboration, challenge, complementary activities, and
consciousness-raising (the "four Cs"). Here, collaboration means working
closely with a particular target institution to achieve a direct change in its
policies, accepting the terms on which the issue is defined by the target institution. Challenge (confrontation, opposition, including passive resistance)
is also aimed directly at changing the policies of a target institution. Complementary activities are projects or programs carried out independently of
government or other decision-makers. Their success can oblige those
decision-makers to change their policy to accommodate the new development. Finally, consciousness-raising involves campaigning work aimed at
indirect influence over the long term through changing public opinion
and norms.

By the mid-1990s, concerns had evolved. NGOs were still expected to
scale up their activities and impact, while maintaining their distinctively participatory mode of engagement with host communities and beneficiaries.
There was now also increasing focus on how NGOs could be accountable
and transparent in their operations (cf. Edwards and Hulme, 1995),
especially since, as public benefit organizations, NGOs are not representative of specific constituencies, which can hold them to account. NGOs
were also asked to reflect critically on their relationships with governments
and donors amid concerns that, collectively, they had become "too close for
comfort" (cf. Hulme and Edwards, 1997).

These approaches to "scaling up" necessarily focused attention on the
political roles of NGOs. In the early 1990s, NGOs were already seen as
important actors in civil societies. However, by the mid-1990s there was a

clearer awareness of NGOs operating on a broader canvas, enmeshed in both complementary and conflictual relationships with a range of other institutional entities including trade unions, peasant associations, interest and consumer groups, and faith-based groups (cf. Clarke, 1998; Van Rooy, 1998; Eade, 2000). In turn, both governmental and inter-governmental organizations began to speak of their engagement with "civil society," rather than only with "NGOs." The implication was that NGOs could be unaccountable and narrowly based[4], and that engagement with institutions representative of the poor requires the inclusion of a broader range of civil society organizations. Increasingly, development NGOs participated in broad-based but issue-specific social movements that campaigned for institutional and policy change in areas such as human rights, rural and urban poverty, the environment, and gender and began to frame their activities in reference to a new and evolving civil society discourse. Often such participation provoked disquiet among left-wing activists wary of what they perceived as key organizational features of such NGOs, including their close relationships with foreign donors, their antipathy to hierarchically structured social movements and to class-based struggle and their commitment to short-term media-centered campaigns (see, for instance, Kothari, 1986; Sethi, 1993; Petras, 1999).

In many respects, development NGOs have responded well to these strategic challenges and met the diverse concerns of governments, donors, and left-wing social movements. In most parts of the world today, NGOs are accepted by governments as legitimate actors in civil society and are protected and encouraged, to varying degrees, by government legislation and policy. Continued growth in aid disbursed through NGOs testifies to enduring donor confidence in NGOs, while in many parts of Asia and Latin America (and to a lesser extent Africa) left-wing political parties have embraced NGOs and now work with them in broad-based social movements. In real sense, the diversity of NGO communities has allowed NGOs to be all things to all people and to create vital links between institutions and between levels of decision-making. NGOs have become the "switch points" of the development aid industry and this perhaps has been their most significant contribution to development.

IV. NGOs and Development Governance

An alternative way of viewing NGOs is in terms of their role in governance, both at national level and globally. Governance, or "the manner in which power is exercised in the management of a country's economic and social resources for development" (World Bank, 1992), is now generally regarded as much broader than just government. Within this broad conceptualization of governance, civil society, and NGOs within it, can play a strong role complementary to that of government and the private sector.

For example, Tandon (2003) suggests a number of roles for civil society in governance in the Indian context, and it is easy to see how NGOs are likely to play a big part in each of these ways in almost any country. First, there is the "self-governance of institutions" — NGOs and other civil society organizations have a role in "ensuring standards of transparency and accountability," as well as "clarity of vision" and "the pursuit of public good," in the way that they govern themselves. Second, there is a role in defining public good — contesting the dominant development paradigm and acting to "influence public negotiations for public good" (Tandon, 2003: 70). Finally, there is what may be called a "watchdog" role — ensuring the accountability of market institutions and of government at all levels, including the legislature and agencies providing state services, as well as monitoring elections and compliance with obligations under international treaties (Tandon, 2003: 71–72).

All of these roles are also important for NGOs at the global level, although there are differences not only of scale and scope but also due to the fact that the global system is one of "governance without government" (Rosenau and Czempiel, 1992). This global governance system is still premised on the sovereignty of each individual state and combines this principle with inter-governmental decision-making. However, although there is no world government, there are areas where the United Nations and other multilateral organizations such as the World Bank and World Trade Organization (WTO) increasingly perform some of the functions that would be expected of such a government.

In fact, NGOs, particularly large Northern-based membership organizations engaged in lobbying on environment, human rights, etc., as well as international federations of trade unions and faith-based organizations, have for many years exerted influence at global level. According to Willetts (1996: 46), NGOs have been involved in the United Nations system from its inception and NGOs now "dominate agenda setting" in world politics. In recent years, development NGOs have also turned their attention to the global level, alongside continuing work at community and national levels, in a process of "scaling up" going well beyond what was generally foreseen in the late 1980s or early 1990s.

Thus NGOs of all types have become increasingly important actors in the evolving system of global governance. The number of NGOs with consultative status with the UN Economic and Social Council (ECOSOC) has increased steadily from about 200 in 1950 to almost 1000 in the early 1990s and 1500 by 1995 (Willetts, 1996: 38), and many exert influence within the key organs and bodies of the United Nations. The UN Commission on Global Governance, which reported in 1995, recommended greater participation by NGOs and other civil society organizations in the running of the UN (Our Global Neighbourhood, 1995: 253–262).

Multilateral organizations such as the World Bank have also promoted multi-stranded relationships with NGOs and have introduced environmental and social reforms to their policies partly in response to lobbying and campaigning by NGOs in concert with grassroots movements (Fox and Brown, 1998). They now acknowledge NGOs as important stakeholders in their policy-making processes. National and INGOs, for instance, have played an important role in the preparation of national Poverty Reduction Strategy Papers (PRSPs) and related plans, which guide the lending and grant-making activities of multi-lateral and bilateral donors. Even the WTO, the intergovernmental organization with arguably the most strained relationship with NGOs and the protest movements in which they often participate, has worked to improve its relationship with them and promote dialogue (cf. Moore, 2003).

These developments testify to a significant "associational revolution" at international level and represent a significant challenge to the dominance of inter-governmental decision-making in the global governance system. It is difficult to estimate the number of national or INGOs that seek to influence inter-governmental bodies or to participate in the activities of international decision-making fora. According to one commentator, however, quoting existing research, over 20,000 transnational civic networks are active on the global stage, 90% of which have been established since 1970 (Gaventa, 2001: 4). NGOs represent the core of these transnational networks, complementing a myriad of other organizational forms including trade unions, professional associations, interest groups, and loose networks of protest groups. As a result, concern has shifted from NGOs' national or sub-national role to their participation in a transnational or global civil society. Commentators have raised a number of concerns about the role of NGOs in global civil society but have also pointed to opportunities for NGOs to make significant and radical contributions to international development.

One key feature of the international community of NGOs is the dominance and concentrated "market share" of a small number of NGOs based in North America and Europe. According to Clark, for instance, ten INGOs or international NGO networks had total income in 1999 of $4.64 billion, equivalent to more than 30% of total development assistance channeled through INGOs (and also equivalent, he adds, to Nepal's GNP ($5.3 billion) or the soft-loan arm of the World Bank ($5.2 billion) and more than the entire UK aid budget) (Clark, 2003: 132–133). In addition, however, NGOs from developing countries are largely excluded from international decision-making fora, compounding the power disparities between a virtual NGO oligopoly and the bulk of NGOs in the developing world.

Of the 1550 NGOs registered with the UN Department of Public Information, for instance, only 251 come from developing countries and the proportion of developing country NGOs with consultative status with ECOSOC is even lower (cf. Gaventa, 2001: 9).

Despite the financial muscle of NGOs working at international level and the influence that goes with it, some commentators argue that NGOs fail to maximize their influence and to translate it into impact. According to Clark, for instance, prominent NGOs are often wary of using their clout for fear of losing support and they frequently fail to act in concert (Clark, 2003: 133). "NGOs" Clark argues,

> are potentially immensely powerful but this power is more latent than actual for several reasons. They aren't sufficiently strategic in using their experience to influence decision-makers and publics. Their competitive instincts impede the cooperation with peers that might lead to achieving big transformations. They are averse to political controversy at home for fear of losing supporters and irritating their governments (this especially applies to US-based international INGOs). And they focus too much on mobilising funds in the North to finance work in the South when the transformations that would have the most poverty-reducing impact are probably in the North (Clark, 2003: 149).

Clark goes on to identify a series of dilemmas facing NGOs in the first decade of the new millennium, some of which echo concerns of the 1990s while others point to a radically new landscape:

■ **The dilemma of scale**
   According to Clark, INGO commitment to eradicate poverty entails not only more and bigger projects but also a commitment to the reshaping of development itself. NGOs, he suggests, have considerable scope to leverage institutional and policy change at international level through coordinated and creative campaigning, often with minimal resources. Jubilee 2000 (the international anti-debt campaign), he argues, operated on a shoe string budget yet "probably contributed more to poor countries financially than all operational NGOs combined by wresting for them up to $100 billion of debt relief from unwilling G7 governments and IGOs [inter-governmental organizations] and by ensuring that much of this was redistributed to basic services in those countries" (Clark, 2003: 137). NGOs therefore need to commit themselves to coordinated engagement with the institutions of global governance

and the Western states which exert disproportionate influence over them.

■ **The dilemma of politics**

NGOs face a political dilemma; projects can dent the structure of poverty, "but reforming global policies can tear it down." INGOs are becoming more advocacy-oriented yet NGOs, for instance, tend to be more critical of soft targets (such as the WTO and World Bank) rather than their own governments or transnational corporations (TNCs). NGOs working at international level, Clark suggests, face political challenges in engaging the institutions that matter, often the ones that are closest to home.

■ **The dilemma of the state**

NGOs face dilemmas that arise from their financial dependence on governmental and inter-governmental sources, a dependency that leads NGOs to operate as contractors to the donor community. This dependence, Clark adds, inhibits international NGO advocacy and raises questions about NGO commitment to working with the poorest of the poor (in circumstances where donors focus on the "middle poor") and about what are optimal state–NGO relationships.

■ **The dilemma of networks**

INGOs operate in a competitive environment and many compete for supporters, funds, and idea leadership. This competitiveness however often undermines the need for networking where significant opportunities exist for NGOs to increase their leverage over the institutional and policy environment, especially in the area of advocacy. "If all the main development INGOs" Clark argues, "were to pull together — for say two years — on a major (but soluble) development problem, they could profoundly influence the issue and so perhaps poverty itself" (Clark, 2003: 142).

■ **The dilemma of ethics**

Finally, Clark argues, NGOs must promote high ethical standards in their own agencies and the sector as a whole as they grow in prominence and official funding. Individual NGOs need to address their governance, culture and focus, especially accountability to partners and the communities they serve and not just to donors.

V. Future Scenarios for NGOs

Generally the huge growth in development assistance channeled through NGOs and in their numbers and influence at national and international level seems destined to continue for the foreseeable future. International commitment to the Millennium Development Goals (MDGs) agreed at the UN General Assembly in September 2000 will require, many commentators agree, a significant increase in development aid (a doubling, according to the British government, from $50 to $100 billion/annum). To the extent that it materializes, NGOs will be important channels of this increased aid and the challenges facing them will grow in tandem.

In turn, NGOs may benefit from new funding mechanisms, which shift emphasis from short-term project-specific funding to broader-based strategic goals. In Britain, for instance, the Department for International Development (DFID) supports Program Partnership Agreements (PPAs) with leading British-based INGOs, which provide funding for strategic initiatives including institutional development. In theory, this provides greater scope for advocacy at international level, but, potentially, it also draws NGOs closer to donors (since donor funding is no longer limited to discrete projects but now embraces the core missions of leading NGOs). This may reinforce the process, identified by some commentators, of increased standardization in terms of virtually forced adoption of certain management techniques such as logical framework analysis and strategic planning, and hence a possible loss of focus on the specific needs of local communities (Wallace et al., 1997).

In the 1980s and early 1990s, NGOs benefited from donor antipathy to the state and from a lack of coordination among multi-lateral and bilateral donors. NGOs working in a particular country, for instance, and focusing on a particular issue (such as health) would have enjoyed a diversity of donor funding streams and programmatic aims for health projects, many of them emphasizing NGO participation. This often led to waste and duplication, stretched the capacity of national ministries tasked with coordination, and undermined the policy influence of donors. NGOs may now suffer, however, as multi-lateral and bilateral donors increasingly coordinate their activities and reengage with central governments through new initiatives such as budgetary support and sector wide approaches (where donors pool resources and channel them to support central departmental budgets).

One of the gravest risks to the immediate future of NGOs working on the international stage stems from the new concern with "security" in the aftermath of the Al-Qaeda attacks on Washington and New York on 11 September 2001, the subsequent war in Afghanistan, and the 2003 invasion of Iraq. According to Naomi Klein, US-based INGOs face a threat on two distinct fronts:

> One buys the silence and complicity of mainstream humanitarian and religious groups by offering lucrative reconstruction contracts [in Afghanistan and Iraq]. The other marginalises and criminalises more independent-minded NGOs by claiming that their

work is a threat to democracy. The US Agency for International Development (USAID) is in charge of handing out the carrots while the American Enterprise Institute, the most powerful think-tank in Washington is wielding the sticks (Klein, 2003).

The threat is by no means limited to US-based NGOs. INGOs generally risk being perceived as an arm of Western governments, both by Western governments themselves who provide funding and expect reciprocity and by governments and communities in developing countries fearful of NGO support for Western intervention outside the authority of the United Nations.

This security concern dovetails uncomfortably with a more general threat to the independence of NGOs. As their resources and influence continue to grow in years to come, NGOs will be forced by critics and supporters alike to subject themselves to enhanced forms of self-regulation; for instance, through codes of conduct (Klein, 2003).[5] Both Michael Moore (Director General of the World Trade Organization, 1999–2002, and a far from sympathetic observer of NGOs) and John Clark (former Head of Policy in Oxfam Great Britain, former manager of the World Bank's NGO and Civil Society Unit, and an enthusiastic champion of NGOs and their role in global civil society) have called on NGOs to guard against a backlash by subscribing to codes of conduct or broader ethical standards (Moore, 2003: 200; Clark, 2003: 172–178). Agreeing such standards will be a significant challenge given the complexity and diversity of the international community of NGOs, yet failure to make progress may well provide ammunition to critics on the left and right alike.

Thus the changing nature of development assistance and the strategic challenges which NGOs face in tackling global patterns of poverty and exclusion may force the most prominent organizations to move upstream by gradually withdrawing from direct socio-economic work with communities and with local-level organizations to focus increasingly on advocacy and on policy and institutional change. At the same time, those NGOs which continue to work in local level development may be increasingly obliged to adopt standardized management practices. NGOs may also be forced into a tentative yet bureaucratic process of self-regulation, which may rob the NGO community of its diversity, dynamism, and political weight. Add to this the complex political landscape of a post-9/11 world.

This suggests a difficult journey. There is potential for NGOs to increase their influence and legitimacy in the institutions of global governance, where the key development battles are fought and won. But the same forces threaten to erode the ties of leading development NGOs with local communities across Asia, Africa, and Latin America, which they have traditionally championed and from which their legitimacy has traditionally derived.

Notes

1. As measured in constant 1990 $billion.
2. Also known as community-based organizations (CBOs) or grass-roots organizations (GROs).
3. See, http://www.brac.net/aboutb.htm (accessed March 9, 2004).
4. See, for instance, http://www.undp.org/governance/civilsociety.htm; or http://www.un.org/partners/civil_society/home.htm.
5. One example of such a code is the *People in Aid* initiative (People in Aid, 1997). Although focused mainly on standards in human resource management, particularly as applied to expatriate aid personnel posted temporarily to developing countries, this code proposes standards of "best practice" in other areas as well.

References

Annis, S., Can small-scale development be a large-scale policy?: The case of Latin America, *World Dev.*, 15 (Suppl.), 129–134, 1987.

Clark, J., *Democratizing Development: The Role of Voluntary Organizations*, Kumarian Press, West Hartford, CO, 1991.

Clark, J., *Worlds Apart: Civil Society and the Battle for Ethical Globalisation*, Earthscan, London, 2003.

Clarke, G., *The Politics of NGOs in South-East Asia: Participation and Protest in the Philippines*, Routledge, London, 1998.

Eade, D., Ed., *Development, NGOs, and Civil Society*, Oxfam GB, Oxford, 2000.

Edwards, M. and Hulme, D., Scaling-up the development impact of NGOs: concepts and experiences, in *Making a Difference: NGOs and Development in a Changing World*, Edwards, M. and Hulme, D., Eds., Earthscan, London, 1992, pp. 13–27.

Edwards, M. and Hulme, D., Eds., *Non-Governmental Organizations: Performance and Accountability — Beyond the Magic Bullet*, Earthscan, London, 1995.

Fowler, A., *Striking a Balance: A Guide to Enhancing the Effectiveness of Non-Governmental Organizations in International Development*, Earthscan, London, 1997.

Fox, J. and Brown, L.D., Eds., *The Struggle for Accountability The World Bank, NGOs and Grassroots Movements*, MIT Press, Cambridge, MA, 1998.

Gaventa, J., Introduction, in *Global Citizen Action*, Edwards, M. and Gaventa, J., Eds., Earthscan, London, 2001, pp. 1–16.

Hulme, D. and Edwards, M., *NGOs, States and Donors: Too Close for Comfort?* Macmillan Press, London, 1997.

Klein, N., Now Bush wants to buy the complicity of aid workers, *The Guardian*, 23 June, 2003.

Korten, D., *Getting to the 21st Century: Voluntary Action and the Global Agenda*, Kumarian Press, West Hartford, CT, 1990.

Kothari, R., NGOs, the state and world capitalism, *Econ. Polit. Weekly*, 21 (50), 1986.

Moore, M., *A World Without Walls: Freedom, Development, Free Trade and Global Governance*, Cambridge University Press, Cambridge, 2003.

Our Global Neighbourhood: The Report of the Commission on Global Governance, Oxford University Press, Oxford, 1995.

People in Aid, *People in Aid Code of Best Practice in the Management and Support of Aid Personnel*, Overseas Development Institute, London, 1997.

Petras, J., NGOs: in the service of imperialism, *J. Contemporary Asia*, 29 (4), 429–440, 1999.

Poulton, R. and Harris, M., *Putting People First: The NGO Approach to Development*, Macmillan, London, 1988.

ROAPE, Editorial, *Rev. Afr. Polit. Econ.* (special issue on Democracy, Civil Society and NGOs), 20 (55), 3–8, 1992.

Rosenau, J. and Czempiel, O., *Governance without Government: Order and Change in World Politics*, Cambridge University Press, Cambridge, 1992.

Sethi, H., Action groups in the new politics, in *New Social Movements in the South: Empowering the People*, Wignaraja, P., Ed., Zed Books, London, 1993, pp. 230–255.

Tandon, R., The civil society — governance interface: an Indian perspective, in *Does Civil Society Matter? Governance in Contemporary India*, Tandon, R. and Mohanty, R., Eds., Sage, London, 2003, pp. 59–76.

Thomas, A., Non-governmental organisations and the limits to empowerment, in *Development Policy and Public Action*, Wuyts, M., Mackintosh, M., and Hewitt, T., Eds., Oxford University Press, Oxford, 1992, pp. 117–146.

Thomas, A. and Allen, T., Agencies of development, in *Poverty and Development into the Twenty-first Century*, Allen, T. and Thomas, A., Eds., Oxford University Press, Oxford, 2000, pp. 189–216.

Thomas, A., Carr, S. and Humphreys, D., Eds., *Environmental Policies and NGO Influence: Land Degradation and Natural Resource Management in Africa*, Routledge, London, 2001.

Van Rooy, A., Ed., *Civil Society and the Aid Industry*, Earthscan, London, 1998.

Vivian, J., NGOs and sustainable development in Zimbabwe: no magic bullets, *Dev. Change*, 25 (1), 167–193, 1994.

Wallace, T., Crowther, S., and Shepherd, A., *Standardising Development: Influences on UK NGOs' Policies and Procedures*, WorldView Publishing (in association with Development Administration Group, School of Public Policy, University of Birmingham), Oxford, 1997.

Willetts, P., *The Conscience of the World. The Influence of Non-Governmental Organizations in the UN Syste*, Christopher Hurst for the David Davies Institute, London; The Brookings Institution, Washington, 1996.

World Bank, *Governance and Development*, The World Bank, Washington, DC, 1992.

World Development, 15 (Suppl.), 1987.

Chapter 24

Nongovernmental Organizations, Governance, and the Development Project

Shelley Feldman

CONTENTS

I. Introduction

The decade of 1990s witnessed the increased significance and active participation of nongovernmental organizations (NGOs) in the aid and development nexus. NGOs are social organizations that are represented by a variety of institutional arrangements, patterns of representation, strategies for program implementation, and diverse goals. As many have noted, there are numerous kinds of NGOs — local, national, regional, and international, which employ diverse mobilization strategies, forms of representation, and implementation schemes (Edwards and Hulme, 1992, 1996b; Gordenker and Weiss, 1995; Fernando and Heston, 1997). Others distinguish the heterogeneous grouping of organizations under the title NGO as beneficiary, mercenary, missionary, and revolutionary, each with a different set of goals, opportunities, and challenges (Malena, 2000). But, by almost all accounts, NGOs share a not-for-profit status and are not formally affiliated with local, state, or federal government or private sector entities. According to Gordenker and Weiss (1995: 358), despite the varied names accrued to NGOs — whether independent or voluntary sector, civic society, grassroots organizations, private voluntary agencies, transnational social movement organizations, or non-state actors — as organizations, they "consist of durable, bounded, voluntary relationships among individuals to produce a particular product using specific techniques." They are devoted to managing resources and implementing projects with the goal of addressing social inequalities, social problems, and short- and long-term crises. Most, although not all, local and national NGOs are ideally concerned with transferring skills, literacy, and credit to those with limited access to such resources and to representing NGO members in national policy discussions. International and transnational NGOs, in contrast, are more likely to focus on mobilizations that provide a voice for the generally invisible and voiceless in international fora where discussion and debate concerns issues of trade, labor, the environment, and human rights.

As already well-acknowledged, the current development agenda of neo-liberal reform includes policies which reduce state controls on private enterprise and promote deregulation, privatization, and reductions in social service expenditures. These economic policy choices are supported by a value shift from community and collective social responsibility to that of individualism, coupled with a commitment to governance and democracy, wherein rights and social obligations are presumed to be negotiated in the absence of a central authority. For some, this shift represents a "break from the conventional wisdom that social development is primarily the responsibility of states and markets," since it is based on the increasing influence of NGOs in the development project (Fernando and Heston, 1997: 1). For others, however, NGO participation in the neo-liberal agenda can compromise their goals and carries with it a loss of autonomy and the possibility of co-option. In this chapter we ask: How do NGOs constitute and adapt to this new economic and political environment? How do NGOs realize their goals in the context of neo-liberal reform and a professed concern with good governance? I suggest that the interests, goals, and strategies of NGOs have a complex and often contradictory relationship to the current and dominant development project of neo-liberal reform. On the one hand, NGOs provide the rhetoric and institutional logic accruing to the concepts of decentralization, participation, and empowerment, each a hallmark of governance interests. On the other hand, the substantive meanings that NGOs may give to such concepts and practices are often compromised in collaborative relations and appropriated by transnational institutions, the donor community, and national policy makers.

The chapter is divided into four substantive sections. In the first, I examine governance as a discourse and practice in the hope of providing a backdrop against which to understand the role of NGOs in the current development project. In the second section, I examine the shifting role of NGOs within the development project to contribute to discussions about their promise as representatives of the disenfranchised and their vulnerability to having their values and interests co-opted. In Section three, I provide a historical view of the shifts that characterize the institutional and organizational capacity of NGOs as well as their critical contributions to contemporary discussions of development as a negotiation between states, markets, and civil society. In the final section, I emphasize the values outlined in an alternative development paradigm to showcase key interests, contradictions, and tensions that arise at the intersection of NGO-governance relations.

II. Governance as Discourse and Practice

Governance refers to the complex processes, institutions, and patterns of negotiation through which citizens and collectivities articulate their interests, mediate their differences, and define and exercise their rights and social obligations. As a social process, the practices of governance incorporate a range of institutional capacities, class and group interests, and in the contemporary development project, the values of western democracy or modernity. When scholars and practitioners refer to "good governance," their concerns include the importance of participation, transparency, and accountability grounded in a liberal view of individuals.[1] They also include a commitment to ensure active and broadly representative negotiations over legitimate forms of behavior, the exercises of power, and the building of consensus over rules and regulations.

Although the evidence is mixed, there is the belief that "good (i.e., democratic) governance is essential for a healthy economy" (Edwards and Hulme, 1996a: 961). Good governance is concerned not only with insuring that states create fair political and legal environments for both citizens and others but also in working with the private sector and popular constituencies to formulate and realize shared goals and standards for living. Implicitly, the goals of good governance are realized when the equitable treatment of people, regardless of economic status, gender, ethnicity, or race, underlie social norms and practices. Theoretically, one might say that good governance is realized when liberal democracy and equality constitute the practice of social life.

From this point of view, it is not surprising that approaches to questions of good governance are increasingly premised on efforts to secure globally the goals of peace and security that include, at least ideologically, the aim of realizing equality, democracy, and individualism. But, it is crucial to emphasize that these global goals complement, rather than displace, the focus of the multi- and bilateral aid community on reconfiguring the capacities of individual nation-states to ensure such goals.

Governance and NGO participation in development initiatives became a focus of concern at the close of the Cold War with the realization of the growing influence of multinational companies, and recognition by the UN that "multilateral agreements [were] reducing the authority of national governments over many areas of policy that [were] crucial to sustainable development" (Bigg, 2000). This recognition helps to situate the UN and other bilateral and multilateral agency's policy commitments to strengthen global governance and to sustain and extend a transnational dialogue among civil society organizations, including the business community, in ongoing policy debates. The new policy commitment is assumed to build good governance by incorporating inter-governmental relations, cross-national institutional exchanges — including the private sector, transnational institutions, and increasingly, NGOs and other transnational collectivities — within broadly conceived grassroots initiatives.

To respond to these goals globally, the UN system, for example, recently re-engaged the NGO community as participants in their global fora,[2] no doubt in partial response to the active role of NGOs as critics at these meetings. Their critique of development strategies and practices includes, among other issues, challenging the social costs of structural adjustment policies, new GMO food production strategies, as well as the limited enforcement or concern with environmental degradation. NGO contributions to the 1995 Social Summit in Copenhagen and the Beijing Women's Conference that same year, as well as at the Rio Summit and subsequently in Seattle, Quebec, Davos, Genoa, and elsewhere, has extended the reach and range of issues to which NGOs lend their support. Importantly, these fora have created new alliances between northern and southern NGOs who share the struggle for social justice. While their interests are diverse and, at times, even oppositional, NGOs recognize that the costs of economic reforms or environmental degradation are often borne unequally and that the interests served by economic restructuring are often those of global capital.[3]

In his comments as chair of a UN panel on civil society and global governance, Fernando Henrique Cardoso (2003: 3) identified four key areas in processes of global integration: (1) citizen participation, (2) the vital role of the UN, (3) risks and opportunities of the present international scenario, and (4) strategic questions for building towards global governance — that center on contemporary tensions between NGOs and governments. As he notes:

> As a consequence of the difficulties to "discipline and democratize globalization," the radicalization of the "anti-globalization movement" led to disruptive forms of public protest and to the questioning by a segment of civil society of the very legitimacy of some multilateral institutions. Many NGOs feel frustrated with the obstacles and barriers to substantive participation in policy decision-making and in the actual implementation of agreed programs ... Conversely, many governments react to increased interaction with civil society, perceiving their growing influence in the decision-making process as a threat to their national interests and sovereignty.

Cardoso's comments are instructive because they center on questions of discipline and democracy, what can arguably be interpreted as the failure of governments to discipline their citizens and subjects by holding opposition in check. Such an interpretation highlights the unequal power relations between representatives of civil society and the interests of those who support particular governments. It also reveals the power of NGOs to demand recognition for critical and challenging positions and to do so on behalf of a presumably large popular constituency. Yet, despite the commitment to good governance and collective negotiation, Cardoso suggests an anomalous understanding of national interests and sovereignty since NGOs are presumed to be outside these interests as governments seek to limit their participation in national decision-making. Negotiation and debate between governments and NGOs, and between NGOs and the aid community, including the UN, thus seek to restrain the full participation of all members of civil society in debate over national policy formation. These relations thus depend on a critical analysis of the question of rights as well as of organizational legitimacy, structure, and strategy. For those concerned with governance and representation it also requires that we ask first, how NGOs and government or multilateral and bilateral agencies collaborate so that the interests of the popular classes can inform policy; second, what the costs of these collaborations are for NGO legitimacy and autonomy; and third, whether NGO representation actually enhances or constrains participation of the popular classes. But, whatever the focus of debate, it is important to stress that even though we treat civil society and government as if they are distinct social configurations; each can only be understood in their mutual constitutiveness.

III. The Emerging Neo-Liberal Agenda

During the 1980s, national capacity building as a focus of development assistance was slowly recast. This is reflected in the growing commitment to the creation of more porous national boundaries, new or reformed global institutions and trade relations, and the enhanced integration of global production.[4] At the policy level, the shift from import substitution to export-led growth was expected to lead to greater export earnings that would ensure debt repayment and solidify a development strategy of comparative advantage. The shift also promoted the denationalization of public sector industries and removal of agricultural subsidies, replacing these with export processing enclaves designed to provide the infrastructural capacity for the incorporation of cheap, third world women's labor into the expanding international division of labor and production. Incorporated as conditions for continued aid, these structural adjustment policies included fiscal reform, institutional reorganization, and the removal of subsidies on agricultural commodities. Policies of this kind altered the sustainability of small family-farm agriculture, a shift that contributed to increased land lessness, forced urban migration, and high rates of under- and unemployment, including among first generation, lower-middle class college graduates.

In southern countries NGOs were also being transformed from loosely organized institutional arrangements to formal organizations that were increasingly regulated by government. Ministerial requirements were instituted, rules and regulations for external support were formulated, and donor agencies, including bilateral aid programs, began to demand formal fiscal and program accountability. The advent of computer technology, record-keeping schemes, and formal proposals and budgets increasingly accompanied competition among NGOs for resources and established new relationships between donors and NGOs. For example, by the 1990s, in the wake of the need for "adjustment with a human face," NGOs were increasingly viewed as important allies to be cultivated, rather than adversaries to be ignored or undermined, in realizing the goals of good governance and liberal reform: they were close to the people, had credibility with the rural and urban poor, and were not only able to provide training and resources to the poor, but also an ideological safety net in securing the legitimacy of their agenda. NGO credibility resided in their clear commitment to gender equity, improving resource access to the poor, particularly of credit, and subsidizing training for low-skilled workers that would prepare them for the global assembly line. Thus, following in their tradition of arbitrating the interest and needs of the poor, NGOs continued to play a critical role in identifying, articulating, and implementing programs that addressed the social and economic costs of structural adjustment for the poor.

These shifts also promoted an ideology of individualism which retained the language of self-reliance embedded in the nationalist development project made popular in the immediate post-colonial period, but which relocated social sustenance as the responsibility of individuals who were to be increasingly expected to join the wage labor market. According to Eade and Ligteringen (2001: 13) and Storey (2001), the new language adopted by both development institutions and international financial institutions actually embraced the language of NGOs — participation, empowerment, and equity[5] — if only "to serve as a rhetorical cloak for their own neo-liberal agendas." Not co-incidentally, in other words, shifts in the practice and strategy of development altered the discourse about development, opened new areas for discussion, review, and policy engagement, and brought to the forefront interest in questions about governance, civil society, participation, and representation. It also centered attention on the salience of decentralization in decision-making and strategies for mobilization, both cross-nationally as well as globally.

What is distinctive about these discussions is that they were of concern, not only to those in the banking, industrial, and manufacturing sectors, but they were also central to NGOs and other civil society groups. In fact, one might say, as Tandon (2001) suggests, that the alternative development paradigm was an important contribution of NGOs to the development debates and practices at the end of the 20th century. This alternative paradigm highlighted three distinct thematic concerns: local-level development, small-scale initiatives, and an integrated approach, the latter demanding that people be understood as embedded in their surroundings and circumstances rather than as isolated individuals. Importantly, the alternative development paradigm emphasized participatory engagement between people and institution but has since become a term with a range of meanings and practices associated with it. It can, but need not be, based on equality among representative voices. Significantly, this new discourse offers an alternative understanding of inter-state relations, one that establishes a context for reframing relations between northern and southern NGOs, broadening their range and representation, and expanding their professed mission.

IV. The Emergence and Institutionalization of NGOs

A broad historical view of the rise of NGOs, signals the institutionalization of informal resource transfers and welfarist approaches to redistribution[6] that has long characterized relations within kin groups and communities (Feldman, 2003). Informal economic transfers generally include local collections for the needy, intra-family exchanges, and individual investments in community development. In countries like Bangladesh, for example, such exchanges take the form of *zakat* (alms) or constructing schools and mosques in order to enhance family status. From the 1950s through the 1970s, national groups built on this tradition by developing organizations to respond to immediate social and economic crises that included war, famines, and earthquakes. By the late 1970s, these so-called relief organizations became increasingly formalized as development NGOs. Framed by the principle of state sovereignty within a global network of inter-state relations, they were incorporated into a broad developmentalist agenda that was characterized by programs that would lead to capitalist modernity centered on the values of national economic self-sufficiency, production, trade and industrial diversity, and self-reliance. Policies supporting these programs promoted nationalization, import substitution, subsidies to agriculture and infant industries, and social welfare interventions for the poor.

During this period, northern NGOs, often with bilateral support, were prominent in the transfer of new agricultural technologies and practices, such as high-yielding rice varieties (HYV), and in developing family planning programs for women. In their shift from relief to development organizations, often with support from foundations rather than bilateral and multilateral agencies, southern NGOs centered their work on humanitarian aid and the distribution of goods and services. They introduced functional literacy, credit, and extended family planning programs for women, all credible programs that enabled the government to respond to new international demands for interventions that had positive gender impacts.[7] Focused on enabling or enhancing the earning capacity and sustainability of small-scale agricultural and non-farm producers, NGO initiatives mediated the costs of growing landlessness and the instability of family-farm production. They also provided local, grassroots institutions that were viewed by many as parallel to those operating at the national level. While national institutions such as the Integrated Rural Development Program sponsored by World Bank supported family planning, credit, and training to rural women, NGOs usually sought support locally and from international foundations.

But, the limited success of many national programs, particularly in alleviating poverty and the conditions necessary for "take-off," eventually led many NGOs to challenge the policies, implementation strategies, and practices of the bilateral and multilateral development agencies. As advocates for the disenfranchised, NGOs were particularly critical of the increasing participation of the donor community in national policy reform, especially early instantiations of structural adjustment lending and tied aid agreements. They also began to query the dependency of countries on donor assistance and the concomitant generalized relations of dependency and inequality that characterized them.[8] Not surprisingly, the primary focus of the NGO challenge during the early 1980s was the complicity of their respective governments in the policies of the World Bank, the International Monetary Fund, and bilateral agencies.[9] As advocates for extending resources and representing the poor in national policy debates, however, some NGOs took the opportunity to negotiate with multi- and bilateral agencies for resources to meet the demands left behind by the state agencies. Others took a strategic distance from the aid community in ways that secured their autonomous actions and acitivites. The donor community, recognizing the short-term costs of structural adjustment lending for the poor, began to court NGOs hoping to utilize the special services for which they had a known advantage: working well with local communities, promoting small-scale initiatives, and knowledge of their membership.

For example, early efforts by national NGOs called for restitution for those who were either left out of development[10] or forced to carry the burden of its supposed "short-term" costs. From the point of view of the World Bank, as Paul Nelson recalls, "there was a growing number of World Bank projects in which NGOs have a role and there is a deepening of these operational relationships" (Nelson, 1995: 1). Some NGOs self-consciously chose to collaborate with the Bank as part of a strategy to pursue reform from within. Others felt that NGOs were better able than state institutions to meet the needs of the poor and supported initiatives that redirected donor assistance from national institutions to their programs. Still others refused multi- and bilateral aid altogether or, drawing distinctions between good and bad donors, accepted assistance from the former while boycotting the latter. Whatever the rationale, relationships between NGOs, donor agencies, and national governments at this historical juncture were significantly recast with relations between NGOs and the development community based more on complementarity than on a critique of the development project as such. Said differently, it is safe to say that at this time in the careers of NGOs, there was no equivalent to the anti-globalization efforts characteristic of recent transnational NGO initiatives.

But notwithstanding the seeming convergence of NGO and bilateral and multilateral aid initiatives, critiques offered by NGOs made their efforts, both programmatically and politically, impossible to ignore. For example, in addition to servicing the needs of the donors, NGOs provided an experimental context in which to test alternative development approaches that focused on small-scale, decentralized, participatory projects. Politically, NGO challenges exposed both the unequal costs of development and the fragility of donor success, which helped to establish a new context for popular mobilization and democratic voice. In short, their critiques of the unequal costs and implementation practices of dependent development positioned NGOs to both view and to respond to the turn towards neo-liberal policy reforms that would shape their future direction. By creating a space in civil society, NGOs implicitly demanded to be taken seriously by the aid community because they offered access to populations of concern to donors and because they challenged the legitimacy and direction that the development project had taken. Yet, in so doing, NGOs raised the issues and concerns that would ultimately be mediated in ways that would compromise and co-opt many of their demands.

V. Interests, Contradictions, and Tensions

Today, NGOs are institutionalized participants in civil society. Organization-ally, they now have formal constitutions, lines of mobility for staff, and competitive hiring practices. They maintain a highly professionalized and well-trained staff and are represented at many national policy-level meetings as well as at international fora. NGOs now offer long-term career employ-ment with opportunities for professional training. Staffs are hired with highly specialized expertise and certification is now available through degree programs in North American and European institutions (Stiefel and Wolfe, 1994). The technical skills of staff include project development and evaluation, program implementation, needs and social impact assessment, and grant-writing, each of which has helped to transform formerly loosely knit communities of humanitarian volunteers working for relatively low wages into highly professionalized organizations with some, if only a few, staff who receive an international wage rate. In Bangladesh, for instance, by 1994, there were approximately 1000 NGOs with more than 120,000 field staff. While not all were staffed by highly trained personnel or had secure funding from the aid community, others have become almost self-sustaining enterprises by operating retail outlets for the sale of NGO-made goods for a large and growing market, managing a hotel and conference center, and providing training both in research and project implementation. Organizations such as the Bangladesh Rural Advancement Committee (BRAC) and the Grameen Bank Project/Trust are supported by research activists and scholars, of which many have graduate degrees from North America.

Important about this process of institutionalization is that large and self-sustaining programs and projects displace small, participatory and represen-tative activities that meet the specific needs of local clienteles. This new focus often leads to bureaucratization, which also undercuts the flexibility that was created by the new institutional structures of the NGO movement. As well, the successful and profitable new enterprises operated by large NGOs are now increasingly dependent on specialized staff for their success. In these situations it might be fair to conclude that NGOs have compromised the values and agendas that were the hallmark of their initial promise — local, small-scale and decentralized decision-making with a diverse membership representing the heterogeneity of civil society.

NGO institutionalization, however, does not only refer to changes in the internal structure of an organization, it also refers to new areas of collaboration between institutions. For example, collaboration between NGOs and various multi- and bilateral agencies has had short- and long-term consequences for NGO autonomy, democratization and governance practices. As Gordenker and Weiss (1995: 368) suggest, "cooperation is not cost-free for NGOs," and as they continue, the opportunity costs include increased pressure on personnel, resources, and perhaps, most importantly, the possibility of diminished credibility. While it is often the case that sharing tasks between the UN or the World Bank and an NGO with whom it may collaborate are generally complementary, the relationship is generally one of dependence and inequality. In most cases, the NGO depends on the bi- or multilateral agency for funding and then generally implements an agency's program. This means that decision-making tends to reside with the donor agency. Such collaborative arrangements increase the likelihood of greater bureaucratic control of the NGO by the donor agency and, in some cases, by the NGO leadership. For the leadership, accountability to the agency may take priority over that to the community they serve since realizing agency goals will more likely sustain funding and more likely ensure program sustainability and job security. Pragmatically, this means that since project funding and extension is usually based on measures of success or completion (number of girls in school, amount of credit extended, or organizing community groups), encouraging processes of collective participation and decision-making among program members, or working with a country's poorest communities, may be of decreasing importance to the NGO. In these circumstances, building democratic participation and representing poor communities in public fora may be thwarted, risking, as well, the hope of NGOs to enhance participation, representation, and good governance.

Another challenge to the democratic and participatory impulse of NGO initiatives is their movement towards offering national programs to primarily poor urban and rural dwellers. These national programs often parallel a country's health care, education, and micro-credit infrastructure. This relatively recent program commitment can actually displace government resources and help the shift towards privatization and reduced support for the national social service sector. Shifting international assistance to the NGO sector to provide these services transforms both the institutional role of NGOs as well as that of the public sector. It also ties NGOs to the need for long-term funding, a position that jeopardizes their flexibility — a feature of NGOs which makes them initially favored by local users — and their ability to both represent their constituents and maintain a critical stance towards public policy. These concerns are well expressed by Farrington and Bebbington (1993: 188) who suggest that "the claim for [NGO] legitimacy comes closer to that of a private sector operator — being able to provide the service at the best price," and raising a deeper set of issues reflected in the possibility of rewriting the "social contract" between government and its citizens.

As resources are privatized using the NGO sector, not only citizen rights are open to question, but issues of accountability can also be compromised, since ensuring accountability may no longer be centrally monitored but fragmented by the implementing NGO. This makes accountability of grassroots staff difficult, even as they reside close to the membership and members have the ability to withdraw or be non-compliant with program goals. Additionally, there is evidence that despite the many achievements of NGOs, they have still failed to reach the world's poorest, the population to whom they ought to be most committed (Streeten, 1997). Since program success as defined by donors relies on quick and visible results, social safety net programs and support for those without initial resources (e.g., literacy, skills, or capital) are not as likely to be supported by NGOs as are micro-credit schemes for those with the promise of success. The result is the continued exclusion of a country's poorest. Such exclusion does not contribute to enhancing the voice and decision-making power from below but reveals the possibility that NGOs may no longer be at the forefront of helping poor communities participate in local fora on their own behalf. As a result, one can conclude, along with Nelson (1995: 177–178), that the increased engagement of NGOs and the World Bank "is changing NGOs more than it is changing the Bank," and in so doing, is compromising "NGOs' potential significance for effective democratization." In such circumstances, institutionalized NGOs, as distinct from transnational social movements, are likely to serve as brokers rather than as catalysts for change, thus compromising their promise to build good governance by creating new relations of representation and voice for those once excluded from decision-making.

VI. Conclusion

NGOs have been of central concern in debates on participation, local decision-making, decentralization, and the spread of good governance. Building on a tradition of informal resource redistribution between communities and kin, NGOs first organized as relief services and then as development organization to help meet the needs of those excluded from the economic benefits of the development project. Since the 1970s, and in the context of changing poverty reduction strategies, NGOs have advocated for the poor in national policy dialogues, eventually becoming instrumental as critics of national policy reform. Building coalitions among NGOs within particular nation-states, they critiqued not only selected policy choices but also ultimately the development project as such. Today, some NGOs operate in parallel with government social service sectors while others join transnational coalitions to seek redress for the poor and against environmental degradation, global fiscal policies, and the growing role and control of multilateral and transnational enterprises.

National governments and the donor community, and increasingly multinational corporations, have had various relationships with NGOs: ignoring them, challenging their right to be included in policy fora, and then forming partnerships with them to draw on their particular expertise — knowledge of their members, small-scale, and participatory practices. By the 1990s, the aid community was collaborating on a variety of projects with a broad range of NGOs, and governments were inviting NGO representatives as participants in national policy dialogue. Not surprisingly, as a result of these collaborations, today many NGOs operate more as brokers than as catalysts for changing the goals and direction of the policies and practices of either the development community or national governments. For some NGOs, these collaborations have compromised their position as critics. For others, they remain ever vigilant that donors will co-opt their partisan representation on behalf of the world's poorest, in exchange for providing them with institutional stability and secure livelihoods, while failing to actually meet the needs of their constituencies.

For still others, they formed alliances with those in the broader southern community and, eventually, with northern NGOs as well. These alliances and exchanges are fashioned in ways that lead to broad-based challenges of the direction and interests of multinational capital and the multilateral agencies that represent them. At the present juncture, transnational social movements, international NGOs, and alliances among northern and southern NGOs continue to be a strong voice in demanding greater participation and recognition of the multiplicity of interests that need to attend to planning for a collective, representative, and participatory global future.

Notes

1. Much of the concern within the international donor community is with issues of corruption as a focus of governance and a growing literature has begun to highlight this focus. It is not, however, the focus of the present paper.

2. UN General Assembly Resolution 1296, agreed on in 1968, has been the basis for determining the official criteria for the participation of NGOs in UN processes. In 1993 there was agreement to review and update the criteria for participation to accommodate NGO interests (Bigg, 1997). There is an enormous literature on NGOs and the UN System. See, for example, Gordenker and Weiss, 1995, particularly their extensive bibliographic references.

3. An entirely new discourse of transnational social movements would appropriately be included in this discussion since they overlap with and also extend discussions of NGOs. Unfortunately, it is impossible to explore the varied ways in which transnational social movements provide a challenge to the interests of global capital, represent a voice of the poor that is not synonymous with nationally based NGOs, and reflect how new forms of global production and capital find their parallel in new social relations.

4. See, for example, the enormous literature on the New International Division of Labor, flexible specialization, and the global assembly line followed by that on the WTO and the GATT. For many southern countries this strategy led to the creation of export processing zones, tax holidays, limits on health and safety standards and rights to organize, subsidized land and electricity, including for the construction of roads and highways to enhance their competitive advantage for DFIs. Few backward linkages were forged to sustain this national development strategy.

5. See, for example, Narayan et al. (2000).

6. Literature on crowding out, that is displacing private resources with public ones, is partially based on the recognition that there continues to be informal transfers between households, especially those between kin and community relations.

7. See, for instance, new U.S. requirements that identified gender impacts as part of specific project and program assistance and which followed the passage of the Percy Amendment in 1975. Other donor countries also enforced requirements for receiving development assistance especially during and after the UN Decade for Women.

8. While there remains disagreement as to the reasons for the shift toward neoliberal policy reform and the social and economic costs of structural adjustment, there is agreement that many of the costs identified fall unequally on the poor. This is suggested in the World Bank response — from rejection to acceptance — to the findings of the now classic *Adjustment with a Human Face* (Cornia et al., 1987).

9. It would be a mistake to homogenize the aid community since debates among them and their varied challenges were carefully noted and negotiated by the NGO community. Differences were also negotiated among donors, forging alliances among some countries to the exclusion of others. See, for instance, the Like-Minded Group — Norway, Sweden, Denmark, Canada, and the Netherlands — who worked together to formulate a health policy (and subsequently other policies) to complement the World Bank focus on population control focus in Bangladesh.

10. This was a phrase often used to justify the emergent women's programs that came to characterize many NGO programs begun during the 1970s. This

phrase is misleading, however, since those excluded from national or NGO resources are nonetheless implicated in the construction and effects of new policies and programs. Said differently, shifts in national policy have consequences for all members of a polity, not only its beneficiaries.

References

Bigg, T., *NGOs and the UN system since the Rio Summit*, www.globalpolicy.org/ngos/ngo-un/gen/2000/1122htm: 1–5 (accessed 27 March 2004), 2000.

Cardoso, F.H., *Civil Society and Global Governance*, www.globalpolicy.org/ngos/ngo-un/gen/2003/0619cardosopaper.htm: 1–8 (accessed 27 March 2004), 2003.

Cornia, G.A., Jolly, R., and Stewart, F., *Adjustment with a Human Face*, UNICEF/Clarendon Press, New York, 1987.

Eade, D. and Ligteringen, E., Eds., *Debating Development: NGOs and the Future Essays from Development in Practice*, Oxfam GB for Oxfam International, Oxford, England, 2001.

Edwards, M. and Hulme, D., *Making a Difference: NGOs and Development in a Changing World*, Earthscan Publications, London, 1992.

Edwards, M. and Hulme, D., Too close for comfort? The impact of official aid on nongovernmental organizations, *World Dev.*, 24, 961–973, 1996a.

Edwards, M. and Hulme, D., Eds., *Beyond the Magic Bullet: NGO Performance and Accountability in the Post-Cold War World*, Kumarian Press, West Hartford, CT, 1996b.

Farrington, J. and Bebbington, A., *Reluctant Partners? Non-governmental Organizations, the State, and Sustainable Agricultural Development*, Routledge, London, 1993.

Feldman, S., Paradoxes of institutionalization: the depoliticisation of Bangladeshi NGOs. *Dev. Pract.*, 13 (1), 5–26, 2003.

Fernando, J. and Heston, A., Introduction, *Ann. Aapss*, 55, 1–17, 1997.

Gordenker, L. and Weiss, T.W., Pluralising global governance: analytical approaches and dimensions, *Third World Quart.*, 16, 357–388, 1995.

Malena, C., Beneficiaries, mercenaries, missionaries and revolutionaries: "Unpacking" NGO involvement in World Bank-financed projects, in *Questioning Partnership: The Reality of Aid and NGO Relations, Institute of Development Studies*, Fowler, A.F., Ed., 31 (3), 19–34, 2000.

Narayan, D., Patel, R., Schafft, K., Rademacher, A., and Koch-Schulte, S., *Voices of the Poor: Can Anyone Hear Us?* World Bank and Oxford University Press, Washington, DC, 2000.

Nelson, P.J., *The World Bank and Non-Governmental Organizations: The Limits of Apolitical Development*, Macmillan Press, Houndmills, Basingstoke, Hampshire, 1995.

Stiefel, M. and Wolfe, M., *A Voice for the Excluded: Popular Participation in Development: Utopia or Necessity?* Zed Books in association with the United Nations Research Institute for Social Development, London and Atlantic Highlands, NJ, 1994.

Storey, A., The World Bank, neo-liberalism, and power: discourse analysis and implications for campaigners, in *Debating Development: NGOs and the Future Essays from Development in Practice*, Eade, D. and Ligteringen, E., Eds., Oxfam GB for Oxfam International, Oxford, England, pp. 104–117, 2001.

Streeten, P., Nongovernmental organizations and development, *Ann. Am. Acad. Pol. Soc. Sci.*, 554, 193–210, 1997.

Tandon, R., Riding high or nose diving: Development NGOs in the new millennium, *Dev. Pract.*, 10, 319–329, 2001.

Chapter 25

Aiding Local Governance: How Effective Are Small Funds

Jo Beall

CONTENTS

I. Introduction

Governments, aid agencies, and development organizations aim for their interventions to help disadvantaged people and enhance their capacity to help themselves. Unfortunately, achieving this outcome can prove elusive. All too often large amounts of money directed at economic development, alleviating poverty, and empowering marginalized people end up in the wrong hands or give rise to ambiguous or contradictory results. The intentions are often good but either the conditions are not propitious or the mechanisms by which funds are disbursed are inappropriate. International agencies have experimented with a wide array of instruments for providing development assistance, ranging from full interest-bearing loans to concession-based finance, tied aid, unconditional grants, and various forms of conditionality. Decisions as to what kind of assistance to provide, where to direct it, and how to deliver it are based on factors such as the priorities and capabilities of recipient countries, what donors want out of the process, what is being done by the private sector, nongovernmental organizations (NGOs), and other donors, as well as changing trends and fashions in development thinking and practice. The latter are often associated with ensuring that the impact of assistance is felt not only on the national level but also on the sub-national, local, and micro-levels.

Since the demise of project-based lending, attention has been most often focused on the macro-level, whether in terms of structural adjustment programs (SAPs), sector-wide approaches (SWAps), or the increasingly popular macro-level aid instrument of direct budget support (DBS). This seeks to provide financial support directly to recipient government budgets which in turn use their own systems rather than conforming to the management and reporting systems of donors. DBS is usually provided by general budget support, which covers financial assistance as a contribution to the national budget, with any conditionality focused only on policy measures related to overall budget priorities. It is also provided by SWAps whereby financial aid is earmarked for a discrete sector and channeled by existing sectoral mechanisms. An important motivation for moving toward DBS, coming in the face of mounting criticism of aid conditionality, is to increase the control and ownership of recipient governments over their country's national development. Nevertheless, even under ideal conditions, DBS or any other form of macro-level aid can never be sufficient or appropriate in all circumstances. In addition, meso- and micro-level instruments will always be needed. It is in recognition of this that local funds have become a favored instrument for targeting assistance at the local or micro-level, as they are thought to ensure overall reach and to be an effective way of meeting pro-poor development goals.

Local funds constitute a wide waterfront including World Bank supported social funds at one end, which actually involve quite large sums of money, and at the other, small grants designed to kick-start a process or to promote engaged citizenship in some way. While the former originated in the 1980s as a way of ameliorating the negative social impact of structural adjustment policies, the latter are as old as politically informed philanthropy itself. Funds are controversial and have been heavily criticized in the development literature, often for good reason. Almost, by definition, they are the product of external agents, and in all cases, the external agents are in a stronger position than the the clients or beneficiaries, simply through holding the purse strings and through information and power asymmetries. Herein lies one of the primary contradictions of funds as a mechanism for development aid, especially if they are intended to empower poor people and communities to engage gov ernment more effectively. More recently, local funds have been designed to address this contradiction and most seek to enhance the livelihood capabilities and rights of disadvantaged people through increasing access to resources, while at the same time, removing the barriers to people's participation in local decision-making. Hence, contemporary local funds are also usually concerned to promote the effectiveness and accountability of governance institutions (Jørgensen and van Domelen, 2001; Beall, 2002; Satterthwaite, 2002).

This chapter is concerned with the evolution and effectiveness of local funds as a means of promoting local governance alongside development. Not easy to define — local funds are both co-financing instruments and funding agencies — local funds are ideally demand driven and partnership oriented, encouraging the involvement of local and other actors, including government, in initiatives designed to disburse modest resources swiftly and simply to where they are needed most. By no means a panacea, they do not always directly reach the poorest, and even indirectly, the interests of disadvantaged people can sometimes be eclipsed. However, local funds can be an effective if not an exhaustive social development strategy and there are a growing number of examples of increased downward accountability as they become more confident and competent in matters of local governance. With this in mind, and highlighting the features that set them apart from conventional methods of delivering aid, the chapter considers the evolution of local funds. It describes some of their more generic features and provides some lessons from implementation of local funds programs in the context of development cooperation.

II. Evolution and Development of Local Funds

Social funds have been a part of the repertoire of international development agencies, particularly the World Bank for almost 20 years, evolving over time and coming in different shapes and forms. There is no universally agreed definition of a social fund, although a useful characterization is provided by Jørgensen and van Domelen (2001: 91):

> We propose to define social funds as follows: agencies that finance projects in several sectors targeted to benefit a country's poor and vulnerable groups based on a participatory manner of demand generated by local groups and screened against a set of eligibility criteria. There are agencies that would meet these criteria but are not called social funds and there are agencies that are called social funds that do not meet these criteria.

Social funds were developed from the early 1980s as a strategy to counteract the social costs of the macro-economic SAPs promoted and supported by the World Bank and the International Monetary Fund (IMF). During the early stages, social funds programs were supposed to compensate those who had been impoverished by adjustment processes through anti-cyclical income maintenance and social expenditure programs. In the later phases, generally the poor were addressed through promotional measures such as employment creation or public works programs and through community-based provision of social services (Cornia, 1999: 2).

The first social funds, known as social emergency funds (SEFs), were implemented during the 1980s in Latin America and Africa with the assistance of the Bretton Woods institutions, notably the World Bank and the Inter-American Development Bank (IADB) as emergency relief funds.[1] SEFs, which were introduced in tandem with SAPs, had the transfer of resources to the poor through multi-sectoral programs as their goal, such as employment generation and support for social services.[2] SEFs were mainly managed outside of state institutions and were entirely reliant on external funding. The emergency funds were presented as an innovative alternative to the conventional welfare systems, which could respond more swiftly and effectively than conventional welfare systems, because of their relative autonomy from governments. With time, it became clear that addressing the social impact of structural adjustment policies was likely to take a long time and SEFs were replaced with social investment funds (SIFs), designed to operate over a longer time horizon and to expand the supply and utilization of necessary infrastructure and social services (Cornia, 2001: 8). They are funded by governments as well as donors and are not necessarily set up as independent organizations. Some are autonomous agencies with nonprofit legal status, while others are located within government ministries. Thus, it was that social funds acquired a more permanent stronghold as a critical social development strategy, with greater emphasis on delivery.

Social funds evolved into local funds, which became an important mechanism for social risk management. This coincided with a turn in development thinking during the late 1990s toward rehabilitation of the state and government institutions (World Bank, 1997). It would probably be fair to say that when social funds were initially conceived, they were seen as vehicles for bypassing ineffective and recalcitrant governments. However, by the end of the 1990s, less emphasis was placed on circumventing or undermining the state and more on eliciting "good governance," a now familiar yet contested notion in the development lexicon that refers to the relationship between governments and local people. In addition to efforts improving the accountability, transparency, and competence of governments, enhanced governance involves increasing the confidence and capacity of local communities to take them on (Devas, 1999: 1). While there is little consensus as to what constitutes good governance, there is general agreement that bad governance is not good for most and especially the poor (Goetz and Gaventa, 2001). Against this background, around the turn of the millennium, there was an expansion of funds that fostered local governance alongside development. For example, the World Bank expanded its social funds portfolio to include municipal development funds (MDFs), which are designed to strengthen institutional capacity at local level, and the UNCDF created the local development funds (LDFs) with similar goals. Even philanthropic organizations such as the Ford Foundation joined in, instituting its Asset Building and Community Development Program. It was at this time that local funds took over from social funds as a primary mechanism for channeling aid resources to the local level.

Another critical influence on the design and delivery of local funds was the challenge fund model. This was a child of the West and more particularly the United States where they are manifold in number and constitute part of the funding repertoire of local authorities, state governments, private companies, charitable trusts, libraries, museums, research organizations, and universities. The idea behind them is to get people, groups, or communities to compete for funds, on the basis of putting forward innovative projects. The idea came to the United Kingdom under Conservative Party rule in the early 1990s in the form of the City Challenge. Bailey et al. (1995: 64) explain what was envisaged and what was new at the time:

> The innovative features of the initiative [City Challenge] were that deprived neighbourhoods were to be targeted by independent regeneration agencies using public money and the leverage of private sources set up to prepare and implement action plans over five years. Action plans were required to identify a "vision" and to specify with clear targets both property-related and "people-orientated" strategies.

Initiatives ranged from quite large area-based projects, such as Enterprise Zones and Urban Development Corporations, right down to neighborhood level and more people-orientated projects. An important part of the idea was that challenge funds would catalyze other resources from the private, public, and voluntary sectors and would stimulate development through enhancing the competitiveness of local areas. Three elements of challenge funds have come to critically inform the development of local funds in international development cooperation. They are the encouragement of inter-sectoral partnerships, competition with local partnerships bidding for funds through the submission of innovative projects, and "hands off" management in the form of "light touch" monitoring and oversight.

Like social funds, challenge funds are not without their critics, particularly in the context of developing countries, where the efficacy of setting up disadvantaged groups and communities in competition with each other is questionable. However, for better or worse, the challenge fund model has increasingly come to influence international development cooperation and local funds. It contains two critical components, which parallel social funds as well as two elements that add something new to the mix. In terms of parallels, like social funds, local funds have a social development or poverty alleviation focus, and this frequently relates to the development of infrastructure and services. In terms of differences, social funds, especially in their earlier incarnation, did not emphasize partnerships and nor were they particularly concerned to involve the private sector. It was these two dimensions that came to inform the evolution of local funds in developing countries. In summary, contemporary local funds have emerged out of the experience of both social funds and challenge funds. They aim to alleviate poverty through the financing of activities that include social service programs and infrastructure, such as schools, clinics, water supply, and sanitation; economic programs such as support to micro-credit, small, medium, and micro-enterprises (SMMEs), and other forms of local economic development; environmental protection; and physical infrastructure such as roads, civil works, irrigation, land reclamation, and natural resource management (Narayan and Ebbe, 1997; Jørgensen and van Domelen, 2001).

Often explained in terms of social risk management, it is believed that through support to such activities through local funds, poor people, and communities will be equipped to exercise greater control over their own lives and leverage over local governments and other institutions. As such, it is argued that local funds can be a tool for the empowerment of poor people and marginalized groups. Development agencies are urging that local people make a greater contribution in planning, designing, implementing, maintaining, and operating small-scale projects (Parker and

Serrano, 2001: 1) and local funds are an important aid instrument toward this end. The MDFs and LDFs are examples of funds with this focus, providing resources and technical and professional assistance toward decentralization efforts (Parker and Serrano, 2001: 32). Hence, the UNCDF (1999: v) is able to declare of its LDFs, "[O]ur local development programs give newly elected officials the resources to govern and invest — while also opening up local planning processes so that ordinary people have a say in the decisions that effect their lives." In theory at least, then, the interactions between confident and empowered citizens and responsive local officials and politicians should create better local governance and guarantee a more enabling environment for local development. However, the challenges encountered in practice are considerable and not all local fund agencies are well equipped to meet them.

III. Characteristics of Local Funds

Local funds are first and foremost a means by which *small resources* are targeted directly toward local communities, according to predetermined local criteria. Although individual grants may be small, considerable amounts of money are spent on local funds. For example, as of May 2001, the World Bank alone had spent $3.5 billion on social funds projects (World Bank, 2002: 1). Secondly, local funds adopt various mechanisms to help ensure that their funds reach those in most need. Local funds should be *swift and flexible*. This imperative derives from their origin with social funds, which, as policy instruments, were designed to transfer resources quickly and efficiently under emergency conditions, "in order to mitigate temporary states of deprivation caused by economic crisis and adjustment" (Fumo et al., 2000: 4). In order to reduce the effort local groups need to make in accessing resources, a lot of time and effort has been spent on simplifying and refining procedures for reviewing, supporting, and funding applications and projects, through capacity building and "light touch" monitoring. There are a number of constraints that serve to impede progress. For example, even with simple procedures, some of the poorest applicants need a lot of support, and on the side of donors and local fund agencies, it is difficult to break the habits of a lifetime and to reduce the levels of managerial scrutiny. The watchwords for successful local funds are oversight, guidance, and stewardship. These more hands-off and arm's length approaches are a departure from conventional administartion of aid instruments but are the crucial elements of good practice in local fund management.

Thirdly, precisely because local funds are local, it is believed that people are better able to decide what they need and to influence what they get.

As such, a critical dimension of local funds is that they are *demand driven* and operate in response to demands arising from local communities. Requests can also come from NGOs working with community-based organizations and from local governments and private firms, as long as they are working directly in partnership with representatives of local organizations and communities. The demand-led feature of local funds is also offered as a mechanism for effective targeting as only those in need will apply. However, in reality, local funds often go to those who know how to apply and to report on their activities according to donor monitoring and evaluation requirements, and they are not necessarily those in need. That is why it is so important that procedures and practices are kept short and simple to ensure that local funds reach down to those places other funding mechanisms cannot reach. Fourthly, local funds are supposed to *stimulate partnerships* that will mobilize or *leverage resources* locally, leading to increased resources and cooperation among multiple local stakeholders.

A fifth feature of local funds is that they usually offer grant funding as opposed to loans but require *co-financing*. In other words, applicant organizations have to provide matching funds. This is believed to limit the benefits to those who actually need the service and to create a sense of ownership among the applicants. This undoubtedly works and has advantages over early models of development that evolved within the context of project aid. However, this also serves to limit those who can take advantage of local funds. At a stakeholder workshop of the City–Community Challenge (C3) Fund in Lusaka, the problems posed by match funding for poor communities were described by one of the participants as follows:

> A chicken and a pig were travelling together. After a hard nights travelling they woke up bright and early. The chicken [read donor] said that they ought to have some breakfast. The chicken said it would contribute an egg. The pig [read community] asked what it was expected to contribute. "Bacon, of course" replied the chicken. "Bacon is not like an egg" said the pig. "To give you bacon for your breakfast I must die."

This poses a problem for donors on two counts in that most international development agencies purport to be driven by pro-poor agendas and as such it is problematic if their grant aid is premised on principles and mechanisms that exclude the poorest. It has been argued in the context of social funds that the requirement of match funding has only transpired in practice in a small percentage of them (Tendler, 2000: 117). However, in the more innovative local funds, of which the C3 pilot project in Zambia is one, creative ways have been developed to measure the contribution, in kind, of community-level partners. These go beyond traditional contributions such as community labor and serve to put a value on local knowledge and expertise.

While all these characteristics are important, the main reason why local funds are popular with donors is that local agencies manage the funds, examine the projects, disburse the money, and monitor and evaluate progress and outcomes. Hence, the transaction costs of overseeing a large number of small projects are transferred from the donor to these agencies, reducing the cost of the intervention. Satterthwaite (2002: 179) has put it well:

> Ask any staff member from an official bilateral agency or the World Bank to manage fifty times the number of projects with an average cost of one-*fiftieth* of their current project portfolio, and they would resign. Any international agency would face an impossible administrative burden and far higher staff costs if its central offices had to support a multiplicity of (often) low-cost, diverse, distant initiatives, especially if each proposal had to be reviewed on the ground and monitored and evaluated to ensure compliance with its initial objectives.

Local funds can be deployed easily and quickly and without the complications and delays attached to bilateral government-to-government aid. As such, they are beginning to replace the "small projects" budgets of many bilateral and multilateral donor agencies. They also fit well with a development cooperation climate, where international donor agencies are criticized for agenda setting and for unwarranted interference in domestic policy agendas. As local fund agencies and trusts are often autonomous organizations, or are designed to become independent at some future stage, donors can be seen to be adopting an arm's length approach while at the same time, directing resources to poor people. For those donor agencies pursuing a policy of DBS, where no strings attached transfers are made to partner governments or sectors, local funds offer a compatible mechanism to channel much smaller amounts to less ambitious and more circumscribed initiatives at the local level.

IV. Experience of Local Funds

This section focusses two local funding mechanisms used as aid instruments by donors in urban development in Africa. The first profile is of the *Agences d'Exécution de Travaux d'Intérêt Public pour l'Emploi* (AGETIPs), which are the executing agencies for funds for public works that operate across many francophone African countries, particularly in West Africa. The World Bank and the International Labor Organization (ILO) fund AGETIPs, with the latter providing support to capacity building, learning, and dissemination of the model and to the international association of AGETIPs called AFRICATIP. AGETIPs developed as a form of social funds but some also have the characteristics of more recent local funds, as is the case with the fund reviewed here, *L'Agence d'Exécution des Travaux Urbains (à haute intensité de main-d'oeuvre)* (AGETUR), which is an urban focused labor-intensive public works program in Benin with a strong emphasis on partnership, notably with the private sector. AGETUR is reviewed primarily in terms of whether it supports the reputation gained by AGETIPs for getting funds to where they are needed most and whether it creates sustainable livelihoods or risk management. The second profile is of the City-Community Challenge Fund, known as C3, a local fund pilot program funded by the United Kingdom's Department for International Development (DFID) in Uganda and Kenya. It is based on the challenge fund model and with the specific goal of creating engaged citizenship and responsive government through partnership in small urban development projects. DFID has been supporting a range of Challenge Fund programs, which act as a complementary aid instrument to DBS and which seek to target aid more directly at the sub-national level. In addition to addressing urban poverty and urban governance, the C3 methodology sought to transfer management responsibility, transaction costs, and capacity building to local partners and to attract other partners to the initiative. The section on C3 focuses on the experience in Uganda and assesses the efficiency of the methodology for supporting large numbers of small-scale community initiated projects in poor urban areas and whether it was able to generate more effective state–citizen interaction.

A. *Francophone African AGETIPs and AGETUR in Benin*

The *Agence d'Execution de Travaux d'Intéret Public* (Public Works and Employment Agency) was the name of the social funds agency set up in Senegal in 1989 and since then the model has been generalized to a number of countries, in francophone Africa, such as Benin, Burkina Faso, Chad, The Gambia, Madagascar, Mali, Mauritania, Niger, Senegal, and Togo. They operate under the name *Agences d'Exécution de Travaux d'Intérêt Public pour l'Emploi,* with the same acronym (AGETIPs). AGETIPs are delegated contract management agencies for public works. While in typical social funds, the social funds agency selects eligible sub-projects and channels funds to them, AGETIPs in addition to performing both of these functions, prepare and execute the elected sub-projects on behalf of the sponsoring agency, which surrenders authority for the execution of the sub-project to the AGETIP management until delivery of the completed works. Hence, the typical AGETIP is a dual agent with responsibilities for providing infrastructure and for implementing projects. They were set up as national executing agencies for these activities, on a competitive basis but in the form of private not-for-profit NGOs. This is because government agencies, were not well equipped procedurally to deal with small entrepreneurs and community contractors who need regular and timely payment, if they are to stay in business and deliver on employment intensive operations.

AGETIPs have a number of critical features. First, they were able to absorb the high transaction costs involved and most have developed considerable contract management expertise by using relatively simple systems and procedures. Indeed, some of them are now sufficiently large and experienced to take on the role of coordination and have delegated execution authority. Secondly, AGETIPs are concerned with poverty alleviation and social protection through employment-intensive programs for public works, usually infrastructure. Thirdly, they use the private sector for community-based urban infrastructure projects, sometimes seeking out small-sized and community contractors or affording a mechanism for participation (so that communities can propose projects). Fourthly, AGETIPs are seen as promoting sound development practice using local-based materials. Indeed, the ILO has worked toward transferring lessons on the technical, social, and economic benefits of this approach not only to other countries but also to government ministries. Finally, because of the rapid spread of AGETIPs since the establishment of the pioneering agency in Senegal, they are regarded as a classic demonstration projects and a good example of "learning by doing." In conclusion, enthusiasts see AGETIPs as multipurpose agencies that involve the private sector in poverty reduction through the provision of employment and infrastructure, that promote community participation, and that offer the prospect of building up competitive small- and medium-sized entrepreneurs in local construction industries.

Detractors of AGETIPs point out that they are still highly dependent on external funding and therefore unsustainable. Secondly, they are said to put in motion a substitution effect whereby governments are allowed to abdicate their responsibility for social protection and poverty reduction because AGETIPs are thought to take care of these areas. A third problem is that because AGETIPs operate outside of the restrictive bureaucratic environment of government, often for very understandable reasons, they can undermine Ministries of Public Works as the main overseers of infrastructure programs. This has the potential of harming long-term relations with politicians and government officials and of compromising government structures. It is perhaps for this reason that recently, AGETIPs are more often focused on the execution of public works, while municipalities are reclaiming responsibility for the selection of projects. Finally, because AGETIPs are agencies that recruit private contractors and are often run by people drawn from the private sector, they are open to accusations of patronage and malfeasance, particularly where there are strong personal networks among the business community. It is for this reason that oversight and procedures have to be firmly executed. For the smaller contractors who are less well equipped to take on and follow through on complicated project management, this can be difficult, laying much of the responsibility on the AGETIPs themselves, which in turn have to be squeaky clean.

The *Agence d'Execution des Travaux Urbain* (AGETUR) in Benin operates in the country's two main cities, Porto-Novo the official capital and Cotonou the seat of government and the economic capital of the country. It was established in 1990 as a legally constituted NGO charged with contracting, overseeing, and managing individual projects concerned with delivering urban infrastructure and services. It employs labor-intensive strategies that provide an income to poor people. The agency is also concerned with the development of small- and medium-sized contractors as well as community contracting. Works carried out through AGETUR are financed by various international financing institutions such as the World Bank, the European Union, the French Agency for Development, the African Development Bank, the West African Development Bank, the Canadian Agency for International Development, Swiss Cooperation, DANIDA, and the International Development Association, along with contributions from the Benin government as well as local neighborhood associations. Hence, AGETUR is highly reliant on external donor funding, even though it is contracted to government and forms part of Benin's poverty reduction strategies (Fanou and Grant, 2000). The country has a number of policies and programs meant to reduce poverty, including the Social Action Program, ILO support to the informal sector, labor-intensive Urban Works Programs, and projects financed through social funds. What binds most initiatives is their focus on either employment creation or assistance to micro-enterprises.

Urban development in Benin comes under the Project of Urban Rehabilitation and Management (PRGU), which was set up to rehabilitate urban amenities such as hospitals and schools and to improve the urban environment and land use. This was in response to Porto-Novo and Cotonou failing to cope with the demands arising out of urbanization. It had a focus from the outset on poverty alleviation, which was to be through remunerated employment for the jobless and the provision of basic infrastructure and services to poor urban communities. The two were linked through a focus on based-intensive construction or maintenance, for example, roads, drains and amenities such as markets, schools, and health centers. Two operational agencies act as project managers on behalf of the government. The first is the *Society d'Etudes Régionales d'Habitat et d'Amenagement Urbain*

(SERHAU-SEM), which carries out all pre-implementation studies for planned projects under the program and assists the municipalities of Cotonou and Porto-Novo. The second is the AGETUR, which had the over-riding objective of providing an income to large numbers of people negatively affected by Benin's first SAP, while at the same time, improving the infrastructure of Cotonou and Porto-Novo.

AGETUR is in charge of executing government works contracts, largely concerned with road and sewerage construction. Work is carried out through local small and medium enterprises which are invited to tender for contracts and who are assessed partly on the basis of the number of skilled and unskilled laborers they employ. Although contracted to government, which identifies the project and holds AGETUR to account, the organization is specifically sponsored by donor agencies. AGETUR works in tandem with the *Centre de Promotion et d'Encadrement des Petites et Moyennes Enterprises* (CEPEPE), which was set up with UNDP funding to build the capacity of local enterprises. Unlike some AGETIPs, AGETUR does not work in isolation from government. It has support from SERHAU-SEM, which is engaged in the identification of priority areas for investment through a range of research activities, including community level research. It also has support from CEPEPE, which plays an essential role in the capacity building of the small and medium enterprise sectors and which is critical to the execution of AGETUR projects. Within AGETUR itself, the relatively small number of staff (26 people) are all Beninese. Before the establishment of the agency, all construction works in Benin were researched and designed by overseas companies (Fanou and Grant, 2000). Now, local companies bid for major public works programs alongside international ones, evidence that the development of AGETUR has enhanced local professional and entrepreneurial capacity in some way.

In reviewing what AGETUR has achieved, operating costs while not among the lowest, were not disproportionately high. Moreover, it seems that AGETUR has escaped the worst excesses of malfeasance with the agency's director having the reputation of being one of the few local organizational heads that "does not automatically receive 10% of all work profits" (Fanou and Grant, 2000: 35). In terms of sustainability, the agency has been regularly commissioned to undertake work directly by donors, giving rise to further job creation opportunities and not all of the projects tendered for have been capital projects. AGETUR also allocates contracts to local firms for maintenance works and services such as waste management, suggesting a level of sustainability in the contracting and employment of some of the activities they oversee. What are these jobs worth and what is their contribution to sustainable livelihoods? Contractors do employ some permanent employees. These are usually for jobs requiring a level of trust, such as tallymen and watchmen and the incumbents are highly dependent on the enterprise in one way or another. They may be indebted to the contractors or owe loyalty on other bases. However, for most jobs, they are temporary and essentially manual in nature. Hence, it is only very low-income people who take them up. Evaluative research shows that the people who avail themselves of jobs on AGETUR projects are those with large families, who generally report poor access to health care and low school attendance on the part of their children. They are all men, mainly of the marginalized Fon and Adja ethnic groups and most are rural migrants to the cities. As workers, they live in makeshift shelters in marginal settlements and lead fairly unstable lives (Fanou and Grant, 2000: 35).

In terms of the employment creation element of AGETUR's goals, it was designed to target the poorest by keeping wages sufficiently low so as not to attract the better-off to the projects. In this, they have been successful and the work opportunities appear to operate primarily as emergency funds or reception funds for migrants to the cities. In other words, they provide a basic level of income for very poor people rather than sustainable jobs with viable wages that could support a worker or even a worker and his or her dependants. It seems, therefore, that AGETUR is better at providing a social safety net for the most needy than sustainable livelihoods and risk management for a large number of poor people. Nevertheless, AGETUR has been more successful in terms of enterprise development. Since its inception, a total of 107 small and medium enterprises have been used to execute its projects, alongside a larger number of sub-contractors who work with the enterprises that win the actual contracts. This suggests that the tendering process works fairly well and that there is a relatively wide-spread of contractors benefiting. Community development projects are also part of its brief and might involve the construction of a local health center, main and feeder roads, and pavements and drains. Community projects have also included waste collection, market gardening, and environmental protection activities as job-creating spin-offs from area upgrading (Fanou and Grant, 2000).

In assessing AGETUR's impact on poverty reduction more broadly, the results are mixed. It is undoubtedly the case that in an infrastructure poor country, the two main cities have not found it easy to keep up with basic service provision and AGETUR fulfils an important role in this regard. In addition to investment in development, the issue of maintenance appears to be well taken care. What is more difficult to discern is whether the quality of the infrastructure will stand the test of time. It can be the case that labor-intensive strategies are often more expensive and less reliable than capital-intensive approaches. For example, machine tarred roads are cheaper than those laid through manual labor. A focus on employment creation can become even more expensive, if there is poor or inexperienced workmanship and the absence of good quality control. These are important issues to bear in mind when local funds are used to support small contractors and low paid workers in construction and infrastructure provision.

B. C3 Pilot Program

The primary aim of the C3 program, which was piloted in Zambia and Uganda, is to assist organizations of the urban poor and their representative local authorities to undertake localized initiatives that provide resources for small-scale innovative activities of broad community benefit. The Infrastructure and Urban Development Division (IUDD) of DFID provided £1 million for a 2-year pilot program, which began in September 2000. An extension phase of a further year was agreed within this budget and another extension was agreed with an increased financial contribution of £300,000 made via UN-Habitat. Critical to the C3 model was the development of effective and transferable mechanisms that could channel multiple small-scale funds to such initiatives, in the context of urban development partnerships involving organized communities, government at different levels, civil society organizations (CSOs), and the private sector. The secondary aim was to assess the viability of challenge funds and more specifically the C3 methodology, as a mechanism for international development agencies to reach and empower the urban poor, within the context of DBS and SWAps. During the pilot phase, the Local Government International Bureau (LGIB) and Care International U.K. (CARE) were the international program managers for Uganda and Zambia, respectively. Their local partners were the Uganda Local Authorities Association (ULAA) in Kampala and the Lusaka-based NGO, Urban INSAKA (UI), both of which now run C3 in the postpilot phase. A Steering Committee and International Project Liaison Unit (IPLU) operated in the United Kingdom and the external evaluator was a participant observer on both. Governance of the program in Uganda was through a National Coordination Committee (NCC) and in Zambia through the National Advisory Group (NAG). In country, C3 was implemented in two cities, Kampala and Jinja in Uganda and Lusaka and Ndola in Zambia. What follows is a discussion of the implementation of C3 in Uganda.

Although predominantly a rural country[4] urbanization in Uganda is growing due to increased population growth and rural-to-urban migration. A city designed for 600,000 residents, Kampala is now estimated to have 1.5 million residents, as well as a much larger daytime population who work and do business in the city and use its infrastructure and facilities. Jinja, although a much smaller city faces different pressures, not the least being economic downturn due to financial and industrial flight during the conflict of the 1980s and high levels of long-term unemployment. In this context, assistance to urban areas is highly necessary. Another important dimension of the overall context in which C3 operates in Uganda is the decentralization process. Until 1986, government was tightly centralized and there was very little role for local government in decision-making over resource use and allocation. Thereafter, local governments were progressively granted more authority but there is still some way to go.[5] With these factors in mind, C3 sought to assist disadvantaged urban communities in improving livelihood opportunities,[6] while at the same time, building their capacity to use decentralization processes more effectively. The flip side of this was to enhance the capacity of local authorities to respond more readily to community demands for development. Under the management of the ULAA and the stewardship of the NCC, the C3 program in Uganda was able to ensure that the city councils of Kampala and Jinja accepted the challenge of involving the poorest sectors of their local communities in decision-making and of themselves devising ways of leveraging new resources.

In Kampala, C3 was piloted in Kawempe Division, which is one of Kampala's four divisions and which embraces the most densely settled part of the capital city. Kawempe has an estimated population of over 200,000 and is a mixed income settlement and infrastructure levels, with the area as a whole not connected to the main sewerage system. Within Kawempe, there are many informal settlements with poor water supply and sanitation, no drainage, inadequate solid waste collection, and minimal amenities. Formal employment is scarce and the majority of low-income residents engage in informal business. The C3 program in Kawempe at first concentrated almost exclusively on micro-credit schemes, despite this not being the intended focus of C3. Nor was this a particularly original approach, undermining one of the principal aims of the pilot — innovation. However, micro-finance initiatives were strongly advocated for by the Local Implementation Unit (LIU) in Kawempe and when projects are demand-driven, people often come up with the ideas they already know about. In this situation, it was difficult for the ULAA and NCC to refuse, despite misgivings about their capacity and expertise in an already crowded field. Grants were provided ranging from the equivalent of around £16 to £800. Projects included fish farming, poultry projects, mirror manufacture and framing, broom making, furniture making, charcoal making, and small fresh produce stalls. An overwhelming proportion of beneficiaries are individuals, and the match-funding element was supposed to take place though returns and onward lending to a new round of beneficiaries. To ensure that this happened, a Beneficiaries' Association was formed to provide a regulatory and coordinating role and to take responsibility for managing the revolving fund.

During the early phases of implementation, C3 in Kawempe exhibited all the classic problems of micro-finance and social funds, including resources not reaching the poorest, elite capture, and unsustainable income-generating projects. Nevertheless, over time a number of changes took place. Strong local level structures ensured that individuals who benefited were held to account and that politicians using C3 for campaigning purposes were exposed. Moreover, through word of mouth, an active LIU and a vigorous local publicity drive, news of the program spread and the rate and coverage of applications and grantees has increased. Moreover, the Kawempe Division was being encouraged to shift its focus toward other areas of support and, following a visit to Mpumudde Division in Jinja, applications for social and other services started coming through. From the viewpoint of government, there is more direct engagement with C3 in Kampala at divisional level. This is understandable given that it is in Kawempe that the most tangible benefits were to be found. These accrued not only to grantees and residents but also to council employees, often hampered in their jobs through lack of resources and poor motivation. For example, the council's community extension workers in Kawempe rarely had the opportunity to move out of their offices before C3 required them to do so and provided some resources with which they could work.

In Jinja, C3 was implemented in Mpumudde Division, recognized as the most disadvantaged and least densely settled of Jinja's three divisions. With a population of over 20,000 and covering an area of 1,156.5 ha, Mpumudde is a relatively sparsely populated peri-urban area of the municipality with the highest level of unemployment. The economy of Jinja was devastated by the factory and enterprise closures that followed the flight of Ugandan Asians who were persecuted by Idi Amin and it has not yet fully recovered. In Mpumudde, the residents identified lack of shelter as a priority need and hence the focus of C3 was primarily on developing a low-cost housing program. This was also not particularly innovative and again the ULAA and NCC had some misgivings. Houses comprise four rooms and are built with a manual sand or cement block press. They are plastered and with corrugated iron roofs. Community members on a rotation basis build them with eight households building a set of eight houses. The average time to construct a house is currently 21 days. Each household is allocated a grant of £1,400. The materials amount to £1,000 per house, plus an additional £200 and each house comes with a further micro-enterprise grant of £200 that householders can use to generate income to repay the costs of building. In addition, individuals have benefited from training in block making and business skills. Grants have also been made to groups, for example, for the repair of septic tanks and for mowing machines to be used in micro-enterprise.

The C3 project in Mapumudde has the advantage of visible delivery and has demonstrated a fairly accountable allocation process. From the outset it was effective in leveraging additional resources through effective engagement with the local authority. Unlike Kawempe, where for a long time the local council simply kept a watching brief, in Mpumudde, the C3 process benefited from strong commitment and oversight from the Assistant Town Clerk who saw in C3 an opportunity for the Jinja Municipality to be responsive to citizen priorities and to leverage additional resources. The Municipality has been proactive in making links between C3 and other projects, programs, and organizations in Jinja. It has leveraged significant funds from alternative sources, while ploughing in additional resources of its own. It is difficult to pinpoint why Jinja outperformed Kampala Municipality. It may be that C3 got off to a more rocky start in Kampala, that personalities such as the Jinja Town Clerk played an important role, or that C3 is seen as relatively small fry in a capital city where there are multiple and sometimes competing interventions and agendas funding governance issues. In contrast, in Jinja, where resources are more limited, the C3 methodology became more swiftly embedded in local authority practice and it had a broader impact on engagement local communities and local government.

If the focus of activities lacks innovation and a decentralization process is already well underway in Uganda, it is worth asking how C3 adds value. It is clear that in both sites C3 was successful in linking local politicians to local citizens and it has facilitated organized citizens in engaging more effectively with their representative local authorities, both in Mpumudde and Kawempe. Having tangible and accessible resources around which to negotiate, however minimal, has been an extremely effective catalyst in this regard. Through C3, people have learnt a range of things from the best price for a bag of cement, to asking for and keeping receipts, to effective routes of access to decision-makers and the issues on their agendas. In terms of the officials of local councils, their image has improved as well, no longer being seen as overwhelmingly preoccupied with "main roads and drains" but also concerned with neighborhoods and people. One of the most positive outcomes of C3 in Uganda has been the impact of the pilot in terms of increased transparency and accountability. Even in the difficult Kawempe Division where political capture saw funds being channeled to party political supporters, many of whom failed to meet even the most lenient poverty criteria, monitoring and capacity building from C3 structures, along with support from council extension workers, served gradually to inform people of the program and its aims. This together with regular publicity, notably through community radio and notice boards, has encouraged grantees and potential grantees to now regularly harass members of the LIU, if there are problems with selection and management of the funds. In the process, they are learning that they can hold their leaders to account.

The C3 structures were developed to encourage upward and downward accountability, notably the presence of C3 representatives on the LIUs and LIU representation on the NCC. In its second phase, C3 is spreading to and being taken up by other urban centers. The focus has shifted toward strengthening the institutional arrangements for enhanced local governance and encouraging the spread of C3 beyond an area-based approach. Here, the potential for linkage into Uganda's Local Government Development Program (LGDP) is great. This operates countrywide and is a program designed to transfer development funds to local governments on a grant basis. As such, C3 as a methodology operates as a useful counterpoint, assisting local people in community organization, in engaging politicians and officials and in holding them to account, at the same time, as addressing immediate material needs. As the shift takes place from implementing a pilot to extending C3 in Uganda, the role of ULAA is changing from one of simply management of funds to one of developing and spreading the methodology. This is a more appropriate activity for an association of local authorities, and ULAA is well placed as an organization to undertake the broad task of disseminating and rolling out the C3 program, given its strategic location representing local governments and the decentralization process in Uganda. On its own, C3 is not very much different from hundreds of other small grant programs. However, in concert with the broad decentralization process in Uganda and the Local Government Development Program, C3 is an essential component of a broader strategy and one that is reaching down to levels where larger programs cannot reach.

V. Opportunities and Limitations of Local Funds

An obvious objection to local funds is that they are open to political interference and manipulation. In a number of contexts, social funds have become a political tool to reward constituents, recruit new voters before elections, or to win back those disaffected by losses suffered under austerity programs. It is no wonder then that Tendler and Serrano (1999) are emphatic that those that work best are the social funds most distanced from and autonomous of government. However, as the experience of C3 demonstrated, *local* funds embedded within a system of decentralization and with the explicit goal of engaging local government, can serve to assist citizens in holding both officials and politicians to account. Moreover, local funds represent a broad church that embraces diverse organizations and institutional set ups. As such, not all of the problems and objections associated with social funds necessarily present as challenges to *local* funds. For example, social funds are noted for being targeted towards the poor. This is also the case for some local funds, but when targeted at deprived areas, they can be more effective. Many local funds are much smaller, less dependent, and more agile than social funds, which, on the contrary, are growing exponentially and becoming increasingly bureaucratized.

A more valid critique of local funds is that they remain heavily dependent on external funding and are therefore not sustainable. For those who are broadly supportive of local funds concerns remain about their sustainability and whether in the absence of donor support local funds can continue over the long-term (Satterthwaite, 2002: 185). This is a particular concern in countries where affordability on the part of poor people makes cost recovery difficult. It is with this in mind that new directions in local funding now include the setting up of national local funding bodies, such as Ford Foundation's Freedom Foundation and the *DFID* human rights and governance fund, Manusher Jonno, both in Bangladesh. The aim here is that local funding bodies are created and endowed, which can set agendas and time frames that are appropriate to local conditions and imperatives.

Although small funds can reach parts that larger funds cannot reach, the examples cited in this chapter and broader experience reviewed elsewhere (Beall, 2005) suggest that local funds are not necessarily a good instrument for targeting poverty. Kanji (2002: 247) suggests with regard to social funds that the key rests with how they articulate with wider national poverty reduction policies, arguing cogently that they "are no substitute for wider economic and social policies which address the distribution of material and social assets in highly unequal societies." The same would hold true for local funds. Tendler (2000) has argued in respect of social funds that they have contributed insignificantly to the reduction in unemployment and to poverty alleviation in the countries where they operate, when compared with other more supply-driven and centralized programs with the same goal. Moreover, she argues that the jobs that are created tend to be of a poor quality, badly remunerated, and often temporary in nature. These observations can be made of AGETUR in Benin, for example, although in the absence of other mechanisms of social protection, local funds might represent a useful option for some and the infrastructure dimension has both a direct and indirect impact on poverty reduction. The important point is that local funds cannot be the last word on poverty reduction and social protection, which as Kanji (2002: 247) points out, "require a wider panoply of policy approaches." When local funds are designed to simultaneously promote participation and good governance, these objectives are not always mutually compatible with those of poverty reduction.

The demand orientation of most aid supported local funds is not without its problems. One problem is that funds have criteria set by the funding agency, which limit the demand-driven nature of local funds because local actors have to choose their activities from within a predetermined set of options (Narayan and Ebbe, 1997: 2). Even when local funds agencies are very open as to what they fund and genuinely try to be responsive to innovations from the ground, as is evident from the C3 experience in Kampala, people only know what they know. In other words, local communities cannot easily envisage what things could be like or what they themselves might achieve with a little assistance. As a result, they only request funding for things they have seen other people do and hence innovation is more limited than is anticipated by those engaged with local funds at the design stage. In real life, local funds client participation often involves them having to choose from a menu of sub-project options or replicating the activities and requests for funding they have seen initiated by a neighbor or another community or group. Another classic problem with demand-driven approaches is that while they may be beneficial to some sections of the client population, they can tend to keep the poorest or most marginalized groups out of the frame. The latter have a more limited capacity to articulate their demands, to come up with match funding and to sustain projects that meet all the criteria and requirements laid down by donors and local fund agencies. As such and due to inevitable power differentials within a locality, it has been argued that local funds often advance the interests of those who are already better-off (Tendler and Serrano, 1999; Fumo et al., 2000). This may be less of a problem if the goals of funds are more toward enhancing local governance than targeting poverty. Nevertheless, the demand orientation of local funds will always be limited as long as local funds depend on the government or external benefactors and donors for resources.

While earlier social funds were singularly unconcerned about participatory approaches, the latter have become articles of faith in many contemporary local funds. The conventional wisdom is that by broadening client participation in the development projects supported by local funds, connection to and ownership of the resulting activities will be built and fostered. Participatory approaches are also thought to ensure that the aims and objectives of projects match those of the people involved with and impacted by them and to increase government accountability through the involvement of active and engaged citizens. Despite the great claims made for participation in development and the fact that for much of the 1980s and 1990s, it was a central tenet of development practice (Chambers and Conway, 1992; Chambers, 1995, 1997; Narayan et al., 2000a, b), there is a new cynicism about the value and purpose of participation (Cooke and Kothari, 2001; Mosse, 2001) and the effectiveness of institutions to deliver on this agenda (Cleaver, 2001). In local funds, the issues around participation are who participates and who benefits. As the experience of C3 in Uganda demonstrates, sometimes conflicts develop between individuals and groups in a community when some use the opportunity to advance their own rather than collective interests, undermining the good intentions informing local funds and the projects they support. Equally, however, the C3 experience shows that those who are given voice through participatory approaches can and do hold others to account.

Participation in local funds is also sought through the principle of co-financing, which is believed to ferment buy-in on the part of those who have raised or provided the match funding. Here, the dangers associated with who participates and who benefits are very real. It is not unknown for the least powerful in a community, often women or the youngest members, to be the ones to provide the time and labor while more powerful members are most likely to benefit. For example, a road may be built with community participation outside of a local notable's house or business. When things like this happen, the empowerment claims of local funds have also to be regarded with circumspection. It is admittedly difficult for funders and sometimes no less difficult for local fund agencies to identify let alone control social relationships and institutions operative at the local level. Nevertheless, as others have pointed out (Uphoff, 1992; Cleaver, 2001), there is a tendency in development more generally to recognize the ways in which informal institutions operate but nevertheless to concentrate on perfecting the operation of formal institutions. This certainly holds true in the case of local funds. Moreover, to the extent that local funds are initiated to promote participation and local governance agendas, this can also be fraught with danger and caution needs to be exercised over the political use made of "the local." As Mohan and Stokke (2000: 263) have argued, "[L]ocal participation can be used for different purposes by very different ideological stakeholders."

This chapter has reviewed some of the challenges facing international development agencies wanting to reach the poorest people and the institutions of governance closest to them. The multilateral and bilateral programs reviewed here are by no means perfect and, in fact, are replete with problems. The AGETIPs have been quite severely critiqued in the literature on social funds and AGETUR in Benin demonstrates clearly the dilemmas associated with combining poverty reduction goals alongside attempts at local economic development and creating public–private partnership. The case of the C3 program in Uganda shows that interventions of this kind require a slow start up and patience, and indeed, it is only now that the methodology is gaining momentum beyond the initial pilot sites. However, the agendas and timeframes of international agencies do not always conform to the pace, progress, and priorities of the experiments they spawn. Nevertheless, under current conditions of aid delivery where the primary focus is on DBS, alongside donors seeking leverage and influence at the policy level, there is a very real danger that knowledge of experience on the ground will be lost. Direct interventions, whether through projects or local funds, give agencies local knowledge and credibility at the operational level. If this is neglected and lost, donors will be engaging in policy dialogue without knowledge or credibility. From the donor's perspective, local funds constitute a useful conduit of information and perceptions of conditions on the ground. For the ordinary people in aid recipient countries, local funds provide an opportunity by which they can harness development resources that may be a long time trickling down from national governments and ministries of finance, while at the same time, honing their capacity to hold their governments to greater account.

Notes

1. In fact, some social funds appeared prior to the 1980s, such as Costa Rica's *Fondo de Desarollo Social Y Asignaciones Familiares* (FODESAF), which was introduced as a welfare measure in 1975, although wider experience during the 1970s was limited. However, during the 1980s, SEFs developed across Latin America in the wake of macro-economic reform.
2. The first SEF was the *Fondo Social de Emergencia* in Bolivia, established in 1987. It had as its objective to address the plight of mine workers who were unemployed as a result of the collapse of tin prices and the closure of state-run mines. The Program of Action to Mitigate the Social Cost of Adjustment (PAMSCAD) was set up in Ghana in the same year, with similar aims.
3. The information and analysis of the C3F is drawn from a process evaluation of the pilot program conducted by the author between 2000 and 2003 on behalf of DFID. Following the pilot phase, the C3F was taken over by UN-Habitat.
4. Of Uganda's estimated population of 22 million, 85% of Ugandans live in rural areas.
5. In 1993, Uganda's National Resistance Movement (NRM) government adopted decentralization as a means to strengthen democracy and improve social service provision in the country. This was formalized by the 1995 Constitution and the Local Government Act of 1997.
6. Livelihood opportunities do not only comprise direct access to income generating activities but access to human development inputs such as education, health care, housing, and services, as well as support to the protection and consolidation of social networks.

References

Bailey, N., Barker, A., and MacDonald, K., *Partnership Agencies in British Urban Policy*, University College London (UCL) Press, London, 1995.

Beall, J., The DFID Supported City-Community Challenge Fund (C3F) Pilot Programme: Lessons from the Interim External Evaluation Report, Presentation to the International Workshop on Reducing Urban Poverty through Innovative Local Funds: Sharing Donor Experiences, held at the London School of Economics, February 28th–March 1st, 2002.

Beall, J., *Funding Local Governance: Small Grants for Democracy and Development*, IT Publications, London, 2005.

Chambers, R., Poverty and livelihoods: Whose reality counts? *Environment and Urbanization*, 7 (1), 173–204, 1995.

Chambers, R., *Whose Reality Counts? Putting the First Last*, IT Publications, London, 1997.

Chambers, R. and Conway, G., Sustainable Rural Livelihoods: Practical Concepts for the 21st Century, IDS Discussion Paper, 296, Institute of Development Studies, Brighton, 1992.

Cleaver, F., Institutions, agency and the limitations of participatory approaches to development, in *Participation, The New Tyranny?* Cooke, B. and Kothari, U., Eds., Zed Books, London, 2001, pp. 36–55.

Cooke, B. and Kothari, U., Eds., *Participation, The New Tyranny?* Zed Books, London, 2001.

Cornia, G.A., Social funds in stabilization and adjustment programmes, WIDER Research for Action Paper 48, World Institute for Development Economics Research, United Nations University, Helsinki, 1999.

Cornia, G.A., Social funds in stabilization and adjustment programmes: a critique, *Development and Change*, 32 (1), 1–32, 2001.

Devas, N., Who runs cities? The Relationship between Urban Governance, Service Delivery and Poverty, Urban Governance, Partnership and Poverty Theme Paper 4, International Development Department, School of Public Policy, University of Birmingham, Birmingham, 1999.

Fanou, B. and Grant, U., Poverty Reduction and Employment generation: the case of Agetur, Benin, Urban Governance, Partnership and Poverty Working Paper 29, International Development Department, School of Public Policy, University of Birmingham, Birmingham, 2000.

Fumo, C., de Haan, A., Holland, J., and Kanji, N., Social Fund: An Effective Instrument to Support Local Action for Poverty Reduction? Social Development Working Paper 5, Department for International Development, London, 2000.

Goetz, A.M. and Gaventa, J., Bringing Citizen Voice and Client Focus into Service Delivery, IDS Working Paper 138, Institute of Development Studies, Brighton, 2001.

Jørgensen, S.L. and van Domelen, J., Helping the poor manage risk better: the role of social funds, in *Shielding the Poor, Social Protection in the Developing World*, Lustig, N., Ed., Brookings Institution Press and Inter-American Development Bank, Washington D.C., 2001, pp. 91–107.

Kanji, N., Social funds in sub-Saharan Africa: how effective for poverty reduction? in *World Poverty, New Policies to Defeat an Old Enemy*, Townsend, P. and Gordon, D., Eds., The Policy Press, Bristol, 2002, pp. 233–250.

Mohan, G. and Stokke, K., Participatory development and empowerment: the dangers of localism, *Third World Quarterly*, 21 (2), 247–268, 2000.

Mosse, D., People's knowledge, participation and patronage: operations and representations in rural development, in *Participation, The New Tyranny?* Cooke, B. and Kothari, U., Eds., Zed Books, London, 2001, pp. 16–35.

Narayan, D. and Ebbe, K., Design of Social Funds Participation, Demand Orientation and Local Organizational Capacity, World Bank Discussion Paper 375, World Bank, Washington D.C., 1997.

Narayan, D., Patel, R., Schafft, K., Rademacher, A., and Koch-Schulte, S., *Voices of the Poor, Can Anyone Hear Us?* The World Bank and Oxford University Press, Oxford, 2000a.

Narayan, D., Chambers, R., Shah, M.K., and Petesch, P., *Voices of the Poor, Crying out for Change*, The World Bank and Oxford University Press, Oxford, 2000b.

Satterthwaite, D., Local funds, and their potential to allow donor agencies to support community development and poverty reduction in urban areas: workshop report, *Environment and Urbanization*, 14 (1), 179–188, 2002.

Tendler, J. and Serrano, R., The Rise of Social Funds: What Are They a Model of? Mimeo for the United Nations Development Programme (UNDP), Department of Urban Studies and Planning, Massachusetts Institute of Technology, Boston, 1999.

Tendler, J., Why are social funds so popular? in *Local Dynamics in the Era of Globalization*, Yusuf, S., Wu, W., and Evenett, S., Eds., The World Bank and Oxford University Press, New York, 2000, pp. 114–129.

UNCDF (United Nations Capital Development Fund), Taking risks. Communications Development Incorporated, Washington D.C., 1999. Document can be accessed through http://www.uncdf.org/english/local_governance/index.html.

Uphoff, N., Local Institutions and Participation for Sustainable Development, Gatekeeper Series 3, International Institute for Environment and Development, London, 1992.

World Bank, *World Development Report 1997: The State in a Changing World*, Oxford University Press, Oxford, 1997.

World Bank, *Social Funds: Assessing Effectiveness*, World Bank Operation Evaluation Department, Washington D.C., 2002.

Chapter 26

Privatization and Development

Roger Wettenhall

CONTENTS

I. Introduction

"Privatization" has been one of the dominant concepts in the discourse of public sector reform in the late 20th century, a clear antidote to the earlier "nationalization," and it has faded only very marginally as the 21st century begins its course. Essentially, the term reflects a belief in the superior economic efficiency of the private sector over the public sector, and in general usage, it is employed to cover a number of processes which involve public-to-private movement. These processes include the sale of public assets such as "state-owned enterprises (SOEs)" (also known as "public enterprises" or sometimes "government-business enterprises"), contracting out, deregulation, and enforcing the public sector to adopt private sector behaviors and processes such as competition, user pays, and other corporate-management systems. Asset selling, contracting out, competition, and corporate management are certainly not new to the public sector, but their incidence has greatly increased under the stimulus of a body of economic theories associated with the so-called "new institutional economics." The sale (or divestment) of SOEs is probably the hardest form of privatization recognized in the reform discourse and that is the principal focus of this chapter.

Over several decades, I have been researching the Australian experience of public enterprise. I have also been actively involved in relevant cross-national research, through several international study associations and often relating to developing countries. As the privatization push has built up around the world, this interest has inevitably extended to the causes, methods, and outcomes of divestment activity. One important finding has been that, in many countries, activity undertaken in the name of privatization has led not to clear-cut transfers from the public to the private sector but to the creation of public–private mixing arrangements of one kind or another. Therefore, "public–private partnership" (although clearly not all the mixes are partnerships) becomes another slogan-term invested with emotional and exhortatory value, just as "nationalization" was at mid-20th century and "privatization" was in late 20th century.[1]

A few other introductory comments are necessary. First, regarding an important issue highlighted in a mid-1990s' World Bank report: while many public enterprises have been unloaded in one way or another in the recent reform period, many remain and they continue to be deserving of analysis and reform attention in their own right. As the World Bank team put it:

> Despite more than a decade of divestiture efforts and the growing consensus that governments perform less well than the private sector in a host of activities, state-owned enterprises (SOEs)

account for nearly as large a share of developing economies today as twenty years ago. (World Bank, 1995: 1)

The second comment draws on an important analysis of western experience, which is equally applicable to developing world experience (Feigenbaum et al., 1999), and from a more general consideration of the connection between privatization and globalization (Farazmand, 2002). Both demonstrate persuasively that, notwithstanding that so much of the early advocacy focused on economic argument, privatization is very much a political phenomenon: it redistributes costs and benefits between different groups. Although it is unlikely to be clearly stated, much of the deliberate planning by governments is to that end, and across countries, there is significant diversity among motives to privatize (Cheung, 1997).

There are other significant limitations in the recent discourse. Thus, while the subject of privatization has spawned a huge international literature, many of those working in the field have been fascinated by the mechanics of divestment and have shown little interest in what is being divested — notably, in the reasons why public enterprises were established and whether they satisfied the public policy prescriptions of an earlier period. Thus, again, and connected to the last, much of this discussion has been overly influenced by two abstract terms introduced by economic theorizing and often not much related to the real causes of public enterprise creation and privatization: "market failure" and "government failure".

Of course, there have, through the 20th century, been vast differences in the relative sizes of public sectors. They have been much bigger in the centrally planned economies and some developing countries modeled on them, so that the case for privatization has been much stronger in some than in others. That too seems often to have been forgotten by many theorists.

Accordingly, this chapter begins with some observations on the public enterprise/development nexus, necessary in my view before we can have any chance of properly understanding the privatization/development nexus, which became a familiar subject for discussion in the later 20th century.

II. Public Enterprise and Development
A. A Note on the Earlier History of Public Enterprise

The significance of the notions of market failure and government failure immediately becomes apparent when we inquire into the history of public enterprise. When the privatizing "bug" gained hold in the 1980s, reformers began to ask why there was such a thing as public enterprise (Wettenhall, 1988). Explanations then produced by economists revolved around the idea of private enterprise failures forcing state intervention, with subsequent failures by government forcing reversal — so giving historical priority to private enterprise or "the market." However, this was essentially a late 20th century construct. It did not allow for the sheer absence of private enterprise capacity that marked so many developing country contexts, which was not really "failure." It also involved the assumption that everything to do with the market was private, which seems to be another outcome of a very short-term perspective. It is instructive to look back to a time before such interpretations became fashionable.[2]

As Ramanadham (1984) reminded us almost a generation ago, public enterprises had two faces, a governmental face (in that they were owned by the state and needed to serve public goals) and an enterprise face (in that they were expected to be business-like in their operations). Whatever the tensions posed by the interaction of these two faces, few then doubted that they were part of the public sector.

When the first public enterprises were established — here we may contemplate the granary department and temple estates administration of Pharonic Egypt or the state iron, salt and alcohol monopolies established in Imperial China in the first and second centuries BC (Erman, 1969: 81, 107; Gernet, 1982: 140, 145, 323) — markets were rudimentary in form. As the first example indicates, it was the state that stored and distributed the staple foods and other necessities on which early civilizations depended. No less, the state was responsible for the planning and construction of vast schemes of flood control and irrigation along the major waterways around which those civilizations grew. Farazmand (2001b: 176) has described the situation in the old Persian empire (see also Farazmand, 1998: 78–79):

> Public enterprises grew dramatically as a result of state policy for thousands of years — partly in competition with the Chinese silk export to the west and partly for economic development and building infrastructure such as roads, bridges, water canals, irrigation systems, textile and silk production, and promotion of commerce.

In earlier times, the church was the only other institution capable of organizing for such large-scale operations. The ability of private enterprise to do so is of much more recent vintage and markets in the modern sense arrived only when this happened.

In the earlier periods, private ventures were to be found mostly in small-scale production and areas like collecting taxes for government, a service remunerated by fees under an early form of contracting out. In his account of Persian or Iranian public enterprise, Farazmand (2001b: 176) asserts that practices such as contracting, partnership-building, and marketization — all involving connections between large government and small businesses — go back as far as the time of the "Great King," Darius, some 2500 years ago. In his Chinese study, Gernet (1982: 140) records that shifts between state and private enterprises in salt and iron mining around the time of the birth of Christ resulted from the instituting and relaxing of state monopolies. Another study concerning what might be thought of as a middle-distance public enterprise (Blanc, 1940) shows how the community of Geneva, with experience of recurring famines, decided in 1628 to make provision for famine-affected years by providing for a publicly owned "chamber" to purchase, store, and distribute corn, and how this chamber prospered through complex relations with individual suppliers, investors, and merchants until rendered impotent in the post-revolutionary French occupation of Geneva in the 1790s. This was public–private mixing *par excellence*.

In western experience, such mixing was often entered into fairly deliberately as part of the strengthening of the state, with its incidence reducing both as state institutions and independent market institutions matured.

B. Variations among States

In this, however, world experience has not followed a single course. It seems to have been more difficult for people in "metropolitan" Anglo-Saxon countries (Britain and the U.S.A.), from which much of the mainline new public management (NPM) and privatization theorizing has emanated, to conceive of public enterprises as inherent parts of the state. For them, these enterprises usually emerged — actually or notionally — through acquisition by the state of firms previously under private ownership and operation but experiencing difficulty, either because of poor management or inclement market conditions (market failure) or because a dominant collectivist political ideology allowed no place for them. It is as though such enterprises were temporarily in state ownership, their proper home was elsewhere, and they would return to it when the time was opportune. Thus, Drucker, who is widely regarded as having coined the word "privatization," actually used "reprivatization" (Drucker, 1969: 218, 220). *Laissez-faire* theorizing, both old and new, emerged easily in this context.

In the major countries of Continental Europe (particularly France and Germany), however, a statist tradition endowed public enterprises with greater respectability and greater centrality.[3] Standing even further away, in much of the rest of the world (*including the colonies of those metropolitan powers*), public enterprise has had a "natural-growth" character: it did not displace private enterprise and it has been an essential ingredient of national development and economic growth. Therefore, there has been no reluctance through much of the world to see it as an integral part of the public sector and of fundamental, rather than marginal, importance to mainline governance arrangements.

The notion of "natural-growth" public enterprise, contrasted with acquisition-by-nationalization public enterprise, actually comes from a Swedish–British comparison (Verney, 1959: 7): even in the smaller states of Western Europe, the emergence of public enterprise is often to be explained by market absence rather than market failure. This was also the case in the old British dominions. As I have argued elsewhere, the large public enterprise network established in 19th and early 20th century Australia put it far apart from the "mother country" and made it effectively a "pioneer among developing countries" (Wettenhall, 1990; 1996). Mainline British observers were then disgusted by its espousal of public enterprise, but how else were infrastructure and services to be developed? However, one British observer found ethical justification in what was happening:

> In the United States and Canada [where American influence had been substantial] companies are brought into existence by enormous prospective gifts of land in return for the performance of certain operations, and most of the various Pacific railroads were made rapidly on this plan. The companies were bribed to make them.... The Australians have more logically, and there is reason to think somewhat more economically, decided to keep public works mainly in the hands of the colonial governments. (Dilke, 1890: 195–196)

The many decisions to use the state thus as the primary instrument of development were taken by administrators schooled in British *laissez faire* philosophy — and, after the Australian colonies mostly became self-governing in the 1850s, by similarly schooled politicians; they simply realized how inappropriate that philosophy was in the circumstances in which they found themselves. Therefore, they innovated greatly in creating a form of "colonial socialism" administered by statutory corporations with a degree of separation from government itself. Their system later had some model value when the mother country moved in the 20th century to establish public enterprises beyond the postal and telegraphic service and looked for an appropriate managerial form.[4]

British administrators were similarly active in establishing public enterprises in basic infrastructure and utility areas in other parts of the empire. Also reflection insists that old third-world states that escaped colonization or emerged out of earlier colonizing eras (such as China, Japan, Thailand, and, to a lesser extent, the countries of Latin America) found no embarrassment in pragmatically deciding to use public enterprises where private enterprise was unavailable or foreign-owned.

C. The Post-World War II Developing World

With the mass movement of former colonies to self-government or independence in the 1950s, 1960s, and 1970s, it was inevitable that there would be much more public enterprise. The new states inherited the public enterprises established by the colonial governments and, where there had been private enterprises in the hands of citizens of the former colonial powers, there was insistent pressure to take them over. There was also insistent pressure to speed up development, establish infrastructure and industries, provide employment for local people, and fill service gaps that might otherwise be taken up by ambitious multinationals. In other cases, as in East Africa and Indonesia, there was compulsory acquisition of businesses and properties previously owned by residents or other interests now unwelcome for one reason or another.

Armies of consultants advised governments on how best to manage their expanded public sectors, with the UN's Technical Assistance Program, the World Bank, the IMF, and regional development banks, all sending streams of advisers and preparing masses of reports directed at improving the quality of management. There were also numerous academic treatises. Hanson's *Public Enterprise and Economic Development* (Hanson, 1959; 1965) was a pre-eminent example: it surveyed the experiences of many developing countries, made recommendations for improvement, and was widely read. However, it was often forgotten that the world was now expecting its new states to achieve a degree of development in 50 years that took 400 years to come in Europe (Hunter, 1968).

As part of a process similar to that which would later be called "corporatization," and similar to that which produced the Australian statutory corporations in an earlier period, attention was now given to building semi-autonomous bodies, sometimes called parastatals, located outside the conventional ministries, to manage and operate these public enterprises:

> For third world countries, they seemed to provide an effective mechanism for reducing foreign control and making up for the lack of an effective private sector. Donors, lenders and investors all encouraged the new solution because essentially it held out the promise of bypassing what were by then widely seen as slow, complex and inefficient bureaucracies. (Hirshmann, 1999: 292)

An International Centre for Public Enterprises in Developing Countries, established in Ljubljana (now the capital of Slovenia) with the support of the old Yugoslavian government, attracted academics and practitioners from many third-world countries. For the Yugoslavs, it presented an opportunity to spread the word about the system of worker control of enterprises then being developed in that country, but for the rest it did much good work in exploring a range of important issues such linkages between governments and the corporate bodies running so many of their enterprises, and the emergence in some countries of "focal points" — specialized sections of central administrations — to coordinate or harmonize government–enterprise relationships (e.g., Suarez, 1985; Vratusa, 1985). The Indian Bureau of Public Enterprise was a leading example of such a focal point; with the world's largest public sector operating in a multi-party democracy, India has been especially productive of innovative mechanisms in this area, other examples being the Standing Conference of Public Enterprises (SCOPE) — bringing together the chairmen and chief executives of major enterprises (Moharir, 1987) — and the training and research Institute of Public Enterprise in Hyderabad.[5]

D. Contrasting Patterns and Influences

In the early World War II period a school of Marxist-oriented Polish scholars presented two models of public sector patterns in third-world economies, the Indian model being contrasted with the Japanese. These patterns, shown in Table 26.1, are instructive because they remind us of approaches as they then existed. The interesting question for me was to consider the "fit" of the Australian experience. At that time, conservative Australian politicians were still expressing the view that public enterprise was justified when it served the role of "development stimulator." In accordance with that view, it was proper for governments to establish enterprises for developmental purposes, but it was also proper, when government entrepreneurship had brought an industry or service to the point where it was profitable, for the enterprise to be sold to private interests. Of course, argument followed: on one hand, why should not the taxpayer, who funded the original investment, continue through ownership to enjoy the benefit of that profitability; on the other hand, if sale did take place, should not the proceeds be reserved for reinvestment in other entrepreneurial asset-building activity? That this perspective existed obviously brought the then Australian situation closer to the Japanese than to the Indian pattern (Wettenhall, 1990: 5–7).

III. Toward Privatization

It hardly needs stating that India, Japan and Australia do not fits these characterizations today; Japan and Australia have been firmly admitted to the category of industrialized, developed countries and India is

Table 26.1 Third-World Public Sector Patterns

Indian Model	Japanese Model
(1) The public sector is given a permanent place in the economy and its rate of growth is to be higher than that of the private sector, to achieve progressively a situation of predominance of the public sector in the whole economy	(1) The public sector is to have a permanent place only in as much as it covers "social overheads" in the field of public utilities and assists in the development of private industries—considered as alternatives to the state entering the field of industrial production
(2) Certain strategic branches of production are reserved for the state, and in these branches, the predominance of the public sector is to be achieved as soon as possible	(2) The state may start new industrial ventures but their privatization is foreseen as soon as they become profitable
(3) As a result of (1) and (2), the development of private monopoly capital will be restricted or at least slowed down	(3) The state pursues a policy of the conscious formation and strengthening of the capitalist class and thus facilitates the formation of monopoly groups
(4) Planned industrialization with the public sector as its main support, and public utility and raw material industries as its main concern, is launched to lay the basis for a self-sustaining growth of the economy and to strengthen the economic independence of the country	(4) Since the domestic capitalist class is weak, an "open-door" policy towards foreign capital is pursued
(5) Comprehensive planning — not only financial but also physical — assumes growing importance	(5) Planning remains embryonic and is generally confined to "programming," based almost exclusively on financial considerations

Source: Adapted from Sachs, I., *Patterns of Public Sector in Underdeveloped Economies*, Asia, London, 1964, pp. 79–80.

probably not too far behind. What is important here is to consider all the shifts that have occurred since the categorizations were developed and the how and why of decisions that have been made about preserving or shrinking public sectors. It would seem that two main interacting factors have been at work in producing the major reorientations of the late 20th century.

First, there has been plentiful evidence of economic underperformance of public enterprises, connecting with the notion of "government failure."[6] There have been indisputably successful, profitable public enterprises, but they have been mostly lost sight of in the ideology-aided dramatization of the negatives, rather than the positives. The underperformance has been especially marked in the poorer, lesser developed countries (World Bank, 1995: 2, 23), with the international aid-giving bodies heavily engaged in shoring up the economies of those countries often in crisis in large part because of that underperformance.

The second factor has been the influence of mainline economic theorizing, which has notoriously produced a movement against the state virtually throughout the western world. Principal-agent theory, public choice theory, and transaction analysis — often collectively referred to as "the new institutional economics" — have all taught that private ownership and enterprise are more efficient than their public equivalents, and they have been embraced enthusiastically by the NPM governance paradigm, which has displaced the more traditional "public administration." Britain and the U.S.A. have been the major sources of all this intellectual activity, with the impact intended mainly for the western societies themselves. As noted earlier in this chapter, the public enterprise climate in these "metropolitan" countries has been vastly different from that in the developing world, and the initial instigators of these theories were not much concerned with those parts of the world which follow a contrasting tradition and so see the whole issue of public enterprise through a different lens. However, Britain and the U.S.A. have been highly influential in the councils of the international aid industry and have thus procured a universalizing of their theories. Therefore, the U.S.A. often imposes anti-public enterprise conditions on its own aid: as Vernon reported (1988: 20), in 1986 the Washington headquarters of the U.S. Agency for International Development commanded each of its overseas missions to generate at least two privatization projects in the following year. The "conditionalities" attached to World Bank and IMF aid have similar effects. The western intellectual activity thus gets imposed on third-world systems through the process known as "policy transfer" (Dolowitz and Marsh, 1996), which Ikenberry (1990: 22) described as "policy bandwagoning" in the specific case of privatization, and it becomes intertwined with the underperformance lesson emerging from the developing countries themselves.

Numerous academic and practitioner reports point to the two prongs of policy development that have emerged from this conjunction: the urge to privatize and the parallel urge to reform enterprises remaining within the public sector (e.g., MacAvoy et al., 1989; Suleiman and Waterbury, 1990; Ramamurti and Vernon, 1991; Farazmand, 2001a). In the already-cited 1995 report, the World Bank subdivided the latter urge by directing attention to:

> ... the five components of reform that economic theorists and reform practitioners widely recommend. These components are divestiture [synonymous with selling public enterprises], competition, hard budgets, financial sector reform, and changes in the institutional relationship between SOEs and governments. (World Bank, 1995: 21)

It saw them not as "separate options" but as "mutually supportive components of an overall strategy": its research team had found that "the more successful reformers made the most of all five components." Some have privatized more than others, and this earns World Bank praise. However, there is also recognition — and this applies to developed as well as developing countries — that some public enterprises remain even in those countries that have become known as keen privatizers. Thus, both strategies remain important, "divestiture alone is seldom enough" and "outgrowing SOEs" — by achieving very rapid private sector growth rather than by disposing of state enterprises — may be a good alternative strategy (World Bank, 1995: 4–5, 71, 75).

Some of the reforming reports have seen privatization and deregulation as twin desirable state-shrinking processes (e.g., Gayle and Goodrich, 1990; Pelkmans and Wagner, 1990; MacAvoy, 1995; O'Connor, 1998), and in Britain, the Thatcher government tried to do both. However, a powerful contrary view insists (a) that the profit-seeking objectives of private capital usually act contrary to the public interest, (b) that, in seeking to protect that interest, the state has two options available, public ownership and public regulation, so that they are constructive alternatives rather than twin evils, and (c) that to abandon both means abandoning hope of protecting the public interest. No doubt there can be better ways of regulating, but on this view it is counterproductive to oppose regulation altogether. Indeed, the Thatcher government found itself having to create new regulatory mechanisms for the industries it had privatized.

A further objection to the effect of mainline privatization policy band-wagoning on developing countries is that it has so often proceeded on the basis of an indiscriminate "one size fits all" approach. There have been tensions within the policy-drivers themselves on this issue, as when serious studies commissioned by the World Bank have called for "empirical rigor" in answering questions about who gains and who loses from privatization, whether it benefits owners and managers at the expense of workers and consumers, and indeed whether privatized firms are really more efficient. Chile under Pinochet rivalled Britain under Thatcher as the world's privatization leader, but one such study concluded that what the Pinochet government was selling with strong U.S. support was "efficient public enterprises in well-regulated markets" (Galal et al., 1994: Foreword and Part III). The World Bank itself has often seemed to forget this message. In the pre-reform Chinese case, much was made of an "overloaded" public sector with a mass of SOEs making huge losses. However, many western analysts entirely overlooked the fact that, in the absence of a western-style welfare state, the SOEs rather than government itself provided welfare services and bore their costs. Any reasonable reform effort had to take that into account, and the Chinese government sensibly adopted "an East Asiatic or Asia Pacific model," which argues "for a collectivist approach to the market place" and involves "a clear rejection of westernized values" (Common, 2000: 27, 29–31).[7]

IV. The Practicalities of Privatization

Through the late 1980s and 1990s, many practical guides appeared, suggesting how a country embarking on a privatization program should develop and define its privatization policy in a systematic way, with the clarification of objectives and establishment of a taskforce to prepare guidelines, strategies, programs, and projects as key beginning steps (see, e.g., Commonwealth Secretariat, 1994; International Finance Corporation, 1995; McMaster, 1996; Welch and Frémond, 1998). Malaysia offered a good example of this comprehensive planned approach; its Privatization Plan explicitly defined the government's policy objectives, provided guidelines, and specified the criteria to be used to select enterprises to be privatized, the means of privatization, and the timetable (Mahathir, 1991).[8] Many factors needed to be considered in the development of such a plan: the opportunities and scope for privatization; areas of highest potential benefit; major constraints, including legal constraints, and political implications; and the political, social, and economic costs and benefits of alternative strategies.

World Bank advice to developing countries, given frequently and in numerous contexts, sought to develop these prescriptions. Thus, at a 1989 meeting in Dakar, Senegal, for officials from the governments of several francophone sub-Saharan African countries, six prior conditions needing to be satisfied before a divestment policy could succeed were spelt out (Table 26.2). There was also advice — monumentally ignored when

Table 26.2   A World Bank List of Pre-privatization Conditions to Be Satisfied

(1) An appropriate macroeconomic framework and a competitive market must exist
(2) Government must possess the administrative resources to implement its privatisation policy to the country's advantage
(3) The enterprises to be privatized should be fit for it — not only politically and psychologically, but also from the standpoint of their material, economic and financial condition at the time of the transaction
(4) A well-designed program should exist to cushion the adverse social effects that privatization can have
(5) There should be buyers acceptable to the general public and the government
(6) The government is able to rely, as an alternative to sale to politically unacceptable ethnic or national political groups, on local financial and capital markets sufficiently developed to allow both identification of the potential buyers and mobilization of the financial resources they will need to purchase the stock

Source: Adapted from Adamolekun, L., Ed., Symposium on Privatization in Africa, World Bank, EDI Working Papers, Washington, pp. 3–5, 1989.

western divestment advocates influenced Russia after the break-up of the Soviet Union — that if these conditions were not present, it might be better to explore alternatives to divestment such as commercialization and joint public–private ventures (Adamolekun, 1989: Preface).

However, often it does not happen in such a planned way, even in developed countries. Thus, privatization came to Britain almost by accident: it emerged as an unanticipated solution to several other identified problems (Heald, 1988). In addition, systemic privatization came gradually in Australia, as the practice of disposing of public enterprises mostly emerged under a Labor government as an answer to other problems rather than as a conscious policy in its own right; then electoral change introduced conservative governments with public sector-shrinking as main aims, but even so political factors rather than economic or managerial rationality usually determined what was to be sold and how it was to be sold (Wettenhall, 2002: 104–106). In developing countries, of course, the external pressures are usually greater, but it would be surprising if such factors were also not operating to lead divestment practice away from rational planning guidelines.[9]

Two principal methods of sale have been used around the world. The first, the trade sale, involves selling an enterprise to an existing firm, usually one already active in the industry or in a kindred industry. The second, the public offering (sometimes "initial public offering" or IPO) or public float, involves selling shares in the enterprise on the stock market and produces a much wider and more diverse ownership structure — in the early, heady days of the privatization boom, it was thought that this method might lead to the creation of a new "people's capitalism." Sometimes, both methods are used in respect of a single enterprise: in the case of Australia's international airline Qantas, the first 25% was sold by a trade sale, but the remaining 75% went by public float. However, it is always going to be more difficult in developing countries, where the private sector will often be weak or have low legitimacy, where the middle income strata with money to invest is small, where shedding costly redistributive programs in the name of efficiency can result in the alienation of traditional bases of political support for governing regimes, and where the requisite administrative skills and planning capacity to value assets, assess bids made by potential buyers and deal with all the complex financial and legal issues involved may be lacking (Bienen and Waterbury, 1989; Woodward, 1990; Gupta, 1996). As one 1990 commentary had it:

> For political leaders in many developing countries, the first wave of privatisation in the early 1980s brought exaggerated expectations as to the ease with which privatisation could be implemented and the size of the potential benefits that would be generated. Under a barrage of overoptimistic claims that privatisation would improve the budgetary situation and raise economic efficiency performance through the discipline of the private sector, a pattern of policy paralysis was induced, with other policy reforms being delayed or abandoned in anticipation of the benefits that would follow.…. (Cook and Kirkpatrick, 1990: 21–22)

A variation of the trade sale produces what is effectively a third method, the management buyout, whereby the managers of an enterprise form themselves into a company which purchases it from the state. Some British and Australian divestments have taken this form, and one of the very few U.S. asset-sale privatizations has done so scandalously (Guttman, 2001).[10] As is well known, it has also loomed large in the Russian privatizations and it is the predominant way in which Chinese town and village enterprises are now being reformed (Li and Rozelle, 2003: 982–983). It may increase efficiency, but it often involves elements of corruption and it does not do much to develop social capital.

Of course there are other variations, probably the most notable being the IPO-Plus scheme used in former Soviet Union countries, under which private interests are allowed to establish special investment funds to buy the shares of enterprises being privatized, and then issue their own "participation shares" to the public (Goldberg et al., 1997). The debt-for-equity schemes developed in Latin America whereby creditors accept equity in heavily debt-laden enterprises in exchange for discharging their debt furnish another example (Basile, 1990; Milman and Lundstedt, 1994: 1667–1670).

Wide and imprecise use of the term "privatization" often hides the fact that often only parts of enterprises are being divested. Back in 1975, to enhance staff performance and commitment, the Singapore government sold some shares of its airline to airline staff as an incentive; later, more shares were sold as a capital-raising device (Thynne and Ariff, 1987). Into the new century, however, Singapore Airlines remains majority government-owned. In the Indian case, a policy of "disinvestment" adopted in 1991[11] saw a minority of shares in many public enterprises disposed of as a way of raising additional revenue to meet the fiscal deficit (Ghuman, 1999: 221–224). Across the world, many actions taken in the name of privatization have produced such public–private mixes. In the Saudi Arabian case, a "privatization policy" launched in 1994 produced a substantial reform of the system of port management; nevertheless, ownership remained with the government. What the change did was to enlist the support of a score or more private companies to operate individual port facilities under management contracts, so another mixing arrangement emerges (Al-Homeadan, 2001).[12]

The changes may generally have come a bit later in those systems committed to "market socialism," but here the effects are not dissimilar. In the 1990s, Vietnam recognized the need to develop a capital market and to diversify ownership of SOEs, while not depriving them of their central place in economic development, and a slow movement towards mixed ownership under a policy described as "equitization" emerged (van Tiem and van Thanh, 1996). In addition, recent reporting of reform action in town and village enterprises in two Chinese provinces shows a range of changes all described as "privatization" — sometimes selling just a few shares, sometimes a majority of shares, and sometimes all shares (Li and Rozelle, 2003: 985, 988). However, whether ownership, especially private ownership, has quite the same meaning in these systems as it does elsewhere is a matter requiring further research, and the question raises serious issues about the maturity of commercial law provision. Private ownership is likely to be a weak concept where laws to protect private property are themselves in weak condition.

V. Pluses and Minuses: How to Work Out the Scorecard?

An accounting proposition directed particularly at third-world readers explains that notionally, "the proceeds from privatization represent the capitalization of future net resource flows achieved by the sale of the asset." In other words, the pure effect of the asset sale should be neutral: "the price at which an asset is sold will (simply) be the sum of the discounted future profits generated by the asset." A sale where there are "fully efficient capital and money markets," "full and costless information," "neutral tax structures," no ideological preferences involved, no parties exerting political pressure to secure advantage, and so on might achieve such neutrality (Adam et al., 1992: 9–11). The problem, of course, is that in real life public-to-private transactions, there is no chance of achieving it. Intentionally or unintentionally, structural and policy distortions will produce all sorts of deviations, so there will be both winners and losers in any privatization "deal."

Numerous studies in both developed and developing countries indicate that in personal terms, the winners are largely the "institutional investors, the executives of privatized companies, the stock exchanges, the experts associated with consultancy firms on privatization and the merchant bankers," while the "common, low-income citizens" are the main losers (from Haque, 1998: 446). Many observers see the development of a local bourgeoisie or "derivative middle class" as a positive effect, the process being slowest in sub-Saharan Africa where the traditional "economy of affection," although it has achieved much, stands in the way of the market economy (Hyden, 1983; Subramaniam, 1988; Vernon, 1988: 7–8).[13] Associated gains include the breakdown of bureaucratic dysfunctions and the building up of private capital and entrepreneurship; balancing losses for individual countries are increased differential between wealth and poverty, erosion of national sovereignty along with more power to the multinationals and international aid agencies, and development of a negative image of the public governance system (Haque, 1998: 445–447).

Obviously, it is not possible to put any precise value on the privatizing effort that has been undertaken in developing countries, and any conclusion needs to recognize that effort has had both good and bad effects. However, there can scarcely be any dispute that all countries need a strong and vigorous private sector, and the countries that are emancipating themselves from acute dependency have recognized the need to move in that direction.

There will always be a need for some public enterprises to lead development in strategic areas, and further shifts between public and private ownership — either way, and into mixes — may be expected. However, they should be undertaken after serious evaluation of the needs of particular situations and not swayed by unhelpful ideological considerations. In many countries, the size of the public sector may be smaller as a result of privatizing action, but the importance of the role of the state as a necessary energizer and regulator has not diminished. This needs to be recognized both by individual states and by the lending agencies and their metropolitan western financiers.

I have read millions of words on public enterprise and privatization and I judge that one of the best rounded treatments I have encountered is that of former Harvard Professor Raymond Vernon in his introduction to the edited collection *Promise of Privatization*. In a lecture to a group of public enterprise managers from developing countries just after the book was published,[14] he explained the problem he had with that title. His publisher was the U.S. Council on Foreign Relations, and it insisted on the *promise*. However, as work on the book progressed, his team came to see mass privatization as introducing just another *problem* for governments to deal with. However, negotiations with the publisher secured only an agreement to add the word *challenge* — in a sub-title of the book and as an accompaniment to *promise* in the title of Vernon's own introductory chapter. This did not stop him from delivering a timely lecture to U.S. policy-makers (Vernon, 1988: 19–22).

Whether it was ever learned is a moot point. Instructions of the U.S.-led Coalition Provisional Authority in Iraq, issued as this book was being conceived, suggest that it was not. Initially, no bids to participate in the reconstruction of Iraq would be entertained from potential contractors that were more than 10 percent-owned by a foreign government; from August 2003, the requirement was relaxed, but even so no bids would be entertained where foreign government participation in a bidding *consortium* exceeded 10%. Thus the bias against public ownership has continued (CPA, 2003).

Notes

1. Some of the background studies which demonstrate this involvement deal separately with public enterprise, privatization, and partnership — on the Australian public enterprise experience, see especially Wettenhall (1987, 1990, 1993, 1996); for some cross-country studies of public enterprise, see O Nuallain and Wettenhall (1987), Wettenhall and O Nuallain (1987, 1990), Corkery et al. (1994), Wettenhall et al. (1997), and Thynne (1998); on privatization generally, see Wettenhall (1983) and de Ru and Wettenhall (1990), on privatization in Australia, see McIntosh et al. (1997) and Collyer et al. (2001a); and on public–private mixing, see Wettenhall (2003). In other studies, however, these interests tend to run together, as in Thynne (1995); Wettenhall and Thynne (2001), Thynne and Wettenhall (2001), Ghuman and Wettenhall (2001), Collyer et al. (2001b). I acknowledge the close and rewarding collaboration I have had with Ian Thynne in many of these works.
2. For an analysis by an economist that acknowledges and critiques these assumptions, see Wolf (1988).
3. With railways as perhaps the leading exhibit, most continental countries moved vigorously in the 19th century to establish state-owned utilities. However, market failure explanations applied to some extensions of their public enterprise networks, as when Italy created its great public holding corporations IRI and ENI as "ambulances for sick industries" in the early 1930s depression.

4. On the British interpretations of the Australian experience, see especially Wettenhall (1970, 1990: 9–10).
5. This Institute publishes a quarterly journal: *Journal of Institute of Public Enterprise*. ICPE also has published its own quarterly journal *Public Enterprise* since 1980, although its present status is uncertain.
6. Although it is important to note the observation of Callaghy and Wilson (1988: 179–180) that in sub-Saharan Africa (which is usually seen as the "basket case" in these matters), some of the "dismal economic failures" have at the same time been "considerable political successes." They have "provided resources, support, and legitimacy in the complicated factional disputes within and between African regimes and have performed important welfare functions."
7. There are numerous studies of how the World Bank and other international aid agencies have proceeded with their tasks. For one essentially sympathetic analysis that nevertheless notes some of the contradictions, see Mosley (1988). For a more critical treatment that attacks both their assessments of need and their lack of accountability, see Hancock (1989).
8. For a serious critique of the Malaysian activity, see Jomo (1995).
9. For an account of the "ritual" dances performed by former Zaire dictator Mobutu in his relationship with the aid agencies, see Callaghy and Wilson (1988: 219–222).
10. U.S. privatization discourse and practice is much more about contracting out than about selling assets.
11. It followed an earlier "parallelization" approach that encouraged the development of private firms to offer competition to SOEs (Goulding, 1997).
12. The practice of state enterprises entering into management contracts with private firms is well in evidence in Africa also: on the Zaire case, see Callaghy and Wilson (1988: 221).
13. For Hyden and Subramaniam, the state corporations or parastatals operating public enterprises also had this effect, suggesting a continuity running between their creation and privatization.
14. Fourteenth International Workshop on Public Enterprise Policy and Management in Developing Countries 1988, conducted by the Harvard Institute for International Development (HIID). I was "guest observer" at this Workshop. Ironically, HIID was itself closed after its dramatic but highly damaging involvement in Russia's privatization program between 1992 and 1997 (Wedel, 2000: 31).

References

Adam, C., Cavendish, W., and Mistry, P.S., *Adjusting Privatization: Case Studies from Developing Countries*, James Currey for Commonwealth Secretariat, London, 1992.
Adamolekun, L., Ed., Symposium on Privatization in Africa, World Bank, EDI Working Papers, Washington, 1989.
Al-Homeadan, A., The Saudi Ports Authority: a case of public ownership but mostly private management, *Asian J. Public Admin.*, 23 (2), 217–228, 2001.

Basile, A., The role of debt-equity conversions in privatization and deregulation processes, in *Privatization and Deregulation in Global Perspective*, Gayle, D.J. and Goodrich, J.N., Eds., Quorum Books, New York, 1990, pp. 139–155.

Bienen, H. and Waterbury, J., The political economy of privatization in developing countries, *World Dev.*, 17 (5), 617–632, 1989.

Blanc, H., A great state enterprise of olden times: the Geneva corn chamber, 1628–1798, *Ann. Collect. Econ.* (now *Annals of Public and Cooperative Economics*), 16 (1), 136–191, 1940.

Callaghy, T.M. and Wilson, E.J., Africa: policy, reality or ritual? in *The Promise of Privatization: A Challenge for American Foreign Policy*, Vernon, R., Ed., Council on Foreign Relations, New York, 1988, pp. 179–230.

Cheung, A.B.L., The rise of privatization policies: similar faces, different motives, *Int. J. Public Admin.*, 20 (12), 2213–2245, 1997

Collyer, F., McMaster, J., and Wettenhall, R., *Public Enterprise Divestment: Australian Case Studies*, Pacific Institute of Management and Development, University of the South Pacific, Suva, 2001a.

Collyer, F., McMaster, J., and Wettenhall, R., Privatization and public enterprise reform in Australia, in *Privatization or Public Enterprise Reform? International Case Studies with Implications for Public Management*, Farazmand, A., Ed., Greenwood Press, Westport, Connecticut, 2001b, pp. 141–171.

Common, R., The competition state in China: Does it fit the global trend? *Public Admin. Policy*, 9 (2), 27–35, 2000.

Commonwealth Secretariat, *Management of the Privatisation Process: A Guide to Policy Making and Implementation*, Commonwealth Secretariat, London, 1994.

Cook, P. and Kirkpatrick, C., *Privatisation Policy and Performance: International Perspectives*, Harvester Wheatsheaf, Hemel Hempstead, 1990.

Corkery, J., O Nuallain, C., and Wettenhall, R., Eds., *Public Enterprise Boards: What They Are and What They Do*, AJPA and IASIA, Hong Kong, 1994.

CPA (Coalition Provisional Authority, Iraq), CPA announces important changes to wireless telephone license requirements, Press Release No. 27, August 8, 2003.

de Ru, H. and Wettenhall, R., Progress, benefits and costs of privatization: an introduction, *Int. Rev. Administrative Sci.*, 56 (1), 7–14, 1990.

Dilke, Sir Charles, *Problems of Greater Britain*, Macmillan, London, 1890.

Dolowitz, D. and Marsh, D., Who learns what from whom? A review of the policy transfer literature, *Political Stud.*, 44 (2), 343–357, 1996.

Drucker, P., *The Age of Discontinuity*, Heinemann, London, 1969.

Erman, A., *Life in Ancient Egypt* (trans. HM Tirad), Benjamin Blom (first published 1894), New York, 1969.

Farazmand, A., Administration of the Persian Achaemenid world-state empire: implications for modern public administration, *Int. J. Public Admin.*, 21 (1), 25–86, 1998.

Farazmand, A., Ed., *Privatization or Public Enterprise Reform? International Case Studies with Implications for Public Management*, Greenwood Press, Westport, Connecticut, 2001a.

Farazmand, A., Privatization and public enterprise reform in post-revolutionary Iran, in *Privatization or Public Enterprise Reform? International Case Studies with Implications for Public Management*, Farazmand, A., Ed., Greenwood Press, Westport, Connecticut, 2001b, pp. 175–200.

Farazmand, A., Globalization, privatization and the future of modern governance, *Public Finance Manage.*, 2 (1), 125–153, 2002.

Feigenbaum, H., Henig, J., and Hamnett, C., *Shrinking the State: The Political Underpinnings of Privatization*, Cambridge University Press, Cambridge, 1999.

Galal, A., Jones, L., Tandon, P., and Vogelsang, I., *Welfare Consequences of Selling Public Enterprises: An Empirical Analysis*, Oxford University Press for the World Bank, New York, 1994.

Gayle, D.J. and Goodrich, J.N., Eds., *Privatization and Deregulation in Global Perspective*, Quorum Books, New York, 1990.

Gernet, J., *A History of Chinese Civilization* (trans. J.R. Foster), Cambridge University Press, Cambridge, 1982.

Ghuman, B.S., Public enterprise in India: phases of reform in the 1990s, *Asian J. Public Admin.*, 21 (2), 220–233, 1999.

Ghuman, B.S. and Wettenhall, R., From public enterprises and privatization towards sectoral mixes: Guest Editors' Introduction, *Asian J. Public Admin.*, 23 (2), 143–166, 2001.

Goldberg, I., Jedrzejczak, G., and Fuchs, M., The 'IPO-Plus': A New Approach to Privatization, World Bank Policy Research Working Paper 1821, Washington, 1997.

Goulding, A.J., Retreating from the commanding heights: privatization in an Indian context, *J. Int. Affairs*, 50 (2), 581–612, 1997.

Gupta, A., Privatisation: an economic device or a political strategy? *Journal of Institute of Public Enterprise* (Hyderabad, India), 19 (1/2), 38–51, 1996.

Guttman, D., The United States Enrichment Corporation: a failing privatisation, *Asian J. Public Admin.*, 23 (2), 247–272, 2001.

Hancock, G., *Lords of Poverty*, Macmillan, London, 1989.

Hanson, A.H., *Public Enterprise and Economic Development*, Routledge and Kegan Paul, London, 1959.

Hanson, A.H., *Public Enterprise and Economic Development*, 2nd ed., Routledge and Kegan Paul, London, 1965.

Haque, M.S., Impacts of globalization on the role of the state and bureaucracy in Asia, *Administrative Theory and Praxis*, 20 (4), 439–451, 1998.

Heald, D., The United Kingdom: privatization and its political context, *Western Eur. Politics*, 11 (4), 31–48, 1988.

Hirschmann, D., Development management versus third world bureaucracies: a brief history of conflicting interests, *Dev. Change*, 30 (2), 287–305, 1999.

Hunter, G., The transfer of institutions from developed to developing countries, *African Affairs*, 266, 3–10, 1968.

Hyden, G., *No Shortcuts to Progress: African Development Management in Perspective*, University of California Press, Berkeley, 1983.

Ikenberry, G., The international spread of privatization policies: inducements, learning, and 'policy bandwagoning', in *The Political Economy of Public Sector Reform and Privatization*, Suleiman, E.N. and Waterbury, J., Eds., Westview Press, Boulder, 1990, pp. 88–110.

International Finance Corporation, *Privatization: Principles and Practice*, The World Bank, Washington, 1995.

Jomo, K.S., *Privatizing Malaysia: Rents, Rhetoric, Realities*, Westview Press, Boulder, Colorado, 1995.

Li, H. and Rozelle, S., Privatizing rural China: insider privatization, innovative contracts and the performance of township enterprises, *China Quart.*, 176, 981–1005, 2003.

MacAvoy, P.W., *Privatization and Deregulation in the United States*, Edinburgh University Press, Edinburgh, 1995.

MacAvoy, P.W., Stanbury, W.T., Yarrow, G., and Zeckhauser, R.J., Eds., *Privatization and State-Owned Enterprises: Lessons from the United States, Great Britain and Canada*, Kluwer, Boston, 1989.

Mahathir, B.M., (Prime Minister), *Privatization Masterplan*, Economic Planning Unit, Prime Minister's Department, Kuala Lumpur, 1991.

McIntosh, K., Shauness, J., and Wettenhall, R., *Contracting Out in Australia: An Indicative History*, Centre for Research in Public Sector Management, University of Canberra, Canberra, 1997.

McMaster, J., Methods of privatization and privatization policy issues, in *Privatisation in Asia and the Pacific: Profiles, Strategies, Results*, McMaster, J. and Samad, S.A., Eds., Asia and Pacific Development Centre, Kuala Lumpur, 1996.

Milman, C. and Lundstedt, S.B., Privatizing state owned enterprises in Latin America: a research agenda, *Int. J. Public Admin.*, 17 (9), 1663–1677, 1994.

Moharir, V., India's SCOPE: Standing Conference of Public Enterprises, in *Getting Together in Public Enterprise*, Wettenhall, R. and O Nuallain, C., Eds., International Institute of Administrative Sciences, Brussels, 1987, pp. 23–33.

Mosley, P., Privatisation, policy-based lending and World Bank behaviour, in *Privatisation in Less Developed Countries*, Cook, P. and Kirkpatrick, C., Eds., Wheatsheaf, Hemel Hempstead, 1988, pp. 125–140.

O'Connor, K., *The New Game: Deregulation, Privatisation and the State of the Airline Industry*, Evatt Foundation and Public Sector Research Sector, University of New South Wales, Sydney, 1998.

O Nuallain, C. and Wettenhall, R., Eds., *Public Enterprise: The Management Challenge*, International Institute of Administrative Sciences, Brussels, 1987.

Pelkmans, J. and Wagner, N., *Privatization and Deregulation in ASEAN and the EC*, Institute of Southeast Asian Studies, Singapore, 1990.

Ramamurti, R. and Vernon, R., *Privatization and Control of State-Owned Enterprises*, World Bank, Washington, 1991.

Ramanadham, V.V., *The Nature of Public Enterprise*, Croom Helm, London, 1984.

Sachs, I., *Patterns of Public Sector in Underdeveloped Economies*, Asia, London, 1964.

Suarez, R.A., Ed., *The Management of Interlinkages*, ICPE, Ljubljana, 1985.

Subramaniam, V., Perspectives on Public Enterprise in the Third World: The Derivative Middle Class, Political Economy and Ideology, paper presented at 13th International Political Science Association Congress, Washington, 1988.

Suleiman, E.N. and Waterbury, J., Eds., *The Political Economy of Public Sector Reform and Privatization*, Westview Press, Boulder, 1990.

Thynne, I., Ed., *Corporatization, Divestment and the Public–Private Mix: Selected Country Studies*, AJPA in conjunction with IASIA, Hong Kong, 1995.

Thynne, I., Ed., Symposium on government ownership and enterprise management, *Public Admin. Dev.*, 18 (3), 217–306, 1998.

Thynne, I. and Ariff, M., Singapore Airlines: a study in the management of privatisation, in *Public Enterprise: The Management Challenge*, O Nuallain, C. and Wettenhall, R., Eds., International Institute of Administrative Sciences, Brussels, 1987, pp. 111–129.

Thynne, I. and Wettenhall, R., Eds., Symposium on turn-of-the-century trends and future prospects in public enterprise and privatization: contexts, structures and dynamics, *Public Finance Manage.*, 2 (1), 1–153, 2001.

van Tiem, P. and van Thanh, N., Problems and prospects of state enterprise reform, 1996–2000, in *State-Owned Enterprise Reform in Vietnam: Lessons from Asia*, Yuen, N.C., Freeman, N.J., and Huynh, F.H., Eds., Institute of Southeast Asian Studies, Singapore, 1996, pp. 3–18.

Verney, D.V., *Public Enterprise in Sweden*, Liverpool University Press, Liverpool, 1959.

Vernon, R., Introduction: the promise and the challenge, in Vernon, R., Ed., *The Promise of Privatization: a Challenge for American Foreign Policy*, Council on Foreign Relations, New York, 1988, pp. 1–22.

Vratusa, A., Ed., *Essays on Relations Between Governments and Public Enterprises*, ICPE, Ljubljana, 1985.

Wedel, J.R., Tainted transactions: Harvard, the Chubais clan and Russia's ruin, *The National Interest*, Spring, 23–34, 2000.

Welch, D. and Frémond, O., The Case-by-Case Approach to Privatization: Techniques and Examples, World Bank Technical Paper 403, Washington, 1998.

Wettenhall, R., *The Iron Road and the State: WM Acworth as Scholar, Critic and Reformer*, University of Tasmania, Hobart, 1970.

Wettenhall, R., Privatisation: a shifting frontier between private and public sectors, *Curr. Affairs Bull.* (Sydney), 60 (6), 14–22, 1983.

Wettenhall, R., *Public Enterprise and National Development: Selected Essays*, Royal Australian Institute of Public Administration (ACT Division), Canberra, 1987.

Wettenhall, R., Why public enterprise? A public interest perspective, *Canberra Bulletin of Public Administration*, 57, 44–50, 1988.

Wettenhall, R., Australia's daring experiment with public enterprise, in *Dynamics in Australian Public Management: Selected Essays*, Kouzmin, A. and Scott, N., Eds., Macmillan, Melbourne, 1990, pp. 2–16.

Wettenhall, R., The globalization of public enterprises, *Int. Rev. Administrative Sci.*, 59 (3), 387–408, 1993.

Wettenhall, R., Australia: a pioneer among developing countries, in *Public Enterprise Management: International Case Studies*, Farazmand, A., Ed., Greenwood Press, Westport, Connecticut, 1996, pp. 237–261.

Wettenhall, R., Public enterprise divestments in Australia: a turn-of-the-century review, in *Reforming Public and Corporate Governance: Management and the Market in Australia, Britain and Korea*, Ahn, B., Halligan, J., and Wilks, S., Eds., Edward Elgar, Cheltenham, 2002, pp. 103–122.

Wettenhall, R., The rhetoric and reality of public–private partnerships, *Public Organ. Rev.*, 3 (1), 77–107, 2003.

Wettenhall, R. and O Nuallain, C., Eds., *Getting Together in Public Enterprise*, International Institute of Administrative Sciences, Brussels, 1987.

Wettenhall, R. and O Nuallain, C., Eds., *Public Enterprise Performance Evaluation: Seven Country Studies*, International Institute of Administrative Sciences, Brussels, 1990.

Wettenhall, R. and Thynne, I., Eds., Symposium: public enterprise systems, performance and change, *Int. Rev. Public Admin.* (Seoul, Korea), 6 (1), 1–48, 2001.

Wettenhall, R., Corkery, J., and O Nuallain, C., Eds., Symposium on public enterprise boards, *Asian J. Public Admin.*, 19 (1), 3–198, 1997.

Wolf, C., Jr., *Markets or Governments: Choosing between Imperfect Alternatives*, MIT Press, Cambridge, MA, 1988.

Woodward, N., Public enterprise, privatisation and cultural adaptation, in *Public Enterprise at the Crossroads*, Heath, J., Ed., Routledge, London, 1990.

World Bank, *Bureaucrats in Business: The Economics and Politics of Government Ownership*, Oxford University Press, New York, 1995.

Chapter 27

Governance for Environmental Planning and Sustainable Development: Asian Perspectives

Peter Hills

CONTENTS

I. Introduction

One of the most striking features of 1990s was the emergence of governance as a key issue in debates about the design and implementation of a wide range of public policies. Much like the concept of sustainable development, governance is a term that is used widely and freely but which carries with it a variety of connotations and meanings. To some, it still appears to be a contemporary term for government itself: better government equates with improved governance and vice versa (Yencken, 2002). Many others, including the Commission on Global Governance (Carlsson and Ramphal, 1995), have emphasized that "governance" means much more than just "government" (Dahle, 1998). There has been much debate about the nature of environmental governance and governance for sustainable development at the macro-level (i.e., internationally, regionally, and nationally) and about how it can and should evolve (e.g., Weale et al., 2000; Anaedu and Engfeldt, 2002; Gardiner, 2002; Lafferty, 2002; OECD, 2002; Dietz et al., 2003; Frickel and Davidson, 2004). There has also been growing recognition of the importance of governance in the context of local intervention (e.g., in creating "sustainable communities" [Roseland, 2000; Stewart, 2000]) and the implications of what has been described as a process of "governance rescaling" in relation to environmental policy and discourse (Gibbs and Jonas, 2000; Jonas and Gibbs, 2003). Governance is also linked with the emergence of new environmental policy instruments (Jordan et al., 2003). Such instruments are not only seen as the outcomes of new approaches to policy making but also as part of the governance process itself.

Governance has also been strongly linked with the discourse regarding "partnerships" — the central theme of the 2002 World Summit on Sustainable Development in Johannesburg — and their role in promoting sustainable development initiatives (e.g., Bleischwitz, 2003; Davies, 2002). Briefly, the contemporary discourse of sustainability which dominates the development agenda cannot be addressed without some consideration being given to the issue of governance and the extent to which changes in modes of governance will facilitate and enhance the effectiveness of sustainable development policies.

II. Governance and Good Governance

As Maseland (2000) observes, governance has been variously described as:

1. "... the science of decision-making"
2. "... the art of public leadership"
3. "... the written and unwritten policies, procedures and decision-making units that control resource allocation within and among institutions"
4. "... how key community objectives are determined and realized, with government, whether central or local, being one, but not the only, possible means through which it may happen"

Numerous attempts have been made to delineate the dimensions of "good governance." The Asian Development Bank (ADB, 2004), for example, emphasizes the importance of four key elements of governance:

1. *Accountability* — making public officials answerable for government behavior and responsive to the entity from which they derive their authority.
2. *Participation* — the involvement of citizens in the development process. Beneficiaries and groups affected by the project need to participate so that the government can make informed choices with respect to their needs, and social groups can protect their rights.
3. *Predictability* — which refers to (a) the existence of laws, regulations, and policies to regulate society and (b) their fair and consistent application.
4. *Transparency* — which refers to the availability of information to the general public about government rules, regulations, and decisions.

The United Nations Development Programme (UNDP) has also enunciated a set of principles of good governance (Graham et al., 2003):

1. *Legitimacy and voice* — which incorporate the concepts of participation and a consensus orientation
2. *Direction* — embracing the idea of strategic vision
3. *Performance* — which links responsiveness, effectiveness, and efficiency
4. *Accountability* — which links accountability and transparency
5. *Fairness* — which emphasizes the importance of equity and the rule of law

As we can observe, there is a considerable overlap in terms of these key criteria or principles.

The emergence of different modes of governance and their classification and characterization have attracted considerable scholarly attention in recent years. DiGaetano and Strom (2003), for example, provide us with some valuable insights into the dimensions of comparative urban governance. Their analysis of the institutional milieu of urban governance in the United States, Great Britain, France, and Germany suggests the existence of five contrasting governance modes: clientelistic, corporatist, managerial, pluralist, and populist. However, as Ng (2004) points out in her discussion of this framework in the context of governance change in Chinese global cities, the modes or models of governance identified by DiGaetano and Strom (2003) are predicated on the assumption that there exists a democratic political system, a form of capitalist, market economy, and a more or less active civil society.

However, in an Asian context as Gouldson et al. (under revision) observe, engaging in civil society in a process of social learning (Glasbergen, 1966) to promote changes in modes of governance raises a variety of conceptual and practical issues. Civil society is not only a "contested concept" but in Asia it is also "very much a received concept" that may be conceptualized in various ways: "a civil society opposed to the state, a civil society assisting a minimal state, and a pluralistic civil society demanding an accountable state" (Zarsky and Tay, 2000: 136).

The financial crisis that struck the region in 1997 intensified interest in civil society. The central question is how governments can "harness the transformative potential of this growing popular consciousness and burgeoning civil society towards greatly improving environmental performance. In essence, this means creatively bringing civil society groups exactly into the task of environmental governance" (Zarsky and Tay, 2000: 138).

What has also emerged in parts of Asia is an interest in subpolitical arrangements (Beck, 1994) that can represent "alternative enforcement and control mechanisms of national environmental policy plagued by limited budgets, manpower, and information" (Phuong and Mol, 2004: 442). These can lead to direct engagement between local communities and industrial undertakings in attempts to resolve local environmental problems, thus giving rise to new and innovative forms of local environmental governance. The existence of these resource constraints, which Phuong and Mol argue, provide a rationale for the existence of such subpolitical arrangements in countries where the state remains dominant and civil society initiatives are constrained.

In much of Western Europe and North America, national and local NGOs have become key players in environmental subpolitics and in governance itself. In contrast, in Vietnam, the analysis of Phuong and Mol (2004) demonstrates how environmental subpolitics can develop around local social organizations and local mass media. The linkages that develop between communities and local industrial polluters appear to emerge largely in a vacuum created by state failure, or at best state acquiescence, and are not themselves driven by the pursuit of cooperative modes of governance between government, industry, and other stakeholders. Sonnenfeld's (2002) analysis of the transformation of pulp and paper manufacturing in Southeast Asia provides further evidence of the distinctive role played by communities and broader social movements in relation to environmental reform processes.

Central to many of these debates about the transformational potential of civil society and local communities and the emergence of new modes of environmental governance is the issue of democracy. Weidner (2002) contends that "development of democratic institutions and rules is a key precondition for building environmental capacity, gaining support of environmental proponents, and creating an opportunity structure to publicly address environmental problems." Such an assertion may be relevant in certain Asian economies such as Taiwan, but does not relate to research findings from elsewhere in the region. The work of Phuong and Mol (2004), for example, demonstrates the potential for alternative transformational potential in a society that is still some way from a western-style democracy.

III. Environmental Governance in Hong Kong

The Hong Kong Special Administrative Region of China extends over an area of 1100 km^2 and has a population of 6.9 million (Hills and Welford, 2002). Formerly a British colony before 1997, Hong Kong's existing economic, legal, and social systems are protected within the PRC until 2047 under the "one country-two systems" framework (Hills and Roberts, 2001). The nature and scale of Hong Kong's environmental problems are extensively documented elsewhere (Hills and Barron, 1997; Welford et al., forthcoming). Its marine waters are badly polluted and its air quality is a serious problem with frequent poor visibility. With a high population density, noise pollution is a common complaint among residents. Over 9 million tons of wastes are produced each year and recent cutbacks in the number and scale of land reclamation projects for which such wastes can be used as fill material have further aggravated the problem. A major study of sustainability indicators for Hong Kong concluded that the SAR is moving away from sustainable development rather than moving closer towards it (Barron and Steinbrecher, 1999).

Environmental policy-making has a relatively short history in Hong Kong. It has been highly centralized and synonymous with environmental protection and has been driven primarily by a command-and-control approach to local pollution problems. Even in 2004, environmental policy remains largely based on to this approach (Hills, 2004) and to a framework that is linked to tackling problems on an environmental media basis (e.g., air quality and water quality). Limited progress has been made with the introduction of environmental taxes and charges and, despite the rhetoric, considerations relating to sustainable development have largely failed to exert much influence on the decision-making process.

As Hills (2004) observes, although sustainable development became an increasingly important focus of environmental discourse in Hong Kong during the 1990s, the Special Administrative Region entered the new millennium still lacking a policy framework for sustainable development, with no binding commitment to Agenda 21 or to Local Agenda 21 initiatives and without the institutions in place to design or implement an effective sustainability strategy.

In 1999, the SAR's Chief Executive announced a number of initiatives in the area of sustainable development (Tung, 1999). These included the establishment of a Council for Sustainable Development (CSD) and a Sustainable Development Unit (SDU) within government. Implementation of these important institutional developments was delayed for some years. The SDU was set up in April 2001, but its influence and impact on the policy-making process has been limited. The Council was finally established in February 2003 and met for the first time on April 1, 2003. Two subcommittees of the Council have been formed (Council for Sustainable Development, 2003). One is working on the development of a sustainable development strategy for Hong Kong with the objective being to complete work on this by late 2004. The other subcommittee focuses on education and publicity and will oversee initiatives aiming at promoting public awareness of sustainable development. It will also assess applications for grants from a Sustainable Development Fund, which will provide financial support for projects that help to enhance public awareness and understanding of sustainability issues.

Research on environmental governance and processes of environmental reform in Hong Kong has been limited. The following discussion reports on some recent research undertaken by the author, which has examined these issues in relation to the applicability of ecological modernization theory as an interpretative framework through which to understand processes of environmental transformation in Hong Kong is understood (Gouldson and Murphy, 1997; Mol and Sonnenfeld, 2000; Hills and Welford, 2002; Welford et al., forthcoming). The research in question involved a survey of 120 informed stakeholders in the environmental policy-making process and was conducted in 2003.

This study was based on the premise that a number of recent policy initiatives in Hong Kong appear to be consistent with the objectives of the ecological modernization model and have brought about improvements in the environmental efficiency of the local economy (Hills and Welford, 2002; Welford et al., forthcoming). There is evidence of a willingness to use various technological measures, incentives, and supporting mechanisms to bring about improvements in the efficiency with which resources are used, to reduce impacts of particular activities, and to bring about improvements in the quality of life. These initiatives address the technical dimensions of ecological modernization. Then, there are indications of a move away from a command-and-control regulatory regime to a broader mix of regulation, economic instruments and voluntary agreements, although such changes are as yet limited. These changes partly reflect the social and institutional transformations that are central to the processes of environmental reform with which ecological modernization theory engages (Mol and Sonnenfeld, 2000).

Our initial research on the technical aspects of ecological modernization in Hong Kong provided us with insights into policy outcomes but not with many insights into issues relating to the dynamics of the policy-making process and the emergence of new modes of environmental governance. To structure our stakeholder questionnaire and to ground it conceptually, we took the themes identified by Mol and Sonnenfeld (2000: 5–7) in their review of the evolution of ecological modernization theory as our starting point. These themes, which reflect the core of ecological modernization research, include:

1. The changing role of science and technology which are evaluated not only with regard to their contribution to the emergence of environmental problems but also for their role in resolving them.
2. The role of market dynamics and economic agents in ecological restructuring and reform.
3. Transformations in the role of the nation state and the shift away from command-and-control regulation to new modes of decentralized, flexible, and consensual governance coupled with the emergence of supranational institutions, which are also having an impact on the nation state's role in environmental reform.
4. Changes in the position, role, and ideology of social movements, which instead of being marginalized, are increasingly involved in public and private decision making on environmental reform.
5. Changes in discursive practices and the emergence of new ideologies that reject the neglect of the environment or the counterpositioning of economic and environmental interests.

For the purposes of the present discussion, we shall focus on the study findings that address issues relating to environmental governance and sustainable development in Hong Kong. More detailed discussion on the survey findings may bc found in Hills (in preparation).

A. Policy Objectives and Policy Instruments

There is general agreement among all stakeholder groups that the main objective of environmental policy in Hong Kong is to control pollution and that the principal policy instruments used are those of a command-and-control type (i.e., ordinances and regulations). However, the view seems to be that environmental policy has not been particularly effective over the years between 1993 and 2003 (Figure 27.1 and Figure 27.2). The promotion of sustainable development comes some way behind pollution control as a policy priority, as does improving the environmental efficiency of the economy, the wording that we used in an attempt to convey the techno-economic essence of ecological modernization. All stakeholders recognize the role of education and moral persuasion as policy instruments used by government. Economic instruments have not, in the view of most stakeholders, played a particularly prominent role in environmental policy nor have voluntary agreements. Many stakeholders believe that Hong Kong must address a number of important factors if economic instruments are to be more widely used. These factors include opposition from the business community, a lack of support from the government and legislature, and a lack of understanding of such instruments in the community (Figure 27.3). In the case of voluntary agreements, a basic problem seems to be a lack of understanding about how such agreements work, as well as opposition from business. Lack of government support and implementation problems are also significant concerns (Figure 27.4).

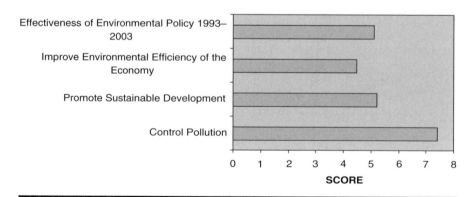

Figure 27.1   Objectives of environmental policy (n = 120).

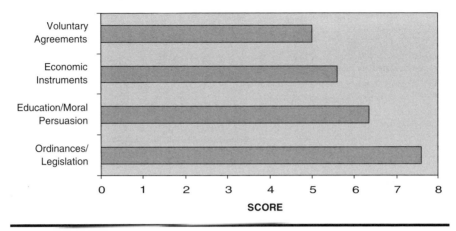

Figure 27.2   The importance of environmental policy instruments (*n* = 120).

These findings indicate that Hong Kong continues to adopt a very conservative and traditional approach to environmental governance, maintaining a strong emphasis on the regulatory control of environmental pollution problems. Ironically, economic restructuring over the past 20 years has seen most of Hong Kong's manufacturing base relocating to the adjacent Pearl River Delta region in neighboring Guangdong province and contributing to the emergence of significant transboundary air and water pollution problems. As the sources of these problems are located outside of Hong Kong's territorial jurisdiction, their mitigation is dependent on cooperation with authorities in the mainland. This is indicative of the need for Hong Kong to develop innovative forms of regional environmental governance in collaboration with mainland authorities.

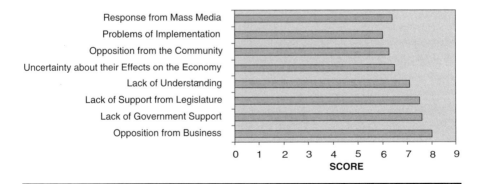

Figure 27.3   Factors preventing the more extensive use of economic instruments (*n* = 120).

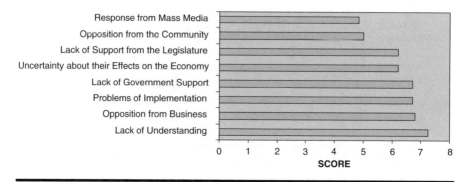

Figure 27.4   Factors preventing the more extensive use of voluntary agreements (*n* = 120).

B. Role of Government and NGOs

There is a broad consensus that environmental policy in Hong Kong has been based on the command-and-control model and that government has tended towards a controller rather than a facilitator state in the way it has tackled environmental problems. Furthermore, government is not generally regarded as being open and responsive to the views of environmental stakeholder groups.

Local environmental NGOs are widely regarded as agenda leaders, independently minded and with reasonably effective community links. They are regarded as technically competent and effective lobbyists, having some influence on the policy-making process. However, stakeholders are generally of the view that NGOs lack a sound financial base (Figure 27.5).

C. Debates and Ideas: Sustainable Development

Our questions concerning the status of sustainable development in Hong Kong produced some interesting responses. Figure 27.6 indicates that

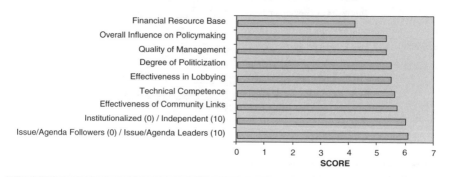

Figure 27.5   Assessment of environmental NGOs (*n* = 120).

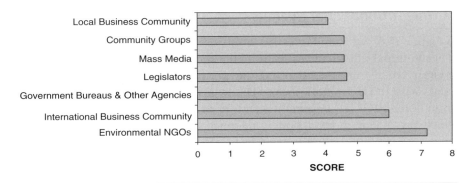

Figure 27.6   Level of understanding of sustainable development among stake-holders (*n* = 120).

environmental NGOs are widely regarded as possessing the best under-standing of the concept of sustainable development, with government and the local business community coming some way behind. The assess-ment of obstacles to promote and achieve sustainable development in Hong Kong clearly indicates that the absence of a sustainable development strategy, lack of understanding of the concept, lack of policy integration in government, institutional effectiveness, and agenda displacement are the key issues (Figure 27.7). There is also a general consensus that the debate about sustainable development has not been well informed, that there is still a pronounced tendency in Hong Kong to counter-position economic and environmental interests in policy discourses, and that Hong Kong is likely to make only limited progress towards sustainable development over the next 10 years.

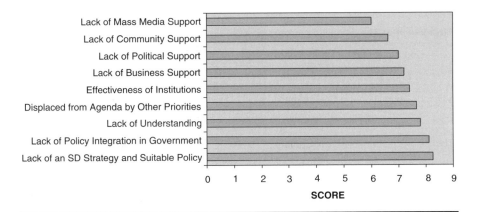

Figure 27.7   Obstacles to promoting and achieving sustainable development (*n* = 120).

D. *Institutional Effectiveness*

In Figure 27.8, we summarize the results of a question addressing the issue of institutional effectiveness in bringing about positive change leading to environmental improvement and the promotion of sustainable development. With the exception of the SDU, which is a government agency, the institutions listed are important statutory or nonstatutory advisory bodies, which provide high-level policy guidance on matters relating directly to environmental and natural resources issues, sustainable development, and town planning. Respondents were asked to make an assessment of the potential effectiveness of each institution (i.e., what it can achieve) and their view as to its actual operational effectiveness (i.e., what it does achieve).

Our findings suggest that most of these key institutions suffer from what might be regarded as a credibility gap. The SDU and the newly established CSD score rather poorly on actual performance. In the case of the SDU, these assessments may reflect the unit's lack of visibility and limited impact on government policy-making processes since its establishment in 2001. The Council was only established in early 2003, and there has been little time to judge its performance directly. The low score awarded for its actual effectiveness by all stakeholders may reflect concerns about the long delay in setting up the body, its membership, and the manner in which it is going about it task.

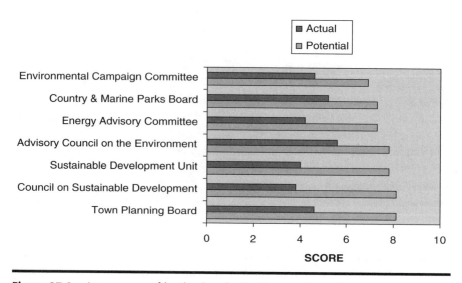

Figure 27.8 Assessment of institutional effectiveness (*n* = 120).

IV. Discussion

Although various policy initiatives in Hong Kong have produced changes in environmental conditions consistent with the technical prescriptions of ecological modernization theory, the results of our survey indicate that as far as the social and institutional transformations associated with ecological modernization are concerned, there is limited evidence to suggest that Hong Kong is actively and consciously engaging in broader processes of environmental reform and moving towards the adoption of new modes of environmental governance.

The use of a conventional command-and-control approach to environmental policy seems to enjoy wide support among stakeholders, and while the role of education and the use of economic instruments are both recognized and broadly endorsed, the move towards more consensual styles of environmental governance based upon voluntary agreements and cooperative environmental management finds only limited support. Many stakeholders still see environmental policy primarily as an exercise in pollution control, even though it is clear that local industrial and agricultural sources of pollution have diminished and that some of the most serious challenges involve transboundary pollution which Hong Kong itself cannot control.

Since the early 1990s, environmental NGOs have been drawn more closely into the policy making process through their membership of a number of advisory bodies, including the Advisory Council on the Environment and the Environmental Campaign Committee, and as informal consultants with government on a wide variety of policy issues and local environmental controversies. Our findings suggest that most stakeholder groups respect the abilities of and the role played by these groups.

Despite the government's efforts to promote sustainable development in Hong Kong (Hills, 2004), the concept remains poorly understood and the discourse is not well informed. Furthermore, the counter-positioning of economic and environmental interests is still evident in this discourse.

Our findings also suggest that various environmental institutions are underperforming in terms of stakeholder expectations. Advisory bodies have long played a key role in governance and the policy process in Hong Kong: as a sounding board for government and as a mechanism by which policy initiatives can be legitimized through their endorsement by supposedly independent, informed, and respected community leaders. These reservations regarding the performance of advisory bodies should be a source of concern to government. However, in a positive sense, this suggests that there is considerable potential in Hong Kong for institutional and governance transformations, which will serve to open up the environmental policy making process and enhance its credibility with key stakeholders. This will require that government itself responds positively to the new macro-political environment that has emerged in recent years, a challenge that will test its ability to adapt and move towards more open, participatory, and consensual modes of governance. At the core of this debate will be the issue of trust (Fukiyama, 1995; Tonkiss and Passey, 2000) between the polity and the community it governs.

V. Conclusions: Social Learning and Governance

This chapter has focused on various dimensions of environmental governance. Using the example of Hong Kong, it has also attempted to illustrate how various social and institutional transformations can facilitate or impede the transition to new modes of governance for the environment and sustainable development. Clearly, Hong Kong may be somewhat atypical in terms of its contextual setting. However, it is also arguable that it may reflect some of the features of more advanced economies elsewhere and the difficulties that such economies can experience in moving from pollution control regimes and their associated institutional structures to modes of environmental governance better suited to the design and implementation of policies for sustainable development.

At the core of this transition is the need for adaptive policy making systems and institutions that evolve in response to a process of societal learning. Glasbergen (1996) has provided an analytical framework that recognizes three basic modes of policy learning: technical, conceptual, and social. These are described in more detail in Table 27.1, which also attempts to relate these modes of learning to the evolution of environmental discourse and governance in Hong Kong.

Environmental pollution control regimes are typically technical in orientation and therefore tend to be driven by the mode of technical learning. The Hong Kong experience clearly fits this pattern. The dominant form of environmental discourse associated with this mode of policy learning is typically administrative rationalism (Dryzek, 1997). Engagement with sustainable development concepts or ecological modernization theory is associated with the emergence of conceptual learning. Again, this has been in evidence in Hong Kong since the early 1990s, although only recently has it played a more prominent role in shaping policy and institutional developments. Improved environmental governance must however rely on the emergence of policy learning, which is clearly shaped by social learning. This not only places greater emphasis on relations between key actors (or stakeholders) in the policy process but also recognizes the need to move beyond models of policy making that are dependent on hierarchies and control regimes to those which recognize the importance of cooperation and shared responsibility for achieving policy goals.

Table 27.1 Modes of Policy Learning in Hong Kong

Mode of Learning	Descriptors	Dates	Examples	Dominant Mode of Discourse
Technical	Search for new policy instruments in context of fixed policy objectives Change occurs without basic discussion of objectives or strategies Policy makers respond to demands for change with more of same kinds of solutions they adopted in first responding to environmental problems: regulation, oversight, and enforcement Government as controller — relations between regulators and their targets are distant, formal, and adversarial Optimism about knowledge and problem solving	Late 1970s–1980s — much of 1990s	Pollution control legislation Creation of environmental protection agency Rational policy techniques	Administrative rationalism (Dryzek, 1997)
Conceptual	Process of redefining policy goals and adjusting problem definitions and strategies Policy objectives debated Perspectives on issues change and strategies reformulated New concepts emerge (e.g., ecological modernization and sustainability)	From early 1990s	1993 2nd Review of 1989 White Paper introduces sustainable development into official policy discourse 1996 3rd Review of 1989 White Paper 1999 Chief Executive's Policy Address (sustainable development, world city status, regional environmental, and sustainability concerns)	Ecological modernization and sustainable development (Hills, 2004)

(Continued)

Table 27.1 *(Continued)*

Mode of Learning	Descriptors	Dates	Examples	Dominant Mode of Discourse
Social	Builds on cognitive capacities of technical learning and rethinking of objectives or strategies in conceptual learning Structural openness Continuous processes of interaction between social actors, groups, and forces and semipublic organizations, institutions, or authorities Emphasizes relations among actors and quality of dialog Hierarchy and control replaced by cooperative model (government, industry and other stakeholders share responsibility for achieving policy goals) Recognition of uncertainty in knowledge of problems and capacity to solve them Precautionary principle — need for communication among stakeholders to determine action in absence of conclusive scientific evidence	After 2001	Greater emphasis on consultation and stakeholder engagement Hong Kong 2030 Planning Study Council for Sustainable Development Strategy Sub-Committee — stakeholder engagement exercise	Improved governance

Social learning as a driver for policy change also offers the potential to engage more effectively with Ratner's concept of sustainable development "as a dialogue of values." Such a concept, Ratner (2004: 64) argues:

> ... impels us to focus our attention on the way that alternative forms of governance structure the possibilities for meaningful and equitable involvement of social actors in decisions over a collective future.... A dialogue of values perspective provides a rationale for seeing participation of actors in deliberating the ends and means of development not only as instrumental in realizing specific development goals, but as *constitutive* of the very meaning of sustainable development practice.

Thus, the comparative study of governance structures is essential to determine how differences in such structures influence collective decision making, the nature of policy decisions, and ultimately policy outcomes at all spatial levels, from the global to the local.

Good governance alone will not guarantee progress towards a sustainable future. Similarly, elaborate policies for enhanced sustainability will not of themselves ensure a successful transition to such a future unless they embody and reflect basic principles of good governance.

Acknowledgments

The research on which this chapter is based was funded partly by the Hong Kong Research Grants Council under grant no. HKU7202/02H. The assistance of Ms Jennifer Zee in the design, administration, and analysis of the questionnaires is gratefully acknowledged.

References

ADB (Asian Development Bank), Elements of governance, ADB website: http://www.adb.org/Governance/gov_elements.asp (viewed 12.8.04), 2004.

Anaedu, O. and Engfeldt, L.-G., Sustainable Development Governance at the International, Regional and National Levels, paper presented at UN Third Summit Preparatory Committee (PREPCOM 3), March 25–April 5, New York, 2002.

Barron, W. and Steinbrecher, N., Eds., *Heading Towards Sustainability? Practical Indicators of Sustainability for Hong Kong*, Centre of Urban Planning and Environmental Management, University of Hong Kong, Hong Kong, 1999.

Beck, U., The reinvention of politics: towards a theory of reflexive modernization, in *Reflexive Modernisation: Politics, Tradition and Aesthetics in the Modern Social Order*, Beck, U., Giddens, A., and Lash, S., Eds., Polity Press, Cambridge, 1994, pp. 1–55.

Bleischwitz, R., Governance of sustainable development: towards synergies between corporate and political governance strategies, Wuppertal Papers 132, Wuppertal Institute for Climate, Environment and Energy, Wuppertal, 2003.

Carlsson, I. and Ramphal, S., Eds., *Our Global Neighbourhood: The Report of the Commission on Global Governance*, Oxford University Press, Oxford, 1995.

Council for Sustainable Development, Terms of Reference of the Council and Establishment of Sub-committees, Paper 01/03, Council for Sustainable Development, Hong Kong, 2003.

Dahle, K., Toward governance for future generations: How do we change course? *Futures*, 30 (4), 277–292, 1998.

Davies, A.R., Power, politics and networks: shaping partnerships for sustainable communities, *Area* 34 (2), 190–203, 2002.

Dietz, T., Ostrom, E., and Stern, P.C., The struggle to govern the commons, *Science*, 302, 1907–1912, 2003.

DiGaetano, A. and Strom, E., Comparative urban governance: an integrated approach, *Urban Affairs Rev.*, 38 (3), 356–395, 2003.

Dryzek, J.S., *The Politics of the Earth: Environmental Discourses*, Oxford University Press, Oxford, 1997.

Frickel, S. and Davidson, D.J., Building environmental states: legitimacy and rationalization in sustainability governance, *Int. Sociol.*, 19 (1), 89–110, 2004.

Fukiyama, F., *Trust: The Social Virtues and the Creation of Prosperity*, The Free Press, New York, 1995.

Gardiner, R., *Governance for Sustainable Development: Outcomes from Johannesburg*, Stakeholder Forum for Our Common Future, London, 2002.

Gibbs, D. and Jonas, A.E.G., Governance and regulation in local environmental policy: the utility of a regime approach, *Geoforum*, 31, 299–313, 2000.

Glasbergen, P., Learning to manage the environment, in *Democracy and the Environment*, Lafferty, W. and Meadowcroft, J., Eds., Edward Elgar, Cheltenham, 1996.

Gouldson, A. and Murphy, J., Ecological modernization: restructuring industrial economies, in *Greening the Millennium? The New Politics of the Environment*, Jacobs, M., Ed., Blackwell Publishers, Oxford, 1997, pp. 74–86.

Gouldson, A., Hills, P., and Welford, R., Ecological modernisation and policy learning in Asia: lessons from Hong Kong, *Geoforum* (under revision).

Graham, J., Amos, B., and Plumptre, T., Principles of good governance for the 21st century, *Policy Brief* 15, Institute on Governance, Ottawa, 2003.

Hills, P., Administrative rationalism, sustainable development and the politics of environmental discourse in Hong Kong, in *Sustainable Development in Hong Kong*, Mottershead, T., Ed., Hong Kong University Press, Hong Kong, 2004, pp. 13–41.

Hills, P., Stakeholder perspectives on environmental reform in Hong Kong: an exploratory study, *J. Environ. Plann. Manage.*, 48 (2), 209–240.

Hills, P. and Barron, W., Hong Kong: the challenge of sustainability, *Land Use Policy*, 14 (1), 41–53, 1997.

Hills, P. and Roberts, P., Political integration, transboundary pollution and sustainability: challenges for environmental policy in the Pearl River Delta region, *J. Environ. Plann. Manage.*, 44 (4), 455–473, 2001.

Hills, P. and Welford, R., Ecological modernisation as a weak form of sustainable development in Hong Kong, *Int. J. Sustainable Develop. World Ecol.*, 9, 315–331, 2002.

Jonas, A.E.G. and Gibbs, D., Changing local modes of economic and environmental governance in England: a tale of two areas, *Social Sci. Quart.*, 84 (4), 1018–1037, 2003.

Jordan, A., Wurzel, R., Zito, A.R., and Brückner, L., European governance and the transfer of "new" environmental policy instruments (NEPIs) in the European Union, *Public Admin.*, 81, 555–574, 2003.

Lafferty, W.M., Adapting government practice to the goals of sustainable development, Proceedings of a Seminar: Improving Governance for Sustainable Development, OECD, Paris, 2002.

Maseland, J., Governance versus government, *Habitat Debate*, 6 (1), 2000. www.unhabitat.org/HD/hdv6n1/feedback.html.

Mol, A.P.J. and Sonnenfeld, D.A., *Ecological Modernization around the World: Perspectives and Critical Debates*, Frank Cass, London, 2000.

Ng, M.K., Mode of Governance and Planning for Sustainable Development: A Comparative Study of Chinese Global Cities, paper presented at the City Futures Conference, University of Illinois, Chicago, July, 2004.

OECD, *Governance for Sustainable Development: Five OECD Case Studies*, OECD, Paris, 2002.

Phuong, P.T. and Mol, A.P.J., Communities as informal regulators: new arrangements in industrial pollution control in Vietnam, *J. Risk Res.*, 7 (4), 431–444, 2004.

Ratner, B.D., "Sustainability" as a dialogue of values: challenges to the sociology of development, *Sociol. Inq.*, 74 (1), 50–69, 2004.

Roseland, M., Sustainable community development: integrating environmental, economic, and social objectives, *Prog. Plann.*, 54, 73–132, 2000.

Sonnenfeld, D.A., Social movements and ecological modernization: the transformation of pulp and paper manufacturing, *Develop. Change*, 33, 1–27, 2002.

Stewart, M., Community governance, in *Sustainable Communities: The Potential for Eco-Neighbourhoods*, Barton, H., Ed., Earthscan Publications Ltd, London, 2000.

Tonkiss, F. and Passey, A., *Trust and Civil Society*, Macmillan Press, Basingstoke, 2000.

Tung, C.H., Quality people–quality home: positioning Hong Kong for the 21st century. Address by the Chief Executive at the Legislative Council meeting on 6 October 1999, Printing Department, Hong Kong SAR, 1999.

Weale, A., Pridham, G., Cini, M., Konstadakopulos, D., Porter, M., and Flynn, B., *Environmental Governance in Europe: An Ever Closer Ecological Union?* Oxford University Press, Oxford, 2000.

Weidner, H., Capacity building for ecological modernization, *Am. Behav. Scientist*, 45 (9), 1340–1368, 2002.

Welford, R., Hills, P., and Lam, J., Environmental reform, technology policy and ecological modernization in Hong Kong, *Develop. Change*, forthcoming.

Yencken, D., Governance for sustainability, *Aust. J. Public Admin.*, 61 (2), 78–89, 2002.

Zarsky, L. and Tay, S.S.C., Civil society and the future of environmental governance in Asia, in *Asia's Clean Revolution: Industry: Growth and the Environment*, Angel, D.P., Rock, M.T., Eds., Greenleaf Publishing, Sheffield, 2000, pp. 128–154.

Chapter 28

E-Government and Development

Ian Holliday

CONTENTS

I. Introduction

The opening years of the new millennium witnessed leading international agencies campaigning proactively for development initiatives to focus on technology, and on ways of harnessing it to the central development goal of poverty eradication. The United Nations (UN) used *Human Development Report 2001: Making New Technologies Work for Human Development* (HDR 2001) to issue a clarion call: "[I]t is time for a new partnership between technology and development. *Human Development Report 2001* is intended as the manifesto for that partnership" (UNDP, 2001: iii). The United Nations Conference on Trade and Development (UNCTAD) followed up by convening the World Summit on the Information Society (WSIS), in Geneva in December 2003 and in Tunis in November 2005. The World Bank launched a website designed to amass and disseminate e-government experience in development contexts. Beyond the UN system, many other high-profile international agencies also began to pay increased attention to the development potential of modern technology. The result was that, despite long-standing skepticism, technology came to rank high on the agenda of key players in the development community.

Debates provoked by this technological turn range across many domains of scientific advance. Biotechnology and nanotechnology particularly are well studied. However, apart from this, one aspect of contemporary experience that is attracting considerable attention is electronic government, or e-government in short. Recent initiatives taken by UN agencies, for instance, focus squarely on e-government, which stands at the heart of HDR 2001, is absolutely central to WSIS, is given a dedicated World Bank website, and so on. At the national level, donor governments are also active in promoting e-government for development. In November 2002, for example, the Korean Ministry of Information and Communication sponsored the launch of the Development Gateway Foundation–Korea Training Center, with the aim of reducing poverty and promoting sustainable development by providing technical training in developing countries. Apart from formal government organizations, initiatives such as the egov4dev website run from the University of Manchester are attracting significant interest. The possibilities of e-government are thus becoming a core theme of international development governance, and are being linked to headline projects such as attainment of the Millennium Development Goals (UNDP, 2001; WSIS, 2003a).

In basic terms, e-government usually comprises public sector use of information and communication technology (ICT), including the Internet, to boost information dissemination, enhance service delivery, and facilitate citizen participation. Though distinct definitions vary in marginal ways, the core idea remains the same. Furthermore, e-government is often divided into stages, such as the five-step progression described in a study co-sponsored by the UN: emerging, enhanced, interactive, transactional and seamless (UN/ASPA, 2002: 2). In the development community, the most frequently stressed feature of e-government is the option it generates for pro-poor development initiatives aimed at empowering individuals and communities, and expanding choice.

There are of course conflicting views about the importance development strategists ought to attach to e-government. At one end extreme, it is held by some to make very little difference to fundamental development challenges. When billions of people live on less than a dollar or two a day, have insecure access to nutritious food, clean water and decent sanitation, and fall prey to fatal yet preventable disease, the invention of the Internet is a matter of strictly marginal significance. At the other end extreme, e-government is said to open up the possibility of radical advance in tackling the governance problems that have always plagued development initiatives.

This chapter takes what is fast becoming an orthodox line in the development community. New technologies can be made to work for human development. However, there is no automatic technological fix. In the sentence that follows its clarion call, HDR 2001 states that "it is also intended as a source of cautionary public policy advice to ensure that technology does not sweep development off its feet, but instead that the potential benefits of technology are rooted in a pro-poor development strategy" (UNDP, 2001: iii). A cautionary approach to e-government directs attention to the conditions in which contemporary initiatives are generating positive cost-benefit outcomes. This chapter therefore begin by giving a quick overview of what e-government currently amounts to. It then examines some of the e-government plans and strategy documents produced notably by international development agencies. It next surveys some current experience in three main domains: e-administration, e-services and e-citizenship. In its concluding evaluation, it argues that e-government is only likely to generate development gains when it is closely adapted to the needs and capacities of the user community.

II. E-Government

In a landmark analysis of the changes wrought by what he calls the Information Age, Castells (2000: 500) holds that the impact of contemporary ICT will be at least as great as that of the industrial revolution. The contention at the core of his thesis is that "as an historical trend, dominant functions and processes ... are increasingly organized around networks." Today, he claims, *"the unit is the network*, made up of a variety of subjects and organizations, relentlessly modified as networks adapt to supportive environments and market structures" (Castells, 2000: 214; author's emphasis). This is extreme, for many pre-existing units such as class, state, nation and culture retain considerable purchase in the contemporary world, and form the basis for much more circumspect analyses (Van Dijk, 1999;

Halavais, 2000; Slack and Williams, 2000; Rantanen, 2001). Nevertheless, it is the networking aspect of e government that constitutes its defining feature. Today, technology raises the prospect of building new networks designed to challenge and re-shape long-standing patterns of exclusion.

That said, it comes as no surprise to find that e-government is most advanced in developed nations. E-governance leaders are found exclusively in advanced countries registering per capita annual incomes in the range of US $25,000 and above, notably Canada, Singapore, the U.S.A. and Australia (Accenture, 2004). Not only do administrations in developed nations have greater resources to pursue the e-government agenda, but also their citizens have better access to ICT. A 2003 UNCTAD report noted that while "OECD countries consistently rank as the best-performing countries in terms of ICT development . . . African countries remain clustered towards the bottom of the distribution" (UNCTAD, 2003: 32–34).

Developed nations are also the focus of much analysis, whether undertaken by public agencies or by private-sector think tanks and consultancies. However, there is a strong argument for saying that the greatest possibilities lie in underdeveloped states, and that e-governance could finally present them with the tools they need to engineer radical change in hitherto under-performing governance structures. According to UN reports, "technology is a tool for, not just a reward of, growth and development" (UNDP, 2001: 27). Furthermore, applications of e-government technology are already happening in many development contexts. In 2001, Heeks (2001: 1) wrote that "e-governance is a current, not just future, reality for developing countries." As time goes by, that statement becomes ever more pertinent.

Indeed, in recent years, there has been an explosion of interest in e-government throughout the developing world, and many determined attempts have been made to move up the e-government hierarchy. Moreover, international surveys indicate the real progress being made in a number of jurisdictions, though not all such surveys look plausible. A 2003 Brown University study ranked Turkey at 6 in the world, Malaysia 8, China 12 and the Philippines 15, all of which seem a little high, but may just about be believable. However, it also ranked North Korea 61, and at the same time placed South Korea at 91, which cannot be right (West, 2003). Nevertheless, even in more credible surveys, some developing countries secure good rankings. The UN survey, undertaken in 2001 as one of the first systematic benchmarking exercises, placed a series of Latin American countries in its top category of "high e-government capacity": Brazil (ranked highest at 18 in the world), Mexico, Argentina, Uruguay and Chile (UN/ASPA, 2002). It also placed Lebanon in this category. A 2003 survey placed Shanghai and Jakarta in the top 20 global cities (EGI/GePeGI, 2003).

However, to develop a real sense of the progress in e-government that is currently made or which may be made in the days ahead, it is necessary to look beyond global surveys to actual experience on the ground. Heeks argues that e-government can be broken into three critical elements: improving government processes (e-administration), connecting citizens (e-citizens and e-services), and building external interactions (e-society) (Heeks, 2001: 4). But the three key dimensions are perhaps better viewed simply as:

1. e-administration, focused on internal government processes (G2G);
2. e-services, focused on government service delivery to citizens and businesses (G2C/G2B);
3. e-citizenship, focused on citizen and business input into governance (C2G/B2G).

Although in practice there is some overlap between these categories, they can be separated for analytical purposes. The central point is that ICT reshapes the tools with which governments can undertake their governing functions, and at the same time generates widespread possibilities for across-the-board transformation of governance arrangements.

Taking these three categories, it quickly becomes apparent that, in both developed and developing contexts, most progress is being made in the first two. On the whole, the governance changes taking place at present are greater for matters flowing out of the public sector than for matters flowing back into it. Although later sections of this chapter evaluate some contemporary developing country experience in all three categories, the major focus lies on the two most advanced areas of e-administration and e-services. Before turning to real-world experience, however, the chapter takes a look at the aspirations articulated by e-government boosters, notably in the reports and strategy documents released by international development agencies.

III. E-Government Aspirations

The international development community rarely lays down e-government aspirations in a comprehensive fashion. While both HDR 2001 and WSIS stake out forward positions on the e-government agenda, neither provides detailed prescriptions for future progress. It is therefore difficult to get a clear sense of what e-government in a development context should look like. Nevertheless, the prominence of initiatives like HDR 2001 and WSIS means that it is necessary to try to work out where they would like e-government to head.

HDR 2001 starts from the premise that "Throughout history, technology has been a powerful tool for human development and poverty reduction" (UNDP, 2001: 1). It notes that "Developing countries may gain especially high rewards from new technologies, but they also face especially severe challenges in managing the risks" (UNDP, 2001: 3). It then outlines the opportunities for empowering individuals and communities throughout the world that are opening up in what it calls "the network age." While noting the considerable problems generated by the digital divide and issues of risk management, it holds that the positive benefits of ICT lie in the barriers to human development that can be dismantled. In particular, barriers to knowledge, participation and economic opportunity can be broken down by a shift to e-government (UNDP, 2001: 35–36). It says little more than that.

WSIS is much more concrete and specific. It identifies its core challenge as harnessing ICT to promote the development goals of the Millennium Declaration, and proposes a plan of action designed to build "an inclusive Information Society" (WSIS, 2003b: 1). The e-government segment of the plan is quite minor, advocating a strategy aimed at promoting transparency, efficiency and stronger relations with citizens, initiatives such as services adapted to the needs of citizens and business, and general support for international cooperation initiatives. However, the plan is also infused with specific e-government targets that considerably extend the agenda. As global targets are to be attained by 2015, it presents a list with clear implications for e-government:

- To connect villages with ICTs and establish community access points.
- To connect universities, colleges, secondary schools and primary schools with ICTs.
- To connect scientific and research centres with ICTs.
- To connect public libraries, cultural centres, museums, post offices and archives with ICTs.
- To connect health centres and hospitals with ICTs.
- To connect all local and central government departments and establish websites and e-mail addresses.
- To adapt all primary and secondary school curricula to meet the challenges of the Information Society, taking into account national circumstances.
- To ensure that all of the world's population have access to television and radio services.
- To encourage the development of content and to put in place technical conditions in order to facilitate the presence and use of all world languages on the Internet.
- To ensure that more than half the world's inhabitants have access to ICTs within their reach (WSIS, 2003b: 2).

It also encourages all countries to develop an e-strategy by 2005, and more generally to expand access, build capacity and enhance confidence in ICTs.

Against this backdrop, what sort of progress are developing countries making in the three major spheres of e-administration, e-services and e-citizenship?

IV. E-Administration

A critical development issue concerns the quality of public administration, with much attention focused on two main areas: basic administrative efficiency and corruption. The shift to e-government generates real possibilities for tackling problems in these linked domains. Even a relatively simple initiative, like creating a government portal and departmental homepages, can boost the information available to citizens. A more ambitious initiative, like offering feedback opportunities or creating an online catalogue of government forms, can reduce many of the bureaucratic hurdles faced by citizens. Making forms downloadable can reduce the hurdles still further. Similarly, the transparency offered by the Internet can increase accountability and cut corruption. How, then, is e-administration progressing in development contexts?

Most governments across the world now have at least a minimal Internet presence. The 2001 UN co-sponsored survey found that only 21 of 190 UN member states had no e-government whatsoever, and the number will have been reduced since then. However, the utility of some sites is minimal, with the Internet serving merely as a vehicle for government propaganda. Real administrative impacts start to be felt when government departments place citizen-friendly information online, open up feedback opportunities, and so on.

A celebrated development initiative is Mexico's Tramitanet portal (www.tramitanet.gob.mx), launched in January 2002, which provides an online catalogue of more than 2000 forms (or *tramites*) available 24 hours a day, 7 days a week. A very small proportion (only around 1% in June 2003) can be downloaded from the site. For the rest, full details of how to obtain and process forms are given. Access is on a registration basis, but the procedure is straightforward. The major problems have been of two kinds. On the one hand, government funding turned out to be insufficient, with the result that ways are now being examined of creating some private-sector participation, and there was a degree of disconnect between federal and provincial action. On the other hand, limited access and a weak digital culture, plus some illiteracy and unfamiliarity with Spanish, generated barriers to popular use of the service. However, the World Bank evaluates that, in a society where very many interactions with government require the filling in and submission of at least one form, the Tramitanet portal constitutes a significant advance (World Bank, 2003).

Large proportions of government forms are available electronically in other jurisdictions. The Sabah Electronic Government Network in Malaysia (www.sabah.gov.my) contains a wealth of forms and licenses available through Kota Kinabalu City Hall. Microsoft reports the case of Lebanon, where in 2001 a team of reformers went "underground" to search for every form produced by the government's 21 ministries and 44 agencies. The team then digitized the documents and placed them on a web portal called Informs (www.informs.gov.lb). Forms can now be accessed online, or through a four-digit telephone hotline (Microsoft, 2002).

Developing nations are also harnessing ICT in the fight against corruption. A leading instance is the website created by the Central Vigilance Commission (CVC) of the Government of India (www.cvc.nic.in), which enables citizens to file online complaints against public servants, and to gather information about public servants convicted of corruption. Established in 1999 in a country then ranked 73 out of 99 on the Transparency International index, the CVC site entered the public consciousness when, in January 2000, it published the names of senior officials charged with violating conduct rules. This in itself is expected to have something of a deterrent effect, and to impact at least to some degree on the wider administrative culture in which corruption has long thrived (World Bank, 2001e). Other developing states have also instituted anti-corruption initiatives, built on the transparency offered by the Internet. In the Philippines, for instance, customs procedures have been made far less corrupt as a result of a migration to online processing (World Bank, 2001a).

In which conditions does e-administration generate benefits? The Mexican Tramitanet initiative is instructive. As has already been mentioned, funding problems placed some limits on the ability of central government and, more particularly, local governments to extend the initiative as far as many would have liked. At all levels, no payment can be made online. At many local levels, forms are still not widely available. However, problems of this kind need not generate a negative cost-benefit evaluation for the costs of translation into an online mode of operation, which are often quite small in comparison with the benefits that can be secured. More serious in this case were limitations outside government, in civil society. In Mexico, Internet access within the general population remains low, and digital experience is limited. Thus, the social penetration of the initiative is restricted. In these circumstances, governments have to think hard about pursuing an e-option. Provided that costs are low, which for initiatives like electronic provision of existing government forms they generally are, the chances of generating a positive utility are high. However, there quickly comes a point where wider social issues need to be addressed, and that can change the cost-benefit calculation quite dramatically.

More widely, a shift to e-administration appears to offer real possibilities for reducing corruption and enhancing accountability. The greater transparency generated by the Internet should, in most contexts, limit the occasions when corruption is possible. The very visible platform it creates for advertising abuses of position and power should, over time, change bureaucratic cultures. This is precisely the claim made for India's CVC. Such a shift would be of great value in development contexts.

V. E-Services

Many governments are nowadays adopting the portal approach pioneered by e-governance leaders such as the U.S.A. (www.firstgov.gov), Singapore (www.gov.sg) and Australia (www.fed.gov.au), in delivering e-services. The aim is to provide a single gateway to all government services available online, and easy pathways to and through them. Developing country examples are legion, and include Brazil (www.brasil.gov.br), India (www.nic.in) and Nigeria (www.nigeria.gov.ng). Microsoft reports the case of Egypt, where efforts have been made over a number of years to reduce red tape and ease citizen interaction with service-delivery departments of government. Nevertheless, a recent Suez Canal University study showed that, on average, citizens have to visit a government department 3.5 times to obtain a service. Many such interactions are extremely complex, involving many government departments and considerable citizen engagement. The Ministry of Communication and IT is therefore building a government portal to link as many service-delivery departments as possible. The hope is that red tape will be cut, productivity will increase, and cost savings will result (Microsoft, 2004). In 2003–2004, one of the two e-government winners of the prestigious Stockholm Challenge Award was Mexico's citizen portal (www.gob.mx), organized thematically around citizen needs, rather than along institutional lines. Again however, potential usage rates are low, with only 6% of the population reported as having access to the portal in the Stockholm citation. Finally, the World Bank reports on the creation of Colombia's government portal (www.gobierno enlinea.gov.co), inspired by the Mexican example. Immediately after the portal launch in August 2002, a presidential decree was issued requiring public agencies to post large quantities of information online. "As a result of this Internet initiative, citizens of Colombia have access to a huge volume of public information related to budgets, government plans, purchasing, etc. All government regulations since 1900 are available online. In addition, businesses (and citizens) can access government procurement information online" (World Bank, 2001d). At the sub-national level, a leading case is Naga City in the Philippines (www.naga.gov.ph), winner of a Cybercity Award from the UNDP's Urban Governance Initiative in 2002.

Again here, access is a critical issue. An instructive initiative from India is Gyandoot (gyandoot.nic.in), "an intranet in Dhar district [in Madhya Pradesh] connecting rural cybercafes catering to the everyday needs of the masses" (Gyandoot, 2004), which was established in January 2000. This initiative has won a number of international prizes, including the Stockholm Challenge Award in 2000. The Stockholm citation lauded the project, calling it "a breakthrough in e-government, demonstrating a paradigm shift which gives marginalized tribal citizens their first ever chance to access knowledge, with minimum investment" (Stockholm Challenge, 2000). The knowledge in question was identified through local villager input at the design stage of the project. Guilty it comprised up-to-date information about agricultural prices, details of land records, and information about application or complaint forms. This sort of information was therefore put online, and made available to villagers through a series of kiosks (initially 20, but quickly expanded to 31), each serving some 25–30 villages and together reaching nearly half-a-million people. The kiosks charge user fees, and are run on commercial lines. Over time, Gyandoot is intended to become driven by private enterprise. In the first year of operation, the system registered around 5000 users per month.

Gyandoot is certainly innovative, and it can claim a number of successes. In 2001, a World Bank report cited a number of improvements registered by villagers, such as better prices for agricultural products, faster official responses to complaints and less corruption (World Bank, 2001b). However, there have also been downsides. Technological problems, notably generated by power supply and connectivity problems, made for difficulties at the start. A shift to optical fiber connections partially overcame them, though problems of intermittent power failure remain. Equally serious were bureaucratic problems, created by local officials who did not always respect the turnaround time commitments made when the service was launched. There were also significant administrative problems within the system itself, notably failures to keep the kiosks open at all the advertised times, and to update fluctuating agricultural prices regularly enough. Finally, cost concerns quickly became a major issue for users, with the telephone often offering a cheaper and more reliable option than networked services.

An overall verdict on Gyandoot was provided by a major evaluation undertaken for the World Bank in April–May 2002: "In achieving its intended objectives, ... Gyandoot cannot be considered a success. In spite of being in existence for more than two years, the usage of the system has remained far below acceptable levels. The current status of the project illustrates that ICT alone cannot improve the service delivery to rural poor. Significant re-engineering of backend processes and introduction of services that directly contribute to the poverty alleviation are needed to make such initiatives sustainable" (Center for Electronic Governance, 2002: 27).

Less ambition, but also path breaking was the Kothmale community radio/Internet project, in Sri Lanka aimed at boosting access for poor and marginalized citizens. This initiative sought to tackle four main problems:

limited access to ICT; linguistic problems for villagers speaking vernacular languages; lack of information in such languages; and limited motivation to make use of ICT. The solution adopted was a "radio browse" model run through a community radio station serving some 200,000 people. Each evening, between 19:00 and 20:00, the radio station browses the Internet on air, often in response to requests for information or topic areas submitted by listeners. Experts are invited to discuss the information found online. Over time, the station has built up a database of information gathered through the Internet. It also provides limited Internet access, and has created some websites of its own. The total investment was around $35,000–$40,000. On this basis, it is estimated that the entire 18 million people of Sri Lanka could be served by a network of community radio stations for a total investment of around $3.6 million (World Bank, 2001c).

In which conditions do e-services generate benefits? It is clear from the contrasting experiences of Gyandoot and the Kothmale community radio/Internet project that technology needs to be introduced in a nuanced and sensitive manner. This is, of course, a lesson already learnt many times over in the development community. The kiosk approach of Gyandoot appears to be a good way forward, until it becomes clear that a basic matter like insecure electricity supply can disrupt the service and significantly reduce its attractiveness as an option for users. At this point, the rather more low technology approach of Kothmale starts to come into its own. In particular, the blending of information age technology with pre-existing technology from the radio age looks like an ideal way of making an incremental shift from one technological platform to another.

VI. E-Citizenship

E-citizenship, understood as the provision of ICT-enabled channels for citizens and organizations in the private and third sectors to feed views into the process of government decision-making, remains in its infancy all over the world. Governments of some developed countries have experimented with e-enabled citizen involvement in planning, implementing and appraising policy, or have also sought to boost citizen participation in the democratic process through use of ICT. In July 2002, for instance, the British government launched a major consultation exercise on e-democracy, creating an informative website (www.edemocracy.gov.uk), feedback opportunities, discussion forums, and so on. Nevertheless, it is hard to say that initiatives like this in themselves constitute a shift to e-citizenship. In all contexts, then, there remains much work to be done.

Experience of e-citizenship is especially limited in developing countries. In the sphere of democracy, Heeks reports the case of South Africa's

Independent Electoral Commission, which made innovative use of ICT to engineer fully democratic procedures in time for the country's second postapartheid election, held in 1999. "The effort included the creation of a nationwide satellite-based wide-area network and infrastructure; a bar-code system used to register 18.4 million voters in just nine days; a geographic information system used to create voting districts; a national common voters' role; a sophisticated election results centre for managing the process; and the training of 300,000 people" (Heeks, 2001: 10). The Commission was awarded the 2000 Computerworld Smithsonian Award for most outstanding government or third-sector program.

Use of ICT to create wider input channels from civil society into government appears to be very thin on the ground at present. The World Bank's website contains case studies on "empowerment through information." However, the case studies reported are government portal of Colombia, Gyandoot and the Kothmale project, none of which really counts as an e-citizenship initiative. As "e-society" initiatives, Heeks (2001) reports the Philippine customs case, and Gyandoot. Again, each is actually rather limited in scope.

More than any other aspect examined here, e-citizenship remains at the level of potential. The technology now exists for governments to create input channels from civil society. Exactly how such inputs might be assembled, managed, processed and used actually to alter existing modes of planning, implementing and appraising policy are all matters that remain to be worked out.

VII. Conclusion

It is still early days for e-government, and yet earlier days for e-government in development contexts. Nevertheless, real progress is being made, and most governments in the developing world now have at least an online presence. Many have a great deal more than that. As with so many other development initiatives, the key to success appears to be close attention to the real needs and desires of citizens on the receiving end of development projects, allied to clear awareness of the technological, cultural and other constraints within which any initiative must inevitably be set. E-government is likely to make the greatest contribution to development when it is built into, and builds out of, existing governance arrangements.

Acknowledgment

The work described in this chapter was partially supported by a grant from the Research Grants Council of the Hong Kong Special Administrative Region, China (Project No. CityU 1199/03H). The usual disclaimer applies.

References

Accenture, *eGovernment Leadership: High Performance, Maximum Value*, 2004. http://www.accenture.com/xdoc/en/industries/government/gove_egov_ value.pdf (accessed July 14, 2004).

Castells, M., The information age: Economy, society and culture, Vol. I, *The Rise of the Network Society*, 2nd ed., Blackwell, Oxford, 2000.

Center for Electronic Governance, Indian Institute of Management, *An Evaluation of Gyandoot*, 2002. http://www1.worldbank.org/publicsector/ bnpp/Gyandoot.PDF (accessed July 14, 2004).

EGI/GePeGI (E-Governance Institute, Rutgers/Global e-Policy e-Governance Institute, Sungkyunkwan University), *Digital Governance in Municipalities Worldwide: An Assessment of Municipal Web Sites Throughout the World*, 2003, http://www.andromeda.rutgers.edu/~egovinst/Website/summary. htm (accessed July 14, 2004).

Gyandoot, *Gyandoot*, 2004. http://gyandoot.nic.in/(accessed July 14, 2004).

Halavais, A., National borders on the World Wide Web, *New Media Soc.*, 2, 7–28, 2000.

Heeks, R., *Understanding e-Governance for Development*, 2001. http://idpm.man. ac.uk/publications/wp/igov/igov_wp11.shtml (accessed July 14, 2004).

Microsoft, *Lebanese Office of the Minister of State for Administrative Reform: Thousands of Government Forms Available from a Single Access Point*, 2002. http://www.microsoft.com/resources/casestudies/CaseStudy.asp? CaseStudyID=12363 (accessed July 14, 2004).

Microsoft, *Egypt E-government*, 2004. http://www.microsoft.com/middleeast/ egypt/english/press/casestudy/egov.aspx (accessed July 14, 2004).

Rantanen, T., The old and the new: Communications technology and globalization in Russia, *New Media Soc.*, 3, 85–105, 2001.

Slack, R.S. and Williams, R.A., The dialectics of place and space: On community in the "information age," *New Media Soc.*, 2, 313–334, 2000.

Stockholm Challenge, *Gyandoot*, 2000. http://www.challenge.stockholm.se/new_ tavlande_index.html (accessed July 14, 2004).

UN/ASPA (United Nations/American Society for Public Administration), *Benchmarking E-government: A Global Perspective: Assessing the Progress of the UN Member States*, 2002. http://www.unpan.org/e-government/Bench marking%20E-gov%202001.pdf (accessed July 14, 2004).

UNCTAD (United Nations Conference on Trade and Development), *Information and Communication Technology Development Indices*, UNCTAD/ITE/ IPC/2003/1, 2003.

UNDP (United Nations Development Programme), *Human Development Report 2001: Making New Technologies Work for Human Development*, Oxford University Press, New York, 2001. http://www.undp.org/hdr2001/comple tenew.pdf (accessed July 14, 2004).

Van Dijk, J.A.G.M., The one-dimensional network society of Manuel Castells, *New Media Soc.*, 1, 127–138, 1999.

West, D.M., *Global E-Government 2003*, 2003. http://www.insidepolitics.org/egovt 03int.html (accessed July 14, 2004).

World Bank, *Philippine Customs Reform*, 2001a. http://www1.worldbank.org/ publicsector/egov/philippinecustomscs.htm (accessed July 14, 2004).

World Bank, *Gyandoot: Community-owned Rural Internet Kiosks*, 2001b. http:// www1.worldbank.org/publicsector/egov/gyandootcs.htm (accessed July 14, 2004).

World Bank, *Kothmale Community Radio/Internet Project: Expanding the Knowledge Base*, 2001c. http://www1.worldbank.org/publicsector/egov/ kothmale_cs.htm (accessed July 14, 2004).

World Bank, *Colombia's Government Portal*, 2001d. http://www1.worldbank.org/ publicsector/egov/colombiaportal_cs.htm (accessed July 14, 2004).

World Bank, *Central Vigilance Commission Website: A Bold Anticorruption Experiment*, 2001e. http://www1.worldbank.org/publicsector/egov/cvc_cs.htm (accessed July 14, 2004).

World Bank, *Mexico's Tramitanet Portal*, 2003. http://www1.worldbank.org/public sector/egov/tramitanet.htm (accessed July 14, 2004).

WSIS (World Summit on the Information Society), *Declaration of Principles: Building the Information Society: A Global Challenge in the New Millennium*, WSIS-03/GENEVA/DOC/4-E, 2003a. http://www.itu.int/dms_pub/itu-s/ md/03/wsis/doc/S03-WSIS-DOC-0004!!PDF-E.pdf (accessed July 14, 2004).

WSIS (World Summit on the Information Society), *Plan of Action*, WSIS-03/ GENEVA/DOC/5-E, 2003b. http://www.itu.int/dms_pub/itu-s/md/03/ wsis/doc/S03-WSIS-DOC-0005!!PDF-E.pdf (accessed July 14, 2004).

Chapter 29

Good Governance, Bureaucracy, and Development: Have the Traditional Bureaucratic Values Become Redundant?

R. B. Jain

CONTENTS

I. Introduction

The advent of the 21st century has been characterized with increasingly poor quality of governance and unsustainable development that have gripped the so-called third-world countries into a new form of maladministration found rampant everywhere. More than a generation has passed since the process of decolonization has changed the contours of the world map and set the emergence of the third-world countries. While the pattern of political change has differed in each of these societies, in most there has been a persistence of juridical states, even if some of these have often lacked effectiveness and internal legitimacy. The image of the state in these societies has, however, varied from one of a strong molding society into new shapes and forms, to one of a weak state virtually helpless in the swirl of dizzying social changes that have overtaken it. However, in all these societies, despite their being limited by the fragmentation of social control, states have grown and have expanded their jurisdiction and resources considerably. Scholars, advocating the concept of "strong corporate" or "bureaucratic authoritarian" states, comment upon the control of state agencies on nearly every aspect of social life. In some societies, the demands on the state by the unorganized and the organized groups have grown to such an extent that the state is said to have become "incapable of governing," despite all the resources and tools that it may be able to command. This inability of third-world states to respond to the demands of their societies has been the one single factor responsible for a deviation from Weberian rational pattern of bureaucratic behavior.

A common feature that has dominated the countries in the third world has been the "ideology of development" incorporating the social and economic progress which determines the boundaries of political and social action, without at the same time specifying the exact form of the machinery for either politics or administrative action. However, bureaucracy as an instrument of state action seems to have become the principal vehicle for the accomplishment of development goals in all third-world countries. Concerns have been expressed about the prospective role of bureaucracies and the possibility that they may stray from their instrumental role to become the primary power holders in the societies. The political role of bureaucracy has been one of the principal issues of discussion in the context of many third-world countries. Many of the characteristics of the colonial governments have permeated the successor states. In addition, because of the growing intervention of the state in most human collective activities and resultant public enterprises, the states of the third world have found themselves deficient in skilled, technically competent, and specialist manpower necessary for their development purposes resulting in low administrative capacities (for details, see Jain, 1989; 362–374).

II. Meaning of Good Governance

The two terms that are very often talked nowadays are governance and corruption, but these not only largely remain undefined, but also even the relationship between the two is either not properly understood or not well defined. While corruption is commonly defined as the abuse of public office for private gains, governance is a broader concept, which is defined as the exercise of authority through formal and informal traditions and institutions for the common good. Governance includes the process of selecting, monitoring, and replacing governments. It includes the capacity to formulate and implement sound policies, and it assumes a respect for citizens. From this framework, governance can be explained as consisting of six different elements: (i) voice and accountability, which include civil liberties and freedom of the press, (ii) political stability, (iii) government effectiveness, which includes the quality of policymaking and public service delivery, (iv) quality of regulations, (v) rule of law, which includes protection of property rights and an independent judiciary, and (vi) control of corruption. In the situation that many countries, especially in the developing world face at the start of the 21st century, combating corruption and improving the quality of governance for sustainable development emerge as the most crucial. The key question therefore is what strategies lower corruption and strengthen quality of governance? (Kaufman, 2001: 1–3).

Improving the quality of governance requires a system of checks and balances in society that restrains arbitrary action and harassment by politicians and bureaucrats, promotes voices and participation by the population, reduces incentives for the corporate elite to engage in state capture, and fosters the rule of law. A meritocratic and service-oriented public administration is a salient feature of such a strategy. However, synthesizing the strategy of key reforms for improving governance and combating corruption is a particularly daunting challenge, as is the task of detailing and adapting a strategy to each country-specific reality. Governance is more than fighting corruption. Improving governance should be seen as a process integrating three vital components: (a) knowledge, with rigorous data and empirical analysis, including in-country diagnostics and dissemination, utilizing the latest information technology tools; (b) leadership in the political, civil society, and international arena; and (c) collective action *via* systematic participatory and consensus-building approaches with key stakeholders in society (for which technology revolution is also assisting). No two countries arrive at the same strategy, but to maximize the prospects of success, any country serious about improving governance for sustainable development must involve all key stakeholders, guarantee a flow of information to them, and lock in the commitment of the leadership (Kaufman, 2001: 6).

III. Emerging Challenges of the "Corporate Millennium" and "Development Management"

The threshold of the 21st century heralds the advent of the corporate millennium. The politico-administrative system in most developing countries has to now face a number of growing challenges of the new corporate millennium. In the coming years, there is likely to be a growing commitment to a free market and global economy, and therefore corporate governance is going to be a crucial factor in efforts to restructure governing institutions. With the end of the Cold War in the 1980s, the victory of capitalism, the emergence of new industrialized countries around the world, and the new technological revolution, political, economic, and social phenomena have in many respects bypassed the borders of the state and acquired a global dimension. Under globalization, citizen demands are more diversified and sophisticated. They want choice, improved responsiveness, and quality of services. With the diminished role of the state, a market-oriented economy supported by a democratic government with an efficient and quality-oriented public administration is conceived as the formula for economic development and well being of the people. Privatization, deregulation, debureaucratization, and decentralization are the current political issues. Performance-oriented governance and management strategies are advocated to improve responsiveness and accountability. No wonder the concept of *development management*, which has gradually expanded to encompass bureaucratic reorientation and restructuring, the integration of politics and culture into management improvement, participatory and performance-based service delivery and program management, community and NGO capacity-building, and policy reform and implementation, is increasingly gaining grounds especially in the context of developing countries (DCs) (Brinkerhoff and Coston, 1999).

Development management specialists now need to hone in on the critical managerial features of the problems that are preoccupying decisionmakers and demonstrate how the discipline is relevant and useful. It is these decisionmakers who must be convinced of the fit between development management and current global issues. Development management has made a difference in the lives of the citizens in the developing world, but continuing to contribute means remaining "in good currency." This is as much a challenge to the subfield as renewing and advancing development management's practical and applied research agendas (Brinkerhoff and Coston, 1999: 357). The policymakers in DCs today face a real formidable challenge in striking this balance as a strategy for good governance. Given the present politico-social scenario of the country, whether the system will respond to these new challenges is a big question that is today agitating the minds of the policymakers as also concerned citizenry in most DCs.

The triumph of corporate millennium and world capitalism has led to a veritable tidal wave of economic and financial reforms in developing and transitional economies in the form of structural adjustment programs. Coupled with the increased financial power of transnational corporations, the pace of technological innovation has led to an increased search for new products, new production methods, and new markets. The revolution in information technology has not only made the world smaller, but has also led to profound changes in the reorganization of production and industrial establishments. Both businesses and governments are under intense pressure and scrutiny because people share instant information through a worldwide telecommunication network. There has been an expansion of world trade on a more competitive basis. The system of American-dominated multinational enterprises is being replaced by a system of multi-national alliances in airlines, telecommunications, banking, insurance, etc. At the same time, the resurgence of massive international migration flows due to the global economic structuring, information, and technological revolutions have caused worldwide demographic changes.

The role of the state has been changing with the global transformation. The trend is to shift from a system where the state is the center of the world to a system where the territorial principle has to come into balance with the interdependency principle. The political power of the states has been weakened by supra-nations, sub-nations, economic forces, and macro-regions. In many countries, traditional bureaucratic public management is under severe criticism and is being gradually replaced by a new perform-ance, result-oriented management along with efforts toward downsizing government bureaucracy, empowering local community, and encouraging private incentives. The tendency both at the national and local level is to evolve a common concept of governance implying a leaner, fairer, and representative government, which allows for more individual freedom and active participation of civil society. Citizens are increasingly coming together and organizing to represent their interests, express their views, and undertake actions to assist themselves, either independent of or in partnership with the government. In the globalizing world of the 21st century, the civil society takes on an increasingly powerful role in development and in influencing policies.

This rearrangement of roles between the market, the state, and people gives more space for the civil society to organize itself to effectively voice the interests of the people and of the common good. It also gives more responsibility to the civil society to take up the interests of the people whose voices would otherwise be overwhelmed and drowned by the powers of business interests of the politically powerful (Fuuda Parr, 1997: 1–2).

A. The Pressures of Globalization

Contrary to widespread pessimism regarding the effects of globalization on nation states and the quality of governance in DCs in the present century, Prof. Harald Fuhr in one of his contribution stresses — somewhat provocatively — that several of its features can be made instrumental, and be beneficial, in terms of improving public policymaking and state capability.

According to him, four "constructive pressures" stemming from globalization could be seized constructively by citizens and governments in the developing world. First, better-informed and better-connected citizens, and an emerging global civil society, demand improvements in service delivery, transparency, and participation. Second, subnational governments, often backed by local non-governmental organizations (NGOs) and businesses, and keen to attract foreign investment, increasingly exert pressure *vis-à-vis* central governments. Third, global investment strategies by private businesses increase the demand for appropriate institutional arrangements within DCs as well as credible government policies. Although with mixed results, fourth, international organizations, in particular IFIs, have been addressing public sector modernization in DCs, also sponsoring global public policy networks in critical areas. Moreover, policy coordination and cooperation between states increases significantly, constraining arbitrary action by governments. Globalization, thus, advances the discussion about, and the demand for, new institutional arrangements, clearly with new opportunities for improvements in state capability and governance (Fuhr, 2003). Developing these new institutional arrangements so as to increase the capability of the state and government is a major challenge faced by the political leaders and policymakers in all developing societies.

IV. Bureaucratic Values and Development: The Experience of a Developing Society — India

The problem of bureaucracy is somewhat complex in DCs where social and political institutions are relatively less developed and where the state has mainly to depend upon the administrative structure for the accomplishments of its goals. Thus, the bureaucracy in India and other DCs have to perform functions, which in developed countries are performed by a variety of other institutions. However, whatever may be the nature of political institutions, all modern bureaucracies do possess some Weberian characteristics to a varying degree. The bureaucracy in India exhibits these characteristics in a number of ways.

Notwithstanding the Weberian characteristics, however, in practical terms, a bureaucrat in India must seek to reconcile the two different worlds in which he works — the little world of his office with its files, rules, and routine procedures which call for his adherence to the Weberian principles and another world of men and women within their growing problems and demands. The environmental constraints of this world and, the special consideration for backward castes, classes and the weaker sections and communities and compulsions of social obligations toward his own friends and family members necessitate deviation in his actual behavior from the strict Weberian model.

To explore the content of values and orientations of the bureaucracy in India, the paper is specifically concerned with an analysis of their perceptions about the kind of Weberian, behavioral, and socio-administrative values that they seem to cherish. It also seeks to examine the social background of officials and the impact of such factors like their training, work experience, psychological makeup, and the political environment on their accomplishment of developmental and nondevelopmental tasks. A further investigation in the nature of commitment of the officials to the traditional values, particularly the ascriptive, and the modern liberal and rational values is also attempted in order to determine if any particular constellation of value orientation affects the functioning of officials in the achievement of the developmental goals. This paper is based on a full-length empirical field study of the bureaucrats involved in both developmental and nondevelopmental tasks, conducted by the author in two different states in India, Madhya Pradesh, an underdeveloped state, and Punjab, a more developed state, which broadly reflects the national milieu (see Jain and Chaudhuri, 1984).

A. Basic Proposition and Findings of the Study

The basic idea underlying the above empirical research study (Jain and Chaudhuri, 1984) is that the old traditional values of the Weberian and colonial bureaucracy place impediments in the achievement of developmental goals, which has been the theme of many learned works in this field. Any meaningful analysis of an administrative system requires a deeper insight into the value orientation of the administrators. Our investigations in this study have focused attention on some of the administrative and behavioral values of the civil services at the grass root level with a view to enquiring into the impact of the bureaucratic values on the administrative performance and to discern whether an antiWeberian model of the administrative system and the process of debureaucratization can help meet the requirements of achieving the developmental goals of a developing society.

The findings of a large number of studies on bureaucratic role in development that have been conducted by various scholars in different settings and ecological framework seem to have firmly established the theory that the band of officials brought up in the traditional administrative culture and wedded to the Weberian model of bureaucracy is totally unfit to perform the responsibilities of development administration. It has been argued repeatedly that the development administrators have to be quite flexible in their approach, shed the existing formalism, be amiable in nature, outgoing, people-oriented, and should be willing to take risks and on-the-spot decisions without worrying for the procedures, and the rules and regulations notwithstanding.

While the empirical study by Jain and Chaudhuri does not attempt to refute this theory, nor do the findings indicate that such an attitude on the part of the officials will not be conducive to attainment of developmental goals, the study does point out certain limitations to a blanket acceptance of the above premises and in the process seeks to answer some questions having certain theoretical implications.

The study clearly demonstrates that the values imparted by the colonial bureaucratic system, so far as its structural organization is concerned, does not necessarily stand in the way of developmental process. The agriculture and industrial progress that took place in the state of Punjab since independence in 1947 has been attained through a hierarchical organization with a system of rules, prescribed individual responsibilities, and the observation of impersonality on the part of the officials. These are not always barriers to development. On the other hand, these values provide a framework for the operation of the officials, without which the accomplishment of developmental goals becomes difficult, if not altogether impossible. However, the very same characteristics tend to become dysfunctional when greater emphasis is laid on their observance instead of making use of them as a tool toward the accomplishment of the tasks. The very fact that the state of Punjab has moved to a position of rapid development and that with all the structural characteristics of bureaucracy, while the Government in the state of Madhya Pradesh has embarked on a program of development show that the bureaucratic system *per se* is not inimical to development.

Similarly, it can also be inferred from the findings of the study that the preindependence bureaucratic traditions train the officials to respect their political masters. To observe a system of rules and to maintain a high standard of integrity of character are not necessarily a stumbling block in the way of development. The high values attached by a very high proportion of the officials to the observance of rules and integrity of character are not necessarily inhibitions in the way of development. These qualities are as much necessary in the public services of a democratic developmental framework as they are supposed to have been the traits of the bureaucracy in India of preindependence days. For one thing, adherence to the rules gives the officials a chance to defend themselves against unwarranted criticisms or attacks, and for another matter, it enables them to maintain impartiality in the face of enormous political and other kinds of pressures as also to apply a small amount of egalitarian treatment in making the fruits of development available to people.

In the same vein, the study does not portray that the attributes of capability and honesty are irrelevant to development. In fact, the findings clearly show a gap between officials' own perceptions of their capabilities and the perceptions of the citizens of their capabilities for development. Thus it appears that the most desirable attribute of a development administrator would be to be inherently capable of performing his development tasks. Here the study certainly reveals the weakness of the officials' capacity to face developmental challenges.

B. Result Orientation of Development Administrators

A lot has been written and said about the result orientation of development administrators. The study does suggest the need for such an orientation on the part of the officials and that such an attitude is necessary for rapid development. If the officials give due consideration to this value, they will be more able to secure the ready cooperation of their own colleagues, of the politicians, and of the masses at large for developmental work. However, this does not mean that in order to achieve this type of orientation, the officials should ignore all rules, regulations, procedures, and norms. Nor does the result orientation mean that the criteria for fairness, just distribution, and allocation of resources be sacrificed on the altar of their being result-oriented. An official possessing the outlook of a result-oriented administrator would be necessarily a person who would have the capacity to face all challenges and opposition from all kinds of social–political environments, but not the kind of person who would sacrifice the prime values of his profession in order to be able to get along with his colleagues, supervisors, and politicians.

C. Theoretical Framework of the Value System of Developmental Bureaucracy

Thus the kind of theoretical framework of a value system that the development officials must possess is the one which to some extent has to be based on conventional bureaucratic characteristics of hierarchy, system of rules, division of labor, and impersonality. The findings of the study do not point out that a completely debureaucratized model of administration is the only alternative for achieving the goals of a development administration. On a theoretical plane, the value system of the officials would have to be geared in a manner in which the negativism of the dysfunctionality of bureaucratization is reduced to the minimum. For this purpose, the conclusions of the study point out that a developmental bureaucracy needs a framework which (a) is flexible in its operation, (b) is pragmatic, that is, able to take into consideration the exigencies of the circumstances from a practical point of view, (c) encourages open decisionmaking processes based on dissent and discussions between colleagues, (d) is centered around client-oriented philosophy, and (e) is loaded with human values of service and sympathy for all especially for the weaker sections of the community.

Various attempts have been made by many theorists, such as Bennis (1969), to evolve a theory of structure that discards bureaucracy in favor of more flexible forms of organization. He paints a picture of a nonhierarchical organization, temporary in its arrangements, governed by ability rather than by authority, with democratic methods of supervision. His model fits well the needs of modern organization with a specific task to perform in rapidly changing environment. Such a model was highly successful in the U.S.A. in putting the man to moon. However, it is doubtful whether Bennis' theory would have equally worked in an environment of development where an amorphous client confronts a fragmented service-oriented institution such as an Electricity Board or an Irrigation Department. Clearly, what is needed is a new version of the postbureaucratic theory appropriate to a client-centered organization. White (1969) came very close to discovering one such alternative. A bureaucracy, in its purely ideal form, treats clients as if they were the last layer in the organizational hierarchy. It groups clients into specialized categories and forces them to adjust to conditions as they exist. Because the bureaucracy suffers from the scarce resources and the clients ask for too much, the bureaucrats treat the clients impersonally. If the client demands special treatment, or does not conform to the organizational definition of proper behavior, the client is not treated well at all. White tried to reverse those patterns and suggested that instead of subordinates, the agency treats clients as peers. However, that could not approximate those ideals any more than traditional organizations could be perfectly bureaucratic. In addition, such an organization was never able to solve the problem of scarce resources, which is the primary cause of bureaucratization in public agencies.

Similarly, another attempt was made by Thayer (1973), a career public executive turned scholar who attacked the principle of hierarchy and suggested that "organizational hierarchy can be made to wither away, disappearing under pressures to devolve decision-making, redesign the assembly line, involve citizen in administration, and plan systems that cut across organizational boundaries." In its place, he sees a "process of *collective will*, where a college of groups, representing the various elements involved in the solution to a problem, would interlock to map out the solution. In a way it is like turning the organization pyramid on its side" (Thayer, 1973).

There is thus a lot of contradiction between the postbureaucratic theorists about the kind of bureaucratic structure that could solve the problems of development of heterogeneous societies like that of India. All these talks about the postbureaucratic organizations are on the leading edge of the administrative research. These can be described as trends extrapolated from real events. Similarly, the Jain and Chaudhuri study suggests that the structural organization that would be more appropriate for developmental work should be such where (a) notwithstanding a rigid hierarchical pattern, the authority flows to the persons with the ability to solve the problems, (b) which can adapt itself to the emerging situations, (c) is client-oriented, (d) encourages open communication and professional mobility, and (e) can embark upon to problem-solving and participative decisions.

V. Development Bureaucracy and the New Public Management

It is now appropriate to consider one of the most crucial and controversial aspects of the administrative innovations of modern times — the conflict between the traditional value systems of bureaucracies in developing societies and the new value systems and cultural perspectives sought to be generated by the new public management (NPM).

A. *New Management Culture and the Development Bureaucracy*

One of the characteristic features of the NPM movement is to put emphasis on a "managerial" approach to the processes of public administration in which the policymaking and policy execution functions get separated. It lays stress on giving more powers to the operational agencies and staff, deregulating departments from the control of central agencies, and establishing a new relationship between the ministers and the departments through the negotiation of "corporate contracts." The aim is to systematically manage the performance of the senior public service through developing clear objectives, carrying performance evaluations, and giving bonuses based upon performance. Corresponding changes in recruitment would entail emphasis upon more external recruiting, short-term contract staff, and higher salaries for senior public servants. The NPM has a preoccupation with the "client-oriented administration," "total quality management" (TQM), "results-based performance" imported from private sector, and to bridge the way to the 21st century by introducing optimal integration and flexibility (Thomas, 1996).

The experience of many DCs has demonstrated that the introduction of a new value system in their governments through the philosophy of NPM has resulted in a kind of conflict with the traditional public service values. Despite the inherent contradiction of the NPM, especially the need for increased control by political leaders and the need to delegate as much as possible, NPM has a bold and coherent philosophy, which is meant to galvanize senior public servants, eliminate the excesses of the bureaucratic model, save money and deliver better services in the emerging system of governance. The new values proposed by the NPM movement seek to stress flexibility, business orientation, results orientation, customer service, innovation, and personal accountability as against the traditional values of the Westminster system, for example, fidelity, discretion, permanence, objectivity, and neutrality. The question that needs to be answered is: to what extent public administration in DCs has succeeded in absorbing this new administrative culture, and with what results? Many scholars argue that these two value systems resulting in two different types of administrative culture should not be seen as contradictory: each is incomplete without the other. For orderly functioning of governance for development, however, the administrative culture in DCs will have to act as the custodian of traditional public administration values and ideals, while accommodating a number of new NPM values (Thomas, 1996: 99).

VI. Concluding Observations

This discussion of the new NPM values and the traditional bureaucratic value system still in existence in most developing societies may *prima facie* seem to be in conflict with each other. However, when we notice that the original component of the NPM is its focus to change from policy-making to management, it will appear that in this sense the role of the bureaucracy is to strengthen government practices and to make institutions perform their duties in the most productive way. From this, it can be argued that rather than being in conflict there is more of convergence between the traditional bureaucratic values ingrained in the well-known Gulick and Urwick's classical POSDCORB model and the modern public management system influenced by the NPM (Charih and Rouillard, 1997; Kernaghan, 1997). While the traditional values will continue to constitute the essence of public bureaucracies and would therefore occupy a central place in a formal statement of principles, careful consideration would have to be given to the status of certain new values of the NPM such as innovation, service, etc., that have in recent years shaken the foundation of the public service. This would require an assessment of the extent to which the so-called new values are fundamentally different from the traditional ones and the extent to which a synthesis of new and old values can be achieved (Kernaghan, 1997: 61).

The findings of the Jain and Chaudhuri study suggest that in the context of administering development programs it is necessary that the officials develop an attitude of "client orientation." Remaining under the law and subject to usual controls of accountability, a development administrator should be forward looking in his approach in respect of decisionmaking, but should also be in close touch with the client groups through a regular pattern of frequent consultation, information, and guidance. The administrator–community relationship has to develop on a note of mutual trust and confidence.

However, for good governance and development it would further be necessary to effect changes in the official's socio-personal, socio-administrative, socio-cultural value systems in order to effect desired changes in his behavior toward his own colleagues, subordinates, the people, and the political leaders with whom he comes into daily contact. A collaborative effort of the officials, the masses, and the public leaders need to permeate the developmental process. For the moral concern and personal responsibility of those exercising the great regulating and coercive powers of the modern state, it is essential that their value systems should undergo some transformation. How could this be achieved is indeed a ticklish problem. If the officials could be made to realize the importance of the ideal of human dignity and social awareness in their dealings, much of the problems arising out of there could be mitigated. This demands, what a public administrator has termed, a sort of creative intelligence both at the administrative and political levels.

Administration is manned by human beings and is the servant of a complex society. It is true that the qualities of an administrator, which motivate him to act toward public good and public interests cannot be either tested at the time of their recruitment or imposed through a rigid set of training programs, although education and training do help in building these values to some extent. However, such values can certainly be inculcated through a well-designed and integrated program of motivation matching their performance with a regular reward and punishment system. In addition, officials would have to be enabled to realize their importance in their work so that they do not feel simply a cog in the organizational machine. A project-team approach in the reorganization of administrative hierarchy would have to be introduced. The bureaucrats have to be enabled to shed out their inhumane, technocratic, impersonal, and faceless image. The officials must fully project their public image of impartial and honest functionaries and at the same time be closer to their subordinates and other segments of the society with whom they have to work without sacrificing their concern for public interest against the individual's interest (Redford, 1975).

In the final analysis, one could conclude that what public bureaucracy in the context of good governance and development needs today is ethical sensitivity in order to serve public interests. If a greater measure of rationality and fraternity are embodied in the order and regularity of bureaucratic processes, the creative intelligence and broad sympathies of public officials working through institutional organizations can help achieve a measure of good governance, public good, and development for the citizens.

References

Bennis, W., Post bureaucratic leadership, *Transaction* 6, 44–51, 1969.

Brinkerhoff, D.W. and Coston, J.M., International development management in a globalized world, *Public Admin. Rev.*, 59 (4), 346–361, 1999.

Charih, M. and Rouillard, L., The new public management, in: *New Public Management and Public Administration in Canada*, Charih, M. and Daniels, A., Eds., The Institute of Public Administration of Canada, Toronto, 1997, pp. 27–45.

Fuhr, H., Constructive pressures and incentives to reform: globalization and its impact on public sector performance and governance in developing countries, in: A Paper Prepared for Presentation in Panel RC 4.2 at the 19th Congress of the International Political Science Association, Durban, S. Africa, June–July, 2003.

Fuuda Parr, S.F., *Sustainable Human Development in a Globalizing World*, Human Development Report Office, New York, 1997.

Jain, R.B., *Bureaucratic Politics in the Third World*, Gitanjali Publishing House, New Delhi, 1989.

Jain, R.B. and Chaudhuri, P.N., *Bureaucratic Values in Development*, Centre for Policy Research and Uppal Publishing, New Delhi, 1984.

Kaufman, D., New empirical frontiers in fighting corruption and improving governance: selected issues, in: A Paper Presented at the OSCE Economic Forum 2001 Brussels, January 30–31, 2001.

Kernaghan, K., Shaking the foundation: the new versus traditional public service values, in: *New Public Management and Public Administration in Canada*, Charih, M. and Daniels, A., Eds. The Institute of Public Administration of Canada, Toronto, 1997, pp. 47–65.

Redford, E.S., *Ideal and Practice in Public Administration*, University of Alabama Press, 1975.

Thayer, F.C., *An End to Hierarchy: An End to Competition*, New Viewpoint, New York, 1973.

Thomas, P., Beyond the buzzwords: coping with change in the public sector, *Int. Rev. Admin. Sci.*, 62 (1), 5–30, 1996.

White, O., The dialectical organization: an alternative to bureaucracy, *Public Admin. Rev.*, 29 (1), 32–42, 1969.

Chapter 30

Public Sector Reforms and Transformation: Implications for Development Administration

Ali Farazmand

CONTENTS

I. Introduction: Public Sector Reforms and Development

The public sector all over the world has undergone profound reforms, changes, and transformations during the last 25 yr. No one can deny this reality; yet, there is no clear agreement over the nature, extent, scope, and normative implications of impacts of the reforms and changes that have caused the transformation of government, public administration, and the issue of service delivery around the globe. Of all the important components of public sector reform worldwide, the foremost has been the phenomenal surge of administrative reforms. Therefore, the term administrative reforms in this chapter reflects the public sector reforms carried out during the last 25 yr or so.

Administrative reform is one of the most frequently exercised plan of action that almost all governments of the world have tried in order to streamline their administrative systems and to carry out public policy choices ever desired or demanded by time and change since the ancient world. Indeed, administrative reform may be considered a hallmark of governmental actions that signal changes and transformation, promises and prospects, and hopes and opportunities. However, reforms may or may not result in promised expectations, and very often reforms fail for a variety of reasons.

In fact, history of administrative reform has shown mixed results on this governmental action. Administrative reform for development of a country, society, or organization is a challenging task that produces high rewards when successful and effective, and major disappointments when they fail. Most studies of administrative reforms report major disappointments with results of the efforts. Yet, the policy choice continues worldwide, and each decade of the last century has shown almost distinct patterns and orientations of administrative reform. However, the reforms of the last two decades or so have been of a different form and nature. They have been structural, systemic, and far reaching as far as economics, society, and public administration are concerned. These reforms have also been process-oriented, with profound value and cultural implications, affecting almost all governments, citizens, and organizations worldwide.

Unlike the reform movements of the earlier decades of the 20th century, which emphasized institution building, bureaucratization, nationalization, and a wide variety of organizational and administrative capacity building for national and economic development, the recent global phenomenon of public sector reform has been in the opposite direction: reversing the traditional role of government, the state, and public administration institutions into one that promotes a private, corporate-driven marketplace dominated by big business elite.

Privatization, commercialization, marketization, and contracting out, together with a number of institutional changes, promote this new ideological trend on a global scale. Under the direct influence of globally dominant superpowers such as the United States and other Western donors, the World Bank (WB), the International Monetary Fund (IMF), and the World Trade Organization (WTO) have forced almost all less developed and developing nations to structurally adjust their governments and administrative systems to these new global trends and conditions that promote globalization of corporate capitalism and enhance the power of the globalizing corporate elite.

This challenge has been even more accentuated by the severity of the problems that face less developed nations. Most of these nations inherited a legacy with significant dependency on colonial powers of the West, and their administrative systems suffer profound deficiencies beyond explanation. However, not all developing nations can be categorized this way. Many of them have gone through major transformations after independence. Some of them have achieved significant development with remarkable effectiveness. Others have lagged behind and remained dependent on external assistance.

This chapter outlines a discussion of public sector reforms with implications for development and its administration. Section II presents a brief theoretical overview of administrative reforms, followed by a discussion of the global trends of reforms and the recent transformation of public administration in Section III. Here, globalization, privatization, and the corresponding managerial system or model, "new public management" (NPM) reforms are also discussed as strategic instruments toward achievement of globalization goals, along with a brief report on the failures of NPM in Europe and Latin America. Finally, Section IV highlights several implications for development administration in the context of public sector reforms.

II. Administrative Reforms and Change: A Theoretical Analysis

Theoretically speaking, three broad approaches to administrative reform may explain some of their intricacies, including who starts and who benefits, who implements and who decides, how reforms take shape and how they are implemented, what makes them succeed or fail, and a host of other questions. These three approaches are top–down, bottom–up or environmentally induced, and institutional or hybrid. Each of these approaches cuts across several disciplinary fields of inquiry, including organization theory and behavior, political science, economics, and public administration.

A. Top–Down Elitist Reforms

This approach to reform and change generally starts from the top leadership of organizations, governing elites, administrative and bureaucratic elites or leaders, executive managers of an enterprise, and Chief Executive Officer (CEO) of a corporation. Problems are detected, needs are identified, and issues are developed by top leadership — as a group, as an individual, or committee — who then decide to launch reforms or change programs. Announcements are made and perhaps deliberations are sought, but leadership decisions are final on changes and reforms. Generally, it is perceived that top leadership has full knowledge of the entire organization, system, and government, and therefore knows the problems and the changes required to solve them. Also, it is argued that top leadership has a full view of the big picture, the authority to make reforms and changes happen, and the financial capacity to fund the implementation of reforms (see Peters, 2002; Farazmand, 2002b).

However, this approach has a key drawback, namely, its complete neglect of some of the real needs, expectations, and preferences of those below: citizens, employees, workers, and the like. It is very easy to misread people's preferences, and it is certainly very difficult to understand them if there is a lack of legitimacy and of close communication between the leaders and the led or followers. Throughout history, politicians and administrators have committed this basic mistake repeatedly.

B. Bottom–Up Reforms

The opposite to the top–down elitist approach to reforms is the bottom–up approach that emphasizes not only marginal inputs or participation from rank-and-file employees in organizations, and, by extension, from citizens in decision making regarding changes and reforms, but also the spontaneously developed movements from the environment of an organization or political system. This means changing dynamics, pressures, demands, and expectations from people, constituencies in a governing system, and, of course, employees or workers of an organization within and from outside the system. That is why the environmental approach is used as way to signify what a system or organization and its leadership need to know on a regular basis, what they must understand by accurate reading of their surrounding changes, and what courses of action are needed to appropriately respond to those preferences, demands, and expectations. Otherwise, the leadership is no longer in a position to lead.

External forces of change driving organizational leadership to perform can lead to three possible forms of responses. One is the leadership's adaptation of those changes and demands from the environment by reflecting them in decision-making and implementation via reforms and changes that would be responsive and adaptive. The second way is to adopt as few as possible the environmentally induced changes in the leadership programs of reforms; and this will be mainly a reactive and passive approach to respond to the environmental demands for change. A third possibility is that in face of realization, by those below, that the leadership — political or organizational — is not genuinely interested in reforms and changes that would reflect their interests, a full take over of the entire system of leadership may be contemplated.

This is, of course, a rare possibility, but it is potent one. Most revolutionary changes result from these sorts of action, and once they happened, it would be too late to think of "reforms," for the entire system is now up for grabs, and revolutionary changes are expected to sweep away the old, ancient regime of order. In such cases, reforms will not satisfy those below, the citizens. Examples include revolutions in Iran, Cuba, Russia, and elsewhere around the world (see Farazmand, 1989, 2002b). A potential drawback of this approach to reform is the possibility of missing the "big pictures" by those below — citizens and organizational members.

C. Institutional and Cultural Reforms

The institutional approach to change and reforms is often viewed, in scholarly research, as a more realistic and comprehensive model. It is viewed as being superior because it combines the advantages of both the top–down and bottom–up approaches.

The argument is that, from an institutional perspective, there are at least three key elements that require close attention: structure, process, and values. Changing structures is fairly easy (not to be confused with structural changes) to pursue by a top–down approach, and process changes require cooperation of the bottom–up approach because it has a better chance of promoting an understanding of what the reforms and changes are all about, and how they can be implemented without threatening the people involved. The third element of this approach is the value or cultural dimension, which is embedded in the institution, in its environment, and in the basic assumptions that form and reform the organization, system of government, and society at large. In short, the institutional approach is considered a more comprehensive model to pursue change and reform, because changing institutionalized orders require institutional approaches.

A drawback of this model is its potential resistance to reforms and changes that may threaten the basic institutional assumptions as well as its structural foundation. For example, capitalism resists revolutionary changes and reforms that tend to challenge its basic assumptions or to bring in the ideas of socialism and nationalization of major properties. Similarly, organizations resist changes that threaten their core foundation. Even revolutionary leaders often find themselves having to go slowly and gradually to transform the already institutionalized systems of old government, bureaucracy, and administration. In short, the institutional theory explains why some reforms fail miserably while others succeed in modern public administration. Today, the concept of "neoinstitutional theory" has a currency hold in scholarship and practice. (For details, see Farazmand, 2002a, Chapter 3; Peters, 2001, 2002).

III. The Global Trend of Public Sector Reforms

This section addresses four components of the global trend of "big-turns." The first is the phenomenon of globalization of corporate capitalism; the second relates to the sweeping structural privatization of the state and public administration and other related reforms to promote globalization; and the third is the massive transformation or re-transformation of governance and public administration in both theory and practice to manage globalization of corporate capitalism. The final trend is the increasing awareness of the disappointment and turn away from these transformations, especially of NPM, with a new search for still new models as well as a return to the classical ones in governance and administration. The future of governing and governance are detailed elsewhere (see Peters, 1996; Farazmand, 2004), and our focus here is instead on key reforms and transformation of public administration.

A. Globalization and Global Reforms

The 20th century was a witness to several trends of administrative reforms around the world. First came the big structural reforms post-World War II on nation-building followed by institution building in the 1960s, both motivated by the necessity of the time — post-colonialism and national independence movements — and structural capacity building for governance and administration in a new world characterized by Cold War dynamics. The world was divided and theories of development, governance, and public administration were equally divided.

The capitalist world led by the West launched massive programs of aid and technical assistance, and projects intended to deter the appeals of socialism and the growing global power of the U.S.S.R., to westernize the third world countries, and to maintain a culturally and institutionally similar, or replica of, capitalist model of government and administration with the private sector playing a key/dominant role.

The post-war efforts at nation-building and institution-building coincided with the global quest of multinational corporations, now mainly controlled and dominated by the United States. Since World War II began, the United States launched a relentless global quest to outdo its rivals, including Great Britain, and to claim global leadership of the Western capitalist world. In the process, empowering the state as the key institutional player in the realms of economic and politics was essential, not only in advanced countries but also in developing and less developed nations. The state provided the most important basis of security for financial capital investments in developing countries; it was the grantor and guarantor of investment returns.

As a consequence, nationalization became a key policy tool in developing countries with massive growth of public enterprise management, as was the case in the developed countries for at least two centuries. (For details on the rationales and factors contributing to the growth of government and public enterprise management worldwide, see Farazmand, 1996, 2001a,b.)

Interestingly, nationalization and public enterprise management gained momentum and grew dramatically during the 1960s and even 1970s. Governments and public management played a fundamental role in economic growth, infrastructure development, national development, income distribution, and redistribution of national wealth. The Western quest for globalization of corporate capitalism was checked and restrained by global socialism and the U.S.S.R., as a superpower, had played a key role in international arena and shaped the world politics. The rise of the welfare state in the West was primarily, in the author's view, a reaction and deterrent to the growing appeal of global socialism, with the U.S.S.R. championing its leadership role for the working class worldwide.

The decline and stagnation of capitalism in the West accompanied by continuous rise in expenditures on arms race, on the one hand, and the growing pressures inwards — for higher wages and participation in management, emerging power of the women workforce, and unions, etc. — inside the industrialized countries of the West, on the other, pushed multinational corporations further outward in search of cheap labor, open markets, and available resources. This time, new technologies aided them to move faster, and to enter into joint ventures with former enemies, such as China and later the U.S.S.R. The fall of the U.S.S.R. gave a golden opportunity to the global corporate capitalist elite to dismantle the welfare state, to turn back decades of achievements in administrative and social reforms on labor and environmental regulations, to keep the working class and average people quiet at home, to move out and outsource jobs to cheap places with little or no regulations, and to exploit new markets in former socialist countries.

With the fall of the U.S.S.R., there was no longer a compelling rationale for the welfare state. The idea that every one must fend for himself or herself in the "new world" with "one market under God" (Frank, 2000) became the new global slogan of corporate capitalism. The ideological underpinning that market is superior to all other forms of social and economic organization (Lindblom, 2001), was coupled with the purported "Western supremacy." As a result, many changes began to flow worldwide, affecting the lives of billions of people. Advancement in technological innovations, almost overnight, also added rapid pace to these changes, and transformation began to take place, some naturally and others by design. Consequently, epochal changes began as humanity entered the new millennium. Yet, these changes must be considered a part, or in a context, of continuity in historical quest of world capitalism for absolute profits or accumulation drive, and the changes only reinforce the strength of global capitalism.

The hallmark of all these changes has been globalization, a term that has captured the topics and subjects of books and publications too many to count. Globalization has been the transcending force that recognizes no national boundaries, no space, no time, and no limit in its process of action. Globalization is a process "through which worldwide transcendence and integration are taking place" (Farazmand, 1999a, b; 2004), enclosing the entire globe under the banner of global capitalism with a self-declared ideological supremacy of market capitalism led by the globalizing corporate hegemony. Discussion of globalization, its causes and consequences, and implications for public management is beyond the scope of this chapter, and have been discussed elsewhere (see Farazmand, 1999).

The bottom line of all these changes — both linear and nonlinear and chaotic — is the continuity and expansion of global capitalism with the corporations positioning themselves toward a global hegemony. Therefore, the close correlation between globalization and its demands for sweeping structural reforms around the world is already established (see Farazmand, 2002a,b; Korten, 2001; Mander and Goldsmith, 1996). Sweeping privatization has functioned as an instrument of implementing the goals of global corporate capitalism. Accompanied by a set of deregulations, devolution, and agencification, sweeping privatization and contracting out have been the most important and structurally comprehensive administrative reforms that have been carried out worldwide. Similarly, NPM, widely introduced and implemented worldwide — mainly by global pressures but also voluntarily as a trend — has also served as a powerful intellectual arm of the globalization of corporate capitalism, with a "one size fits all" ideology of capitalism.

The approaches used in launching and implementing reforms, right from the initial to the most transformational stages, have been predominantly top–down, with some environmentally induced models serving for justifications for change. The processes of radical, systemic as well as pragmatic and tactical privatization from introduction to implementation in most countries, including industrially advanced countries of the West, but especially developing and less developed, has been a response to two fundamental forces of change: one internal and the other external. Internally, the initial policy design of the Reagan and Thatcher regimes in the U.S.A. and U.K., respectively, set the whole motion of massive privatization in the early 1980s, a macro organizational redesign of the government–society–private sector. Reagan and Thatcher were the key governmental instruments of initiating and implementing by design the privatization policies to achieve the goals of the globalizing corporate power elite. Both regimes represented the core of the globalizing corporate elites and their interests using the institutional channels and budgetary powers of the state to accomplish the goals of global capitalism.

Subsequently, the international/foreign arms of these two governments of the North expanded the deliberate policy of globalizing "restructuring" into the developing and less developed countries, most of whom are highly dependent on them and had no choice but to adopt the reform policy. Foreign aid and other economic and technological exports accompanied the "new conditions" of structural reforms. These external forces of reforms were reinforced by a host of other international and globalizing institutions such as the United Nations and its strategic organizational entities, namely, IMF, WB, and WTO, and others that have systematically pushed for fundamental structural reforms of the public sector with privatization and devolution as a key condition for technical assistance and financial aid. The keywords of the 1980s were "structural adjustment programs" (SAPs) supplemented by the words "good governance" and "public–private partnerships" of the 1990s that have entered the new millennium. Today, a true transformation has taken place in public administration.

B. Public Sector Privatization and Globalization

The privatization policies that have been pursued during the last two decades or so have covered almost every function and activity, including those always considered the core and heart, of governments around the world for millennia. The entire public sphere has been taken over for profit and capital accumulation by corporate business organizations.

Therefore, a fundamental reconfiguration has taken place in public–private sector relations worldwide; everything in society has been claimed by business corporations for profit purpose, including prisons, mental hospitals, healthcare, and security areas. There has been a *fundamental restructuration* in public–private sector relations, and structural *reconfiguration* has resulted in macro-reorganization of the ways in which economy, society, and governance administration function.

The role of government and society has been redefined by the new ideological reform of capitalist organization and philosophy. The role of the state has been pulled back, or forced to "retreat" (Strange, 1996), and reduced to providing law and order (system maintenance), or social control, to promote the goals of capital accumulation and facilitation of corporate sector ideals. Structural and systemic privatization has been accompanied by massive deregulation, devolution, and deconcentration of some functions while centralizing others, especially the commanding ones. Therefore, while there are many paradoxes in the reforms movement, the overall structural changes are a reality that has taken place to position the corporate sector in a commanding status of governance, administration, and management, as well as of policy and economy worldwide. This has been accomplished by a top–down approach, with a combination of some bottom–up or environmentally induced changes.

Although the forms of privatization have varied — from *partial privatization* to *contracting out*, and *outsourcing* — *systemic privatization* has been the most dominant form, especially in developing nations, with tactical and *pragmatic privatization* to follow. *Systemic privatization* has structurally altered the public–private sectors configuration as a macro public policy, with profound implications for governance, administration, and citizens. Thus, privatization has effectively served the interests of globalization of corporate capitalism, its local political–military–corporate/business elites (which the author has called "*agents of global corporate elites*," hence *agencification*; see Farazmand, 2002b).

C. Globalization and the NPM

Thus, concurrent with the sweeping privatization reforms that resulted in structural changes in the public sector, a new ideologically oriented managerial theory has been developed. Dubbed as NPM, this new theory is constructed on business management models, with the conservative neoclassical economic theory of "public choice" of the 1960s (see Buchanan and Tullock, 1962), as its theoretical underpinning that considers citizens as consumers, public managers as "agents" serving consumer "principals" and business models as the best and only best models of managing any organization anywhere around the world; hence the ideological concepts of "managerialism," "subsidiarity," "agencification," and "principal–agent relations" (see Jensen, 1983; Williamson, 1985; Hood, 1991) were born on the alter of modern public administration.

The initial idea of the public choice theory — already discredited in the age of globalization of large-scale corporate organizational systems due to the concept of "voting on foot" and efficiency achieved through small scale, overlapping jurisdictions — was now supplanted by the freshly supplied and refined models of "transaction cost" and "principal–agent" of organization theory with a root in sociology (Williamson, 1985). This new ideological, managerialist, and entrepreneurial model of organization in public management has since the 1990s been at the forefront of governmental reforms to run governments and public organizations as private enterprises, with maximum managerial flexibility. The traditional models of public administration and management have been rejected as inefficient, inflexible, and too regulatory and procedurally oriented. Efficiency and cost-cutting imperatives have replaced concerns for equity, equality, and fairness. The concept of managerialism, therefore, is claimed to have the capacity of an "ideal" model for all organizations (see, e.g., Hood, 1991; Barzelay, 2001).

NPM, therefore, represents a new "orthodoxy" of one size fits all in public management administration. Ironically, its proponents claim NPM to be a response to the failing and discredited "old orthodoxy" of the bureaucratic models of administration. Subsequently, what we have in hand today is a new ideologically oriented, neoconservative political–economic model of organization and management that purports to solve old problems while NPM has become a new orthodoxy itself, with too many promises and few achievements. This new one size fits all model of public management is in fact more rigid and inflexible than any previous model, so much so that it allows no tolerance of any alternatives to its market-oriented supremacy in theory and practice. The reason for this self-declared supreme model of managerialism is its attachment to the globalization of corporate capitalism discussed earlier.

Therefore, the new ideologically oriented model of public management has risen as an "intellectual arm" of corporate globalization of capitalism, serving its goals of profit maximization and accumulation of capital, as well as its military–political hegemony of the world as a new "global empire."

D. Disappointment and the Search for New Models

Disappointments with sweeping privatization policies, massive market reforms, and NPM have been growing significantly during the last decade, at an alarming frequency. Critics, this author included, have from its inception warned against the flaws of this new orthodoxy that range from promising too much to its impracticability, antidemocratic and inequality driven premises, as well as ethical and accountability problems that it carries in both theory and practice. Reports of the failures of administrative reforms — with privatization and adoption of NPM as their key features — in Latin America have been presented at the CLAD conferences (Latin American Conferences on Public Administration Reforms) since the mid-1990s. As a result, most Latin American countries have either abandoned NPM or modified its application to the point that it has become almost irrelevant to public management. The overriding concern of these countries has been the issues of fairness, equity, and equality, as well as accountability that NPM cares less about.

In fact, NPM's overriding interest is managerial flexibility and cost efficiency without concern for fairness, equity, transparency, and accountability. Ironically, much of the failure of the sweeping privatization and NPM reforms have been reported in Latin American countries, a region which is highly dependent on the globalizing corporate forces of North America, namely the United States. Others (see, e.g., Wettenhall, 2001, 2003) have also warned against the serious flaws of sweeping privatization, public–private partnerships, and NPM).

The most recent reports of NPM's failures have been documented in two European countries of Switzerland and the Netherlands (see Noordhoek and Saner, 2005). Loss of democratic control by citizens as well as equity is cited as a key reason for cancellation of NPM in these countries.

Why are NPM and sweeping privatization being pursued forcefully, even to the extent of aggressive efforts (examples include Iraq and former Yugoslavia) worldwide? This can be explained with reference to the intimate relationship between globalization and systemic privatization and similar reforms, with NPM acting as an intellectual arm of globalization promoting its goals in both academia and governments. Most governments in developing countries are under a heavy burden of financial, political, and military dependency on global capitalism and powers of the North. They have little or no choice but to accept what the global corporations, powerful governments of the North, and other supra-national institutions such as IMF, WB, WTO, and the United Nations tell or advise them to do as a condition for international assistance. Others, like Iran, are following suit to meet the conditions of joining the WTO, with the objective of emerging as one of the major economic powers in the region, if not the world.

IV. Conclusions: Some Implications for Development and Administration

The discussion of public sector reforms in this chapter renders several implications for development policy and administration. Elsewhere, the author has outlined a detailed analysis of these implications for developmental states and public administration (see Farazmand, 2001a, b, as well as Farazmand, 2002a, b, and c). Some of which are as follows:

The first implication is that globalization of corporate capitalism signals the end of any alternative model of economic, politics, and administrative systems. The welfare state has been replaced by the new welfare-corporate state with the task of facilitating and promoting capitalist economy and society globally integrated to the world system under corporate hegemony and the superpower United States and Western Europe.

The second implication by extension is that neither new model nor the old model of socialism or even semisocialism is acceptable to corporate capitalism under globalization of capitalism. The only ideology is the ideology of "one God, one market system," and the rest will be crushed under the new labels of terrorism and subversion.

Third, this means the world is moving toward a new "global tyranny and bondage" characterized by wars, conflicts, counter-conflicts, and a vicious circle of global repression and further insecurity. All human questions of nationalism, self-determination, justice, and economic fairness, or alternative modes of development are subsumed under this new global super model of market capitalism, serving its goals of surplus accumulation.

The whole process is protected and enhanced by the emerging "global empire" of the United States, that, due to its military might and an absence of the global counter-balanced power of the U.S.S.R., tends to claim the entire globe as its private domain for economic and political and military operation. Such global pretension will obviously generate its own antithesis of global insecurity as the will of democratic self-determination and freedom from global bondage will increasingly mount among the suppressed and exploited people and nations around the world. The result will be a vicious cycle in which no one will feel secure in the world. Injustice, exploitation, repression, poverty, colonial occupation — directly or indirectly — are the root causes of terrorism and insecurity.

The next implication is for developmental policy and administration. The clear message of globalization is to abandon all former models of development, such as self-governing organizations of cooperatives, self-help urban centers, socialist theories, and models of development, and welfare-state or mixed state models of governance and administration, and states are encouraged to enter into "subsidiarity and agencification pacts" with the global corporations, rely on the WTO, WB, and IMF for policy, reform blueprints, and administrative instructions.

Sixth, by extension, the implication for development administration is to rigorously adopt the market models of Western capitalism with its values of consumerism, be export-orientated, supply cheap labor to globalizing corporations, and maintain law and order for security of the market functions. Development administration must be streamlined through both education and training, teaching the capitalist model of the West, and development of the skills needed to operate national economies accordingly.

Seventh, the combined impact of the abovementioned implications will lead to deepening dependency, thickening poverty and underdevelopment, and larger gaps between the developed and developing countries. In no time, the developing countries will turn into "junkyards" of the developed nations, in which no one can live any more.

Eighth, to escape from the above consequences of the public sector reforms and globalization of corporate capitalism and the "emerging global tyranny," several policy options are conceivable and available. As the author has outlined in his earlier works (Farazmand, 2001a), these policy options include: (1) acceptance and adoption (do nothing policy); (2) resistance policy; (3) resistance and adaptation policy; (4) partnership-based strategies to resist while adapting; and more. Addressing these policy options is beyond the scope and limits of this chapter; it requires a separate presentation.

References

Barzelay, M., *The New Public Management*, University of California Press, Berkeley, CA, 2001.

Buchanan, J. and Tullock, G., *The Calculus of Consent*, University of Michigan Press, Ann Arbor, MI, 1962.

Farazmand, A., *The State, Bureaucracy, and Revolution in Modern Iran: Agrarian Reforms and Regime Politics*, Praeger, New York, NY, 1989.

Farazmand, A., *Public Enterprise Management*, Greenwood Press, Westport, CT, 1996.

Farazmand, A., Globalization and public administration, *Public Adm. Rev.*, 59 (6), 509–522, 1999a.

Farazmand, A., Privatization or reform: public enterprise management in transition, *Int. Rev. Adm. Sci.*, 65 (4), 551–567, 1999b.

Farazmand, A., Globalization, the state, and public administration: a theoretical analysis with implications for developmental states, *Public Organ. Rev. Global J.*, 1 (1), 437–464, 2001a.

Farazmand, A., *Privatization Or Reform?: Implications for Public Management*, Greenwood Press, Westport, CT, 2001b.

Farazmand, A., Privatization and Globalization: a critical analysis with implications for public management education and training, *Int. Rev. Adm. Sci.*, 68 (3), 355–371, 2002a.

Farazmand, A., Globalization, privatization and the future of governance: a critical assessment, *Public Financ. Manage.*, 2 (1), 125–153, 2002b.

Farazmand, A., *Administrative Reform in Developing Nations*, Greenwood, Westport, CT, 2002c.

Farazmand, A., *Sound Governance: Policy and Administrative Innovations*, Praeger, Westport, CT, 2004.

Frank, T., *One Market Under God: Extreme Capitalism, Market Populism, and the End of Economic Democracy*, Doubleday, New York, NY, 2000.

Hood, C., A public management for all seasons?, *Public Adm.*, 69 (3), 3–19, 1991.

Jensen, M., Organization theory and methodology, *Account. Rev.*, 8 (2), 319–337, 1983.

Korten, D., *When Corporations Rule the World*, 2nd ed., Kumarian Press, West Hartford, CT, 2001.

Lindblom, C., *The Market Systems*, Yale University Press, New Haven, CT, 2001.

Mander, J. and Goldsmith, E., Eds., *The Case Against Globalization and for a Return Toward Local*, Sierra Club Books, San Francisco, CA, 1996.

Noordhoek, P. and Saner, R., Beyond new public management: answering the claims of both politics and society, *Public Organ. Rev.: Global J.*, 5 (1), 35–54, 2005.

Peters, B.G., *The Future of Governing*, University of Kansas Press, Lawrence, KS, 1996.

Peters, B.G., From change to change: patterns of continuing administrative reform, *Public Organ. Rev. Global J.*, 1 (1), 41–54, 2001.

Peters, B.G., Government reorganization: theory and practice, in *Modern Organizations: Theory and Practice*, 2nd ed., Farazmand, A., Ed., Praeger, Westport, CT, 2002, pp. 159–180.

Strange, S., *The Retreat of the State: Diffusion of Power in the World Economy*, Cambridge University Press, Cambridge, UK.

Wettenhall, R., Public or private? Public corporations, companies, and the decline of the middle ground, *Public Organ. Rev.*, 1 (1), 13–36, 2001.

Wettenhall, R., The rhetoric and reality of public–private partnerships, *Public Organ. Rev. Global J.*, 3 (1), 77–108, 2003.

Williamson, O., *The Economic Institutions of Capitalism*, The Free Press, New York, NY, 1985.

Chapter 31

Public Service Reform

Gerald E. Caiden

CONTENTS

I. Introduction

Public service reform never goes out of style. How public services are performed and who performs them are topics of everyday discussion. When done well, people tend to take them for granted. When things do not go so well, people turn on those they hold blameworthy and demand instant rectification. Therefore, public authorities everywhere have to ensure that public servants are capable of providing satisfactory service, making improvements, planning ahead to meet most contingencies, and keeping up with the state of the art. In short, public service reform, which tries to head off crises in the capacity to govern (Dror, 2001), should command attention everywhere. But it cannot be divorced from everything that public servants touch, which these days is about whatever occupies public attention.

Inevitably, public service reform is highly complicated and emotional. It is bound up with ideology and values, not with just techniques and processes, and includes not mere detail but key societal issues. What should be considered public and how far should public intervention go? How should public goods and services be provided and delivered and to whom? How should public organizations be run and by whom? What should be the social standing of public servants and what should their duties and obligations cover? To whom and how should they be accountable and for what? What should be considered fair compensation to them? Who should be denied public office or removed from office for what offences? How is performance, capacity, talent to be measured, by whom and for what purpose? Indeed, the range of inquiry can wander over the whole spectrum concerning the nature and future of humanity and planet Earth.

Although these universal questions may have some universal answers, the circumstances of every country, every public sector within a country, and every public organization within the public sector is such that most answers need to be tailored to specifies. What works in one place may well be applicable elsewhere but usually things are not so simple. There may be similarities, but usually there are just too many differences. Redesigning, adjusting, and alterations are required to make a better fit with local conditions. This pragmatic approach is more in line with an evolutionary perspective which is much more realistic of human nature and social systems. It avoids the "erroneous view that human resource interventions operate independently of context and of the personal interests of people using them and that, therefore, they can be surgically installed in any organization." (Colareli, 2003: 316)

> Interventions operate in complex social systems, with their
> attendant conflicts, disparate interests, loose connections, and

long and multifaceted causal chains . . . [reducing] our capacity to predict and control behavior. This is bad news for managers who are looking for interventions that will produce specific, intended effects. It is also bad news for social scientists who believe they can develop such interventions and for those who are laboring under the delusion that the interventions they already developed work like that. And it is bad news for consultants who want to sell neat solutions and quick fixes. (Colareli, 2003: 318)

An evolutionary perspective does not provide human resources practitioners with the comfort of a best way or with the illusion of certainty . . . [It] settles, instead, for improving adaptive processes, maintenance, and limited improvement, ever mindful of context and conflict. (Colareli, 2003:321)

Public services seem to have taken a beating over the past few decades virtually all over the globe. Fortunately in some places, particularly among the developed countries that have the means and administrative ability, adjustments are being made, reforms implemented, and rethinking done about what is further needed to attract and retain talent in public service. In them, people complain about their public services and their public servants but on the whole they have been shielded from most calamities that might have befallen them had they not been so well served.

This is not the case in other places, particularly in the less developed countries, where no matter what has been tried to prevent deterioration, little seems to have worked as it should have done. All too frequent crises occur in many public services, bordering on calamity. In a few places, where public authority itself has all but collapsed, the decline or actual absence of public services has turned whole societies into shambles. There, terrible atrocities are taking place beyond the ability of international relief efforts to prevent. Warlords step in and provide what governance exists for reasons of self-aggrandizement, greed and profit in lawless, arbitrary, violent, and corrupt proceedings.

Given such disparities, from the reasonably tolerated to the inhuman, there can be little relief unless something is done immediately to restore public service where it has suffered the most. Public servants who are unhappy where they are seek to move on where they believe or hope their talent might better be appreciated. In the case of the less developed countries, they move on to international organizations and welcoming developed countries as part of the international brain drain. There is virtually negligible reverse flow outside international relief organizations whose staffing is largely temporary. Their field turnover is high as their employees and volunteers become too frustrated in the adverse circumstances to continue to provide what semblance of public service they can. In the more developed countries, the exodus out of public service is into the more rewarding private sector, depending on employment prospects in it. In short, no public authority anywhere can afford to be complacent; there is no telling when or where it may suddenly find itself losing the talented employees it would like to keep and unable to replace them. The central focus of public service reform rightly remains the transformation of the conditions of employment of career public officials who occupy key positions in government organizations so as to enable public authorities to attract, retain and reward talented professionals.

This is best illustrated by the recent report issued at the beginning of 2003 by an eminent committee in the United States, a successor to another such committee headed by Paul Volcker some 13 yr earlier. The 1989 committee had been stringent enough and made a dire warning then that the federal government had been experiencing a severe shortage of talent at the top and the situation would rum catastrophic if nothing was done. Reforms were made but they fell well short of what had been needed. The result was spelt out by the National Commission on the Public Service (2003).

> Trust in government ... has eroded. Government's responsiveness, its efficiency, and too often its honesty are broadly challenged as we enter a new century. The bonds between our citizens and our public servants, essential to democratic government are frayed even as the responsibilities of government at home and abroad have increased. Government work ought to be a respected source of pride. All too frequently, it is not.
>
> Evidence points unambiguously toward certain conclusions:
>
> - *Organization* — A clear sense of policy direction and clarity of mission is too often lacking, undercutting efficiency and public confidence. As a result there is a real danger of healthy public skepticism giving way to corrosive cynicism.
> - *Leadership* — Too many of our most competent career executives and judges are retiring or leaving early. Too few of our most talented citizens are seeking careers in government or accepting political or judicial appointments.
> - *Operations* — The federal government is not performing nearly as well as it can or should. The difficulties federal workers encounter in just getting their jobs done has led to discouragement and low morale. (National Commission on the Public Service, 2003: iii–iv)

There was deep disaffection within. Public servants were unhappy with their situation, frustrated and fatigued, and lacked the resources to do their jobs. Outmoded systems prevented them from fully developing and utilizing their talents. The vast majority knew the system was not working and needed repair (National Commission on the Public Service, 2003: 12). Things could be turned around if an elaborate reform agenda, which it proposed, were adopted. So far, there is little evidence to show that the United States Government has listened. If anything, the situation continues to deteriorate and several recent changes in direction appear to worsen it (Oman et al., 2003).

II. Tackling the Task of Reform

In the first subsection, some general comments about public service reform are made, emphasizing past experience, the need to be pragmatic rather than idealistic, the mudding of the waters by the New Public Management (NPM) movement, and the damage resulting from the imposition of universal, solutions unfitted and unsuitable to local circumstances. In the second subsection, we will return to some universal problems facing public service reformers all around the globe.

A. The Lessons from Past Reform Movements

Most adjustments take place through evolutionary change. Whenever something better appears, people adopt it. The beauty of bureaucracy and why most public administration is bureaucratic or has strong bureaucratic features (and has done so for some thousands of years) is that bureaucracy is designed for change. Once bureaucracies decide on change, change is incorporated and the whole system adjusts accordingly. Unfortunately, bureaucracies, especially large ones, also have attributes — bureaupathologies (Caiden, 1991) — that tend to obstruct or block changes that should be made. Things still work and even work well but in time performance suffers, perhaps imperceptibly at first until a breakdown occurs that can no longer be ignored. Something more than change is required and that is reform.

Reform implies imposition, forced change, against natural inclinations. Opposition of some kind has to be expected and overcome. Opposition cannot be dismissed as mere conservatism. True, people may not like change but they adjust and get used to it. Opposition indicates that there may well be good reasons why reforms should be resisted. Such resistance needs to be studied to discover whether there are legitimate grounds and sound reason for resistance or whether there is misunderstanding, misinterpretation, groundless suspicion, or unreasonable objection. For reform to succeed, resistance has to be overcome by winning opponents over. Gaining their cooperation and wholehearted participation is essential. More radical measures should be unnecessary when it comes to administrative changes but occasionally they have to be held in reserve and used when there seems no other way. The continuity of governance demands that extreme measures be avoided and only used in die last resort. Any disruption of public services has adverse social consequences that may not be immediately apparent. Even poor performance is better than no performance at all.

Public service reform is not as daunting as political, economic, and social reforms. The same administrative system or bureaucratic forms can be employed to carry out quite different programs and policies. The same public servants can generally be trusted to do what they are instructed to do. Few resign in protest or sabotage operations from within. Most acknowledge that they are indeed *servants*, not masters; they are on tap not on top. Their job is to help, assist, guide, warn, protest, and perhaps even substitute for public leaders when they fall to lead, but not take over altogether and run the show. They may drag their feet but it is rare for them to down tools altogether.

Incoming revolutionaries who distrust the officials of the former regime may well purge them, but this does not happen overnight. Providing public servants demonstrate the same willingness and loyalty to serve the newcomers as they did their predecessors, they are likely to retain their positions. Sudden, quick and unexpected administrative revolutions are quite rare and most public servants are talented enough to adjust to new circumstances. Anyway, incoming revolutionaries are unlikely to command sufficient administrative competence to readily replace them. The priority of revolutionaries is getting and consolidating power not starting from scratch or fighting with their public servants.

Despite all the build-up that accompanies them, public service reforms rarely succeed as evidenced by numerous failures to come oven close to their initial intentions. To contrast themselves with the status quo, public service reformers tend to exaggerate the defects of the status quo and exaggerate the potential benefits of their proposals. Sometimes, things are so bad that they do not need to exaggerate. However, when it comes to the inner workings of government, many people are ignorant or just do not understand exactly what is involved, and this also includes many insiders who have become so accustomed to things as they are that they cannot conceive how things could be different. To make things look better, reformers have to present a more dramatic picture, one that catches people's curiosity. So they take things out of context choose extreme (and possibly rare) examples, and distort, or manufacture evidence; and they are not beyond cheating and sheer invention. They do the same but in the opposite direction when it comes to their own proposals. They also select, bend, manipulate, and even idealize how different things are going to be, should their reforms be adopted. Probably the truth lies in between. The status quo is not so black as it is painted while the promised benefits are unlikely to materialize as predicted. But no matter what happens, reforms will make a difference and there can be no going back to the status quo ante.

But whether they will make *that* much of a difference, there is no telling. Reform is a risk. Things may not rum out to be much of an improvement worth the whole exercise, just change for the sake of change. Worse still, they may not work at all. Events may move too fast and overwhelm them before they have had any chance to take effect. Unforeseen events may intervene to kill any chance of success. The assumptions on which reform was based may prove quite mistaken, even with the best available intelligence. In other words, even with the best of intentions, the reformers through no fault of their own may find that the new course they embarked upon turns out irrelevant. Too often they needlessly blame themselves and turn on one another in their frustration. Just as often they blame every thing but themselves when in fact they ignored warnings and pushed ahead regardless, so convinced that they knew better. They misdiagnosed, prescribed the wrong treatment, and misunderstood signals. They unwisely experimented; they risked too much; they aggravated too many; they overreached. They were their own worst enemies especially when they actually adopted reforms that had failed before (Horton, 2003).

Although nobody really knows beforehand what is likely to occur, there are pointers from successful reforms and reformers, that is, from reformers who did achieve most of what they set out to do, did transform the public service in some way that could not be reversed, and did improve public service performance in a measurable way, that reduced the risks of failure.

First, there has to be wholehearted support from public leaders assured in turn of wider public support. Mere lip service means little. Public leaders say what they like (or say what they are told to say) and just as quickly reverse themselves at the first hint of trouble. Reform is bound to be troublesome. It is inconvenient, even unpleasant for some. It is not always a win–win situation, which is what distinguishes reform from change. There are winners and losers and the losers do not go down without a fight. As public servants are talented, the fight can he bitter and drawn out, no place for the faint hearted. Public leaders have to show their backing by word and deed and if need be rally public opinion behind reform. They should identify with reform and behave as if reform was their own personal project, as long as they remain convinced that reform will produce better results. Reform is doomed when it is suspected that public leaders are merely going through the motions, and. they have little public support.

Second, reform is an investment and has to be considered like any other investment. Before embarking on the enterprise, careful research has to be done to see whether it is likely to be fraudulent or reckless; there has to be some assurance of a positive gain. Reform uses scarce resources that have many alternative uses. It is costly and expensive and not easily abandoned once set in motion. If insufficiently funded, all may be lost. Initial homework has to be followed up with periodical monitoring to see whether things are working out as originally anticipated and whether adjustments have to be made. The enthusiasm that accompanies reform often turns out to have been over optimistic and the reforms oversold, projections too wide off the mark, the real costs hidden, and more resources have to be found from somewhere. If additional resources cannot be rustled up, the whole venture may run out of steam and doom reform before it produces adequate returns.

Third, reform takes time. Reasonable time must be allowed for it to work. But the public, public leaders, reformers, and public servants are impatient. Their time horizons are short. They want instant results. Given the complexities and intricacies of public service reform, sufficient breathing space is at a premium. To keep everybody on board, there have to be some quick results, however contrived. Occasionally, progress reports have to show real progress has been made and persists. Nothing succeeds like success, not manufactured success, sounding flimsy if not phoney, that spells doom. Behind the build-up, there has to be real evidence of progress that enable all concerned to feel pride and optimistic that the best is yet to come. Lack of time makes reform particularly hazardous.

Fourth, no matter how successful is public service reform, there will always be criticism and complaints, just as is with the weather. Nobody ever seems satisfied, whatever is achieved. There are always going to be some people who believe that the public service is too big, too costly, too wasteful, too unproductive, too inefficient, certainly too ineffective than it should be and that public servants are parasitic, incompetent, rude, too officious, mean, spiteful, and abusive. Any defects in performance are seized upon and touted as typical. No mistakes are forgiven or forgotten. Of course it is true that nothing less than perfection will satisfy. Unfortunately, public servants and the systems in which they work are only human. No matter how well reforms succeed, there will always be room for improvement.

The reality is that not everything can be done at once. Priorities have to be chosen and it is better that the big problems get tackled before the small, annoying problems. All the time, in public administration, the unexpected happens and problems need to be solved before they become unmanageable. Attention gets diverted and reform may have to be put on the back burner for the time being. In the best of circumstances, some folks will have legitimate gripes. The question is how serious are their complaints and what further reforms may be needed to silence serious critics. The most serious critics to whom attention should be paid are not the perennial public service bashers but the internal professionals who really know what is going wrong, are jealous about their professional reputation and believe that nobody is taking them seriously enough. They tell anyone who will listen that if they had to choose again, they would not enter public service, and they would not recommend it to anyone. When things get this bad, public service reform is imperative.

B. Pragmatism — It All Depends

It would be wonderful if the would-be public service reformer could just reach out to the nearest bookshelf or dial into a computer to find an encyclopaedia that records the latest research findings, outlines what can and does go wrong, and lists all the possible remedies and treatments. Unfortunately, no such single source exists. There are many scattered sources and several international agencies such as the International Institute for Administrative Sciences, the United Nations Development Program, the World Bank and other international development banks, the Organization for Economic Cooperation and Development, and the United Nations Department of Economic and Social Affairs together with publishing houses such as Marcel Dekker, Sage and Cass are filling the vacuum. Despite their handbooks and guidebooks being useful, they are usually unbalanced, over generalized, and outdated before they appear. Just as medical practitioners and legal consultants have to know how to interpret their knowledge, public service reformers too have to confront an ongoing working public service system that has been in existence for sometime, is currently operating in some fashion, and is unique.

No matter how much public service systems may resemble one another, none exactly mirrors another. Each is quite distinct and results from a singular shifting combination of history, culture, politics, economics, sociology, ideology, and values. Each has its own idiosyncratic traditions. Each has to be approached differently. Each requires its own special diagnosis and treatment. The surface symptoms may look the same, but the underlying causes may be different. A remedy may work in one case but not in another; it fails for no apparent reason. In public service reforms, there are no universal formulae, no infallible remedy, no one best way. Each public service system has its own way of going about its business and doing things. Each has to be respected and studied in its own right. Each presents its own surprises, its unexpected relationships, its good and bad aspects, its contradictions and uncertainties. Little can be taken for granted or left unquestioned.

Nonetheless, for any action to be taken, assumptions have to be made and people of action (like reformers are), it is to be hoped, would be blessed with judgment and insight that enable them to make correct choices and right decisions. Rarely, as pointed out earlier, is a total radical departure from the past called for, except where public authority is breaking down, public services are on the point of collapse where they have not already done so and public servants, or what remain of them, are in despair and willing to try anything to improve the situation. Otherwise, practical and feasible reforms are the order of the day. Perhaps, the best guide in this is the prevailing tradition of governance (Bevir et al., 2003) by which public service reform is seen as a bargain between the polity and the public bureaucracy, between public leaders and career officials, in developed countries between elected politicians and other political actors and senior public managers analogous to a thermostatic vision of control over public bureaucracy (Hood, 2002).

A simpler approach would be to divide public organizations into instrumental and institutional bureaucracies. In the instrumental bureaucracy, the master is the politician and the public servants are definitely servants. The former command the latter and impose whatever reforms they choose to, although presumably it would be more beneficial if the public servants had their say and participated fully in implementation. In contrast, institutional bureaucracies have independent power, having developed an expression or significance value for themselves and the community. They are not dispensable tools but valued as having intrinsic worth, and their survival assumes greater importance than economy and efficiency. They can be created as assigned autonomous entities free from political interference, like independent agencies established apart from partisan political control, or they develop accrued autonomy over time by outlasting several generations of political and administrative leaders and mediating between competing social interests. Their autonomy is supported by voluntary associations and professional groups which have grown around them over many years of stable relationships and reciprocal support. They are supported by tradition and widespread societal legitimacy. They are powerful enough to block the creation of rivals and carefully guard their status in the community, thereby perpetuating their self-serving concerns (Bjur and Caiden, 1977).

The reality is that most public bureaucracies eventually shift from being somewhat instrumental to somewhat institutional as each shares some features of the other. The difference is degree gauged by age, lack of political responsiveness, lack of public accountability in decision making, application of administrative law, tenure rights, and moral strength. Clearly, institutional bureaucracies do not respond to reform in the same way as instrumental bureaucracies because they can resist imposed changes by rallying supporters to their defense against external interference and they are masters in their own household and political leaders are wary of taking on organizations held in high esteem. Strong-arm measures are met with resistance and subterfuge making for lower morale and lower productivity to the detriment of the bureaucracies' clients. Reform is thus more political than managerial and specific to each bureaucracy. As long as institutional bureaucracies do not feel threatened, they have little incentive to change but as long as they need to maintain legitimacy they are vulnerable. The key to reform is to keep questioning their legitimacy and placing them under strict open scrutiny to expose any shortcomings, any administrative complacency, and internal self-perpetuation. Independent audits are indispensable, as are client watchdogs, in exposing failure. Once discredited, institutional bureaucracies lose their protection against imposed reform in which even professional pride can be incentive enough to encourage rethinking and change to avoid losing their autonomy and credibility. Their ability to determine what constitutes their own success should be strictly circumscribed, as it should be for all public organizations.

C. The NPM Menu

This latest approach to public service reform has international organizations looking to those reforms that have been tried by the developed countries over the past 20 yr or so. For the sake of convenience, these will be grouped under the heading of the NPM movement. For many decades, the business community has been critical of public administration and has believed that its management techniques could be applied to the public sector and improve government performance. Business consulting firms have eyed the public sector as a possible profitable avenue in their belief that management techniques are universal and apply to any organization. The opportunity arose when incoming British Prime Minister Margaret Thatcher employed a successful businessman, Derek Rayner (of Marks and Spencer), to conduct a series of detailed efficiency scrutinies into government agency work. These went well beyond the usual management services approach and cost reduction exercises to ask "What is it for? What does it cost? What value does it add?" Raynerism was soon institutionalized to change the culture and attitudes of the senior civil service in the U.K. and was copied in other developed countries.

However, NPM was also part of a new political agenda that went far beyond the housekeeping functions of government to question the basis of the administrative state, what it should do, how it should operate, and how its performance was to be measured. It was assumed that the government had grown too big, that it ought to shed activities that other institutions could perform. Indeed it would be better if these other institutions and individuals assumed more responsibilities for themselves. Government should be brought closer to citizens and consider things from their view, not just from its own superior vantage. Business methods were probably superior to traditional bureaucratic processes. Many public servants were parasitic, unproductive, and superfluous. The principle of efficiency should be as important to public administration as it was in business. As numerous reforms had been proposed but few had been adopted, public servants had grown too secure, unimaginative, and complacent. The prosperous times, which had shielded them had faded. Expenditures were now exceeding income. Things would have to be different. Any proposal for the improvement in the delivery of public goods and services had to be considered. Nothing would remain sacrosanct.

To NPM practitioners, the idea of public service, while noble in theory, was suspect in practice. Why should any job in the public sector be any different from any job in the private sector? The so-called merit systems and other public personnel practices protected the incompetent, the unfit, the inefficient, the lazy, the burnt out, even the corrupt and the criminal. Such public employees had to be cleared out. Public personnel practices had to be overhauled to allow greater competition. Indeed, all public management practices needed to be rethought to bring them more in line with good business practice. Privatization would automatically take care of this but where it was unlikely business practices should be adopted and public organizations should be reshaped to run more on the lines of their business counterparts. This NPM program was actually only a part of a much bigger scheme to transform government and promote debureaucratization, deregulation, output, financial viability, downsizing, client service, innovation, and entrepreneurship.

What NPM offered was a wide menu from which public service reformers could pick and choose. It included a slew of techniques and approaches, some old and some new, such as job rotation, job enrichment, total quality management, project teams, strategic planning, performance budgeting, and reengineering, familiar in international businesses but actually rare in large public bureaucracies (Golembiewski et al., 2002). Public service reformers have selected and implemented their favorites possibly with greater success in the developed countries than in the less developed countries (Polidano and Hulme, 1999) although it is still difficult to make assessments because other public service reforms have been implemented at the same time. Many of these reforms are quite new and experimental. Performance measures are inadequate and omit adverse effects and unintended consequences, and cheating occurs.

The less developed countries have lacked the resources and managerial capacity to adopt these rather sophisticated reforms. When they have relied on foreign experts, the outsiders have too often ignored domestic circumstances and confused matters by incorporating their foreign values. Even the developed countries have experienced mixed results with some notable successes and some bad failures. Imposed reforms (by elites) have been formally adopted but informally evaded. Governments have been managerially decentralized but politically centralized. Improved public service employment conditions have been negated by inflation, corruption, and nepotism, and even better conditions in the private sector. Yet, scattered successes have created isolated islands where local talent, dedication, enthusiasm, and loyal public support have transformed local public services and entrenched competence and integrity in a sea of mismanagement and venality that shows what can be done when people are serious about public service reform.

In this paradigm, the reform of state institutions is the central objective, driven by the thrust for contracting services, flexible and performance-based managerial structures, provision for less stringent rules for hiring and firing, and a gradual dismantling of the Weberian prescriptions for a permanent career civil service. The exercise is introvert and government-focused, while the citizens are, at best, a secondary priority. The citizens feature in these calculations as consumers of public services and tax payers, who would benefit from improved governance through the economic benefits of efficiency gains, leaner structures and improved financial management.

Internal evaluations of aid agencies like the World Bank and country examples demonstrate the limitations of NPM and reinvention models in improving administration and civil service performance in developed countries as also the fallacy of efforts to transfer western models to developing countries (World Bank, 1999). What is of greater importance is the demonstrable increase in public disenchantment and distrust in government in OECD countries, and the evidence of alienation and apathy of the citizens in developed and developing countries alike. The benefits of economic and administrative reform and the gains from alternative service delivery and competition are not self-evident to ordinary citizens, especially the poor and marginal groups.

In many developing countries, the government is still perceived as distant, unaccountable, and unresponsive (and corrupt, though to a lesser degree in Western countries than in the developing countries). Officials are considered to be self-interested and motivated by job security and monetary gains rather than by public service ethos and standards of integrity. *The Voices of the Poor* drew on interviews in 23 countries to conclude that state institutions are neither responsive nor accountable to the poor, and that poor people see little recourse to injustice, criminality, abuse, and corruption by institutions. Another study in the U.K. by the Rowntree Foundation referred to the lack of public commitment to local democracy and the alienation of citizens.

Internal evaluations of aid agencies like the World Bank and country examples demonstrate the limitations of NPM and reinvention models in improving administration and civil service performance in developed countries as also the fallacy of efforts to transfer Western models to developing countries (World Bank, 1999). What is of greater importance is the demonstrable increase in public disenchantment and distrust in government in OECD countries, and the evidence of alienation and apathy of the citizens in developed and developing countries alike. The benefits of economic and administrative reform and the gains from alternative service delivery and competition are not self-evident to ordinary citizens, especially the poor and marginal groups.

D. No Choice

When it comes to public service reform, the developed countries have many advantages. They have an assured capacity to govern, a competent public bureaucracy, investment resources, and a deeply rooted tradition of governance. They can afford occasional lapses in public service performance and they are better equipped to embark on public service reform. Less developed countries are much more fragile; they live closer to the edge; they lack the ability to mobilize resources. They cannot provide the same level or quality of public goods and services and they are more prone to interruptions in public services and the exploitation of public office. Their administrative deficiencies are more obvious but they lack the ability to tackle them. They know they need public service reform but political circumstances are such that by challenging vested interests in the public bureaucracy, from entrenched elites to powerful public service unions to dependent clients, the political price may be too high to pay, despite the bureaucratic drag on national progress. And all this is apart from the problems caused by political instability, incompetence, and irresponsibility.

For reasons unknown, less developed countries tend to employ proportionately more in military and police services, view government employment as an end in itself (being prestigious, secure, soft, opportunistic), see public funding as a prize, and rarely balance budgets, spending more than they collect. Short of money, most have to borrow from lenders who impose conditions. The International Monetary Fund did so in its structural adjustment programs some 20 yr ago not on a pragmatic country-by-country approach but more on universalistic ideological grounds. It wanted to liberalize the world economy by reducing government intervention and replacing government as *the* engine of development by private enterprise. It insisted on the downsizing of the public sector and public employment, the privatization of public enterprises and the corporatization of other government organizations, deregulation and the general easing of government controls, and tightened administrative controls over public budgeting, staffing, and auditing to safeguard public monies and improve public service productivity and performance. Borrowing countries had no choice but to comply. These were externally imposed reforms with little domestic input and little regard for local circumstances; they were coercive transfers.

Such externally imposed public service reforms were resented by borrowing countries and considered the bad medicine they were meant to be for overblown, costly, and inefficient public services. The borrowers bit the bullet and formally at least complied. They liberalized their economies, reduced their public sectors, tightened public expenditures, and slashed public employment. The experience has left behind a bad taste and a reluctance to repeat the experiment. First, it resulted in much misery and suffering as the anticipated economic miracle did not occur. Many borrowers found themselves worse off than before with their subservience to globalization, foreign penetration, and loss of self-protection. Second, the downsizing of the administrative state undermined the capacity to govern. Law and order, never well enforced, further declined accompanied by social strife, violence, insurrection, and civil war. Organized crime and gangsterism took stronger hold. Third, public services declined as witnessed by increasing power and water shortages, overcrowded transportation, worsening slums, inadequate schools and hospitals, and poorer refuse collection. Fourth, privatization often failed to raise expected public funds, fulfill promised business economies, and generally bring the vaunted superiority of private enterprise. Fifth, public service deteriorated. While ghost positions and deadwood may have been eliminated, employment opportunities, employment conditions, and prospects for promotion diminished. Talented officials with opportunities elsewhere left while newcomers were discouraged by the genteel poverty of the public sector. Public service was left much worse off than it was before, which might have been the intention of the free enterprise ideologues who did not disguise their contempt for government and public employees.

The bad feeling generated by the structural adjustment programs has left lasting scars. The hope is that the experiment will never be repeated and that the ill-fated borrowers will have learnt their lesson, weathered the storm, and rebuilt themselves for another day. The International Monetary Fund has since changed its policies. The international community has realized that the capacity to govern has to be restored and strengthened and the emphasis has now been put on good governance, democratization, human rights, and restoring the appeal of public service.

Blanket approaches and imposed reforms are out. Idiosyncratic solutions with input from targeted countries and partnership in implementation are in. The meat axe is reserved only for the really tough cases where self-reform looks hopeless. Public service reform in less developed countries is becoming more of a shared venture, recognizing the importance of domestic input identification and execution, the injection of external resources and expertise, and the ongoing commitment of the international community. An excellent example of this new approach is provided by the U.S. Agency for International Development's Center for Democracy and Governance project Implementing Policy Change where the emphasis is now on policy assistance, legitimation, constituency building, resource accumulation, organization design, mobilization, and monitoring (Brinkerhoff, 2000).

III. Some Current Universal Issues

What should public service reformers consider right now, given that it takes time to change current trends? Some reforms being implemented need to be reinforced and encouraged. Others may need to be halted and a new course charted. In some destabilized countries, violence has to be reduced, order restored and government rebuilt from its very foundations through international emergency missions. In other parts of the globe, professionalization is the priority to place public service on a permanent competent and moral basis. Almost everywhere, the reputation and attraction of public service has to be restored to prevent exodus and induce talent.

A. The Future Shape of Public Service

One would expect from the campaigns to restrict government intervention, reduce the administrative state, downsize the public sector, and transform the nature of public management, that public services have been trimmed and are leaner and meaner than they were some 20 yr ago. But this has not occurred. Public expenditures have hardly been dented and have risen in real terms. More is spent on outsourcing and less on the direct delivery of public goods and services. Former public employees now work in other organizations, sacrificing their public service rights, and benefits for a different package of employment conditions.

While governments may have shed some activities, they have also added new ones such as environmental protection, market regulation, consumer protection, tourism, sport, and research and development. Traditional activities such as external and internal security, international relations, crime prevention, and revenue raising have all demanded modernization, revitalization, and reinvention. Population pressures and migration have increased the demand for public goods and services. Strengthened democratization has intensified pressures to improve the quality of life for all citizens and extend public benefits to every person. Also, at the back of people's minds is the idea that when unemployment reaches intolerable levels, the government is the employer of last resort and should instigate projects as there is still so much that needs to be done for the underprivileged.

In short, the era of Big Government has not yet come to an end. Big business has grown but only on its own terms. It has not been willing to take over government responsibilities, sticking to its traditional view that the business of business is business not social concerns although many corporations are more willing to share and to participate in communal activities. Nonetheless, they have returned to the government privatized enterprises when these have failed to make sufficient profits. International business has been tarnished by notorious business failures and shortcomings, the excesses of corporate executives and business exploitation of the weak and defenseless. Thus, business is less attractive than it once was and public service can bounce back providing it can regain its credibility. The opportunity is there to appeal to people of talent to shift back from the private to the public sector now that openings and rewards have diminished in the former while the public service will be tying to replace many of its old time careerists who are rapidly approaching retirement.

B. Reversing the Erosion of Public Service

The image and reputation of public service has suffered over the past 20 yr. During this time, the ideological hostility to government and public service has been relentless, but it may have gone too far and is probably toning down; nonetheless it will continue to damage. Although government may have been disappointed, no other institution seems to have done much better. The once roaring success of business has been subdued by world economic difficulties, the uneven effects of globalization, the scandalous behavior of corporate executives, the excesses of and the misuse and abuse of private power. The nongovernmental organizations have been a mixed bag, ranging from the excellent that have combined the best of government and business to the corrupt and unproductive which have combined their worst features. The worst aspect for public agencies is the bad mouthing by insiders who did opt for government, devote their careers to public service, and try to modernize administrative systems. They are aging and choosing early retirement but they are also discouraging successors from following in their footsteps.

Restoring the image and reputation of public service will not be easy or quick; it requires a concerted effort. Public leaders who criticize have to be reminded that they only worsen the situation. It is not the public servants who are so much the fault as the conditions under which they labor, faulty policies and contrived arrangements, and the systems imposed on them. Many public leaders know how much they depend on their public servants, how hard working, self sacrificing, devoted and unassuming they are, and how unfairly they are publicly maligned by colleagues who should know better. The emphasis should be placed on the constructive and the positive. Public leaders should distance themselves from (and speedily disown) unwarranted criticism. They should not be too busy to acknowledge their debt to public servants, praise good performance and recommend public service to younger generations as a force for good and a contributor to public well being par excellence. This message should be repeated by anyone who influences public opinion, from the mass media communicators to the local school teacher and clergy who are public servants themselves and should be allowed every so often to blow their own trumpet. Sophisticated public relations should also be employed but the best image builder is good performance.

C. Fragmentation

Contemporary government has become highly specialized. It contains a wide variety of public and semipublic organizations. The old idea that there should be one unified public service, governed by uniform rules, centrally administered, and presenting a common front to the polity and the public is fast disappearing. Governments, the world over, are bent on bringing themselves closer to the public they serve. They are devolving power, deconcentrating responsibilities, decentralizing administration, and delegating authority, to take the pressures off the apex and enable local authorities to deal with the public directly. As a result there are now many different and distinct public services (military, civil, foreign, legal, judicial, health, education, social service, police, etc.) at different levels of government. There are many different and distinct specializations with separate career paths. Each public organization has its own culture and within that several subcultures. Attempts to restore and strengthen unity and interchangeability have fared badly. More and more countries are accepting the reality of fragmentation and are moving toward the business model of corporatization whereby each public organization will go its own way and make its own managerial and staffing arrangements, free to operate in the labor market within general employment laws and labor–management relations.

None has yet gone that far but the idea is to discard the negatives of public personnel administration for the positives of human resources development. Out go all those complications and restrictions that have been the bane of public service and in come the new entrepreneurial freedoms that business enjoys. This way, each public organization can develop its own image (or brand), choose its own employment conditions, adopt its own strategic planning, concentrate on its own staffing needs, grant portable benefits, improve the quality of work life, invest in its own training facilities, apprenticeship schemes, and career development, and inculcate its own organization culture, without bothering anyone else or awaiting somebody else's permission. The old paper pushers are replaced by new go-ahead professionals or chief human capital officers (James, 2002).

Undoubtedly, the overcentralized public service systems that governments inherit need a drastic overhaul; they are obsolete in many respects and they need to be more flexible and innovative. But fragmentation overlooks why the central systems were first introduced when before the merit system, public service was rife with incompetents, favoritism, arbitrariness, nepotism, corruption, discrimination, and venality. Public servants had few rights and were exploited, victimized, and treated unfairly. The description of spoils system was appropriate and it was abandoned even though its replacement had imperfections.

Nobody expects the bad old days to return but experience with fragmentation suggests that politicization and cronyism may well return and that competition creates disparities and inequalities, introduces some of the undesirable aspects of business entrepreneurialism, reduces loyalty and commitment, actually widens the gap between good and bad performance, compromises full accountability, weakens public service unionism, downgrades training, and encourages disobliging parochialism. The real issue is just how much can individual public organizations be entrusted to manage staffing themselves, how much should still be left to a central monitoring agency to retain a certain degree of uniformity and enforce safeguards, and how desirable a common pool of system wide talent should be maintained.

What concerns some observers about fragmentation and internal rivalry within the public service is the temptation to frequent job switching when talented public servants move quickly between positions with one foot out the door as they move upwards. How much commitment do they have to their current organization and how long will they stay? Government-wide needs are subordinated. Strategic planning is compromised. Investment in training and career development is wasted. Costly outreach programs, for example, may attract talent that is then poached by another organization. Classification systems are wrecked with frequent turnover in positions which are often being renegotiated. The principle of equal pay for equal work evaporates. Perhaps more significantly, will the high flyers have the needed energy to perform effectively and will that energy be guided by a commitment to their current organization?

> Commitment also matters because energy must be part of a broader effort and applied to some purpose. Commitment involves an impulse, and to some extent a decision, to engage in work for some purpose beyond the self. This "commitment to" must involve some element of public interest and requires that public servants have a sense of connectedness or relationships to communities. Most important, commitment embeds public servants in concrete relationship with the political system their agency, programs, and the people they serve. (Lane et al., 2003: 134)

Without improvements in accountability, downsizing and more adequate incentives may result in a small and well-paid but no less inefficient or corrupt civil service, as has happened, for instance, in India where substantial salary increases have hardly improved public sector productivity.

D. Compensation

Few employees consider that they are fairly compensated, senior public servants included. Their ceiling is usually fixed by their political masters whose official and legal compensation is often well overshadowed by the money made by business and entertainment celebrities. Without corruption and underhanded deals, public service is rarely highly lucrative. It pays moderately well, a decent even comfortable living, enough to take care of most needs and provide some economic security. Perhaps employees lower down the public hierarchy may be badly rewarded and may not even earn a living wage; therefore, they have to resort to cheating their public employers or fleecing their clients but this is rarely the case for senior public servants. Responsible governments try to treat them fairly by aiming to be competitive in the local labor market for the talented professionals they seek. By competitive they mean a good employer, certainly in the top half.

Being within the top half of employees is not so easy. First, private employers are not transparent and pay research units which try to find out how much others pay and are not so open either. Whereas public service unions open the whole bargaining process to public scrutiny, senior public servants are not so protected and for many the process remains mysterious unless they set their own conditions or these are set by apolitical independent bodies. On the other hand, they know that whenever the pay scales and other employment conditions for their subordinates get adjusted, theirs' will follow accordingly just to keep the margin. So, senior public servants have an interest in seeing that their subordinates receive decent and adequate compensation although this does not quite settle the issue for them.

Second, often, nongovernmental organizations, particularly in business, professions and entertainment, provide perquisites and extras that no public employer can possibly match without widespread public protest. This is the trade-off that public servants have to make, namely, to be satisfied with what they get with little prospect of short-term improvement or to switch and enjoy comforts and advantages beyond anything they can expect in public employment. The trade-off that public employers have to make to retain top talent and keep their seniors satisfied is to keep their jobs interesting and honor beneficial retirement packages to prevent revolving departures, especially toward career's end when public servants believe they have to make up for lost time.

Third, even within the same general public service tradition, there are wide variations. Some public organizations, especially near the apex of political power, allow so many hidden extras and rewards (intangible and informal as well as tangible and formal) that their official compensation can actually become a secondary consideration. Among these perquisites can be such things as access to privileged information, networking with the powerful and well connected, "honest" graft, tax avoidance, insider trading, tolerated corruption, and exceptional access, for themselves and more importantly for their friends and family too (Hood et al., 2003). Moreover, just as in the private sector, there seems little or no relationship between levels of compensation on the one hand and output, performance, efficiency, venality, and commitment on the other. What seems to count more when it comes to fixing individual compensation packages are such things as elite cohesion, social values (particularly egalitarianism and asceticism), charisma, degree of risk, extent of responsibility, peer recognition and reputation, personal drive and energy, political skills, and vision.

Fourth, there are circumstances which preclude public employers ever being considered good employers even if they want to be. Some are just too poor and do not have the resources to compete in the local labor market dominated by foreign and international employers. Every time they raise their compensation, their rivals follow suit. They never seem to be able to catch up. Fortunately, public service has its own rewards as noted earlier, such as being close to public power, being in a position to make a real difference or contribution in public policy, commanding a high social status, loving the work, ideological pull, religious compulsion, and altruism. Not everyone embraces materialism or enjoys business or wants to join a selfish rat race. These are the very people that public service needs, who are attracted to it, and whose genuine inner spirit sees them through the toughest challenges with grace, modesty, and self-satisfaction. Too much emphasis is put on material compensation and too little on these intangibles in attracting and retaining talent in public service.

E. Diversity

Diversity has emerged as a key issue in the initiative to reassess the role of government. Demands for equality, equity, and fairness in a time of growing demographic diversification indicate a parallel need to diversify public organizations. A diverse public service integrates individuals from different racial, religious, and ethnic backgrounds and also men and women, the elderly and disabled, and those with different sexual orientation. Diversity means opportunities for all groups in the community to be hired, to advance and to value their differences.

The senior ranks of public organizations have been accused of being too long unrepresentative of the general public, being overly confined to one or another entrenched group who distort procedures to favor people like themselves. Diversity requires reforms in hiring and promotion as well as structural changes to ensure mobility and opportunity for previously excluded or under-represented groups to challenge narrow power over policy making, bureaucratic isolation, secrecy, hierarchy, over reliance on rigid rules, insensitivity to those excluded, and lack of responsiveness. Public service reforms that promote diversity also encourage other reforms, such as broader participation in policy making, stronger community linkages, improved information flow, greater openness and transparency, more humane operations, and enhanced capacity for decision-making and implementation.

Theoretically, merit systems open up public service careers to all qualified citizens. But who qualifies? Whole categories of people are excluded from eligibility such as foreigners, nonresidents, health risks and disabled persons, undesirables, nonbelievers, the poorly educated, the elderly married women, and the like. Even when eligible, cultural prejudices, legal restrictions, and inflexible working conditions often rule out women and minorities or relegate them to low level positions. As they are now fast becoming the majority of the work force, to take advantage of available talent and to utilize it effectively, public organizations have to take deliberate measures to encourage the recruitment and advancement of a heterogeneous pool of labor, including all under-represented groups. Changes need to extend from practical physical accommodations and work schedules to the transformation of organizational cultures.

Diversity is justified on the following grounds:

- *A highly qualified work force* — government needs to draw on a wider pool of talent and cannot afford to exclude groups because of discrimination and prejudice.
- *Social equity* — public service is a public resource not a political prize or instrument for any particular group and should be model for fairness and nondiscrimination.
- *Human capital* — public service should deliberately attract neglected and underrepresentative groups and offer career paths to enable diversity at all levels.
- *Innovation and problem solving* — public services need to develop capacity to relate, understand, and cooperate with all groups, improve cultural sensitivity toward client groups and incorporate a greater variety of viewpoints.
- *Organizational culture* — public organizations need to change the way they go about their business.
- *Nation building* — public services cannot stand aloof behind a neutral façade of technical competence from the vicissitudes of the wider society and should conduct themselves to reduce conflict and integrate communities.

The management of diversity presents difficulties. Other public service reforms such as cutbacks, greater professionalization and computer expertise may actually reduce diversity. Equality of opportunity may be restricted by narrow job description and inflexible work facilities. Formal job qualifications may be distorted by prejudice and cronyism. Poor public education may create a most uneven playing field between rich and poor, rural and urban, men and women, conformists and nonconformists. Attempts to favor previously under-represented groups may provoke a backlash and may bring in incompetence and double standards. One problem is who is being kept unfairly out of public employment. Another is, who is allowed in public employment, who is qualified and competent but does not come from a small inner circle. Diversity requires the backing of laws that prohibit unfair discrimination and prejudice, encourage equal opportunity, and promote affirmative action, public education that inculcates a multicultural vision of society that values all groups, cultural awareness training and leveling up, structural changes to create career paths, job enrichment, job rotation, and removal of formal barriers within hierarchies, and political support for the wider social aim of diversity which is social justice, the end to false stereotyping, empowering weak groups and changing the bureaucratic mindset.

F. Corruption

Corruption virtually kills reform. While the reformers do their best to improve things, the corrupt who benefit from leaving things as they are do their best to obstruct and sabotage reform. The worst form of corruption is institutionalized, where things work the opposite way round to what they should and everyone caught within it has no alternative but to conform or exit which just reinforces wrongdoing. The whole system is rotten and is self-perpetuating. Individual corruption can be tackled and rooted out providing wrongdoing is condemned and the structure is in place to expose it. However, institutionalized corruption needs whistleblowers prepared to defy insiders and undergo terrible trials until they find outsiders who believe them and back them to the bitter end. Cursed is the country where institutional corruption infects the very public authorities that people expect to tackle wrongdoing, the misuse and abuse of public power and office, theft of public resources, nonapplication or bending of the law, distortion of public policies and regulations, nepotism, and public leaders who place themselves beyond public accountability. Corruption is infectious; if not treated, it spreads and contaminates everything it comes into contact with. It never goes away but always lurks in the background ready to strike again whenever the opportunity presents itself. Before they set out to embark on their enterprise, public service reformers should give high priority to reducing corruption if their reforms are to stand any chance of lasting impact.

G. Where to Begin?

Everyone complains about their public goods and services and about public officials from top to bottom. The public will always have complaints as long as public service is imperfect. Even supposing that their complaints are justified (ombudsman offices find that only about one fifth are), they may not have any solutions or the right solutions. But at least their complaints indicate what most concerns them and where if something meaningful is done to reduce their dissatisfaction, they would be less critical. They see public service from a different angle than insiders and they may well identify shortcomings that too often are overlooked or downplayed. Mass media critics exploit public grievances. Bad scintillating news is better than boring good news as it grabs more attention and much good news about public service is boring. But good investigative reporting assisted by screened or secret whistleblowers exposes failings that otherwise would never come to light. Yet, once again, finding fault is quite a different exercise than coming up with practical solutions. Foreign experts and domestic researchers are more valuable but they do not have the responsibility of implementing their solutions and escape blame when their reforms fail. Nonetheless, they are useful sounding boards and catalysts that should be part of the reform process.

It is best to begin with the people who really know from the inside what is wrong, what needs to be done to improve matters, and whose professional pride give them incentive to risk changes and tackle vested interests. These constitute the core senior public servants who hold up public organizations and work hard to keep things from deteriorating. They are found in all public organizations, devoted professionals all and secretly admired by those who see what they do day in and day out. They know or can make shrewd guesses why talent is scared off and why colleagues contemplate getting out. They know whether lower level staff are qualified and experienced enough to take over, whether they lack sufficient mobility, opportunity, training, or career development, whether they are dissatisfied with their employment conditions and what specifically might improve commitment and morale. They know to whom they lose talent, and what might be done to reduce the flow. They know the structural obstacles, what poaching takes place, and the political limitations under which they operate. Their proposals may not be as academically attractive or politically appealing as those of outsiders, but they have a better idea of what is feasible and might actually work. Yet they may be part of the problem too; therefore, their reforms need to be considered and appraised by outsiders and expert consultants lest they too go off the rails. Just as they can give corrective advice to outsiders, so outsiders can ram the favor given their knowledge of other situations and applications. Correct diagnosis goes hand in hand with effective remedies. No one has a monopoly over inventiveness, creativity, and innovation which can come from the most unlikely sources. In any event, should the selected reforms fail to satisfy, the choice remains open to try something else from the long menu of public service reform.

References

Bevir, M., Rhodes, R.A.W., and Weller, P., Traditions of governance: interpreting the changing role of the public sector, *Public Adm.*, 81 (1), 1–17, 2003.

Bjur, W. E. and Caiden, G. E., Administrative reform and institutional bureaucracies, in *Dynamics of Development: An International Perspective*, Sharma, S.K., Ed., Concept Publishing Company, Delhi, 1977, pp. 365–378.

Brinkerhoff, D.W., Policy implementation in developing and transitional countries: past lessons and future challenges, inPaper Presented at the 61st National Conference, American Society for Public Administration, San Diego, CA, 2000.

Caiden, G.E., *Administrative Reform Comes of Age*, De Gruyter, Berlin, 1991.

Colareli, S.M., *No Best Way*, Praeger, Westport, CT, 2003.

Dror, Y., *The Capacity to Govern*, Frank Cass, London, 2001.

Golembiewski, R.T., Vigoda, E., and Sun, B.-C., Cacophonies in the contemporary chorus about change at public worksites, as contrasted with some straight talk from a planned change perspective, *Int. J. Public Adm.*, 25 (1), 111–137, 2002.

Hood, C., Control, bargains, and cheating: the politics of public service reform, *J. Public Adm. Res. Theory*, 12 (3), 309–332, 2002.

Hood, C., Peters, B.G., and Lee, G., Eds., *Reward for High Public Office: Asian and Pacific Rim States*, Routledge, London, 2003.

Horton, J., Yesterday's failure is tomorrow's reform, *Los Angeles Times*, M3, August 17, 2003.

James, K.C., The HR paradigm shift and the federal human capital opportunity, *Public Manager*, Winter, 13–16, 2002.

Lane, L.M., Wolf, J.F., and Woodard, C.A., Reassessing the human resource crisis in the public service, 1987–2002, *Am. Rev. Public Adm.*, 33 (2), 123–145, 2003.

National Commission on the Public Service (Volcker), *Urgent Business for America: The Federal Government for the 21st Century*, The Brookings Institution, Washington, DC, 2003.

Oman, R.C., Gabriel, R.L., Garrett, J.J., and Malmberg, K.B., An assessment of a drastically changed federal workplace in the United States, *Int. J. Public Adm.*, 26 (10–11), 1099–1104, 2003.

Polidano, C. and Hulme, D., Public management reform in developing countries: issues and outcomes, *Public Manage.*, 1 (1), 121–132, 1999.

World Bank, *Civil Service Reform: A Review of World Bank Assistance*, The World Bank, Washington, DC, 1999.

Chapter 32

Capacity Development and Good Governance

Kempe Ronald Hope, Sr.

CONTENTS

I. Introduction

Since the 1990s, capacity development has become recognized as a necessity for underpinning a number of critical prerequisites for sustaining development in the developing world. High on the list of those prerequisites is good governance. Without good governance, as will be demonstrated subsequently, the quest for development is a fruitless goal. Consequently, capacity development has taken on added importance, both by the international development community and by the developing countries themselves, as a vital aspect of policy change for growth and development. Indeed, the international development community and the developing countries all tend to invoke capacity problems to explain why policies fail to deliver or why development assistance is not leading to positive sustainable outcomes.

The lack of good governance in most of the developing world has been demonstrated to have corrosive effects on the development process. Such poor governance has been shown, among other things, to undermine democracy, subvert the rule of law, entrench corruption, scare off foreign investment and foreign aid, and obstruct the implementation of poverty alleviation and development policies. Improving the governance environment in the developing world is therefore a major priority on the development agenda and the capacity to do so must be enhanced. Good governance is essential for sustaining economic transformation in developing countries. This chapter conceptualizes capacity development and good governance and discusses the role and importance of the former in the process of achieving the latter in developing societies.

II. Conceptualizing Capacity Development

There are several definitions of capacity development. However, a logical starting point here is to address the meaning of capacity. According to UNDP (2003), capacity is the ability of individuals, organizations, and societies to perform functions, solve problems, and set and achieve goals. The emphasis here is on having a certain level of individual and institutional capability and the appropriate resources to bring about sustainable impacts. This is referred to by Land (2000) as the instrumental notion of capacity.

A similar instrumental notion of capacity has been put forward by the World Bank (1996), which defines capacity as the ability to perform appropriate tasks effectively, efficiently, and sustainably through the combination of human resources and institutions that permit countries to achieve their development goals. It engenders the self-reliance that comes with the ability of people to make policy choices and take actions to achieve the objectives they set for themselves, including the ability to identify and analyze problems, formulate solutions, and implement them.

Another approach offered by Land (2000) is termed the dynamic perspective. In this approach, capacity is viewed as a continuous process by which individuals, groups, institutions, organizations, and societies enhance their abilities to identify and meet development challenges in a sustainable manner. There is a greater emphasis placed here on issues related to role and relationships, attitude, and responsibilities at the interorganizational and societal levels (Land, 2000).

Bolger (2000), for the Canadian International Development Agency (CIDA), provided a much more sweeping definition of capacity. In his view, capacity should be regarded as the abilities, skills, understandings, attitudes, values, relationships, behaviors, motivations, resources, and conditions that enable individuals, organizations, networks/sectors, and broader social systems to undertake functions and achieve their development objectives over time. Although sweeping, this definition offers a comprehensive approach for translating and transitioning into the next levels of defining and proposing principles and policies for the development of capacity.

The foregoing definitions of capacity cover a wide spectrum although the basic elements are essentially the same. In the context of development, and for this chapter, capacity is being defined as the competency of individuals, public sector institutions, private sector entities, civil society organizations, and local communities to engage in activities in a sustainable manner that permit the achievement of beneficial goals such as poverty reduction, efficient service delivery, good governance, economic growth, effectively facing the challenges of globalization, and deriving the greatest possible benefits from such trends as rapid changes in information technologies and science.

Having established what is meant by capacity, we can now move on to the concept of capacity development. From the perspective of the United Nations Development Program, capacity development is about promoting learning, boosting empowerment, building social capital, creating enabling environments, integrating cultures, and orienting personal and societal behavior (UNDP, 2003). It is a process that should build on and harness indigenous capacity rather than replace it (UNDP, 2003).

Cheema (2003) regards capacity development as the central process of long-term development that involves the acquisition of ability by an institution, organization, group, or individual to perform a function or group of functions. And, it allows them to do this regularly in an efficient, effective, and sustainable manner. Both quality and sustainability are significant elements in this formulation.

For Wangwe and Rweyemamu (2001), capacity development, as particularly applied to the African region, is a comprehensive process including the ability to identify constraints and to plan and manage development. It involves both the development of human resources and institutions and a supportive policy environment. In this definition, the issues of creating the capacity, effectively mobilizing and using existing and newly created capacities, establishing ways to bridge the gap between existing and required capacity, and sustaining the capacity over time are important (Wangwe and Rweyemamu, 2001).

On the basis of a review of the literature through to the end of the 1990s, Lusthaus et al. (1999) found capacity development to be an elastic concept which can be grouped into four perspectives or approaches: organizational, institutional, systems, and participatory. The organizational approach sees an entity, organization, or a set of organizations as the key to development. It applies to work with governments, nongovernmental organizations, as well as other civil society and community organizations and focuses on identifying and improving the elements or components of capacity within those organizations. In this perspective, organizations are regarded as processing systems that change individual and system capacities into organizational results (Lusthaus et al., 1999).

The institutional approach attempts to set out a clear distinction between organizations and institutions. It is concerned with building capacity to create, change, enforce, and learn from the processes and rules that govern society. This approach is deemed to be better able to deal with the issues which underlie most development problems such as cultural values, norms, beliefs, and incentive systems due to its macro perspective (Lusthaus et al., 1999).

The systems approach to capacity development refers to a framework that is multilevel, holistic, and interrelated with each system or part being linked to another. In the systems approach, capacity development should build on what is found to exist in order to improve it, rather than to create new systems. It is considered as a dynamic process in which individuals, communities, groups, and organizations attempt to improve their capability to achieve their goals through their own initiatives as well as through the support of outsiders (Lusthaus et al., 1999).

The participatory approach emphasizes the importance of the means used to achieve the goals of development. It is people-centered and non-hierarchical and based on the idea that unless the ultimate beneficiaries of the process are empowered and feel a considerable degree of ownership, the required results will not emerge. In this approach, it is deemed desirable, for example, that local expertise be identified and used rather than the imposition of foreign experts (Lusthaus et al., 1999).

Another definition of capacity development, gaining currency with development practitioners, recognizes the concept as being fundamentally about change and transformation at the individual, institutional, and societal levels. Bolger (2000), for example, notes that capacity development refers to the approaches, strategies, and methodologies used by developing countries and external stakeholders, to improve performance at the individual, organizational, network/sector, or broader system level. This definition recognizes that capacity development occurs not just in individuals, but also between them, and in the institutions and networks they create within the society. Furthermore, it also reflects the importance of the need to be responsive to the interrelationships among them (Bolger, 2000).

Fukuda-Parr et al. (2002) further elaborated this view. They contend that capacity development needs to be addressed at three levels: individual, institutional, and societal. The individual level entails enabling individuals to engage in a continuous learning process which allows them to build on existing knowledge and skills, and to be able to expand these into new directions as additional opportunities arise. The institutional level pertains to the building of existing institutional capacity rather than trying to create new institutions that may be based on foreign models. The societal level involves the society as a whole for development transformation. It includes creating opportunities in both the private and public sectors to allow people to use and expand their capacities to the fullest for the benefit of the society in general (Fukuda-Parr et al., 2002).

From the foregoing, it is obvious that there are numerous interpretations of capacity development. However, the emerging dominant approach, being adopted by both developing countries and donors, negates the traditional approaches which have concentrated only on the individual and the organizational levels and has embraced a much more integrated approach that also recognizes the societal dimension which encompasses the facilitatory processes, such as ownership, which enable people to use and expand their capacities to the fullest (Browne, 2002).

In this chapter, capacity development is defined as the enhancement of the competency of individuals, public sector institutions, private sector entities, civil society organizations, and local communities to engage in activities in a sustainable manner for positive development impacts such as poverty reduction, improvements in governance, and generally meeting the millennium development goals. For most developing countries, donor support and other technical assistance will be required to both assist with developing capacity as well as retaining it. Nonetheless, for capacity development to be sustainable and also contribute to sustainable development, the process must be owned and managed by the developing countries and not their external partners.

III. Conceptualizing Good Governance

Governance is about power, relationships, and accountability — who has influence, who decides, how citizens and other stakeholders have their say, and how decision makers are held accountable (Schacter, 2000). In this chapter, good governance is defined as the existence of political accountability, bureaucratic transparency, the exercise of legitimate power, freedom of association and participation, freedom of information and expression, sound fiscal management and public financial accountability, respect for the rule of law, a predictable legal framework encompassing an interdependent and credible justice system, respect for human rights, an active legislature, enhanced opportunities for the development of pluralistic forces including civil society, and capacity development (Hope, 2002).

Developing countries have to be particularly concerned about good governance in the political, economic, and corporate realms. Indeed, these three areas of governance are somewhat interdependent. It is not possible, for example, to have good economic and corporate governance in an environment of poor, bad, or deteriorating political governance. In other words, it is good political governance that will influence all other facets of governance in any society. Also, good political governance is a prerequisite for either good economic or good corporate governance (Hope and Hamdok, 2002).

Good political governance is a societal state epitomized by, among others, the following characteristics: predictable, open, and enlightened policy making; a bureaucracy imbued with a professional ethos; a strong civil society participating in public affairs; adherence to the rule of law, respect for basic human rights and freedoms, and judicial independence; and consistent traditions and predictable institutions that determine how authority is exercised in a given nation–state including (1) the process by which governments are selected, held accountable, monitored, and replaced; (2) the capacity of governments to manage resources efficiently and formulate, implement, and enforce sound policies and regulations; and (3) the respect of citizens and the state for the institutions that govern economic and social interactions among them (Hope and Hamdok, 2002).

Good economic outcomes are derived from good economic governance. Good economic governance is defined as the existence of institutions of government that have the capacity to manage resources efficiently; can formulate, implement, and enforce sound policies and regulations; can be monitored and be held accountable; exhibit respect for the rules and norms of economic interaction; and in which economic activity is unimpeded by corruption and other activities inconsistent with the public trust. The key elements contributing to an environment of good economic governance are transparency, accountability, and an enabling environment for private sector development and growth, and institutional development and effectiveness (Hope and Hamdok, 2002).

Corporate governance refers to the mechanisms through which corporations (whether private, publicly traded, or state-owned) and their management are governed. Good corporate governance is defined as entailing the pursuit of objectives by the board and management that represent the interests of a company and its shareholders including effective monitoring and efficient use of resources. Good corporate governance is influenced by a number of factors, primary among which is the nature of the overall institutional and legal framework that has been established by governments to effect such good governance (Hope and Hamdok, 2002). In attempting to effect good corporate governance structures, developing countries would therefore be primarily concerned with creating an enabling environment for all types of commercial entities to flourish within well-defined and predictable applications of rules.

IV. Developing Capacity for Good Governance

Sustainable growth and development in developing countries cannot be achieved in the absence of good governance. Among other things, good governance ensures the most efficient utilization of already scarce resources in the promotion of development; enhances participation, responsibility, and accountability; and has the potential to emancipate people from poverty as state legitimacy is recognized and entrenched. In fact, any effort to reduce poverty and sustain development in developing countries must be built upon a foundation of good governance.

Good governance, in all its facets, has been demonstrated to be positively correlated with the achievement of better growth rates, particularly through the building of institutions in support of markets. Recent empirical analysis suggests a positive correlation between democratic governance and the levels of income, investment, human capital, economic liberalization, and distributive income growth in society (Tavares and Wacziarg, 2001). In particular, a political system characterized by freedom and stability is best suited to promote a growth-oriented economic agenda.

Feng (2003), for example, has demonstrated that institutions do matter in their influence on economic growth. Political repression, political instability, and policy uncertainty all define and constrain an individual's economic decisions in the marketplace. Consequently, they have significant dampening effects on a nation's economic development. The effect of democracy on growth is therefore positive (Feng, 2003). Several other analysts and policymakers have also drawn the link between good governance and sustainable development.

According to the United Nations Secretary General Kofi Annan, good governance is perhaps the single most important factor in eradicating poverty and promoting development (United Nations, 1998). Saitoti (2002) has also noted that good political and economic governance underpins sustainable development. Kabbaj (2003) has emphasized that good governance is not only a worthy goal *per se*, but also a prerequisite for sustainable development and poverty reduction in long-term. Bhagwati (2004) has argued that the link between development and the rise of democracy is robust. There is, therefore, a growing consensus in the literature that development is impossible in the absence of democracy, respect for human rights, and generally good governance.

However, in the majority of developing countries, the capacity for sustaining good governance is very weak and that, in turn, means that the capacity for sustaining development is also weak and needs to be developed. Indeed, there seems to be a real consensus that development cannot be achieved by throwing money and external know-how at problems. It is the product of each country's historical and cultural circumstances and involves a fundamental society transformation process (ECDPM, 2003). It has to be based on the particular circumstances of each country and requires openness to the lessons of experience, and the flexibility to modify approaches as required (Bolger, 2000).

Both the demand and opportunities for capacity development have never been greater. After decades of approaching capacity development as just the enhancement of skills through training and institutional strengthening, developing countries, and donors alike have now come to the realization that their approach ignored the reality that capacity development also entailed the achievement of societal objectives with a systems approach that allows for the setting of objectives, the drawing up of action plans, the development and implementation of appropriate policies and programs, the design of regulatory and legal frameworks, the building and management of partnerships, and the fostering of an enabling environment for the civil society and the private sector (Cheema, 2003).

In the context of achieving good governance for sustainable development, the objectives of capacity development must include:

- Ensuring that there exists a relationship of trust between governments and the citizenry.
- Empowering those who are most affected by bad governance and poverty.
- Creating an enabling environment for competition and a plurality of ideas.
- Providing equal opportunities for citizens to access resources and to participate in political processes.
- Mobilizing respect for human rights, freedoms, and the rule of law.
- Enforcing ethical behavior among public servants and political leaders.
- Strengthening public financial management.
- Enhancing institutional reforms that should focus primarily on the administrative and civil services, the strengthening of parliamentary oversight, the promotion of participatory decision-making, the adoption of effective measures to combat corruption, the undertaking of judicial reforms, and the promotion of an enabling environment for the private sector and civil society to flourish.

To achieve the foregoing objectives of capacity development, and in championing the process toward capacity development for good governance, developing countries and donors should also follow a set of fundamental principles. Those principles for capacity development should include, among others:

- Being locally owned and controlled by those committed to the objectives of the capacity development initiative as well as those who will be responsible and accountable for it. External partners cannot create the levels of ownership and commitment required for capacity development efforts to be successful.
- Being addressed as a continuous, dynamic, and long-term process.
- Having the requisite amount of financial resources to ensure that the initiative can be implemented to its fullest potential.
- Building on the existing local capacity across the public, private, and civil society sectors. Foreign expertise should not be substituted. The lack of local capacity has been cited as both a cause and a consequence of poor governance and failed attempts at governance support in some developing countries (Schacter, 2000; Hope, 2002).
- Involving a broad-based and participatory approach. This will increase awareness and understanding of the capacity development initiative and improve its chances of acceptance and success across the public, private, and civil society sectors.
- Being comprehensive in approach, to the extent possible, so that the primary and support personnel, institutions, and communities are able to simultaneously benefit from the capacity development initiative in a strategic systems management manner.

With the foregoing principles being observed, the key areas in which most developing countries appear to suffer from serious capacity gaps and deficiencies with respect to good governance, and for which sustainable capacity development is therefore required, among both their state and nonstate actors, are the following:

- The legislative bodies which are experiencing difficulties in exerting their oversight and control functions due to their limited capacity in terms of policy analysis and review, budget control, initiation of new bills, and the development and enforcement of codes of conduct.
- The justice systems which require reforms to address the burdensome judicial procedures, the inadequate human resource recruitment and management methods, and issues of judicial independence.

- The civil services which require reforms to fill existing gaps in capacity in the executive branch where flawed incentive structures and employment methods, weak leadership and management, dysfunctional organizational structures, outdated procedures, archaic equipment, poor expenditure management and policy analysis skills, and corruption are adversely affecting the implementation of government policies and the delivery of public services.
- The local governments which need to better respond to the needs of the citizens, particularly in those developing countries where decentralization efforts have been undertaken or are being contemplated.
- The civil society organizations (including political parties and the media) and private enterprises both of which need to improve their analytical, strategic, service delivery, policy advocacy, and partnership capabilities.

Ideally, developing countries should try to establish a capacity development facility through which their capacity development initiatives will be implemented. Such a facility should be established as a semi-autonomous entity. Such semi-autonomous entities — unlike government agencies and specialized training institutions — have demonstrated higher degrees of institutional ownership, better governance, professionalism, performance and output utility, and better prospects of sustainability (Wangwe and Rweyemamu, 2001). In addition, semi-autonomous entities are better suited for developing countries to benefit from partnership arrangements with both internal and external partners. At the same time, the external partners will have greater confidence that the assistance (technical and financial) they provide will be more efficiently and appropriately utilized.

V. Conclusion

This work has conceptualized capacity development and good governance in the context of the developing world and discussed the role and importance of developing capacity for achieving that good governance. It also indicates the basic objectives, principles, and the key areas of capacity development for improving governance.

Good governance is a critical prerequisite for achieving sustainable development. Much has been observed and volumes have been written about the deleterious effects of bad governance in the developing world. Very clearly, growth and development cannot be achieved where governance is bad. Good governance can therefore be also regarded as governance on behalf of development-oriented policy.

In pursuing capacity development for improving governance, developing countries must also ensure that such initiatives are comprehensively designed to be simultaneously related to change and transformation at the individual, institutional, and societal levels. Moreover, such initiatives are likely to be more successfully implemented if done through semi-autonomous entities.

References

Bhagwati, J., *In Defense of Globalization*, Oxford University Press, New York, NY, 2004.

Bolger, J., Capacity development: why, what and how, *CIDA Occasional Series*, 1 (1), Canadian International Development Agency (CIDA), Ottawa, 2000.

Browne, S., Rethinking capacity development for today's challenges, in Browne, S., Ed., *Developing Capacity Through Technical Cooperation: Country Experiences*, Earthscan Publications, London, 2002, pp. 1–13.

Cheema, G.S., Capacity development at the country level: a ten-point agenda for action, Paper Prepared for Presentation to the Workshop on Capacity Building: Lessons and Future Directions, Bellagio Study and Conference Centre, Italy, December, 2003.

European Centre for Development Policy Management (ECDPM), Building capacity: how can it be done? *InfoCotonou*, 2 (1), 1–2, 2003.

Feng, Y., *Democracy, Governance, and Economic Performance: Theory and Evidence*, MIT Press, Cambridge, MA, 2003.

Fukuda-Parr, S., Lopes, C., and Malik, K., Institutional innovations for capacity development, in Fukuda-Parr, S., Lopes, C. and Malik, K., Eds., *Capacity for Development: New Solutions to Old Problems*, Earthscan Publications, London, 2002, pp. 1–21.

Hope, K.R., *From Crisis to Renewal: Development Policy and Management in Africa*, Brill Publishers, Leiden, 2002.

Hope, K.R. and Hamdok, A., *Guidelines for Enhancing Good Economic and Corporate Governance in Africa*, United Nations Economic Commission for Africa, Addis Ababa, Ethiopia, 2002.

Kabbaj, O., *The Challenge of African Development*, Oxford University Press, New York, 2003.

Land, A., Implementing institutional and capacity development: conceptual and operational issues, *Discussion Paper* 14, European Centre for Development Policy and Management (ECDPM), Maastricht, 2000.

Lusthaus, C., Adrien, M.-H. and Perstinger, M., Capacity development: definitions, issues and implications for planning, monitoring and evaluation, *Occasional Paper* No. 35, Universalia, Montreal, 1999.

Saitoti, G., *The Challenges of Economic and Instutional Reforms in Africa*, Ashgate Publishing, Aldershot, 2002.

Schacter, M., *Monitoring and Evaluation Capacity Development in Sub-Saharan Africa: Lessons from Experience in Supporting Sound Governance*, ECD Working Paper Series Number 7, World Bank, Washington, DC, 2000.

Tavares, J. and Wacziarg, R., How democracy affects growth, *Eur. Econ. Rev.*, 45, 1341–1378, 2001.

United Nations, *Annual Report of the Secretary-General on the Work of the Organization*, Document A/53/1, United Nations, New York, NY, 1998.

United Nations Development Programme (UNDP), Capacity Development, Available at http://www.undp.org/capacity, last accessed on December 3, 2003.

Wangwe, S.M. and Rweyemamu, D.C., Human resource and institutional development in Africa: an overview, Paper Presented at the First Pan African Capacity Building Forum, Bamako, Mali, October, 2001.

World Bank, *Partnership for Capacity Building in Africa*, World Bank, Washington, DC, 1996.

Chapter 33

A Short History of Failure? Development Processes over the Course of the 20th Century

Michael Jennings

CONTENTS

I. Introduction

The 20th century has been a century of development. Over the course of the last 100 yr or so, governments at the national and the international levels have increasingly sought to directly intervene in shaping the social and economic prospects of citizens around the world. Public expenditure has been channelled, in an unprecedented level, into improving production; raising living standards; providing basic welfare services, education, health, and so on. The primary duty of governments across the world has increasingly focused on guaranteeing the welfare of its citizens, and increasingly that of members of distant countries. As the world experienced unparalleled divergence in rates of economic growth, individual and national income, life-expectancies and social well-being, the question of how to better integrate those regions of the world traditionally thought of as peripheral became central to international political-economy.

Yet, for all the effort expended over the decades, the analysis of how development as a process occurs, and the institutions and initiatives designed to raise the standards of living of the poorest and reduce absolute levels of poverty, we live today in a world more divided than ever. The "development paradigm" as it appears, failed in its mandate. Yet, it has not been a grand failure — 100 yr of hope dashed as the old century turned into the new. It has been a series of failures and shortcomings, of shifts and changes in how development has been implemented and (perhaps more crucially) how it has been understood. As the hopes of the early 20th century faded, the dominant discourses were challenged and produced the modernity and positivism of the 1950s. Economic collapse in the 1970s gave way to structural adjustment in the 1980s. The story of development is not one of a single process, but a series of inextricably entwined discourses, processes, and paradigms, each feeding off the perceived failure of its predecessor and swinging the pendulum from one theory to another. It is an unfinished story, perhaps, but nonetheless an important one if we are to truly understand how we choose to define the word "development" today, and why interventions are designed in the way that they are.

For many authors and practitioners working in the field, the modern era of "development" began in the aftermath of the Second World War. Development, and the related concepts of "underdevelopment" were "invented" (Esteva, 1993: 6) in the post-war period with the establishment of international organizations dedicated to promoting economic growth and lessening poverty in a newly defined "less developed" and later "third" world. Marshall Plan aid from 1948 suggested the positive impact that large injections of capital might have on re-starting faltering economies and possibly kick-starting into life underdeveloped ones. Consultants, development experts, and the rise of the new breed of non-governmental organizations dedicated to poverty-alleviation and improving living standards appeared to indicate something new running through the international community, as development interventions gradually began to replace colonial interventions in the economies of large parts of Africa, Asia, and Latin America.

Much of the analysis of shifting development policies has similarly focused on the post-1945 world, and in particular on the ideology of development itself: the concept of the "state" and its role and responsibility in developing national economies and societies; the place of the "market" in fostering growth and freedom, or in limiting freedom and diversity; the rise of civil society and its place in development processes. Much of this analysis has focused upon development as a manifestation of western hegemony: the imposition of discourses that both help establish and reinforce western (or perhaps northern) dominance of the international political and economic system. The very idea of "developed" — with its co-dependent terminology of "developed," "underdeveloped," "least developed" — reinforces models of societies that hold up the dominant industrial or liberal democratic powers (essentially Western Europe and the United States) as benchmarks against which the rest of the world is valued.

Such structural analyses give supremacy to the international (and "western" dominated) developmental institutions: the International Monetary Fund, World Bank, European Union, and other United Nations agencies. It is in these institutions and in the academies of the developed west that "development" as a process is forged and disseminated. The analysis tends, therefore, to suggest two key elements: "development" began after 1945; and "development" is largely an unchanging discourse. Individual policies might change, but the fundamental nature of what is understood and promoted as development remains the same, and continues to reinforce western dominance.

What is missing from these depictions is the so-called "periphery": the nations, communities, societies that are "being developed." The periphery has been excluded from the analysis, with interventions designed and implemented in the field portrayed as reflecting (rather than shaping) discourses and paradigms at the center. This perception is being increasingly challenged, in particular by a growing literature on the history of development in sub-Saharan Africa. Monica Beusekom (2002: xxi) notes that the practical development initiatives of the 1920s and 1930s in French Niger directly influenced post-war agricultural and development policies. Other writers have similarly focused on the importance of the inter-war period as critical in shaping colonial administrative attitudes to the economic and productive capacities and potentials of their territorial possessions (Tosh, 1980; Anderson, 1984; Fruend, 1984).[1]

The emergence in the 1920s and 1930s of a distinctive "development ideology" in inter-war Africa was as important in shaping post-war theories and discourses as were the works of Walter Rostow and Paul Baran and the emergence of the Bretton Woods Institutions in the 1940s and 1950s. The first official "decade of development" may have begun in the 1960s, but colonial administrators, planners and officials had been wrestling with similar concepts and notions for some 60 yr prior to its official inauguration. Development in the early 21st century reflects not simply the modern era of post-1945 development initiatives and theory, but that of the entire 20th century. In particular, it reflects the efforts of those early colonial development planners who, in a different context and different political structure, sought to bring the societies and polities they acquired through blood and intrigue into what they perceived as the modern world. Despite the shifts in particular paradigms and individual theories, the language of development has remained remarkably constant over the past 100 yr. Ever since planners have sought to manufacture and transplant the conditions and patterns of economic and social change that occurred in Industrial Revolution Europe into pre-industrial economies, the language of "developed" and "undeveloped" has existed. In seeking to create the conditions for socio-economic change, the precise requirements for that change have been debated, evolved, and transformed as planners have been confronted with the realities of attempting to mechanically engineer such change.

II. The "Dual Mandate": Understandings of "Development," 1900–1945

With the onset of the last stage of European colonial expansion in the late 19th century, the crucial question exercising colonial planners was how to make the colonies pay for themselves. "Development" as a concept was understood in strictly narrow terms as economic growth: through the encouragement of increased production in the new colonies, government income would rise, allowing for the provision of basic and subsequently improved infrastructure, feeding in turn further growth in production.

Two questions exercised the development planners of the early 20th century: upon what sector or sectors was the growth-oriented "development" to be based; and who was responsible for implementing and regulating intervention processes? The key to much colonial development was to be agriculture. On the basis of the understanding of complementary economic systems, the colonies would export raw commodities and import manufactured imports (thus benefiting both the colonizer and the colonized alike). By the 1920s, such notions had become part of the "dual mandate"

(Lugard, 1922): the belief that colonialism and colonial development would be equally positive for all. Development discourse throughout the period was fundamentally a technical question of how best to promote agricultural production. Export production was to be the foundation stone of increased public revenues and hence investment in economic and social services, and the key to improving the quality of life of those producers.

In managing the process of development the role of the state was held to be minimal. Development was to stem, as it had appeared to do in the European Industrial Revolution, from private investment. The British government, for example, made little in way of financial investment to the development of its colonies until the 1920s. Between 1896 and 1923, over 90% of government funds for colonial development went to construction of the railways (largely in East and Central Africa). Only 2% of the funding was in the form of grants, the rest made on the basis of loans with interest rates applying from the moment the loan was made (Havinden and Meredith, 1993: 140–141).

By the 1920s, both the narrow definition of what constituted "development," and the understanding of agency, was starting to shift. The Colonial Development Act of 1929 was the first major act that committed the British state, and the money of British taxpayers, to overseas development. The Treasury Department was empowered to advance money to British territories for development, in the form of either loans or importantly grants. Initially, economic development was the prime focus with the transport and communications infrastructure as the main recipient of funds. Nevertheless, debates in the 1930s brought about a shift in the understanding of "development," and what development constituted, to include an element of social welfare. Some 16% of colonial development fund allocations were for health care schemes (the second largest allocation by type). This new concern for welfare was carried into the post-war period, and the new Colonial Development and Welfare Act (CDWA). While the CDA failed in its application as a means to develop colonial economies, it did serve to re-orient official British and colonial government policy towards a focus upon the social aspects of development: education, health, improvement in living standards, etc.

Moreover, the development acts made the role of the state more important to the process of development, accompanying and informing the growing trend towards central planning of economies and hence, development itself. The state had assumed the responsibility for development — both economic and increasingly social — and thus positioned itself as the natural engine driving the process forward.

For much of the inter-war period, the basic development question was essentially a technical one: how best to promote and increase agricultural production. If the new colonies were to be fully incorporated into the world capitalist system, capitalist market economies needed to be established. The rural sector was identified as the sole sector, which could provide any realistic opportunities for economic development. Export crops were the foundations of economic (and hence, socio-political) growth. The process was inherently interventionist: European cultivation and livestock management methods were assumed without question to be superior to the traditional African systems. Development initiatives were largely therefore, a technical application of measures to overcome bottlenecks that inhibited further growth: a conservative peasantry unwilling to accept change and modernization; an environment hostile to agriculture and worsened through poor ecological management from African systems of agriculture; and the failure of market-relations to penetrate traditional society. The inevitable result was a bureaucracy that regarded its developmental mission as something that had to be imposed from above on unwilling recipients. It was an administrative task, not a consensual process. Strategies were decided by the administration, with advice from the relevant experts, and then expected to be implemented by the people, under supervision from the administrative masters.

Thus, over the course of the inter-war period, two paradoxical processes were in operation. The sphere of what development constituted was widened, while at the same time, the number of actors associated with control over that development was radically narrowed. When, in the aftermath of the Second World War, private industries and manufacturing was more actively promoted, it was nevertheless firmly within a government-defined space. With the outbreak of World War II, the concept of "development" inferred more than purely economic advancement. Improvements in living standards, in literacy and health rates, and so forth, were considered intrinsic elements — albeit as mechanisms for improving production and hence economic growth. Parallel to this process, development became less of an interaction between the voluntary, private, public, and civil society sectors. It consisted of fixed policies, set by the state and largely implemented by that state. The colonial inheritance was a system of central planning that had evolved in the war, and continued to centralize over the remaining decade and a half of colonial rule.

III. The Supremacy of Development Planning

In 1949, President Harry Truman heralded the emergence of the modern development era in his inauguration address. He declared: "we must embark upon a bold new program for making the benefits of our scientific advances and industrial progress available for the improvement and growth of underdeveloped areas" (Truman, 1949). So began, according to conventional wisdom, the "development path" that envisioned the rise of "underdeveloped" nations from reliance on agricultural production to rapid industrialization, economic growth and hence, the rise to "developed" status along the lines of the already industrialized west. Of course, such sentiments had been expressed throughout the 20th century, largely in the context of colonial domination.

What was, perhaps, new was the dominance of modernism and positivist theories as applied to the notion of development: the potent belief in the power of technology; blind faith in "progress"; and willingness to intervene more proactively in the lives of peasant farmers, small-scale producers, communities, societies and nations in order to shape the brave new worlds that were to be created. As independence swept across Asia and Africa, old nomenclatures of colonizers and colonized began to be replaced by the new terms "developed" and "underdeveloped." International organizations gradually took over the main responsibility for devising national development plans in the newly independent nations. The World Bank report on the economic development of Tanganyika reflects this dichotomy of the old and new merging: prepared at the request of the British colonial administration in 1960, yet forming the blue-print for national development in the first five years of independence, it reflected older colonial policy framed in a new context (World Bank, 1961). In its plans for agricultural development it mirrored Tanganyikan colonial agricultural development policy from the late 1950s, merely changing names to the more modern sounding twin-strategies of "transformation" and "improvement" approaches. Yet, it moved beyond colonial policy in its stress on industrialization, and desire to use increased agricultural production to fund the industrialization policy on a larger scale. It was, in essence, a compromise of both old and new, reflecting the paradoxes of the shifts in broader development processes themselves.

The economic-growth fuelled optimism of the 1950s brought forth the "decade of development" in the 1960s. The apparent success of Marshall Plan aid, established in 1948 to assist in the reconstruction of European war-ravaged economies and societies, seemingly asserted the validity of the principle of vast injections of capital to unblock the bottle-necks holding back the economic growth that was an economy's natural state. The post-war period saw the emergence of "development" and development economics as academic and professional disciplines. The interventionists had won the battle over whether intervention was required to promote development: the state (and increasingly from the late 1940s multiple states acting through international organizations) was to be the engine and main promoter of development, not private enterprise. Development could, it appeared, be achieved through influxes of capital, through parliamentary and representative body acts. Moreover, the scope of what that intervention was designed to achieve was widening beyond strictly economic concerns. The era of modern development had truly begun.

IV. Agency

As with the pre-World War II period, the central debates around development processes focused on the two essential questions: agency and purpose. As Hyden (1994: 310) notes in his depiction of the iterative nature of development, the issues of agency to the mid-1970s had been resolved in favor of the state. Development was to be state-directed, and in large part implemented by that state. Development assistance in the form of grants and loans was directed to national governments, and development planning conducted through the auspices of ministries, departments and local governments.

By 1945, "development" as a process was one over which the state was to exert total control. The era of command economies saw states asserting their authority over marketing and pricing policies, over the minutiae of reforming cultivation and other production practices, of directing and planning development interventions and projects, controlling, in short, all aspects of the development process. Central planning on a scale unknown prior to 1939 ensured the dominant position of the colonial state in directing overseas development, a mantle subsequently adopted by the governments of the newly independent nations in the 1960s. The failure of the central state institutions to match the economic growth of the 1950s led to a shift in policy towards decentralization of authority towards local government institutions.

By the end of the 1970s, the era of central planning was under attack with the onset of structural adjustment programs and rolling back of the state. The dominant development paradigm, questioning the failure of states to successfully oversee a transition to modern industrialized economies and rapid economic growth, turned away from the state towards the market as Reaganite and Thatcherite free-market economics came to dominate the issue of agency in development. State's were no longer to be the dominant actors in development policy (in terms of both planning and implementation), and official development assistance was correspondingly diverted to a succession of new players: private companies inheriting the old parastatals, non-governmental organizations rapidly springing up to take advantage of the increased aid flows to their sector, and multinational corporations pushing for decreased restrictions on investment and profit flows, tariffs and a general opening up of the market.

The end of the century has witnessed a resurgence of the state. Development actors have called for the state to be re-integrated as the key element within development planning and intervention. The rise of sector-wide approaches, the poverty reduction strategy papers, and other key elements of modern development strategies have placed the state back at the heart of the process. The era of central planning has not fully returned, and greater consideration is given to civil society actors in the formulation and implementation of development planning. Nevertheless, the shift from the beginning of the 20th century towards state-directed development has been maintained.

V. What is Development?

The rise of "social development" has largely been attributed to the post-war period, especially from the 1970s with Robert McNamara's "dethronement of GNP" and the United Nations International Development Strategy adopted in 1970. However, as has been seen, the broadening out of what constituted "development" from simply economic indicators to social occurred in the late 1930s with the CDW Acts and Hailey's (1938) influential *African Survey*. Nevertheless, there was an increase in both financial and institutional support for social development. As the debates on agency and structure turned towards grassroots and civil society participation in development planning, implementation, monitoring and evaluation, so too the inclusion of what was deemed part of the developmental mandate widened. The human rights discourse of the late 1970s and 1980s, and the conventions and international instruments that emerged from those debates, have similarly widened understandings of the responsibility of the development industry. Indeed, rights have now become essential to modern development processes (in terms of both designing interventions and in their intended outcomes). Of similar importance has been the redefining of "poverty" over the past decade or so: shifting away from narrow interpretations based purely on economic standing to including notions such as insecurity, vulnerability, access to power, and the presence of and access by individuals to social capital within communities. As the definition of "poverty" has widened, so too has that of "development" and what particular interventions are intended to achieve. Economic development and growth have not been abandoned (as seen in the dominance of market-based strategies and the rise of the World Trade Organization), but neither have they reigned unchallenged by current development discourses.

Paradoxically, the "rolling back of the state" in the 1980s witnessed resurgence in market- and growth-based notions of development. However, economic growth alone was no longer posited as the ultimate goal of development. For those pushing free-market-based development, the fruits of economic growth would allow for social development to occur. In other words, social development, while an important and increasingly predominant objective, could only emerge from increased national and individual productivity and incomes. GNP had had its crown restored, albeit under a different constitution.

VI. Conclusion

So where has a century of shifts, turns and redefinitions of the developmental mandate left the process? The dominant paradigm established by the 1950s has largely remained intact: national governments are the main actors in development, assisted and informed by an industry that has grown up around the efforts to modernize and instill social change in the poorest countries of the world; "development" is understood as being wider than purely economic growth and indicators (however important those indicators remain in assessing levels of "development" and "progress"); and the international community continues to establish successive targets, reflecting the continued failure to resolve the dilemmas of development.

Does this sound unduly pessimistic? Are current development process and paradigms essentially repetitions of past endeavors and failures? Perhaps yes. But perhaps it is also an indication of how far we have come, and how great the challenge truly is. For today no one would accept the narrow position of early 20th century development planners: that all can be resolved by private enterprise; that simply increasing production and hence income is enough. Development has not failed over the course of a century, but has faced new challenges, new complexities. For the very notion of "development" is not a fixed concept. It can never be truly reached. As technology and science advance, as societies find new ways to function, they continue to develop in new forms. Nations and societies, as with organisms, only cease developing when they die. The development paradigm we currently possess, re-shaped to meet new challenges, has been forged by our predecessors. It is a never-ending process, and as such its shifts and turns should be welcomed. For as long as it continues to evolve, for as long as it seeks to address the needs of the world's poorest, it is in some way fulfilling its purpose. For the developmental mandate is unchanging in one key and fundamental aspect: whilst there are people dying from preventable diseases, whilst people suffer insecurity and vulnerability from human and environmental crises, and when more than one billion people live on less than $1 a day, development planning has one simple aim, to raise livelihoods and remove people from the daily realities of their poverty. It is an aim that might never be realized. In this sense, "development" is not an outcome, it is a process, and for all its shortcomings, its failures, its near and total misses, it remains a process worthy of remaining engaged in.

Note

1. Importantly, the initiative of African producers working within colonial development policies, but more significantly often *despite* colonial interventions, has been a major focus of much work on African colonial development in this period.

References

Anderson, D., Depression, dust bowl, demography, and drought: the colonial state and soil conservation in East Africa during the 1930s, *Afr. Affairs*, 83, 321–343, 1984.

Esteva, G., Development, in *The Development Dictionary*, Sachs, W., Ed., Zed Books, London and New Jersey, 1993, pp. 6–25.

Fruend, B., *The Making of Contemporary Africa: The Development of African Society Since 1800*, Macmillan, London, 1984.

Hailey, W.M.H., *An African Survey: A Study of Problems Arising in Africa South of the Sahara*, Oxford University Press, London, 1938.

Havinden, M. and Meredith, D., *Colonialism and Development: Britain and its Tropical Colonies, 1850–1960*, Routledge, London and New York, 1993.

Hyden, G., Changing ideological and theoretical perspectives on development, in *African Perspectives on Development: Controversies, Dilemmas and Openings*, Himmelstrand, U., Kinyanjui, K., and Mburugu, E., Eds., James Curry, London, 1994, pp. 308–319.

Lugard, F., *The Dual Mandate in British Tropical Africa*, William Blackwood and Sons, Edinburgh and London, 1922.

Tosh, J., The cash crop revolution in tropical Africa: an agricultural reappraisal, *Afr. Affairs*, 79, 78–94, 1980.

Truman, H.S., *Inaugural Address*, 1949. http://www.american presidents.org/inaugural/32.asp (accessed March 27, 2004).

van Beusekom, M.M., *Negotiating Development: African Farmers and Colonial Experts at the Office du Niger 1920–1960*, James Currey, Oxford, 2002.

World Bank, *The Economic Development of Tanganyika: Report of a Mission Organised by the International Bank for Reconstruction and Development at the Request of the Governments of Tanganyika and the United Kingdom*, Johns Hopkins Press, Baltimore, 1961.

Chapter 34

Managing Development in Africa: How Many More False Starts?

Diana Conyers

CONTENTS

I. Introduction

In 1962, Réne Dumont, a French agronomist-cum-social scientist, wrote a book entitled *L'Afrique Noire est Mal Partie*, which was later published in English as *False Start in Africa* (Dumont, 1966). The book, which examines the first few years of post-independence development effort in Francophone Africa, is a catalogue of development disasters — inappropriate and unworkable policies and projects, which failed to address basic needs or create sustainable development. Dumont blamed the colonial administrations for institutionalizing a eurocentric model of "development," and the new African governments for adopting it unquestioningly. He advocated an alternative approach, based on the principle of African solutions for African problems, and maintained that, if this approach were followed, "underdevelopment" could be conquered in 20 years.

However, 40 years later, it is evident that Dumont's optimism was unfounded. During those 40 years there have been many more "false starts" in Africa. In the late 1960s and 1970s, approaches similar to the one he advocated were attempted in a number of countries under the label of "African socialism," but failed to bring about significant economic growth. The "neoliberal" free market, capitalist model imposed by the International Monetary Fund (IMF) and World Bank, succeeded them in the 1980s and 1990s, but in most countries this merely changed the nature and impact of the problems. Today, 30 of the 34 countries with the lowest index of "human development" are in Africa (UNDP, 2003), while the proportion of the population living on less than U.S. $1 a day in the 29 poorest African countries actually increased from 56% in 1965–1969 to 65% in 1995–1999 (UNCTAD, 2002: 8–9).

If Dumont were to visit Africa today, he would find as many failures as he did in the 1960s. He would find rural water supplies that have been rehabilitated by donors time after time because no effective maintenance system has ever been established, irrigation schemes that have been abandoned as the costs of maintaining them exceeded the value of the crops produced, and schools and health services that lack the basic inputs necessary to function. He would also find "capacity building" projects that have undermined the organizations they were supposed to have strengthened, "co-management" projects that have disempowered local communities and legitimized the exploitation of natural resources, "decentralization" projects that have succeeded only in strengthening national control or "passing the buck" to impoverished local authorities, "structural adjustment" projects that have destroyed domestic industries and increased poverty and unemployment, and "poverty reduction support" projects that have been captured by national or local elites.

This chapter explores the reasons why so many interventions have failed to result in sustainable development. In line with other chapters in this section of the book, it focuses on the operational or "management" aspects. It argues that:

1. "Development" has proved to be a far more complex and elusive goal than originally thought;
2. The elusiveness of development has necessitated long-term dependence on international aid, resulting in undue external influence and insufficient local ownership of development initiatives;
3. Most international aid has taken the form of "projects," the management of which has contributed to the lack of sustainable development;
4. Lack of institutional learning, especially in international aid agencies, has resulted in repeated mistakes over and over again; and
5. In recent years, the introduction of "new" approaches to public sector management has exacerbated many of the existing problems.

These arguments are discussed in turn below.

II. The Elusiveness of Development

Not only in Africa but in the world as a whole, "development" has proved to be a much more complex and elusive phenomenon than once envisaged — so much so that writers like Escobar (1995), Rist (1997) and De Rivero (2001) question whether it is a viable objective or even a valid concept. De Rivero (2001: 110), describes development as "one of the most persistent myths of the second half of the 20th century." Its origins, he argues, "lie in our western civilization's ideology of progress," which was "born during the Age of Enlightenment," "fostered by the Industrial Revolution" and "buttressed by the narcissism implicit in Darwin's theory of evolution, which suggested that the human species was the most apt of all the species on the planet, due to its capacity to adapt itself to any natural habitat and always to achieve progress." He maintains that the many "developing" nations that have made little or no progress over the last 40 years should accept their fate. They should acknowledge that they are "non-viable national economies" with no prospects of reaching the economic and social standards of the "developed" world and focus their attention on survival rather than "development."

One does not have to be as pessimistic as de Rivero to acknowledge that the poorest nations of the world, and African countries in particular, are facing enormous development problems, for which there are no easy or obvious solutions. They include internal problems related to the integrity and accountability of African governments and external ones resulting from global trade and aid policies. Discussion of these problems is beyond the scope of this chapter. In fact, many are covered in earlier chapters. The aim here is merely to point out that the widespread failure of development interventions is not just a "management" problem; it indicates a need to re-examine the basic assumptions underlying the concept of "development."

III. External Influence and Lack of Local Ownership

Although, most African countries have been politically independent for three or four decades, very few have succeeded in becoming financially independent. At first, external financial assistance was seen as a short-term solution, part of the "package" of measures that would lead to economic growth and thus to financial independence. However, when the unrealistically high expectations that existed at independence failed to materialize, African governments found themselves becoming more and more dependent on international aid. For this reason, De Rivero (2001: 114) aptly describes such aid as "the daughter of the myth of development."

As already indicated, aid is a part of the complex set of problems facing the poorest countries. It makes a country not only financially dependent but also dependent on external conceptions of "development" and of the means of achieving it. This has become increasingly problematic in the last two decades. During the immediate post-independence period, African countries could at least choose between two alternative development models: "capitalism" from the west and "socialism" from the east. Moreover, many donors were prepared to support indigenous development policies, such as the various versions of "African socialism." However, since the end of the Cold War and the apparent failure of both the conventional "socialist" model and its African variants, there has been little choice. Any country that requires substantial external assistance is required to subscribe to the orthodox model promoted by most multilateral and bilateral aid agencies, which comprises not only the package of economic and financial reforms known as *structural adjustment*, but also a western-style "democratic" system of government (which boils down to little more than the holding of multi-party elections) and the adoption of "new" approaches to public sector management.

In reality, therefore, African countries have had little more control over their models of development during the post-independence period than they did during the colonial era. The process of "development" has been a constant struggle between the realities of Africa's physical, socio-economic and political environment and the aspirations and demands generated by the external forces. This has hampered development management in three ways.

First, interventions continue to be inappropriate to the local environment and thus fail to have the intended impact. One of the most obvious and damaging examples of this is structural adjustment. It is now widely acknowledged that many aspects of the standard structural adjustment package were inappropriate and unworkable in Africa and elsewhere. Joseph Stiglitz, a former World Bank economist, has made a damming critique of IMF interventions, including structural adjustment programs, crisis intervention in South-East Asia and Latin America, and the transition to market economies in Russia and other former eastern bloc states. He concludes (Stiglitz, 2002: 19, 96) that "the result for many people has been poverty and for many countries social and political chaos" and that "the IMF itself [has] become a part of the countries' problems rather than part of the solution." The situation is similar when one looks at community level projects. For example, the large number of abandoned or non-viable irrigation projects in Africa stems in large part from their inappropriateness in the local socio-economic environment. Recent research in central and southern Africa suggests that small-scale community gardens, developed around natural water sources or domestic water points, are often far more cost effective than commercial irrigation projects (Lovell, 2000).

Secondly, the dominance of external forces has resulted in lack of local *ownership*, which in turn means that the commitment necessary to guarantee successful implementation is lacking. Although, the importance of *ownership* is now widely recognized in development practice, its full implications are often either misunderstood or ignored. In the context of project aid, the term is generally used to mean merely that the participants or beneficiaries have acknowledged a need for the project, formally agreed to it, and (preferably) made some sort of financial or other commitment to it. However, in order to be effective, *ownership* must mean more than this. It must mean that the initiative emerges from the beneficiaries' felt needs, that the beneficiaries discuss alternative ways of addressing these needs before deciding what to do, and that they play a leading role in both the design and implementation of the initiative. In other words, as Unsworth (2001: 11) says, local ownership should mean local *leadership*.

Lack of political commitment, due to lack of ownership, has contributed to the failure of many externally-supported national policy interventions in Africa, including structural adjustment and poverty reduction support programs, decentralization initiatives, and other measures designed to promote "democracy." Such interventions require institutional change and, to quote Unsworth (2001: 13) again, "building institutions involves establishing ("institutionalizing") different ways of conducting public business, and legitimizing this involves an internal political process." Community-level interventions have suffered a similar fate. Over the last decade or so — and thanks in particular to the work of Chambers (1994, 1997), participatory planning methodologies have been widely promoted as a means of encouraging community ownership and commitment. In some instances, these have been effective. For example, in the Binga District of Zimbabwe, a community-based organization that was genuinely locally-owned succeeded, with appropriate external assistance, in raising political awareness and promoting local socio-economic development (Conyers and Cumanzala, 2004). However, there are also many cases where participatory methods have been abused by donors and non-government organizations (NGOs) to manipulate local people to accept external agendas (Cooke and Kothari, 2001). Recent research by the World Resources Institute has identified this problem in many attempts to decentralize natural resources management to local communities in Africa (Ribot, 2004).

The third way in which external influence has hampered development management is by increasing the pressure on local management capacity. For reasons that I will elaborate later, donor-funded projects inevitably consume more time and effort than locally funded initiatives and each donor has its own specific requirements. Therefore, in a country that is heavily dependent on external aid, a large proportion of public officials' time is spent planning, justifying and monitoring donor projects. This is the situation in Uganda (Amis, 2002), which has attracted a particularly large amount of aid (U.S. $37 per capita in 2000, compared to U.S. $20 in the region as a whole) (World Bank, 2003), due partly to genuine need but also to its reputation among donors as a success story. In a study on decentralization in Uganda in 2002, colleagues and I concluded that the capacity to absorb external support for decentralization was saturated (DIP, 2002a: 34).

IV. Concept of a Development Project

If international aid is the daughter of the myth of development, then development projects are the granddaughters, since the concept of a "development project" is a product of such aid. The term "project" is used here to mean any intervention that is *discrete*, in the sense that it has a clearly identifiable objective, set of resources, and implementation plan. This is a broad definition, which includes relatively large and complex interventions that tend to be referred to as "programs" rather than "projects." During the colonial and immediate post-colonial period, most external funding was provided in the form of "budget support" — that is, a block grant that was combined with local sources of revenue to fund the overall national budget. However, as independent governments began to develop their own policy agendas, external agencies had to be able to account for the funds that they were giving or loaning. "Project aid" thus emerged and, as the volume of external assistance increased, such funding became increasingly important and project planning methods increasingly complex.

Project aid has had some positive effects on development management. It has encouraged a more vigorous approach to the planning and implementation of development activities, through, for example, introducing the concept of a "project cycle" and the use of "logical frameworks," emphasizing the importance of monitoring and evaluation, and promoting the participatory planning methods mentioned earlier. However, it has created a number of problems that have contributed to the lack of sustainable development.

First, there has been a tendency for "projects" to be planned without sufficient consideration of the macro-environment in which they have to operate. Although project planning should take account of the wider environment, in practice this does not always occur, especially when projects are "driven" by donors who have their own agendas. In such situations, the project frequently fails because the environmental conditions necessary for its success are absent. The U.K. government's recent experience in Nigeria is an interesting case in point (Heymans and Pycroft, 2003). Following the election of a civilian government in Nigeria in 1999, the U.K. Department for International Development (DFID) embarked upon a number of projects designed to support "pro-poor" public sector reform in four pilot states. The rationale underlying the projects was that the transfer to a "democratic" government would be sufficient to provide an environment conducive to such reform. However, four years later, DFID had to review its overall strategy in Nigeria because, despite the change in government, Nigeria's public sector continued to be so beset by patronage and corruption that the projects were making little headway.

Second, because project aid is basically a tool that enables donors to know how their money is going to be spent, project planning tends to be "blueprint" planning (Lecomte, 1984). The project document must spell out in great detail what is going to be done, where, when and by whom, and project implementation is measured against this blueprint. This approach works reasonably well for physical construction projects undertaken by a single agency in a predictable macro-environment. But in other situations it has major defects. It is inflexible, thus making it difficult to accommodate delays or changes in plans due to unexpected events, and it emphasizes physical outputs and expenditures, rather than changes in attitude or behavior that are more difficult to measure. It is particularly inappropriate for community-based activities and for interventions designed to bring about institutional change, because in both cases it is impossible to plan everything in advance and, in the latter case, the objectives are attitudinal and behavioral rather than physical or financial. This problem has long been recognized and has resulted in the promotion of more flexible, "process" approaches to project planning and implementation (Korten, 1980; Lecomte, 1984; Conyers et al., 1988; DIP, 2002b). However, such approaches create fundamental problems for donors, because they no longer know exactly how, when and where their money is going to be spent.

Third, the separation of "projects" from "normal" activities, and thus "project management" from "normal management," has resulted in dual management standards and parallel management systems. Donors demand much more rigorous standards of planning and management than those adopted for "normal" administrative purposes, so donor projects tend to be more thoroughly planned and managed than other activities and, as noted earlier, to absorb so much time and effort that public officials are forced to neglect their other duties. Similarly, donors frequently require the establishment of special administrative units to implement "their" projects. As these units are funded by the donor as part of the project package and salaries are usually pegged above normal civil service rates in order to attract good staff, they drain resources from "normal" government agencies, thereby reducing the capacity of the permanent civil service structure. Donors are most likely to demand the establishment of special units in countries where management capacity is lowest, thus creating a long-term "chicken-and-egg" type of problem. In Uganda, for example, donors adopted this approach in the late 1980s, when the public service was in a state of virtual collapse, and now, nearly 20 years later, the situation is virtually unchanged: permanent government agencies continue to lack funds and qualified committed staff, and most externally-supported activities continue to be managed by special units established and funded by donors.

In the last few years, some external agencies have shown signs of moving away from project aid to budget support, initially for specific sectors and, more recently, for the budget as a whole. This move is ostensibly motivated by the need to address the above problems and increase local ownership. However, one cannot help wondering, whether it may not also reflect an element of desperation on the part of donors, who have witnessed the failure of so many projects that they are at a loss as to what to do next. Furthermore, budget support tends to come with so many strings attached, including technical assistance to the ministry of finance (Amis, 2002), that it is not really so different from project funding.

V. Lack of Institutional Learning

When one compares Dumont's *False Start in Africa*, with the situation today, it is evident not only that the answers to Africa's development dilemmas have yet to be found but also that the same mistakes have been made over and over again. This suggests that the various organizations involved in African development, and especially the external funding agencies that continue to have such an influential role, are failing to learn from past experience.

There are three inter-related aspects of this problem. First, there is a tendency for aid agencies to neglect the lessons of history, including the history of the countries in which they are working and their own national histories. DFID's frustrated attempts to promote "pro-poor" development in Nigeria, mentioned earlier, illustrate this point (Mellors and Conyers, 2004). It is evident from Nigeria's history that it was unrealistic to expect the transfer to civilian rule in 1999 to result in an immediate or dramatic change in public sector performance; history shows that there have been several earlier transfers to civilian rule, none of which resulted in any significant improvement, and that the country's governance problems are deeply entrenched, with roots going back to pre-colonial and colonial times. Moreover, it is equally evident from European history that the evolution of western democracy was a complex and long-term process; as Unsworth (2001: 5) says, "some of the key concepts which underpin our view of good government were constructed over time and are not universal." This suggests that African countries need time and space to evolve sustainable systems of democratic governance.

Second, there is a gap between the theory and practice of "development." In other words, there is insufficient interaction between the academics involved in the study of African history and development and the practitioners employed in governments and aid agencies. In some respects, this gap is surprising, as many academics are employed as development consultants and many development practitioners attend courses in development policy and management. The problem appears to be that academics and practitioners operate in different "organizational cultures." Chambers made this point 20 years ago. He maintained (Chambers, 1983) that academics are good at identifying and analyzing problems but poor at providing the solutions that practitioners need. Moreover, in the academic world it is important to collect and analyze all relevant material before reaching a conclusion, while in the practitioner's world there is never time for such rigor.

The third aspect of the problem is that, in both the theory and practice of development, there is a tendency to invent new ideas rather than utilize old ones. Academics gain repute by inventing new theories, and practitioners get jobs and funding by claiming to have new solutions to old problems. This has hampered development management in two ways. First, theories or practices that do not have immediate or dramatic results tend to be abandoned and replaced by new ones, rather than monitored and modified in the light of experience. For example, integrated rural development projects were very popular during the 1970s but, by the mid-1980s, they had failed to deliver the expected results. Some analysts argued that the answer was to give more attention to organizational and institutional development and adopt a more flexible, "process" approach (Conyers et al., 1988), but most donors chose to abandon such projects altogether and revert to conventional sectoral approaches. Second, old theories and practices tend to be re-introduced under new names. For example, the participatory planning methodologies promoted in the last decade or so have generated volumes of literature and endless training courses; but they are not really new. The strengths, weaknesses and limitations of participatory planning were presented decades earlier in Arnstein's (1969) seminal article and in the work of Cohen and Uphoff (1977, 1980), while participatory planning methods have been used by many generations of sensitive community-based development workers. This tendency to re-invent the wheel, which is related to the wider problem of "managerialism" discussed in the next section, creates confusion and discourages institutional learning.

VI. New Approaches to Public Sector Management

One of the main tenets of the "neoliberal" approach to economic growth and "development" that has been promoted worldwide over the last 20 years is that public sector organizations are less efficient than those in the private sector. This has had a major impact on public sector management. All governments have been under pressure to privatize as many public sector organizations as possible and, in those organizations not privatized, many functions have been either "contracted out" to the private sector or decentralized to local levels of government, while new management practices, based largely on those in the private sector, have been introduced in order to improve performance.

These changes in public sector management have influenced development management in two main ways. First, a large part of international development assistance work has been contracted out to the private sector. Most development agencies, including bilateral and multilateral government organs and NGOs, now contract out the planning, implementation and evaluation of their development projects to private consultants, rather than doing the work "in house" or employing long-term technical assistance personnel. This practice has fuelled an enormous growth in the development consultancy industry — so much so that development consultants might be described as the great-granddaughters of the myth of development. And, more significantly, it has contributed to the poor quality of project management. Because of the nature of the consultancy business, consultants are forced to undertake as many projects as they can in the shortest possible time, while aid agencies are primarily concerned with getting the best value for money. In other words, project management has become commercialized and "profit" rather than "development" has become the main motivating factor. The fact that consultants are only involved in certain stages of the "project cycle" and have no responsibility for project implementation as a whole, has also had a negative impact on project management. Moreover, the extensive use of consultants has also added to the problems of institutional learning. It has widened the gap between academics and practitioners, as professional consultants (although often once academics) seldom have time to keep up with developments in the academic world, and, as very little project management work is now done "in house," the wealth of experience that used to exist within development agencies themselves is no longer there.

Second, development management has been hampered by the new management practices that have been introduced into the public sector in an attempt to improve performance. These practices, which are intended to make public sector organizations operate like those in the private sector, are characterized by the promotion of "management" and its separation from technical functions, the widespread use of performance monitoring systems, and constant changes in "fashions" and "jargon." The use of these "managerialist" practices in the "developed" world has been widely criticized (e.g., Protherough and Pick, 2002). They have proved to be expensive and time-consuming, and to increase rather than decrease central government control. Moreover, as already noted, the constant changes in fashion and jargon cause confusion and hamper institutional learning. In "less developed" countries the problems have been even more glaring. As Manning (2001) points out, the success of such practices is dependent on there being an established "public service culture" and a "social contract" between government and civil society, both of which are frequently lacking in African countries. Uganda's Local Government Development Project (LGDP), a largely World Bank funded initiative that provides capital funds for local governments subject to their meeting certain performance standards, provides a good example (DIP, 2002a). The performance monitoring procedures are so complex that neither central nor local governments can handle them without external support, thus defeating the objective of creating a sustainable system of local government management.

VII. Conclusions

The above analysis suggests that, in order to bring about sustainable development in Africa, some radical changes in development management are required. It suggests the need to:

- ■ Recognize that there are no easy or obvious solutions to the profound development problems facing most African countries;

- Review the nature and role of development assistance in this light and give African countries time and space to evolve their own models of development;
- Adopt a flexible, "learning process" approach to project management, in which external inputs merely support internal initiatives and facilitate the development of indigenous capacity;
- Learn from history and build upon the lessons of good practice rather than constantly reinventing the wheel; and
- Abolish the current practice of contracting out most development assistance functions to consultants and put management back in its rightful place as a means of improving performance rather than an end in itself.

These prescriptions resemble those of Dumont in many respects, especially in the emphasis on indigenous African solutions; but the result would be a much slower and more modest rate of "development" than that which he anticipated.

However, the analysis also suggests that these relatively modest aspirations are just as un-realistic as those of Dumont. The reason for this is that "development management" is not just a set of techniques that can be taught in a course or written in a manual. It is a flourishing international "development" industry, and there are many individuals and organizations in this industry that are benefiting from the present management practices and have too much at stake to abandon them. Moreover, it is a product of the world in which we currently live: a world in which economic and political forces, both global and local, are increasing the gap between rich and poor.

Acknowledgments

The author would like to thank David Pudsey, Rob Mellors and Raymond Apthorpe for contributing to the ideas in this chapter and commenting on an earlier draft.

References

Amis, P., *Uganda: A Country Case Study*, Report Prepared for OECD/DAC Task Force on Donor Practices, 2002.

Arnstein, S., A ladder of citizen participation, *J. Am. Inst. Plann.*, 35, 216–224, 1969.

Chambers, R., *Rural Development: Putting the Last First*, Longman, London, 1983.

Chambers, R., The origins and practice of participatory rural appraisal, *World Dev.*, 22, 953–969, 1994.

Chambers, R., *Whose Reality Counts?* Intermediate Technology Publications, London, 1997.

Cohen, J.M. and Uphoff, N.T., *Rural Development Participation: Concepts and Measures for Project Design, Implementation and Evaluation*, Cornell University, Center for International Studies, Ithaca, Monograph 2, 1977.

Cohen, J.M. and Uphoff, N.T., Participation's place in rural development: seeking clarity through specificity, *World Dev.*, 8, 213–235, 1980.

Conyers, D. and Cumanzala, F., Community empowerment and democracy: a case study from Binga District in Zimbabwe, *Soc. Policy Admin.*, 38 (4), 383–398, 2004.

Conyers, D., Mosely, P., and Warren, D.M., Eds., Integrated rural development: lessons of experience, *Manch. Papers Develop.*, 4 (1), (special issue), 1988.

Cooke, B. and Kothari, U., Eds., *Participation: The New Tyranny*, Zed Books, London, 2001.

De Rivero, O., *The Myth of Development*, Zed Books, London, 2001.

DIP (Development in Practice), *Formation of a Programme in Support of Decentralization in Uganda*, 9th EDF, Report Prepared for Government of Uganda and European Commission, 2002a.

DIP (Development in Practice), *Capacity Building for Decentralised Local Governance in Zimbabwe: Lessons from PDSP and RDCCBP*, Nottingham, 2002b.

Dumont, R., *False Start in Africa*, Andre Deutsch, London, 1966.

Escobar, A., *Encountering Development: the Making and Unmaking of the Third World*, Princeton University Press, Princeton, NJ, 1995.

Heymans, C. and Pycroft, C., *Drivers of Change in Nigeria: A Preliminary Overview*, Abuja, DFID Nigeria, 2003.

Korten, D., Community organization and rural development: a learning process approach, *Public Admin. Rev.*, 40 (5), 480–511, 1980.

Lecomte, B., *Project Aid: Limitations and Alternatives*, Organization for Economic Cooperation and Development, Paris, 1984.

Lovell, C., *Productive Water Points in Dryland Areas: Guidelines on Integrated Planning for Rural Water Supply*, Intermediate Technology Publications, London, 2000.

Manning, N., The legacy of the new public management in developing countries, *Int. Rev. Admin. Sci.*, 67 (2), 297–312, 2001.

Mellors, R. and Conyers, D., *Mapping the Local Government Electoral Process in Nigeria*, Report Prepared for IFES Ltd., and DFID Nigeria, 2004.

Protherough, R. and Pick, J., *Managing Britannia*, Imprint Academic, Exeter, 2002.

Ribot, J., *Democratic Decentralization of Natural Resources: Encountering and Countering Resistance*, World Resources Institute, Washington, DC, 2004.

Rist, G., *The History of Development*, Zed Books, London, 1997.

Stiglitz, J., *Globalization and its Discontents*, Penguin Books, London, 2002.

UNCTAD, *The Least Developed Countries Report 2002: Overview*, New York and Geneva, 2002.

UNDP, *Human Development Report 2003*, New York, 2003.

Unsworth, S., *Understanding Pro-poor Change: A Discussion Paper*, Prepared for DFID, London, 2001.

World Bank, *World Development Report 2003*, New York, 2003.

Chapter 35

Strategic Planning in Development

Mark Turner

CONTENTS

I. Introduction

The 1950s was a time of optimism. The Second World War had been concluded, Europe was being re-built at a rapid pace, and former colonies were achieving political independence and setting out on the road to development. But how were they to achieve the ambitious socioeconomic goals they had set themselves? The answer was planning. The scientific application of knowledge to development problems was seen to have worked wonders in rehabilitating Europe and in the rapid industrialization of the Soviet Union. Planning was thus identified as the principal way in which developing countries could achieve economic rapid and sustained growth and improvements in welfare. Such planning could be at a macro-level involving a comprehensive national development plan through to small-scale projects in villages. While the scope and scale of planning may have varied, all planning initiatives involve making decisions about how best to use resources to achieve particular aims some time in the future.

Development planning may also be seen to have a strategic dimension, a characteristic that has become more prominent over the years. It can be summed up in three simple questions:

- Where are we now?
- Where do we want to be in a given number of years?
- How do we get there from here?

Answering these questions requires a clear understanding of the internal situation of the organization, state apparatus and society, particularly strengths and weaknesses. More importantly, the strategic orientation focuses attention on the complex environment in which development planning must take place.

Planning may be conceptualized from two major perspectives — technical and political. The dominant technical perspective is built on the rational assumption that trained planners can calculate the outputs and outcomes of their considered actions. Scientific methodologies of planning can thus be used to direct and organize the development of economies and societies towards desired goals. For developing countries this optimistic view of planning was tempered by the turbulence of their organizational environments, resource constraints and the urgency of the problems faced. Thus, a more "bounded rationality" was adopted in which it was acknowledged that choices were limited and data imperfect. The second planning perspective focuses on the political interactions of stakeholders who bargain, coalesce, lobby and maneuver to achieve their desired planning decisions. Thus, decisions made during the planning cycle are less the result of technical calculation and more a function of power and the pursuit of particular interests. In practice, both approaches to planning operate simultaneously.

II. National Development Planning

National development planning is a

> deliberate governmental attempt to coordinate economic decision-making over the long run and to influence, direct, and

in some cases even control the level and growth of a nation's principal economic variables (income, consumption, employment, investment, saving, exports, imports, etc.) to achieve a predetermined set of development objectives (Todaro, 1994: 566).

The initial logic behind national development planning was that developing countries were suffering from bad cases of market failure. This affliction inhibited efficient resource allocation and restrained economic growth. The theorists saw markets in developing countries as, at best, rudimentary but often non-existent. Infrastructure was poor, information was lacking and rural populations lived according to traditional cultures that hindered them from entering into market relations. Planners were viewed as the specialists who could change all this. They had two major options. On the one hand they could suppress the market and attempt to reach national goals by command. This type of planning was best exemplified in the "directive planning" of the Soviet Union and Eastern Europe. In contrast was "indicative planning" based on price signals. This involved government "supplement[ing] the market through taxes and subsidies so that prices reflect "true" social costs and benefits" (Chowdhury, 2002: 35). If there was no market for a desired product or service then government should provide incentives.

In the 1950s and 1960s, developing countries began setting up planning ministries, bureaux, offices and commissions which busied themselves in the preparation of national development plans. They generally adopted a five-year frame for the plans, which at first, in countries such as India, Ghana and Tanzania, reflected the influence of directive planning and relied on large public sectors. However, they varied from the Soviet model in that sectoral targets were indicative. This varied combination of directive and indicative planning was retained at least until the 1990s. Even in the high-growth Asian economies such as Korea, Indonesia, Malaysia and Thailand "economic planning is widely practiced as an instrument of government intervention" (Chowdhury, 2002: 36).

According to Lewis's (1966: 13) manual on development planning, a country's development plan should contain "any or all" of the following:

- A survey of current economic conditions
- A list of proposed public expenditures
- A discussion of likely developments in the private sector
- A macroeconomic projection of the economy
- A review of government policies

In the 1950s and 1960s there was strong belief in the necessity and efficacy of national development planning. For example, Myrdal (1971: 135) thought development unlikely "unless, the new element, state planning is vigorously applied." But other voices began to express doubts about national development planning on both empirical and theoretical grounds. A mid-1960s survey found that "among developing nations with some kind of market economy and a sizeable private sector only one or two countries seem to have been consistently successful in carrying out plans" (Waterston, 1966: 91). Killick (1976: 161) judged that "medium-term development planning has in most less developed countries (LDCs) almost entirely failed to deliver the advantages expected of it." Caiden and Wildavsky (1974: 288) bluntly stated that "formal planning fails ... in virtually all poor countries most of the time," a sentiment echoed by Bauer (1976: 92) who claimed that "comprehensive planning has not served to raise general living standards anywhere." Even Lewis (1966: 7) noted that, "the secret of successful planning lies more in sensible politics and good public administration."

Six major reasons have been advanced for the poor performance of development planning (Turner and Hulme, 1997). First, plans were over-ambitious about rates of development and overestimated the degree of state control over resources and the private sector. Second, the data used by planners was poor resulting in planning guided by intuition and guess-work rather than by scientific calculation. Third, the analytical methods, while sophisticated, still failed to do justice to the complexity of the economy and society. Fourth, rigid plans were unable to deal with un-anticipated shocks such as oil price rises in 1974 and 1979. Fifth, plan implementation suffered from the weakness of public sector organizations. Finally, planning's reliance on technical rationality overlooked the crucial role of politics in determining decision-making about resource allocation.

While these factors led to a consensus on the feasibility of comprehensive development planning this did not lead to a total rejection of national development plans. They were re-conceptualized as "development policy management" in which the principal objectives were

> to provide a stable macroeconomy, coordinate public policy, use public expenditure efficiently, anticipate problems and changes in the external and internal environments, ensure competitive markets and stimulate market development (Turner and Hulme, 1997: 138).

The "strategic" elements of planning were emphasized within frameworks that saw the state's principal role as providing an enabling environment for development. State intervention was not rejected. Indeed, the development of human capital in such areas as education, health, public administration, and regulatory and legal infrastructure was acknowledged as important tasks to be planned by the state. Also, it was appreciated that greater attention needed to be paid to budgeting with the result that many countries "now link their annual budgets to modest medium-term rolling plans for capital expenditure and new recurrent expenditure" (Turner and Hulme, 1997: 138–139). While the rationalist ambitions of the early development planners have been discarded, national development planning is still an important state activity, which provides direction to development and identifies what the state should do in order to create the conditions, which are at once indicative of development but more importantly that will lead to development.

National poverty reduction strategies are a recent manifestation of macro country-wide planning. The impetus for this renewed thinking and action on poverty alleviation derives from earlier disappointments with efforts in this field. Agreement on setting up national poverty reduction strategies was announced at the annual meeting of the World Bank and IMF in 1999, and by January 2003, 21 countries had submitted Poverty Reduction Strategy Papers (PRSPs) containing the national strategy for poverty alleviation.

The World Bank identifies five core principles for the development and implementation of poverty reduction strategies (PovertyNet)

- Country-driven — involving broad-based participation by civil society and the private sector in all operational steps
- Results-oriented — focusing on outcomes that would benefit the poor
- Comprehensive — in recognizing the multidimensional nature of poverty
- Partnership-oriented — involving coordinated participation of development partners (bilateral, multilateral and non-governmental)
- Based on a long-term perspective for poverty reduction

In recognition of the different circumstances and capacities of poor countries flexibility has been built into the design of the poverty reduction strategy. However, the World Bank has set out "core principles" indicating what a PRSP should contain (PovertyNet). These include:

- A description of the participatory process that was used
- Comprehensive poverty diagnostics
- Clearly presented and costed priorities for macroeconomic, structural, and social policies
- Appropriate targets, indicators, and systems for monitoring and evaluating progress

An emerging area of interest is scenario planning, a technique for planning in unpredictable futures. The idea of scenario planning is not new but its suggested application to national development planning would be novel. Back in 1949, Lippit was urging people to look to "images of potential" as the starting points for change (Manning and Curtis, 2003). Royal Dutch Shell were already using scenario planning in the 1970s while in the early 1990s Stewart developed the methodology of "future state visioning" to help organizations identify "what and where you want to be in the future" (van Maurik, 2001: 187). According to current thinking on scenario planning, plans are "bundles of options" which are constantly reviewed and updated. For this to be of use the organization should be clear on its mission, purpose and values. It must also develop expertise in understanding its environment. With these elements in place the organization can then construct scenarios, prioritizing options, which seem to work in several imagined futures. Investigation also looks at where alternative futures diverge and what actions can be taken to deal with them. Among the claimed advantages of scenario planning are that, it is appropriate for uncertain environments, it avoids rigid strategies and reactive decision-making, encourages participation and cooperation, and provides the impetus for developing learning organizations.

III. Project Planning

In order to convert national development plans and policies into practice governments and donors have relied heavily on projects. These programmed interventions were described as the "cutting edge of development" (Gittinger, 1982). Development projects could be in a vast range of field such as education, health, infrastructure, resettlement, poverty alleviation, public administration reform, agriculture and business development. They were the means by which traditional societies would be modernized and human welfare be improved. Projects could be of any size ranging from massive road or dam building enterprises to small-scale community development initiatives. But whatever the field or size, projects needed planning, and methodologies emerged to ensure that intentions were turned into reality. Indeed, there was considerable optimism in the 1960s and 1970s that increasing methodological sophistication "encouraged a belief, particularly amongst donors, that projects could be selected and planned in ways that almost guaranteed results" (Turner and Hulme, 1997: 140). Planners produced precise "blueprints," like engineers or architects, in which the specifications and steps were clearly marked for the implementers to follow.

The methodological core of all project activities has been and remains the project cycle. This construct is highly rational in that it conceptualizes projects as a sequenced set of activities, which if pursued correctly, will produce desired results. For example, AusAID, the Australian government's development assistance agency notes that its project cycle "assists AusAID to deliver assistance effectively, efficiently and sustainably" (AusAID, undated a). While there is some minor variation between the project cycles employed by different organizations they all contain the same fundamental elements:

Identification: a development problem or opportunity is identified, normally by government or donor.

Data Collection: project planners assemble the available data on the problem or opportunity as the basis for informed decision-making. In many project cycles, this stage is incorporated into the next one.

Data Analysis, Project Selection and Preparation: the data is analyzed and alternative actions to address the problem or opportunity are considered. What is judged to be the most appropriate course of action is selected, and the project is designed using tools such as cost-benefit analysis and feasibility studies.

Project Appraisal: the project plans are assessed in terms of costs, benefits, feasibility and risks. Modifications may be made before final approval is granted. Where donors are involved there will be negotiations between donor and recipient government about the terms and conditions of the loan or grant before both parties sign the agreement.

Implementation: specialist managers and technical personnel are recruited to oversee and implement the activities identified in the project plan. They must also follow specific guidelines of donor agencies and governments on such matters as procurement of goods and services. Progress of the project should be monitored through regular reporting.

Evaluation: often at the mid-point of a project, but always at its conclusion there will be thorough evaluation of the experience. Costs, benefits and other aspects of the project are reviewed in order to gather lessons to feed back into the project cycle for future projects.

It should be appreciated that most projects in low-income countries have been funded by donors including multilateral agencies such as the World Bank and Asian Development Bank and bilateral agencies such as AusAID. They have each developed their own versions of the project cycle but all have shared a common concern for the need to undertake detailed planning before approval for implementation is given. The aid agencies demanded quantitative evidence that projects would provide the desired results. Thus, it became necessary to apply techniques such as cost-benefit analysis, measuring the rate of social return, market and needs analysis, and technical feasibility studies. According to Rondinelli (1993: 55) the World Bank "believed that the more elaborate and detailed the feasibility and appraisal analyses, the greater the probability that the projects would be implemented successfully." However, skilled planning personnel were frequently in short supply in low-income countries necessitating the employment of expatriate specialists to apply the sophisticated planning techniques.

Despite the optimism accompanying the application of increasingly rationalist techniques to project planning the results have frequently disappointed. A World Bank (1988) study revealed that 51% of its rural development projects between 1965 and 1985 did not achieve the 10% rate of return, which the Bank had set as the minimum acceptable standard. Other research also indicated that the promises of project planners were not being fulfilled in practice. For example, the complex integrated rural development projects which were funded across the developing world in the 1970s produced meager returns (*Manchester Papers on Development*, 1988). A detailed study of one of these — the Margarini project in Kenya — gives a particularly detailed account of planning failure (Porter et al., 1991). However, it should not be thought that all projects were going wrong and failing to provide substantial welfare benefits. There are examples of success — land settlement in Malaysia, village water supply in Malawi, oral rehydration in Bangladesh (Turner and Hulme, 1997). However, concern was spreading among donors, governments, academics and civil society organizations that the scientific techniques of project planning were performing well below expectation. Researchers now began to investigate the reasons for this.

Turner and Hulme (1997) have summarized the findings of this body of research, identifying six reasons for project planning underperformance:

> *The Nature of Development Problems*: rationalist planning techniques were seen as unsuitable for the "ill-structured" problems found in developing countries, particularly in rural areas (Johnston and Clark, 1982). For example, addressing poverty could not simply be "thought through" with the aid of the sophisticated technology of blueprint planning. There are too many interacting variables to cope with especially as many of them may be poorly understood. In such circumstances problems such as rural poverty have to be "acted out" through social experimentation and interaction. Incremental gains can then be expected from these efforts to "adjust present difficulties."
>
> *Poor Data*: the planning techniques exported to the developing world from rich-country settings had large appetites for data including a strong preference for accurate data. Unfortunately, in many developing countries such data had not been collected and collated. Thus,

planners often worked on assumptions about such things as crop yields, the rates of behavioral change, costs and time needed for particular actions. They also overlooked the local knowledge of intended beneficiaries. This was a result of "normal professionalism" which valued "the thinking, values, methods and behavior dominant in a profession or discipline" over indigenous technical knowledge (Chambers, 1993: 3). In practice, the latter demonstrated a better understanding of local diversity and complexity, just the data planners should use when designing projects.

Uncertainty: in the pursuit of precision and calculability the sophisticated techniques of rational project planning overlooked the nature of environments in developing countries. Typically, these environments were uncertain and turbulent and not necessarily amenable to the finely tuned methods of the project planners. Such things as droughts, earthquakes, civil wars, lawlessness and hyperinflation were irregular but all too frequent occurrences in developing countries. They demanded flexibility in planning techniques, a quality that was often lacking.

Separation of Planning from Management: the nature of project planning methodologies separated the planners from the managers. The planners held the power. They had the analytical and predictive tools, which determined the design of projects. The managers assumed secondary roles of simply implementing the plans. This attribution of low status did little for the morale of project managers but more importantly it underestimated the role of good management in determining project success. In practice, project managers were faced with numerous decisions about resource allocation. They had to deal with un-anticipated events and a politics of implementation. Good managers actually undertook planning on the run, demonstrated flexibility and were adept at interpersonal relations. Gradually, the importance of such management skills and the complexity of project management began to be appreciated (Gow and Morss, 1988; Carvalho and White, 1996).

Lack of Beneficiary Participation: orthodox project planning was based on the assumed superiority of rational planning techniques. It was the business of trained specialists. This meant that the beneficiaries were frequently overlooked. They may have been consulted in the sense of being told information or to hear a few opinions from the grassroots. However, they rarely participated in the sense of influencing decisions concerning the design, implementation and evaluation of the project. This neglect of beneficiary participation could result in beneficiary dependency, lack of beneficiary commitment to projects and feelings among beneficiaries that they were simply onlookers not owners of projects (Korten and Klauss, 1984; Chambers, 1993; Rondinelli, 1993).

Projects and Politics: The conventional methodologies of project planning are built on assumptions of technical rationality, which omit or greatly underestimate the importance of political factors. However, actual project experience indicates that political interactions occur at all stages in the project cycle. The interactions are between a variety of actors who pursue their own particular interests in choosing, shaping and implementing projects (Grindle, 1980; Hulme, 1994). These actors may include, among others, national politicians, subnational politicians, local elites, government departments and sections of those departments, intended beneficiaries, particular social classes, donors and civil society organizations. "By avoiding political analysis, conventional methodologies facilitate the concealment of partisan behavior and reduce the opportunity for the powerless (i.e., the intended beneficiaries) to gain influence over the project process" (Turner and Hulme, 1997: 144).

IV. Alternative Approaches to Project Planning

Disappointment with the blueprint approach to project planning did not lead to the abandonment of project planning. It was still perceived as an essential activity in the development process. Cernea (1991: 8) observed that, "no effective alternatives have emerged, and projects are likely to remain the basic means for translating policies into action programs." Thus, the urgent task was not to dispense with project planning but to find more effective methods for design and implementation. Two distinctive approaches derived from this search for project planning alternatives: refinement of existing methodologies and process planning. The latter referred to the recognition that "there are many unknowns in planning, that multiple actors have competing interests and that the challenges of development are "messes" that require experimentation and learning with those involved" (Bond, 2002: 425).

Refining Existing Approaches: This strategy has been adopted by most aid donors. It does not challenge the project cycle but augments it with additional methods and disciplines where problems or gaps are identified. For example, the logical framework approach (LFA) has proved particularly popular with donors. This is a tool which helps planners and managers:

■ Analyze the existing situation during project preparation
■ Establish a logical hierarchy of means by which objectives will be reached

- Identify the potential risks to achieving the objectives, and to sustainable outcomes
- Establish how outcomes might best be monitored and evaluated
- Present a summary of the project in a standard format
- Monitor and review projects during implementation (AusGUIDE undated b)

The outcome of the various analytical exercises comprising the LFA is expressed in a matrix (Logframe) which contains "what the project intends to do and how, what the key assumptions are, and how outputs and outcomes will be monitored and evaluated" (AusGUIDE undated b).

A complementary initiative has been the insertion of new "sub-disciplines" into the project cycle. These include such things as social development appraisal, environmental impact assessment, gender planning and institutional analysis. Planners have incorporated these methodologies into their calculations and justifications for projects thus making project preparation a more complex procedure. For example, planners would need to investigate and account for the effect of an educational project on gender equity. They would need to demonstrate that an agricultural development initiative would not have adverse consequences for the environment. The creation and modification of these sub-disciplines can make it difficult for planners and observers to keep abreast of what is happening or available in the realm of project planning.

Process Planning: The process planning methodologies have two underlying conceptual bases. The first focuses on the role of project management and looks for improvement in the implementation phase of the project cycle. This is best demonstrated in Rondinelli's (1993) "adaptive administration." The second seeks to involve beneficiaries or communities in all stages of the project cycle and is manifested in approaches such as "participatory rural appraisal" (PRA) and "objectives-oriented project planning" (ZOPP) (World Bank, 1996).

Rondinelli (1993: 118) argues that adaptive administration

> sees planning and implementation as the art of creating problems that can be solved through informed experimentation. Courses of action are shaped from lessons of past experience as well as from a more realistic understanding of current and emergent conditions.

He characterizes the environments in which development projects take place as uncertain, high risk, limited data and open to political manipulation. From this he argues that specific capacities are required for effective projects—learning experimentation, creativity, organizational flexibility and access to local knowledge. Taking these considerations into mind Rondinelli comes up with a four-stage process for project planning and implementation but notes that his framework should only be used as "an aid to judgment" in the pursuit of better and more responsive decisions. The first stage consists of "experimental projects" which are "generally small-scale, highly exploratory, risky ventures" (Rondinelli, 1993: 119). Immediate results should not be expected but planners and managers should acquire knowledge, which they can use to improve the project design and operation. Successful experimental projects form the basis of "pilot projects" which disseminate the model to a larger constituency and test it in different environments. If a pilot project works well it can be converted into "a demonstration project to show that new technologies, methods or programs are better than traditional ones because they increase productivity, lower production costs, raise income or deliver social services more efficiently" (Rondinelli, 1993: 139). Even at this stage there is still risk thus necessitating continued experimentation and adaptation. The few projects that graduate from this demonstration stage can now be disseminated and replicated. Care must be taken to ensure appropriate scheduling, coordination, finance and institutional capacity, and to avoid the assumption that they can be replicated anywhere in a country according to a standard blueprint.

For some critics of orthodox planning models the major shortcoming is the lack of beneficiary involvement. These writers and organizations, often NGOs, wish to see beneficiary participation in all stages of a project, from identification through preparation and implementation on to evaluation. A fundamental assumption of this approach is that local knowledge is a valuable commodity which if mobilized will ensure that planned activities are consistent with resource endowments. There is the additional objective of empowering disadvantaged groups to enable them to determine decisions, which affect their everyday lives.

These objectives form the basis for the panning approach known as participatory rural appraisal (PRA). It has grown out of rapid rural appraisal (RRA) a method of concise but focused inquiry into rural conditions initiated to overcome outsider misinterpretation or ignorance (Carruthers and Chambers, 1981). The major difference between the two approaches is that "RRA is extractive with outsiders appropriating and processing the information, PRA is participatory with ownership and analysis more by the local people themselves" (Chambers, 1993: 97). There is no one standard mode of PRA. It is even transferable to urban areas. PRA is a collection of techniques including open meetings, semi-structured interviews, focus group discussion, preference ranking, mapping and modeling, and seasonal and historical diagramming. A typical PRA initiative would involve "a team of people working for two to three weeks on workshop discussions, analyses and fieldwork" (World Bank, 1996: 191). The outsiders act as facilitators in a process of shared learning that can be presented as a series of reversals, for example, from individual to group, from verbal to visual, from top–down to bottom–up (Francis, 2001). However, questions have arisen as to whether bureaucrats can embrace the ideology of PRA, whether the notion of "community" is sometimes oversimplified in PRA methodologies, whether in practice inequitable power relations are changed, and whether some of the participation lies at the weaker end of the participatory spectrum (Cooke and Kothari, 2001).

Also deriving from the "participatory enquiry paradigm" is participatory poverty assessment (PPA). It originated in the World Bank in the early 1990s as an aid to country poverty assessments. However, it was highly quantitative in nature and was criticized as inadequate to capture a range of significant dimensions of deprivation (Norton, 2001: 8). This shortcoming led to the development of a second generation of PPA which, like PRA, sought to give voice to the poor and vulnerable, and to take that voice seriously in planning for poverty alleviation. Norton (2001: 13) has summarized the emerging areas of PPA as

- A view of poverty and deprivation as being multidimensional in character — an interlocking set of factors which reinforce ill-being in individuals and communities.
- A concern with understanding the nature of poverty as poor people see and report it.
- A concern with powerlessness as a determinant and consequence of deprivation.
- A concern with the dynamic dimensions of poverty, and issues of vulnerability to shocks, cyclical deprivation (e.g., seasonal hunger and disease) and long-term trends.
- An emphasis on understanding the key assets which poor individuals, households and communities use to face up to threats and build their livelihoods.
- A view of assets which comprises social dimensions (networks, the capacity to make claims), as well as financial, material, environmental and human dimensions.
- A concern to differentiate between dimensions of poverty which apply at different levels of organization — for example, the community as against the household or individuals.
- A concern with intra-household dimensions of poverty — especially gender.

Demands from policy-makers have entailed that PPA is also concerned with establishing the priorities and preferences of the poor, the socially constructed profiles of vulnerable individuals and the constraints facing the poor when attempting to access public services.

V. Putting Blueprint and Process Together

Despite the differences between blueprint and process approaches to planning there appears to be room for utilizing "temporal or hierarchical combinations of the two" (Bond, 2002: 425). In particular circumstances it may be opportune to mix or sequence both blueprint and process approaches to achieve project effectiveness. Thus, Bond (2002: 428) lists the following possible combinations and the conditions under which they would be appropriate:

- *Blueprint then process*: quick, efficient pre-planned improvement of key services followed by longer-term participatory program to improve livelihood.
- *Process then blueprint*: participatory analysis and experimentation to establish local needs and effective responses followed by conventional series of projects to expand impact.
- *Blueprint/process continuum*: a selection from both approaches blended to fit the situation.
- *Blueprint in process*: a process approach to a program made up of smaller blueprint projects.
- *Process in blueprint*: a clear, pre-determined program structure with considerable flexibility as to the means of operationalization at field level.

Bond (2002) also identifies another possible synthesis of apparently opposing methodologies — competition and cooperation. He sees possibilities for chaordic organizations, which straddle the boundary between chaos and order and reflect the complexity of that boundary. The adaptive, non-linear, complex self-organizing characteristics of chaordic organizations could make them suitable for dealing with the ill-structured problems which confront development planners.

VI. Conclusion

Planning still remains a central activity in the development process. While the technical rationality which dominated development planning in the 1950s and 1960s has been challenged and moderated there is still considerable faith in the capacity of good planning to produce desired developmental outcomes. New methods have been introduced into the conventional project cycle, national plans are now oriented to development policy management, flexibility is recognized as a key quality of good planning and there is greater participation in the planning process by actors including project beneficiaries, civil society and the private sector. There is an overall realization that planning development is much harder than initially thought. The uncertain and turbulent environments of developing countries cannot be controlled by planners but must be taken into account by them whether through the rigors of logical framework analysis or the experimentation of process approaches. New ideas about planning and development are still being produced such as varying combinations of blueprint and process approaches, PRSs and scenario planning. There are also emerging areas. For example, rapid urbanization has emphasized the urgent need for urban planning to ensure the creation of effective infrastructure to make cities viable and to enable them to fulfill their growth potential (Sachs, 2003). Planning will continue to be a fundamental element for initiatives aimed at improving human welfare and reducing poverty and vulnerability whether undertaken by the World Bank, a national government, local council, NGO or people's organization. All need some systematic way of trying to understand their current situation, where they want to progress to and how they can best get there.

References

AusGUIDE (undated a). http://www.ausaid.gov.au/ausguide/ausguidelines (accessed April 13, 2004).

AusGUIDE (undated b). http://ausaid.gov.au/ausguide/ausguidelines (accessed April 13, 2004).

Bauer, P.T., *Dissent on Development*, 2nd ed., Weidenfeld and Nicolson, London, 1976.

Bond, R., Planning and managing development projects, in Kirkpatrick, C., Clarke, R., and Polidano, C., Eds., *Handbook on Development Policy and Management*, Edward Elgar, Cheltenham, 2002, pp. 421–433.

Caiden, N. and Wildavsky, A., *Planning and Budgeting in Poor Countries*, Wiley, New York, 1974.

Carruthers, I. and Chambers, R., Rapid appraisal for rural development, *Agric. Admin.* 8 (6), 407–422, 1981.

Carvalho, S. and White, H., *Implementing Projects for the Poor: What Has Been Learned?*, World Bank, Washington, DC, 1996.

Cernea, M., *Putting People First: Sociological Variables in Rural Development*, Oxford University Press, New York, 1991.

Chambers, R., *Challenging the Professions: Frontiers for Rural Development*, IT Publishers, London, 1993.

Chowdhury, A., Economic planning: theory, practice and experiences, in Kirkpatrick, C., Clarke, R., and Polidano, C., Eds., *Handbook on Development Policy and Management*, Edward Elgar, Cheltenham, 2002, pp. 32–41.

Cooke, B. and Kothari, U., Eds., *Participation: the New Tyranny?* Zed Books, London, 2001.

Francis, P., Participatory development at the World Bank: the primacy of process, in Cooke, B. and Kothari, U., Eds., *Participation: the New Tyranny?* Zed Books, London, 2001, pp. 72–87.

Gittinger, J.P., *Economic Appraisal of Agricultural Projects*, Johns Hopkins University Press, Baltimore, 1982.

Gow, D.D. and Morss, E.R., The notorious nine: critical problems in policy implementation, *World Develop.*, 16 (1), 1399–1418, 1988.

Grindle, M.S., Ed., *Politics and Policy Implementation in the Third World*, Princeton University Press, Princeton, 1980.

Hulme, D., Projects, politics and professionals: alternative approaches for project identification and project planning, *Agric. Syst.*, 47 (2), 211–233, 1994.

Killick, T., The possibilities of development planning, *Oxford Econ. Papers*, 28 (2), 161–184, 1976.

Korten, D.C. and Klauss, R., *People-Centered Development*, Kumarian, West Hartford, 1984.

Johnston, B.F. and Clark, W.C., *Redesigning Rural Development*, Oxford University Press, Oxford, 1982.

Lewis, W.A., *Development Planning: the Essentials of Economic Policy*, George Allen and Unwin, London, 1966.

Manchester Papers on Development, Special issue on integrated rural development, 4 (1), 1988.

Manning, G. and Curtis, K., *The Art of Leadership*, McGraw-Hill Irwin, Boston, 2003.

Myrdal, G., *Asian Drama: an Inquiry into the Poverty of Nations*, Abridged student edition, Vintage Books, New York, 1971.

Norton, A., *A Rough Guide to PPAs: Participatory Poverty Assessment: an Introduction to Theory and Practice*, Overseas Development Institute, London, 2001.

Porter, D., Allen, D., and Thompson G., *Development in Practice: Paved with Good Intentions*, Routledge, London, 1991.

PovertyNet (World Bank), Overview of poverty reduction strategies. http://www.worldbank.org/poverty/strategies/overview.htm (accessed April 19, 2004).

Rondinelli, D., *Development Projects as Policy Experiments: an Adaptive Approach to Development Administration*, 2nd ed., Routledge, London, 1993.

Sachs, J.D., The new urban planning, *Development Outreach*, November 2003. http://www1.worldbank.org/devoutreach (accessed April 8, 2004).

Todaro, M., *Economic Development*, 5th ed., Longman, London, 1994.

Turner, M. and Hulme, D., *Governance, Administration and Development: Making the State Work*, Macmillan and Kumarian, Houndmills and West Hartford, 1997.

van Maurik, J., *Writers on Leadership*, Penguin, Harmondsworth, 2001.

Waterston, A., *Development Planning: Lessons of Experience*, Johns Hopkins University Press, Baltimore, 1965.

World Bank, *The World Bank Participation Sourcebook*, World Bank, Washington, DC, 1996.

World Bank, *Rural Development: World Bank Experience 1965–1986*, World Bank, Washington, DC, 1988.

Chapter 36

Implementing Development Programs: "The Reality on the Ground"

Donald E. Klingner

CONTENTS

I. Introduction

"Democratic governance," "development administration" and "sustainable development" are each a focus of research and practice in contemporary public administration. Taken together, they are a whole whose sum is greater than its parts — a collective hope of achieving economic development through a system of governance that is effective, transparent and accountable. Program implementation is a tool of international development governance that depends upon clear conceptual understanding, an understanding of issues, and specific sector applications. This chapter will: (a) establish the importance of program implementation to governance, particularly in development administration; (b) review the criteria for successful program implementation in a development context; (c) present and discuss workable program implementation techniques; and (d) discuss their applicability to specific sectors of development administration.

II. Program Implementation and Governance in Development Administration

After World War II, the success of the Marshall Plan at rebuilding Europe and a global interest in economic development for least developed countries (LDCs) led to the creation of a new field of study and practice (Seely, 2003). Development administration emerged as an amalgam of development economics and public administration aimed at improving economic conditions and governance systems in LDCs by replicating Western concepts and techniques. It generally presumed that the laws, policies, structures and procedures in developed Western countries were superior to those indigenous to developing countries because of their greater rationality, efficiency and relationship to democratic ideals (Rostow, 1971; Fredland, 2000). Their diffusion and adoption was considered both automatic (given the "evolutionary superiority" of reforms introduced by Western consultants) and purposive, in that Western lenders often mandated administrative reforms as a condition of continued credit (Adamolekun, 1999).

But this traditional notion of economic development has by and large been abandoned because it did not achieve the desired results (Heady, 1998). It did not decrease the gap between rich and poor nations, nor reduce global poverty (UNDP, 1998). One scholar clearly summarizes this failure as reported by the UN:

> The United Nations' *Human Development Report, 1999*, notes that between 1980 and 1996 gross national product (GNP) per capita declined in no less than fifty-nine countries. It reports that the income gap between the fifth of the world's population living in the richest countries, and the fifth in the poorest widened from 30 to 1 in 1960 to 74 to 1 in 1997" (Hoogvelt, 2001: xiii).

Three analytically separate yet interdependent approaches have emerged in response to the now discredited traditional approach to development administration: comparative administration, development management, and international public management. Comparative administration began as a social science discipline intent on correcting the two fundamental intellectual flaws of traditional development administration: ethnocentrism and ignorance (Riggs, 1968; Klingner and Washington, 2000). Its adherents are primarily scholars and researchers who believe that traditional development administration failed because development administrators tended to automatically and erroneously assume that Western techniques and structures were superior to their indigenous counterparts (Fredland, 2000); and because they were unaware of the unique historical factors that had led to the success of Western management techniques (Riggs, 1968). In contrast, comparative administration is the more value-neutral study of public administrative systems across countries and cultures (Riggs, 1980, 1991; Rutgers, 1998). It examines alternative governance models as outcomes of cultural contexts (historical, economic, political and social), and evaluates the relative capacity of administrative systems based on underlying trends and conditions (Peters, 1988; Van Wart and Cayer, 1990; Heady, 1996). Its intellectual antecedents are political science and sociology. Its primary purpose is to compare alternative systems in order to understand how they have evolved and why they function as they do, rather than to evaluate them, describe their shortcomings, or prescribe recommendations to improve them.

The sub-field of development management, which encompasses the management of particular development efforts as well as the indigenous process of development, broadened in the 1990s. With the collapse of the Soviet Union in 1989, the underlying structural mechanism for international economic development changed fundamentally from politically motivated state-to-state aid, to market-oriented economic transactions by transnational corporations (Fredland, 2000). But while capitalism has clearly triumphed globally as a system of production, some of its more negative consequences (e.g., inequitable distribution of wealth and a focus on economic rather than social, political or environmental objectives) led detractors to question the underlying assumptions of globalism and to suggest structural alternatives, appropriate technologies, sustainable development and non-economic criteria for assessing development (Schumacher, 1973; Korten, 1995). Thus, development managers adopted many of the insights learned from comparative administration. First, they recognized that macroeconomic growth is not the sole or even the primary goal of development. Other valued outcomes are balanced economic development, the growth of civil society as measured by such factors as citizen participation, the development of non-governmental organizations as a supplement to the public and private sectors, and strengthening public administrative capacity so as to increase public confidence in government policies and administrative capacity. Second, they explicitly recognized that strengthening the capacity of government agencies and NGOs was not only a desirable antidote to the dominance of market-based structural responses to globalization (Farazmand, 2002), but also a prerequisite to development (Werlin, 1990). Third, these development managers formed new alliances with international donor organizations and became, in effect, a global industry with different clients, sponsors and objectives than in the Cold War era (Brinkerhoff, 1996; Brinkerhoff and Coston, 1999).

Throughout the world, demands for development and democratization have pressured governments to make good policy decisions and use scarce resources effectively (Dilulio et al., 1993). Government capacity — or the lack thereof — is perhaps the most obvious factor affecting perceptions of governance (Klingner et al., 2002). In developed countries, governance usually means *maintaining* government's ability to coordinate policy, gather information, deliver services through multiple (often nongovernmental partners), and replace hierarchical bureaucracies with more flexible mechanisms for managing indirect government (Brudney et al., 2000; Kettl, 2002). In developing countries, it probably means *establishing* government's ability to deliver vital public services (through core administrative functions like budgeting, human resource management and program evaluation) while simultaneously focusing on more fundamental changes (e.g., citizen participation, decentralization, innovation and entrepreneurial leadership (Kettl, 1997) necessary for effective political systems. In developing countries lacking a strong culture of either autonomous government or indigenous markets (Klingner and Pallavicini Campos, 2002), global markets tend to dominate — or even undercut, per Friedman's (2000) "golden straightjacket" — national economic and political systems.

In sum, international economic development has evolved over the past 50 years from relatively simplistic and patronizing efforts to develop LDCs by transplanting Western technology (including administrative systems and processes) to a more complex and interactive global network (Keohane and Nye, 2000; Kahler and Lake, 2003).

III. Successful Program Implementation in a Development Context

Developed countries generally have more money than developing ones, but this is not always the critical difference. A country rich in oil or other natural resources may have a high average income, but still suffer from political, economic or social conditions that lead to its being classified as "developing." Thus, macro-economic data may mask deficiencies in political culture, laws, government agencies or procedure necessary for economic (and hence, political and social) development. Following Huddleston's (1999) dictum that we "learn anatomy before practicing surgery," we need to examine the prerequisites for successful program implementation in a development context.

While administrative systems in developing countries tend to evolve towards increased rationality and transparency, this process is not uniform: in some cases, it stops, skips steps, or changes their order (Kiggundu, 1989). Administrative systems are generally robust in developed countries, but their viability in developing countries is more problematic (Heady, 1996). These countries may lack not only administrative capacity, but also the conditions in civil society and government that engender it. Table 36.1 shows these conditions and measurement criteria.

Privatization and other market-based public service delivery mechanisms are frequently regarded — particularly by macroeconomists — as critical tools for decreasing government spending and increasing its effectiveness. Yet, everything we have learned from 30 years' experience with these mechanisms in developed countries indicates that privatization outcomes are more likely to be positive if there are competitive bidders,

Table 36.1 Development Indicators

	Negative	Positive
Political Freedom (Speech and Media)	Low	High
Economic Growth and Development	Export-based	Balanced
Racial and Ethnic Discrimination	High	Low
Basis of Political Leadership	Charismatic	Issues and parties
Electoral Process	Inadequate	Functional

a public policy process that relates government effectiveness to larger societal issues, and a cadre of professionally and technically qualified public administrators to develop adequate contract specifications and monitor private sector performance. Absent these conditions, privatization has high risks of crony capitalism, military diversification into the civil economy, or administrative formalism (Welch, 1998; Hodge, 2000).

Less developed countries may be characterized by factors—mostly beyond their control—that make it difficult to establish conditions developing countries take for granted: a national identity, the rule of law, and a self-sufficient economy. Even the development of stable patronage systems may be hampered by societal conditions such as non-functional justice systems, inability to meet even minimum standards of education and health care, political leadership based on "cults of personality" rather than pluralist political parties, and overly centralized and authoritarian political systems (Klingner, 2000). These conditions generally impede the evolution of rational administrative structures and systems (Ruffing-Hilliard, 1991). For example, organizations in many less developed countries share common structural and managerial attributes that differ from those typically found in North America, Europe, and Japan: *low* levels of role specialization, formalism, and morale; *high* levels of centralization, paternalism, authoritarian leadership, rigid stratification, and dysfunctional conflict (Kettl, 1997).

IV. Program Implementation Guidelines and Techniques

While much of the public management and development literature focuses on defining and identifying best practices that may be applied in other contexts, we think the term "smart practice" (Bardach, 2000: 72) is better suited to the context of establishing security and supporting development in Iraq, Afghanistan and other highly security risk unstable nations. Smart practice analysis attempts to identify the "... causal mechanisms and processes that allow particular processes to counteract the tendency of political, technical, and organizational systems in the public sector to perform unsatisfactorily with respect to evolutionary adaptation" (Barzelay and Campbell, 2003: 14).

Within this general history and context, we may present several key guidelines that apply to successful development program implementation efforts. These relate to: (a) time orientation; (b) sovereignty and capacity; (c) empowerment and accountability; (d) adaptability, flexibility and incrementalism; and (e) sustainability.

A. Time Orientation

The length of time required for implementing development programs depends upon the nature of the objective and the circumstances. The nature of the objective is discussed below. Circumstances relate to those environmental factors discussed in the previous section. Within these contexts, it is important to remember that successful development program implementation, even under favorable circumstances, usually takes years, and often decades. Thus, organizational commitment to policy objectives almost always extends beyond the involvement of any one program director or elected official. Where occupation appears necessary to achieve security and stability: accurately assess and report all the costs of military occupation and state building. Particularly in the case of high security risk development-assisted nations like Iraq and Afghanistan, it is important to resist political pressure that would lead to premature withdrawal of security, economic and political support prior to the point where high security risk nations are capable of governing themselves (Klingner and Jones, 2004).

B. Sovereignty and Capacity

Creating new national sovereignty is different from, and harder than, building government capacity (Pollitt and Bouchaert, 2000; Kettl, 2002). Evidence compiled by the Congressional Research Service (Pei, 2003) indicates that the type of intervention attempted by the U.S. in Iraq is perhaps the most difficult, costly and potentially frustrating of the available alternatives, since it requires regime change, deployment of large numbers of U.S. ground troops to provide security so that basic public services can be restored, and active participation by U.S. military to obtain civilian personal security to support a post-conflict administration.

The ideal form of political transition involves the drafting of a constitution and establishment of elected government prior to transfer of power to legitimately elected leaders. Consequently, we argue for example the requirement of creating a satisfactory enough political critical mass of participants composed of all necessary and appropriate stakeholders to draft a constitution and to construct rule of law. However, even after an occupation of several hundred years, with political consolidation and the establishment of a common legal framework, national sovereignty may be negatively affected by cultural and religious factors, as was the division of India into two separate countries — India and Pakistan — with its independence from Britain in 1947. The lesson: emphasize diplomatic efforts to secure accommodation of various stakeholders sufficient to permit compromise leading to formation of an independent government.

Building government capacity, though a much simpler objective than nation building, typically requires years rather than months of patient assistance and financing. The objective here is to maintain a near-term focus on establishing and enhancing governance capacity so as to achieve social stability and stable economic growth.

C. Empowerment and Accountability

Several interrelated concepts are critical here: governance (discussed previously), empowerment and accountability (Blair, 2000; World Bank, 2002).

Empowerment is the increased ability of the poor to make political, social, or economic choices, and to act on those choices (Kabeer, 1999; Narayan, 1999). This ties with accountability because it relates to results-oriented and customer-focused applications of New Public Management to managing development programs (Hirschman, 1999). The key to both is to develop a multi-lateral development assistance plan and a multi-national, multi-institutional framework for financing development over a long period of time (Brinkerhoff and Coston, 1999), all supported by a participative and client-centered development management process (Dale, 2003).

D. Adaptability, Flexibility, and Incrementalism

Development occurs within the context of complex systems that are increasingly difficult to model with any accuracy. The more a policy decision is imbued with values, the less applicable the rational method, where inputs cannot be quantified as accurately. Another duality to ponder is that of theory vs. practice. While theoreticians look for an all-encompassing model, a practitioner might find other processes to be more efficacious. Borins (1998) and others (Jones and Kettl, 2003) argue that although problems seem similar across nations, types of solutions that are effective in one public sector context may not succeed in another political, economic or social setting. Lindblom (1959/1997) assesses rational models of the decisional processes of government; rejects the notion that most decisions are made by rational, total-information processes; posits that the policy making process is defined by a series of incremental decisions as a response to short term political goals; and argues that decision-making is much more dependent on events and circumstances than the will of policymakers.

More to the point, however is that in Iraq, Afghanistan and other high security risk settings, the composition of the critical mass of stakeholders is specific to the context and may not be generalized for application elsewhere beyond a few observations. In this respect, Bardach (2000) and Barzelay and Campbell (2003) argue that "smart practice" development program administration is not so much a "tool kit" of ideal practices, but as an operational guideline that emphasizes reducing mechanisms and factors that inhibit adaptation to contingency. In high security risk environments adaptation to contingency is essential — without it little or no progress will obtain and the policy context will be appropriately characterized as fraught with wicked problems that by definition defy resolution (Roberts, 2000).

E. Sustainability

Widespread recognition in development circles that macro-economic growth was not the primary or most relevant indicator of successful development (Korten, 1995; Stiglitz, 2001) led to the development of more broadly based (i.e., political, social, cultural and environmental) variables, and of performance indicators for them, under the general heading of sustainability (Simons, 1999; World Bank, 2003).

According to Hart (cited in Simons, 2001) sustainability is based on community capital and carrying capacity. Community capital is the combination of natural, social and built capital. Natural capital includes natural resources, ecosystems and the beauty of nature. Human and social capital is composed of persons' individual competencies and the social connections among them. Built capital is human-made materials or assets. Placing a value on built capital is rather straightforward. It is more difficult to determine the dollar value of a healthy, happy child, the ability to read, clean air to breath, or an effective system of government. Thus, determining appropriate indicators, ones that quantify gains and losses in natural or social capital, presents a challenge.

Carrying capacity is the size of a population that can be supported indefinitely by the resources and services provided by the supporting ecosystem. The limits of the ecosystem are dependent upon the level of community capital, and therefore, subject to available natural resources, social capital, and the consumption rate of that population.

Effective indicators as described by Hart have been used in the public and private marketplace for systems evaluation and management for years (Rosen, 1993). Sustainable community indicators however, must also meet additional criteria. According to Hart they must address community carrying capacity; highlight interdependencies between community economy, society, and nature; be usable by the general populace; have a long-term perspective; and evaluate local sustainability in the context of global sustainability.

Operationally, with respect to Iraq, Afghanistan and other high security risk development assisted nations, sustainability means continued emphasis on social stability and stable economic growth under self-governance to prevent economic exploitation. Operationally, it means placing as high a priority on preventing looting of the National Museum of Antiquities, as on protecting oil industry infrastructure.

V. Development Sector Applications

The following are examples of what might be termed "smart practice" development management program implementation, organized by sector and geographic area.

- Despite the prevalence of rhetorical support for empowerment, the effectiveness of efforts to encourage participation in India's Employment Assurance Scheme (EAS) depended heavily on idiosyncratic village social structure and power relationships (Williams et al., 2003).

- International development specialists' experience in Cambodia from the 1970s and 1990s demonstrates that, at least in failed states, effective humanitarian aid requires multi-national, long-term cooperation across governments and sectors (Chong, 2002).

- Experiments with rural land reform in Tanzania demonstrated that mixed ownership models (under which villagers own their own homes but cultivate land held in common) could be an effective community development model, particularly in settings without great disparities of wealth and power (Huizer, 1973).

- AID experiences in eight countries (Bangladesh, Cape Verde, Mozambique, Nicaragua, Tanzania, Uganda, Vietnam and Zambia) indicates that policy conditionality — setting policy requirements as a precondition for aid — is generally less effective than applying general policy criteria afterwards (Dijkstra, 2002; Singh, 2002).

- Assessment of 40 AID projects indicates that Impact assessments provide information on expected consequences of a potential project or program to serve three policy needs. They help determine whether a project should be implemented or not; they can guide the design of the project to make it more effective and better fit its natural and social environment; and they can lead to the development of mitigation measures that minimize negative impacts (Finsterbusch and Van Wicklin, 1988).

- Zimbabwe's experiences with implementing quantitative assessment tools like the "advocacy index" indicates that despite the necessity to combine them with qualitative measures, they can be useful as tools for measuring managerial and policy effectiveness (Hirschman, 2002).
- South Africa's experience with rural water development projects indicates that while outside non-governmental donor organizations in theory support community-based decentralization, in practice they are more likely to favor state-centric decentralization, or even centralization, because they favor communication and control over empowerment and participation (Galvin and Habib, 2003).
- Information is a key to development. Yet, the most useful model for information management views it not as something that can be transferred and absorbed, but as something that requires self generation and strong local roots (Samoff and Stromquist, 2001).

VI. Conclusion

Program implementation is a tool of international development governance that depends upon clear conceptual understanding, an understanding of issues, and specific sector applications. It is conceptually related to governance, particularly building capacity in developing nations. Successful development program implementation depends upon a range of factors comprising natural and social capital. Because development is an indigenous process rather than one of transfer and absorption, it is best viewed as some "smart practice" guidelines rather than as a uniform toolkit. These guidelines involve: (a) time orientation; (b) sovereignty and capacity; (c) empowerment and accountability; (d) adaptability, flexibility and incrementalism; and (e) sustainability.

References

Adamolekun, L., Ed., *Public Administration in Africa: Main Issues and Selected Country Studies*, Westview Press, Boulder, 1999.

Bardach, E., *Practical Guide for Policy Analysis: The Eightfold Path to More Effective Problem Solving*, Chatham House, New York, 2000.

Barzelay, M. and Campbell, C., *Preparing for the Future: Strategic Planning in the U.S. Air Force*, Brookings Institution, Washington, DC, 2003.

Blair, H., Participation and accountability at the periphery: democratic local governance in six countries, *World Dev.*, 28 (1), 21–39, 2000.

Borins, S., Lessons from the new public management in Commonwealth nations, *Int. Public Manage. J.*, 1 (1), 37–58, 1998.

Brinkerhoff, D., Ed., Implementing policy change, *World Dev.*, 24 (9), 1393–1559, 1996.

Brinkerhoff, D. and Coston, J., International development in a globalized world, *Publ. Admin. Rev.*, 59 (4), 346–361, 1999.

Brudney, J., O'Toole, L., Jr., and Rainey, H., *Advancing Public Management: New Developments in Theory, Methods, and Practice*, Georgetown University Press, Washington, DC, 2000.

Chong, D., UNTAC in Cambodia: a new model for humanitarian aid in failed states?, *Dev. Change*, 33 (5), 957–978, 2002.

Dale, R., The Logical Framework: an easy escape, a straightjacket, or a useful planning tool, *Dev. Pract.*, 13 (1), 57–70, 2003.

Dijkstra, A., The effectiveness of policy conditionality: eight country experiences, *Dev. Change*, 33 (2), 307–334, 2002.

Dilulio, J., Garvey, G., and Kettl, D., *Improving Government Performance: An Owner's Manual*, Brookings Institution, Washington, DC, 1993.

Farazmand, A., Ed., *Administrative Reform in Developing Nations*, Praeger, Westport, 2002.

Finsterbusch, K. and Van Wicklin III, W., Unanticipated consequences of A.I.D. projects: lessons from impact assessment for project planning, *Policy Stud. Rev.*, 8 (1), 108–118, 1988.

Fredland, R., Technology transfer to the public sector in developing states: three phases, *J. Technol. Transfer*, 25, 265–275, 2000.

Friedman, T., *The Lexus and the Olive Tree: Understanding Globalization*, Bantam, New York, 2000.

Galvin, M. and Habib, A., The politics of decentralisation and donor funding in South Africa's rural water sector, *J. South. Afr. Stud.*, 29 (4), 865–884, 2003.

Heady, F., *Public Administration in Comparative Perspective*, 5th ed., Marcel Dekker, New York, 1996.

Heady, F., Comparative and international public administration: building intellectual bridges, *Publ. Admin. Rev.*, 58 (1), 32–40, 1998.

Hirschman, D., Development management versus third world bureaucracies: a brief history of conflicting interests, *Dev. Change*, 30 (2), 287–306, 1999.

Hirschman, D., "Implementing an indicator": operationalising USAID's "advocacy index" in Zimbabwe, *Dev. Pract.*, 12 (1), 20–32, 2002.

Hodge, G., *Privatization: An International Review of Performance*, Westview, Boulder, 2000.

Hoogvelt, A., *Globalization and the Postcolonial World: The New Political Economy of Development*, 2nd ed., Johns Hopkins University Press, Baltimore, 2001.

Huddleston, M., Innocents abroad: Reflections from a public administration consultant in Bosnia, *Publ. Admin. Rev.*, 59 (2), 147–158, 1999.

Huizer, G., The Ujamaa village program in Tanzania: new forms of rural development, *Comp. Int. Dev.*, 8 (2), 183–207, 1973.

Jones, L. and Kettl, D., Assessing public management reform in an international context, *Int. Publ. Manage. Rev.*, 4 (1), 1–16, 2003.

Kabeer, N., Resources, agency, achievements: reflections on measures of women's empowerment, *Dev. Change*, 30 (3), 435–464, 1999.

Kahler, M. and Lake, D., Eds., Globalization and governance, *Governance in a Global Economy*, Princeton University Press, Princeton, NJ, 2003, pp. 1–30.

Keohane, R. and Nye, J., Jr., Introduction, in *Governance in a Globalizing World*, Nye, J. and Donahue, J., Eds., The Brookings Institution, Washington, DC, 2000, pp. 1–41.

Kettl, D., The global revolution in public management: driving themes, missing links, *J. Policy Anal. Manage.*, 16 (3), 446–462, 1997.

Kettl, D., *The Transformation of Governance*, Johns Hopkins University Press, Baltimore, 2002.

Kiggundu, M., *Managing Organizations in Developing Countries: An Operational and Strategic Approach*, Kumarian Press, West Hartford, CT, 1989.

Klingner, D., South of the border: problems and progress in implementing new public management reforms in Mexico today, *Am. Rev. Publ. Admin.*, 30 (4), 365–373, 2000.

Klingner, D. and Jones, L., Smart practice development administration in Iraq and other high security risk nations: lessons from colonial experience, *Int. Publ. Manage. Rev.*, 5 (1), 41–57, 2004.

Klingner, D. and Pallavicini Campos, V., Human resource management reform in Latin America and the Caribbean: what works and what doesn't, *Publ. Org. Rev.*, 2, 349–364, 2002.

Klingner, D. and Washington, C., Through the looking glass: realizing the advantages of an international and comparative approach for teaching public administration, *J. Publ. Affairs Educ.*, 6 (1), 35–43, 2000.

Klingner, D., Nalbandian, J., and Romzek, B., Politics, administration, and markets: conflicting expectations and accountability, *Am. Rev. Publ. Admin.*, 32 (2), 117–144, 2002.

Korten, R., *When Corporations Rule the World*, Kumarian Press, New York, 1995.

Lindblom, C., The science of "muddling through," in *Classics of Public Administration*, Shafritz, J. and Hyde, A., Eds., Harcourt Brace, Fort Worth, 4th ed., 1959/1997, pp. 177–249.

Narayan, D., Can anyone hear us? voices from 47 countries, Voices of the Poor Volume 1, World Bank Poverty Group, PREM, The World Bank, Washington, DC, 1999.

Nye, Jr. J. and Donahue, J., Eds., *Governance in a Globalizing World*, The Brookings Institution, Washington, DC, 2000.

Pei, M., Lessons of the past, *Foreign Policy*, 137, 52–55, 2003.

Peters, B.G., *Comparing Public Bureaucracies: Problems of Theory and Method*, The University of Alabama Press, Tuscaloosa, 1988.

Pollitt, C. and Bouchaert, G., *Public Management Reform: A Comparative Analysis*, Oxford University Press, Oxford, 2000.

Riggs, F., Administration and a changing world environment, *Publ. Admin. Rev.*, 28 (4), 348–361, 1968.

Riggs, F., The ecology and context of public administration, a comparative perspective, *Publ. Admin. Rev.*, 40 (2), 107–115, 1980.

Riggs, F., Public administration: a comparativist framework, *Publ. Admin. Rev.*, 51 (6), 473–477, 1991.

Roberts, N., Wicked problems and network approaches to resolution, *Int. Publ. Manage. Rev.*, 1 (1), 1–19, 2000.

Rosen, E., *Improving Public Sector Productivity, Concepts and Practice*, Sage Publishers, Thousand Oaks, CA, 1993.

Rostow, W., *The Stages of Economic Growth: A Non-Communist Manifesto*, Cambridge University Press, New York, 1971.

Ruffing-Hilliard, K., Merit reform in Latin America: a comparative perspective, in Handbook of Comparative and Development Public Administration, Farazmand, A., Ed., Marcel Dekker, New York, 1991, pp. 301–312.

Rutgers, M., Paradigm lost: crisis as identity in the study of public administration, *Int. Rev. Admin. Sci.*, 64 (4), 553–564, 1998.

Samoff, J. and Stromquist, N., Managing knowledge and storing wisdom: new forms of foreign aid, *Develop. Change*, 32, 631–656, 2001.

Schumacher, E., *Small is Beautiful: Economics as if People Mattered*, Harper and Row, New York, 1973.

Seely, B., Historical patterns in the scholarship of technology transfer, *Comp. Technol. Trans. Soc.*, 1 (1), 7–48, 2003.

Simons, R., *Performance Measurement and Control Systems for Implementing Strategy*, Prentice-Hall, Upper Saddle River, NJ, 1999.

Singh, A., Aid, conditionality and development, *Develop. Change*, 33 (2), 295–305, 2002.

Stiglitz, J., *Globalization and its Discontents*, W.W. Norton, New York, 2001.

UNDP (United Nations Development Program), *Latin America: poverty up close*, Choices 6 (April), 16–18, 1998.

Van Wart, M. and Cayer, N., Comparative public administration: defunct, dispersed, or redefined?, *Publ. Admin. Rev.*, 50 (2), 238–248, 1990.

Welch, E., Public administration in a global context: bridging the gaps of theory and practice between Western and non-Western nations, *Publ. Admin. Rev.*, 58 (1), 40–50, 1998.

Werlin, H., From an LDC to an MDC: Lessons for American public administration, *Publ. Admin. Rev.*, 50 (4), 477–479, 1990.

Williams, G., Véron, R., Corbridge, S., and Srivastava, M., Participation and power: poor people's engagement with India's employment assurance scheme, *Dev. Change*, 34 (1), 163–192, 2003.

World Bank, *World Development Report 2002: Building Institutions for Markets*, Oxford University Press and The World Bank, New York, 2002.

World Bank, *World Development Report 2003, Sustainable Development in a Dynamic World*, Oxford University Press and The World Bank, New York, 2003.

Chapter 37

Policy Evaluation: From Managerialism and Econocracy to a Governance Perspective

Des Gasper

CONTENTS

I. Introduction

The conceptual field of governance has grown partly as an acknowledgment of major gaps in traditional treatments of development policy and management. We see the insufficiency of focusing only on government as the state, and the need for a wider perspective of governance, understood as "array of ways in which interplay between the state, the market, and society is ordered" (*Insights*, September 23, 1997). In addition, we realize now how ineffective or disaster-prone public policy can be when key factors conducive to effective policy formation and implementation are absent, including sufficient political legitimacy and accountability, an adequately functioning legal apparatus, systems for public expression and social learning, and peace rather than war.

A governance perspective brings an expectation of a more complex approach to policy evaluation than approaches which assume no substantial interplay between state, market, and society; more complex, for example, than the assessment of projects with saleable inputs and outputs as if market-based or market-inspired criteria suffice. Similarly, the significance of legitimacy, accountability, and public feedback has implications for the content and procedural design of policy evaluation.

The usage of "policy" and "evaluation" will be as follows. *Policy* covers project and program levels, as well as those of strategy and framework. It concerns activities in the name of or directed to the benefit of the polis, the political community; in other words, our focus is on public policy, with the public as the populace or citizenry ("public" derived from the Latin "pubes," meaning adult). This concern stands in contrast to the market principle of *consumer* sovereignty. Some citizens have no power as consumers in the market, while some others have enormous market power. *Evaluation* covers the normative assessment of public policy activities, whether prospective or retrospective (see, e.g., Scriven, 1991; Fischer, 1995). It is not used to cover every review of experience regardless of the purposes or type of questions; only normative questions and grading purposes are considered here, but for both before and after implementation (thus both *ex ante* and *ex post* evaluation). Evaluation in this normative sense requires the use of normative values.

This chapter examines some methods that are prominent in or promising for policy evaluation for developing countries. It relates them to various desiderata, including some implied by a governance perspective, such as attention to the interactions between markets and their social, political, and natural environments, the importance of political and social "infrastructure," and the inclusion of all citizens.

"Effectiveness" and "efficiency" are perhaps the most used terms within policy evaluation in development management circles. We will look at concepts and practices around *effectiveness*, with special reference to "the logical framework approach" and its successors, then at *efficiency*, with special reference to economic cost–benefit analysis (CBA), and finally, at more open and exploratory approaches or frameworks for multi-criteria evaluation and structured democratic policy discourse.

Figure 37.1 gives a "family tree" of some methods, from simple unstructured checklists through more sophisticated checklists and multi-criteria methods to (monetary) CBA. Generally speaking, as one proceeds from top to bottom in the figure, the methods become more complex, and at the bottom, as one proceeds from left to right, the methods involve more aggregation, culminating in CBA, which reduces its assessment of a proposal ultimately to a single figure.

We look at three broad styles of practice. In "managerialism" (Pollitt, 1992), criteria are set by managers and political masters and are supposed to determine choices. In mainstream economics and "econocracy" (Self, 1975), the criteria, again supposed to determine choices, are set by purchasers and, in the background, also by economists. In "democratic pluralism," the criteria and choices are negotiated between multiple stakeholders, subject to rules about accepted procedures (such as voting).

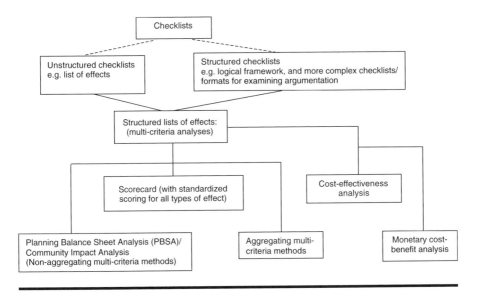

Figure 37.1 **"Family-tree" of some methods in policy evaluation.**

II. Effectiveness and Evaluation in Terms of (Pre-) Set Objectives

Effectiveness means producing approved effects. Nowadays, this is typically interpreted as fulfilment of objectives. Two sets of questions arise: effectiveness in what, that is, which types of effects are included as objectives, and effectiveness for whom, that is, whose objectives. In a private producer context, the determiner of values, the "principal", is more obvious — the enterprise owner — so effectiveness is a more straightforward concept. The objectives that are set before an activity and those that have emerged after the activity are of interest, but the latter have priority. There is no reason to screen out the principal's later thinking. In a public policy context, these questions become more difficult, but are fundamental. The range of stakeholders increases, so roles and rights can be obscure or disputed. An external funder may insist on evaluation in terms of originally set objectives rather than those which emerge through experience, because of fear that the implementing agents diverge from an earlier agreement. Evaluation can then be conducted in terms of outdated criteria.

Managerial approaches in public policy can conceal or sideline the question of "whose objectives" with regard to "the project's objectives" and "the policy's objectives." They typically presume that managers/ leaders/experts set the objectives. Market-based approaches to evaluation assume that consumers set the objectives, in proportion to their financial strength. Participatory approaches aim to derive objectives for all citizens (or in global public policy, for all persons), by some legitimate processes of expression, representation, and aggregation. Human rights and related ethics-driven approaches hold that many key objectives are embedded in actual or virtual constitutions and similar binding commitments like the Universal Declaration of Human Rights and that these should give major direction in policy evaluation. In all stances, the choice about which objectives will be considered flows from the decision on whose objectives. The citizen- and human-oriented stances differ significantly from the manager- or consumer-oriented stances, which have predominated in practice in development policy (see, e.g., Narayan and Patel, 2000). Growth of conscious attention to governance might enhance the more citizen-oriented stances.

Growth of global citizen-oriented perspectives in policy evaluation is also happening, although more slowly. Most policy evaluation remains emphatically national in perspective or follows the form of globalism that is used in the market: effects on anyone, anywhere, will be considered, according to the amount that those people pay to receive or avoid the effect. If they can pay little, they will be considered little, and if they cannot pay at all, then they will be ignored (Gasper, 2004).

Within development policy, the effects and aspects which are included in evaluation were, for long, biased towards economic output. The unpaid time of women, for example, was often treated as a free and abundant resource, so that its saving or expenditure was not counted (see, e.g., Crewe and Harrison, 1998). General evaluation of the impacts of international assistance has been preoccupied with its effects on economic growth, to the relative neglect of other possible desirable and undesirable effects; for example, the extraordinary health impacts that have been realized in some cases (see, e.g., CMH, 2001). UNDP's Human Development approach and the Millennium Development Goals represent counters to the preoccupation with economic growth. Yet, in practice, matters such as leisure, quality of family life and physical environment, participation, and the meaningfulness of work and life as a whole still receive relatively little attention in much development policy evaluation. A focus only on the monetizable, or even only on the measurable, is not only unbalanced but also suicidal if the neglected and disvalued areas include those fundamental for societal continuity. "Rationalizing" methods can prove to be socially irrational when extended beyond their particular niches to try to order whole societies.

III. "Logical Framework Approach" and Successors

The logical framework approach (LFA) is a method which specifies, across a set of levels (typically inputs–activities–outputs–purpose–goal), a project, program, or policy's objectives and thus what *effectiveness* means in a particular case. It is part of the family of methods for analyzing, specifying, and measuring objectives (e.g., as part of program budgeting and via performance indicators) that has grown since the 1950s. Such methods emerged since many objectives cannot be reduced easily or at all to the fully monetized terms of CBA and many expenditures (e.g., most recurrent expenditures) are too small for an analysis as complex as CBA to be worthwhile. In addition, the ideology of "managerialism" has held that there are universal principles of good management, which apply equally in private and public contexts and which the public sector should imitate from the private, including the ideas, especially in work influenced by American sources, that management centrally involves the setting and following of precise, measurable objectives, and that evaluation centrally involves identification of their achievement.

LFA has spread greatly since 1970, especially in international-aid projects, including under newer product labels (ZOPP — objectives-oriented project planning, project cycle management, and results-based management). Its rationale is that, even for monetizable expenditures or policies, sophisticated calculations are futile if the means-to-ends logic and other background assumptions behind a design are flawed. LFA pays attention to these features, as well as to making objectives clear and precise. A matrix is prepared, in which the intended means-to-ends narrative is first clarified by specifying the links expected from controllable means to priority ends; secondly, operationalized, in terms of performance indicators; thirdly, tested, in terms of its implied assumptions including about contextual factors.

A logical-framework matrix is still a very limited format of policy argument. It excludes reference to alternatives, to "side effects", and to normative debate about objectives and "whose objectives?"; it is in danger of marginalizing assumptions analysis since the assumptions column is illogically located at the far right of the matrix. For *ex post* evaluation in a public policy context, the neglect of side effects and unintended effects is particularly defective. It implies managerial indifference to others' objectives or ignores what may be the main effects (Gasper, 2000a).

Thus, LFA's appropriate role in policy evaluation is for clarification of a design and for initial screening of proposals and routine internal monitoring. It can, in principle, be employed in more participatory fashion, not only for top-down management, and for example, become a tool to truly probe and debate assumptions, although this would be facilitated by relocation of the assumptions column to next to the objectives column.

Simple assessments of effectiveness rarely suffice for decision-making. Assessment in relation to costs and in terms of the impacts on multiple objectives is needed. Therefore, more summative concepts are sought, of the efficiency in achieving multiple objectives in relation to (multiple) costs. However, the same questions should remain central: efficiency in terms of which objectives and costs and in terms of whose objectives and costs.

IV. Efficiency and the Perspective of Evaluation through Markets

The term *efficiency* refers to maximum fulfilment of one's objectives from given resources. The idea comes from engineering, but acquired new variants in economics. "Cost effectiveness" is one type of efficiency criterion: the productivity of given resources in achieving a given type of value, for example, the health achievements of a specified type, which are obtained per unit of resources. Usually, the resources are measured in financial terms, but this is not essential, and other types of cost-effectiveness measure exist: the ratio of a non-financial output to a non-financial input and the ratio of a financial output to a non-financial input. Figure 37.2 presents these families of measure.

	Non-monetized outputs	Monetized outputs
Non-monetized inputs	Physical ratios (e.g. ratio of graduates per year to the number of teachers)	The least common family of cost-effectiveness indicator
Monetized inputs	The most common type of cost-effectiveness indicator	"Cost-benefit analysis", as understood in mainstream economics

Figure 37.2   Cost-effectiveness analysis and CBA.

The efficiency label has been extensively misused. It is a relational concept: efficiency is only efficiency in terms of certain values (beliefs concerning what is valuable). Different values can lead to different conclusions about what is efficient (Shubik, 1978; Richards, 1985; Le Grand, 1991). Various perspectives seek however to capture the concept's authority to endorse the fulfilment of their particular values alone. The leading example is the misuse of efficiency to refer to what should at most be labeled "economic efficiency": the maximization of net output as measured in monetary terms, for those things which can be monetized and according to the willingness-to-pay (WTP) principle. It excludes attention to all objectives other than those measured in terms of money and measures the fulfilment of those in proportion to how much people pay; therefore, it excludes attention to equity. The objectives of people who have no money are not measured and the objectives of the rich are magnified according to their purchasing power.

Veiling this practice in economics-oriented policy evaluation is the doctrine of "Pareto efficiency": that any situation where nobody can be made better-off without making another person worse-off is a Pareto-efficient point (Stiglitz and Driffil, 2000). Economics-led policy goes much further than this. The WTP criterion is used to justify changes that make many people worse-off, by use of the principle of potential compensation: that those harmed could have been adequately compensated — whether or not they actually were (Alvares and Billorey, 1988; Cernea, 1999; Gasper 2004).

Figure 37.3 suggests the relations between concepts of economic efficiency, effectiveness, and equity — "the three Es" that have commonly figured in economics-based treatments of policy evaluation. Inputs are used to obtain outputs; the first level of effectiveness concerns this attainment of outputs. Output-to-input ratios measure technical productivity. Economists then look at monetary valuation of both outputs and inputs and their

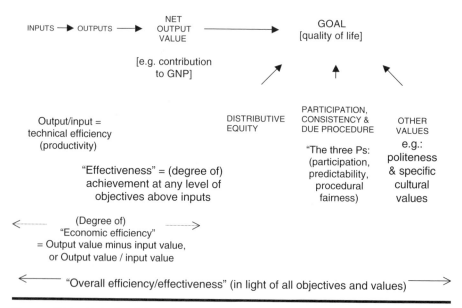

Figure 37.3 **Relationships of concepts of efficiency, effectiveness, equity, and quality of life.**

proportion or difference; the difference in the case of monetized products constitutes the contribution to national product. In the case of nonmonetiz-able outputs such as health, measures of cost-effectiveness are possible. Equity objectives are typically treated separately, even though by definition efficiency depends on what one's values are — Efficiency in what? — and those values could include equity. Further, there are other objectives that should be included in policy evaluation, notably "three Ps": participation, predictability or consistency, and procedural fairness (Nagel, 1984). Any consideration of efficiency, which excludes equity objectives, many other end-state objectives, procedural objectives, and achievements in terms of overall quality of life, is extremely limited. It becomes misleading unless it makes clear which objectives or values it has taken into account and which it has not.

V. Economic CBA

In contrast to the simplicity of LFA, CBA is an ambitious and synthetic method, for comprehensive and rigorous assessment of investments and even policies. It involves monetizing the impacts not only on the agency which makes the expenditure but also on all (significant) agents in a nation. It was thus a tool of national economic planning that emerged as an identified method from the 1930s and spread especially in the 1960s and 1970s. It calculates the value of net output in terms of modified market criteria, not effectiveness in terms of an agency's own objectives; thus, it is "goal-free evaluation" not "goal-based evaluation", to use the terms of Scriven (1991). It is relevant only if nearly all impacts are monetizable or only for the monetizable aspects.

Economists' CBA is based on private financial analysis methods, but takes into account a wider range of impacts — in other words, it considers the social importance of "external costs and benefits," by inclusion of some additional monetizable costs and benefits. Then, it adjusts for some other failures of market prices as measures of societal costs and benefits, by modification of the prices and monetary weights attached to some types of cost and benefit (use of "social prices"). Therefore, it makes limited adjustments to the style of calculation of a modern capitalist business. Relatively speaking, it is more appropriate for public sector commercial projects or enterprises. Overall, the method shares most of the assumptions of market economics. Its merit is to provide a theory-based approach for systematic, case-by-case analysis, in place of choice by rule-of-thumb or sweeping generalizations.

It has major shortcomings as a primary model in public policy evaluation, although they can, in principle, sometimes be counteracted and compensated for. It tries to measure all costs and benefits in monetary terms and tends to ignore other social and political effects. It suggests that in each case, there is one correct choice, which can be found by its procedure of measurement and calculation. It is in practice usually blind to interpersonal distribution of costs and benefits, in the same way as is the criterion of economic efficiency.

The underlying philosophy of CBA varies according to the detailed variant, but is basically a liberal version of utilitarianism (MacIntyre, 1977), interpreted largely by the WTP criterion. In the background is a picture of society as a set of individuals and of individuals as a collection of appetites or preferences, utilities or satisfactions, and maximization programs. In the foreground, utilitarianism in policy and ethics has three explicit components (Sen, 1984). First, consequentialism, that is, assessment of acts by looking at their consequences. Besides the problems of identifying these, the approach leaves gaps concerning the valuative significance of past events and commitments. Secondly, "utility base," that is, the principle of specifically looking at utility consequences, operationalized via measurement of WTP. This monetizing method not only faces measurement issues but also brings a bias to more affluent people and the danger of invasion of market valuation into spheres of life that should never operate on such principles (Walzer, 1983; Staveren, 2001), as illustrated perhaps in the trade in human organs. Thirdly, sum ranking, that is, ranking options according to the sum of net benefits across all people. CBA does include all people in its calculations, but with no equity constraints concerning individuals' gains or losses, instead only the principle of potential compensation, on top of the principle of WTP, so that people's wishes are weighted according to how wealthy they are and those who cannot pay are forgotten.

Figure 37.4 indicates assumptions and debates for this type of policy evaluation. The format is a modification of the Toulmin–Dunn approach for describing policy arguments (Dunn, 1994; Gasper, 2000b; 2002). Warrants 1–3 are predictive and warrants 3–6 are normative.

As a liberal philosophy, CBA starts from the normative principle of consumer sovereignty. The objectives to be accomplished are those which consumers express in the market or simulated market. Economists have often taken a don't-want-to-know, sometimes even nihilist, approach to ethics and discussions of values, and as a result confused the acceptance of all wants with the adoption of a value-neutral stance (Rhoads, 1985). The

The structure of argumentation behind the proposal to accept the results of economic cost-benefit analysis for making resource allocation decisions	Possible counterarguments (to the data provided, or the warrants; or of other types)
[CLAIM:] I PROPOSE THAT This activity is worth doing	• (But not if:) You have ignored vital process values (e.g. due consultation, majority rule)
GIVEN THAT [DATA] It is profitable, as calculated using adjusted prices and an adjusted rate of interest, set by public authorities	• Your calculations are wrong (e.g. your projections are too optimistic, or you used a wrong without-project case to compare against) • You have only corrected some monetizable omissions, and still exclude many important costs and benefits • The rate of interest used and/or the process of discounting is unacceptable
AND GIVEN THE PRINCIPLE(S)/WARRANT(S) THAT 1. Markets are Pareto-efficient, after corrections for major externalities and distortions (e.g. monopoly prices) 2. Minor omissions will not make a difference 3. All the omissions and problems are just as bad for the alternative you offer (if any) 4. State authorities (e.g. central bank, Ministry of Finance) are the legitimate decision-makers 5. Consumers should get what they want and can pay for 6. Existing incomes and property rights are just [or the poor are given priority within the C-B analysis].	• Pareto-efficiency is an insufficient criterion; (insofar as) you have still ignored those who cannot pay, which is not just. • The omissions are not minor. • There is a better alternative. • State authorities take too narrow a view (and sometimes are interested-parties) • You are too liberal about consumer wants [unless "merit goods" are given priority within the C-B analysis] • Existing property rights derive from unjust past processes of expropriation.

Figure 37.4   Identification and testing of assumptions in economic CBA.

consumer sovereignty principle should instead be assessed for what it is, a value stance. One defense is to argue that in general, consumers make good choices. There are numerous counterexamples, however, in which use of "social prices" appears justified, and economic CBA can make provision for this. A second possible defense is to argue that in general, the alternative measures are worse in outcome than would be allowing people to decide for themselves, given the dangers of authoritarianism and state failure. A third is to openly defend the value of "the right to make one's own mistakes."

By trying to frame questions of social choice largely along the same lines as the investment choices by a self-interested businessman, CBA may unreasonably distort some aspects of policy. Environmentalists argue that this is seen in its adoption in a central role of the discounting of future costs and benefits by use of a rate of interest ("rate of discount"), to reduce policy evaluation to the calculation of a rate of (social) profit. This is the same procedure as for a single self-interested capitalist computing his choices in the context of an economy with growth potential. Use of a rate of discount of 10%, as is common, or even 5%, makes basically irrelevant the effects on one's grandchildren and later generations. The procedure appears quite inappropriate for a community determining its future. We need then to set constraints to guide and restrain the use of techniques such as discounting; for example, the sustainable development requirement that projects must leave the environment as good as they found it, or, more stringently and better, must clean up after themselves, rather than discount-away the damage that they leave for future generations. This need to set a restraining framework applies to CBA as a whole. Not all monetizable activities should be monetized.

Other major issues arise in the practice of a sophisticated method such as CBA. Its formal complexity brings various possibilities. It can be misused and manipulated, especially by the powerful, and with too much attention given to refining details rather than focusing on basic questions such as: What would be the conditions and trends without the policy or project? What is the relevant without-project case? CBA can be used as a ritual of legitimation to justify prearranged choices by a screen of calculations (Gasper, 1987; Porter et al., 1991). Sensitivity analysis, seeing the effect of varying the assumptions, is essential but frequently done superficially when compared with the huge divergences that often emerge in reality. One should still assess CBA by comparing with how decision-making would be in its absence. Arguably, that would sometimes be more ritualistic and even more manipulated by the powerful, wielding tools of political rhetoric and influence. Some authors see CBA as potentially a forum, an opportunity, and a set of rules of argumentation which set some burdens of proof — testable, measurable, and quasi-inclusive — rather than following pure rhetoric and power. To reap such potentials requires a very active polity, which provides information and monitoring, pressure and competition; and which also sets limits to the power of WTP. Economics has long considered itself "The Queen of the Social Sciences," but CBA should always be advisory rather than determinant and seen as one among a set of different, complementary methods; one of the servants, never a queen.

VI. Multi-Criteria Evaluation: Policy Evaluation Potentially as Regulated Democratic Political Discourse

Policy evaluation centrally involves the analysis and preparation of arguments in which ideas about values/objectives/priorities are combined with claims about facts and cause-effect linkages, to produce valuations about past or possible future actions by public agencies. Each approach in policy evaluation is a particular style of building arguments, which selects and handles ideas and data in its own distinctive way and tends to emphasize different values. Figure 37.4 illustrated this for economic CBA. To see policy evaluation as the conscious building of arguments, open to the full range of relevant considerations, not only to the aspects that an approach like economics or LFA finds comfortable to handle, is a perspective that comes from law and philosophy. William Dunn and others have called it a jurisprudential approach. It guides, for example, Dunn's classic textbook, *Public Policy Analysis* (2004), which highlights the range and variety of types of argument in policy analysis, and the work of Fischer (1980; 1995), which goes considerably further than Dunn to give a sophisticated but manageable framework for broad-vision policy analysis. Here, we will consider another set of methods — those of multi-criteria evaluation — and how they may fit in an approach of conscious public construction and testing of broad based policy arguments. They bring in a wider range of factors than in CBA and leave more space for public debate about relative weights and implications.

Methods of multi-criteria evaluation have been developed for contexts where one or more of the following aspects are felt to be very important: unmeasurables and incomparables; interpersonal or intergroup distribution; and procedural legitimacy based on procedural fairness and procedural rationality (Nijkamp et al., 1990). Such methods do not attempt the same precision as CBA. They are less precise in weighting effects and in aggregation over time. They offer tools not for optimizing but for "satisficing" — reflective, semi-intuitive, good-enough choice — and "justifying," the establishment of political acceptability. (Both labels build from the verb 'to suffice'.) Thus, they are especially suited for complex, ramifying choices with high uncertainty, where the "*pro memoria*" items (aspects "to be remembered," which cannot presently be well specified) are so many and important that the apparent precision of CBA or similar methods is seriously misleading; and for political circumstances where certain groups (politicians/other top decision makers/other stakeholders/publics) have to be consulted frequently by planners, for example, because many strong voices represent the potential losers and non-economic goals, and yet the divisions are not so deep as to prevent useful debate.

For those purposes, non-aggregating multi-criteria analysis is sometimes enough. A rich picture of diverse effects is provided and mulled over (e.g., Dietz and Pfund, 1988). Often, in fact, disaggregation is taken further, to present the different impacts on different groups or regions, as in so-called Planning Balance Sheet Analysis or Community Impact Analysis (e.g., Lichfield, 1996). However, complex nonaggregated lists of effects and impacts can become baffling and even misleading. We must be careful how the categories for classifying effects are chosen, to reduce overlap. Therefore, we often wish to do additional processing and grouping, by relating the categories to policy criteria and by grouping together all categories which concern the same broad type of policy objective.

Aggregating multi-criteria analysis, just like CBA, estimates effects, applies value-weights, then aggregates scores to give an overall judgment, which it checks through sensitivity analysis. However, it operates in the dramatically different context that we described, avoids the pseudo-objective language of money, and emphasizes debate and analysis of assumptions.

The range of both non-aggregating and aggregating multi-criteria methods is enormous and cannot be surveyed here (see, e.g., Nijkamp et al., 1990). We can instead relate such methods to recent work on reconceptualizing development. The UNDP's conception of human development has taken us away from seeking a single policy evaluation measure like GNP per capita or a small number of monetized or narrowly economic measures like the share of people in waged employment. The Human Development Index, which takes into account some aspects also of health and education, shows that GNP per capita is an unreliable measure of the quality of life. It does not itself purport to be a sufficient single measure. UNDP directs our attention instead to a wide range of relevant human functionings, which need disaggregated attention. The Human Development Reports have the enormous advantage of looking directly at categories of human "functionings" (Sen, 1999) which economic calculation of GNP and benefit-to-cost ratios have raced past: at life expectancy, physical and mental health, mobility, ability to participate, felt satisfactions, quality of family life, and much more; not merely at the associated or supposedly associated money flows.

Much attention has been given to how closely correlated the HDI is with GNP per capita. Since a third of the weight of the HDI is provided by GNP per capita and since financial capacity is relevant to provision of educational and health services, substantial correlation is no surprise. More interesting are the many major discrepancies. Further, the correlation of GNP per capita and recorded subjective satisfaction is weak. Even if there were perfect correlation, with subjective satisfaction always changing by a consistent predictable amount whenever per capita GNP rose, the strength of the connection is extremely limited after countries reach a middle-income level (around $6000 per capita in 1991 prices, according to the World Values Survey). This finding, regularly reconfirmed since the 1960s, is known as "the Easterlin paradox" (see, e.g., Easterlin, 2002). Organizing and evaluating policy by a goal of economic growth beyond a middle-income level may have low justification. Cost-effectiveness analyses which look directly at the valued human functionings attained in monetarily already rich countries often show little or no progress, and sometimes regress, for periods in which GNP per capita recorded massive further increase (Crocker and Linden, 1998; Lane, 2000). In addition, on the other hand, per capita GNP sometimes greatly understates progress.

In addition, the interaction of different systems within society as a whole — economy, polity, families, civil society, culture and values, and physical environment — is more complex than we can measure and model. The more important we find these interactions to be, the less can policies be appropriately judged by overwhelmingly economic calculation. We have sobering examples from Rwanda, the former Yugoslavia and elsewhere in the 1990s of the devastation that can result from adjustment policies driven by economic calculation alone (Eriksson et al., 1996; Woodward, 1995). Thus, the conceptions of sustainable development, sustainable human development and human security in effect adopt multicriteria methods of policy evaluation and set frameworks to constrain economic calculation, such as the principles of precaution and sustainability (see, e.g., Pearce et al., 1990; Söderbaum, 2000).

The methods described in this chapter have their own advantages and disadvantages, areas of greater and lesser applicability, and different degrees of compatibility with various sets of political principles.

References

Alvares, C. and Billorey, R., *Damming the Narmada*, Third World Network, Penang, Malaysia, 1988.

Cernea, M., Development's painful social costs, in *The Development Dilemma — Displacement in India*, Parasuraman, S., ed., Macmillan, Basingstoke, 1999, pp. 1–31.

Commission on Macroeconomics and Health (CMH), *Macroeconomics and Health: Investing in Health for Economic Development*, World Health Organization, Geneva, 2001.

Crewe, E. and Harrison, E., *Whose Development? An Ethnography of Aid*, Zed, London, 1998.

Crocker, D. and Linden, T., Eds., *The Ethics of Consumption*, Rowman and Littlefield, 1998.

Dietz, T. and Pfund, A., An impact identification method for development project evaluation, *Policy Stud. J.*, 8 (1), 137–145, 1988.

Dunn, W.N., *Public Policy Analysis*, Prentice-Hall, Englewood Cliffs, NJ, 2004 (3rd edition).

Easterlin, R., Ed., *Happiness in Economics*, Edward Elgar, Cheltenham, 2002.

Eriksson, J., Kumar, K., and Borton, J., *The International Response to Conflict and Genocide: Lessons from the Rwanda Experience — Synthesis Report*, Steering Committee of the Joint Evaluation of Emergency Assistance to Rwanda, Copenhagen, 1996.

Fischer, F., *Politics, Values and Public Policy*, Westview Press, Boulder, CO, 1980.

Fischer, F., *Evaluating Public Policy*, Nelson Hall, Chicago, 1995.

Gasper, D., Motivations and manipulations: some practices of appraisal and evaluation, *Manch. Papers Dev.*, 3 (1), 24–70, 1987.

Gasper, D., Evaluating the "logical framework approach", *Public Admin. Dev.*, 20 (1), 17–28, 2000a.

Gasper, D., Structures and meanings: a way to introduce argumentation analysis in policy studies education, *Africanus*, 30 (1), 49–72, 2000b.

Gasper, D., Fashion, learning and values in public management, *Africa Dev.*, 27 (3), 17–47, 2002.

Gasper, D., *The Ethics of Development: From Economism to Human Development*, Edinburgh University Press, Edinburgh, 2004.

Lane, R., *The Loss of Happiness in Market Democracies*, Yale University Press, New Haven, 2000.

Le Grand, J., *Equity and Choice*, Harper Collins, London, 1991.

Lichfield, N., *Community Impact Evaluation*, UCL Press, London, 1996.

MacIntyre, A., Utilitarianism and cost–benefit analysis, in *Values in the Electric Power Industry*, Sayre, K., Ed., Notre Dame University Press, Notre Dame, IN, 1977, pp. 217–237.

Nagel, S., *Public Policy*, St. Martin's Press, New York, 1984.

Narayan, D. and Walton, M., Eds., *Voices of the Poor: Can Anyone Hear Us*, Oxford University Press, New York, 2000.

Nijkamp, P., Rietveld, P., and Voogd, H., *Multicriteria Evaluation in Physical Planning*, Amsterdam, North-Holland, 1990.

Pearce, D., Barbier, E., and Markandaya, A., *Sustainable Development*, Earthscan, London, 1990.

Pollitt, C., *Managerialism and the Public Sector*, 2nd ed., Blackwell, Oxford, 1992.

Porter, D., Allen, B., and Thompson, G., *Development in Practice: Paved with Good Intentions*, Routledge, London, 1991.

Rhoads, S., *The Economist's View of the World*, Cambridge University Press, Cambridge, 1985.

Richards, H., *The Evaluation of Cultural Action — A Study of the Parents and Children Program*, Macmillan, London, 1985.

Scriven, M., *Evaluation Thesaurus*, 4th ed., Sage, Newbury Park, 1991.

Self, P., *Econocrats and the Policy Process*, Macmillan, London, 1975.

Sen, A., *Choice, Welfare and Measurement*, Blackwell, Oxford, 1984.

Sen, A., *Development as Freedom*, Oxford University Press, New York, 1999.

Shubik, M., On concepts of efficiency, *Policy Sci.*, 9 (2), 121–126, 1978.

Söderbaum, P., *Ecological Economics: A Political Economics Approach to Environment and Development*, Earthscan, London, 2000.

Staveren, I., *The Values of Economics: An Aristotelian Perspective*, Routledge, London, 2001.

Stiglitz, J. and Driffill, J., *Economics*, W.W. Norton, New York, 2000.

Walzer, M., *Spheres of Justice*, Basil Blackwell, Oxford, 1983.

Woodward, S., *Balkan Tragedy: Chaos and Dissolution after the Cold War*, Brookings, New York, 1995.

Chapter 38

Beyond the Horizon: Policy Learning and Development

Richard Common

CONTENTS

I. Introduction

Prior to the intensification of globalization in recent years, it was generally assumed that policy-making was unique to the individual nation state, with some exceptions, including colonial administrations. The recent growth in interest in policy learning appears to reflect the internationalization of policy knowledge, which, in theory at least, allows governments to engage in continuous improvement in relation to their "successful" counterparts. However, when applying the concept to development administration, the results of policy learning can have the opposite effect. Governments appear to be too quick to learn from others without clearly understanding the process of learning and the feasibility of implementation. Undue haste to seize on policies and programs developed in other countries may reveal scant appreciation for the potential consequences of importation and transplantation. The demands of development governance also require a thorough examination of the political, social and economic context in which learning takes place. Moreover, the generally uncritical acceptance of learning from developed countries by emerging countries is regarded by Minogue (2001: 39) as "disturbing."

Given the deep problematic context of policy learning for developing countries, the chapter begins by attempting to explain the apparent "boom" in policy learning within the wider context of the processes of globalization. This is followed by an investigation of the institutional conditions necessary for policy learning based on the work of Rogers (1995). Finally, the chapter looks at how the U.K. government has formalized its processes of policy learning. The aim of this chapter therefore, is to allow implications to be drawn for developing countries; that policy learning will only be effective if the institutional context within which that learning takes place is fully understood.

II. The Policy Learning "Boom"

The interest in policy learning that has accumulated since the late 1980s has been coterminous with the development of the governance perspective. Both perspectives share an interest in improved policy-making over narrower managerial concerns. So, what is policy learning? Ikenberry (1990: 103) regards it as "social learning," which involves "the spread of new information with which governments make policy choices." Busenberg (2001: 173) defines policy learning as "a process in which individuals apply new information and ideas to policy decisions." However, only when governments convert that information to "knowledge" can they be said to "learn."

The scope for policy learning also appears to be infinite. As Rose (1993: 3) observes "easy access to information about what other governments are doing" has facilitated what he terms "lesson-drawing" between nations. The ease of access to information about other government's public policies has been facilitated by technology but also by the ease of international travel and access to various media. These factors have provided opportunities for policy makers in developing countries to absorb first-hand lessons from abroad, or to find themselves under pressure from an increasingly mobile middle-class who are able to make comparisons with what they experience at home. Thus, access to international networks facilitates policy learning by internationally mobile elites. Ikenberry (1990: 101) observes that "elites monitor policy change abroad and, seeking similar successes, import the appropriate policies." For instance, this has been the case with Britain promoting the export of New Public Management and privatization in the 1980s (Common, 2001: 17).

However, policy learning presupposes proactivity on the part of governments. Governments may have formal processes for policy learning, which allows and encourages them to emulate or learn from policy developments in other countries. For example, Malaysia's "Look East" policy of 1981 took a systematic approach to policy learning from Japan, and to a lesser extent South Korea and Taiwan (Common, 2001: 169). However policy learning tends to be unsystematic and ad hoc for most countries. It is the demand of globalization that have compelled states into monitoring the activities of their economic competitors, thus policy learning appears as "vital" in achieving global competitiveness. Thus, developing countries are particularly vulnerable to policy learning from developed countries, which come to be regarded as "exemplars." As economic competition increases, so does policy learning activity, particularly where the policies of one region or country attract business and commerce at the expense of its neighbors.

Bennett (1991: 36) considers the influence of exemplars in the process of policy learning. For instance, Sweden was long regarded as the exemplar of the welfare state, Germany and Japan for their economic and management success, Britain as the leading exponent of privatization. Thus, developing countries are encouraged to look to these states from which to draw lessons and experience, often due to the imperatives of international competitive pressures. In this scenario, policy makers may simply emulate successful policy innovations in expectation of similar rewards received by the policy innovator. Policy makers are also likely to be convinced by "demonstration effects," which rapidly assist in the dissemination of policy innovations.

For Rose (1993: 28) the object of policy learning is to find "a program that 'works.'" Governments may be forced into learning activity in the international environment if immediate solutions to pressing policy problems are demanded. Bennett (1991: 35) argues that states might consider policy learning when "domestic pressures are such that swift action is needed to deal with a problem" as "incentives might be quite high to utilize a program from elsewhere as a ready-made solution." Engaging in rapid searches for suitable "fixes" can thus mollify political pressure for reforms. On the other hand, policy learning can be a proactive process, to improve existing policies or to seek policy innovations to augment existing programs. In such cases, policy learning implies an improved understanding on the part of government elites about a particular problem but policy learning can only occur if decision makers have the "ability to draw lessons about policy problems, objectives or interventions" (May, 1992: 333). It is the ability to learn, which depends upon institutional capacity, and the ability to manage new information effectively that make policy learning a complex and resource intensive process.

The globalization of certain practices and policies may also be the result of enforced conformity resulting from coercive pressures in the international environment, rather than deliberative policy learning. Of relevance here is "New Institutionalist" theory, which espouses the concept of "isomorphism." Isomorphism may be the result of policy learning activity from dominant models or institutionalized practice. Organizations may also be induced or coerced to follow leading or "cutting-edge practice" exhibited by certain high profile organizations. Thus Strang and Meyer argue that "the homogenizing effects of coercive pressures" comes from "dominant organizations within the field." However this "enforced conformity" thus denies organizations the opportunity to "calculate individually optimal strategies" (Strang and Meyer, 1993: 491), which runs counter to genuine policy learning. Furthermore, international intervention or "external inducement" occurs when one state (or its agents) provides incentives or inducements that lead other states to adopt the preferred policy. External inducements can range widely in their severity, from overt coercion to the loose structuring of incentives and sanctions. It is with no surprise that the accusation of "coercion" has been leveled at the major aid donors such as the World Bank and the International Monetary Fund (Common, 2001: 71).

Although policy learning occurs within networks and as a response to political events, a key learning process is "through the diffusion of innovations and experiences between different jurisdictions and policy domains" (Busenberg, 2001: 175). Busenberg also adds that learning can only be understood in terms of its institutional context. In the next section of this chapter, the institutional conditions for cross-national policy learning are explored from the perspective of the diffusion of innovations literature. Policy learning of this nature goes beyond experiential learning or the accumulation of historical experience (March and Olsen, 1984: 745) to "vicarious experiences with ... policy change" (Barzelay, 2003: 273). However accounting for policy change as a result of policy learning is a difficult enterprise to test empirically.

III. Institutional Conditions for Policy Learning

The ability to draw lessons from elsewhere is not a straightforward process. The first condition is the desire to learn, as Stone (1996: 89) points out, "the receptivity of decision-makers to new ideas or scientific insights is not automatic." Understanding the context of policy learning is crucial as "the lessons drawn are significantly influenced by political institutions and legacies, and the current situational context of reform and learning processes" (Olsen and Peters, 1996: 33). Whether governments choose to engage in policy learning or have policies thrust upon them, policy learning can only take place under certain conditions.

Moreover, as policy learning is a difficult and resource intensive enterprise, not all the necessary conditions may be in place at the same time. In this section, the main institutional conditions for learning are identified. This is based on Rogers' (1995: 15–16) analysis of the diffusion of innovations, which can be extended to that of policy learning, with the resulting adoption of policy innovations. The first institutional characteristic identified by Rogers (1995) is the relative advantage or *the degree to which an innovation is perceived as better than the idea it supersedes.* Therefore, the incentive to learn about a policy is dependent on the policy in question being demonstrated to be a proven success elsewhere. However in a discussion of the diffusion of pay-for-performance programs, Ingraham (1993: 348) notes that despite the apparently widespread acceptance of such programs,

> the diffusion of pay-for-performance has been based less on careful analysis and evaluation than on a perception of success in other settings, informal communication among bureaucratic and elected decision makers and perhaps wishful thinking.

Ingraham's assessment is consistent with the dynamics of emulation where a pay-for-performance system has a powerful "demonstration effect." Thus, a key dynamic in the process is the incentive to learn. As Strang and Meyer (1993: 488) point out, "practices are adopted to the extent that they appear more effective or efficient than the alternatives." It can be assumed that learning occurs when considerable benefits are perceived for both the disseminators of "new" information about policy innovations and the recipients of that information. The export of New Zealand's "model" of public management is one such example (Schwartz, 1997).

Rogers' (1995) next characteristic is that of compatibility, or the degree to which an innovation is perceived as being consistent with the existing values, past experiences, and needs of potential adopters. Strang and Meyer (1993: 490) stress the importance of cultural linkages for learning to occur: "the cultural understanding that social entities belong to a common social category constructs a tie between them." Policy learning is dependent on "perceptions of similarity" between prior and potential adopters. Therefore, we could predict that policy learning only takes place between "similar systems." Although no two countries in the world are exactly alike, it is the perception that they are similar that assists in the process of learning. Policy makers will do nothing rather than attempt the complexities of policy learning from outside a group of nations that are considered to be structurally similar.

Wolman (1992: 33) also observes that policy learning is based on patterns of information flows, geographic propinquity or linguistic or cultural similarities. Rose (1993) labels this "social psychological proximity" where such similarity is perceived. In short, countries look at how similar the problem is in the originating country to that of their own, how successful was that policy, and how the policy setting in the originating country compares to their own. However, perceptions can be misleading. For instance, when accounting for urban policy learning between Britain and the U.S.A., Hambleton and Taylor (1993: 247) concluded that although cities in the U.S.A. and the U.K. shared similar problems, policy settings turned out to be notably different between the two countries.

A third characteristic identified by Rogers (1995) is complexity, or *the degree to which an innovation is perceived as difficult to understand and use.* On the one hand, an ambiguous innovation increases the possibilities for diffusion as "experts" claim specialist knowledge in "interpreting and resolving such ambiguity" (Scarborough and Swan, 2001: 8) but is likely to be adopted more slowly. It is also more likely that only certain parts of a policy or a program will attract attention. On the other hand, simplicity assists the more rapid diffusion of an innovation, especially if "communicated by best practice examples" (Scarborough and Swan, 2001: 8). O'Neill et al. (1998) also argue that there is a distinction between "administrative innovations" and "strategy"; innovations may have a marginal impact on organizational performance, whereas strategic change, such as privatization, subjects organizations to "potentially rapid and visible" shifts in performance.

Fourth, Rogers (1995) discusses observability, which *is the degree to which the results of an innovation are visible to others.* It is important for government legitimacy to learn from a policy that can be easily evaluated and thus proved to be a success. "Demonstration effects" are an important consideration here, especially when provided by organizations or governments that are regarded as "exemplars" who appear to be coping well with economic uncertainty. However, the demonstration of success is not always necessary for diffusion to occur, inefficient innovations may be adopted by a fear that other organizations may use them successfully (O'Neill et al., 1998).

Although the perception of similarity is a powerful mechanism for learning, some countries are more prepared to look outward, and to borrow others' innovations. Countries are highly individualistic in their approaches to policy learning, and there are varying degrees of formality in the ways in which the search for the "best policy" is conducted. On the one hand, small states, including ex-colonies such as Singapore, appear to instinctively scan their environment to learn from elsewhere. For example, shortly after independence Singaporean officials looked to Switzerland, among other countries, for inspiration, as it was perceived to be the most comparable country to their own (Common, 2001: 203). On the other hand, countries such as the U.K. with long histories and traditions tend to export policy rather than learn from others who are perceived to have a political culture different from their own. For example, Rose (1993: 107) notes that Britain tends to ignore nearby Ireland and France, whereas "British policymakers often look across the ocean to the U.S.A. or Canada, or even further away to Australia." However, until recently, policy learning, in the U.K. at least, has remained informal and ad hoc.

A. Policy Learning in the U.K. Government

The U.K. government embarked on a systematic approach to policy learning in the wake of the *Modernising Government* White Paper (Cabinet Office, 1999a). Located in the U.K. Cabinet Office, the Centre for Management and Policy Studies (CMPS) established an International Comparisons in Policy Making Project in 2001 to run to 2004 as a direct consequence of the White Paper. The aim of the project is:

> To help improve the quality of public policy development and delivery by promoting the use of international examples where relevant, easing access to reliable information about international policy-making experience, and increasing the capability of practitioners to learn useful lessons from that experience (Wyatt and Grimmeisen, 2002).

Officials engaged on the project have produced a "toolkit"; to act as practical guidance for U.K. policy-makers engaged in policy learning, with a view to eventual policy transfer. Alongside the toolkit, the "Policy Hub" web site has been developed by CMPS to act as a resource base and to manage the knowledge derived from overseas learning as well as providing an example of an attempt to develop an "intelligent search engine" (Rajan et al., 1999) to assist with the learning process. In effect, The Policy Hub is an IT system that facilitates the exchange of knowledge between specialists and which can be accessed from both within and outside CMPS. For example, links to web sites hosted by international organizations such as the OECD and other governments are featured within Policy Hub. Knowledge management of the kind manifested by the Policy Hub in theory at least should support the problem-solving orientation of policy learning in the U.K. public sector by the "strategic use of information to resolve problems in service delivery" (Brown and Brudney, 2003: 31).

The toolkit developed by CMPS appears to distinguish between learning *about* and learning *from* cross-national experience by presenting these processes as two broad stages in policy learning. First, learning about other countries consists of scanning, selecting and understanding to identify policy innovations from a range of developments in different countries. A process of assessment leading to recommendation follows this stage, which attempts to learn from the experience of others. Then, decisions are made about the innovation or program ranging from outright rejection to "aiming to copy it as closely as possible" (Wyatt and Grimmeisen, 2002).

However, in a critical review of a U.K. Cabinet Office report *Professional Policy-Making for the Twenty-First Century* (Cabinet Office, 1999b), Parsons (2001) discusses the problematic nature of "outward-looking policy-making," which is manifested in the International Comparisons project. Parsons' criticism is based on concerns that good policy-making is about dialogue, whereas the government, although prepared to learn from the experiences of others, seems to be more concerned with "controlling the message than communicating — as in listening — to those outside government" (Parsons, 2001: 101). Inevitably, of course, politicians will always be selective in their judgments based on the advice they receive from their officials.

The International Comparisons in Policy Making Project appears to be a radical departure for the U.K., who had hitherto been generally regarded as a policy "exporter." Hood (1996: 69) links the willingness to learn with ideology: "conventionally, it is argued that ideology hinders learning, but in other ways, ideology may provide a clear and stable political framework within which learning can take place." The impact of "Third Way" politics on the Labor government's willingness to learn is a moot point, but as the Director of the U.K. Strategy Unit remarked at the launch of the toolkit, "the governments which are quickest on their feet, most willing to adapt and learn, will be the ones that serve their citizens best" (Mulgan, 2002). The urge to "look beyond the horizon" has the implicit aim of establishing processes within the U.K. government that ultimately lead to recommendations put to policy executives, including ministers. However, with regards to the Project, the CMPS recognizes that "ultimately, the knowledge gathered from international comparisons is only one source among many of evidence that will inform policy decision making" (Wyatt and Grimmeisen, 2002).

IV. Conclusion

It is clear that in a globalized environment, increased uncertainty has influenced the impulse to learn, but for policies and programs to be adopted from other countries or jurisdictions, certain conditions must be met. As Strang and Meyer (1993: 488) point out, diffusion is facilitated by "exchange dependence" based on familiarity, for example, "businesses benefit when they buy the kind of keyboards secretaries are familiar with, and typewriting schools benefit when they train secretaries to use the kinds of keyboards businesses own." It is often the perception of similarity between nations that is the most important dynamic of policy learning. Therefore, for instance, it is unlikely that the U.K. "International Comparisons" project will learn from beyond the Anglophone or OECD nations. Policy learning also appears to offer a clear account of how various agents actively disseminate policy innovations and why governments choose whether or not to adopt the innovation. When learning from abroad, policy makers need to be assured that a program has a strong probability of success when introduced.

However one of the limitations of the policy learning concept in the public sector is the assumption that adoption and non-adoption is a clear-cut process. In terms of adopting a particular piece of equipment or scientific invention, the outcomes of learning are more easily measured, but to account for the diffusion of management practices or public policies, important political and socio-economic contextual detail may be missed. Although the processes of learning can help to explain policy adoption, the demands for effective policy learning also involve an understanding of the mechanisms of adopting and evaluating policy innovations. However, as successful innovations enter the public domain with the consequence that other organizations attempt to mimic the innovation, the intrinsic value of the innovation becomes dissipated. This is often a consequence of bandwagon effects where the high rate of policy adoptions means that the intrinsic properties of the innovation are largely ignored. More negatively, research may well prove that policy learning will always fall short of expectations; rather than bringing about genuine and continuous changes in public institutions.

Finally, the impulse to learn from the so-called "developed" countries brings with it particular problems for development governance. For example, the current and popular drive towards "e-governance" faces considerable obstacles in emerging countries, which may lack the basic infrastructure to support such initiatives (Ferguson and Masters, 2004). Given that the U.K. government has devoted considerable resources to its International Comparisons project and the Policy Hub, for the developed countries, the opportunity to learn may be a luxury that only they can afford.

References

Barzelay, M., Introduction: the process dynamics of public management policymaking, *Int. Publ. Manage. J.*, 6 (3), 251–281, 2003.

Bennett, C., How states utilize foreign evidence, *J. Publ. Policy*, 11 (1), 31–54, 1991.

Brown, M. and Brudney, J., Learning organizations in the public sector? a study of police agencies employing information and technology to advance knowledge, *Public Admin. Rev.*, 63 (1), 30–43, 2003.

Busenberg, G., Learning in organizations and public policy, *J. Publ. Policy*, 21 (2), 173–189, 2001.

Cabinet Office, *Modernising Government* (Cmnd. 4310), The Cabinet Office, London, 1999a.

Cabinet Office, *Professional Policy Making for the 21st Century*, The Cabinet Office, London, 1999b.

Common, R., *Public Management and Policy Transfer in Southeast Asia*, Ashgate, Aldershot, 2001.

Ferguson, M. and Masters, R., E-merging with e-governance, *Int. Develop. Rev.*, 1 (2), 51–53, 2004.

Hambleton, R. and Taylor, M., Reflections on transatlantic policy transfer, in *People in Cities A Transatlantic Policy Exchange*, Hambleton, R. and Taylor, M., Eds., SAUS, Bristol, pp. 235–248, 1993.

Hood, C., UK: from second chance to near-miss learning, in Olsen, J. and Peters, B.G., Eds., *Lessons from Experience: Experiential Learning in Administrative Reforms in Eight Democracies*, Scandinavian University Press, Oslo, pp. 36–70, 1996.

Ikenberry, G., The international spread of privatization policies: inducements, learning and policy 'bandwagoning,' in Suleiman, E. and Waterbury, J., Eds., *The Political Economy of Public Sector Reform and Privatization*, Westview, Oxford, pp. 88–110, 1990.

Ingraham, P., Of pigs in pokes and policy diffusion: another look at pay-for-performance, *Publ. Admin. Rev.*, 53 (4), 348–356, 1993.

March, J. and Olsen, J., The New Institutionalism: organizational factors in political life, *Am. Political Sci. Rev.*, 78 (3), 734–749, 1984.

May, P., Policy learning and failure, *J. Publ. Policy*, 12 (4), 331–354, 1992.

Minogue, M., Should flawed models of public management be exported?, in *The Internationalization of Public Management*, McCourt, W. and Minogue, M., Eds., Edward Elgar, Cheltenham, pp. 20–43, 2001.

Mulgan, G., International comparisons in policy making: the view from the centre, Speech delivered to the *International Comparisons in Policy Making Project Conference*, Lancaster House, London, 19 March 2002.

Olsen, J. and Peters, B.G., Learning from experience?, in *Lessons from Experience: Experiential Learning in Administrative Reforms in Eight Democracies*, Olsen, J. and Peters, B.G., Eds., Scandinavian University Press, Oslo, pp. 1–35, 1996.

O'Neill, H., Pouder, R., and Buchholtz, A., Patterns in the diffusion of strategies across organizations: insights from the innovation diffusion literature, *Acad. Manage. Rev.*, 23 (1), 98–115, 1998.

Parsons, W., Modernising policy-making for the twenty first century: the professional model, *Publ. Policy Admin.*, 16(3), 93–110, 2001.

Rajan, A., Lank, E., and Chapple, K., *Good Practices in Knowledge Creation and Exchange*, Focus/London Training and Enterprise Council, London, 1999.

Rogers, E., *Diffusion of Innovations*, 4th Ed., Free Press, New York, NY, 1995.

Rose, R., *Lesson Drawing in Public Policy*, Chatham House, Chatham, NJ, 1993.

Scarborough, H. and Swan, J., Explaining the diffusion of knowledge management: the Role of Fashion, *Brit. J. Manage.*, 12, 3 12, 2001.

Schwartz, H., Reinvention and retrenchment: lessons from the application of the New Zealand model to Alberta, Canada, *J. Policy Anal. Manage.*, 16 (3), 405–422, 1997.

Stone, D., Capturing the Political Imagination, Frank Cass, London, 1996.

Strang, D. and Meyer, J., Institutional conditions for diffusion, *Theor. Soc.*, 22 (4), 487–511, 1993.

Wolman, H., Understanding cross national policy transfers: the case of Britain and the US, *Governance*, 5 (1), 84–100, 1992.

Wyatt, A. and Grimmeisen, S., Background to the development of the Toolkit, in *International Comparisons in Policy Making: Toolkit*, CMPS, Cabinet Office, Centre for Management and Policy Studies, Ascot, 2002.

DEVELOPMENT SECTORS

Chapter 39

Rethinking Industrial Policy

Sanjaya Lall

CONTENTS

I. Introduction

Industrial policy has two approaches: *neoliberal* and *structuralist*. The former argues that the free markets optimize resource allocation and dynamic advantage and the only legitimate role for the state is to provide a stable macro-economy, an open economy and basic public goods. The *structuralist* view puts less faith in free markets and more in the need for governments to mount interventions. Accepting the mistakes of past industrial strategies, it argues that globalization needs a more active role for the government. The controversy on industrial policy is not new; it goes back to decades or even centuries (Reinert, 1995; Chang, 2002). We show why this is the case and suggest that the case for policy is becoming stronger with technical change and globalization.

II. New Dimensions of Industrial Competitiveness

Technical change is shifting industrial and trade structures towards more complex, technology-based activities. Table 39.1 shows the growth of manufacturing value added (MVA) for three sets of activities: resource based (RB), low technology (LT) and medium and high technology (MHT).[1] For exports the data allows us to show high technology products separately.

Organizational structures and the location of production are changing in response to technical change. Industrial firms are becoming less vertically integrated and more specialized by technology, scouring the world for more economical locations. Shrinking economic space allows them to locate functions in far-flung corners of the globe. Some facilities are under the control of transnationals from the industrialized countries but others are independent, interwoven with the leaders in intricate relations. "Fragmentation" is rewriting industrial geography.

Table 39.1 Growth of Manufacturing Value Added and Manufactured Exports by Technology (% Per Annum, 1980–2000)

Activity	World (%)	Industrialized Countries (%)	Developing Countries (%)
Manufacturing value added			
Total MVA	2.6	2.3	5.4
RB MVA	2.3	1.8	4.5
LT MVA	1.7	1.4	3.5
MHT MVA	3.1	2.6	6.8
Manufactured exports			
Total manufactured exports	7.6	6.6	12.0
RB manufactured exports	5.6	5.2	6.7
LT manufactured exports	7.4	8.4	11.4
MHT manufactured exports	8.4	7.3	16.5
o/w Hi-tech exports	11.5	9.9	20.2

Source: Calculated from UNIDO and Comtrade data.

Globalization transfers productive factors more rapidly but not evenly. Factors reach where competitive production is possible, where there are inputs and institutions to complement them. It requires new industrial capabilities (Best, 2001). However, industrial capabilities develop in a cumulative and path-dependent manner, with agglomeration economies. Industrial performance can continue diverging over time, with no inbuilt forces towards convergence.

Let us examine how developing regions are doing in this scene.[2]

MVA: The developing world performed well between 1980 and 2000. Its share of global MVA rose by 10% points (from 14 to 24%) and its annual rate of growth (5.4%) was over twice the 2.3% recorded by the industrialized world. Success in the developing world was very concentrated (Figure 39.1). East Asia dominated raising its world share from around 4% to nearly 14% — exactly the 10-point rise for the developing world as a whole. EA, while strongly export-oriented, was not "liberal" in the Washington consensus sense.[3] LAC, the region that liberalized the earliest and the fastest, was the worst performer.

LAC and East Asia illustrate the issues nicely. The regions had different industrial policies, initially to develop industry[4] and later to liberalize — EA always had more *strategic* policy. The resulting differences are interesting. LAC started the 1990s with considerable slack engendered by the "lost decade," which better macro policy and liberalization should have allowed it to exploit. However, the region continued to perform poorly: LAC2 had

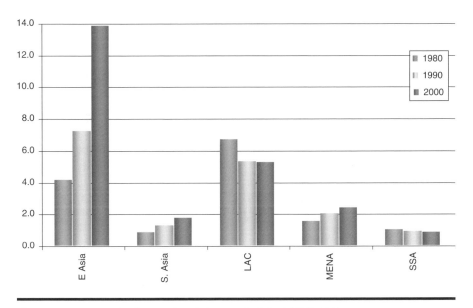

Figure 39.1   Developing regions' shares of global MVA (%).

MVA growth of only 1.9% per annum, much lower than developing countries as a whole (6.4%) or East Asia (9.5%). Mexicans robust growth of 4.4% was largely a consequence of trade privileges over other developing regions under NAFTA — hardly a neoliberal recipe. In any case it did not match EA2 (6.7%) or China (13.1%), and this despite the fact that the 1990s were a bad period for EA2, reeling from the effects of the 1997 financial crisis.

Export performance: East Asia accounted for 18.4% of world-manufactured exports in 2000, up from 6.8% in 1981. Within it, EA2 raised its share from 5.8 to 12.0% and China from 1.0 to 6.5%. LAC lost world market share in 1981–1990 (from 3.2 to 2.4%) then raised it over the next decade to 5.1%. The initial fall was due entirely to LAC2 (from 2.7 to 1.9%), with Mexico steady at a 0.5% share. Other regions were relatively stagnant, though each did better in the 1990s than the 1980s. Thus:

- MVA performance is correlated with manufactured exports, though the fit is not perfect.
- Neither MVA nor export growth is related to liberalization in the Washington consensus sense.
- Industrial success remains concentrated. Liberalization is not leading to convergence, contradicting the neoliberal premise that liberalization *per se* would promote industrial growth and competitiveness.

III. Why the World Differs from the Neoliberal Ideal

Neoliberals accept a government role in providing public goods, law and order and macro management. Selectivity (the support of particular activities) is taboo. Their early interpretation of East Asian success, that it was due to non-interventionist policies, was subjected to intense criticism. It was noted that most successful countries had been very interventionist in trade, FDI, technology and domestic resource allocation.[5] The neoliberals responded with a "*moderate neoclassical*" stance that tried to explain why selectivity, was redundant and unnecessary in spite of its existence (World Bank, 1993). They admitted *some* market failures and *some* role for the state, but only as long as interventions were functional. This "market friendly" approach segmented market failures not according to whether market failures existed but according to the level at which policies affected investment.

This distinction arises from the *political premise* that governments *cannot* mount effective selective interventions. The World Bank (1993) admitted that some selectivity worked in East Asia, but argued that the circumstances were unique. Other governments did not and *could not* have the capabilities needed. The moderate position retained the assumptions that technology markets were "efficient." Efficiency has stringent theoretical requirements: product markets give the correct signals for investment and factor markets respond to these signals. There are no scale economies or externalities. Firms have perfect information, foresight and knowledge of all available technologies. They choose the right technology and, having selected the right technology, use it at "best practice." There are no significant learning processes, risks, externalities or deficiencies in skills, finance, information and infrastructure.

In this model, any policy intervention is distorting.[6] The critical assumption concerns *learning and capability building* and changing it yields different conclusions. But demonstrating market failures does not establish the case for selectivity. It is also necessary to show that such failures are important in practice and that governments can effectively remedy them. Both *can* be shown, and the transition from a neoclassical world to a universal neoliberal policy *diktat* is not justified in theory, history or practice.

How enterprises in developing countries use technology is analyzed by the technological capabilities literature.[7] The literature is mainly empirical, drawing on the evolutionary approach of Nelson and Winter (1982). It argues that industrial success in developing countries depends on how enterprises manage the process of mastering, adapting and improving upon existing technologies. The process is difficult and prone to diffuse market failures. Technology has "tacit" elements that need the user to invest in new skills, routines, and technical and organizational information. Such investment faces market and institutional failures. Many interventions *have* to be selective: technologies differ in their tacit features and externalities.

Capability development can face market failures in building initial capacity and in subsequent deepening. Both need support, *functional* and *selective*. Support entails a mixture of policies apart from infant industry protection.[8] Free markets may not give correct signals for investment in new technologies when there are high, unpredictable learning costs and widespread externalities. Added to this, the extra handicaps facing firms in developing countries: unpredictability, lack of information, weak capital markets, absence of suppliers, poor support institutions and so on. Exposure to full import competition is likely to prevent entry into activities with difficult technologies. Yet, these are the technologies that are likely to carry the burden of industrial development and future competitiveness.

Why should interventions be *selective*? Offering uniform protection to all activities makes little sense when learning and externalities differ by technology. In some activities the need for protection is low because the learning period is brief, information easy to get and externalities limited. In complex activities or those with widespread externalities, newcomers may never enter unless measures are undertaken to promote the activity. The only complex activities where investments may take place without promotion are those based on local natural resources, if the resource advantage is sufficient to offset the learning costs. However, the processing of many resources calls for strong capabilities; both Africa and Latin America have large resource bases but advanced processing has only taken root in the latter, based on decades of capability building under import-substitution.

Infant industry protection is only one part of industrial policy, and *by itself can be harmful and ineffective.* First, protection cannot succeed if not offset by competitive pressures: cushioning the costs of capability building can remove the incentive for undertaking it. But it is possible to provide incentives by strengthening domestic competition, setting performance targets and, most effectively, by forcing firms into export markets. Many such measures also have to be *selective*, since the costs of entering export markets differ by product.

Secondly, there is a need to *coordinate protection with factor markets.* Firms need new inputs for learning: new skills, technical and market information, risk finance, or infrastructure. Unless factor markets respond, protection cannot allow firms to become competitive. Factor market interventions also *have to be selective as well as functional,* for three reasons. First, several factor needs are specific to activities and have to coordinate to learning needs. For instance, the skill needs of electronics may not be fully foreseen by education markets,[9] or the financial needs emerging new technologies may not be addressed by capital markets. Second, government resources for supporting factor markets are limited, and allocating them among competing uses entails selectivity at a high level (say, between education and other uses). Third, where the government is already targeting particular sectors in product markets, factor markets have to be geared to those activities if the strategy is to succeed.

The *deepening* of capabilities faces similar problems. The more complex the functions, the higher the costs involved and the greater the coordination required. Getting into production may be easy compared to design, development and innovation. Neoclassical theory accepts that free markets fail to ensure optimal innovative activity because of imperfect appropriability of information. However, developing countries face an additional problem. It is generally easier to import foreign technologies fully packaged than to develop an understanding of the basic principles involved — the basis of local design and development. "Internalized" technology transfer takes the form of wholly foreign-owned direct investment. This is an effective and rapid way to access new technology, but it may result in little capability acquisition in the host country apart from production skills. The move from production to innovative activity involves a strategic decision that foreign investors tend to be unwilling to take in developing countries. While some relocation of innovative activity *is* taking place (UNCTAD,

2002), it is largely in advanced countries and a few newly-industrializing economies.

Most countries that have built strong innovative capabilities have done it in local firms, often by selectively restricting FDI. Some have done it by stimulating foreign investors to invest in R&D, but this also involved selective intervention. Thus, complete openness to internalized technology imports may not be a good thing if it truncates the process of technological deepening and internalized transfers may need to be subjected to interventions to extract greater technological benefits.

IV. Industrialization Strategies in Asian Tigers

There was no generic "East Asian model." Each country had a different model within the common context of export orientation, sound macro management and a good skill base. As a result, each had a different pattern of industrial growth, reliance on FDI, technological capability and enterprise structure (Table 39.2). However, for none was "getting prices right" sufficient for industrial success.

Hong Kong was nearest to the neoliberal ideal, combining free trade with an open door policy to FDI. However, its success does not provide many lessons to other countries. Hong Kong had unique initial conditions and its industrial performance, after the initial spurt, was weak. It had a long *entrepôt* tradition, global trading links, established infrastructure of trade and finance, presence of large British companies with spillovers in skills and information, and influx of entrepreneurs, engineers and technicians from the mainland. This let it launch light export-based manufacturing: other *entrepôt* economies in the developing world have similar environments but not similar success. Moreover, the government did help industry by allocating land to manufacturers and setting up support institutions. The absence of industrial policy constrained industrial development as capabilities were "used up." Hong Kong *started with and stayed with* light activities. There was progress in terms of product quality and diversification, but little technological deepening. Hong Kong de-industrialized as costs rose; manufacturing is now less than 5% of GDP compared to over 25% at the peak.

Singapore used interventionist policies to promote and deepen industry in a free trade setting, showing how industrial policy takes many forms apart from import protection. With half the population of Hong Kong, even higher wages and a thriving service sector, Singapore did not suffer a similar "hollowing out." Its industrial structure deepened over time, allowing it to sustain rapid industrial growth. It relied heavily on TNCs but the government targeted activities for promotion and aggressively used FDI to achieve its objectives (Wong, 2003).

Table 39.2 Industrial Policy Objectives of NIEs

	Deepening Industrial Structure	Raising Local Content	FDI Strategy	Raising Technological Effort	Promotion of Large Local Enterprises
Hong Kong	None	None	Passive Open Door	None except technology support for SMEs	None
Singapore	Very strong push into specialised high skill/tech industry, without protection	None, but sub-contracting promotion now started for SMEs	Aggressive targeting and screening of TNCs, direction into high value-added activities	None for local firms, but TNCs targeted to increase R&D	None, but some public sector enterprises enter targeted areas
Taiwan	Strong push into capital, skill and technology intensive industry	Strong pressures for raising local content and sub-contracting	Screening FDI, entry discouraged where local firms strong. Local technology diffusion pushed	Strong technology support for local R&D and upgrading by SMEs. Government orchestrated high tech development	Sporadic: to enter heavy industry, mainly by public sector
Korea	Strong push into capital, skill and technology intensive industry, especially heavy intermediates and capital goods	Stringent local content rules, creating support industries, protection of local suppliers, sub-contracting promotion	FDI kept out unless necessary for technology access or exports, joint ventures and licensing encouraged	Ambitious local R&D in advanced industry, heavy investment in technology infrastructure. Targeting of strategic technologies	Sustained drive to create giant private conglomerates to internalise markets, lead heavy industry, create export brands

Note: SMEs, small and medium enterprises; FDI, foreign direct investment; TNCs, multinational corporations; R&D, research and development.

Singapore started with some capabilities in *entrepôt* trading and ship servicing. After a decade or so of light industrial activity, the government acted to upgrade the industrial structure. It guided TNCs to higher value-added activities, integrated into their global operations. It intervened extensively to create the skills needed (Ashton et al., 1999) and set up public enterprises to undertake activities where foreign investment was unfeasible or undesirable. Such reliance on FDI reduced the initial need for technological effort. Over time, however, the government induced TNCs to establish R&D and foster innovation in local enterprises (Wong, 2003). This strategy worked well, and Singapore now has the third highest ratio in the developing world of enterprise financed R&D in GDP, after Korea and Taiwan (UNIDO, 2002).

Korea and *Taiwan* adopted the most interventionist strategies, spanning product and factor markets. Local firms, backed by policies, including FDI restrictions that allowed them to develop impressive technological capabilities, led their export drive. The domestic market was not exposed to free trade; quantitative and tariff measures were used to give infant industries "space" to develop capabilities. The deleterious effects of protection were offset by strong export incentives.

Korea went much further in heavy industry than Taiwan. To compress entry into complex, scale and technology-intensive activities, its interventions were far more detailed and pervasive. Korea relied primarily on capital goods imports, technology licensing and OEM agreements to acquire technology. It used reverse engineering, adaptation and R&D to build upon arm's length technology imports and develop capabilities (Amsden, 1989; Westphal, 2002). Its R&D expenditures are now the highest in the developing world, ahead of all but a handful of leading OECD countries. Korea accounts for some 53% of the developing world's total enterprise-financed R&D (UNIDO, 2002).

One of the pillars of Korean strategy, and one that marks it off from the other Tigers (but mirrors Japan), was the deliberate creation of large conglomerates, the *chaebol*. The *chaebol* were hand-picked from successful exporters and were given various subsidies and privileges, including the restriction of TNC entry, in return for furthering a strategy of setting up capital and technology-intensive activities geared to export markets. The rationale for fostering size was obvious: in view of deficient markets for capital, skills, technology and even infrastructure, large and diversified firms could internalize many of their functions. They could undertake the cost and risk of absorbing very complex technologies (without a heavy reliance on FDI), further develop it by their own R&D, set up world-scale facilities and create their own brand names and distribution networks.

This was a costly and high-risk strategy. The risks were contained by the strict discipline imposed by the government: export performance, domestic competition and interventions to rationalize the industrial structure. The government encouraged the diffusion of technology, putting pressures on the *chaebol* to establish supplier networks. The government also provided selective and functional support by building a technology infrastructure and creating skills. Its enrolments in technical subjects at the tertiary level are over twice the ratio in the OECD. Even more striking was its promotion of industrial R&D. Enterprise financed R&D in Korea as a percentage of GDP is the second highest in the world, after Sweden, and exceeds such technological giants as the US, Japan and Germany. Such R&D has grown dramatically in the past two-and-a-half decades as a result of the promotion of the *chaebol*, export orientation, incentives, skill availability and government collaboration.

Taiwan's policy encompassed import protection, directed credit, selectivity on FDI, support for indigenous skill and technology development and export promotion (Wade, 2003). Taiwan did not promote giant conglomerates, nor did it attempt a drive into heavy industry. Taiwanese industry remained largely composed of SMEs, and, given the disadvantages to technological activity inherent in small size, it supported industry by R&D collaboration, innovation inducements and extension assistance. Taiwan has probably the developing world's most advanced system of technology support for SMEs. It also built a large public sector to set up facilities where private firms were unwilling or unable to do so.

In the early years, Taiwan attracted FDI into activities in which domestic industry was weak, and used a variety of means to ensure that TNCs transferred technology to local suppliers. Like Korea, Taiwan sought FDI where local firms lacked world-class capabilities. The government helped SMEs to locate, purchase, diffuse and adapt new foreign technologies. Where necessary, it entered into joint ventures, in technologically difficult areas like semiconductors (Mathews and Cho, 1999).

The success of industrial policy in the Tigers suggests that there is no ground for a general case against selective interventions. The outcome depends not on *whether* but *how* governments intervene. The Asian experience has the following lessons:

- Selectivity (picking a few activities at a time) rather than promoting all industrial activities indiscriminately and in an open-ended way.
- Picking activities and functions that offered significant technological benefits and linkages.
- Forcing early entry into world markets, using exports to discipline bureaucrats and enterprises.
- Giving the lead role to private enterprises but using public enterprises as needed to fill gaps and enter exceptionally risky areas.

- Investing massively in skill creation, infrastructure and institutions, coordinated with interventions in product markets.
- Using selectivity in FDI help build local capabilities (by restricting FDI or imposing conditions on it) or to tap into dynamic, high technology value chains.
- Centralizing strategic decision making in competent authorities who could take an economy-wide view and enforce policies on different ministries.
- Improving the quality of bureaucracy and governance.
- Ensuring policy flexibility and learning, so that mistakes could be corrected *en route*, and involving private sector in strategy formulation and implementation (Lall and Teubal, 1998).

V. Industrial Policy for the New Era

What difference do technical change and globalization make to industrial policy?

Technical change: The rapid spread of information technology, shrinking economic distance and the skill and institutional needs of new technologies have made competitiveness more demanding. Minimum entry levels in terms of skill, competence, infrastructure and "connectivity" are higher. All these raise the need for support of learning by local enterprises. Low wages matter for unskilled labor, but they matter less. Only natural resources give an independent competitive advantage, but only for extraction; subsequent processing needs competitive capabilities.

The policy needs of capability building have not changed. They are *direct* — the infant industry case to provide "space" for enterprises to master new technologies — and *indirect*, to ensure that factor markets meet their needs. There is also a need to *coordinate learning* across enterprises and activities, when these are linked in the production chain and imports cannot substitute effectively for local inputs. At the same time, technical change makes it necessary to *provide more access to international technology markets*; it also makes it more *difficult to anticipate which activities are likely to succeed*. The information needs of industrial policy rise in tandem with technological change and complexity.

The greater complexity of technology does not make selectivity unfeasible. Detailed targeting of technologies, products or enterprises may be more difficult because of the pace of change, but targeting at higher levels is feasible and more necessary. Technological progress may actually make industrial policy easier in some respects: information on technological trends and markets is more readily available, more is known about the policies in successful countries and benchmarking is easier.

With weak local capabilities, industrialization has to be more dependent on FDI. But FDI cannot drive industrial growth without local capabilities, for several reasons:

- FDI concentrates in technology and marketing intensive activities and does not cover large areas of manufacturing with mundane skill, marketing and technological requirements.
- Attracting manufacturing FDI into complex activities needs strong local capabilities, without which TNCs cannot launch efficient operations.
- Retaining an industrial base with a strong foreign presence needs rapidly rising capabilities as wages rise and skill demands change.
- FDI is attracted increasingly to efficient agglomerations or clusters of industrial activity.
- The cumulative nature of capabilities means that once FDI takes root in particular locations, it becomes difficult to newcomers to break in, particularly in the more complex activities and functions.
- It is difficult to see how countries can tap FDI potential fully without local content rules, incentives for deepening technologies and functions, inducements to export and so on.

Globalization: The spread of integrated systems makes it *more difficult and risky* to take the autonomous route of Korea or Taiwan. It is much easier for countries to attract segments of TNC activity and build upon these. Most later entrants into globalized systems, from Malaysia to Mexico and Costa Rica, have gone the FDI route. *Globalization does not do away with the need for all selective industrial policies*; it only reduces the scope and raises the potential cost of some. FDI is complementary to local enterprises and capabilities after a certain level of development. Strong local capabilities raise the possibility of attracting high value systems and of capturing skill and technology spillovers; these need selective policies. Attracting export-oriented FDI requires selective promotion and targeting; the most effective targeting is undertaken by advanced economies.

How far *can* globalized production spread across the developing world? Fragmentation is feasible only when production processes are separable in technological terms. In low technology activities, it is strong in clothing, footwear, sports goods and toys; in high technology, it is strong in electronics; in medium technology industry, it is strong in automobiles (UNCTAD, 2003). This leaves a broad range of industries in which production and exports are not driven by global systems. Where such systems exist, they are likely to continue relocating to lower wage countries in only some activities. Low technology industries are the best candidates because of low entry requirements, but here the abolition of the Agreement on Textiles and Clothing (formerly MFA) raises the risk that garment production will shift back to East Asia. In high technology systems like electronics the picture is different. Entry levels are higher than in the late 1960s when the industry first moved to Southeast Asia. Production techniques have advanced and manufacturing systems have "settled down" in their new locations, with established facilities, logistics, infrastructure and support institutions. If these systems grow, they are likely to cluster around established sites rather than spread to new, less-developed ones. The prospects of complex global production systems spreading to Africa, LAC, South Asia or MENA are dim.

New systems may emerge to catalyze the growth of FDI-driven production in new sites but they may not transform competitiveness in poorer economies. Those in resource-based activities are likely to be demanding in skills, technology and infrastructure. Industrialization in the developing world thus continues to face many of the same constraints that it did before integrated systems. The need to foster the development of local capabilities remains the "bottom line" and globalization offers an alternative route only in some activities, to some countries and even to these only for some time.

WTO rules do not prohibit all selective interventions, only those that affect trade. However, other forces making for liberalization are less formal (structural adjustment programmes, bilateral trade and investment agreements and pressures by rich countries) but they are as powerful. Some constraints may be useful and may prevent the more egregious interventions that led to inefficiency, rent-seeking and technological sloth. They are also beneficial to countries with strong capabilities developed behind protective barriers: India, Brazil or China should accelerate liberalization if they can combine this with a strategy to restructure activities and enter promising new activities.

It is still possible to selectively promote skills, technology, innovation financing, FDI and infrastructure. These tools are used vigorously by industrialized countries and most semi-industrial countries, but not by less-developed countries (on Africa see Lall and Pietrobelli, 2002). The permissible tools are not enough, however, to foster the rapid development of technological capabilities. They may force countries with weak industrial bases to become over-dependent on FDI. This cannot meet their full industrialization needs. Even countries able to plug into global production systems can only do so as providers of the low-level labor services; subsequent deepening may be held back by constrictions on capability development. For developing countries with a capability base the rules can deter diversification into new technologies.

In general, the rules threaten to *freeze comparative advantage* in areas where capabilities exist at the time of liberalization, yielding a relatively short period of competitive growth before the stock is "used up." It is time to seriously rethink the whole theoretical basis of neoliberal policies.

Notes

1. For a description of the categories and the rationale behind the classification see Lall (2001).

2. The regions are: "East Asia" or EA includes China and all countries in the Southeast Asian region apart from Japan, while EA2 excludes China. "LAC" (Latin America and the Caribbean) includes Mexico and LAC2 excludes it. South Asia includes the five main countries in that region. "MENA" (Middle East and North Africa) includes Turkey but not Israel (an industrialized country). "SSA" (Sub-Saharan Africa) includes S. Africa except in SSA2.

3. Most East Asian economies used infant industry protection, export subsidies and targets, credit allocation, local content rules and so on to build their industrial capabilities, disciplining the process by strong export orientation (Amsden, 1989; Wade, 1990; World Bank, 1993; Stiglitz, 1996; Westphal, 2002). China combined different strategies, some similar to its neighbors and others, like public enterprise restructuring, uniquely its own (Lall and Albaladejo, 2003).

4. In the first phase, LAC, in common with other developing regions, relied heavily on protected import-substitution, sheltering enterprises from international competition but failing to offset this with incentives or pressures to export. It did little to attract export-oriented FDI (in EPZs) and so missed the surge in global production systems in electronics. It did not deepen local technological activity (by encouraging R&D) or develop the new skills needed for emerging technologies. In concert with widespread macroeconomic (and in some cases political) turbulence, this meant that LAC failed to develop a broad base of industrial capabilities that would drive competitiveness as it liberalized. As a high wage region, LAC needed competitive advantages in complex activities to offset wage disadvantage *vis-a-vis* Asia. Despite its tradition of entrepreneurship and base of skills, it failed to foster the necessary capabilities. There were exceptions, such as the automotive industry in the larger economies and resource-based activities more generally, but many such activities are not growing rapidly in world trade. LAC failed to raise export market shares rapidly, the exception being Mexico, due to NAFTA than to strategy.

5. The objections to the strong neoliberal position came from such authors as Westphal (1982, 1990), Pack and Westphal (1986), Amsden (1989), Wade (1990), and Lall (1992).

6. Neoclassical economists admit the possibility of market failure arising from monopoly, public goods and externalities, but treat failures as special cases rather than the rule. The failures that may call for selective interventions are capital market deficiencies, scale economies and externalities arising from the imperfect appropriability of investments in knowledge, technology, and skills. However, the admission that these possibilities exist does not translate into recommendations that government mount selective policies to overcome them. Moreover,

the neglect of firm-level learning processes means that the list of market failures remains incomplete; the most critical ones for developing countries are ignored. See Lall and Teubal (1998).
7. See Lall (1992, 1996, 2001), Westphal (2002), and UNIDO (2002).
8. See the contributions by Wade (2003) and Lall (2003).
9. On the selectivity of education and training policies in East Asia, and their intimate relationship to industrial policy more narrowly defined, see Ashton et al. (1999).

References

Amsden, A., *Asia's Next Giant*, Oxford University Press, Oxford, 1989.

Ashton, D., Green, F., James, D., and Sung, J., *Education and Training for Development in East Asia*, Routledge, London, 1999.

Best, M., *The New Competitive Advantage*, Oxford University Press, Oxford, 2001.

Chang, H.-J., *Kicking Away the Ladder*, Anthem Press, London, 2002.

Lall, S., Technological capabilities and industrialization, *World Develop.*, 20 (2), 165–186, 1992.

Lall, S., *Learning from the Asian Tigers*, Macmillan, London, 1996.

Lall, S., *Competitiveness, Technology and Skills*, Edward Elgar, Cheltenham, 2001.

Lall, S., Roberts on infant industry protection: another comment, in Symposium on Infant Industries, Wood, A., Ed., *Oxford Develop. Stud.*, 31 (1), 14–17, 2003.

Lall, S. and Albaladejo, M., *China's Export Surge: The Competitive Implications for Southeast Asia*, Queen Elizabeth House, report for the World Bank East Asia Department, Oxford, 2003.

Lall, S. and Pietrobelli, C., *Failing to Compete: Technology Development and Technology Systems in Africa*, Edward Elgar, Cheltenham, 2002.

Lall, S. and Teubal, M., "Market stimulating" technology policies in developing countries: a framework with examples from East Asia, *World Develop.*, 26 (8), 1369–1385, 1998.

Mathews, J.A. and Cho, D.S., *Tiger Technology: The Creation of a Semiconductor Industry in East Asia*, Cambridge University Press, Cambridge, 1999.

Nelson, R.R. and Winter, S.J., *An Evolutionary Theory of Economic Change*, Harvard University Press, Cambridge, MA, 1982.

Reinert, E., Competitiveness and its predecessors: a 500-year cross-national perspective, *Struct. Change Econ. Dyn.*, 6, 23–42, 1995.

Stiglitz, J.E., Some lessons from the East Asian miracle, *The World Bank Res. Obser.*, 11 (2), 151–177, 1996.

UNCTAD, *World Investment Report 2002*, United Nations, Geneva, 2002.

UNCTAD, *World Investment Report 2003*, United Nations, Geneva, 2003.

UNIDO, *Industrial Development Report 2002/2003*, United Nations, Vienna, 2002.

Wade, R., Reply to John Roberts on infant industry protection, in Symposium on infant industries, Wood, A., Ed., *Oxford Develop. Stud.*, 31 (1), 8–14, 2003.

Wade, R.H., *Governing the Market*, Princeton University Press, Princeton, 1990.

Westphal, L., Technology strategies for economic development in a fast changing global economy, *Econ. Innovation New Technol.*, 11, 275–320, 2002.

Wong, P.-K., From using to creating technology, in *Competitiveness, FDI and Technological Activity in East Asia*, Lall, S. and Urata, S., Eds., Edward Elgar, Cheltenham, 2003, pp. 191–238.

Wood, A., Ed., Symposium on infant industries, *Oxford Develop. Stud.*, 31(1), 3–20, 2003.

World Bank, *The East Asian Miracle*, Oxford University Press, Oxford, 1993.

Chapter 40

Agriculture and Economic Development: A Review of Policies and Issues in Developing Asia

Akhtar Hossain

CONTENTS

I. Introduction

> Most of the people in the world are poor, so if we knew the economics of being poor we would know much of the economics that really matters. Most of the world's poor people earn their living from agriculture, so if we knew the economics of agriculture we would know much of the economics of being poor. Schultz (1993: 13)

> Economic improvement may call for greater industrialization, but this should be a natural growth, appropriately facilitated by government but not maintained under hothouse conditions. In many countries, the most promising field for rapid economic development lies in agriculture ... There are no inherent advantages of manufacturing over agriculture, or, for that matter, of agriculture over manufacturing ... The choice between expansion of agriculture and expansion of manufactures can for the most part best be left to the free decisions of capitalists, entrepreneurs, and workers. Viner (1953: 53)

Most developing economies in Asia are agricultural. Although there has been a significant economic transformation in Asia since the 1950s, agriculture remains an important, if not the dominant, sector in terms of its contribution to output or employment or both. For example, in six large Asian countries (Bangladesh, India, Indonesia, Pakistan, Philippines, and Vietnam), the average share of agriculture in GDP during 2001 was about 22%. The share of agriculture in employment in these countries was much higher, somewhere in the range of 40–50%. In contrast, in some large and populous Asian countries, such as China, South Korea, Malaysia, and Thailand, the share of agriculture in GDP has declined sharply to about 10%. The share of agriculture in employment, especially in China and Thailand, however, remains at a much higher level. However, in most low-income countries in Asia, such as Cambodia, Lao PDR, Myanmar, and Nepal, agriculture remains the predominant sector in terms of its contribution to both GDP and employment. Thus, despite having different social structures, resource endowments, and levels of development, Asian developing countries in general have undergone a significant structural transformation since the 1960s. In the most successful economies of Asia, the phenomenon of economic transformation has indeed been consistent with the established pattern that, as an economy develops, the share of agriculture in both GDP and employment declines.[1]

One key issue in development economics is concerned with the role of agriculture. Unfortunately, as a historical legacy, agriculture's role in economic development remains unappreciated and somewhat misunderstood. The origin of the ambivalent attitude of the *elite* toward agriculture as a growth-promoting sector can be traced to classical economics. Having observed the British agriculture dominated by *landed-gentry* and the fact that agriculture faces strong diminishing returns, David Hume, Adam Smith, and David Ricardo had the view of agriculture as an unprogressive sector in comparison to manufacturing.[2] This attitude of classical economists toward agriculture perpetuated in different forms and influenced many economists and policymakers until the mid-20th century. The structuralist views of Prebisch (1950) about the declining international terms-of-trade for agricultural products and the importance Hirschman (1958) attached to linkages to industrial activities further diminished the rationale for agricultural investment. The Russian economist Preobrazhensky (1965) went one step further and argued for turning the internal terms-of-trade against agriculture to achieve capital accumulation by the state. The urban elites of the newly independent developing countries of Asia, who had little experience of farming and were contemptuous of the rural folk, shared the prevailing intellectual view that agriculture is a reservoir of resources and that industrialization, meaning economic development, requires the exploitation of agriculture in a static sense (Timmer, 1988, 2001).

Accordingly, the two methods suggested for transferring resources from agriculture to the industrial sector were imposition of heavy taxes (direct and indirect) and turning the internal terms-of-trade against agriculture (Kaldor, 1965; Wald, 1965; Meier, 1970). The Japanese agricultural taxation during the Meiji period (1868–1911) was interpreted as a case example of agricultural taxation-led economic development. Likewise, the former Soviet Union was considered the classic example of how agriculture could be exploited for industrialization through turning the internal terms-of-trade against agriculture. In fact the Soviet strategy of development via forced industrialization caught the imagination of most developing countries of Africa and Asia and it was all intents and purposes a squeeze on agriculture in a static sense. The 1950s and early 1960s were therefore the periods when most developing countries of Asia used policy instruments to squeeze agriculture for industrial growth (Koo, 1968; Dorner, 1969; Lee, 1971; Reynolds, 1977; Moon, 1991; World Bank, 1992; Hossain and Rashid, 1996; Buch-Hansen, 2000).

The economic rationale for squeezing agriculture did not last long. By the mid-1960s, some prominent economists forcefully argued against the view that agriculture is a reservoir of resources waiting for exploitation. They viewed agriculture as a resource-generating sector and that industrial development should be preceded or at least accompanied by agricultural development (Southworth and Johnston, 1967; Hayami and Ruttan, 1985; Mellor, 1991). Lewis (1954: 133) put this in precise form in his classic model of economic development:

> Now if the capitalist sector produces no food, its expansion increases the demand for food, raises the price of food in terms of capitalist products, and so reduces profits. This is one of the senses in which industrialization is dependent upon agricultural improvement; it is not profitable to produce a growing volume of manufactures unless agricultural production is growing simultaneously. This is also why industrial and agrarian revolutions *always* go together, and why economies in which agriculture is stagnant do not show industrial development.

Historically, as Nurkse (1953) pointed out, the industrial revolution in England was preceded by agricultural revolution. The effective blow to the orthodox view that farmers are unprogressive and unresponsive to incentives came somewhat later from Schultz. He helped to establish the modern view that peasants are poor but efficient. And they respond to incentives because, like the rich people, they are concerned about improving their lot and that of their children (Schultz 1964, 1993). Farmers are therefore agents of economic growth and agriculture should be treated as the integral part of an economic system. In the same spirit and a broader sense, Kuznets (1961) and Johnston and Mellor (1961) identified specific channels through which agriculture can contribute to economic growth: a product contribution by providing food and raw materials; a factor contribution by supplying labor; an investment contribution by generating savings and providing taxes to the government; a market contribution by stimulating domestic demand; and a foreign exchange contribution by raising agricultural exports. They cited historical evidence on agriculture-led economic development in Europe, Japan, and the United States, where a dynamic agriculture accompanied — and in some instances led — industrialization and growth.

Economic development in the modern sense entails a long-term structural transformation of the economy in which agriculture plays an important part, although it destroys its own existence in the process[3] (Johnston, 1970; Syrquin, 1988; Timmer, 1988). Looking from a general equilibrium perspective, agricultural policy encompasses a wide range of macroeconomic and microeconomic policy measures and strategies that cross the boundaries of fiscal, monetary, exchange rate, and commercial policies. Moreover, sustainable agriculture incorporates technological and environmental issues and policies. Given the limited scope, this chapter does not cover all policies and issues in agriculture. Instead, it describes the importance of agriculture in development and provides an overview of selected agricultural policies and issues in developing Asia and draws policy lessons that may help to develop institutions and programs for agriculture-led/supported sustainable development. Contemporary development literature indeed emphasizes the importance of balanced development in which agriculture not only contributes significantly to the overall economic growth but also promotes equitable distribution of income and reduces rural poverty. In a broad sense, raising economic well being of the rural poor leads to an increase in human capital via quality education and healthcare services. In the end, this may raise social and political consciousness of the people, which could be manifested in various forms, including environmental protection and respect for human rights. As economic equity, social justice and political participation remain an integral part of good governance of a modern state, the formulation and implementation of economic policies in general and agricultural policy in particular carries an extra importance. They underwrite the long-term social and political stability in a developing country and determine the viability of its development strategy. The remaining chapter is organized as follows. Section II reports the pace and extent of agricultural transformation in developing Asia. Section III discusses the patterns of agricultural and economic growth in developing countries of Asia. Section IV reviews selected agricultural policies and issues in developing Asia. Section V draws some policy lessons and identifies current issues and challenges.

II. Agricultural Transformation in Developing Asia

Empirical studies by Clark (1940), Kuznets (1956–1967), and Chenery and Syrquin (1975, 1986) found that the process of economic growth brings structural change in output and the labor force. Modern economic growth in turn depends much on structural change in output, employment, and foreign trade.[4] Typically, the share of agriculture in both output and employment declines rapidly during the early stages of economic development. The share of manufacturing in both output and employment correspondingly rises initially but is superseded by the share of services as the economy reaches an advanced stage of development. The declining importance of agriculture in terms of its share in both output and employment remains pervasive, uniform, and universal (Timmer, 1988).

As economic growth (or industrialization) originates from both the demand and supply sides, the phenomenon of structural change in both output and the labor force can be analyzed in conjunction with changes in the structure of final and intermediate demand, changes in the composition of foreign trade, and changes in the rates of sectoral capital accumulation and technological progress. Empirical studies consistently show that with economic growth, the demand for final and intermediate products, and the composition of foreign trade, shifts towards nonagricultural products (Syrquin, 1988). The structural change in output from the supply side originates from differential rates of expansion of inputs and total factor productivity across sectors. As economy progresses, the rates of capital accumulation and total factor productivity growth in the nonagricultural sector exceed those in agriculture and bring a structural change in output.[5] Syrquin (1988) points out that even though the supply side analysis of sources of growth focuses on the growth of factor productivity, at the aggregate level productivity growth depends much on demand-induced resource shift from sectors with lower to sector with higher marginal productivity.

In general, workers attached to slow growing sectors lose out relatively to those in faster growing sectors. In most countries, sectoral productivity and wage gaps are created with economic growth in such a way that induces agricultural workers to move from the slow growing farm sector to the rapidly growing nonfarm sector.[6] Such a shift in labor manifests an efficient resource allocation through market forces and thereby raises the rate of aggregate productivity growth. However, the structural change in the labor force is a slow process and lags behind the structural change in output (Syrquin, 1988).

There has been a significant structural change in both output and the labor force in developing countries of Asia since the 1960s (see ADB, various years-a; ADB, various years-b; World Bank, various years; Wilson, 2002). As the structural change in output and the labor force has been associated with sustained economic growth (see; ADB, 1983; Chowdhury and Islam, 1993; Hossain and Rashid, 1996: 7, 16; Blarel et al., 1999: 30), especially since the early 1980s, it can be considered durable or irreversible. However, Asian developing countries remain at different stages of development, have different structural characteristics and adopted different development strategies and policies and therefore the pace of structural transformation has not been uniform across countries. In the relatively slow-growing South Asian countries (Bangladesh, India, Pakistan, and Sri Lanka), the share of agriculture in output declined at a slow pace from about 50% in the 1960s to about 20% in 2001. The share of agriculture in employment in these countries during the same period declined even at a slower pace from about 80 to 50%. Unlike these countries, the share of agriculture in both output and employment in Bhutan and Nepal remains at a much higher level.

In East and Southeast Asian countries there are sharp variations in the shares of agriculture in output and employment. There are some countries, such as China, South Korea, Malaysia, and Thailand, where the share of agriculture in output has declined to the level of about 10%. Singapore and Taiwan are two successful mature economies that do not have much output originating from agriculture. However, in low-income Southeast Asian countries, such as Cambodia, Lao PDR, and Myanmar, agriculture remains the predominant sector in terms of its contribution to both output and employment.

III. Agriculture and Economic Growth in Developing Asia

Asia has a long history of settled and organized agriculture. It has been producing both food and nonfood crops over a few thousand years with techniques developed and adapted to local traditions and customs and to soil, weather, and climatic conditions (Robinson, 1989). However, until the 1960s, agriculture in most Asian developing countries (except the rice exporting countries, such as Myanmar, Thailand, and Vietnam) was subsistence in nature. The objective of agricultural production was primarily to feed the growing population, rather than to raise their standards of living in a modern sense. The situation was precarious as most of these countries were not self-sufficient in food production, required food importation, and that had serious balance-of-payments consequences, especially for years when there were harvest failures. Therefore, for most low-income countries of Asia, there existed some form of a Malthusian balance between food production and population and food security was almost nonexistent.

Given the subsistence nature of agriculture, there was slow transformation of Asian developing economies during the 1950s and early 1960s. As indicated earlier, the nationalist leaders of newly independent countries of Asia did not consider agriculture the right candidate for leading their nations to economic prosperity. Instead, an industrial-oriented import-substituting development strategy was considered appropriate. In the absence of large agricultural investment and price incentives, there was no major technological progress and agricultural diversification. The result was that Asian peasants lived what Schultz (1993) termed a "niggardly life" in the same way as Europeans scratched out their subsistence from poor soil and lived under the Ricardian shadow before the industrial revolution. They were neither organized nor politically powerful enough to oppose those economic policies that discriminated agriculture. The resulting agricultural stagnation broke the back of the rural people in Asia, as in other developing countries of Africa and Latin America (see ADB, 1983; Chowdhury and Islam, 1993; Hossain and Rashid, 1996: 7, 16; Blarel et al., 1999: 30; Todaro and Smith, 2003: 422).

By the late 1960s most developing countries started to question the rationale behind import-substituting strategy of development, as most manufacturing industries established under heavy protection started to show signs of problems. Although it was expected that the manufacturing sector would pull the economies of the newly independent countries out of stagnation, it did not become dynamic, generate investable resources, and created much employment. It relied heavily on government subsidies and tariff protection and over time, created vested interest groups and ultimately turned into a den of corruption. Whatever social objectives were behind the import-substituting development strategy remained unrealized, as it stifled economic efficiency and growth (Balassa and Associates, 1971; Islam, 1981; Ahluwalia, 1985; Hossain and Rashid, 1996).

Some prominent economists therefore started to challenge the import-substituting strategy of development on the ground that it was based on some unsustainable assumptions, such as inelastic international demand for exports (elasticity pessimism) and the secular deterioration in the terms-of-trade of developing countries (Balassa, 1968, 1983; Bhagwati and Srinivasan, 1975). While they generally advocated for an outward-oriented development strategy, agriculture was assigned an important role for both economic and socio-political grounds. By then it became obvious that the poverty situation in developing Asia aggravated due to policies that promoted capital-intensive industrialization and discriminated against agriculture,[7] both of which slowed economic growth and raised income inequality (Bhagwati, 1984, 1988). Lipton (1977) showed that there was indeed an urban-bias in the development strategies of developing countries. There was urgency for poverty alleviation and this called for a major change in development strategy in favor of agricultural and rural development and that required a sharp increase in investment in the rural areas (Chenery et al., 1974).

By late 1960s most East and Southeast Asian countries effectively broke away from import-substituting industrialization strategy and during the next decade or so made a phenomenal economic progress under an export-oriented strategy of development (World Bank, 1993). In some of these countries agriculture came under pressure and was accorded adequate protection with the objective of maintaining equity, social harmony, and food security (Anderson, 1983; Anderson and Hayami, 1986). In South Asia, there was no major shift in development strategy but it took a modified form that aimed at achieving food self-sufficiency without an abandonment of the import-substituting industrialization strategy (Hossain and Rashid, 1996). The public appreciated the idea of food self-sufficiency because the fear of famine perpetuated as an age-old phenomenon. There was also an element of economic nationalism hidden inside the idea of food self-sufficiency on the ground of national security (Gillis et al., 1992). One practical way of achieving food self-sufficiency was the introduction of the seed–fertilizer–irrigation technology in agriculture. This technology was available by the mid-1960s. Compared with the traditional agriculture, it substantially raised the yields of rice and wheat. However, as there were various risks involved, the rate of adoption of the technology was slow at the early stage. This induced the governments of South Asian countries to provide subsidies on fertilizers, seeds, irrigation, and pesticides.

Table 40.1 shows that agricultural growth rate in most Asian developing countries was impressive during the 1970s given the background of agricultural stagnation during the 1950s and early 1960s. This turnaround of agricultural performance was remarkable given that it was achieved despite

Table 40.1 Economic versus Agricultural Growth in Developing Countries of Asia: 1971–1982*

Region/ Country	Economic Growth: 1971–1982	Agricultural Growth: 1971–1981	Food Production: 1971–1981	Cereal Production: 1971–1981	Irrigated to Arable Land	Agricultural Exports to Agricultural GDP
	Average Annual Growth Rate (%)				Ratio (%)	Ratio (%)
South Asia						
Bangladesh	5.7[a]	2.9	3.0	3.4	11.8	3.0
India	2.7[b]	2.9	3.1	2.8	19.4	3.4
Nepal	2.7	1.2	1.3	0.9	5.9	3.5
Pakistan	4.1	3.2	3.7	4.6	67.9	13.8
Sri Lanka	5.5[b]	3.8	6.0	3.8	49.1	60.6
Southeast Asia						
Indonesia	7.6	3.7	3.8	5.2	34.6	14.7
Malaysia	7.5	4.7	5.9	2.6	27.5	67.8
Myanmar	4.5[b]	3.4	3.4	6.0	8.6	8.7
Philippines	5.7	4.9	4.9	4.6	12.1	22.8
Thailand	6.7	6.0	6.4	4.6	16.9	39.2

Note: *Refers to available data nearest to the reference period. [a]1972–1982; [b]1971–1981.
Source: Author's compilation based on Vyas (1983: 28, 31) and ADB (various years-b).

unfavorable domestic and international conditions. Agriculture made a substantial contribution to overall economic growth. Its satisfactory performance also had a number of favorable consequences. First, traditional food surplus countries, such as Myanmar and Thailand, increased their food surpluses, while the food deficit countries, such as Bangladesh, India, and Sri Lanka, reduced their dependence on food imports. Second, there were increases in the production of agricultural raw materials and export crops, such as cotton, jute, sugarcane, and coconut. The improved supply situation of food grains and export crops allowed the food-deficit countries to pay more attention to other agricultural subsectors, such as fisheries, forestry, and livestock. Finally, the reduction of food imports and the increase in agricultural commodity exports imply that the agricultural sector made a positive contribution to the improvement of the balance-of-payments situation (ADB, various years-a; Vyas, 1983).

The agricultural growth momentum that was built in the 1970s in response to relatively agriculture-friendly policies as part of various IMF–World Bank supported structural adjustment and reform programs improved overall macroeconomic performance in Asian developing countries during the 1980s and 1990s. As Table 40.2 shows, agriculture's contribution to economic growth in most Asian countries throughout this period was significantly high.[8] In South and Southeast Asian countries, agricultural output grew at an average annual rate of about 2.5% since the early 1980s. Agricultural performance in some populous countries of Asia over the past 5 years was indeed impressive. This reflects an emerging consensus for a balanced development strategy that puts an emphasis on both agriculture and manufacturing within an open economy set-up. This has been a significant strategic policy decision that was influenced by two recent factors. First, the Asian currency crisis in the late 1990s raised the incidence of poverty in affected countries and shifted their policy emphasis on poverty alleviation through a broad-based development strategy that favors the poor. Second, under the IMF–World Bank supported *Poverty Reduction and Growth Facility* programs, most low-income Asian developing countries have undertaken economic reforms and reoriented their development strategies for poverty alleviation and social development through agricultural and rural development.[9]

IV. Agricultural Policies and Issues

Having found that agriculture remains an important sector for economic development, this section reviews selected agricultural policies and issues in developing Asia. In general, agricultural policies and issues are wide-ranging and can be organized under some interrelated heads, such as land

Table 40.2   Economic Growth versus Agricultural Growth in Developing Asia*

Region/ Country	Average Annual Economic Growth Rate (%)			Average Annual Agricultural Growth Rate (%)		
	1980–1990	*1990–1995*	*1997–2004*	*1980–1990*	*1990–1995*	*1997–2004*
South Asia						
Bangladesh	4.3	4.1	5.3	2.7	1.1	3.8
Bhutan	n.a.	n.a.	6.8[a]	n.a.	n.a.	3.5[a]
India	5.8	4.6	5.5	3.1	3.1	1.3
Maldives	n.a.	n.a.	5.9	n.a.	n.a.	3.7
Nepal	4.6	5.1	3.5	4.0	1.5	3.2
Pakistan	6.3	4.6	3.6	4.3	3.4	2.3
Sri Lanka	4.2	4.8	4.2	2.2	2.4	2.1
East Asia						
China	10.2	12.8	7.7	5.9	4.3	3.0
South Korea	9.4	7.2	4.7	2.0	1.3	1.1
Mongolia	5.5	−3.3	3.4	2.9	n.a.	−5.2[a]
Taipei, China	n.a.	n.a.	3.9	n.a.	n.a.	−0.2
Southeast Asia						
Cambodia	n.a.	6.4	5.3	n.a.	2.1	2.2
Indonesia	6.1	7.6	1.5	3.4	2.9	1.6
Lao PDR	n.a.	6.5	5.8	n.a.	n.a.	4.9
Malaysia	5.2	8.7	3.5	3.8	2.6	0.4
Myanmar	n.a.	n.a.	9.4[b]	n.a.	n.a.	7.7[c]
Philippines	1.0	2.3	3.6	1.0	1.6	2.5
Singapore	6.4	8.7	3.8	−6.2	0.5	−3.0
Thailand	7.6	8.4	1.8	4.0	3.1	2.1
Vietnam	n.a.	8.3	6.2	n.a.	5.2	3.4

Note: *Refers to available data nearest to the reference year; n.a. denotes that data are not available; [a]1997–2002; [b]1997–2001; [c]1997–2000.
Source: ADB (various years-a); World Bank (various years).

ownership and land reform, the seed–fertilizer–irrigation technology, taxation, wages and employment, pricing and subsidies, and multifunctionality and agricultural trade. Some long-standing agriculture issues are structural and developmental and debated along political lines. There are other regional and country-specific issues, including those related to international trade and environment that have arisen lately with globalization. Given that Asian developing countries are at different stages of development and have significant structural differences in resource endowments, socio-cultural practices and economic openness, the review undertaken here is less rigorous and databased than is warranted for sake of completeness.

A. Land Ownership and Land Reform

One common characteristic of developing countries is the prevalence of moderate to extreme inequality of land ownership. There are complex historical, political, and economic reasons behind the evolution of land ownership distribution in developing countries in favor of a relatively small number of households. Ray (1998: 445) remarks that "Why the ownership of land is distributed as it is ultimately is a historical question?" The situation, however, varies from region-to-region and from country-to-country. This is revealed in the summary data of Table 40.3 for selected countries of Asia and Latin America. The Gini coefficient measure for land-ownership distribution suggests a moderate degree of inequality of land distribution in Asia in comparison with that of Latin America. However, the average farm size in Asia is much smaller than that in Latin America. In two populous countries of Asia (Bangladesh and Indonesia) the average farm size is just about 1 ha. The corresponding figure for Brazil is about 60 ha.

Table 40.3 Farm Size and Land Tenure in Selected Developing Countries in Asia and Latin America

Country/ Region	Year of Survey	Average Operational Farm Size (ha)	Gini Coefficient of Land Concentration	Percentage of Tenanted Area in Total Farmland	
				Pure Tenancy	Total*
Asia					
Bangladesh	1976–1977	1.6	0.42	n.a.	20.9
India	1970–1971	2.3	0.62	2.4	8.5
Indonesia	1973	1.1	0.56	2.1	23.6
Nepal	1971–1972	1.0	0.56	1.5	13.2
Philippines	1971	3.6	0.51	21.4	32.8
Thailand	1978	3.7	0.45	6.0	15.5
Latin America					
Brazil					
Costa Rica	1970	59.7	0.84	6.1	10.2
Colombia	1973	38.1	0.82	1.2	9.0
Peru	1970–1971	26.3	0.86	5.3	11.5
Uruguay	1970–1971	16.9	0.91	4.5	13.6
Venezuela	1970	214.1	0.82	19.1	46.3
	1971	91.9	0.91	4.5	2.4

Note: *Area in pure tenant farms plus area in owner cum tenant farms.
Source: Otsuka et al. *J. Econ. Lit.*, 30, 1965–2018, 1992.

Given such landownership distribution, the institution of sharecropping is widespread in both Asia and Latin America. Under sharecropping a tenant farmer uses a landlord's farmland in exchange for a predetermined share of output produced in the land. In general, this share varies from one third to two thirds of output produced, depending on many factors including whether the landlord shares costs of seeds, fertilizer, and credits. The factors that are used to explain the presence of sharecropping in developing countries are the general risk aversion of peasant farmers and the prevalence of absentee landlordism that practically separates cultivators from landowners. The high incidence of rural poverty and the lack of alternative employment opportunities force landless farmers to engage in farming under sharecropping arrangements. Sharecropping is generally considered an inefficient institution (Stiglitz, 1988). However, its long survival is considered a proof that it serves the interests of both landlords and tenants (Rashid and Quibria, 1995)

Inequality of land ownership is not an innocuous issue, rather it has given rise to a set of economic, administrative, and political questions (Ray, 1998; Rashid and Quibria, 1995): (i) Is unequal distribution of land compatible with productive efficiency? (ii) If there is an efficiency loss, can it be restored through land rental markets? (iii) If land rental markets are not adequate to restore efficiency, would land sales from rich to poor spontaneously redress the balance? (iv) If neither land rental markets nor sales markets are sufficient, what would be the role of land reform? and (v) If land reform is desirable, how could it be implemented without production loss given that the socio-political and administrative structure remains inegalitarian and is sympathetic towards large landowners? In the context of developing Asia the debate is whether or not the existing land tenure system is a constraint on agricultural modernization. The debate is also about the question of equity and social justice in traditional societies.

In the debate the term land reform is used in two broad senses — land redistribution in favor of landless and near-landless farm households and tenancy reforms in favor of sharecroppers or other tenants. Having seen the successful land reforms in South Korea and Taiwan in the late 1940s and early 1950s, there is a body of literature that suggests the need of radical land reform for agricultural modernization and poverty alleviation.[10]

Two economic arguments are given for redistributive land reform. First, land productivity on small farms is higher than that on large farms. Second, small farms employ more labor per unit of land than large farms. Small farms are therefore considered appropriate for both increasing agricultural production and reducing rural unemployment.

There are also economic arguments for tenancy reforms. The economic case against share tenancy is based on the Marshallian argument that it is inefficient in both the static and dynamic sense. It is inefficient in the static sense because, given the production technology, output produced under share tenancy is lower than that under owner cultivation. It is inefficient in the dynamic sense because it may inhibit investment and technological progress (Taslim, 1995).

It was Sen's (1964) study, which used the Indian farm management data, that started the debate on the size–productivity relation in agriculture. He found that output per acre is inversely related to the farm size. In later studies for India and other developing countries, his finding was vindicated. A number of plausible explanations were given why the small farms are more efficient than the large farms. First, the land of small farms is more fertile than that of large farms. It follows from the observation that, when in economic distress, the poor farmers sell inferior-quality land to the large landowners and this lowers the average productivity of land as the farm size increases. Second, the small farms are more productive because they use labor intensively and more efficiently than the large farms. Large farmers usually use hired labor and employ it according to the principle of profit maximization, that is, employment is determined at the level where the marginal productivity of labor equals the real wage rate. In contrast, the small farms use family labor up to the point where the marginal productivity of labor is zero or close to zero. Third, supervision of hired labor is a consideration for economizing labor by large farmers. Hired labor has a tendency to shirk and does not deliver full effort, unless it is supervised. The severity of the supervision problem increases with the increase in the amount of hired labor (Taslim, 1995). Unlike the large farm households, the small farm households do not face the supervision problem because the latter work under the pressure of what may be called "survival algorithm."

Unlike the case of static inefficiency, there are no convincing reasons for dynamic inefficiency of large farms. Available evidence from South Asia does not point to dynamic inefficiency of large farms. For instance, both small and large farms in South Asia have adopted the seed–fertilizer–irrigation technology and there is no systematic difference in the rate of adoption by farm size. There are areas where the small farms adopted the technology more rapidly than the large farms and there were cases where the large farms adopted the technology more rapidly than the small farms (Asaduzzaman, 1979; Hayami and Ruttan, 1984; Hossain, 1988). For Bangladesh, Hossain et al. (1994: 122) find that "the dominance of small farms and the widespread practice of tenancy do not impede technological progress in agriculture." There has also been rapid adoption of the new agricultural technology in the small farms of Indonesia. In fact, since the 1950s the Indonesian government encouraged intensive production by providing direct incentives, such as subsidies for fertilizer, pesticides, irrigation and credit, and indirectly by supporting the provision of research and extension services. During its rapid growth phase beginning from the late 1960s to the late 1990s agricultural growth rate was about 3.5% per annum. Agriculture thus played an important role in the country's economic success (Suryana and Erwidodo, 1996).

The argument that share tenancy is inefficient is based on the theoretical rationale that a tenant does not have an incentive to work as hard when he receives only a fraction of increased output as he would do when he receives the whole amount. A landlord cannot remove this incentive problem for tenants by stipulating the efficient level of labor-intensity and then observing and monitoring the tenant's effort. In reality, there are at least two solutions for the incentive problem — cost-sharing and offering a short lease. Both these practices exist in Asian agriculture. Given the relatively high incidence of poverty in developing countries of Asia, the landowners remain in a dominant position and they do not compromise on anything that may dilute their ownership of land.[11] Therefore, strategically, they dictate the length of land lease. In general, the length of lease does not exceed one crop or more than 1 yr, although it is renewed for the next crop or year. This type of rolling of the lease keeps tenants on their toes and acts as a disciplinary measure that keeps the tenants under the landowners' effective control.[12]

Is share tenancy dynamically inefficient? Bhaduri (1973) developed a model where he argued that landlords who provide credits to tenants do not wish them to adopt technological innovations because a richer tenant would break free from the bonds of indebtedness. This argument is weak, at least empirically (Feder et al., 1985). Tenants do not necessarily borrow from landlords[13] and not many tenants are dependent on landlords. In addition, many tenants are not so weak as portrayed.

In essence, share tenancy is not as inefficient as it is perceived. The longevity of share tenancy is considered a valid evidence of its efficiency and fairness (Bliss and Stern, 1992; Rashid and Quibria, 1995). This implies that the existing land tenure system may not be a major constraint on agricultural modernization.

What about the prospect of redistributive land reform in developing Asia? It is widely acknowledged that there were wide ranging benefits from land reform in South Korea and Taiwan. For example, the small farmers were generally better off from land reform in these countries. Later they played a key role in promoting agricultural research and technology, introducing modern inputs and provisioning extension services (Fei et al., 1979; Ray, 1998). Nevertheless, there remain uncertainties that other countries would generate similar benefits from any redistributive land reform. After all, the conditions that prevailed in South Korea and Taiwan immediately after World War II were different from those currently exist in most developing countries of Asia. Islam (1974) argues that under certain circumstances, a redistributive land reform may even lead to a fall in output.[14] Similar concern has also been expressed by Todaro and Smith (2003), who suggest that land reform could be ineffective and perhaps counterproductive unless there are corresponding changes in rural institutions that control production (banks, money lenders, seed, and fertilizer distributors), in supporting government aid services (technical and educational extension services, public credit agencies, storage and marketing facilities, rural transport and feeder roads), and in government pricing policies with regard to both inputs (removing factor-price distortions) and outputs (paying market-value prices to farmers).

At a practical level, there is general concern that a redistributive land reform would not be feasible in most Asian countries on both administrative and political ground. Land reform efforts undertaken so far in Asia have failed because the governments bowed to political pressure from landowning interests (including legislators). Land reforms undertaken in Japan, South Korea, and Taiwan were the product of political upheavals. Political upheavals have the advantage that large landowners are often viewed as enemies or collaborators with the previous regime and so there is popular support for land reform. For developing countries of Asia, which are otherwise politically and socially stable, it would require tremendous political will to implement a redistributive land reform program. It is doubtful that when most East and Southeast Asian countries have moved to middle-income levels without much change in their land ownership structure, they or even-low income countries in this region would take the risk of undertaking programs that may lead to economic, social, and political chaos and disruption. Therefore, instead of raising expectations of the rural poor, the governments of developing countries in Asia should better aim at raising economic growth as an effective solution to poverty and inequity (Rashid and Quibria, 1995). Stiglitz (1988: 124) notes that even a redistributive land reform may not necessarily lead to a durable egalitarian land ownership system.

> A land reform, which redistributed the land which each tenant worked to the tenant, would, unless the supply curve of labor is backward bending, cause output to increase. Of course, even after a land reform, as time evolves some farmers will work harder, be smarter, or be luckier, and accumulate wealth, purchasing land from those who do less well. Inequality of land ownership — and sharecropping — might re-emerge. Policies, which attempt to limit land ownership, are not only often of limited effectiveness, but they weaken the incentives for exerting effort and for saving.

B. The Seed–Fertilizer–Irrigation Technology

Despite the adoption of the seed–fertilizer–irrigation technology since the early 1970s, agriculture in most Asian developing countries remains traditional at the core. Land, labor (family or hired), and traditional capital are the key factors of production. Most farm households own basic farming tools and inputs required for cultivation. Under the traditional technology, land is the scarcest factor and the binding constraint on agricultural production and employment. Traditional capital consists mainly of ploughs, shovels, bullocks, and homemade irrigation implements. In farms where the seed–fertilizer–irrigation technology has been adopted, modern inputs, such as high-yielding seeds, chemical fertilizers, irrigation, and insecticides, complement the traditional inputs of production. However the use of chemical fertilizer is not restricted to farms, which have adopted the irrigation technology. Chemical fertilizers are also used in the production of crops under the traditional technology. The intensity of fertilizer use, however, varies from region-to-region and from country-to-country depending on the stages of adoption of the technology and the level of development of the country. The use of modern tractors has been very limited in most Asian developing countries. South Korea and Japan are the only two users of modern tractors in this region (World Bank, 2004).

Note that in traditional agriculture, the uses of land, labor, and capital are well-defined, in the sense that they are used more or less in fixed proportions and that there is not much scope for factor substitution among primary inputs. As Sen (1960) points out, there are certain primitive capital items like shovels, bullocks, and ploughs without which there cannot be agricultural production. In traditional agriculture, land, labor, and capital can therefore be considered complementary inputs and given that land and capital are limited in supply, employment cannot be increased beyond a certain limit, unless there is such a technological change that augments land and capital in efficiency units. Technological change can alter factor proportions and create scope for factor substitution.

One controversial issue in Asian agriculture is whether the adoption of the seed–fertilizer–irrigation technology (or simply the new technology) increases the inequality of income and the incidence of absolute poverty. Economists participating in the debate are polarized into two camps (Chambers, 1984). The protagonists of the new technology emphasize that it can dynamically redistribute income through agricultural growth and may alleviate poverty on a sustained basis. In land scarce countries in Asia, the new technology is appropriate because it is land-augmenting and labor-using. The new technology is labor-using because it requires intense cultivation practices at all stages of the production process and most agricultural operations can be performed by labor without much application of mechanical power. The yield effect of the new technology could be substantial, especially during the early stages of adoption of the technology (World Bank, 1991; James et al., 1987).

Both the rich and poor farmers gain from the new technology in agriculture. The poor gain from the technology through the workings of both the product and labor markets (Hossain, 1988). Nevertheless, the consequences of the new technology that have received prominence in the literature are the proletarianization of the peasantry and the consequent rise in the number and proportion of landless farm households, a growing concentration of land and assets in fewer hands, a widening disparity between the rich and poor households and a rise in the incidence of absolute poverty. The suggested reasons for any adverse effects of the new technology on poverty and income inequality are the faster rate of adoption by large compared with small farms or by owners compared with tenants, a labor-saving bias in the technology that reduces labor's income share, the nonadaptability of technological innovations to all geographic areas, the availability of public services to large farmers but not to small, and incentives for landlords or wealthy farmers to consolidate small holdings into larger units through eviction of tenants and the buying out of small and marginal holdings (Falcon, 1970; Griffin, 1974; Pears, 1980; Staub and Blasé, 1974).

Most of such criticisms of the new technology, however, are not valid empirically. Hayami and Ruttan (1984) strongly oppose the view that the new technology is biased against the poor, although they admit that there were some cases where small farmers lagged behind large farmers in the adoption of the new technology. This was due to institutional rather than technical bias. Any adverse effect of the new technology on income distribution may therefore be a consequence of institutional factors rather than the technology itself. Even when the new technology increases the degree of income inequality, it may be tolerable in a society where the poor gain in absolute terms and expect to gain in the future (Sundrum, 1983). The significance of this technology has indeed been far reaching. Hayami and Ruttan (1984) pointed out that, if there had been no biological–chemical technology in agriculture, most developing countries, especially those in Asia, might have moved several steps closer to the Ricardian trap of economic stagnation and there might have also been greater stress on the distribution of income.

One important feature of the new technology is that it has been easily adaptable to small-scale farming in Asia without a major change in the agrarian structure. It also fits well with a market-oriented development strategy that emphasizes agricultural growth and the redistribution of income through growth. Such a development strategy is appropriate for Asian developing countries because it can benefit the poor without seriously hurting the interests of rich. There are also other benefits from the adoption of this technology. Any major technical change in agriculture, by creating dynamic economic and social forces, can induce changes in social institutions and create social consciousness. The poor may then be able to remove the yoke of the rural power structure, which is repressive and degrading to them. Critics of the new technology often fail to take account of such non-economic benefits associated with the new technology. The alternative to the new technology is sheer economic and social stagnation and that would mean the confinement of the poor in the rural areas to poverty and hopelessness. Within the traditional economic and social system, the richer section of the community continues to dominate the rural power structure and institutions and thereby exploit the poor.

On the whole, whatever may be the complexion of the debate, the controversy over the question of whether the new technology is a contributor to poverty and income inequality is more a political issue than an economic issue. The debate is political in the sense that the new technology, by raising income and employment of the poor, has reduced the pressure on policymakers for structural and institutional change, such as land reform, that may benefit the poor more. There is, however, one economic question that needs to be addressed. As the new technology helps the poor through market mechanisms (both labor and product markets), whether farm workers benefit from any increase in demand for farm products depend largely on the nature of labor markets in developing countries. This issue is taken-up next.

C. Agricultural Wages and Employment

Rural unemployment remains a major problem for some Asian developing countries, especially in South Asia. Although there are difficulties in measuring unemployment in family-oriented farming, the bulk of rural unemployment is seasonal in nature. Underemployment is also prevalent among family workers. Therefore, one desirable property of any development strategy in Asia should be the reduction of rural poverty through income generation via paid employment. The beneficial trickle-down effect from growth would work better if both employment and real wages respond positively with the rise in demand for labor. That is, the issue is whether the supply curve of labor is upward-sloping in apparently overpopulated Asian developing countries.

In the traditional theories of agricultural wage determination, it is assumed that there is an excess supply of labor in the rural areas of developing countries and that the supply curve of labor is perfectly elastic at a subsistence wage level. This is at odds with the fact that agricultural real wages are not fixed and that they fluctuate widely and have an upward trend in most developing countries. In a developing country like India, the agricultural labor supply curve has been found positively sloped rather than perfectly elastic at a subsistence wage level.[15]

The recent literature on rural labor markets suggests that there exists a large army of unemployed in developing countries is an exaggeration. To understand why, a distinction needs to be made between the voluntarily and the involuntarily unemployed, and between wage laborers and family laborers. There is also a need to analyze the supply behavior of each category of laborers in different agricultural seasons and at different wage rates. An involuntarily unemployed person is a person who is willing to work at the prevailing wage rate but does not get work. A voluntarily unemployed person is a person who is not seeking (wage) employment at the going wage rate, possibly for noneconomic reasons. A wage laborer is a person who hires out labor in exchange for wages (paid in cash or kind); and a family laborer is a person who works on his/her family farm and does not receive wages as remuneration but shares output with other members of the family on an egalitarian basis.

In the rural areas of Asia, wage laborers are the constant source of labor supply and the part of the labor supply that is constituted by family laborers varies significantly in different seasons depending on prevailing wage rates and the levels of farm and nonfarm activities. Wage laborers mainly come from the landless and marginal farm households. The main sources of income for the landless farmers are wage employment and earnings from nonfarm activities, such as fishing, weaving, petty business, boatcraft, and housecrafts. As nonfarm activities are not in abundance and are not available in all seasons and in all places, the landless wage laborers seek employment in the farm sector throughout the year. These groups of people mostly live in poverty and are desperately in need of work for their livelihood. Therefore, when they are found unemployed, it is mainly due to lack of work; most of them cannot afford to remain unemployed voluntarily even for a week.

The second group of wage laborers come from the marginal farm households, and they supplement their farm income by hiring themselves out. However, many potential wage laborers belonging to this group sometimes prefer to remain unemployed voluntarily for a certain period of the year if their own farms are not large enough to provide them with full employment. This is because working as a wage laborer is nonprestigious and usually degrades one's social status (Ahmed, 1981; Bliss and Stern, 1992). In his study for the Indian State of West Bengal, Bardhan (1984) found that hiring out behavior is negatively related to the size of land cultivated by the household, the level of living, and the education level of adults in the household. For the same reason, most potential family laborers in rich households refrain from manual work voluntarily at least during the off-peak season, or work far less than the normal working hours and employ themselves in nonfarm activities. Thus, in short, in a typical rural area of developing countries in Asia, a substantial number of (potential) rural workers (this number varies in different agricultural seasons) either remain voluntarily outside the actual rural labor force or work less than the normal working hours. This is one reason for agricultural labor shortage during a peak season in apparently labor surplus countries such as Bangladesh and India.

Once the different groups of farm labor are identified, it is possible to explain real wage movements in terms of the demand for and supply of labor. However, there are in fact two extreme views on wage determination in agriculture. One view is that there does not exist any rural labor market and nonmarket institutions and relations determine both wages and employment. The alternative view is that in the absence of trade unions, minimum wage laws, and any market imperfections, there exist competitive rural labor markets that determine both wages and employment. The truth is perhaps somewhere in between the two — there exists an active, but somewhat imperfect, rural labor market (Bardhan, 1980).

Within the two extreme views on wage determination, there are a number of propositions on wage determination in rural labor markets, such as the subsistence wage theory, the efficiency wage theory, and the neoclassical wage theory. The traditional subsistence and nutrition-based wage theories are, however, inadequate, although not irrelevant, for determining agricultural wages. In these theories, it is expected that at least in the long run, the real wage rate would remain more or less stable at the subsistence or efficiency level, and would not fluctuate much due to changes in labor demand and supply conditions. However, empirical studies provide consistent evidence that over time real wage rates show substantial variations and fluctuate significantly during the peak and slack seasons. These variations and fluctuations in real wage rates can be explained in terms of the demand and supply factors of labor (Ahmed, 1981; Squire, 1981; Hossain, 1995).

For India, Bardhan (1979b) developed a wage model along the line of a traditional labor-contract theory. His model is more applicable to permanent wage laborers, who enter into long-term contracts with employers. But, according to his findings, contract laborers (both formal and informal) are only a small part of the total agricultural labor force. In fact, Bardhan conceived of an imperfect rural labor market, where employers have some monopsonistic or oligopsonistic power and which they frequently exert when fixing the terms of labor contracts. He essentially reiterated the popular patron–client relationship in rural societies, which brings economic and noneconomic benefits to both parties. For Bangladesh, Cain and Majumdar (1980) found no evidence in support of monopsonistic power of landowners along the line suggested by Bardhan.

Rosenzweig (1978, 1980) and Evenson and Binswanger (1984) used the supply–demand framework to explain wage determination in India. They suggest that the variability in wage rates over time and across space is explained to a considerable degree by variations in demand for and supply of labor and that the competitive model of labor market cannot be readily rejected. Bliss and Stern (1992) observed no surplus labor in an Indian village, and this is what one would expect in a competitive labor market — neither an employer nor a worker has the power to change the wage rate or employment, whereas both these variables are determined by the market forces of demand and supply. If this interpretation is accepted, it would imply that agricultural growth through investment and technology would benefit the poor through the labor market.

Given a competitive agricultural labor market, an increase in demand for rural labor would raise both employment and real wages and this may reduce the incidence of rural poverty. This has indeed been the case for successful countries of East and Southeast Asia. The East Asian countries have demonstrated the possibility of poverty alleviation through a labor-intensive outward-oriented industrialization strategy that emphasizes agricultural development for absorption of rural surplus labor. As the demand for labor increased rapidly in the rural and urban areas of these countries, there was a sustained increase in both employment and the wage rate. However, as the wage growth was somewhat moderate due to the governments' policies to keep wage costs under control, the employment growth was substantial in both rural and urban areas. The dividends of economic growth were thus distributed equitably between workers and capitalists and this served these countries well, economically, socially, and politically (World Bank, 1993). Malaysia, South Korea, and Thailand have already experienced shortages of agricultural labor. In South Korea, the sharp rise in farm wages and costs in the 1980s and 1990s has created a strong pressure on the government, through farm organizations and elected members of the National Assembly, to restrict the importation of beef and rice and other agricultural products. South Korea's farm lobbies have now become as strong as those in Japan.

However, in most low- and middle-income countries, such as Bangladesh, Cambodia, India, Indonesia, Lao PDR, Pakistan, and Philippines, there are still considerable rural unemployment problems. To mitigate these problems, these countries should aim at raising economic growth through institutional reforms, infrastructural development, and further opening up their economies. Note that China's phenomenal economic success over the past two decades was initially fueled by institutional reforms in the rural areas, such as freeing the markets of agricultural products and decollectivization of the rural society. Rural workers in China have benefited immensely from such changes. Traditionally, rural public works programs remain one way to mitigate rural unemployment problems of low-income countries. However, by nature, these are short-term programs; there is no alternative to modernization of agriculture that would create sustained employment for the rural workers in agricultural and agro-industries, preferably export-oriented as occurred in Thailand.

D. Agricultural Taxation

For sustained economic development, agriculture has to play an important role. Agricultural economists suggest that any resource transfer from agriculture for economic transformation would require agricultural modernization in the first place, so that any adverse welfare costs to the rural community of resource transfer can be kept to a minimum level (Hayami and Ruttan, 1985; Syrquin, 1988; Timmer, 1988). However, agricultural modernization requires large investment. A capital poor country cannot mobilize adequate investable funds from outside agriculture. Being the dominant productive sector, agriculture remains the major potential source of government revenues in poor countries.

How should agriculture play a developmental role without being discriminated against or exploited in a static sense? When agriculture develops, its fiscal contribution to the government could be considerable. In any agriculture-led and supported development process, the tax system can act as a conduit through which resources may be transferred out of agriculture. What should be the appropriate form of taxation, however, depends on the structure of the economy and the type and efficiency of the existing tax administration system.

The major taxes in agriculture are export taxes, land taxes, and income taxes. Traditionally, export taxes were dominant in developing countries, while land and income taxes were modest. This reflects the ease at which export taxes were collected *vis-à-vis* land and income taxes. For example, Vietnam, currently the second largest rice exporter in Asia after Thailand, exports rice through its state food companies, which reap big profits by paying low prices to producers. In general, an overemphasis on export taxes has been counterproductive, as it created disincentives to production of exportables. On the part of government, there were also no major efforts to collect land and income taxes. Therefore, an emerging view is that developing countries should make efforts to collect taxes directly, say, as land taxes, rather than impose implicit taxes on exportables. Unlike land taxes, the collection of agricultural income taxes remains difficult in developing countries, and there is a need for modernization of agriculture before income taxes can be collected efficiently (Mellor, 1966).

Historically, land taxes were the major source of government revenues in South Asia during the Mughal and British rule (Mukherjee, 1933). This was also the case for Japan (Mellor, 1966). Because land is the major taxable asset in agriculture, fiscal economists have long recognized the suitability of land as the base of agricultural taxation. A case for land taxation can be made on the grounds of the following desirable properties. First, land taxes may be designed in such a way that productive incentives are not much affected and that they raise productivity. Land taxes may increase agricultural output by raising the supply of labor, although for this to occur, the suppliers of labor must be the owners of land (Rao, 1989). Second, land taxes are not in general shiftable.[16] As landowners themselves pay land taxes from their unearned income or rent, land taxes may not have adverse effects on agricultural production. Third, land taxes can be a substitute for agricultural income taxes. Land taxes may indeed be superior to taxes on agricultural income on both efficiency and equity grounds. Fourth, land taxes can be seen as a politically safe and viable alternative to any radical redistributive land reform when landowners are too influential to be dispossessed. Politically, incremental land taxation may avoid the confrontational, and even violent, effects of land reform while achieving the ultimate goal of redistribution of wealth in an otherwise inegalitarian society. From the viewpoint of equity and efficiency, land should therefore be viewed as the natural base for agricultural taxation (Bird, 1974a,b; Ahmad and Stern, 1989).

The main factor that explains the opposition to agricultural and land taxation in developing countries is the political power of landowners at both the apex and the base of public administration. Politicians of all persuasions, many of them often are large landowners, block all forms of land taxation. Resource mobilization from agriculture would thus require an accelerated growth in agriculture and a genuine commitment from politicians to tax agriculture in an enlightened fashion. Until then the question remains why would politicians impose taxes on agriculture when such taxes are likely to hurt them economically, socially, and politically? Politicians, just like other interest groups, are unlikely to give up their economic, social, and political interests unless they are forced to do so. But who would compel them to do so under a democratic political system where those who are in power and those who are in opposition, but aspire to be power, have common self-interests?

In addition to the lack of political commitment, there are administrative difficulties in taxing agriculture. Bird (1974a,b) suggests that land taxes, which could be designed somewhat easily, should be in the *in rem* form to be effective in raising revenues. Land taxes should also be collected and administered by local governments and preferably should be invested in the rural economy. Such a sectoral approach to taxation makes sense because the local government, say, at the village level may be able to implement and adjust land tax policies because it can acquire detailed information on the farm size and land productivity for each and every farm household within its area of jurisdiction. Knowing that land tax revenues would be spent in the rural economy, landowners may be willing to bear a higher tax burden and comply with tax obligations. The central government, by shifting the authority of tax collection to the local government and providing it the power to invest tax revenues in the rural areas, can lower the heat of land taxation in national politics.

Summing up, given the importance of agriculture in developing Asia, it should make its contribution to capital accumulation and development. Efforts should be made to identify agricultural surplus and then to mobilize it for investment, initially in the agricultural sector itself. Agricultural surplus may be created by raising the level of productivity, which does not necessarily require the adoption of capital-intensive methods of production. Any transfer of resources from a dynamic agriculture is unlikely to worsen the living standards of farmers. When agricultural and land taxes are fixed judiciously and collected efficiently, they would not reduce incentives for agricultural production. Historically, Japan mobilized large resources from agriculture for public investment. The government took away about one third of agricultural output in the form of land taxes (FAO, 1964). However, as Mellor (1966: 85) points out, this was possible in a dynamic agriculture that generated income before it was subject to heavy taxation:

> Japan represents the classic case of a low-income, high-population-density country which relied heavily on the agricultural sector for capital in its early stages of development ... As development gained momentum, the importance of agriculture's contribution declined. The substantial contribution in early stages was made at the same time that the agricultural sector itself was experiencing significant technological change and increasing production and productivity at a rapid rate.

E. Agricultural Pricing and Input Subsidies

Most governments in developing countries intervene in agricultural markets to set or influence both input and output prices. There are various cases of market failures that are sometimes used to justify agricultural intervention (Stiglitz, 1987). Food prices in particular are generally controlled in food deficit countries to achieve, often conflicting, economic, political, and social objectives (Mellor, 1978, 1988a,b; Ahmed and Mellor, 1988). The conventional wisdom behind the control of prices of food and other agricultural products and an overvalued exchange rate is to promote industrialization by keeping the costs of industrial production low. The high profit margins of industrial producers are also raised by import controls and subsidies to manufacturing exports. These policies are often considered costless to agriculture on the assumption that agricultural production does not respond to price incentives and that resource transfer from agriculture to the industrial sector originates from large farmers who produce marketable crops and livestock while small farmers produce food for their own consumption.

Unlike such simplistic assumptions, agricultural price distortions have profound effects on equity, income distribution, consumption, production, and development (Ahmed and Mellor, 1988). Low regulated food prices have universally found to lower incentives of farmers to increase food production. This creates food shortage and raises food prices in open markets. Somewhat ironically, high food prices lower food consumption of the very poor who are supposed to be benefited from regulated food prices. The situation becomes worse in countries that discriminate against the poor through a subsidized food rationing system. For example, in South Asia, the rural poor do not have protection from high food prices, although the urban residents (rich and poor alike) are generally protected through food rationing and other measures. This and the fact that the urban public employees and the military have a disproportionate political influence result in the government controlling food prices to benefit the urban constituency at the expense of farmers and the rural poor.

The effect of overvaluation of the exchange rate of domestic currency on agriculture deserves special mention because at the early stages of development agriculture is the largest source of employment in developing countries. Both an overvalued exchange rate and import controls provide industry high protection. Consequently, agriculture is discriminated against and suffers from negative protection. In general, there are a number of implications of such discrimination against agriculture. First, as the poorest people live in the rural areas and remain dependent on agriculture, any discrimination against agriculture hurts the poorest most. A neutral real exchange rate in contrast can raise rural income, reduce income inequality and raise overall economic growth. Second, a rise in the incidence of rural poverty, caused by discrimination against agriculture, can increase the rural-to-urban migration, demand for imported foodstuffs and put pressure on the balance-of-payments. Third, where agriculture is a dominant sector, a slow growth of agriculture, caused by disincentives relative other activities, may lower overall economic growth (Brown, 1977; Todaro and Smith, 2003).

In recent years, there has been an increasing support for pricing policy that favors agriculture. At least two reasons can be identified for this policy shift. First, most developing countries have given greater emphasis on poverty reduction through employment generation and the reduction of income inequality. Second, those countries, which discriminated against agriculture by suppressing agricultural prices, have experienced slower growth. Adequate price incentives to farmers are now considered necessary for rapid growth. High agricultural prices generally encourage agricultural research, use of new production techniques and inputs, on-farm investment and development of rural infrastructure. Farm prices that are not artificially depressed also reduce income disparity in part by raising rural incomes (Brown, 1977). For example, export taxes on rice that depressed food prices in Thailand and export restrictions in Vietnam affected both rural and urban poor but benefited the relatively skilled workers and capital owners (Anderson, 2002).

For the relatively advanced countries of Asia, the problem is the opposite. Like other advanced countries, South Korea, for example, provides high levels of assistance to farm producers while taxing consumers. South Korea adopted high pricing policy for rice and barley in 1968 in order to achieve self-sufficiency in food and livestock production and the related goal of greater parity between rural and urban incomes. Food self-sufficiency is considered strategically important in South Korea because it remembers the deleterious effects of food shortages under the Japanese colonial rule and later during the Korean War (Anderson, 1983; Evans, 1991).

1. Input Subsidies

Subsidies on modern inputs, especially chemical fertilizers, irrigation water, pesticides, and bank credits are a common phenomenon in developing countries. This has usually been part of the adoption of modern technology in agriculture. Subsidies are also provided to promote agricultural diversification, as it may reduce production and other risks. However, whether input subsidies are necessary for raising farm production and diversification remain a debating issue. In addition to adverse budgetary implications, they have adverse effects on rural income distribution (Alamgir and Ahmed, 1988). A strong case can indeed be made against input subsidies on the following grounds. First, subsidized inputs discriminate against small farmers because the access to subsidized inputs depends on the size and tenure of landholdings. Second, subsidized inputs instead of being optimally utilized are wasted and induce a substitution of these inputs for labor. Third, because the costs of certain inputs (for example, water and fertilizer), even without a subsidy, is a small proportion of costs of production, the removal of subsidies may not increase the cost burden of producers. Fourth, the withdrawal of input subsidies would release substantial resources that can be used for extension services, research, and infrastructural development.

2. Subsidized Bank Credits

A related policy issue that has remained unresolved is the desirability of providing subsidized bank credits to farmers. Such subsidies have a great deal of political appeal and have been provided through specialized agricultural banks in developing countries. Adams et al. (1984) have strongly criticized the provision of subsidized credits to farmers. In general, all credit subsidy programs are justified on the ground that they provide relief to small farmers. However, they always go to the relatively large farmers. This and the fact that farmers, in collusion with bank officials, have created a loan-defaulting culture in most developing countries are enough to justify termination of most, if not all, subsidized credit programs.

3. Subsidies, Pesticides, and Environmental Damage

Under the new agricultural technology, there has been a rapid increase in the use of pesticides in most Asian countries over the past two decades. A number of reasons can be identified for this increase. First, pesticide-intensive crops, vegetables, and fruits are highly value-added. As farmers have gradually switched from low value-added to high value-added crops, the use of pesticides has increased. Second, to raise crop yields, farmers have generally intensified the use of pesticides without adequate assessment of their effective costs and benefits. Third, the real prices of pesticides have fallen over the years and this has caused their increased demand. Fourth, the government policies have generally encouraged the use of pesticides and chemical fertilizers.

Although the increased use of pesticides has been helpful to raise agricultural production, the current usage of pesticides has been inefficient and also damaging to human health and natural environment. The high-dose application of pesticides generally affects consumers through chemical residues in food. Asian farmers often spray highly concentrated pesticides with little intervals between spraying rounds. Chemical residues in food therefore remain high. There is evidence on the harmful effects of pesticides on farmers' health. For example, the use of excessive pesticides has been harmful to cotton pickers in Pakistan. Similarly, the standing water in paddy farms contaminate with fertilizers and pesticides leads to dermatology problems for farmers. Such contamination kills fish. The indiscriminate spray of pesticides, especially on vegetables and fruits, badly affect consumers of fruits and vegetables. The pesticide-related environmental degradation has also been considerable. It includes the contamination of groundwater, the reduction of biodiversity and the destruction of beneficial insects, which help control pests.

Given such adverse effects on both humans and environment, one policy suggestion has been to withdraw subsidies on agricultural inputs, such as fertilizers and pesticides. Although the rates of subsidies have been falling in most developing countries as part of rationalization of fiscal policy measures, not all countries are prepared to abolish subsidies all together as they may have adverse effect on food production. Some argue that reduction of subsidies may raise input prices, lower production, and lead to higher levels of poverty. This, in turn, may lead to farming of marginal lands, worsening environmental problems (Buch-Hansen, 2000; Todaro and Smith, 2003).

F. Multifunctionality of Agriculture and Agricultural Trade

Agriculture has come a long way from not too important to so special that it deserves intervention and protection. This is an idea that has now been floated in many advanced countries and the related issues are debated under the World Trade Organization (WTO) and environmental forums. The protagonists — under the catchall phrase *multifunctionality of agriculture* — have produced various documents to support that agriculture not only produces direct products but also generates a host of positive externalities, such as food security, biological diversity and environmental conservation, beautiful rural landscape and lifestyles, and vibrant rural communities and cultural heritage. Therefore, only counting the market value of agricultural products would overlook this sector's contribution to the economy and society. Under the classic market failure argument, the government is then justified to intervene in agriculture to ensure whatever it might consider the adequate supplies of positive externalities.

However, the idea of multifunctionality of agriculture has become a contentious international issue and stifled international trade negotiations. The European Union, Norway, Japan, South Korea, Poland, and other East European countries claim that this concept is part of the nontrade concerns alluded in the Article 20 and the Preamble of the Agreement on Agriculture and must be included in topics for trade negotiations. The Cairns Group[17] and the U.S. oppose granting any independent role for multifunctionality of agriculture in the conceptual framework for the WTO negotiations. Developing countries, including those in Asia, have taken different views on the issue of multifunctionality of agriculture, depending on their status as agricultural net exporters or importers (Anderson, 2002; Diaz-Bonilla et al., 2002).

The opponents of the notion of multifunctionality of agriculture argue that showing a productive sector, in this case agriculture, has positive externalities for the rest of the society does not necessarily imply that it is special and deserves protection and encouragement beyond the level that it would attain under no intervention. Agriculture may have negative externalities as well, such as the damage that it causes to the natural environment. Moreover, subsidizing agriculture to expand its production beyond its normal level would increase its use of resources to the level that may raise the costs of production of nonagricultural products unless the resources used were idle. An induced expansion of agricultural production may therefore contract other sectors, which may have their positive externalities, and thereby create a lopsided economy.

Traditionally, Asian developing countries relied heavily on agricultural exports until the 1960s. As most of them were food importers, their agriculture was concentrated heavily on food production and some exportable cash crops. Since the 1970s, there has been a significant structural change in trade in most Asian developing countries. While the newly industrializing economies of East Asia have been the most successful, other countries have increased their exports of labor-intensive manufacturing, especially clothing, textiles, footwear, and light electronics, and also reduced food importation. This has allowed some of these countries to diversify their agricultural production and exports, which now include vegetables, fruits, fish, and dairy and forestry products. Given their relatively high-income elasticities, the potential for these exportables remains high. Much would, however, depend on their continuing trade and economic reforms and correcting of anti-agricultural policies. Opening up their own markets and the reduction of agricultural subsidies in rich countries under the ongoing WTO negotiations would create agricultural market opportunities for some net-agricultural exporters of Asia. However, low-income food-importing countries of Asia remain uncertain whether to support liberalization of agricultural trade (McCalla, 2000; Anderson, 2002).

The share of agriculture in exports has fallen in some large developing countries of Asia. This decline has been rapid in economies that have been most open and have grown fast and the least has been in India. The value of the revealed comparative advantage index is above unity for all, except Singapore. Except for India, this value has, however, declined in all countries since the late 1960s. The agricultural net export index shows that, except for Bangladesh and Pakistan, all other countries have a positive value, that is, they are net exporters of agricultural products (see Balassa, 1965; Anderson, 2002).

As far as agricultural tradability and food import financing capacity for selected countries of developing Asia are concerned, Sri Lanka, South Korea, Malaysia, Thailand, and Vietnam have relatively open agricultural trade regimes, while India and Lao PDR have been the two relatively closed economies. Thailand has the highest food import financing capacity, while Cambodia has the least. Thailand has a relatively low share of agriculture in GDP, but a large share of its agricultural products is exported.

Thailand thus appears to have a clear competitive advantage in agricultural exports and would be a major beneficiary of opening for agricultural trade. Vietnam and Sri Lanka would be other beneficiaries from opening up of agricultural trade (Wilson, 2002).

In the ongoing WTO trade negotiations, there are a large number of proposals from member countries. They are related to market access, export subsidies, domestic support programs, and sanitary and phytosanitary standards. In general, elimination of export subsidies and domestic support of export partners would raise the relative competitiveness of exporting countries. Such reforms would directly benefit the net agricultural exporters of Asia. As world prices of previously subsidized products may rise, this may hurt net agricultural importers but not in a significant way, as most of them have achieved near full-sufficiency in food production. Even countries that are food importers may have better food security if they remain open to food imports.[18]

Thus, as members of the WTO, Asian developing countries have a large stake in trade negotiations over a host of policies and issues, including price support programs, export competition rules, sanitary and phytosanitary standards, food safety rules, and the use of genetically modified organisms. To the extent recognition of nontrade concerns provides additional channels through which trade is restricted in agricultural commodities, net agricultural-exporters from developing countries would be adversely affected (Wilson, 2002)

V. Policy Lessons and Implications

Poverty remains a major problem for developing Asia. Rapid economic growth is a necessary, if not a sufficient, condition for sustained reduction of poverty. As pointed out at the outset, agriculture can make a substantive contribution not only to economic growth and poverty alleviation but also human development by raising demand for quality education and health-care services. As most of the poor people live in the rural areas, agricultural development is broadly synonymous with empowerment of the rural poor in economic, social, and political sense. In fact, any political development along a democratic path cannot be sustained for long or even be meaningful without empowering the majority, which constitutes the rural poor. Sound economic policies and strategies that promote or at least allow agriculture to grow can create a foundation for sustainable development and thereby improve governance of the state by ensuring economic equity, social justice, and political stability.

Although Asian agriculture remains exposed to natural shocks, its long-term performance has been linked to economic policies. In particular the major constraint limiting agricultural development in low-income countries has been policies that discriminated against agriculture and thereby impeded technical and institutional innovation. Therefore the factors needed for inducing agricultural transformation involve a complex mix of appropriate agricultural technology, flexible rural institutions and a market orientation that offers farmers material rewards for their physical effort in the field and the risks they face from nature and markets. A successful economic transformation in the end is also a painful process for the agricultural sector. The question is whether agricultural support programs are necessary at the expense of consumers and taxpayers in order to mitigate the suffering of the rural folk. This issue has already arisen in some successful countries of Asia, such as Japan, South Korea, and Taiwan. In this respect the experiences of advanced countries with respect to social, political, and economic stresses caused by a declining role of agriculture have lessons for latecomers (Hayami and Ruttan, 1985; Timmer, 1988).

Asian agriculture has reached at the critical juncture of development. Over the past two decades agricultural growth in most populous countries of Asia was at the steady rate of about 3% per annum. The food crops sector has performed particularly well. Myanmar, Thailand, and Vietnam have turned out to be the three large food exporters. In South Asia, Bangladesh, India, and Pakistan have achieved near food self-sufficiency. They have the potential to become regular food exporters. The seed–fertilizer–irrigation technology has played the critical role in raising food production in these countries. Fortunately, this technology became available at a time when in Asia's high population growth interacted with moderate to high economic growth and increased demand for food at a rapid rate. The drive to food self-sufficiency by most countries in Asia was appropriate, as it contributed to social and political stability and removed the age-old fear of famine and food insecurity.

However, the race between food production and population growth is not yet over. Given the shortage of farmland, the populous Asian countries have a disadvantage in food production by raising crop acreage. To meet the increasing demand for food and other crops, they have to raise farm productivity through technological innovation and adaptation. As Asian agriculture remains undiversified, domestic consumption-oriented, and prone to natural disasters, the governments have to continue supporting agriculture to modernize. It is well established that agricultural production responds to both sectoral and macroeconomic policies. Therefore, trade, exchange rate, monetary, and fiscal policies remain important for agricultural development. In general, economic policies create the environment that determines the incentive patterns for agricultural growth, diversification and sustainability.

The policies and issues reviewed in this paper lead to a number of general policy lessons for developing Asia.

- *Agriculture-led or supported growth*: There is an inherent tension between a static or short-term view of agriculture as a reservoir of resources that need to be squeezed for current investment and a dynamic or long-term view of agriculture as a sector to be invested in and encouraged for generation of future investment (Ray, 1998). There is evidence that developing countries that invested in agriculture and allowed it to grow without hindrance achieved higher and balanced growth (World Bank, 1992).
- *Bias against agriculture*: Discrimination against agriculture cannot be justified from the viewpoint of economic efficiency, equity, and growth. To achieve economic prosperity, a developing country should not discriminate against agriculture relative to other sectors. To be specific, it should not turn the domestic terms-of-trade against agriculture and impose heavy implicit taxes. Elimination of bias against agriculture would generally require the removal of controls over agricultural prices and other policies and measures, such as overvaluation of the exchange rate, for industrial protection.
- *Agricultural reforms*: For raising efficiency and growth, agricultural reform programs should reduce taxes on exportables, remove controls over imports and dismantle quotas, licenses, and state trading companies. Other reforms should be in areas of land, rural finance, marketing and transport, and communication. Agricultural reforms would give high dividends if they become part of overall economic reforms. Most Asian developing countries have undertaken various IMF–World Bank-supported agricultural reform measures with the aim of removing bias against agriculture. Although much has been achieved in the policy arena, the aim should be to consolidate the development policy framework on a firm footing that would provide agriculture a space to develop on a sustainable basis. This would lead to an efficient use of natural resources and reduce pressure on the environment.
- *Agricultural diversification*: Agriculture's contribution to both output and employment declines with development. This is one of the "iron laws" of economics. As workers start to leave agriculture, agricultural mechanization would follow and productivity may rise. Agricultural diversification becomes necessary with the rise in per capita income. With the relative decline in demand for cereals and other staples, agricultural diversification takes the form of increased production of fruits, vegetables, oilseeds, and

livestock. This leads to a diversified agriculture. This process is typical but not inevitable because exports and imports play a role in changes in production patterns (Schuh and Barghouti, 1988).

■ *Technology*: Agricultural productivity has remained relatively low in developing Asia. The seed–fertilizer–irrigation technology has been a major breakthrough and has made a contribution to agricultural development. However it has its own constraints and limitations. Lately, environmental concerns have been loud and clear. Therefore, Asian developing countries need to embark upon a technological adaptation and development path for agricultural and rural development that would give high priority to environmentally friendly technologies without sacrificing growth of production and incomes of the rural people. Such technologies do exist but may to be adapted to local conditions. The idea should be to raise productivity by combining efficiently chemical and natural inputs and resources on a sustainable basis. Promising technologies include improved land management methods, water saving and drainage technologies, recycling of animal waste and by products of agricultural industries, integrated pest management, and integrated plant nutrition management, all of which can combine agricultural growth with improved resource management (Todaro and Smith, 2003). Thai farmers have already started what they call natural farming where they do not use chemical inputs and ecologically favorable techniques, although they are yet to receive institutional support (Buch-Hansen, 2000).

■ *Institutional development*: Any large-scale adoption of environmentally sustainable farming techniques rests on a favorable institutional framework in an open-economy set up that would reduce price distortions and remove discrimination against agriculture in combination with rules and regulations for proper use of scarce resources by internalizing environmental costs. In general, while institutional reforms remain imperative for agricultural development, what form they should take place is an area of intense debate. In principle, mere transplantations of successful institutions from developed countries to less developed countries are not enough. As Lin and Nugent (1995) point out, where to start and how to bring out institutional reforms in a country are questions that can be answered only with serious considerations of the country's existing institutional structure and human and physical endowments. Institutional development is also an endogenous process that remains associated with a country's economic, social, and political development.

Notes

1. Data used in this paragraph are drawn from ADB (various years-a); ADB (various years-b), World Bank (various years) *World Development Report*; and Wilson (2002).

2. David Hume accused the farm people of having a "predisposition to indolence," while Adam Smith and David Ricardo saw agriculture as "the sinecure of an unprogressive landed aristocracy" (Schultz, 1987: 22). However, although classical economists did not consider agriculture a progressive sector, they acknowledged that agricultural stagnation could be a constraint on economic growth. In his *Principles of Political Economy and Taxation*, David Ricardo believed that the growth rate of agricultural production sets the upper limit to the growth of the nonagricultural sector and to capital formation for economic growth. Adam Smith had a similar view (Lewis, 1988).

3. The recent literature sees agriculture within a general equilibrium perspective, recognizes the importance of macroeconomic policy for agricultural performance, acknowledges the necessity (and feasibility because of the potential for technical change) of agricultural growth to deal with poverty and hunger, and emphasizes the superior performance of trade- and market-oriented systems for achieving rapid economic growth (Meier and Rauch, 2000: V1.8).

4. Abramovitz (1983), Chenery (1979), and Kuznets (1971) emphasized the interdependence between economic growth and structural change. For Kuznets, a structural change in social institutions and beliefs is required for modern economic growth.

5. This follows the classic growth accounting approach of Solow (1956).

6. Even though in the structural transformation model resources first shift from agriculture to manufacturing, they may shift from agriculture to services if the latter is the leading growing sector of the economy. Whether resources would shift from agriculture to manufacturing could depend much on the structure of manufacturing production and employment. If there are rigidities in manufacturing production and employment, the services sector may take the lead and attract resources from the agricultural sector. When both manufacturing and services grow rapidly, agricultural resources may move toward both the manufacturing and services sectors. Therefore, the sectoral growth patterns and the relative rigidities in the structures of production and employment in the manufacturing and services sectors determine the direction of labor mobility. The change in the structure of the labor force, however, is not instantaneous and generally lags behind the structural change in output (Timmer, 1988).

7. Anti-agricultural bias is reflected in the negative value of the protection indicator. This was extreme in South Asia in the prereform years beginning from the 1950s to mid-1980s. High indirect disprotection for agriculture originated from the high level of protection of manufacturing and the associated overvaluation of the exchange rate and a lesser extent of direct disprotection originated from export controls and taxes (Blarel et al., 1999).

8. The relatively poor agricultural performers, such as South Korea, Malaysia, and Singapore, have already transformed into industrial economies and lost their comparative advantage in agriculture.

9. For official documents on this topic for Asian developing countries, see both the World Bank and IMF websites available at http://www.worldbank.org and http://www.imf.org, respectively.

10. The debate has been intense in South Asia. Intellectuals, particularly in Bangladesh and the Indian state of West Bengal, recommended nothing but a radical redistributive land reform. There are historical reasons behind this. In Bengal, peasant protests against large landowners began during the British rule. Following the "Permanent Settlement" in Bengal in 1793, which created a Calcutta-based absentee landlord class, peasant protests became militant and organized and took various forms — anti-British, anti-landlord, and anti-moneylender (Chakraborty, 1992). In the process, support for land reform became an intellectual tradition. And only a reactionary could have opposed it.

11. Landowners are well aware that a long lease of land will dilute their ownership of land. Given the political rhetoric of the need for redistributive land reform, landowners, large or small, remain in fear of losing land. This explains why tenancy reform is counterproductive and leads to eviction of tenants.

12. Rashid and Quibria (1995: 134) have explained this phenomenon as follows:

> If the tenant has no long-term security of tenancy, then the tenant will work hard to keep up to the average standard. In most agrarian economies, social interactions are constant and all information is virtually public. Even if the landlord is not in a position to monitor shirking and cheating by the tenants, the neighbors of the tenant can, through *peer monitoring*, often detect dishonest behavior. The defaulter can suffer loss of reputation and any future contracts will likely be extremely difficult to obtain. Finally, in many poor economies where unemployment is widespread, tenancy is a reliable source of employment. As there is no unemployment insurance, the tenants are not likely to shirk, because it might imply the ignominious fate of being unemployed.

13. Bliss and Stern (1992) did not find evidence from an Indian village in support of the Bhaduri model.

14. This may happen for at least two reasons. First, a redistribution of land to the landless laborers, many of whom for years may not have been engaged in farming operations and have lost skill in cultivation, may lead to less efficient and careful cultivation. Second, a transfer of land to small farmers may have adverse effects on output and production, if small farmers do not have necessary access to agricultural inputs or financial resources.

15. For example, based on a large-scale employment and unemployment survey of households in West Bengal, Bardhan (1979a: 73) writes: "my evidence seems to be against the standard horizontal supply curve of labor assumed in a large part of the development literature." His estimated wage elasticity of the supply of labor is between 0.2 and 0.3 for casual farm workers and small farmers, which is certainly low compared with an infinite elasticity presumed in the horizontal supply curve of agricultural labor.

16. The idea that land tax is paid by landowners presupposes an inelastic supply of land, which is also fully employed. When land is underutilized and landowners have localized monopoly, the imposition of land tax may lower the utilization of land, reduce output and increase the rent and prices, and shift a part of tax burden to laborers and consumers. The land tax may also be shifted when custom or law regulates tenancy and land rents: any rise in land tax may provide an opportunity for landowners to raise the customary rent (Rao, 1989).

17. The Cairns Group was established in Cairns, Australia in 1986 with the objective of agricultural trade liberalization in the Uruguay Round and subsequent multilateral trade negotiations. Its membership comprises the following WTO members: Argentina, Australia, Bolivia, Brazil, Canada, Chile, Colombia, Costa Rica, Fiji, Guatemala, Indonesia, Malaysia, New Zealand, Paraguay, Philippines, South Africa, Thailand, and Uruguay (Anderson, 2002).

18. Anderson (2002: 79) explains this as follows:

> Does growth in food import dependence by developing (or other) countries represent a decline in their food security? ... the answer is not "necessarily." The level of consumption is the issue, and that critical level may be met without the food having to be produced domestically. For example, imports of food may be more affordable because of rapid domestic growth in nonfood agricultural output and/or nonagricultural production. In such cases the only reasons for concern about food security are (a) if the imported food supplies are less reliable than domestically produced food in terms of price or quantity uncertainty/variability, or (b) the benefits of economic growth are so skewed (after taking into account changes in fiscal transfers) as to make some marginal households worse off to the point of forcing them into food insecurity.

References

Abramovitz, M., Notes on international differences in productivity growth rates, in *The Political Economy of Growth*, Mueller, D.C., Ed., Yale University Press, New Haven, CT, 1983, pp. 79–89.

Adams, D.W., Graham, D.H., and Von Pischke, J.D., *Undermining Rural Development with Cheap Credit*, Westview Press, Boulder, CO, 1984.

ADB, *Asian Development Outlook*, Asian Development Bank, Manila, various years-a.

ADB, *Key Indicators of Developing Asian and Pacific Countries*, Asian Development Bank, Manila, various years-b.

Ahluwalia, I.J., *Industrial Growth in India: Stagnation Since the Mid-1960s*, Oxford University Press, New Delhi, 1985.

Ahmad, E. and Stern, N., Taxation for developing countries, in *Handbook of Development Economics*, Vol. II, Chenery, H.B. Srinivasan, T.N., Eds., Elsevier Science Publishers, Amsterdam, 1989, pp. 1005–1092.

Ahmed, I., Wage determination in Bangladesh agriculture, *Oxford Econ. Papers*, 33, 298–322, 1981.

Ahmed, R. and Mellor, J.W., Introduction: agricultural price policy — the context and the approach, in *Agricultural Price Policy for Developing Countries*, Mellor, J.W. and Ahmed, R., Eds., Johns Hopkins University Press, Baltimore, MD, 1988, pp. 1–10.

Alamgir, M. and Ahmed, S., Poverty and income distribution in Bangladesh, in *Rural Poverty in South Asia*, Srinivasan, T.N. and Bardhan, P.K., Eds., Columbia University Press, New York, NY, 1988, pp. 11–38.

Anderson, K., Growth of agricultural protection in East Asia, *Food Policy*, 4 (8), 330–336, 1983.

Anderson, K., *Agricultural Trade Liberalization: Implications for Indian Ocean Rim Countries*, Centre for International Economic Studies, University of Adelaide, Adelaide, 2002.

Anderson, K. and Hayami, Y., *The Political Economy of Agricultural Protection: East Asia in International Perspective*, Allen and Unwin, Sydney, 1986.

Asaduzzaman, M., Adoption of HYV rice in Bangladesh, *Bangladesh Dev. Stud.*, 7 (3), 23–52, 1979.

Balassa, B., Trade liberalization and "revealed" comparative advantage, *Manch. School Econ. Soc. Stud.*, 33 (2), 99–124, 1965.

Balassa, B., *Economic Growth, Trade and the Balance of Payments in Developing Countries, 1960–65*, IBRD, Washington, DC, 1968.

Balassa, B., Outward versus inward orientation once again, *World Econ.*, 6 (2), 215–218, 1983.

Balassa, B. and Associates, *The Structure of Protection in Developing Countries*, Johns Hopkins University Press, Baltimore, MD, 1971.

Bardhan, P., Labor supply functions in a poor agrarian economy, *Am. Econ. Rev.*, 69, 73–83, 1979a.

Bardhan, P., Wages and unemployment in a poor agrarian economy: a theoretical and empirical analysis, *J. Political Econ.*, 87, 479–500, 1979b.

Bardhan, P., Interlocking factor markets and agrarian development: a review of issues, *Oxford Econ. Papers*, 32 (1), 82–98, 1980.

Bardhan, P., *Land, Labor, and Rural Poverty: Essays in Development Economics*, Columbia University Press, New York, NY, 1984.

Bhaduri, A., A study in agricultural backwardness under semi-feudalism, *Econ. J.*, 83, 120–137, 1973.

Bhagwati, J.N., Development economics: what have we learned? *Asian Dev. Rev.*, 2 (1), 23–38, 1984.

Bhagwati, J.N., Poverty and public policy, *World Dev.*, 16 (5), 539–555, 1988.

Bhagwati, J.N. and Srinivasan, T.N., *Foreign Trade Regimes and Economic Development: India*, National Bureau of Economic Research, New York, 1975.

Bird, R., *Taxing Agricultural Land in Developing Countries*, Cambridge, Harvard University Press, MA, 1974a.

Bird, R., Agricultural taxation in developing countries, *Finance Dev.*, 11 (3), 35–43, 1974b.

Blarel, B., Pursell, G., and Valdes, A., *Implications of the Uruguay Round Agreement for South Asia: The Case of Agriculture*, World Bank/FAO Workshop, May 1996, World Bank, Washington, DC, 1999.

Bliss, C.J. and Stern, N.H., *PALANPUR: The Economy of an Indian Village*, Clarendon Press, Oxford, 1992.

Brown, G.T., Agricultural pricing policies and economic growth, *Finance Dev.*, 14 (4), 42–45, 1977.

Buch-Hansen, M., Is sustainable agriculture in Thailand politically feasible? 2000, Available at http://www.globasia.dk/papers/MBH(01-00)2.htm.

Cain, M. and Majumdar, A.B.M.K.A., Labor market structure, child employment, and reproductive behavior in rural South Asia, *Centre for Policy Studies Working Papers*, No. 56, 1980.

Chakraborty, R.L., Rural indebtedness, in *History of Bangladesh 1704–1971, Vol. 2, Economic History*, Islam, S., Ed., Asiatic Society of Bangladesh, Dhaka, 1992, pp. 600–636.

Chambers, R., Beyond the Green Revolution: a selective essay, in *Understanding Green Revolutions*, Cambridge University Press, London, 1984, pp. 362–379.

Chenery, H.B., *Structural Change and Development Policy*, Oxford University Press, New York, 1979.

Chenery, H.B. and Syrquin, M., *Patterns of Development 1950–1970*, Oxford University Press, London, 1975.

Chenery, H.B. and Syrquin, M., Typical patterns of transformation, in *Industrialization and Growth*, Chenery, H.B., Robinson, S., and Syrquin, M., Eds., Oxford University Press, New York, NY, 1986, pp. 37–83.

Chenery, H.B., Ahluwalia, M., Bell, C.L.G., Dulloy, J., and Jolly, R., *Redistribution with Growth*, Oxford Uiversity Press, New York, 1974.

Chowdhury, A. and Islam, I., *The Newly Industrialising Economies of East Asia*, Routledge, London, 1993.

Clark, C., *The Conditions of Economic Progress*, Macmillan, London, 1940.

Diaz-Bonilla, E., Robinson, S., Thomas, M., and Yanoma, Y., WTO, agriculture, and developing countries: a survey of issues, *TMD Discussion Paper* No.81, International Food Policy Research Institute, Washington, DC, 2002.

Dorner, P., Review of Anthony Y.C. Koo: the role of land reform in economic development: a case study of Taiwan, *Am. J. Agric. Econ.*, 5 (3), 710–712, 1969.

Evans, J.A., Government intervention in South Korean agriculture, *World Agric.*, 1991, Available at http://www.findarticles.com.

Evenson, R.E. and Binswanger, H.P., Estimating labor demand functions for Indian agriculture, in *Contractual Arrangements, Employment, and Wages in Rural Labor Markets in Asia*, Binswanger, H.P. and Rosenzweig, M.R., Eds., Yale University Press, New Haven, CT, 1984, pp. 263–279.

Falcon, W., The Green Revolution: generations of problems, *Am. J. Agric. Econ.*, 52, 698–710, 1970.

FAO, The role of agricultural land taxes in Japanese development, in *Readings on Taxation*, Bird, R. and Oldman, O., Eds., Johns Hopkins University Press, Baltimore, MD, 1964, pp. 436–449.

Feder, G., Just, R.E., and Zilberman, D., Adoption of agricultural innovations in developing countries: a survey, *Econ. Dev. Cult. Change*, 33 (2), 254–298, 1985.

Fei, J.C.H., Ranis, G., and Kuo, S.W.Y., *Growth with Equity: The Taiwan Case*, Oxford University Press, New York, 1979.

Gillis, M., Perkins, D.H., Roemer, M., and Snodgrass, D.R., *Economics of Development*, W.W. Norton and Company, New York, 1992.

Griffin, K., *The Political Economy of Agrarian Change: An Essay on the Green Revolution*, Macmillan, London, 1974.

Hayami, Y. and Ruttan, V., The Green Revolution: inducement and distribution, *Pakistan Dev. Rev.*, 23 (1), 37–63, 1984.

Hayami, Y. and Ruttan, V., *Agricultural Development: An International Perspective*, Johns Hopkins University Press, Baltimore, MD, 1985.

Hirschman, A.O., *The Strategy of Economic Development*, Yale University Press, New Haven, CT, 1958.

Hossain, A., *Inflation, Economic Growth and the Balance of Payments: A Macroeconometric Study of the Bangladesh Economy*, Oxford University Press, Delhi, 1995.

Hossain, A. and Rashid, S., *In Quest of Development: The Political Economy of South Asia*, University Press Limited, Dhaka, 1996.

Hossain, M., *Nature and Impact of the Green Revolution in Bangladesh*, Research Report 67, International Food Policy Research Institute, Washington, DC, 1988.

Hossain, M., Mannan, R., Rahman, H.Z., and Sen, B., Bangladesh, in *Rural Poverty in Developing Asia*, Quibria, M.G., Ed., Oxford University Press, Hong Kong, 1994, pp. 73–187.

Islam, N., Introduction, in *Agricultural Policy in Developing Countries*, Islam, N., Mellor, J. W., and Johnston, B.F., Eds., Macmillan Press Limited, London, 1974, pp. xv–xxxi.

Islam, N., *Foreign Trade and Economic Controls in Development: The Case of United Pakistan*, Yale University Press, New Haven, CT, 1981.

James, W.E., Naya, S., and Meier, G.M., *Asian Development: Economic Success and Policy Lessons*, University of Wisconsin Press, Madison, NJ, 1987.

Johnston, B.F., Agriculture and structural transformation in developing countries: a survey of research, *J. Econ. Lit.*, 8, 369–373, 1970.

Johnston, B.F. and Mellor, J., The role of agriculture in economic development, *Am. Econ. Rev.*, 51 (4), 566–593, 1961.

Kaldor, N., The role of taxation in economic development, in *Joint Tax Program: Fiscal Policy for Economic Growth in Latin America*, Johns Hopkins University Press, Baltimore, MD, 1965, pp. 70–109.

Koo, A.Y.C., *The Role of Land Reform in Economic Development: A Case of Taiwan*, Praeger, New York, 1968.

Kuznets, S., Quantitative aspects of the economic growth of nations (a series of 10 articles,), *Econ. Dev. Cult. Change*, 1956–1967.

Kuznets, S., Economic growth and the contribution of agriculture: notes on measurement, *Int. J. Agrarian Aff.*, 3, 56–75, 1961.

Kuznets, S., *Economic Growth of Nations: Total Output and Production Structure*, Harvard University Press, Cambridge, MA, 1971.

Lee, T.H., *Intersectoral Capital Flows in the Economic Development of Taiwan, 1955–1960*, Cornell University Press, Ithaca, NY, 1971.

Lewis, W.A., Economic development with unlimited supplies of labour, *Manch. School Econ. Soc. Stud.*, 22, 139–191, 1954.

Lewis, W.A., The roots of development theory, in *Handbook of Development Economics*, Vol. I, Chenery, H. and Srinivasan, T.N., Eds., Elsevier Science Publishers, Amsterdam, 1988, pp. 27–37.

Lin, J.Y. and Nugent, J.B., Institutions and development, in *Handbook of Development Economics*, Vol. IIIA, Behrman, J. and Srinivasan, T.N., Eds., Elsevier, Amsterdam, 1995, pp. 2300–2370.

Lipton, M., The new economics of growth: a review, *World Dev.*, 5 (3), 267–270, 1977.

McCalla, A.F., What the developing countries want from the WTO? in *Agricultural Trade Liberalization: Can we Make Progress*, Paper Presented at the Canadian Agri-Food Trade Research Network Workshop, Quebec City, Quebec, 2000

Meier, G.M., *Leading Issues in Development Economics*, 2nd ed., Oxford University Press, New York, 1970.

Meier, G.M. and Rauch, J.E., *Leading Issues in Economic Development*, 7th ed., Oxford University Press, New York, 2000.

Mellor, J.W., *The Economics of Agricultural Development*, Cornell University Press, Ithaca, NY, 1966.

Mellor, J.W., Food price policy and income distribution in low income countries, *Econ. Dev. Cult. Change*, 27, 1–26, 1978.

Mellor, J.W., Food production, consumption and development strategy, in *The Indian Economy: Recent Development and Future Prospects*, Lucas, R.E.B. and Papanek, G.F., Eds., Westview Press, Boulder, CO, 1988a, pp. 53–76.

Mellor, J.W., Food and development: the critical nexus between developing and developed countries, in *The Agro-Technological System Towards 2000*, Antonelli, G. and Quadrio-Curzio, A., Eds., North-Holland, Amsterdam, 1988b, pp. 175–183.

Mellor, J.W., Emphasizing agriculture in economic development — is it a risky business? in *Risk in Agriculture*, Holden, D., et al., Eds., World Bank, Washington, DC, 1991, pp. 3–16.

Moon, P.L., A Positive Grain Price Policy (1969) and agricultural development, in *Economic Development in the Republic of Korea: A Policy Perspective*, Cho, L.J. and Kim, Y.H., Eds., University of Hawaii Press, Honolulu, 1991, pp. 371–404.

Mukherjee, M., *Land Problems in India*, Longmans and Green, London, 1933.

Nurkse, R., *Problems of Capital Formation in Underdeveloped Countries*, Oxford University Press, New York, 1953.

Otsuka, K., Chuma, H., and Hayami, Y., Land and labor contracts in agrarian economies: theories and facts, *J. Econ. Lit.*, 30 (December), 1965–2018, 1992.

Pears, A., *Seeds of Plenty, Seeds of Want: Social and Economic Implications of the Green Revolution*, Clarendon Press, Oxford, 1980.

Prebisch, R., *The Economic Development of Latin America and Its Principal Problems*, U.N. Department of Economic Affairs, Lake Success, NY, 1950.

Preobrazhensky, E.A., *The New Economics*, Clarendon Press, Oxford, 1965.

Rao, J.M., Taxing agriculture: instruments and incidence, *World Dev.*, 17 (6), 809–823, 1989.

Rashid, S. and Quibria, M.G., Is land reform passe? With special reference to Asian agriculture, in *Critical Issues in Asian Development*, Quibria, M.G., Ed., Oxford University Press, Hong Kong, 1995, pp. 127–159.

Ray, D., *Development Economics*, Princeton University Press, Princeton, NJ, 1998.

Reynolds, L.G., *Image and Reality in Economic Development*, Yale University Press, New Haven, CT, 1977.

Robinson, F., Ed., *The Cambridge Encyclopedia of India, Pakistan, Bangladesh, Sri Lanka, Nepal, Bhutan and the Maldives*, Cambridge University Press, Cambridge, 1989.

Rosenzweig, M., Rural wages, labor supply and land reform: a theoretical and empirical analysis, *Am. Econ. Rev.*, 68, 847–861, 1978.

Rosenzweig, M., Neoclassical theory and the optimizing peasant: an econometric analysis of market family labor supply in a developing country, *Q. J. Econ.*, 94, 31–55, 1980.

Schuh, G.E. and Barghouti, S., Agricultural diversification in Asia, *Finance Dev.*, 25 (2), 41–44, 1988.

Schultz, T.W., *Transforming Traditional Agriculture*, Yale University Press, New Haven, CT, 1964.

Schultz, T.W., Tensions between economics and politics in dealing with agriculture, in *Pioneers in Development* (second series), Meier, G.M., Ed., Oxford University Press, New York, 1987, pp. 17–38.

Schultz, T.W., *The Economics of Being Poor*, Blackwell, Oxford, 1993.

Sen, A.K., *Choice of Techniques*, Blackwell, Oxford, 1960.

Sen, A.K., Size of Holdings and Productivity, *Economic and Political Weekly*, 16 (annual number), February, 1964.

Solow, R.M., A contribution to the theory of economic growth, *Q. J. Econ.*, 70, 65–94, 1956.

Southworth, H.M. and Johnston, B.F., Eds., *Agricultural Development and Economic Growth*, Cornell University Press, Ithaca, NY, 1967.

Squire, L., *Employment Policy in Developing Countries: A Survey of Issues and Evidence*, Oxford University Press, New York, NY, 1981.

Staub, W. and Blasé, M., Induced technological change in developing agriculture: implications for income distribution and agricultural development, *J. Dev. Areas*, 8, 581–596, 1974.

Stiglitz, J.E., Some theoretical aspects of agricultural policies, *World Bank Res. Observer*, 2 (1), 43–47, 1987.

Stiglitz, J.E., Economic organization, information, and development, in *Handbook of Development Economics*, Vol. I, Chenery, H. and Srinivasan, T.N., Eds., North-Holland, Amsterdam, 1988, pp. 93–160.

Sundrum, R., *Development Economics: A Framework for Analysis and Policy*, John Wiley and Sons, New York, NY, 1983.

Suryana, A. and Erwidodo. (1996). *Agricultural Policy Reforms in Indonesia: Accelerating Growth with Equity*. Bogor, Indonesia, Center for Agro-Socioeconomic Research. http://www.fftc.agnet.org/library/article/CB434.html#0.

Syrquin, M., Patterns of structural change, in *Handbook of Development Economics*, Vol. I., Chenery, H. and Srinivasan, T.N., Eds., North-Holland, Amsterdam, 1988, pp. 203–273.

Taslim, M.A., Agricultural land tenancy in Bangladesh: a review, in: *Bangladesh Economy: Evaluation and a Research Agenda*, Rashid, S., Ed., University Press Limited, Dhaka, 1995, pp. 64–80.

Timmer, C.P., The agricultural transformation, in *Handbook of Development Economics*, Vol. I, Chenery, H.B. and Srinivasan, T.N., Eds., Elsevier Science Publishers, Amsterdam, 1988, pp. 275–331.

Timmer, C.P., Agriculture and economic growth in Vietnam, in Paper Presented at the Conference on Vietnam in 2001: Prospects for Economic and Social Progress, November 16–17, 2000, The Kennedy Auditorium, Washington, DC, 2001.

Todaro, M.P. and Smith, S.C., *Development Economics*, Pearson-Addison Wesley, New York, NY, 2003.

Viner, J., *International Trade and Economic Development*, Clarendon Press, Oxford, 1953.

Vyas, V.S., Asian agriculture: achievements and challenges, *Asian Dev. Rev.*, 1 (2), 27–44, 1983.

Wald, H.P., Reform of agricultural taxation to promote economic development in Latin America, in *Joint Tax Program: Fiscal Policy for Economic Growth in Latin America*, Johns Hopkins University Press, Baltimore, MD, 1965, pp. 326–358.

Wilson, J.S., Liberalizing trade in agriculture, *Policy Research Working Paper* 2804, Development Research Group-Trade, World Bank, Washington, DC, 2002.

World Bank, *The Political Economy of Agricultural Pricing Policy*, Oxford University Press, New York, 1992.

World Bank, *The East Asian Miracle*, Oxford University Press, New York, 1993.

World Bank, *World Development Indicators*, 2004, Available at http://0-devdata.worldbank.org.

World Bank, *World Development Report*, Oxford University Press, New York, various years.

Chapter 41

Issues in Water Resource Management

C.J. Barrow

CONTENTS

I. Introduction: Water as a Resource

The demand for freshwater is always on the rise, as it is vital for the survival of humans and many other organisms and is a key element in development. Roughly 70% of freshwater worldwide goes to irrigate crops and produce about 40% of all food (FAO, 2001). Water can be a sustainable resource, as long as the rate at which it is consumed is lesser than the rate at which it is replenished, and provided nothing is done to negatively affect its quality or movement. Poor management can lead to temporary or permanent, partial or total loss of water resources. Water is often a common resource, not owned or controlled by any one individual or nation, but used by many. Under conditions of relative abundance this is unlikely to cause difficulties. However, if there is scarcity, and such situations are increasing, use must be regulated or degradation and possibly conflict will occur.

Some water supplies are not recharged fast enough to satisfy the demand. These finite water resources include groundwater, which accumulates slowly or was collected in the past when environmental conditions were different from those of today's. A renewable groundwater supply can become permanently finite if the aquifer collapses or is clogged, thereby preventing recharge, or if there is pollution or saltwater intrusion.

"Adequate water" means enough of a suitable quality, when it is wanted and where it is wanted and satisfactory disposal of any surplus. Managers increasingly have to deal with water quality as well as quantity issues, and water shortages will prompt more wastewater reuse. Supplies are commonly contaminated with human waste, livestock waste, agrochemical or industrial effluent, sediment (resulting from soil erosion), and from sources over which water managers may have little control, for example, acid deposition. Provision of effective basic sanitation is a priority — in 2001, around 2.4 billion people lacked basic sanitation and many suffered illness as a consequence.

A. The Increasing Demand for Water Supplies

Water is required for drinking, washing, cooking, industry, agriculture, power generation, navigation, conservation, fisheries, sewage disposal, and recreational use. Some current estimates suggest that by 2025 around 2 billion people will live in areas with absolute water scarcity (Hunt, 2003).[1] Those managing water must not assume present precipitation quantity and temporal and spatial distribution are stable (Shiklomanov, 1998). There are periodic climatic fluctuations, notably ENSO[2] events, and there is the threat of more permanent and less predictable shifts through global warming. There have been proposals for a "water poverty index" to give a more integrated assessment of scarcity (Sullivan, 2002). Rising water demand and increasing pollution have led some to declare a water crisis (Postel, 1992; Gleick, 1993). Also, large companies have been taking over water supplies in developed and developing countries — some forecast that water will be as profitable in the 21st century as oil is now (Barlow and Clarke, 2002).

Since the 1960s there has been huge investment in irrigation. Much of the irrigation water applied to cropland is wasted, and any surplus returned to streams or groundwater is usually contaminated with agrochemicals and salts. The impact of irrigation can be huge; the Aral Sea has shrunk catastrophically because water has been extracted from inflowing rivers; worldwide there are problems with waterlogging and salinization, and even pollution of marine ecosystems. Sustaining large-scale irrigation is a challenge, and it is not unusual for it to fail to repay its investment costs before falling into disrepair. Easily developed sites with suitable water have already been heavily exploited; therefore, the costs of established methods of irrigation have been rising and the area of irrigated land per person (worldwide) has shifted from marked increases between the 1960s and 1990s to decline (Postel, 1992: 50–51). Current irrigation methods are being questioned because of pollution and because the ratio of available water-to-water demand looks likely to fall considerably.

Thus far most manipulation of the hydrological cycle has taken place at the streamflow and groundwater storage phases. Desalination of brackish groundwater and seawater is not usually economically feasible and salt-tolerant crops are still being developed. Technological advance may make these practical one day, but in the foreseeable future water will come from streamflow or groundwater sources.

B. The Watershed and River Basin Ecosystem

The term watershed is sometimes used to refer to the catchment boundary (or divide) which borders a river basin; however, it is widely taken to indicate the catchment area of a river basin. The watershed/river basin is a biogeophysical unit with recognizable boundaries. It is not ephemeral in the way administrative districts might be, there are seldom gaps between basins, few parts of the world lack them, and much human development activity takes place close to rivers. The river basin is an ecosystem in which the living and nonliving environment functions together, with water being an integrative element. Such an ecosystem can be monitored and modeled without resorting to impossibly detailed studies of interacting subsystems and their components. Therefore, it makes an ideal management unit.

II. Managing Water Resources

Many identify water supply as *the* environmental and social challenge of the 21st century; however, people take water for granted. The world is entering a new era, which contrasts with times when damming rivers and drilling wells was relatively straightforward "engineered." The coming generation will face more limits and constraints: political, environmental, and economic. Since the late 1990s a number of lobby groups have been trying to stimulate concern, notably the World Water Council, the International Water Management Institute, the Global Water Partnership, the World Water Council, the World Commission on Dams, and the World Commission for Water in the 21st Century (Abu-Zeid, 1998). Biswas (2001) warned of the vital need to breakaway from just focusing on the present to look more to the future. An International Year of Freshwater in 2003 emphasized supply and access. UNESCO (2003) published the stock-taking *World Water Development Report*, which was the result of combined efforts of 23 UN agencies and some other bodies. The International Conference on Water and the Environment (Dublin 1992) produced principles which are widely advocated at present and the *World Development Report 2003* has stressed the need for better water management which is environmentally and socially responsible (World Bank, 2003).

Current practices tend to see nature and human usage as competing and seek division of supplies between the two these demands have to be better integrated. Hunt (2003) stressed the need to manage ways that maintain the water cycle and the ecosystems that support it. Adams (1992: 16) also argued for "a new approach to development, embracing integrated natural resource management with realistic socio-economic goals" (Adams, 1992: 16). Three guiding principles are gradually spreading from environmental management to natural resource management, and are important if sustainable development is a goal: the Polluter Pays Principle; the Precautionary Principle; and Proactive Approach. The first implies that the costs of environmental damage are borne by those responsible; the second, that developers err on the side of caution; the third, that implications are assessed in advance and efforts are made to avoid or minimize problems.

A. Watershed/River Basin Management

Development within a watershed/river basin affects that ecosystem. For example, alteration of vegetation will affect the local microclimate and possibly regional climate; groundwater accumulation; and the quality, intensity, and quantity of streamflow. Change of the vegetation cover of a watershed also affects overland flow and infiltration rates, altering erosion and affecting soil moisture retention. Changes made in one part of a basin can have an impact on many people, especially downstream; the installation of land drains and channelization of flow are likely to mean more extreme floods downstream; poor upper basin land husbandry usually means silt problems. Pollution may cause problems for hundreds of kilometers below the point of release, and barriers in lower reaches can disrupt fish migration upstream. Therefore, water management in a basin needs to adopt an integrated and basin-wide approach (Biswas and Tortajada, 2001). Water resources cannot be adequately managed in isolation from soil management, agricultural development, urban planning, and so on (Calder, 1999).

Frequently, water is put to multiple uses: for domestic supply, for livestock, for irrigation, for hydroelectricity, for dilution and disposal of industrial wastes or sewage, for fishing, for recreation, for navigation, and so on. These demands are often incompatible — if one user alters water quality or restricts flows, it affects others. Simply dividing and sharing the resources cannot solve the problems. Water resources managers must ensure that various uses are compatible, and if not, weigh the costs and benefits and decide how to get trade-offs agreed; this can be easier if a basin-wide approach is adopted.

The flow pattern of a river — the level to which water rises and the consequent flood risk, whether the flows are erratic or moderated, their quality (whether there are heavy loads of silt or pollutants), and groundwater recharge — can be modified, regulated, or controlled by watershed management. This also involves promoting good husbandry, maintaining natural vegetation cover, preventing overgrazing or severe fires, and constructing terraces or other soil conservation techniques. In practice, river flows are more usually regulated by constructing dams or barrages to provide irrigation water and hydroelectric power and regulate floods. Barrages are less disruptive, but cannot store water for times of shortage as can dams. Huge sums have been spent on dams and barrages since the 1930s; however, without adequate watershed management, reservoirs are likely to become silted, perhaps even before construction costs are recouped. Large dams have been built on virtually all major rivers since the 1920s. The period between 1956 and the early-1990s was marked by numerous large dams in developing countries. The construction of large dams reached a peak during the 1970s and there has been a slower rate of increase since, partly because of strong criticism (McCully, 2001). However, at the 2003 World Water Forum there were calls for more (Pearce, 2003). Before embarking on huge, costly, and probably inflexible river impoundment or transfer schemes, it should be asked whether a better approach would be to control water wastage and discourage further growth in the water scarce areas.

More water management should take place before runoff reaches rivers or groundwater because this costs less, benefits people often bypassed by large dams, and is potentially more sustainable (Barrow, 1999). Of the estimated 110,000 km^3 of precipitation which falls on the lands of the world, 70,000 km^3 never reaches streams or groundwater, being lost to evaporation. Better watershed management could tap that "lost" moisture for crops, but it has had far less attention and funding than have large dams or barrages. As land use intensifies and competition for water resources increases, it seems likely that developers will be forced to remedy this neglect.

B. Managing Water Resources Systems

To be successful, water resources management must be aware of the linkages between land-use, streamflow, and groundwater storage. In the last few decades, understanding of the structure and function of tropical environments has been improved by work carried out during the International Biological Programme, the International Hydrological Decade, and more recently the UNESCO Man and Biosphere Programme. In spite of the advances there is still inadequate understanding of tropical ecosystems' productivity, resilience to change, and the subtle relationships between environment and humans.

The water resources manager must be capable of assessing, exploiting, and allocating supplies, and maintaining their quality and quantity. The problems involved in developing and managing water resources are complex, extend across discipline boundaries, are often politicized, and depend on sound institutional developments — a multidisciplinary, comprehensive, and integrated approach is therefore widely advocated (Thana and Biswas, 1990). By manipulating land-use and developing the appropriate "mix" of sources, it is often possible to ensure supplies for agriculture, industry, and domestic consumption. Having developed a water supply it must be delivered to the crops, livestock, industry, or human consumers; often, but not always, this involves a conveyance system and arrangements for allocation and distribution. If the maximum benefit is to be obtained from a water supply it must be used in the most appropriate manner with minimum wastage, and surplus water must be disposed of or reused satisfactorily. Many systems leak badly, distribution is often inequitable, and surplus water is lost before it can be reused. There is great potential for improvement.

C. The Need to Avoid Unwanted Impacts

It is difficult to separate planning and management; managers are seldom confined to dealing with care of established systems, they help decide future developments. Once the management identifies the objectives that are to be met, there should be adequate predevelopment appraisal sufficiently in advance to ensure that problems which might arise are identified and can be dealt with. Impact assessment should compare all the consequences of every strategy available to achieve the objectives. Efforts should also be made to research and evaluate relevant hindsight experience and, wherever possible, genuinely consult with the people likely to be affected. This should ensure that they are at least aware of the situation, are able to adopt improvements and innovations, and identify socio-economic or socio-cultural factors which might hinder or aid management; it should also establish what they want and need. The goal of participation and empowerment is often expressed, but seldom adequately achieved (Boelens and Hoogendam, 2002).

Once a particular strategy is selected it has to be implemented and then maintained. Effective ongoing monitoring is required to do this satisfactorily. Without adequate monitoring it is difficult to identify whether it is necessary (and practical) to alter the plan or program, should conditions or demands change or unforeseen problems arise. And without monitoring, it would be difficult to assess the degree of success of the development. The assumption of course is that the project or program is sufficiently flexible to be able to adapt, often that is not the case.

D. Managing Shared Water Resources as Demands upon Them Increase and with the Possibility of Environmental Change

Increasingly, water resources development involves the use of rivers, lakes, or groundwater shared by more than one user, region, state, or country. Even within one region different, often conflicting interests may wish to develop water, for example, hydroelectric generation may compete with urban supply, fisheries, or irrigation needs. To develop such resources fully, and to minimize harm to any of the parties involved, maintaining, and where necessary improving, flows and quality is likely to require inter-regional, interstate, or international cooperation. Large natural lakes have suffered in the last few decades in developed and developing countries as a consequence of pollution with sewage, industrial effluents, and agrochemicals; the introduction of alien species of plants and animals; diversion of inflowing rivers; over-exploitation of fish, game, and other animals; and disturbance related to tourism.

Since the 1930s, a number of countries have sought to use a river basin planning approach to resolve these problems (Saha and Barrow, 1981; Barrow, 1998). Integrated river basin planning and management sets out to use water as an engine for socio-economic development as well as managing the physical resources — revenue from hydroelectricity or tourism could be reinvested away from the watercourse to improve land husbandry, reduce erosion, and so forth. Integrated river basin development is also seen by many as a practical strategy for pursuing sustainable development.

River basins should be managed by a suitable multidisciplinary team of specialists and administrators — a river basin development commission or authority composed of representatives from the interested regions, states, or countries and possibly representatives from international bodies. River basin development commissions can oversee water resources development and, if wished, pursue comprehensive or integrated planning and management using water resources as a "tool" to achieve much wider regional development goals. Crucially, the authority should have jurisdiction over the entire basin, the power to enforce not just advise, and a management team capable of implementing decisions. Often, some or all of those qualities are deficient.

In 1993, there were over 280 internationally shared river basin bodies and it is likely that over 50% of the world's people live in one. If tension grows over a shared river there are two possible ways forward: (1) consultation, agreement, and cooperation and (2) power politics ("hydropolitics") and possibly conflict (Ohlsson, 1995; Klare, 2001; Ashton, 2002; Uitto and Wolf, 2002). A somewhat sensationalist literature has been warning of the risk of "water wars" since the 1970s. Swain (2001) noted that agreements on sharing rivers may be possible while say 80% of total flows run to the sea, but if future demands rise, and if environmental change and pollution cut supplies, agreements may not hold and new ones are less likely. Much of the negotiation so far has focused on quantity of flows, yet the problem of contamination is growing. A Convention on the Protection of Transboundary Watercourses and International Lakes was signed in 1996, but is only a start to resolving contamination problems.

Some international river basin authorities have been successful as vehicles for water sharing and integrated development; however others, despite grandiose plans and considerable investment, seem to have achieved little. Overall, one can argue that, so far, management of shared basins has been successful in that inter-state conflicts (but by no means arguments) over river flows have been rare.

E. Laws Controlling the Use of Water Resources Shared by More than One Country

Law is an instrument which can be used to smooth out conflicts of interest generated in the sharing of water resources. It also provides guidelines for ordering future conduct. Law can be determined by court action(s), which set precedence that becomes a "guideline" for future cases (the process of common law in the west). Law may also come from legislation where an administrative body, for example a government, passes a statute when it sees a need. In many countries a constitution affects water rights and water management because it binds legislation and common law or its equivalent. The present international law concerning use of water resources is the product of centuries of endeavor towards formulating a set of substantive principles and procedural instruments to balance and harmonize divergent national interests (Caponera, 1992). While there is no formally ratified rule of international law prescribing that a basin state must have the prior consent of other basin states to use and develop the waters of an international drainage basin within its own territory, there is a legal duty to give notice in the cases where such use is likely to seriously affect the rights or interests of another basin state. The International Law Association has introduced the concept of the international drainage basin: *the aggregate of both surface and groundwater* within *a given geographic area flowing into a common terminus.* The rights of basin states (those sharing a common basin) have been outlined by the 1966 Helsinki Rules (Zaman et al., 1981: 181–221). There are also a number of important propositions with the status of principles or rules (Hayton, 1983: 197). A review of law covering international rivers, particularly the Nile, Niger, and Senegal was provided by Godana (1985: 21–77).

F. Laws Controlling Water Use Within Countries

Laws and traditions controlling water use within developing countries are often outmoded, may be inadequate, unsuitable for introductions, are often ignored, or are unenforceable. Laws inherited from colonial governments may have worked under such administrations, but after independence have become obsolete or may remind people of foreign rule and be scorned. Much depends upon the attitude of people regarding law; where laws are disregarded even the best water control regulations will be ineffective. Fair, rigorous, and swift enforcement is important in maintaining or improving adherence to laws.

Enforcing law may be difficult in rural areas. People are often suspicious of outsiders, and family and tribal loyalties can outweigh the sense of responsibility to wider social groups. The lack of roads, communications, lighting at night, and adequate policing makes theft of water and disagreement over land difficult for the authorities to spot, let alone solve. Data collection, gathering water charges, land consolidation, and other important tasks are hindered by inadequate documentary evidence of land-ownership, vague terms of tenure and unclear rights to water.

Most excolonial countries still adhere to laws at least in part derived from Western (European) legislation. Western law distinguishes three principal doctrines relating to the distribution of water: (1) the riparian rights doctrine, (2) the correlative rights doctrine, and (3) the prior appropriation rights doctrine.

Riparian rights involve basically the permission to use water as a consequence of owning land bordering a watercourse; the doctrine has spread from the U.K. to the U.S.A. and Australia and from France to parts of Africa. The major features are that: (a) it should give equal rights of use to owners of land which borders on or touches a stream or across which a stream flows; (b) a riparian right is "attached" to land ownership — a user can take up the right to use water at any time even if he/she had not done so before and to do so affects existing users. The owner does not own the water (the resource itself can belong to the state or some other authority), only the right to use it. Thus, one who enjoys riparian rights should receive flows from upstream landowners(s) without material change in quality or quantity and should ensure that downstream owners enjoy the same. Use of water for anything other than household consumption plus a few livestock is likely to be regarded as excessive, and nowadays in most countries would be controlled — licensed by the state.

Riparian rights allow extraction of groundwater from under land without restriction irrespective of its effect on others or on the conservation of groundwater resources. At its roots, the riparian rights doctrine is archaic and really suited only where water is not scarce. For surface water riparian rights go to those who have the watercourse on their land, and those away from it have no rights.

The correlative rights doctrine is basically a modification of riparian rights to include some consideration of parties other than the holder of the rights. The doctrine was developed in California after a 1903 court case and was an improvement on the situation, which allowed landowners to exploit groundwater with no consideration for others. Under the correlative rights doctrine: (i) if groundwater demand exceeds supply, all overlying landowners must reduce use on a coequal basis; (ii) where water supplies are in excess of reasonable needs of those overlying them, water may be put to nonoverlying uses, i.e. piped or led away. Where correlative rights are enforced, access to water can be restricted by the state in times of water shortage — a considerable improvement over the situation with riparian rights.

Prior appropriation rights state the earliest appropriator has a claim superior to later appropriators (i.e., historical precedence). Later appropriators get what is left, and at times may be deprived. Under prior appropriation rights a person occupying land can take groundwater irrespective of others, because water is regarded under the prior appropriation rights doctrine as a saleable commodity separate from the land. The doctrine is suited to situations where there are water shortages and if the water is to be diverted, for example, from one river basin to another. Prior appropriation rights have been blamed for encouraging excessive use of water resources, because if flows are not being used, rights to it may be forfeited.

Administrative disposition of water-use rights is tending to supersede the three doctrine just described. Under administrative disposition, water is controlled fully or partly by the state, which then grants permits or licenses to users. In some countries, the state now controls all surface waters; for example, in Peru the 1969 General Water Law made water and the channels containing it, without exception, the property of the state. Many argue the best water resources management is exercised where water is the property of the state and all utilization is controlled by license for beneficial use.

Some countries follow Islamic law and common sense born out of years of experience of using water in drylands (Faruqui et al., 2001). According to Islamic law, water is divided into three categories: (1) rivers; (2) wells; and (3) springs. Rivers are further subdivided into greater and lesser rivers. Great rivers are deemed sufficient for all the needs of cultivation and from which anyone can lead off water without much affecting neighbors, they are owned in common by all Muslims. Lesser rivers are further divided into: (a) those which have sufficient water to be diverted without the need for storage dams to irrigate the land situated along their course (and from which canals can be led off to water more distant plots), provided such actions do not prejudice the position of lands situated along river banks; (b) those across which barrages or dams have to be built. When the latter is the case, lands situated higher up the watercourse have a prior right to water. This makes sense because any other distribution would involve passing limited water supplies further and thereby incurring greater wastage. The amount of water users can extract from smaller rivers depends upon circumstances, local needs and custom. Islamic law regards canals dug to bring water to otherwise barren land as belonging to those who dug them.

There are some countries operating indigenous water laws; for example, Indonesia. Shallow groundwater has proved difficult to manage in a number of countries, largely because it is often considered a common resource and is easy to access.

III. Hindrances to Water Resources Development Due to Management Faults

Choice of strategy, timing, and administration of water resources development are more often than not subject to political and bureaucratic pressures. Such pressures may well cause hindrance and be more difficult to overcome than environmental and technical problems. Politicians, economists, and engineers have generally dominated water resources planning and management, and "success" has commonly been judged on economic or technological criteria. Prediction of environmental and socio-economic impacts may be seen as "soft science," a delay, and a waste of funds, so gets minimal attention. Concern for the aptitude, attitudes, and needs of the people affected by development has often been inadequate, yet consideration of such factors is critical if water resources development is to succeed.

Developing countries for a variety of reasons are frequently unable or unwilling to find suitable expertise for what have often been slow, costly, and complex preproject, in-project, and postproject studies. Studies must be speeded up and funds must be made available to pay for them, and whenever possible indigenous planners and managers, rather than foreign consultants, should be used to do the job. Getting such personnel may not be easy; professionals are often lost in a "brain drain" to richer nations, and those who do remain tend to concentrate on "safe" issues or prestigious issues and may be reluctant to leave the cities. A consequence of the shortage of skilled manpower in developing countries is that there is often inadequate data for the planner and manager, and secondly a shortage of trained personnel to interpret and use what is available.

Often key management positions are held by persons without sufficient experience or who are in some other way unable to make satisfactory decisions. Even where managers may have the ability to make decisions, they may not have the authority to do so; decisions are seldom made on the spot by officers who can act appropriately, sensibly, and swiftly when action is needed. Administrators based in a city many kilometers away make decisions and, frequently there is little consultation with agronomists, ecologists, or social scientists.

Management in developing countries is blighted by lack of funding, inadequate experienced manpower, and no mandate to act without reference to superiors who are slow to respond. Bureaucrats in many countries have a rapid turnover: an election defeat or career ambitions frequently mean replacement of planning or management teams, or sudden changes in the terms of reference and policy guidelines. The time horizon for planners and managers is rarely greater than 5 yr, commonly much less. Inevitably planning, implementation, and management reflect this uncertainty and need for haste.

Flexibility is important when developing resources with inadequate data to safely forecast and plan ahead. Projects are often large and inflexible and planners and managers can do little to adapt to unforeseen difficulties. As funds commonly run out on completion of the infrastructure, there is little available to pay for the rectification of faults, ongoing management, modification, and refurbishment. Money may be found for infrastructure, but for less "concrete" things, like training managers, there may be a reluctance to provide funds. Engineering structures give physical testimony of a backer's support, but even very successful management has far less publicity value.

A wise course of action before the implementation of a large and costly project or program is to proceed with a pilot test. However, these have been unpopular despite their value in "trouble-shooting," training, and gathering data. Pilot studies are especially important if new techniques are being introduced to see how they fit local conditions before full installation.

From farmer up to senior agricultural administrators, irrigation planners, and water resource managers, there is a need to stimulate more experimentation and to draw away from the unquestioning adoption of western ideas or accepting the status quo. *Cautious* innovation — the adoption, and if need be, the adaptation of new ideas — should be encouraged. Those planning water resources development now often places emphasis on less expensive, "appropriate technology." Narain (2000) has reviewed the role of Water User Associations in India as a way of improving governance, coordination, and getting stakeholder cooperation; the approach may have value elsewhere. Water is "flexible," when in short supply there can be ways of substituting for it. For example, some countries have responded to water supply problems by importing cheap foreign grain and neglecting their agriculture (Yang and Zehnder, 2002).

One of the key issues discussed during the 2002 sustainability summit at Johannesburg was the problem of providing sufficient clean water for all as soon as possible. It will be interesting to see if such a goal attracts investment — poor people are not likely to offer much profit for investors. Estimates suggest that current population growth and water supply trends will result in perhaps half the world population living in water scarce areas by 2025 — most being developing country citizens.[3] In the 1950s, only a few developing country cities had water supply problems, now at least 26 have serious difficulties and shortages affect more than 300 million.

Notes

1. Postel (1992: 28) defined "water scarce" as anywhere with less than 1000 m^3 per person per day — effectively most of the South.
2. El Niño Southern Oscillation (ENSO) is a huge global ocean-atmospheric circulation system, which manifests in the Pacific and Southern Ocean a quasi-periodic

shift in ocean waters which affects climates across the globe for several months after. First noted as a recurrent diminution of cold upwelling off the coast of Peru, Chile, and Ecuador. The system is now sufficiently understood to enable long-term forecasting; for example, an ENSO ocean change forewarns of more storms or droughts in distant parts of the world, which may occur many months later.

3. Worldwide at least 1.2 billion people did not have access to safe domestic supplies in 2002. A large proportion of illness in developing countries (perhaps over 80%) is water-related.

References

Abu-Zeid, M.A., Water and sustainable development: the vision for world water, life and the environment, *Water Policy*, 1 (1998), 9–19, 1998.

Adams, W.M., *Wasting the Rain: Rivers People and Planning in Africa*, Earthscan, London, 1992.

Ashton, P.J., Avoiding conflicts over Africa's water resources, *Ambio*, 31 (3), 236–242, 2002.

Barlow, M. and Clarke, T., *Blue Gold: The Battle Against Corporate Theft of the World's Water*, Earthscan, London, 2002.

Barrow, C.J., River basin development planning and management: a critical review, *World Dev.*, 25 (1): 171–186, 1998.

Barrow, C.J., *Alternative Irrigation: The Promise of Runoff Agriculture*, Earthscan, London, 1999.

Biswas, A.K., World Water Forum: in retrospect, *Water Policy*, 3 (2001), 351–356, 2001.

Biswas, A.K. and Tortajada, C., Eds., *Integrated River Basin Management: The Latin American Experience*, Oxford University Press, New Delhi, 2001.

Boelens, R. and Hoogendam, P., Eds., *Water Rights and Empowerment*, Koninklijke von Gorcum BV, A.A. Assen, 2002.

Calder, I.R., *The Blue Revolution: Land Use and Integrated Water Resources Management*, Earthscan, London, 1999.

Caponera, D.A., *Principles of Water Law and Administration: National and International*, Brookfield (VT), A.A. Balkema, 1992.

FAO, *The State of Food & Agriculture 2001*, Food and Agriculture Organisation of the UN, Rome, 2001

Faruqui, N.I., Biswas, A.K., and Bino, M.J., Eds., *Water Management in Islam*, United Nations University Press, Tokyo, 2001.

Gleick, P.H., Ed., *Water in Crisis: Guide to the World's Water Resources*, Oxford University Press, Oxford, 1993.

Godana, B.A., *Africa's Shared Water Resources: Legal and International Aspects of the Nile, Niger and Senegal River Systems*, Frances Pinter, London, 1985.

Hayton, R.D., The law of international resource systems, in *River Basin Development*, Zaman, M., Biswas, A.K., Khan, A.H., and Nishat, A., Eds., Proceedings of the National Symposium on River Basin Development, Dacca, December 4–10, 1981, Tycooly International, Dublin, 1983, pp. 195–211.

Hunt, E., *Thirsty Planet: Strategies for Sustainable Water Management*, Zed Press, London, 2003.

Klare, M.T., *Resource Wars: The New Landscape of Global Conflict*, Henry Holt, New York (NY), 2001.

McCully, P., *Silenced Rivers: The Ecology and Politics of Large Dams*, Updated ed., Zed Press, London, 2001.

Narain, V., India's water crisis: the challenges of governance, *Water Policy*, 2 (6), 433–444, 2000.

Ohlsson, L., Ed., *Hydropolitics: Conflicts over Water as a Development Constraint*, Zed Press, London, 1995.

Pearce, F., Dismay over call to build new dams, *New Scientist*, 177 (2387), 11, 2003.

Postel, S., *Last Oasis, Facing Water Scarcity*, W.W. Norton, New York (NY), 1992.

Saha, S.K. and Barrow, C.J., Eds., *River Basin Planning: Theory and Practice*, Wiley, Chichester, 1981.

Shiklomanov, I.A., *World Water Resources: A New Appraisal and Assessment for the 21st Century*, UNESCO-IHP, Paris, 1998.

Sullivan, C., Calculating a Water Poverty index, *World Dev.*, 30 (7), 1195–1210, 2002.

Swain, A., Water wars: fact or fiction? *Futures*, 33 (2001): 769–781, 2001.

Thana, N.C. and Biswas, A.K., Ed., *Environmentally-Sound Water Management*, Oxford University Press, New Delhi, 1990.

Uitto, J.I. and Wolf, A.T., Eds., Special issue: Water wars? geographical perspectives, *Geographical Journal*, 164 (4): 289–378, 2002.

UNESCO, *The UN World Water Development Report 2003*, 2003, Available at http:www.unesco.org/water/wwap or http://www.berghornbook.com.

World Bank, *The World Development Report 2003*, Oxford University Press, New York (NY), 2003.

Yang, H. and Zehnder, A.J.B., Water scarcity and food import: a case study for southern Mediterranean countries, *World Development*, 30 (8), 1413–1430, 2002.

Zaman, M., Biswas, A.K., Khan, A.H., and Nishat, A., Eds., *River Basin Development*, in Proceedings of the National Symposium on River Basin Development, December 4–10, 1981, Dacca, Tycooly International, Dublin, 1981.

Chapter 42

Governance, Technology, and Development

Laurids S. Lauridsen

CONTENTS

I. Introduction

The significance of technological change for economic and wider social development has been acknowledged for decades, and "technology issue" belongs to the classic themes of development studies (development economics). During the 1960s and 1970s, thinking about technical change in developing countries (DCs) was guided by linear models of innovation and by a strong distinction between innovation and diffusion. DCs were in principle in the position to benefit from the high-productivity technologies that were already available in the advanced industrialized countries. Rather than needing "to reinvent the wheel," DCs could grow and develop by increasing physical capital accumulation and technology transfer via foreign direct investments (FDIs), licensing, and so on. This then led to debates on the costs of technology transfer (pricing of technology packages, technology clauses), on the appropriateness of transferred technologies (processes and products), and on the wider implication of foreign technology (technology dependency and a truncated production structure). When the governance issue was raised, it was either considered as being unproblematic or dealt with as a matter of local state versus Transnations Corporations (TNCs).

During the 1980s and 1990s, the focus has shifted from the technology providers to the technology receivers. Technology transfer was now seen as a complicated matter because technology was tacit and not fully embodied. Local technology efforts were considered as a necessary condition for successful technology transfer and for local technological upgrading. As a result, scholars introduced new core concepts — corporate competencies, technological capability (TC), learning, absorptive capacity, path dependency, innovation system, etc. A central feature in these new approaches was governance — both authoritative regulation (technology policy) and broader network governance in the private sector as well as across the public and private sectors.

Nowadays, there is a renewed interest in the technology transfer issue — "FDI-driven" development (Lall, 2002) and learning-through-global commodity chains (Gereffi, 1999) or global production networks (Ernst and Kim, 2002) — but there is also a strong interest in the developmental role of the local technological infrastructure (including human resources). Therefore, dynamic technological development has moved to the forefront in development policy in many DCs. This is strongly the case in semi-industrialized middle-income countries that fear they will be "sandwiched" between upcoming low-cost industrializers (e.g., China) and advanced, high-technology OECD (Organisation for Economic Co-operation and Development) countries. However, this is also the case in many low-income countries that have been forced to open their economies and fear that an open economy will just result in closing down of enterprises. Only by improving the ability of its firms to compete against imports in the domestic market and against other manufacturers in foreign markets will economic development be able to improve the relative income of a country.

The new focus on technological change and international competitiveness has also resulted in a renewed interest in governance issues. "Governance pessimists" argue that the growing complexity in modern production and the competence gap between public officials and private entrepreneurs leave little, if any, room for state intervention. While neoliberals tend to recommend an ungoverned technology search process, other pessimists highlight the role that can be played by private consultancy firms, by business associations, and by a range of inter-firm arrangements, including technology-relevant linkages (spillovers) between TNCs assemblers or foreign buyers and their local suppliers. In contrast, "governance optimists" argue with reference to countries such as Taiwan, Singapore, and Ireland that goal-oriented technology policies when implemented skillfully can play a crucial role in economic transformation processes (Meyer-Stamer, 1999).

This chapter takes a governance optimistic view as point of departure. We dismiss the view that the development process can be reduced to factor accumulation plus a sound institutional environment and focus on the potential role of state governance in relation to technological advance. We are concerned with the policy measures (content) and with the formulation and implementation of policies (processes) in the technology field. What is an adequate technology policy in a DC and what are the institutional requirements for such a policy at the level of formulation and implementation? We deal with *industrial technology policy*, which aims at fostering a more advanced and competitive industrial structure, and the focus is technological advance and organizational learning, making it possible to master more complex technological activities within industries.

Section II examines the notions of technology and innovation in relation to development. Section III looks upon the notion of technology and innovation from a policy perspective. Section IV addresses TCs, learning, and national innovation systems (NISs). Section V deals with potential governance failures along the policymaking process and with the institutional preconditions for effective (technology) policymaking.

II. Technology, Innovation, and Development Policy

There is no agreement on about what technology and innovation are, and how they are related to economic development. More *orthodox* contributions consider technological change to be an exogenous and mostly disembodied factor. In the neoclassical textbook universe, technology is considered as a public good — dissociated from the process of accumulation. As firms are assumed to have full knowledge of all possible technologies, technology is a public good that firms can choose from a "shelf of techniques" and the acquisition is assumed to be costless ("costless technology choice"). By further de-emphasizing the time dimension and allowing for almost instantaneous technology acquisition, technology absorption takes place without further risks, costs, and efforts. The core concern is not technological development, but effective utilization of technologies. Consequently, there is neither need for much technological effort at the firm level in DCs nor for particular political and institutional support (Cypher and Dietz, 1997: 402ff; Lall and Teubal, 1998: 1371).[1]

The *heterodox* theories of technological development have a different notion of technology and its role in industrial development. We will in particular draw upon and combine elements taken from evolutionary, (neo-)structuralist, and broader NIS approaches. Rather than presenting and comparing various heterodox contributions, the aim (in this and in the following sections) is to discuss the most important policy implications following from selected insight in these approaches (Dosi, 1988; Dosi et al., 1994: 35ff; Lall and Teubal, 1998: 1371ff; Felker and Jomo, 1999: 11ff). The heterodox theories are concerned with the innovative creativity and adaptive learning of firms, with processes of economic change, and with market competition as an instrument for transfer of change-impulses and a selection process.

The focus is on *technical change* that according to Fransman (1985: 584) refers to "improvements in the transformation of inputs into outputs, including improvements in the quality of outputs." *Technology* is not to just understood as fully transmittable codified information, but encompasses all the activities (including organization and knowledge) involved in this transformation process. Bell and Albu (1999: 1717) describe technology as a complex and interconnected bundle of knowledge "with much of it embodied in a wide range of different artifacts, people, procedures, and organizational arrangements."

Dosi's (1988: 222) broad definition of *innovation* as "the search for, and the discovery of, experimentation, development, imitation, and adoption of new products, new production processes, and new organizational set-ups" demonstrates the many different activities involved. It should be noticed that there is no sharp distinction between innovation and diffusion because both the adoption and the postadoption phases of even simple technologies require creative problem solving leading to incremental developments and modifications. Moreover, the definition includes technological and organizational innovations. The wide spectrum of technological changes and their location at all points in the production chain imply that technology policy should not focus exclusively on promotion of autonomous R&D but support all the activities involved in continuous improvement of production of industrial goods.

From a policy perspective, this leads to considerable scepticism toward technology policies that give priority to formation of public research laboratories that are involved in the production of totally new technology rather than diffusion of known technology to the private sector. The point is not that R&D is unimportant but that its relative importance varies across industries and levels of industrialization. Broader innovation policies are even more important in late-industrializing countries. Here, search for new products and processes, adaptation of product and processes to local conditions, and minor improvements in existing products and processes are the main innovation activities.

III. TC, Learning, and NISs

Thus latecomers which import huge amounts of technology *cannot* cost-free access and absorb new technologies. One aspect is that codified knowledge is becoming increasingly constrained by intellectual property rights and other means of "high tech neomercantilism" (Ernst and Lundvall, 2000). Another aspect — which is focused here — is that because much of the relevant skills and knowledge exist in a tacit or semitacit form (e.g., rules of thumb) embodied in persons rather than being embodied in machinery or available in machine manuals, textbooks, and blueprints (codified knowledge), they have to be learned through practice. Firms in DCs must eventually develop the tacit knowledge component to be able to use, adapt, and modify the imported technology.

The notion of TCs is to attempt to capture the great variety of skills and stocks of knowledge required to efficiently utilize such new equipment and technical information. These capabilities are located in the technology-using firms. Lall (1993: 720) defines TCs in industry as "the skills — technical, managerial, and institutional — that allow productive enterprises to utilize equipment and technical information efficiently. Such capabilities are firm-specific, a form of institutional knowledge that is made up of the combined skills of its members accumulated over time."

There is a range of subdivisions of TCs, and many scholars combine a range of functional competence related to the activities they serve (investment, process engineering, product engineering, industrial engineering) with levels of capability according to technological complexity or depths (simple-routine activities, adaptive-duplicative activities, innovative-risky). The depths or "innovativeness" of TCs are of particular importance. The definition of capabilities encompasses both the capabilities to operate existing facilities and capabilities related to technological change. It is generally acknowledged that firms in DCs could achieve considerable productivity gains by investing more in developing their operating skill and know-how (higher static efficiency), but long-term dynamic efficiency can only be achieved if there is an accumulation of the skills and knowledge needed to generate and manage technological change (Bell and Pavitt, 1993; Lall, 2000).

The process of acquiring and accumulating TCs is in itself a complex process, sometimes referred to as *learning* (or technological accumulation)

(Bell and Pavitt, 1993: 164). Learning takes not just efforts but also *time* to succeed. Newer innovation research stresses that there is still considerable uncertainty and complexity in the process of acquiring and adapting imported technology. Further when changing input conditions, changing market conditions, variable consumer tastes, and other dynamic factors are taken into account, it becomes clear that there is a need of continuing, incremental technological change and thus for the intangible and tacit skills and knowledge that makes such change possible. Finally, when a fast-moving technology-frontier, growing complexity of technologies, still shorter product cycles, and a growing global "scientification" of technology development are considered, catching-up strategies in DCs are confronted with considerable "late-industrialization penalties". Hence there is a need for forceful capability development efforts, including policy and institutional support. In a policy perspective, this means that there exists a valid argument for promoting, subsidizing, and protecting learning in new industries. This in turn raises the issue of how to manage policy-created learning rents (Amsden, 1989, 1997; Chang and Cheema, 2002).

It is also worth stressing the strong element of *diversity and plurality* in learning processes as well as in policies. Learning processes varies according to firm, industry, country, and level of development. There is no uniform well-known learning curve for a given technology, and so much depend on the point from where a firm starts (path dependency) and the character of its efforts (Wong, 1999: 56ff). Further, different industries or rather industry segments tend to have different technology-specific features, which in turn result in different learning requirements. Countries have a different mix of industries and typical learning trajectories. Then from a policy perspective, it is important that technology policy reflects such diversity being adequate in relation to the specific learning trajectories.

Finally, and partly related, there exist a range of *sources or mechanisms for learning.* These various mechanisms or sources can be divided into those that are intra-firm sources (encompassing both internal technological activities and human capital formation at the firm level) and those that are extra-firm (Chantramonklasri, 1990; Lall, 1993: 722ff; Goldman et al., 1997, 20ff; Bell and Albu, 1999: 1724ff; Metcalfe, 1995: 32).

The firm-centered accumulation of technological skills, knowledge, and experience can be acquired through *firm-internal learning.* Though some passive learning may appear as a by-product of routine production activities ("learning by doing production"), newer innovation studies generally suggest that effective learning requires deliberate and costly efforts even at that level, and that technology-changing capabilities are mostly acquired accumulation through "learning by doing technological change" and "learning by doing investment." Directed, internal learning may be organized around formal R&D activities but as mentioned earlier, knowledge can also be acquired from involvement in repair and maintenance of equipment, from trial and error experimentation, from reverse engineering, and so on. A second major firm-centered form of technology accumulation relates to human resource formation at the firm level, which refers to internal training activities or to recruitment of personnel that already have the relevant knowledge from education, training, and working elsewhere (including inter-firm migration of science and technology [S&T] personnel). It should also be noticed that the importance of (the most relevant type(s) of) internal learning effort varies according to industry sector and level of industrial development. As firms — especially those located in DCs — often fail to invest sufficiently in TCs, in general, and in the deeper forms of capabilities, in particular, there is a strong case for policy intervention. Then from a policy perspective, a technological learning approach must give priority to public policies that raise firm-level awareness of the role of technology development ("learning-to-learn"), and stimulate the demand for firm-centered technology development activities and human resource development.

Although internal efforts are important in building a stock of TCs, firms do not accumulate stocks of knowledge in isolation but utilize a variety of firm *external sources* in this process. Of particular importance are *inter-firm relationships* ("learning from each other") — comprising transfer of knowledge and skills from long-term suppliers of machinery, from intermediate-goods producers, from foreign licensers, from customers, from consultants and from private contract facilities. Movement of staff among firms is another important form of spillover. Because the network of specialized S&T agents involved in capability development is "thinner" in DCs, and because many industrial enterprises are simply not aware of their technology problems there is a stronger need for public policy and institutional support in these countries.

First, "policies that encourage companies to learn from their domestic and overseas customers and suppliers (and more indirectly to export) clearly enhance a country's accumulation of technological capability" (Goldman et al., 1997: 3). Second, it is important to introduce policies that support inter-firm knowledge flows and collective learning, extending technological learning beyond the firm that acquired the knowledge in the first place. Third, public policies can support and stimulate flows of knowledge carried by people moving from one firm to another or from an existing firm to a new spinout firm. Fourth, public technology institutions may play a particular role in fostering inter-firm cooperation/collective learning. Finally, policies may be designed to promote the formation of private intermediate technology agents — consultants, contract research organizations, technology service providers training institutes, and so on — all of which may serve as repositories of selected capabilities and as important mechanisms of knowledge diffusion (Teubal, 1998a,b; Teubal and Andersen, 2002).

Another important external source of knowledge and skills is *public or quasi-public technology institutions* (such as universities, technical colleges, research laboratories, standard setting bodies, etc.). Most studies show that firms which have strong in-house capabilities are more likely to search for and use external sources, and that external sources cannot substitute for internal intangible technology resources (Bell and Pavitt, 1993: 176; Goldman et al., 1997: 1, 21). The notion of "absorptive capacity" is often used to describe this complementarity between the internal capability of firm and its external sources. The policy implications are: it is difficult for public technological institutions to reach and help smaller enterprises that often lack internal capabilities; many enterprises may have difficulties in absorbing more advanced knowledge provided by science and technology institutions (STIs).

Altogether, although individual companies are the primary actors in the generation of technological artifacts and in the accumulation of capabilities, they are deeply interwoven in the broader socio-economic fabric and they draw upon other firms as well as the broader private, semiprivate, and public S&T infrastructure.

The interactive character of learning and the governance issues involved has been developed further in system of innovation approaches, in which scholars emphasize that there exist systematic interactions and interdependencies that cannot be reduced the actions of individual firms or to competition between economic actors. Some scholars argue that the nation state constitutes a nonreductive level of analysis, while others refer to the local level ("clusters") or to sectoral systems.

The former group has advanced the concept NIS (Lundvall, 1992; Nelson and Rosenberg, 1993; Dahlman, 1994; Metcalfte, 1995). The performance of the individual firm depends on a well-functioning NIS. The definition of NIS varies considerably but they all describe NIS as a system of interconnected institutions involved in creating, storing, and transferring the knowledge, skills, and artifacts of new technologies. Moreover, they all include as important components: private firms, inter-firm relationships, universities and other national education and training establishments, public research laboratories, and private intermediate organization (i.e., they encompasses the firm-external sources of learning referred to earlier). Finally, they share the view that despite the fact that processes of sub-national regionalization and supra-national globalization/regionalization take place there is a determining national quality in the innovation system.

The systemic nature of learning processes calls for a "systemic" *policy approach* that ensures a balance and coherence in the range of (technology) policies that affect the industrial learning process. What is needed is a well-timed and well-coordinated policy deployment that simultaneously aims at promoting innovation and diffusion processes in the business sector (direct policies), and at influencing (strengthening) the facilitating infrastructure of (mostly) nonbusiness institutions and organizations (indirect policies). It should be noticed that an NIS approach does not imply a centrally driven conception of the innovation process and technology policy. The policy focus is rather on supporting the many sources of innovation (learning) with an emphasis on the diversity at the microlevel. The NIS approach therefore tends to downplay the planning role of the state at the macrolevel and to emphasize the enabling role of the state in relation to the functioning of the individual components of the NIS system as well as the system as a whole.

It is important to have in mind *that different (types of) countries have different systems of innovation.* As mentioned previously, countries have a different mix of industries and typical learning trajectories. To enhance learning and capability building, industrial technology policies must take the sectoral specialization and the specific production/innovation strategies of firm into account. Conversely, firm strategies tend to reflect, the broader institutional environment and the dominant mode of S&T policy. Gu (1999) suggests that when applied in a DC context, an NIS approach to policy must take into account the particular problems of late entry: the particular role of institutions and engineering specialists that support cross-border knowledge flows; the role of incentives to induce active learning at the enterprise level; the discontinuity involved in imitative learning when moving from lower imitative stages (e.g., assembly work) to higher stages; the role of external network linkages in technology diffusion; the role of initial technology choices on later choices (path dependence); the role of science and R&D for catching-up; and the particular nature and role of the S&T infrastructure in a late-industrializing country.

Finally, it might well be that emerging clusters of innovation activity and weak domestic institutions do not yet add up to an NIS, so that the issue is one of creating such a system. Rather than relying on a single policy package, the policy portfolio must differ across countries (and sectors) just as it has to evolve over time (Teubal, 1998a,b).

IV. Policy Formulation, Policy Implementation, and Institutional Set-Up

Design and implementation of a set of coherent and credible technology policies is not an easy matter, and the benefits of state intervention must be analyzed against the costs of policy failure. Technology upgrading is a complicated process, and to be effective in influencing the pace and direction of this process, a well-informed, skilled, disciplined, and connected government and administration is needed. Obviously, technology policies can fail as can technology strategies at the firm level, and failures can appear at all levels of the policy process.

In the interface between *agenda setting and policy formulation* phases, there may be a lack of a strategic vision and a preference for status quo "compromise" solutions. This is especially crucial when the simple and easy modes of technological learning are used up, and when there is a risk that the country is "locked into" a specialization in low-value-added products in which its competitiveness is challenged "from below". Lall and Teubal (1998: 1376) correctly stress that development trajectories are created, not found as logical outcomes "endowments" in the conventional static sense.

In the *policy formulation* phase, there may well be a lack of know-how among policymakers about the actual working of the private sector. There may also be inconsistency between evolving priorities and the portfolio of policies and programs suggested. There may be a subversion of policy processes to narrow — but strong — private interests, making it difficult to discipline nonperformers and to distribute subsidies (temporal protection, directed credits, etc.) conditional upon learning. There may — due to private sector pressure — be a preference for supporting existing firms rather than emerging firms with a higher potential. There may be a preference for assisting large firms — that often (but not always) are in a position to advance technologically by drawing upon own resources and inter-firm collaboration — while neglecting laggards and small and medium-sized enterprises (SMEs). There may be a lack of balance between the supply side and demand side of technology development. There may be a lack of coordination of technology policies with industrial and trade policies ensuring a high demand for technology development in the private sector. There may be a lack of balance between support for enterprise R&D and for the broader technological infrastructure. There may be an insufficient attention to policies that support firm-level capability accumulation and in particular inter-firm flows of knowledge. There may be an emphasis on hard technologies at the expense of the just as important organizational and managerial ones. There may be a preference for (too) technical sophisticated projects with a low market potential and low profitability (Rothwell and Zegveld, 1988: 26ff). Henceforth, reasonable choices and careful design of policies is required for industrial technology policy to succeed in accelerating and changing technological development. Furthermore, policies ought to be subject to learning themselves. The high degree of uncertainty and context specificity involved gives a premium to policies that are flexible and exper-imental — allowing for adjustments and learning from mistakes.

At the level of *implementation*, there is similarly a strong need for responsiveness and flexibility. Extensive policy coordination is also required both in relation to individual programs and between different, but systemically related, policy areas (e.g., between FDI policy and skill development plus S&T education policy). Functional duplication and contradictory initiatives in various parts of the bureaucracy can delay and invalidate well-designed policies. In order to ensure that policy implementation is adequate for the particular circumstances at a particular time, correct timing and sequencing of programs are also crucial. Further, the role of the government as catalyst and broker for collective learning processes is conditional upon interactive learning processes between public sector employees and private entrepreneurs or industry associations. At the same time, the bureaucracy must also demonstrate a certain "long-termism" because it also has to address the future demand of the less advanced enterprise segments, and take into account that lack of awareness and weak capabilities at the enterprise level makes policy support extremely difficult and may result in nonresponse to even well-designed technology policies. Therefore, policy implementation will also be about "building demand" for more advanced technological efforts. Finally, the technology institutes and even industry associations play a double role as being both an object of policy (setting up institutions) and a decentralized implementer of industrial technology policies.

The policy impact is determined, only in part, by policy design and the manner in which the policies are implemented. Even a well-designed and well-implemented industrial technology policy may have limited impact (1) if the resources, incentives (incl. competitive pressure), and capabilities of private enterprises are weak, (2) if industrial and trade policies undermine such policies, (3) if there is no mechanism for mitigating social resistance to change by compensating the looser, and (4) if the power and ideological hegemony in society work against industrial technology upgrading.

Thus while industrial technology policy constitutes a still more important part of strategic industrial policy in late-industrializing countries, it is also a policy, that due to its sector-specific nature, is particularly difficult to perform well and which is institutional demanding. The question about what constitute an appropriate technology policy has to take into consideration whether *the institutional and political conditions* for such a policy is present.

At the overall level, there is a need for an institutional innovation to support the above-mentioned "vision" for a national technology policy and to make interdepartmental coordination between a wide range of public agencies and institutions possible and effective. In particular, technology policies and institutional support have to be integrated into a broader set of trade and industrial policies ("the incentive environment") that reward firms who invest in technology development and penalizes firms that make few or inappropriate technology efforts. Therefore, it is always a risk if technology issues are "parked" in second-rank ministries with no voice in the broader industrial policymaking or spread over a number of disconnected agencies. The organizational form of the industrial technology agency may vary but an effective interface between bureaucratic and political forces and strong analytical backing are needed. Owing to the highly complex, multifaceted, and uncertain nature of policymaking in this field, a highly qualified bureaucracy with "multidisciplinary skills involving knowledge of technology, economics, management, and public policy skills" are needed (Justman and Teubal, 1995: 276). Furthermore, priority setting must also draw upon external expertise — in Academia, in technical associations, in trade associations, etc. Such linking activity is particularly important when the country shift from a low-technology trajectory to a higher technology trajectory ("path-shifting") because the coevolution of policy initiatives and the responses of economic agents cannot be totally planned in beforehand but has to be adjusted when information on prior experience is fed back into the policy process ("policy learning").

In order not to be "captured" by existing enterprises produced by existing technologies and often passively dependent on importing foreign technologies, the state must retain sufficient autonomy. Conversely, it must also be sufficiently connected or embedded in strong policy networks and intermediate institutions that link the state apparatus and the private sector. Such embedded autonomy (Evans, 1995) is particularly important in relation to an uncertain and feedback-intensive policy field such as technology policy. At the stage when targeting policies become an indispensable part of the policy portfolio, insularity and weak policy networks make effective implementation extremely difficult because of the lack of feedback from stakeholders. Consequently, delegation of programming and implementation functions to industry associations or regional institutions which is widespread in advanced economies might also be helpful in ensuring both feedback information and broad-based political support in late-industrializing countries. Institutional reform, therefore, is an integral part of an effective industrial technology policy portfolio.

In summary, effective industrial policymaking requires both adequate information and bureaucratic capabilities, including the ability to monitor policies and rectify mistakes, and the ability to work in close consultation with the industries and firms concerned. This is also the case when STIs are involved in decentralized implementation of policies. The STIs have to be well managed and with a staff whose skills and expertise match the needs of the sector or clients they serve, and in order to obtain constant information flows, serve actual client needs, build demand for new technological services, and catalyze collective learning processes, they need both operational autonomy and social embeddedness, too. In general, the public agencies involved have to be "learning institutions" themselves (adaptive policymaking). They have to be able to design and implement not the "perfect reform" but a set of strategic — yet flexible and responsive — policies.

Note

1. Although technological innovation is increasingly taken up in explaining economic growth, it merely takes the form of additional nontradable inputs stemming from the autonomous "R&D sector" and autonomous "education sector." For an overview of more dynamic neoclassical models, see for example, Chang and Cheema (2002: 372–375). On endogenous growth theory that allows productivity increases to be generated internally through positive externatilities or though increasing returns to scale, see for example, Cypher and Dietz (1997: Chapter 8) and Fine (2000).

References

Amsden, A., *Asia's Next Giant: South Korea and Late Industrialization*, Oxford University Press, New York and Oxford, 1989.

Amsden, A., Editorial: Bringing production back in: understanding government's economic role in late industrialization, *World Dev.*, 25 (4), 469–480, 1997.

Bell, M. and Pavitt, K., Technological accumulation and industrial growth: contrast between developed and developing countries, *Ind. Corporate Change* 2 (2), 157–210, 1993.

Bell, M. and Albu, M., Knowledge systems and technological dynamism in industrial clusters in developing countries, *World Dev.*, 27 (9), 1715–1734, 1999.

Chang, H.-J. and Cheema, A., Conditions for successful technology policy in developing countries: learning rents, state structures, and institutions, *Econ. Innovation New Technol.*, 11 (4–5), 369–398, 2002.

Chantramonklasri, N., The development of technological and managerial capability in the developing countries, in *Technology Transfer in the Developing Countries*, Chatterji, M., Ed., Macmillan, London, 1990, pp. 36–50.

Cypher, J.N. and Dietz, J.L., *The Process of Economic Development*, Routledge, London and New York, 1997.

Dahlman, C.J., Technology strategy in East Asian developing economies, *J. Asian Econ.*, 5 (4), 541–572, 1994.

Dosi, G., The nature of the innovative process, in *Technical Change and Economic Theory*, Dosi, G., Freeman, C., Nelson, R., Silverberg, G., and Soete, L., Eds., 1988, pp. 221–238.

Dosi, G., Freeman, C., and Fabiani, S., The process of economic development: introducing some stylized facts and theories on technologies, firms and institutions, *Ind. Corporate Change* 3 (1), 1–41, 1994.

Ernst, D. and Kim, L., Global production networks, knowledge diffusion and local capability formation, *Res. Policy*, 31, 1417–1429, 2002.

Ernst, D. and Lundvall, B.-A., Information technology in learning economy: challenges for developing countries, East-West Center Working Paper 8, Hawaii, 2000.

Evans, P., *Embedded Autonomy. States and Industrial Transformation*, Princeton University Press, Princeton, NJ, 1995.

Felker, G.B. and Jomo, K.S., Introduction, in *Technology, Competitiveness and The State: Malaysia's Industrial Technology Policies*, Jomo, K.S. and Felker, G.B., Eds., Routledge, London and New York, 1999, pp. 1–37.

Fine, B., Endogenous growth theory: a critical assessment, *Camb. J. Econ.*, 24 (2), 245–265, 2000.

Fransman, M., Conceptualising technical change in the Third World in the 1980s: an interpretive survey, *J. Dev. Stud.*, 21 (4), 572–652, 1985.

Gereffi, G., International trade and industrial upgrading in the apparel commodity chain, *J. Int. Econ.*, 48, 37–70, 1999.

Goldman, M., Ergas, H., and Felker, G., Technology institutions and policies. their role in developing technological capability in industry, World Bank Technical Paper 383, The World Bank, Washington, DC, 1997.

Gu, S., Implications of national innovation systems for developing countries: managing change and complexity in economic development, UNU-INTECH Discussion Paper Series 1999-3, United Nations University Institute for New Technologies, Maastricht, 1999.

Justman, M. and Teubal, M., Technological infrastructure policy (TIP): creating capabilities and building markets, *Res. Policy*, 24, 259–281, 1995.

Lall, S., Understanding technology development, *Dev. Change*, 24 (4), 719–53, 1993.

Lall, S., Technological change and industrialization in the Asian newly industrializing economies: achievements and challenges, in *Technology, Learning, and Innovation. Experiences from Newly Industrializing Countries*, Kim, L. and Nelson, R.R., Eds., Cambridge University Press, Cambridge, 2000, pp. 13–68.

Lall, S., FDI and development: research issues in the emerging context, in *Foreign Direct Investment. Research Issues*, Bora, B., Ed., Routledge, London and New York, 2002, pp. 325–345.

Lall, S. and Teubal, M., "Market-stimulating" technology policies in developing countries: a framework with examples from East Asia, *World Dev.*, 26 (8), 1369–1385, 1998.

Lundvall, B.-Å., Introduction, in *National Systems of Innovation. Towards a Theory of Innovation and Interactive Learning*, Lundvall, B.-Å., Ed., Pinter Publishers, London, 1992, pp. 1–19.

Metcalfe, J.S., Technology systems and technology policy in an evolutionary framework, *Camb. J. Econ.*, 19 (1), 25–46, 1995.

Meyer-Stamer, J., Technology, competitiveness and governance, in *Technology, Competitiveness and The State. Malaysia's Industrial Technology Policies*, Jomo, K.S. and Felker, G.B., Eds., Routledge, London and New York, 1999, pp. 38–52.

Nelson, R.N. and Rosenberg, N., Technical innovation and national systems, in *National Innovation Systems. A Comparative Analysis*, Nelson, R.N., Ed., Oxford University Press, New York and Oxford, 1993, pp. 3–21.

Rothwell, R. and Zegveld, W., An assessment of government innovation policy, in *Government Innovation Policy: Design, Implementation, Evaluation*, Roessner, J.D. Ed., St. Martin Press, Hong Kong, 1988, pp. 19–35.

Teubal, M., Enterprise restructuring and embeddedness: an innovation perspective, CRIC Discussion Paper 15, CRIC, The University of Manchester, 1998a.

Teubal, M., Policies for promoting enterprise restructuring in national systems of innovation, Triggering Cumulative Learning and Generating System Effects, STI Review 22, OECD, Paris, 1998b.

Teubal, M. and Andersen, E., Enterprise restructuring and embeddedness: a policy and systems perspective, *Ind. Corporate Change*, 9 (1), 87–111, 2000.

Wong, P.K., Technological capability development by firms from East Asian NIEs: possible lessons from Malaysia, in *Technology, Competitiveness and the State. Malaysia's Industrial Technology Policies*, Jomo, K.S. and Felker, G., Eds., Routledge, London and New York, 1999, pp. 53–64.

Chapter 43

Health, Development, and Governance

James Warner Björkman

CONTENTS

I. Introduction

The fact that health policy affects the living conditions and life chances of people is not new. What is new today is an effort to make the impact of health policies explicit and, where necessary and possible, to alter the policies in the direction of emerging health paradigms. Health policy is an integral part of development, which is guided by sound governance. Strengthening core public health functions by reforming policies and institutions has become a significant element in development governance, and the Millennium Development Goals "provide a chance to refocus health policy on health outcomes and the major determinants, core interventions, and delivery strategies" (Wagstaff and Claeson, 2004: 45).

This chapter explores the health domain and some of its relevant aspects and their relation to the formulation and implementation of health policy. It describes the context of health policy and the process of actors playing roles in local, national, and international governance. Public health, the "new" public health, and health promotion are highlighted to understand their contributions within changing models of development and governance.

The concept of health has many variations. Different societies, cultures, groups, and individuals perceive health in different ways, and they differ in the meaning of disease and ill health. Beliefs about health, disease, and illness also differ according to socioeconomic status, gender, profession, and role. As definitions of health change over time, the perceived health needs of people also change. Paradigms on what constitutes health and how to understand it from different perspectives have been broadened by scientific investigations, as well as by the emergence of new ideas (Curtis and Taket, 1996).

Health is a policy area of global concern. Efforts to promote health cannot be restricted to a particular country because diseases do not confine within geographical borders. They are transferred from one place to the other through travel, migration, social exchange, and commerce. Efforts to prevent disease and to promote health require cooperation and collaboration of agencies at local, national, and international levels. By emphasizing ecological perspectives, modern health paradigms urge wider involvement by various actors and people. Consequently, conceptual consistency in developing health policies, programs, and strategies at various levels is important (Barker, 1996).

Awareness of concepts and understanding of modern health paradigms are important for development. Guided by modern health paradigms, national health policies address problems of disease and ill health. By focusing on the determinants of health, such paradigms help national authorities to integrate health programs, projects, and strategies at local, national, regional, and international levels. Knowledge of health practices encourages policymakers to invest to combat health problems and improve life chances (Green, 1996).

II. Health Domain

The word "health" derives from an Old English word "heal" (*hael*) which means "whole"; it signals that health concerns the whole person and his integrity, soundness, or well-being. However, health represents different things to different people at different times in different situations. All who engage in health promotion start with a more or less specific view on health. The following definitions provide a range of representative concepts.

> Health is complete physical, mental, and social well-being and not merely the absence of disease or infirmity. (WHO, 1947)

> Health is the expression of the extent to which the individual and the social body maintain in readiness the resources required to meet the exigencies of the future. (Dubos, 1962)

> Health is a state of optimum capacity of an individual for the effective performance of the roles and tasks for which he has been socialized. (Parsons, 1972)

> Health is a relative state that represents the degree to which an individual can operate effectively within the circumstances of his hereditary and his physical and cultural environment. (McDermott, 1977)

The World Health Organization (WHO) definition is a positive definition characterized by absoluteness. It has been criticized for including the word "complete" because this concept is without boundaries and therefore unattainable. Nevertheless, the interaction between physical, mental, and social spheres to achieve well-being has been recommended (de Leeuw,

1989). Parsons' functionalist definition has also been criticized because it prescribes an optimal capacity to be measured in terms of achieving desired goals. The optimum in itself is a relative concept meaning, in this context, most favorable for a certain individual under given circumstances. Dubois's definition emphasizes the ability of individuals as well as groups to adapt to change; like McDermott's definition, it is a relative concept. While the latter takes only individuals into account, it stresses the relativism of human health. Dwore and Kreuter (1980) integrate these definitions and define five "irreducible minima of health":

■ The ability to adapt to changing situations
■ The capacity to perform valued tasks
■ Varying degrees of positive and negative states
■ Multidimensional causality
■ A relative state

The WHO health promotion movement defines health as "the extent to which an individual or group is able, on the one hand, to realize aspirations and safety needs, and, on the other hand, to change or cope with the environment" (Kickbusch, 1986). Others argue that health is holistic and includes different dimensions, each of which need to be considered (Aggleton and Homans, 1987; Ewles and Simnett, 1999). Holistic health takes account of the separate influences and interaction of these dimensions.

The scientific or "biomedical paradigm" of health, which constitutes the dominant tradition in the health professions, has two components: a disease component which holds that illness results from pathological processes in the biochemical functions of the body and an engineering component that regards the body as machine to be repaired by technical means (Commers, 2001). Throughout the 20th century, a key aim of health policy was to ensure that the results of medical science were available to the population through hierarchies of regionally organized services. Specialist hospital services have been major components in these hierarchies (Ham, 1992).

However, the scientific model came under attack during the last decades of the 20th century. Lalonde (1974), Blum (1974), McKeown (1976), and Hancock (1986) spearheaded the attack on medical dominance by questioning the significance of medical science in bringing about improvements in health. They sought to demonstrate that improved nutrition, safe water supply, behavioral changes, better spacing of births, and improved sewerage systems have been primarily responsible for the advances in health. These factors contributed significantly to the decline in infectious disease, and, more than clinical medicine, assisted in reducing death rates, and increasing life expectancy.

A. *Sociocultural and Personal Perceptions of Health*

Societies, cultures, and groups perceive health in different ways and have their own ways of talking about health. Precise meanings of the terms "health" and "disease" differ from one social group to another and even from person to person (Dubos, 1962; Commers, 2001). Many conclude that public beliefs about health and lay concepts of health differ because of socioeconomic status, cultural values, and gender (Herzlich, 1973; Blaxter, 1990). Stacey (1988) identifies three continua of health: individual versus collective health, functional fitness versus welfare, and preventive versus curative. In western societies, the individualistic concept of health dominates and is associated with ideas of functional fitness and curative approaches (Radley, 1994). This concept seeks the causes of illness within the biological system of individuals, and it attempts to provide a specific cure for the illness to make individuals fit for work.

III. Towards a Unified View of Health

Different definitions and concepts of health have enriched the knowledge, skill, and competence of health professionals to combat health problems and improve life chances. Governments and international organizations have attempted to unify the concepts of health to standardize policy interventions for development. As a consequence, the idea of positive health has grown increasingly popular. One source of such interest is the trend toward preventive and community-oriented medicine, which rejects the traditional medical focus on persons already ill.

Seedhouse (1986) combines different views into a unified concept of health by arguing that health is a means to an end rather than a fixed state toward which a person should aspire. Provided certain central conditions are met, people can be enabled to achieve their basic human needs, to access information about factors influencing health, and to develop skills to use that information. In addition to the individualistic concept of health, Stacey (1988) notes the existence of a collective concept that emphasizes the importance of prevention. The collective concept seeks the causes of illnesses within the environmental, economic, and social systems in which people live and attempts to prevent illness by tackling the unhealthy aspects of those systems.

The WHO has played an important role in advancing the debate about definitions of health throughout the world to unify the concept of health. In 1984, WHO presented a unified definition:

> Health is the extent to which an individual or group is able, on the one hand, to realize aspirations and satisfy needs, and, on

the other hand, to change or cope with the environment. Health is, therefore, seen as a resource for everyday life, not an object of living; it is a positive concept emphasizing social and personal resources, as well as physical capacities. (WHO, 1984)

This definition emphasizes the dynamic and positive nature of health. It implies that health is a fundamental human right, as well as a sound social investment. This view has been affirmed by the five international WHO conferences on health promotion between 1984 and 2000.

A. Public Health

The history of health is as old as human beings are (McNeill, 1997). Rosen (1958), an eminent medical historian, published *A History of Public Health* in which he suggested that "the protection and promotion of the health and welfare of its citizens was considered to be one of the most important functions of the modern state." Rosen provided a chronological account of social progress and the technological advance of science and medicine in combating endemic and epidemic diseases.

In tracing the history of public health, most authors emphasize the 19th century when rapid industrialization, urbanization, and overcrowded slums led to new health problems. Florence Nightingale, Simpson, Virchow, Lister, Koch, Roentgen, Lansteiner, and many others conducted scientific investigations that led to public health movements as a solution to the new health problems. Edwin Chadwick, the principal architect of British public health, worked energetically as commissioner of the General Board of Health in the United Kingdom. In 1842, he published his *General Report on the Sanitation of Great Britain*. In 1850, in the United States, Lemuel Shattuck published his *Report of the Sanitary Commission of Massachusetts*. These 19th century leaders and others succeeded in linking the growing body of science — particularly bacteriology or sanitary science — with public health (Mullan, 2000).

In the mid-1970s, a clear separation of medicine from the broader views of public health emerged as it became evident that the sociocultural, political, economic, industrial, environmental, and behavioral determinants of health were beyond the limits of biomedical interventions. It became evident that clinical services alone could not combat the emerging health problems or improve life conditions. During the past half-century, the world has seen tremendous gains in health due to advances in science, technology, medicine, expanded infrastructures, rising incomes, improved nutrition, better sanitation, literacy, and opportunities for women (WHO, 1997a, b, c). Given such a comprehensive consciousness about public health, governments and international organizations as well as health professionals began to realize that health promotion is well beyond the scope of medical care.

The causes of health are complex, and the sources for health problems are numerous, varied, and interdependent (Milio, 1986). To address this complexity, epidemiologists can determine many causes for only one health condition and toxicologists may unravel the health-damaging effects of a single substance (de Leeuw, 1989). However, until the late 1970s, it remained a big challenge for health planners to develop a clear health policy that addressed the complexity of health problems caused by various interdependent sources and linked with humankind, habitat, and wealth.

In 1977, the WHO initiated its concept of health for all (HFA) by the year 2000 as a goal for all societies. In 1978, WHO launched Primary Health Care at the Alma Ata Conference as a strategy to attain the goals of HFA. The HFA strategy advanced a vision to attain a level of health that would permit all people universally to lead socially and economically productive lives. This strategy has helped to unify the comprehensive health field, to articulate clear health policy goals and to develop interventions in a more integrated way.

In 1974, Marc Lalonde introduced a conceptual framework for subdividing health into principal elements to organize the pieces into an orderly pattern, which was both intellectually acceptable and sufficiently simple to permit a quick location of any idea, problem, or activity related to health. As a sort of map of the health sector, his framework comprises four broad factors: human biology, environment, lifestyle, and health care organization. These four elements were identified by examining the causes and underlying factors of sickness and death in Canada and by assessing the extent to which these elements affect the level of health (Lalonde, 1974).

The human biology category includes all aspects of health, both physical and mental, that are developed within the human body as a consequence of basic biology and the organic make-up of the individual, the process of maturation and aging, and the complex internal systems in the body, such as skeletal, nervous, muscular, cardio-vascular, endocrine, digestive, and so on. These elements contribute to all kinds of ill health and mortality, including many chronic diseases (such as arthritis, diabetes, arteriosclerosis, and cancer) and others (genetic disorders, congenital malformation, and mental retardation). Health problems originating from human biology cause untold miseries and cost billions of dollars in treatment services.

The environment category includes all matters related to health which are external to the human body and over which the individuals have little or no control. Individuals cannot by themselves ensure that foods, drugs, cosmetics, devices, water, and noise pollution are controlled; that the spread of communicable diseases is prevented; that effective garbage collection and sewage disposal are carried out; and that the social environment, including rapid changes in it, does not have harmful effects on health.

The lifestyle category consists of the aggregated decisions by individuals which affect their health and over which they have more or less control. Personal decisions and habits that are bad from a health point of view create self-imposed risks. When those risks result in illness or death, the individual's lifestyle can be said to have contributed to, or caused, his own illness or death.

The health care organization consists of the quantity, quality, arrangement, nature, and relationships of people and resources in the provision of health care. It includes medical practice, nursing, hospitals, long-term care, pharmaceuticals, public and community health care services, ambulances, dental treatment, and other health services such as optometry, chiropractic, and pediatrics. This fourth element is generally defined as the health care system and is more directly relevant to development governance.

B. Redesigning the Model

Despite its innovative character, the Lalonde model was criticized because it made no attempt to clarify the interrelations of different components and their relative weights (Hancock, 1986). For this purpose, Hancock redesigned the model into an ecological "Mandala of Health" (Figure 43.1).

Hancock believes that the environment as determinant of health cannot be restricted only to the physical environment. In this regard, he goes beyond Lalonde by including the human-made environment as a significant determinant of health. The political, economic, and cultural environments also influence the health and well-being of a population.

Neither the health field concept nor the mandala of health is an adequate conceptual model for health because they do not discriminate among the various components. Furthermore, they do not operationalize or quantify their components and variables. These weaknesses restrict the potential of the models for designing interventions to combat health problems. Nevertheless, they provide a good impression of the complexities within the health sector (de Leeuw, 1989; Barker, 1996).

C. Blum's Force Field and Well-Being Paradigms of Health

At the same time as the Lalonde Report, Henrik Blum (1974) set the pace for a new approach to health planning with his book *Planning for Health*. His health planning theory relies on three premises:

- An understanding of the force field and well-being paradigms of health.

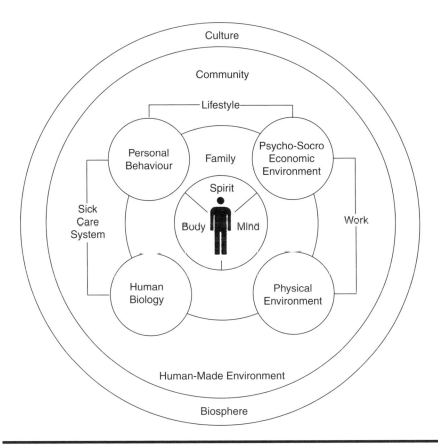

Figure 43.1 Hancock's mandala of health. (From Hancock, T., Lalonde and beyond: looking back at 'a new perspective on the health of Canadians', *Health Promotion: Int. J.,* **1 (1), 93–100, 1986. With permission.)**

- Insight into the complex nonsubstantive, and therefore political, nature of health, and health sector problem issues.
- The need for rational analysis of the problem as well as rational planning and implementation approaches. The theoretical angle chosen for this approach is the systems theory.

Blum visualizes these substantive factors at work in the model presented in Figure 43.2.

The outer ellipse represents the "force-field paradigm" of health, and the inner circle represents the "well-being paradigm" of health. The components of the force-field paradigm resemble the four components of the health field concept (Figure 43.1): human biology, lifestyles, environment, and organization of medical care. The relative weights of the components

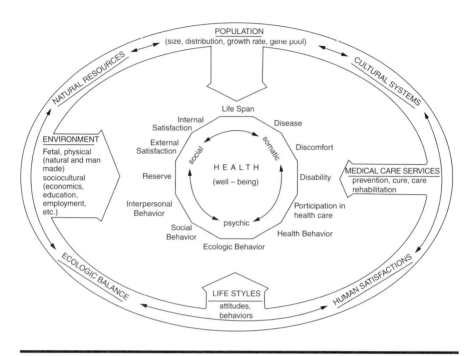

Figure 43.2   Blum's force-field and well-being paradigms of health. (From Blum, H., *Planning for Health: Development and Application of Social Change Theory,* **Human Sciences Press, New York, 1974. With permission.)**

are represented (the width of the four force arrows) as well as their inter-relations (the ellipse itself): the whole field of forces symbolizes the ecological view of what affects health. The inner circle is the "well-being paradigm." The basic notion is that health is holistically determined. The aspects of health such as psychic, social, and somatic health could not be separated from each other. In addition, this holistic well-being view includes determinants of health such as political, socio-cultural, and economic conditions.

In Blum's view, a thorough step-by-step systems analysis of the problem would produce ways of dealing with those complex problems. Since it is clear from his premises that health cannot be isolated from society or the social process, he tries to establish a framework for publicly planned deliberate social change. Assessment of the current situation — that is, identification of health needs and translation of those into health goals — is a first step. Problems and goals analysis should subsequently give weighted priorities to a range of intervention types. Blum asserts that establishing an implementation mechanism is a crucial step in the development of health policy, and part of that step is to create a responsible planning body. Finally, evaluation is required to adjust both goals and means to the changing conditions (Blum, 1974).

Blum's work is a landmark work in health policy. It provides suggestions for the creation of an integrated health policy, although its rational-deductive framework to plan for health has never been tested. Nevertheless, this seminal work has influenced health planners and other stakeholders in considering health comprehensively (de Leeuw, 1989; Collins et al., 1999).

IV. New Public Health

The concept of "new public health" emerged in the early 1980s as a revival of interest in public health by reframing and broadening its boundaries and by acknowledging the influence of economic, environmental, and social factors on health. During the 19th century, the view of public health was dominated by the impact of the physical environment, whereas the new public health is ecological in perspective. Governments and international organizations now argue for the comprehensiveness of health concepts and the importance of ecological perspectives to develop health promoting policies that focus on all determinants of health.

At the national level, for example, the Swedish government issued a health policy document in 1980, which concluded that it does not make sense to treat a wide range of health conditions in a reductionist way (HS90, 1984). In 1988, the Acheson Report in England defined public health as the science and art of preventing disease, prolonging life, and promoting health through the organized efforts of society. What has been called the "new" public health also means statutory and voluntary agencies working together to assess the implications for health in all public policies such as agriculture, energy, transport, defense, economic development, employment, housing, education, and leisure. Such a comprehensive view to develop strategies, program, and policies in partnerships with communities was adopted in making Liverpool a healthy city (Naidoo and Wills, 2000).

The new public health drew on WHO programs that set targets for healthy environments in its HFA European Region targets (WHO, 1985b). The 1986 Ottawa Charter identified healthy public policy as a central plank for health promotion. One of the aims of health promotion is to focus on public health issues such as pollution, occupational hazards, housing, and settlements (WHO, 1986a). The Adelaide Conference defined healthy public policy as an explicit concern for health and equity in all areas of policy and to create a supportive environment, which enables people to live healthy lives or to make the healthy choice an easier choice (WHO, 1988). In 1991, WHO organized its Third International Conference on

Health Promotion at Sundsvall, Sweden. In 1992, the Association for Public Health, a multidisciplinary organization to promote public health policy, was created.

The United Nations Earth Summit on the Environmental and Development in 1992 in Rio de Janeiro launched Agenda 21. This agenda charted a program of actions for sustainable development into the 21st century, which addressed environmental, social, and economic aspects of development. The Rio declaration stated that human beings are at the center of concerns for sustainable development and entitled to a healthy productive life in harmony with nature (United Nations, 1992a, b). Agenda 21 committed all signatory governments to the objectives of meeting the basic essentials for health — namely, safe food and water, sanitation and housing, controlling communicable diseases, protecting vulnerable groups such as children, and reducing the health risks caused by pollution, excessive energy consumption, and waste.

In 1995, WHO renewed its commitment to HFA. While there has been progress in disease prevention, control, and worldwide decline in communicable diseases (WHO, 1997b), new and old infectious diseases remain important threats to global health. There is uncertainty in projections for the future because of the potential for travel and trade, urbanization, migration, and microbial evolution to amplify these diseases and to create conditions for their re-emergence. HFA in the 21st century presents the values and principles to guide action and policy for health at global, regional, national, and local levels (WHO, 1997b, c). The goals that the renewed HFA strategy seeks to achieve are an increase in healthy life expectancy for all people, access for all to adequate health care of good quality, and health equity among and within countries. These goals must be realized through the implementation of three policy directives: embracing the values of HFA, making health central to development, and developing sustainable health systems.

Organized by WHO in 1997 in Jakarta, the Fourth International Conference on Health Promotion viewed health promotion as a comprehensive, multistrategy approach that used diverse strategies and methods in an integrated manner (WHO, 1997a). The conference evaluated the impact of health promotion and identified innovative strategies to achieve success in health promotion. In the same year, the U.K. appointed a minister for public health and introduced a white paper to improve local health promotion programs. The Fifth Global Conference for Health Promotion in Mexico City in 2000 sought to demonstrate how health promotion strategies add value to the effectiveness of health and development policies, programs, and projects, particularly those that aim at improving health and quality of life of the people living in adverse circumstances. The conference tried to place health high on the development agenda of international, national, and local agencies and to stimulate partnerships for health between different sectors and at all levels of society (WHO, 2000).

The rise of the environmental movement and of "Green" politics has raised the profile of public health through the concepts of globalization and sustainability. The globalization of economic activities has meant that nation states no longer control those activities affecting their physical and social environment. For example, pollution from industrialized countries leads to climate change and the international money market affects employment patterns worldwide. More directly, through their management of developing countries' debts, the World Bank and the IMF have been accused of stifling social economic and health development in these countries (Macedo, 1988; Anyinam, 1989; Kanji and Manji, 1991; Loewenson, 1993; Kolko, 1999; Abbasi, 1999b; Henry, 2003).

Public health work includes raising the profile of health in a community or in a society by drawing attention to and by carrying out research. Working in one organization to create health awareness or working collaboratively with others to identify shared projects is also public health work. Public health therefore includes research, partnership, intersectoral collaboration, and advocacy as well as lobbying for policy changes. Many health practitioners may have aspects of public health work as a part of their role (Naidoo and Wills, 2000).

Public health has been defined as both a resource and an activity (Taylor et al., 1998). As a resource, public health includes gathering health information and statistics (epidemiology) to underpin decisions and interventions that impact on health status. Epidemiology has a long history and high credibility. There are efforts to broaden epidemiology to include lay views and priorities and to acknowledge the effect of social factors on health (Naidoo and Wills, 1998). Public health action refers to activities undertaken by international agencies, governments, professionals, nongovernmental organizations, communities, families, and individuals, all of which promote health (de Leeuw, 1999; Naidoo and Wills, 2000). The core principles that underpin the synergy of public health and development are participation, equity, and collaboration.

A. Participation

The concepts of empowerment and participation are defined as the "twin pillars" of the new health promotion movement (WHO, 1986b; Robertson and Minkler, 1994; Minkler, 1999). Health professionals recognize the need to build on a population's understanding about its unique resources and goals. Participatory and empowerment initiatives, which connect with pre-existing public knowledge in this regard, have been shown to generate more effective and widespread participation (Björkman, 1995; Eisen, 1994).

Participation has been effectively used to combat environmental degradation (Clarke, 2001; Boyce, 2002). It successfully targeted young people in combating problems of tobacco and alcohol use (Campbell and Mzaidume, 2001). Participation can more effectively address the issues of access, inclusion, equity, and collaboration (Cockburn and Trentham, 2002). In addition, it makes health programs more effective and improves safety (Howat et al., 2001). It is broadly accepted that the public should have the right to be consulted and provide inputs in the policy-making process. The means of public consultation range from formal to informal, one-off events to ongoing contacts, and reactive to proactive procedures. Activity undertaken to increase public participation and involvement is a form of public health work (Naidoo and Wills, 2000).

B. Equity

A wealth of evidence supports the proposition that social, economic, gender, territorial, and professional inequalities reflect health inequalities (Conley, 2001; Devlin and Appleby, 2001; Goddard and Smith, 2001; Gwatkin, 2001; Hjortsberg and Mwikisa, 2002). The Black Report and the Acheson Report highlighted the link between poverty and ill health. More deprived and disadvantaged groups suffer higher levels of ill health and premature death than affluent and advantaged groups. There is also evidence that people living in societies with greater inequality experience poorer health when compared with more egalitarian societies. This evidence provides a strong argument for advocating greater social and economic equity as a means of promoting health.

Equity refers to material resources, power, specific status, and environment that enable people to achieve desired goals and services (Sen, 2001; Starfield, 2001). Equity is an important objective in the health field and its importance can be argued from various points of view (Ngom et al., 2001). Equity, or being fair and just, is not the same as equality, which is the state of obtaining similarity of condition (Björkman, 2003). While substantive equality is impossible to achieve, procedural equality through the provision of equal services for people with equal needs and working to reduce known inequalities in health are realistic endeavors (Perez et al., 2001; Vernon and Sherwood, 2001; Cockburn and Trentham, 2002).

C. Collaboration

Collaboration means working together with others on shared projects. Collaboration is essential since many sectors, agencies, and people are involved in health related issues. In a government, for example, diverse authorities and sectors take decisions that affect health directly or indirectly — such as agriculture, housing, energy, sanitation, water, labor, transport, trade, finance, education, environment, justice, and foreign affairs. Developing collaboration and working together with other sectors and actors can induce fundamental changes with great potential to promote health (Gilson et al., 1994).

It is the basic responsibility of the health sector to develop collaboration and to ensure effective linkages among its various departments such as well ministries, other sectors, groups, organizations, actors, and communities to achieve the goal of good health (Scholes and Endacott, 2001; Dehlippi, 2002). Collaboration enhances the performance of health professionals, contributes to successful implementation, makes services more accessible, and helps to solve problems of resource constraints (Cockburn and Trentham, 2002).

V. Health Promotion

Health promotion and the *new public health* share many principles and strategies. The principles and content of modern health promotion are identical to those of the new public health (MacDonald, 1998). In the same way, many health workers have a public health role — for example, community nurses, health promotion specialists, environmental health officers, social workers, community health workers, drug inspectors, and many others. The term health promotion is the central force in the new public health movement. Paralleling the growth of interest in health promotion in recent years has been a resurgence of interest in public health (Downie et al., 1999; Naidoo and Wills, 2000).

The term health promotion is used in a number of ways. While there is no agreed consensus on what health promotion is or what health promoters should do to promote health, health promotion includes a range of interventions focusing on healthy lifestyles, access to services, involvement in decisions, and health education. In the past, most health promotion interventions were described as health education and the practice was almost exclusively located in preventive medicine or, to a lesser extent, education. The terms health education and health promotion are often used interchangeably but health education is a component of a broader concept of health promotion. Health promotion is an umbrella term under which health education functions as a part that depends on the variety of action areas within the scope of that umbrella (Green and Kreuter, 1999).

Health promotion encompasses different political orientations, which can be characterized as individual versus structural approaches. Health promotion involves lobbying and political advocacy, but it may easily involve working with individuals and groups to enhance their knowledge and understanding of the factors affecting their health (Tones and Tildford, 1994). As a set of values and principles to be incorporated in all health and welfare work, health promotion comprises efforts to enhance positive health and to reduce the risk of ill health through the overlapping spheres of health education, prevention, and health protection. Crib and Dines (1993) argue that finding ways to promote health is more important than fixing the definition and domain of health promotion. To accept such a definition implies no boundaries to health promotion, since any question or event between client and practitioner has the potential to be health promoting (Naidoo and Wills, 2000).

According to the WHO, health promotion is the process of enabling people to increase control over as well as to improve their health. To reach a state of complete physical, mental, and social well-being, an individual or group must be able to identify and realize aspirations, to satisfy needs, and to change or cope with the environment. Health is, therefore, a resource for everyday life, not the objective of living. Health is a positive concept that emphasizes social and personal resources as well as physical capacities. Health promotion is thus not only the responsibility of the health sector but also requires healthy life-styles for well-being (WHO, 1985a). Peace, shelter, education, food, income, stable ecosystem, sustainable resources, social justice, and equity are fundamental conditions to improve health. The Ottawa Charter in 1986 identified five action areas to promote health: build healthy public policy, create supportive environments, strengthen community actions, develop personal skills, and reorient health services. Three ways in which practitioners can promote health through their work and thereby contribute to development are advocacy, enablement, and mediation.

A. Advocacy

As a major resource for social, economic, and personal development, good health is an important dimension for quality of life. Political, economic, social, cultural, behavioral, environmental, and biological factors can favor health or harm it. Health promotion seeks to make these conditions favorable to health through advocacy. Advocacy means representing the interests of disadvantaged groups and speaking on their behalf as well as lobbying to influence policy. It includes any attempt to insist policymakers to rationalize the nature of health disadvantage. For example, evidence of individual and community health needs should be collected to demonstrate the implications for health of social and political issues (WHO, 1986d).

People's knowledge and understanding of factors that affect health should be increased and health promoters should work to empower people so they may argue their own right to health and negotiate changes in their personal environment. Advocacy has proved to be an effective way to combat various health problems and to control smoking (Vaught and Paranzino, 2000; Raviglione and Pio, 2002). Advocacy helps to improve knowledge, enhance capabilities of health professionals, and develop communication among health professionals and patients (Olsen, 2001; Hewitt, 2002).

B. Enablement

Health promotion focuses on achieving equity in health. It aims at reducing differences in health status and at ensuring equal opportunities and resources to enable people to achieve their fullest health potential. Preconditions include a secure foundation in a supportive environment, access to relevant information, life skills, and opportunities for making healthy choices. People cannot achieve their full health potential unless they are able to control those things that determine their health. This applies equally to women and men.

Health promoters work to increase knowledge, understanding, and coping strategies of individuals and communities. In attempting to improve access to health, health promoters work with individuals and communities to identify needs and to develop supportive networks in the neighborhood (Bracht, 1999). Enablement is an essential core skill for health promoters since it requires them to act as catalyst and then stand aside, giving control to the community (Heaney et al., 2002). Enablement helps to develop coordination as well as collaboration among the variety of health professionals and patients in seeking improved ways of treatment and to empower health professionals and patients to develop "adult-to-adult" rather than "adult-to-child" relationships that accept as well as enable autonomy, accountability, fidelity, and humanity (Mantle, 2002).

C. Mediation

The prerequisites and prospects for health cannot be ensured by the health sector alone. Health promotion requires coordinated action by all concerned: governments, health and other social and economic sectors, nongovernmental and voluntary organizations, local authorities, industry, and the media. People in all walks of life are involved as individuals, families, and communities. Professional and social groups and health personnel have a major responsibility to mediate among differing interests in society for the pursuit of health. It is important for mediation to develop health strategies and programs adaptive to the local needs and possibilities of individual countries and regions to take into account differing social, cultural, and economic systems (WHO, 1986c).

Many studies reveal the advantages and benefits of mediation to the users and patients. Mediation plays an important role in making health promotion strategies effective and in strengthening positive, healthy, and cooperative relationships between patients and health professionals (Saulo and Wagener, 2000; Brandon et al., 2001). Mediation helps to develop healthy behavior and explores to overcome resource constraints (Ennett et al., 2001; Sussman, 2001).

VI. Governance, Development, and Health

"Healthcare systems play a significant role in why we get well when we are sick; social environments play a significant role in why we are healthy or why we become sick in the first place" (Lavis and Sullivan, 1999: 312). The link between development and health policy requires governance at two levels. First, governance must secure mechanisms that help people to get well when they are sick. Second, it must foster socio-economic environments that keep people healthy or stop them from becoming sick in the first place. While governance for the health sector must provide specific medical interventions to tackle challenges such as tuberculosis, malaria, and HIV/ AIDS, it must also address the challenge of social transformation. To be effective in this era of globalization, when "the fundamental social, economic, and environmental determinants of population health are becoming increasingly supranational" (McMichael and Beaglehole, 2000), governance must advance both of these aspects simultaneously.

In 1981, the World Health Organization's World Health Assembly endorsed the "HFA by the year 2000" strategy to translate the Alma Ata Declaration of 1978 into a policy reality. The earlier declaration had enshrined health as a fundamental human right, to be secured by a participatory process of comprehensive primary health care in the context of multi-sectoral development. Health had earlier appeared as a fundamental human right in the UN Covenant on Social, Economic, and Cultural Rights. Both the UN Covenant and the Alma Ata Declaration recognize the central responsibility of the state and the international community for ensuring realization of the human right to health. However, Alma Ata also emphasized the community and the household for sustainable health.

Given the current health situation around the world, it is clear that HFA was not achieved at the second millennium. Moreover, at the international level, health goals have been revised and are now defined much more narrowly around specific diseases and specific quantitative goals, rather than in terms of universal human rights and socioeconomic transformation. Whereas the achievement of HFA as envisioned at Alma Ata required health to be treated as a public good, the neo-liberal development orthodoxy of the 1980s and early 1990s interpreted it instead as a private good. This development strategy affected health both indirectly and directly. The role of the market in determining entitlement to health increased while the role of the state diminished (Drache and Sullivan, 1999).

The realization during the 1990s that this process of economic globaliza tion was accompanied by an uneven distribution of economic benefits produced a modification of the overarching global development policy to ameliorate its worst effects. There was a greater emphasis on targeted poverty reduction through such mechanisms as safety-nets and microcredit, public–private partnerships, and debt relief through the Heavily Indebted Poor Country Initiative (HIPC). The notion of "good governance" became fashionable, and greater efforts were made by multilateral institutions to involve civil society in policy development and implementation. During this period, the WHO lost ground to the World Bank as the latter became the main source of funding of the health sector and set the main multilateral agenda in this field (Buse and Gwin, 1998; Abbasi, 1999a).

This modification in the overarching development strategy of the "Washington Consensus" and the changing relations between key multilateral institutions were reflected in health policy. Official policy circles realized that a better balance had to be struck between the goals of economic growth and social and environmental goals, including health. In 1993, the World Bank published its report, *Investing in Health*, which reiterated the importance of growth with equity. While the subsequent emphasis has been to involve a wide range of stakeholders through public–private partnerships, these "partnerships" are rarely based on equality and those in whose interest they are avowedly developed are generally excluded from their negotiation. For partnerships to be effective, health partners need to make policy as well as binding budgets together (Stott, 1999: 822).

The neo-liberal policy approach has argued that new ways of financing the tackling of health problems are necessary because of the failure of states. The idea of the failure, or at least the inefficiency, of states had been implicit in the World Bank's 1993 report. Yet, the market had also failed. Market entitlement increasingly meant that those who needed drugs and health services did not have access to them unless they could afford to buy them in the marketplace, but many if not most people throughout the world did not have sufficient wherewithal. Because the dominant policy consensus seeks to minimize the role of the state, the concept of public provision (national or global) has become an unfashionable alternative.

Since 1990, the presentation of the relationship between ill health and poverty has changed. Ill health contributes to poverty because, when people are ill, they are less productive. When they are less productive, they become poorer; when they become poorer, they suffer more ill health. However, the presentation of this relationship has shifted from ill health as a result of poverty, prevailing socio-economic structures and the dominant model of development, to health as an opportunity for poverty reduction and development. Whereas poverty was portrayed as the primary cause of ill health, the emphasis has shifted so that ill health is presented more as a key cause of poverty.

As seen in Section II, there is a wealth of evidence that socio-economic factors influence health and well-being more than medical intervention. Indeed, it has been suggested that "the strongest factor affecting health is the size of the gap between the rich and the poor" (Bezruchka, 2000: 322). Beaglehole and Bonita (1998: 590) argue:

> The main variations in health status among countries result from environmental, socio-economic and cultural factors, and medical care is of secondary importance. Poverty is the most important cause of preventable death, disease, disability, although only a low level of income per person is required to achieve acceptable life expectancy at the national level. Literacy, access to housing, safe water, sanitation, food supplies, and urbanization are also important determinants of health status that interact with poverty.

The 1993, World Bank Report acknowledged that "government policies which promote equity and growth together will therefore be better for health than those that promote growth alone" (World Bank, 1993: 7). Moreover, the better health of the population contributed significantly to further economic growth. Medical interventions are absolutely necessary to deal with the problems of infectious diseases and acute ill health, but greater socio-economic equity is vital to tackle the challenge of health.

VII. Conclusion

The human right to health requires political commitment at all levels to remove global, national, and local inequities, including unequal access to health services and medical care. Without such political commitment, the socioeconomic conditions that make HFA realizable do not and cannot exist. Action is needed far beyond health policy because health inequalities are rooted in socioeconomic structures.

The need to understand modern health paradigms and their impact on development has many reasons. These purposes include reaching an agreed health concept, developing relevant and appropriate health policy, implementing health policies effectively, and analyzing the health policy context as well as the roles of various actors influencing the health of the population. It is particularly important to develop a clear conceptual framework to promote health effectively. Such a framework must be adjustable to changes in ideas, investigations, or proposed interventions and must be ensured by political commitment.

In the pursuit of equitable development, modern health paradigms denote new ecological perspectives of disease prevention and protection, enhancement, and promotion of health globally. These health paradigms help to formulate viable health policies. These paradigms elaborate and integrate international health strategies such as HFA, primary health care and population planning with national health plans. They resolve conflicts and debates among actors involved in the health policy process at different levels. Through these paradigms, policymakers and professionals, groups and individuals understand the root causes of health problems and identify solutions. Knowledge and awareness of modern health paradigms help to ensure development.

References

Abbasi, K., The World Bank and world health: changing sides, *Br. Med. J.*, 318, 865–869, 1999a.

Abbasi, K., The World Bank and world health: focus on South Asia, I and II, *Br. Med. J.*, 318, 1066–1069, 1132–1135, 1999b.

Aggleton, P. and Homans, H., *Educating about AIDS*, NHS Training Authority, Bristol, 1987.

Anyinam, C.A., The social costs of the International Monetary Fund's adjustment programs for poverty: the case of health care developments in Ghana, *Int. J. Health Serv.*, 19, 531–547, 1989.

Barker, C., *The Health Care Policy Process*, Sage, London, 1996.

Beaglehole, R. and Bonita, R., Public health at the crossroads: Which way forward? *Lancet*, 351, 590–592, 1998.

Bezruchka, S., Is globalization dangerous to our health? *Western J. Med.*, 172, 332–334, 2000.

Björkman, J.W., Developmental lessons of Sri Lanka's health system: instruments and options in 'healthy' implementation, in *Public Policy Analysis and*

Design, Agnihotri, V.K., Ed., Concept Publishing Company, Delhi, 1995, pp. 133–159.

Björkman, J.W., *Policy Criteria for Human Development: Efficiency, Equity, Parity, Equality*, Oswaldo Cruz Foundation, Rio de Janeiro, 2003.

Blaxter, M., *Health and Lifestyles*, Tavistock/Routledge, London, 1990.

Blum, H., *Planning for Health: Development and Application of Social Change Theory*, Human Sciences Press, New York, 1974.

Boyce, W.F., Influence of health promotion bureaucracy on community participation: a Canadian case study, *Health Promotion Int.*, 17 (1), 61–68, 2002.

Bracht, N., *Health Promotion at the Community Level*, Sage, Newbury Park, 1999.

Brandon, S., Clarke, D., George, A., Jensen, J., Interns, T., and Paul, C.A., Survey of attitudes to parent–doctor conflicts over treatment for children, *New Zeal. Med. J.*, 114 (1145), 549–552, 2001.

Buse, K. and Gwin, C., World health: the World Bank and global cooperation in health: the case of Bangladesh, *Lancet*, 351, 665–669, 1998.

Campbell, C. and Mzaidume, Z., Grassroots participation, peer education and HIV prevention by sex workers in South Africa, *Am. J. Public Health*, 91 (12), 1978–1986, 2001.

Clarke, N., Training as a vehicle to empower careers in the community: more than a question of information sharing, *Health Social Care Community*, 9 (2), 79–88, 2001.

Cockburn, L. and Trentham, B., Participatory action research: integrating community occupational therapy practice and research, *Can. J. Occup. Ther.*, 69 (1), 20–30, 2002.

Collins, C., Green, A., and Hunter, D., Health sector reform and the interpretation of policy context, *Health Policy*, 47, 69–83, 1999.

Commers, M., *Determinants of Health: Theory, Understanding, Portrayal, Policy*, Unigraphic, Maastricht, 2001.

Conley, J.F., Of professional policy and equity, *J. California Dental Assoc.*, 29 (12), 801–802, 2001.

Crib, A. and Dines, A., Eds., *Health Promotion Concepts and Practice*, Blackwell Scientific, Oxford, 1993.

Curtis, S. and Taket, A., *Health and Societies: Changing Perspectives*, Arnold, London, 1996.

Defilippi, K., Collaboration: a challenge, *Int. J. Palliative Nurs.*, 8 (2), 56, 2002.

de Leeuw, E., *The Sane Revolution. Health Promotion: Backgrounds, Scope, Prospects*, Van Gorcum, Assen, 1989.

de Leeuw, E., Healthy cities: urban social entrepreneurship for health, *Health Promotion Int.*, 14, 261–269, 1999.

Devlin, N. and Appleby, J., Data briefing: equity in healthcare, *Health Serv. J.*, 111 (5782), 27, 2001.

Downie, R.S., Tannahill, C., and Tannahill, A., *Health Promotion: Models and Values*, Oxford University Press, New York, 1999.

Drache, D. and Sullivan, T., Eds., *Market Limits in Health Reform: Public Success, Private Failure*, Routledge, London, 1999.

Dubos, R., *The Torch of Life: Continuity in Living Experience*, Simon and Schuster, New York, 1962.

Dwore, R.B. and Kreuter, M.W., Update: reinforcing the case for health promotion, *Family Plann. Community Health: J. Health Promotion Maintenance*, 2, 103–119, 1980.

Eisen, A., Survey of neighborhood-based, comprehensive community empowerment initiatives, *Health Educ. Quar.*, 21, 235–252, 1994.

Ennett, S.T., Bauman, K.E., Pemberton, M., Foshee, V.A., Chuang, Y.C., King, T.S. and Koch, G.G., Mediation in a family-directed program for prevention of adolescent tobacco and alcohol use, *Preventive Med.*, 33 (4), 333–346, 2001.

Ewles, L. and Simnett, I., *Promoting Health: A Practical Guide to Health Education*, Harcourt, Edinburgh, 1999.

Gilson, L., Sen, P.D., Mohammed, S., and Mujinja, P., The potential of health sector non-governmental organizations: policy options, *Health Policy Plann.*, 9 (1), 14–24, 1994.

Goddard, M. and Smith, P., Equity of access to health care services: theory and evidence from the UK, *Social Sci. Med.*, 53 (9), 1149–1162, 2001.

Green, A., *An Introduction to Health Planning in Developing Countries*, Oxford University Press, Oxford, 1996.

Green, L.W. and Kreuter, M.W., *Health Promotion Planning: An Educational and Ecological Approach*, Mayfield Publishing Company, Mountain View, 1999.

Gwatkin, D.R., The need for equity-oriented health sector reforms, *Int. J. Epidemiol.*, 30 (4), 720–723, 2001.

Ham, C., *Health Policy in Britain: The Politics and Organization of the National Health Service*, Macmillan, London, 1992.

Hancock, T., Lalonde and beyond: looking back at 'a new perspective on the health of Canadians', *Health Promotion: Int. J.*, 1 (1), 93–100, 1986.

Heaney, D.J., Walker, J.J., Howie, J.G.R., Maxwell, M., Freeman, G.K., Berrey, P.N.E., Jones, T.G., Stern M.C., and Campbell, S.M., The development of a routine NHS data-based index of performance in general practice (NHSPPI), *Family Practice*, 19 (1), 77–84, 2002.

Henry, J.S., *The Blood Bankers: Tales from the Global Underground Economy*, Four Walls Eight Windows, New York/London, 2003.

Herzlich, C., *Health and Illness*, Academic Press, London, 1973.

Hewitt, J., A critical review of the arguments debating the role of the nurse advocate, *J. Adv. Nurs.*, 37 (5), 439–445, 2002.

Hjortsberg, C.A. and Mwikisa, C.N., Cost of access to health services in Zambia, *Health Policy Plann.*, 17 (1), 71–77, 2002.

Howat, P., Cross, D., Hall, M., Iredell, H., Stevenson, M., Gibbs, S., Officer, J., and Dillon, J., Community participation in road safety: barriers and enablers, *J. Community Health*, 26 (4), 257–270, 2001.

HS90, *The Swedish Health Services in the 1990s*, Government Printing Office, Stockholm, 1984.

Kanji, N. and Manji, F., From development to sustained crisis: structural adjustment, equity and health, *Social Sci. Med.*, 33, 985–993, 1991.

Kickbusch, I., Health promotion: a global perspective, *Can. J. Public Health*, 77, 321–326, 1986.

Kolko, G., Ravaging the poor: the International Monetary Fund indicted by its own data, *Int. J. Health Serv.*, 29, 51–57, 1999.

Lalonde, M., *The Health Field Concept. A New Perspective on the Health of Canadians*, TRI-Graphic Printers, Ottawa, 1974.

Lavis, J. and Sullivan, T., Governing health, in *Market Limits in Health Reform: Public Success, Private Failure*, Drache, D. and Sullivan, T., Eds., Routledge, London, 1999, pp. 312–328.

Loewenson, R., Structural adjustment and health policy in Africa, *Int. J. Health Serv.*, 23, 717–730, 1993.

MacDonald, T.H., *Rethinking Heath Promotion: A Global Approach*, Routledge, London, 1998.

Macedo, R., Brazilian children and the economic crisis: evidence from the state of Sao Paulo, in *Adjustment with a Human Face*, Vol. 2, Cornia, G., Jolly, R., and Stewart, F., Eds., Oxford University Press, Oxford, 1988, pp. 22–56.

Mantle, F., Complementary therapies and health promotion, *Br. J. Community Nurs.*, 7 (2), 102–107, 2002.

McDermott, W., Evaluating the physician and his technology, *J. Am. Acad. Arts Sci.*, 106 (10), 1, 1977.

McKeown, T., *The Role of Medicine: Dream, Mirage or Nemesis?* Nuffield Provincial Hospitals Trust, London, 1976.

McMichael, A. and Beaglehole, R., The changing context of public health, *Lancet*, 356, 495–499, 2000.

McNeill, W.H., *Plagues and People*, Anchor Press/Doubleday, Garden City, New York, 1997.

Milio, N., Multisectoral policy and health promotion: where to begin, *Health Promotion*, 1 (2), 119–132, 1986.

Minkler, M., *Community Organizing and Community Building for Health*, Rutgers University Press, New Brunswick, 1999.

Mullan, F., Public health then and now. Don Quixote, Machiavelli and Robin Hood: public health practice past and present, *Am. J. Public Health*, 90 (5), 702–706, 2000.

Naidoo, J. and Wills, J., *Practicing Health through Public Policy*, Canadian Public Health Association, Ottawa, 1998.

Naidoo, J. and Wills, J., *Health Promotion: Foundations for Practice*, Bailliere Tindall, London, 2000.

Ngom, P.F., Phillips, J.F., Pence, B., and Macleod, B., Demographic surveillance and health equity in sub-Saharan Africa, *Health Policy Plann.*, 16 (4), 337–344, 2001.

Olsen, D.P., Protection and advocacy: an ethics practice in mental health, *J. Psychiatr. Mental Health Nurs.*, 8 (2), 121–128, 2001.

Parsons, T., Definitions of health and illness in the light of American values and school structure, in *Patients, Physicians and Illness: A Source Book in Behavioral Science and Health*, Jaco, E. and Gartley, E., Eds., Collier Macmillan, London, 1972, pp. 97–117.

Perez, C.C., Herranz, E., and Ford, N., Pricing of drugs and donations: options for sustainable equity pricing, *Trop. Med. Int. Health*, 6 (11), 960–964, 2001.

Radley, A., *Making Sense of Illness: The Social Psychology of Health and Disease*, Sage, London, 1994.

Raviglione, M.C. and Pio, A., Evolution of WHO policies for tuberculosis control, 1948–2001, *Lancet*, 359 (9308), 775–780, 2002.

Robertson, A. and Minkler, M., The new health promotion movement: a critical examination, *Health Educ. Quart.*, 21 (3), 295–312, 1994.

Rosen, G., *The History of Public Health*, MD Publications, New York, 1958.

Saulo, M. and Wagener, R.J., Mediation training enhances conflict management by healthcare personnel, *Am. J. Manag. Care*, 6 (4), 473–483, 2000.

Scholes, J. and Endacott, R., Competence and collaboration: rhetoric or reality? What makes critical care education effective? *Intens. Crit. Care Nurs.*, 17 (4), 188–189, 2001.

Seedhouse, D., *Health: Foundation for Achievement*, John Wiley, Chichester, 1986.

Sen, A., Gender equity and the population problem, *Int. J. Health Serv. Plann., Admin. Eval.*, 31 (3), 469–474, 2001.

Stacey, M., *The Sociology of Health and Healing*, Unwin Hyman, London, 1988.

Starfield, B., Improving equity in health: a research agenda, *Health Serv. Plann., Admin. Eval.*, 31 (3), 545–566, 2001.

Stott, R., The World Bank: friend or foe? *Br. Med. J.*, 318, 822–823, 1999.

Sussman, S., School-based tobacco use prevention and cessation: where are we going? *Am. J. Health Behav.*, 25 (3), 191–199, 2001.

Taylor, P., Peckham, S., and Turton, P., *A Public Health Model of Primary Care: From Concept to Reality*, Public Health Alliance, Birmingham, 1998.

Tones, B.K. and Tildford, S., *Health Education: Effectiveness, Efficiency and Equity*, Chapman and Hall, London, 1994.

United Nations, *United Nations Conference on Environment and Development, 1992: Agenda 21 — Action Plan for the Next Century*, UNCED, Rio de Janeiro, 1992a.

United Nations, *Rio Declaration: Environment and Development*, United Nations, New York, 1992b.

Vaught, W. and Paranzino, G.K., Confidentiality in occupational health care: a matter of advocacy, *J. Am. Assoc. Occup. Health Nurses*, 48 (5), 243–254, 2000.

Vernon, C. and Sherwood, J., Heart hospitals should have physician equity, *Health Care Strateg. Manage.*, 19 (12), 1, 16–19, 2001.

Wagstaff, A. and Claeson, M., *The Millennium Development Goals for Health: Rising to the Challenges*, The World Bank, Washington D.C., 2004.

WHO, *Preamble to the Constitution of the World Health Organization*, World Health Organization, Geneva, 1947.

WHO, *Health Promotion: A World Health Organization Discussion Document on the Concept and Principles*, World Health Organization, Copenhagen, 1984.

WHO, *Targets for Health for All: Targets in Support of the European Strategy for Health for All*, World Health Organization, Copenhagen, 1985a.

WHO, *Targets for Health for All*, World Health Organization, Copenhagen, 1985b.

WHO, First International Conference on Health Promotion: 'The Move Towards a New Public Health', Ottawa, Canada, November 17–21, World Health Organization, Geneva, 1986a.

WHO, *Health Promotion: Concepts and Principles in Action — A Policy Framework*, World Health Organization, Copenhagen, 1986b.

WHO, *Intersectoral Action for Health*, World Health Organization, Geneva, 1986c.

WHO, *Ottawa Charter For Health Promotion, 1986*, World Health Organization, Geneva, 1986d.

WHO, Second International Conference on Health Promotion: 'Healthy Public Policy', Adelaide, Australia, April 5–9, World Health Organization, Geneva, 1988.

WHO, *Fourth International Conference on Health Promotion: 'New Partners for a New Era — Leading Health Promotion into the 21st Century'*, Jakarta, Indonesia, July 21–25, World Health Organization, Geneva, 1997a.

WHO, *Health for All: HFA Policy*, World Health Organization, Geneva, 1997b.

WHO, Intersectoral Action for Health: A Cornerstone for Health-for-All in the Twenty-First Century, Report of an International Conference, Halifax, Nova Scotia, Canada, April 20–23, World Health Organization, Geneva, 1997c.

WHO, Fifth Global Conference for Health Promotion: 'Bridging the Equity Gap,' Mexico, June 5–9, 2000, World Health Organization, Geneva, 2000.

World Bank, *World Bank Development Report 1993: 'Investing in Health,'* Oxford University Press, Oxford, 1993.

Chapter 44

Health Systems and Development

Geoffrey Meads and Michiyo Iwami

CONTENTS

I. Introduction

In this chapter, we adopt a contemporary and international perspective. Drawing specifically upon our recent fieldwork in twenty countries where health care has been subject to policies for its "modernization" (Meads et al., 2004), we examine how their development is influenced by alternative constructs of systems and, in particular, by different approaches to governance. The opportunities for transferable learning between both these countries, and others with comparable parallel developments, are considered. Given the different but complementary strengths of governance arrangements in states with widely varying levels of economic status, this transferable learning can be viewed as an essentially even exchange, between the less well-developed and more prosperous nations. Although the former offer the more creative models of community governance, and the latter are often characterized by more robust frameworks for corporate governance, it is in the middle ground of effective clinical governance that the shared experiences and learning may be most reciprocal. The impact of globalization on health systems is a change process that provides rich pickings for those engaged in development.

II. Context

Collaboration is the key concept for development and the governance for all contemporary health systems, regardless (almost) of particular national structures for health service delivery. Moreover, through collaboration and its expression in different forms of governance, the health care sector not only develops but also expands. The universal imperative behind modern health systems is better resource utilization, through both increased inputs and outputs (and preferably improved outcomes as well). Integral to the throughput process between the two, in pursuit of sustained public health improvement on the one hand and a productive mixed economy of provider enterprises on the other hand, are new forms of collaboration. These are not only between healthcare professions, in both public and private agencies, but also between political authorities and the popular representatives of the patients' interests. In this context, governance has emerged as the principle which underpins the regulation of collaborative relationships. It is a direct response to the international trend in favor of partnership-based systems, where networks have replaced the vertical and horizontal modes of interaction that were fundamental features of past health care institutions and markets, respectively.

As such governance is a modernizing concept which stands alongside decentralization, national stewardship and social justice (Giddens, 1998) in placing the development design of health systems at the heart of participatory democracy. In practice, the two may be mutually dependent. Especially in Latin America, locally generated health care reforms have been instrumental over the past decade in the reconstruction of democratic national governments (Bosser, 1997; Meads and Iwami, 2003); whereas in countries of Europe such as Italy, the Netherlands and Finland, it has been national government-led changes that have re-drawn and blurred the boundaries among politicians, professions and patients in the health care environment (Ritsatakis et al., 2000; Lieverdink, 2001).

For Italian doctors, this has meant operating within a corporate governance framework of new regional regulation alongside new semi-professional colleagues in private providers, who combine traditionally separate health and social care functions, as a result of national government policies for resource supplementation and role substitution (WHO, 2001). For their Dutch counterparts the advent of hybrid health insurance organizations as a consequence of the merger of provincial and private Sickness Funds has led to the application of commercially derived criteria for "public trust" (Straten et al., 2002); whereas in Finland, we found that leading medical professionals had responded to the State's comprehensive delegation of health systems governance responsibilities to management at elected municipality levels, by forging influential new alliances for knowledge management with such independent third sector agencies as STAKES, the Helsinki-based national research and development institute (Wild et al., 2003).

In each of these European examples, corporate governance has been the starting point for development and progress on the principle of participatory democracy. Innovations have been applied to health care drawn from outside what was previously understood as the public service sector. Through these applications, the health care environment has been radically re-conceptualized as a new system in which non-governmental organizations (NGOs) are core components. In contrast, in Latin America the aims of programs for effective governance of health systems, through community organizations as their source, were established as deliberate policies for development designed to sidestep the sometimes stifling constraints of powerful corporate interests. Such a deeply conservative culture of "Coronelismo" may be dominated by the vested interests of external donors, multinational companies and even self-serving governmental bureaucracies (Atkinson, 2002). By 2002, there were approaching 10,000 funded local health committees in Brazil, Peru and Colombia alone, each combining lead local clinicians with a majority of elected and appointed popular representatives (Cortez and Phumpiu, 1999; Collins et al., 2000; Hearst and Blas, 2001). Bolivia, Venezuela and Chile have also pioneered similar initiatives in South America (de Kadt, 1997, 1998; Morgan, 2001) and globally the significance of placing "Community" before "Profession" as the vehicle for wider value based participation in health care has been appreciated by such countries as Indonesia (Shiffman, 2002), Guinea (Haddad et al., 1998), and El Salvador (Spickard and Jameson, 1995). In every case, the wider network of collaborative relationships has served either to extend the resource base — with, for example, local health care levies now almost matching national taxation in such countries as Sri Lanka and The Philippines (Meads, 2003) — or to legitimize the assumption at community levels of discretionary powers for prioritizing particular local needs. Typically, these may mean the setting up of clinics in local neighborhoods within official health center boundaries, as in Bolivia (de Kadt, 1997, 1998); or sliding scales for prescription charges and treatment fees as in Peru (Altobelli and Pancorvo, 2000).

Governance founded on community organization and development, like that derived from corporate sources in more economically developed countries, crosses the clinical interface. As Table 44.1 illustrates, there is a convergence, with the particular form that clinical governance takes requiring a cultural compatibility that, in contemporary health care systems, is especially dependent on the role played by NGOs. Accordingly, we now turn to four countries as, in international terms, leading examples of distinct NGO development trends, with each significantly shaping both a host national health system and its governance arrangements. The four countries deliberately cover the full range of developed and developing country categories. They are Peru, Uganda, Greece, and the United Kingdom. We begin with the last and proceed in reverse order.

III. Case Studies

A. United Kingdom

We begin with our host country not because it is, in its own terms, a "beacon site" (Secretary of State for Health, 1997) for any particular mode of development governance, but rather because its recent policy initiatives offer globally some of the best articulated approaches to this subject. Since 1997, when the new Labor government, led by Prime Minister Tony Blair, came into office, the "new" National Health Service (NHS) has been in the process of recreating itself through a comprehensive program of modernization. Governance has been integral to the cultural transformation envisaged by policy and in many areas, progressively effected in practice. Integral to the adoption of governance principles has been a willingness to move towards a "learning organization" *modus operandi* (Iles and Sutherland, 2001) in which any useful source of intelligence may be

Table 44.1 Governance and Contemporary Health Systems Development

	Mode: Definition	Principal Focus/ Accountability	Lead Country Examples	NGOs
"First World" ←	**Corporate** System by which organisation is directed and controlled in compliance with required standards (NHS Executive 1999a)	Performance management	Chile, France, Norway, Sweden, U.K.	Commercial enterprises, financial institutions, external donors, multinational corporations
	Clinical Framework of accountability for continuous clinical quality improvement and the maintenance of high standards through a supportive culture (NHS Executive, 1999b, p. 3)	(Multi) Professional quality	Finland, Netherlands, New Zealand, U.K., USA	Research institutes, alternative providers
"Third World" →	**Community** Arrangements driven by frontline health and social care needs that genuinely reflect shared responsibilities of patients, public and partners with sufficient local flexibility within a national model (Department of Health, 2001)	Public involvement	Bolivia, Mexico, Peru, Venezuela	Rights movements, aid charities, faith based agencies, civic associations, municipal/rural councils

Source: Geoffrey Meads/Michiyo Iwami, Centre for Primary Health Care Studies, University of Warwick, U.K.

adopted regardless of whether or not it comes from within the confines of the public service sector at home or abroad. As an illustration of this official open-mindedness, it was the U.K. Ministry of Health which originally supported the international fieldwork and literature searches on which this chapter is, to a large extent, based. It is also, arguably, the U.K. Department for International Development (DFID) which, in terms of developing countries, has promoted most vigorously the concept and practice of the Sector-Wide Approach.

In the United Kingdom, the starting point for the assertion of a stakeholder NHS was the shift to corporate governance that accompanied the establishment of more managerially autonomous primary care and hospital provider NHS Trusts during the 1990s. The source materials for this shift were codes of conduct which arose from a series of committee inquiries into corporate malpractice mostly in the private commercial and financial sectors (e.g., Cadbury Committee, 1992; Turnbull Committee, 1999). With the emphasis on reviewable risk management procedures, this led to "good corporate governance" in the NHS being defined in relation to "fundamental" features: "internal financial controls; efficient and effective operations; and compliance with applicable laws and regulations" (NHS Executive 1999b: Part 1[1]).

With a series of national enquiries exposing procedural and multiprofessional failures in the NHS and its social care counterparts (e.g., Kennedy, 2001; Laming, 2003), the Blair government proved adept at taking the political opportunity these supplied to quickly implement what it termed "a comprehensive control framework (in which) the common thread linking clinical governance and wider controls assurance is risk management" (NHS Executive, 1999a: 3). Within this framework, all U.K. health care professionals found themselves subject to national quality standards set by a new National Institute for Clinical Excellence with delivery of quality standards monitored through a new statutory Commission for Health Improvement and rigorous NHS Performance Assessment Framework; together (significantly) with the first national survey of patient and user experience (Department of Health, 2001a: 3).

For the first time, as a result, clinical quality became a collective as well as an individual professional responsibility. The Board of the health care unit, as the definition provided in Table 44.1 indicates, is transparently accountable: clinical failure is now a resigning matter for chief executives in the United Kingdom. Moreover, in the progression from corporate to clinical governance a role for non-NHS and lay "stakeholders" beyond the boundaries of health care professions and bureaucrats had been introduced. The need for feedback from patients and users (and partners) was cleverly appended to clinical governance policy statements, taking full advantage of public disquiet at the apparent lack of systems capable of detecting, for example, more than two hundred patient deaths of ordinary men and women at the hands of their local general medical practitioner and notorious serial killer, Dr. Harold Shipman.

The way was cleared for a policy of community governance in the U.K. health system in which (since 2001) all health care units by law have a statutory duty to make arrangements to involve and consult patients and the public:

- Not just when a major change is proposed, but in ongoing service planning.
- Not just in the consideration of a proposal, but in the development of that proposal.
- In decisions about general service delivery, not just major changes (Department of Health, 2004: 4).

The practical expression of this governance framework is now through a nationwide infrastructure of local Patient and Public Involvement Forums, Patient Advice and Liaison Services in every health care provider, and Independent Complaints Advocacy Services set up under the 2001 Health and Social Care Act. The national monitoring role this time goes to another independent body with systems wide performance management functions: the Commission for Patient and Public Involvement in Health. Alongside a revised cross-sectoral Commission for Health Audit and Inspection, the National Patient Safety Agency and the National Care Standards Commission this reports directly to the Minister. For Care Trusts and other emerging NHS organizational enterprises community governance, U.K. style, is explicitly "inside" the NHS (Department of Health, 2001b: para 18), and so are their NGO constituents too.

This location and the progression from corporate through clinical to community governance reflects the position of NGOs in the United Kingdom and their relative influence. In a NHS which remains universal and public taxation funded the role of voluntary agencies, local civic groups and faith-based contributors is relatively marginal in policy making and understated in practice. In contrast, financial institutions, commercial enterprises and multinational corporations together are a major force in, for example, ensuring that the United Kingdom is a global leader in pharmaceuticals, privately financed health care capital projects and information technology based health information advice and treatment (e.g., NHS Direct). For a government looking to develop a modernized health system with new clinical collaborations at its heart, the corporate sector has been the only viable source for development mechanisms that can break the mould of past professions, and then move on towards public participation. Accordingly, while the United Kingdom has processes that provide an international development exemplar of articulated policies across the range of governance, in practice it has developed its health systems approach more through vertical than lateral partnerships. As a result, British clinicians still feel very much subject to top down pressures and performance accountabilities.

B. Greece

Although, like the United Kingdom, a member of the European Union Greece possesses many of the characteristics of a developing country, including considerable constitutional deficits. As a case example of a country in transition to developed status, it is of particular interest and value. Relationships are so multidimensional within the Greek health care system that it is often difficult to know their direction. Rarely are they in a straight line, as a result of the multiple forms of finance that apply virtually throughout the country's seventeen administrative health regions (Periferiaka Systimata Ygias). These were created in 2001 as an attempt to establish a framework of consistent development governance for the disparate corporate contributors to health care. The intention was to establish a system which sustained the principles of universal coverage and equity of access defined by the founding statutes of the Greek National Health Service (ESY) in 1983, while also promoting public health and protecting private enterprise (Tountas et al., 2002; Sissoras and Souliatis, 2003).

The last are critical for both Greek patients and health care professionals. During an average month, a Greek doctor will be paid by his patient through a direct fee for service, or in kind; by a range of long established occupational insurance schemes each with their own terms; by the Ministry of Social Affairs through its national social insurance program for contracted specialists operating in local hub and spoke service models, as well as by the ESY, which will actually allow him to treat his private patients most afternoons in the public hospitals in return for a 40% levy, to augment his state salary. In such a system, corporate NGO interests are dominant, with the role of professions interwoven into the fabric of private and voluntary organizational developments. In the Crete Region in 2003, for example, the Regional President also headed the Medical School in Heraklion where the largest local Medical Centre is a collaboration with the largest local Bank; and the Vice President was a General Medical Practitioner who promoted the creation of local health facilities by employing what one Hospital Chairman described to us as the normal Greek tactic of "pulling strings from behind the curtain." So effectively has he operated that the combined resources of the Greek Orthodox Church, Municipal Mayors and local farmers' representatives (OGA) have been pooled with

European Union project support to take forward a range of primary care gate keeping and integrated home care schemes of genuinely pioneer proportions (Meads, 2003).

In Greece, as in the United Kingdom, health systems and development derive chiefly from corporate interests. But Greek NGO arrangements are much more informal and in tune with an infinitely more flexible cultural fit. As a result, governance is in a different style. Legislation is permissive, with long lead in times and frequent opt-out clauses (e.g., in relation to draft Law 2889 and the "requirement" for specialist access via general medical practitioners). The Regional role is limited to information gathering, problem solving and service safety net. On clinical quality, even in Crete where evidence-based primary care and quality standards are a particular priority, regional participation takes the form of distributing up-to-date academic texts and support for a basic physical premises only licensing policy at municipal levels. Regulation is light touch and where the United Kingdom relies on the vertical demands of general management and the legitimate controls of national government, in Greece corporate governance interfaces with clinical relationships through its mechanisms of citizen consumer rights with their mix of competition and collusion. Service equity is sacrificed in the pursuit of social marketing and several sponsors (Liaropoulos and Tragakes, 1998). The consequence is relationships termed "circles of influence" often at least a decade old, comprising "who we know and who we like." Governance comes down in the Greek health care professional's most common phrase to whoever, at any time for any given purpose is "my very good friend" (Meads, 2003). For Greek clinicians the pressures are informal and the accountabilities mixed. For those engaged internationally in development the dangers of an unbalanced approach to governance are apparent. Transparency, a policy consensus that sticks and, above all, accountability are each still core elements of development which are notable for their absence at this stage of Greece's transition to developed country status.

C. Uganda

As in many other parts of Africa (e.g., Ghana, Zambia, Eritrea) and the economically less well-developed world (e.g., Nicaragua, Bolivia, The Philippines), the concept of governance comes from a very different direction. Here the behavior of clinicians is more directly affected by their relationships with communities. What distinguishes Uganda is its successful introduction of a five level system of decentralized health service provision to deliberately coincide with parallel elected and representative local political structures. Accordingly, the foundation of the health care system is the nursing auxiliary post or station at the level of Uganda's 39,200 villages, representatives of which elect the next parish level management committees for the basic health centers. These receive funds from the Level 3 counties which can raise local taxes and resources to supplement those received through central allocations. These payments are attached to the minimum national 13-item health care package at the public health assessment level of the sub-district. This usually administers to around 100,000 people. Most of the country's 56 "top" level Districts contain four such sub-districts and these are the catchment areas for its own inpatient community hospital facilities.

At every level, governance is determined by community interests and it is in this context that clinical, and even corporate contributions are considered. At all levels the role of NGOs is important and influential. For example nationally the unified regulatory framework for nurses and midwives, dental practitioners and allied health professionals, regardless of their employment status, was a direct by-product of the new National NGO Panel in 1996. The latter signed up to the 1997 National Poverty Eradication Plan (PEAP) a year later (Njie, 2001). This was heavily influenced by the World Bank and its promotion of combined economic and social policies for health investment (World Bank, 1993; Hill, 2002) paved the way for major external donors and charities to underwrite Uganda's systematic approach to community development. The Rockefeller Foundation, for instance, originally sponsored the combined academic and administrative committee at Makerere University which has redesigned the curricula for doctors and health care professionals and established new local educational centers (e.g., Gulu) in response to decentralization. At the District level, this has led to locally defined Masters in Public Health programs, and at this level too there are NGO Panels to coordinate local plans and provision, and to ensure appropriate representation on the nine person local management committees for health care facilities, alongside the District Medical, Vector Control, Health Education and Drugs Inspection Officers (Birungi et al., 2001). The infrastructure for this sector-wide collaboration has received support from, *inter alia*, the U.K. DFID, USAID and their German, Norwegian and Danish counterparts, with the last, for example, overseeing the creation of a national drugs procurement and prescribing program (Okuonzi and Birungi, 2000; Kipp et al., 2001).

In a country where four out of five health care contacts have been outside the remit of government funded services such coordination is crucial. At the five levels within each District, it means that clinicians work with tribal chiefs as "accounting officers" and local "kings" as health educators, sometimes with UNICEF and EU support, to combat the epidemics of HIV/AIDS and malaria. It means that even at the County level health committees appoint their own Ministers of Health, to genuinely "minister."

Such ministry reflects the accountability to faith based communities and traditions on the one hand and political structures on the other hand. Its style is a mixture of pastoral care and performance management, and local clinics see nurses and doctors drawing on a pot pourri of Christian and Muslim mottos alongside lists of quality standards and practice protocols. Their daily lives are spent with volunteer community health workers nominated by the 40,000 plus village health management units which are authorized to set local fees and raise local funds. These volunteers often wear their titles on their t-shirts: for example, "Mobilizer," "Watchdog," "Health Promoter" and "Counsellor." They are the framework for governance in the health care system. Legitimized by communities in which NGOs are the expression of local voices, they are the resources for its development and for its improvement as well. Uganda, through a seven year training partnership with its NGOs will double its level of qualified health care staff (to 65%) in 2005, drawing heavily for its student intakes on its volunteer workforce. Clinical progress here is a product of frameworks for effective community governance and the pressures and accountabilities for clinicians come from their positions of community leadership within these.

D. Peru

Over the past decade, community arrangements in Peru have developed in parallel to those of Uganda. In 1994, the government of then President Fujimori introduced its national health plan entitled Programa de Salud Basica para Todos. This was designed to ensure universal access to basic health services. The administrative structure of decentralization which has subsequently emerged is, at least superficially, similar to that of Uganda. The latter's Districts are mirrored by Peru's regional Departments within which there are 194 provinces and 1812 sub-provinces. The latter are the equivalent to counties in the sub-Saharan counterpart. But there the similarities end. Whereas in Uganda the health care reform process is centrally designed by government as a Sector-wide Approach (Jeppsson, 2002) to restore public administration and local authority across the country, in Peru the new Local Committees for Health Administration (CLAS or Comités Locales de Administración de Salud) have developed "bottom up" essentially with an "alternative" or "oppositionist" character (Cortez and Phumpiu, 1999; Iwami and Petchey, 2002).

Here these community-based organizations, frequently born out of women's rights and seniors movements, have become responsible for over nine million people or a third of the population (Díaz, 2001; ForoSalud, 2003). Their governance is central to the wider agenda for development and designed accordingly to help in the establishment of civil society across the country. Government itself has been left to play catch up in this process.

By 2003, over 780 CLAS associations were operating 2089 health posts and centers: setting the budgets, priorities and payment schedules. With external donor support from the U.S.A., Japan and Europe such major NGO sponsors as MaxSalud, Future Generations and Movimiento Manuela Ramos have effectively bypassed provincial and local tiers of government to develop a national Forosalud movement that currently has witnessed from 2000 to 3000 delegates at its national and regional assembly health conferences. Many of these come from the seven person CLAS management groups that each comprises a clinical director plus six locally elected lay representatives.

This insistent outpouring of community governance has through its critical mass, shaped the response of the Ministry of Health (MINSA) and thence of the health care professions themselves. Historically, both belonged to an exclusive institutional "machismo" culture, characterized by vertical relationships and "clientelismo" controls of public involvement, sometimes backed by conservative church groups and defensive medical unions (Crabtree, 1998). However, by 2003, 15 of Peru's 24 regions possessed decentralized Forosalud governance frameworks that include three year CLAS/MINSA Shared Administration Contracts and CLAS General Assembly approved annual Local Health Programs as the basis for clinical management agreements and nationwide public health programs targeting poorer communities. These are supported by the inclusion of informal sector workers who are in the remit of the National Institute of Social Security (EsSalud), with a newly integrated health insurance program (SIS) designed to subsidize disadvantaged groups, thereby redistributing in effect both wealth and health.

Peru is participatory democracy in action through its health systems development. The level of participation is impressive and the experience of rapid resource dependency on national government experienced elsewhere in Latin America has been largely avoided (Zakus, 1998). However, community-based development governance in Peru has its downside. Nationally in 2004/2005, service provision seems not only fragmented but also still inequitable. As stakeholder arrangements are vibrant with, for example, the management committee for the two MaxSalud sets of clinics in Chiclayo and Cuzco possessing no fewer than 14 different agency representatives (including now MINSA itself), mechanisms for supervision and standards monitoring are weak. Public accountability is as elusive as it is in Greece with the low politics of personal networks as apparent as they are in the Aegean. Without the coordination of NGOs achieved in Uganda at the parallel structural levels of its decentralized health system and professional relationships, community governance in Peru has served, as in

Uganda, to empower patients as citizens — perhaps more so — but without necessarily the same dividends for clinical progress, and probity. For Peruvian clinicians, the pressures and accountabilities are those of grass-roots power, and not infrequently in the form of conflict.

IV. Discussion

The four case studies describe how alternative frameworks for governance have the common goal of enhanced collaboration and resource partnerships both within health systems and beyond. Their different sources, however, both reflect and help to form distinct political constituencies and cultures for each country, in which the changing role and responsibilities of NGOs appear to be increasingly influential factors. For those engaged in development, it is important to recognize that the nature of modern NGOs and power in contemporary health systems development may be viewed as a direct relationship; and one that increasingly determines how the State, its health care professions and their patients relate to one another.

As authentic new stakeholders in governance arrangements, NGOs are now in a position to not only receive but also to share power with others. The Ugandan panels and partnerships with health districts, sub-districts and counties are examples of how this power sharing can l-egitimately assist in holistic health systems and wider civic development. But even in Uganda there are charities, missions and businesses which are resolutely resistant to collaborative overtures and determined to go their own way. Third sector organizations themselves often possess a diffuse complex of internal stakeholders and for some the mandate of founders or sponsors may be paramount. Such is the case in Peru for a number of both liberal and right wing religious NGOs involved in health care. For them, governance appears as a partisan political item on the development agenda, and the extension of NGO roles from technical assistance and safety net service provider to public knowledge management and community change agent can mean the opportunity to function in quasi-State fashion. Whether informally as in Greece or more formally as in the Peruvian civil society movement power can either be transferred to patients or the public; but it can also be exercised over them. In the United Kingdom, with its strong traditions of volunteerism and voluntary organizations in advocacy and campaigning roles, the potential dangers in these new kinds of vertical relationships have been recognized and countered through policies for the inclusion of community representatives within the NHS corporate and clinical governance arrangements.

The level of professional compliance with political authority enjoyed by the central administration in London is not, however, the international norm, and certainly not in developing countries. Elsewhere the acceptance by health care professionals of community participation in governance has required at best crisis pre-conditions (de Kadt, 1997, 1998), or at worst policies of decentralization that amount to little more than "deconcentrated" dumping (Goicoechea, 1995). Similarly, attempts to introduce governance through the corporate route has not always been effective, even in Europe and North America with professions opting out of, for example, competitive quality assurance approaches in Germany and Canada (Naylor, 1999; Riemer-Hommel, 2002). Accordingly, the assertive steward-ship role of the modern State in managing cross boundary issues is critical (Saltman, 2003), and the necessarily "experimental" (Widdus, 2001) development of health systems with sustainable governance models requires, at governmental level "Collective Mediators" (Frenk, 1994) with both political skill and cultural sensitivity of a high order.

V. Conclusion

Nevertheless this development process remains an imperative. Building the necessary extra capacity required of health systems requires ever expanding partnerships and processes of collaboration. A recent WONCA statement accurately recognized the "main challenge" for those working to improve health systems as:

> the reconciliation of divergent viewpoints and entrenched interests among a variety of partners. Government health authorities, health service managers, health professionals, academic faculty members and community representatives each provide indispensable contributions for the development of a coherent, responsive and sustainable health system. To build productive relationships among these partners, strategies are needed to address differences in perspectives and to resolve conflicts that often result in fragmented, dysfunctional health systems (Boelen et al., 2002: 5).

Good governance guards against the development of such under performing health care systems. On the one hand, these systems have often in the past become fragmented and dysfunctional because of short-term project, patriarchal and pressure group NGO activities. On the other hand, these activities have often coincided with resistance to development itself from the preservation instincts of professional classes. In the future, as the contribution of the third sector expands and development depends on the positive recruitment of middle and higher income interests, the development of integrated and functional health systems will depend on the quality of collaboration and frameworks of local governance that effectively harness the potential in all its available resources.

Thus development governance will clearly benefit from an eclectic attitude to its corporate, clinical and community modes. A wide range of reform strategies are required. As Berman has noted there are "important connections among health, the health sector, and the broader goals of human development," which require responses "based on analysis by international organizations and recent national experience in (both) the richer and poorer countries" (Berman 1995). This chapter has sought to offer one contribution to such an analysis.

References

Altobelli, L. and Pancorvo, J., El desafío de la reforma en salud: alcanzando a los pobres, programa de administración compartida y Comités Locales de Administración de Salud (CLAS) en Peru, in Proceedings of El Foro de Europa y las Américas sobre Reforma del Sector Salud, Costa Rica, San José, May, 2000.

Atkinson, S., Political cultures, health systems and health policy, *Soc. Sci. Med.*, 55, 113–124, 2002.

Berman, P., Health sector reform: making health development sustainable, *Health Policy*, 32, 13–28, 1995.

Birungi, H., Mugisha, F., Nsabagasani, X., Okuonzi, S., and Jeppsson, A., The policy on public-private mix in the Ugandan health sector: catching up with reality, *Health Policy Plan.*, 16 (Suppl. 2), 80–87, 2001.

Boelen, C., Haq, C., Hunt, U., Rivo, M., and Shahady, E., Improving health systems: the contribution of family medicine, WONCA, Geneva, 2002.

Bosser, T., Decentralization: a governance option for health care policy, in Proceedings UNDP Conference on Social Policy, Poverty Alleviation and Governance, Harvard Institute for International Development, Boston, U.S.A., Nov., 1997.

Cadbury Committee, Financial aspects of corporate governance, Association of Chartered and Certified Accountants, London, 1992.

Collins, C., Araujo, J., and Barbosa, J., Decentralising the health sector: issues in Brazil, *Health Policy*, 52 (2), 113–127, 2000.

Cortez, R. and Phumpiu, P., The delivery of health services in centres jointly administered by the community and the State: the case of Peru, in Proceedings of CIUP International Seminar on Reform of Social Policy in Latin America, May, Washington, DC,1999.

Crabtree, J., Neo-populism and Fujimori Phenomenon, in *Fujimor's Peru: The Political Economy*, Crabtree, J. and Thomas, J., Eds., Institute of Latin American Studies, University of London, London, 1998, pp. 7–23.

de Kadt, E., Thematic lessons from the case studies, in *The Public-Private Mix in Social Services: Health Care And Education In Chile, Costa Rica And Venezuela*, Zuckerman, E. and de Kadt, E., Eds., Inter-American Development Bank, Washington, DC, 1997, pp. 127–159.

de Kadt, E., Mixed experiences: assessing public-private approaches to social service provision in Latin America, http://www.id21.org/insights/insights27/insights-iss27-art02.html (accessed 24 March 2004), 1998.

Department of Health, *National Service Framework for Older People*, Department of Health, London, 2001.

Department of Health, *Care Trusts. Emerging Framework*, Department of Health, London, 2001b.

Department of Health, *Patient and Public Involvement: The New Arrangements*, Department of Health, London, 2004.

Díaz, R., CLAS: Una experiencia para decentralizar servicios de salud (summary), *Gestión Médica*, 226 (6), 18–19, 2001.

Forosalud, Salud para todos como derecho ciudadano http://wari.rcp.net.pe/FRE/forosalud/index.html (accessed April 28, 2004), 2003.

Frenk, J., Dimensions of health system reform, *Health Policy*, 27, 19–34, 1994.

Giddens, A., *The Third Way. The renewal of democracy*, Polity, Oxford, 1998.

Goicoechea, J., *Primary Health Care Reforms*, WHO, Copenhagen, 1995.

Haddad, S., Fournier, P., Machouf, N., and Yatara, F., What does quality mean to lay people? Community perceptions of primary health care services in Guinea, *Soc. Sci. Med.*, 47 (3), 381–394, 1998.

Hearst, N. and Blas, E., Learning from experience: research on health sector reform in the developing world, *Health Policy Plan.*, 16 (Suppl. 2), 1–3, 2001.

Hill, P., The rhetoric of sector-wide approaches for health development, *Soc. Sci. Med.*, 54 (11), 1725–1737, 2002.

Iles, V. and Sutherland, K., *Organisational Change: Managing Change in the NHS*, National Coordinating Centre for NHS Service Delivery and Organisation Research and Development, London School of Hygiene, London, 2001.

Iwami, M. and Petchey, R., A CLAS act? Community-based organisations, health service decentralisation and primary care development in Peru, *J. Pub. Health Med.*, 24 (4), 246–251, 2002.

Jeppsson, A., SWAp dynamics in a decentralized context: experiences from Uganda, *Soc. Sci., Med.*, 55 (11), 2053–2060, 2002.

Kennedy, I., Final report. Bristol Royal Infirmary Inquiry, HMSO, London, 2001.

Kipp, W., Kamugisha, J., Jacobs, P., Burnham, G., and Rubaale, T., User fees, health staff incentives, and service utilisation in Kabarole District, Uganda, *WHO Bull.*, 79 (11), 1032–1037, 2001.

Laming, H., The Victoria Climbié Inquiry Report, Stationery Office, London, 2003.

Liaropoulos, L. and Tragakes, E., Public/private financing in the Greek health care system: implications for equity, *Health Policy*, 43 (2), 153–169, 1998.

Lieverdink, H., The marginal success of regulated competition policy in the Netherlands, *Soc. Sci. Med.*, 52 (8), 1183–1194, 2001.

Meads, G., It's all Greek to me. International options for Primary Care Trust finance, *Primary Care Rep.*, 5 (14), 20–25, 2003.

Meads, G. and Iwami, M., Latin lessons give a grassroots insight, *Primary Care Rep.*, 5 (2), 17–20, 2003.

Meads, G., Wild, A., Iwami, M., and Pawlikowska, T., International primary care in the twenty first century, Centre for Primary Health Care Studies: University of Warwick, U.K., 2004.

Morgan, L.M., Community pariticpation in health: perpetual allure, persistent challenge, *Health Policy Plan.*, 16 (3), 221–230, 2001.

Naylor, C., Health care in Canada: incrementalism under fiscal duress, *Health Aff.*, 18 (3), 9–26, 1999.

NHS Executive, Governance in the new NHS: controls assurance statements 1999/2000: risk management and organisational controls, Department of Health, Wetherby, 1999a.

NHS Executive, Clinical Governance. Quality in the new NHS, Department of Health, London, 1999b.

NHS Executive, Governance in the new NHS: background information and guidance on the development and implementation of controls assurance for 1999/2000, Annex A. Leeds: NHS Executive, 1999c.

Njie, A.B.H., Poverty and ill health: the Ugandan national response, *Development*, 44 (1), 93–98, 2001.

Okuonzi, S. and Birungi, H., Are lessons from the education sector applicable to health care reforms? The case of Uganda, *Int. J. Health Plan. Manage.*, 15 (3), 201–219, 2000.

Riemer-Hommel, P., The changing nature of contracts in German health care, *Soc. Sci. Med.*, 55 (8), 1447–1455, 2002.

Ritsatakis, A., Barnes, K., Dekker, E., Harrington, P., Kokko, S., and Makara, P., Exploring policy development in Europe, WHO, Copenhagen, 2000.

Saltman, R., Melting public–private boundaries in European health systems, *Eur. J. Pub. Health*, 13, 24–29, 2003.

Secretary of State for Health, *The New NHS. Modern, Dependable*, HMSO, London, 1997.

Shiffman, J., The construction of community participation: village family planning groups and the Indonesian state, *Soc. Sci. Med.*, 54 (8), 1199–1214, 2002.

Sissoras, A. and Souliatis, K., Eds., Health, health care and welfare in Greece, Hellenic Republic Ministry of Health and Welfare, Athens, 2003.

Spickard, J. and Jameson, M., Postwar health care in rural El Salvador: healing the wounds, in *Global Perspectives on Health Care*, Gallagher, E. and Suedi, J., Eds., Prentice-Hall, Englewood Cliffs, New Jersey, 1995, pp. 213–229.

Straten, G.F.M., Friele, R.D., and Groenewegen, P.P., Public trust in Dutch health care, *Soc. Sci. Med.*, 55 (2), 227–234, 2002.

Tountas, Y., Karnaki, P., and Pavi, E., Reforming the reform: the Greek national health system in transition, *Health Policy*, 62, 15–29, 2002.

Turnbull Committee, *Internal Controls Guidance on the Combined Code*, Institute of Chartered Secretaries, London, 1999.

Widdus, R., Public-private partnerships for health: their main targets, their diversity, and their future directions, *WHO Bull.*, 79 (8), 713–720, 2001.

Wild, A., Iwami, M., and Meads, G., Different systems, same issues, *Primary Care Rep.*, 5 (16), 14–19, 2003.

World Bank, *World Development Report: Investing in Health*, Oxford University Press, New York, 1993.

WHO (World Health Organisation), *Health Care Systems in Transition*, WHO, Geneva, 2001, pp. 97–112.

Zakus, J.D.L., Resource dependency and community participation in primary health care, *Soc. Sci. Med.*, 46 (4–5), 475–494, 1998.

Forosalud, Salud para todos como derecho ciudadano http://wari.rcp.net.pe/FRE/forosalud/index.html (accessed April 28, 2004), 2003.

Chapter 45

Rural Development and Governance: Can Democracy Rescue a Stalled Enterprise?

Harry Blair

CONTENTS

I. Introduction

Since the 1950s, "rural development" has constituted a core component of both analysis and practice within the international development community. However, by the end of the century, it seemed to have run out of steam — to the point that some observers find a "crisis in rural development reflect[ing] a loss of confidence in the rural development 'project,' which has for long been central to the [overall] development effort." (Ashley and Maxwell, 2001: 395). Even the World Bank, for many years one of rural development's most stalwart promoters, had begun by the new millennium's opening to wonder publicly what had gone amiss with this massive enterprise that had been the object of so much of its investment over the decades (World Bank, 2003). Some things have improved in the rural areas of the world, the Bank asserted, but rural poverty itself has continued as an abiding problem essentially unameliorated by rural development approaches.

As virtually all those in the development community realize, however, rural development can scarcely be abandoned. Some 75% of the world's poor still live in rural areas,[1] so any serious effort just to begin to meet the UNDP's Millennium Development Goal of halving world poverty by 2015 will necessarily have to involve rural development in some form or other.

Is there hope for relief? Improved governance entered the development community as the major new theme of the 1990s, and perhaps it can provide a remedy to reinvigorate what seems a stalled rural development enterprise. Its prospects for doing so comprise the central focus of this essay.

This chapter starts with by defining "rural development" and "governance." Next, looking at trends in these two sectors in recent decades, as rural development has apparently crested and declined, while governance has risen into new prominence. Finally, it attempts to assess the promises and dangers involved in wedding good governance approaches to the rural development enterprise.

II. Definitions

"Rural" can most easily be defined as whatever is nonurban, but it is more helpful to define it as pertaining to the countryside generally,[2] with an emphasis on agriculture as the chief economic component, though it is important to recognize that the nonfarm economy even in the poorest nations generates a significant share of rural income — from 30% in parts of South Asia to more than 40% in areas of Latin America and sub-Saharan Africa (Start, 2001: 408). "Rural development," then, must mean improving conditions in the countryside, but does this mean economic growth, or equitably distributed economic growth, or something broader, like human development? The World Bank tends to pursue the growth goals, while the United Nations Development Programme emphasizes its Human Development Index (HDI), with each organization seeing the other's main goal as really being a means to its own (Mawdsley and Rigg, 2003: 278–279). This chapter interprets rural development to mean movement toward a higher HDI.[3]

The term "governance" may well be even more vague than "rural," but usually can be taken to mean how the political systems (state, political parties, legal framework, etc.) of a country fit together into some kind of overall structure. Somewhat easier to deal with is the notion of "good governance," which the Development Advisory Committee (DAC) of the Organisation for Economic Cooperation and Development has (after great deliberation among its member states) defined as including "the rule of law, responsible leadership, and effective systems for public management, transparency, and accountability." (DAC, 1997: 11). DAC has combined this with "participatory development," "democratization," and "human rights" to form its concept of "participatory development and good governance" or PD/GG, but many if not most players in the international donor community appear to have accepted the whole package under the rubric of "good governance," so we will use that term to include the entire bundle of PD/GG elements. Accordingly, "good governance" here will mean:

■ A state strong enough to respond to citizen needs and demand
■ Active participation and accountability through elections and civil society
■ A legal environment guaranteeing civil liberties and political rights[4]

III. Trends in Rural Development and Governance

Rural development's trajectory can be traced in terms of both donor funding support and theoretical interest. On the funding side, the agricultural sector can be used as a proxy for rural development. Admittedly less than perfect as a measure, as rural development comprises a good deal more than agriculture alone (especially if we employ our HDI-oriented definition), it can nonetheless give us a rough idea how things have fared over time.[5] As is evident in Figure 45.1, at one point in the late 1970s, the World Bank as the world's largest developmental sponsor devoted almost 40% of its lending to agriculture, but since then the Bank has constantly reduced its emphasis on agriculture to the point where it received less than 10% around the turn of the millennium.[6] Other donors have not maintained

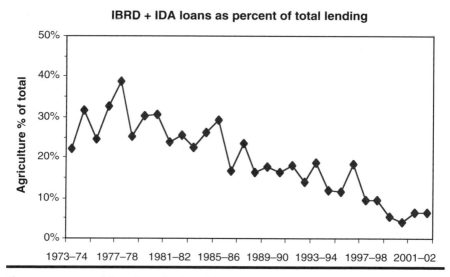

Figure 45.1   World Bank agricultural loans, 1974–2003.

such consistent categories and recording as the Bank, so it is very difficult to track support to rural development, but anecdotal evidence indicates that we can probably assume they have followed a similar pattern.[7]

The literature on rural development shows a similar rise and fall, as is clear in Figure 45.2, which depicts books in rural development over a 37-year period held by year of publication at Cornell University's library system. As the site of the New York State College of Agriculture and Life Sciences, Cornell University would be expected to house as large a collection on rural development as could be found anywhere. Here we see a

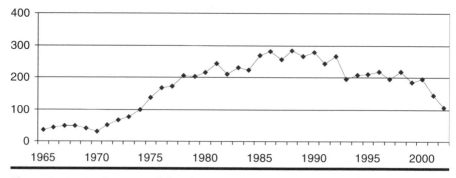

Figure 45.2   Books on rural development at Cornell University libraries by publication year, 1965–2002.

gradual rise in the 1970s and early 1980s, peaking out at 283 volumes published in 1986 and then declining to 144 in 2001 and 106 in 2002.[8] It is interesting to note that the literature's overall trend tends to follow the Bank's by several years, indicating a perhaps not surprising connection between Bank funding and research interests.

In contrast with rural development, donor funding in the governance sector proves much harder to track, as figures under the latter heading (especially using the definition employed here) are generally unavailable for any time period longer than a couple of years. Carothers (1999: 48–54) provides some good data for USAID allocations to what it called the "democracy and governance" sector as it was rapidly expanding in the 1990s, but after that the agency changed its reporting, so his series cannot easily be carried over to subsequent years. Fortunately, the literature in governance is less problematic to follow, as we see in Figure 45.3.[9] For more than a quarter century, "governance" was a nontopic in the academic world,[10] and only in the 1990s did it begin to pick up, as democracy came to be a major focus area in the international donor community.

IV. Themes in Rural Development over 50 Years

Over its 50-year career in the international development community, rural development has seen many paradigms and models come and go. Some of the more prominent ones are shown in Table 45.1.[11] In the early postwar years, donor approaches emphasized Western technology and economies of scale, like the East African groundnut scheme, but then in the late 1950s and 1960s, community development came into prominence, demanding attention to villagers' "felt needs" and offering expertise through the state

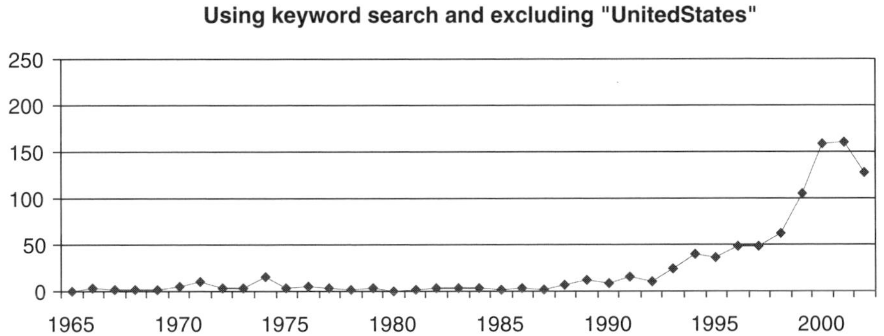

Using keyword search and excluding "UnitedStates"

Figure 45.3   Books on governance at Cornell University libraries by publication year, 1965–2002.

bureaucracy to meet those needs.[12] Enthusiasm for community development declined in the 1960s, as dissatisfaction mounted with its clumsy, top-down bureaucratic approach. As community development was declining in donor eyes, though, the small farmer emerged as rural development's hero, wresting higher yields from his holdings than larger landowners, mainly because of the extra labor he put into his fields, a practice spurred by a constant labor surplus in the rural area and consequent downward pressure on rural wages. In other words, because he had nowhere else to apply his labor, the small farmer poured it into his land, even well past the point of diminishing returns. By the standard input and output gauges of economic efficiency, such practices did not measure up very well, but in terms of yield per acre they promised to become the central engine of rural development.[13]

About the same time as small farmer enthusiasm was sweeping the field, the Green Revolution began to swing into high gear, with its new high-yielding varieties that did not require economies of scale to grow and accordingly could be adopted by small farmers just as well as large ones.[14] The obvious policy implication of all these developments would have been land reform to place more farmland into the hands of smallholders who could farm it more productively, and in a few places land reform was attempted. In general, however, Cold War exigencies stayed the hand of donors more concerned to maintain regimes in place as a bulwark against perceived insurrectionary threats, which meant in many cases backing autocratic regimes dependent on the support of large landholders whose allegiance would be forfeited if land reform were to take place.[15]

Also in the 1970s, some donors, most notably the United States, began to insist on greater participation in the development process, particularly on the

Table 45.1   Rural Development Themes, 1950–2000

1950s — Large-scale modernization

1960s — Community development, small farmer mobilization, Green Revolution begins

1970s — Green Revolution ongoing, development participation, integrated rural development

1980s — Participatory development, despair with the state, structural adjustment, training and visit

1990s — NGOs replacing state, governance (democratic participation, empowerment, decentralization)

2000s — Governance and NGOs ongoing

Source: Derived from Ellis, F. and Biggs, S., Evolving themes in rural development 1950s–2000s, *Dev. Policy Rev.*, 19 (4), 437–448, 2001. With permission.

part of small farmers. Involvement of intended beneficiaries in all phases of the project cycle became a pervasive mantra at USAID.[16] One prominent approach that could control participation was integrated rural development, which combined input provision, credit, education, health, infrastructural investment, and agricultural extension. However, the integrated rural development experience proved an unhappy one, especially for its major backer, the World Bank, largely because of problems in gaining state commitment, coordinating implementing ministries at the field level, and inducing beneficiaries to participate in its programs (Parker, 1995: 12–16).

In the 1980s, a new approach to participation emphasizing local people's knowledge as central to development in contrast to the kind of abstract and often inappropriate technology pushed by central ministries of agriculture. This bottom-up orientation, pioneered by Chambers (1983), led to efforts to incorporate more local expertise and energy into the development process. In a parallel trend, donors became increasingly disaffected with the state as the primary engine of rural development at a time when conservative political movements assumed power in both Washington and London. Structural adjustment now became the donor goal, demanding state downsizing and a more market-based approach to agricultural policy. The World Bank quickly became the lead donor agency making structural adjustment the cornerstone of its lending policy, and it soon encountered a storm of criticism (see, e.g., Dasgupta, 1998; Mohan et al, 2000). By the later 1990s, self-criticism on the practice became common at the Bank (e.g., Dollar and Svensson, 1998).

As donors became disenchanted with state ability to promote rural development, they turned increasingly in the 1990s to non-governmental organizations (NGOs), both international and domestic, to take up the slack. Thus increasing proportions of what had by now become a steadily shrinking pie of donor support for rural development went to NGOs. Instead of channeling virtually all their assistance through line government agencies, donors came to rely more and more on NGOs as their main organizations to promote rural development.

V. Introducing Democracy

The virtual absence of any democratic approach that would promote citizen input into policymaking (as opposed to participation in project or program implementation) or citizen capacity to hold government to account for its policy decisions is noteworthy among the rural development themes discussed so far is. Two principal factors explained most of this donor reluctance to move in a democratic direction, but both began to change during the later 1980s. First there was the bilateral donors' Cold War preference for reliable allies in the competition against the Soviet bloc. From Marcos to Mobutu, a reliable dictator was almost always to be preferred to risking global strategic interests by betting on any potential democratic movements. The beginning of a change in this posture first appeared in Central America in the mid-1980s, as it became tactically expedient in the context of American domestic politics to add a democratic gloss to U.S. support for heavy-handed proxies in the Cold War.[17] In addition, as the decade wore on, the "Third Wave" of democratization identified by Huntington (1991) began to mount, fueled by transitions in places like the Philippines and culminating in the collapse of the Soviet bloc in 1991.

Second, the World Bank, which had seen itself being strictly prohibited by its charter from engaging in any sort of "political" activity,[18] had by the early 1990s begun to view "good governance" as within its permissible purview. Specifically, the Bank came to see public administration, transparency, rule of law, and (a narrowly defined) accountability as legitimate areas to work in. The Bank's definition at this stage did not stretch so far so justify directly supporting democratization, but the introduction of governance as a topic did represent a significant change in its thinking.[19]

In the course of the 1990s, as support for agriculture and rural development declined, interest in governance picked up. Virtually all the bilateral donors geared up democracy programs,[20] as well as some multilaterals like the UNDP, and a good number of them crafted democracy initiatives to operate in the rural area, especially efforts focusing on decentralization. However, perhaps owing to the general decline of interest in rural development *per se*, there was no articulated strategy to harness governance to the cause of rural development, except at the World Bank.

By the mid-1990s, the Bank had begun to think of accountability and participation as reaching beyond their earlier confines. Parker (1995: 35) wrote that "there needs to be a proper system of accountability for decentralized institutions to each of their different constituents, and some system of sanctions that penalizes institutions that fail to carry out their functions appropriately." Such a prescription went quite a way beyond previous formulations insisting that institutions should be accountable to donor institutions in managing project resources. On the participation side, an official bank publication in 1996 specified "giving rural people a voice," insisting that the poor be "listened to, learned from, and engaged with" in "a bottom-up approach in which communities are actively involved in designing, implementing, and monitoring projects ..." (World Bank, 1996: 35). In some ways, such statements did not go very far at all beyond what the Cornell rural development participation team was laying out in the late 1970s,[21] for they did not directly specify that institutions of governance in rural development be accountable democratically to the citizenry, but for the Bank it represented a major step beyond the ways in which it had previously considered accountability and participation.

In October 1997, after much introspection and discussion, the Bank issued a formal "sector strategy" paper titled *Rural Development: From Vision to Action* (World Bank, 1997). The report stated that rural development as a sector was not proceeding well in reducing poverty because of declining commitment from both donors and developing country governments, owing partly to past achievements and declining food prices giving rise to complacency, but also due in part to a lack of rural political voice, especially among the rural poor. The answer was to reinvigorate the sector, moving beyond agriculture to encompass the entire range of productive activities, to focus on neglected issues like land reform and food consumption, and to involve local communities through decentralization initiatives. However, these initiatives were not spelled out with any real detail in the report itself.

Six years later, the Bank found it necessary to issue a new rural development strategy paper. The new report declared that the 1997 approach had yielded "mixed results." While some objectives (such as urban food security) had been largely met, the rural advancement envisioned in 1997 had not materialized. Priorities and program management within the Bank were partly to blame for the shortfall (continued decline in lending to agriculture, lack of rural development baseline data, and outcome indicators), but there were substantive issues as well, notably a lack of "focus on the neglected *political voice of the rural poor*" (World Bank, 2003: 13).

The remedy, in the Bank's view, was to address the two "critical foundations ... namely, creating an investment climate conducive to rural growth, and empowering the poor to share in the benefits of growth" (World Bank, 2003: 21). Empowering the poor directly was to come mainly through political decentralization, in which the Bank would support administrative capacity building, devolution of both power and resources, enhanced accountability to the citizenry, and participatory approaches, in which stakeholders would "influence and share control over priority setting, policymaking, resource allocations, and access to public goods and services" (World Bank, 2003: 38). Similarly at the national level, the Bank would "foster ... strong advocacy processes in the client countries," with the object of "strengthen[ing] the voice of the rural poor, in national processes for strategy formulation." Such strengthening would entail partnering *inter alia* with organizations of producers, women's organizations, and local NGOs (World Bank, 2003: 76).

The Bank did not go so far as to say that it would press for democratic accountability through local (or other) elections, and its ideas for supporting advocacy at the national level seemed somewhat on the tepid side. As of the

2003 report, advocacy for the Bank comprised "organization of stakeholder workshops and consultation processes, the preparation of policy notes, undertaking diagnostic, analytical, and strategic work on rural issues focused on poverty reduction" (World Bank, 2003: 76). It did not include what might be called more "advanced" advocacy approaches such as lobbying, petitioning, launching public relations efforts, mobilizing voters, or accessing the media, to say nothing of demonstrations or protests. Still, the overall concept represented a significant departure from earlier prohibitions on any kind of direct political involvement on the part of the Bank. The World Bank had now come to view improving governance as a fundamental and necessary principal component of rural development strategy, and it had come to see advocacy for the poor as a centerpiece of the governance component.

To sum up the period from the 1950s to the 1990s, rural development thinking within the international development community — as exemplified primarily in the approaches taken by the World Bank — had moved along several broad and in some respects parallel tracks:

- From top-down to bottom-up.
- From state-centered to market-oriented to NGO-led.
- From macro to micro.
- From viewing the rural poor first as target, then as passive participant, and finally as community becoming empowered to advocate for its own cause in policymaking.
- From seeing the political side of rural development as a sector to be avoided or ignored to understanding it as one to be harnessed to promote rural development.

Will including a good governance component prove sufficient to salvage the rural development enterprise and get it on track to "reach the rural poor," as the World Bank now puts it? Answering this question will form the focus of the following section.

VI. The Promise of Good Governance for Rural Development

Good governance's prospect for moving rural development in directions that can bring lasting benefits to the rural poor lies in its potential to increase the poor's participation in public policy decisionmaking and to use this enhanced participation to make that decisionmaking more accountable to citizens in general and the poor in particular. In addition, this in turn will have to come largely through advocacy — both the more modest approaches suggested by the Bank in its 2003 report (workshops, consultations, strategic analyses, etc.) and most especially the more advanced forms mentioned earlier such as lobbying, energizing constituencies, petitioning, and the like.

At both macro- and microlevels, advocacy would mean affecting public decisionmaking to increase policy outputs in two directions — initiatives benefiting the entire rural population, both poor and nonpoor, and programs favoring the poor in particular. Policies impacting all rural citizens would come in areas such as primary education, public health (drinking water, epidemiological protection), and transportation, while those primarily affecting the poor would include minimum wage protection, tenancy rights, land reform, and microcredit. Advocacy can be undertaken at the macrolevel though efforts to affect national institutions and processes — legislatures, elections, cabinet ministers, bureaucracies. At the microlevel, to the extent that significant power is actually devolved to local governmental tiers at the province, district, county, township and village, these same advocacy approaches can also be used.

The key concept here is "empowerment" — an impressively plastic term that can (and has been interpreted to) mean anything from an individual wearing more attractive personal makeup to the former employees of a corporation assuming its ownership and management. Often in the development field, empowerment has meant individual self-betterment, and programs to promote such ends have in many cases proven quite effective in empowering large groups of people as individuals. A good number of microcredit initiatives have produced salutary outcomes in this regard, enabling their participants — especially poor rural women — to escape (or at least ameliorate) economic and even social dependence to achieve self-reliance.

However, for the poor to acquire and build an ability to advocate in their own behalf will require some kind of collective or group empowerment, which means organized effort. This is a great deal more difficult than empowering individuals and much more hazardous. It is also something that is most unlikely to emerge from the rural poor themselves; some outside guidance and nurturing will be needed, in all likelihood in the form of NGOs.[22] Preferably these outside NGOs will be indigenous to the country itself, though not to the rural areas where they operate, for the rural poor can scarcely be expected to have in place *ex nihilo* the skills needed to mobilized themselves and launch advocacy campaigns. In some cases, these NGOs might have to originate from outside the country, at least in the initial stages.

For any of this scenario to occur, an "enabling environment" must be in place, that is, there must exist an enforceable legal framework guaranteeing the political freedom and civil liberties that need to be used to engage in advocacy: free speech, the right to assemble, organize, petition, demonstrate, etc. This enabling environment took many decades and even centuries to construct in the Western countries; the grave setbacks and difficulties that accompany attempts to replicate such an environment in the developing countries should occasion no surprise.

A suitable enabling environment need not take multiple decades and centuries to move into place, however. Though the track record is an uneven one, to say the least, quite a number of countries have managed to do so over the last 20 years or so. The Philippines and Thailand in Asia, Bolivia and El Salvador in Latin America, Mali and Senegal in Africa, and many states in the former Communist Bloc all provide examples of countries that have moved from autocratic forms of governance to transitional democracies over this timeframe.[23] Some of these would have to be counted as "electoral democracies" in which leaders can be and are unseated in elections, political speech is more or less free, and citizens can mobilize for advocacy, but where patron–client ties[24] continue as the normal mechanism linking citizen and state, the judiciary is largely corrupt, human rights are frequently abused, and power tends to be highly centralized. These states have not progressed to the point of becoming "liberal democracies," characterized by civil society as the normal linking mechanism, a judiciary operating by the rule of law, and human rights guaranteed for all and especially for minorities.[25]

However, even in the electoral democracies, there often remains considerable scope for citizen activism. Rural people can organize, craft policy agendas, make themselves heard, demand greater transparency from authorities, affect policy decisions, monitor implementation, and even gain concrete benefits from engaging in public affairs. Thus in India, which has wavered along the line between electoral and liberal democracy for most of the last three decades, farmer groups lobby for higher subsidies and crop prices, while landless laborers campaign for better minimum wage protection.[26] In Brazil, which has seen a similar wobbling around this same line, ranchers have won government assistance for clearing land, while the rural poor have gained some government support for improved public health programs.[27] In short, the poor can gain some advantages through civil society activism from even the limited quantum of good governance to be found in the electoral democracies, just as they can in the liberal democracies, though the chances of success will surely be smaller in the former, as the main difference between a liberal democratic governance structure and an electoral democratic regime is the much larger role of reactionary elites in the latter, that is, power groups (like the Brazilian ranchers mentioned just above) opposed to changes that will benefit the poor.

VII. Pitfalls on the Road to Rural Development through Good Governance

It should be clear from the very brief account given in the previous section that good governance strategies do not offer anything like an easy path to rural development that will bring much benefit to the poor. Constraints and obstacles will be many and profound.

Arguably the major constraint will be that old obstacle that has stood in the way of fundamental reform since time out of mind, political will. Can regimes dominated by elites dependent for their power on maintaining their roles at the top of patron–client systems bring themselves to give up some of that power? Certainly this is true at the macrolevel. Most elites see power as a zero-sum game, in which anything gained by one player must mean a loss for another one. Thus for those at the bottom to gain anything will imply a loss for others higher up. The challenge, then, will be for the rural poor to convince elites either that the power lost will be so negligible it can be discounted or that any possible loss will be compensated by even larger gains. Microcredit programs empowering poor rural widows could easily fit into the innocuous category, while female literacy initiatives might not, especially in some Muslim countries. However, if some elites might be persuaded that a literate cohort of younger women would vote for them and against other elites in an election, they might decide to support such literacy drives. Or a pro-poor organization might ally with one elite faction by supporting it in election against another faction. There are possibilities here, even as there are also perils (e.g., that the pro-poor organization would be coopted by its would-be elite ally and simply used by it, getting no benefits at all for its members).

At the local level, political activism as an engine of poverty reduction becomes even more problematic. Clients tend to be more existentially aware of their dependence on patrons, and accordingly less likely to risk what present security they have for uncertain future benefits.[28] In addition, if pro-poor groups can overcome their understandable anxieties and their general transaction costs to engage in political activism, chances are great that elites will either oppose them directly or take them into camp, just as at the macrolevel. Thus while decentralization schemes have long been touted as key to reducing rural poverty, their track record has not proven very successful.[29] It can still be argued that there is hope for local-level activism on behalf of the poor (see Blair, 2005 in a Bangladesh context), but the case has to be a carefully crafted one.

A second problem lies in the whole issue of accountability on the part of the NGOs that will have to become the main engines driving any civil society advocacy efforts at macro- or microlevel. While governments in a democratic setting must answer to the electorate at periodic intervals, and businesses in a free market economy must satisfy enough customers to remain in operation, NGOs as the "third sector" are for the most part accountable to their funders rather than their constituents or beneficiaries. The latter can exercise some agency by leaving an NGO or ceasing to participate in its programs, but usually have little chance to exercise much if any control over basic policy or its implementation. To be sure, elections are at best an exceedingly blunt instruments for holding political leaders to account, even assuming that the polling is "free and fair" (which of course often it is not). Nor does the marketplace exercise much of its alleged magic when prices are fixed or competition is stifled as so frequently happens. But even so, states and businesses tend to be more accountable than NGOs. Indeed, NGOs can become patron–client mechanisms similar to the structures they are designed to help people escape from. They can relate to their constituents as patrons to clients (Lewis, 2004), and they can develop their own internal patron–client relationships, just like the bureaucracies they so often replace as service delivery institutions (Wood, 1997).

Finally, the whole idea of "participation" — whether of the 1970s variety discussed earlier in this paper or the more democratic kind of more recent vintage — needs to be examined with some skepticism. When it seems to be succeeding, does it really constitute genuine inputs from below, or does it rather amount to engineering consent with a better sheen? Are villagers in effect going along for the ride in some western vehicle that may convey them to a more desirable place but they will be the same villagers tied into the same moral economy when they get deposited at their destination with a little more rice or a little better health? And if they do get changed in the process, is the transformation that has taken place a genuine conversion from within, or is it more nearly a new form of westernization that has been imposed from the top downward?[30]

These are all good questions, some of them with applicability far beyond the rural fastnesses of developing countries. How much, for example, do the employees of a large Western corporation actually "participate" by taking on new personal values when management puts them through a 3-day workshop to instill the latest wisdom from a business school guru with a trendy new motivation-building model to sell? Could democratic governance simply be the latest in the long series of approaches to rural development that seem like panaceas when getting adopted but soon fade and when observed through the rear-view mirror have become the discredited fads of the past?

Still, despite the many cautions we should entertain about democracy as an engine of rural development, it is surely worth trying. Among the many approaches essayed so far, it is the only one that seeks to hold governments accountable to the people they are supposed to be serving. If rural poverty is to be seriously alleviated in the next several decades, democratic governance would appear to hold more promise as the critical mechanism than any suggested to date.

Notes

1. IFAD (2001: 15–16) defines poverty as per capita income below US $1 per day. In this essay, the terms "poverty" and "the poor" (i.e., those who are in poverty) will use this baseline measure.
2. A "nonurban" approach is slightly disingenuous, in that different countries define "urban" quite differently (see IFAD, 2001: 17–18). "Countryside" implies a more commonsense orientation.
3. One of the HDI's three components is per capita income, the other two being life expectancy and an education index combining adult literacy and school enrollment. See UNDP (2003: 340–341).
4. It follows that "governance" by itself would refer to these characteristics in a descriptive rather than the normative sense that informs the concept of "good governance." To talk of "governance" in a place, then, would mean to deal with the state, participation, accountability, and the legal environment, however beneficial or malignant they might be.
5. For the last decade, the World Bank has tracked lending to agriculture and rural development separately in its annual reports. Some things included in "rural development" (rural roads, rural primary education) evidently are not included in "agriculture," while other things that are included in "agriculture" (urban food processing and distribution programs) appear to be excluded from "rural development." Exactly how the two categories are composed is not clear from the Bank's annual reports, q.v. Even so, the trajectories exhibited by the two categories have been very roughly similar over the past decade.
6. Plotting the dollar amount of actual loans over the period rather than the percentages presented in Figure 45.1 would show the high point achieved in the mid-1980s, with a rapid decline since then. The difference from the high mark of Figure 45.1 in the 1970s stems from the Bank's expansion of overall lending in the 1980s.
7. See also IFAD (2001: 41, 66) for confirming evidence in this regard. On the quantitative side, OECD data for 2002 show member countries allocating less than 5% of their bilateral aid to agriculture (for details, see http://www.oecd.org/dataoecd/52/11/1893159.xls).
8. A "keyword" search was employed to identify books dealing with RD. As a good part of the RD literature in the United States focuses on domestic American issues, the term "United States" was excluded as a keyword in the search. Such an approach did not eliminate works about all advanced countries (e.g., analyses of rural transport networks in Ireland) or even the United States in particular (e.g., books about agricultural extension in California that did not include the term "United States" anywhere in the library catalogue

entry), but it should give a good approximation of the overall trajectory of books published on the general RD topic focusing on the developing world.

9. As a check on the Cornell collection (the eleventh largest university collection in North America), I ran an analogous exercise for the Yale University collection (second largest), which showed an almost identical pattern for books with a "governance" keyword. The Yale collection also paralleled Cornell's in RD, though with fewer volumes acquired each year.

10. Before 1990, most of the few books dealing with "governance" (Cornell averaged about three a year up through the late 1980s) focused on university settings, where the term became a popular word in the 1970s. Only later did it emerge into widespread usage in other contexts.

11. For an excellent discussion of these trends, see Ellis and Biggs (2001).

12. As with so many of the RD trends, community development was pushed the farthest by both donors and host country government in India (see Holdcroft, 1978; also Blair, 1982).

13. The small farmer's case was championed most effectively by Schultz (1964) and Mellor (1966, 1976).

14. Brown (1970) was the most eloquent early evangelist for the Green Revolution.

15. Thus land reform's most persistent advocate, Roy Prosterman, was never able to get much traction among policymakers (see, e.g., Prosterman and Riedinger, 1987).

16. The literature on participation in rural development became a large one, especially through the efforts of Cornell University's Rural Development Participation Project (see, e.g., Cohen and Uphoff, 1977; Uphoff et al., 1979).

17. The most dramatic instance was the murder of four American nuns, apparently at the hands of Salvadoran military allies. One major U.S. response to this and other instances of unacceptably autocratic behavior in Latin America was to provide support for judicial reform and accountability — its Administration of Justice program, the precursor to what later became USAID's "Rule of Law" initiative.

18. Economic policy was interpreted by the Bank as "technical," so it saw itself as having a free hand in this area (ignoring the fact that such policies as structural adjustment had immense political effects in the countries pressured into imposing it).

19. See World Bank (1991, 1992). "Accountability" at this time was given a fiscal, economic, and institutional interpretation, meaning essentially accountability to donor agencies (see World Bank, 1991: 8–10).

20. See, for example, Robinson's (1998) account of civil society programs. The best analysis of a single donor's work in the democracy sector remains Carothers (1999).

21. See Note 16 above.

22. The structure of my thinking on empowerment is much indebted to Moore (2001).

23. Progress toward (as well as away from) democratization is summed up every year in an annual survey conducted by Freedom House. In its 2003 survey, Freedom House provided data on 192 countries, finding 46% of them to be "free," up from 33% twenty years before (Freedom House, 2003: 9).

24. Traditional patron–client systems are built around a mutual (but unequal) exchange in which patrons provide security (employment, food, protection) while the client offers labor and loyalty. Patrons can be landlords, politicians, or bureaucrats, among other things, while clients could be landless workers, peasants with land, or subordinates in a political machine, depending on context. For a good overview of the topic, see Eisenstadt and Roniger (1984: 43–50).
25. See Diamond (1999, Chapter 2, 2002).
26. Rudolph and Rudolph (1987) present the classic analysis of farmer lobbying in India. On advocacy efforts from the lower classes and castes, there are many studies. Alexander (1989) and Omvedt (1993: 47–75) provide two good examples.
27. See, for example, Hecht and Cockburn (1989) and Tendler (1998).
28. This "Faustian bargain" the poor find themselves involved in is analyzed by Wood (2003).
29. See Johnson (2001) for an extended discussion of these issues.
30. See Mawdsley and Rigg (2003: 281) and more generally the essays in Cooke and Kothari (2001).

References

Alexander, K. C., Class mobilization and class consciousness: the emergence of agrarian movements in Kerala and Tamil Nadu, in: *Dominance and State Power in Modern India: Decline of a Social Order*, Frankel, F. and Rao, M. S. A., Eds., 2 Vols., Oxford University Press, New Delhi, 1989, pp. 362–413.

Ashley, C. and Maxwell, S., Rethinking rural development, *Dev. Policy Rev.*, 19 (4), 395–425, 2001.

Blair, H., *The Political Economy of Participation in Local Development Programs: Short-term Impasse and Long-term Change in South Asia and the United States from the 1950s to the 1970s*, Monograph Series 4, Cornell University, Center for International Studies, Rural Development Committee, Ithaca, NY, 1982.

Blair, H., Civil Society and pro-poor initiatives at the local level in rural Bangladesh: finding a workable strategy, *World Dev.*, 33(6), 921–936, 2005.

Brown, L., *Seeds of Change: The Green Revolution and Development in the 1970s*, Praeger, New York, 1970.

Carothers, T., *Aiding Democracy Abroad: The Learning Curve*, Carnegie Endowment for International Peace, Washington, DC, 1999.

Chambers, R., *Rural Development: Putting the Last First*, Longman, London, 1983.

Cohen, J. M. and Uphoff, N. T., *Rural Development Participation: Concepts and Measures for Project Design, Implementation and Evaluation*, Monograph Series 2, Cornell University, Center for International Studies, Rural Development Committee, Ithaca, NY, 1977.

Cooke, B. and Kothari, U., Eds., *Participation: The New Tyranny?* Zed Books, London, 2001.

DAC (Development Assistance Committee), Final Report of the Ad Hoc Working Group on Participatory Development and Good Governance, Organization for Economic Cooperation and Development, Paris, 1997.

Dasgupta, B., *Structural Adjustment, Global Trade and the New Political Economy of Development*, Zed Books, London, 1998.

Diamond, L., *Developing Democracy: Toward Consolidation*, Johns Hopkins University Press, Baltimore, 1999.

Diamond, L., Thinking about hybrid regimes: elections without democracy, *J. Democracy*, 13 (2), 21–35, 2002.

Dollar, D. and Svensson, J., *What Explains the Success and Failure of Structural Adjustment Programs?* Policy Research Working Paper 1938, World Bank, Development Research Group, Macroeconomics and Growth, Washington, 1998.

Eisenstadt, S. N. and Roniger, L., *Patrons, Clients and Friends: Interpersonal Relations and the Structure of Trust in Society*, Cambridge University Press, Cambridge, 1984.

Ellis, F. and Biggs, S., Evolving themes in rural development 1950s–2000s, *Dev. Policy Rev.*, 19 (4), 437–448, 2001.

Freedom House, *Freedom in the World 2003: The Annual Survey of Political Rights and Civil Liberties*, Rowman and Littlefield, Lanham, MD, 2003.

Hecht, S. and Cockburn, A., *The Fate of the Forest: Developers, Destroyers and Defenders of the Amazon*, Verso, London, 1989.

Holdcroft, L. E., *The Rise and Fall of Community Development in Developing Countries, 1950–1965: A Critical Analysis and an Annotated Bibliography*, MSU Rural Development Paper 2, Michigan State University, Department of Agricultural Economics, East Lansing, MI, 1978.

Huntington, S., *The Third Wave: Democratization in the Late Twentieth Century*, University of Oklahoma Press, Norman, OK, 1991.

IFAD (International Fund for Agricultural Development), *Rural Poverty Report 2001: The Challenge of Ending Rural Poverty*, Oxford University Press, Oxford, 2001.

Johnson, C., Local democracy, democratic decentralization and rural development: theories, challenges and options for policy, *Dev. Policy Rev.*, 19 (4), 521–532, 2001.

Lewis, D., On the difficulty of studying 'civil society': Reflections on NGOs, state and democracy in Bangladesh, *Contrib. Indian Sociol.*, 38(3), 299–322, 2004.

Mawdsley, E. and Rigg, J., A survey of the World Development Reports II: continuity and change in development orthodoxies, *Progr. Dev. Stud.*, 3 (4), 271–286, 2003.

Mayer, A., *Pilot Project India: The Story of Rural Development at Etawah, Uttar Pradesh*, University of California Press, Berkeley, 1958.

Mellor, J. W., *The Economics of Agricultural Development*, Cornell University Press, Ithaca, NY, 1966.

Mellor, J. W., *The New Economics of Growth: A Strategy for India and the Developing World*, Cornell University Press, Ithaca, NY, 1976.

Mohan, G., Brown, E., Milward, B., and Williams, A. B., *Structural Adjustment: Theory, Practice and Impacts*, Routledge, London, 2000.

Moore, M., Empowerment at last? *J. Int. Dev.*, 13 (3), 321–329, 2001.

Omvedt, G., *Reinventing Revolution: New Social Movements and the Social Tradition in India*, M. E. Sharpe, Armonk, NY, 1993.

Parker, A. N., Decentralization: the way forward for rural development? Policy Research Working Paper 1475, World Bank, Agriculture and Natural Resources Department, Sector Policy and Water Resources Division, Washington, 1995.

Prosterman, R. L. and Riedinger, J. M., *Land Reform and Democratic Development*, Johns Hopkins University Press, Baltimore, MD, 1987.

Robinson, M., What is the aid system doing? in: *Civil Society and the Aid Industry*, Van Rooy, A., Ed., Earthscan Publications, London, 1998, pp. 55–68.

Rudolph, L. I. and Rudolph, S. H., *In Pursuit of Lakshmi: The Political Economy of the Indian State*, University of Chicago Press, Chicago, 1987.

Schultz, T. W., *Transforming Traditional Agriculture*, Yale University Press, New Haven, 1964.

Start, D., The rise and fall of the non-farm economy: poverty impacts and policy options, *Dev. Policy Rev.*, 19 (4), 491–505, 2001.

Tendler, J., *Good Government in the Tropics*, Johns Hopkins University Press, Baltimore, MD, 1998.

UNDP (United Nations Development Programme), *Human Development Report 2003*, Oxford University Press, New York, 2003.

Uphoff, N. T., Cohen, J. M., and Goldsmith, A., *Feasibility and Application of Rural Development Participation: A State-of-the-Art Paper*, Monograph Series 3, Cornell University, Center for International Studies, Rural Development Committee, Ithaca, NY, 1979.

Wood, G., States without citizens: the problem of the franchise state, in: *NGOs, States and Donors: Too Close for Comfort?* Hulme, D. and Edwards, M., Eds., Basingstoke, Macmillan, Hampshire, 1997, pp. 79–92.

Wood, G., Staying secure, staying poor: the Faustian bargain, *World Dev.*, 31 (3), 455–471, 2003.

World Bank, *Managing Development: The Governance Dimension: A Discussion Paper*, World Bank, Washington, 1991.

World Bank, *Governance and Development*, World Bank, Washington, 1992.

World Bank, *Rural Development: Putting the Pieces in Place*, World Bank, Washington, 1996.

World Bank, *Rural Development: From Vision to Action*, Environmentally and Socially Sustainable Development Studies and Monographs Series 12, World Bank, Washington, 1997.

World Bank, *Reaching the Rural Poor: A Renewed Strategy for Rural Development*, World Bank, Washington, 2003.

Index

A

absolutely fixed exchange rates (AFER), 259
academic environment
  creation, 142
accountability, 273–275
  answerability, 270
  defining elements, 270–271
  definition, 270–273
  definitions, 276
  exercise, 271–273
  good governance, 270
  illustrative examples, 273
  increase, 275–285
  increase enforcement, 280–285
  increasing enforcement guidelines, 282–284
  institutions, 273
  links, 276
  mechanisms, 274
  negative publicity, 271
  options, 277
  positive publicity, 271
  state institutions, 271
  types, 276
Acheson Report, 787
Adelaide Conference, 787
adequate water, 746
administrative reforms, 574

analysis, 547–548
history, 546
World War II, 550
administrative system
  Weberian model, 535
administrators
  orientation, 537–538
advocacy
  health promotion, 792
advocacy index, 651
Afghanistan
  development program
    implementation, 647
Africa
  agricultural stagnation, 708
  civil society, 242
  decentralization, 394
  institutional learning, 618–619
  and local funds, 453–454
  managing development, 611–621
  ownership, 615
  recession, 393
  WBES survey, 293
African Charter on Human and People's
    Rights, 158
African civil societies
  apartheid, 246
  nonprofit NGO sector, 244
  private sectors, 243
  weaknesses, 243

D

Human Development Index (HDI), 175,
667, 823
United Nations (UN), 291
Human Development Report, 32, 667
*Human Development Report
2001:Making New Technologies
Work for Human Development,*
516
human factor (HF), 129
centered reform program
objective, 142
children socialization, 140
composition, 138
engineering
human-centered development,
144
primary tasks, 137
process, 140
quality, 139–143
engineering quality, 141
key cluster foundation, 136–139
related programs, 144–145
significant engineering, 136
human factor decay (HFD), 139
HF engineering activities, 139
human rights
abuses, 157
citizen familiarity, 151
governance, 151–161
negative rights, 153
positive rights, 153
human welfare
development, 38
Hurd, Douglas, 57
hyperinflation
developing countries, 263
fiscal control, 264
monetary control, 264

I

ideology, 530
1920s and 1930s, 602
implementation, 770–771
improvement, 605
inclusive embeddedness, 29
income disparities
poverty statistics, 223

income inequality
agriculture technology, 719
Independent Complaints Advocacy
Services, 809
Independent Electoral Commission, 526
India
agricultural exports, 730
bureaucracy, 534
CVC, 523
decentralization, 395–396
developing society, 535–536
Employment Assurance Scheme, 650
Gujarat, 280
Mazdoor Kisan Shakti Sangathan
(MKSS), 411
and NGOs, 421
political accountability, 396
rural unemployment problems, 722
traditional labor-contract
theory, 721
wage model, 721
Weberian characteristics, 534
Indian Bureau of Public Enterprise,
478
indicative planning, 627
individual level
of capacity development, 591
Indonesia, 106, 627
dependent, 107
dependent countries, 112–113
Dutch company, 79
economic reverse, 112
Environmental Impact Management
Agency, 190
FDI, 112
financial crisis, 114
indigenous water laws, 755
Plaza Accords, 107
presidential regime, 119
rural unemployment problems, 722
state capacity, 121
Indonesia Bank Restructuring Agency
(IBRA), 113
Indonesian Legal Aid Foundation, 192
industrial competitiveness
new dimensions, 686–687
Industrial Environment Management
Project, 187

UNESCAP, 188
Unification Treaty, 340
United Kingdom
  conduct codes, 281
  Department for International
    Development (DFID), 617, 808
  health systems case studies,
    806–810
  policy learning, 675–677
  privatization, 553
United Nations (UN), 516
  Framework on Climate Change, 187
  High Commission on Human Rights,
    84
  Human Development Index (HDI),
    291
  Human Development Report, 643
  women
    childbirth, 383
United Nations Conference on
    Environment and Development
    (UNCED), 37
United Nations Conference on Trade and
    Development (UNCTAD), 516
United Nations Development Program
    (UNDP), 21, 84, 129, 243, 306,
    332, 497, 569
United Nations Earth Summit, 788
United Nations General Assembly, 155,
    306, 316
United Nations High Commissioner for
    Human Rights (UNHCHR), 159
United Nations International
    Development Strategy, 607
United States
  Agency for International
    Development, 187
  Agency for International
    Development's Center for
    Democracy and Governance, 576
  agriculture-led economic
    development, 704
  arms race, 98
  cooperative states, 83
  e-governance leaders, 523
  global empire, 557
  poverty, 223
  privatization, 553

United States Agency for International
    Development (USAID), 332
United States-Asia Environmental
    Partnership, 187
United States Development Program
  capacity development, 589
Universal Declaration, 156, 158
Universal Declaration of Human Rights,
    20, 155
universality
  definition, 152
unrealistic vision
  corruption flaws, 315–316

V

Venezuela
  health systems, 805
vertical accountability, 272
vertical social structure
  authority relations, 364
Vienna Convention for the Protection of
    the Ozone Layer, 187
Vietnam
  agricultural exports, 723, 730
Voices of the Poor, 573
voluntary agreements
  prevention factors, 504

W

Wade, Robert, 206
wage laborer
  definition, 720
  types, 720
Wall Street Journal, 309
Wallace, George, 94
Washington Connection, 99
Washington Consensus, 52, 58–59, 91,
    94, 232, 795
  American neoliberalism, 103
  cold-war ideology, 100
water
  increasing demand for, 746
water resource, 746–747
  development
    hindrances to, 756–757
  laws for, 753–755

0 1341 1321408 1

RECEIVED

JUN 03 2011

HUMBER LIBRARIES
LAKESHORE CAMPUS